THE NAMES *of* GOD

THE NAMES *of* GOD

Poetic Readings

in Biblical Beginnings

HERBERT CHANAN BRICHTO

New York   Oxford   •   Oxford University Press   1998

BS
1235.2
.B73
1998

Oxford University Press

Oxford   New York
Athens   Auckland   Bangkok   Bogota   Bombay   Buenos Aires
Calcutta   Cape Town   Dar es Salaam   Delhi   Florence   Hong Kong
Istanbul   Karachi   Kuala Lumpur   Madras   Madrid   Melbourne
Mexico City   Nairobi   Paris   Singapore   Taipei   Tokyo   Toronto   Warsaw

and associated companies in
Berlin   Ibadan

Copyright © 1998 by Herschel D. Brichto

Published by Oxford University Press, Inc.
198 Madison Avenue, New York, New York 10016

Oxford is a registered trademark of Oxford University Press

All rights reserved. No part of this publication may be reproduced,
stored in a retrieval system, or transmitted, in any form or by any means,
electronic, mechanical, photocopying, recording, or otherwise,
without the prior permission of Oxford University Press.

Library of Congress Cataloging-in-Publication Data
Brichto, Herbert Chanan.
The names of God : poetic readings in biblical beginnings
p.   cm.
Companion vol. to the author's Toward a grammar of biblical poetics, 1992.
Includes bibliographical references and index.
ISBN 0-19-510965-1
1. Bible. O.T. Genesis—Criticism, interpretation, etc.
2. Bible. O.T. Genesis—Authorship.   I. Title.
BS1235.2.B75   1998
222'.1106—dc20   96-10381

1 3 5 7 9 8 6 4 2

Printed in the United States of America
on acid-free paper

FOR

Herschel Sarah Kathryn   Johanna   Baruch Naphtali
Eric Alexander Joseph Isaiah   Yeshuah Yirmi Chaim Rivka
Brichto   Rabenstein

and every nin

and neched

to come

PREFACE

This book is a companion volume to *Toward a Grammar of Biblical Poetics: Tales of the Prophets*. It is, in purpose and substance, by initial and continuing design, the goal and consummation of the first volume. The primary objective of both volumes is not to contribute to the theoretical debate on the proper (or preferable) objectives and methodologies of literary criticism, but to enlist generally agreed-upon poetic principles and foci of literary analysis in the interest of interpreting the text we call Scripture, or (as many would prefer) the texts that constitute Scripture. To put the matter differently: my interest is not in such differing schools as, for example, Aristotelian, the Old or New, Structuralist, Deconstructionist, or Postmodern criticism; it is, rather, to draw on the strengths of literary-critical insights, whatever their derivation or provenance, to achieve such persuasive expositions of a text's meaning(s) as are designated in biblical circles by exegesis and in broader contexts by *explication du texte*.

I suggested in *Toward a Grammar* that the literary analyses or explications of texts coming down to us from antiquity are of a different order in some respects than those practiced on more recent compositions. They differ, in the main, in the far greater role of two factors in the criticism of ancient literature: assumptions as to the genre of that literature (e.g., is it fiction or history, a hard disjunction) or, a meta-literary factor, judgments on the part of the critic as to the differing capacities or inclinations of the ancient as against the modern mind (e.g., in regard to naïveté and sophistication, literal or figurative intent). My concern with this difference, which holds in respect to ancient literatures, be they the classics or those written in cuneiform or hieroglyphic scripts, focuses primarily on Scripture.

Here, as in the study of Homeric epic, inconsistencies and contradictions in a composition that has come down to us as a single work (e.g., the *Iliad*, the Book of Genesis) have led scholars to question long-held assumptions of single authorship; and, indeed, to raise such questions as to the existence in it of various strata owing to earlier writings or preliterate traditions, or as to whether the term *author* should not yield to *editor* or *compiler* for the individuals responsible for the literary corpus we have received. Further questions posed with respect to both Hebrew and Greek literary traditions are the degree of autonomy enjoyed by the ancient author or editor, and the extent to which the fetters of tradition are responsible for the literary hash that lies before us. If I may extend this culinary metaphor in a jocose observation: what is most remarkable about this hash is that for all the admitted incompatibility of its constituent ingredients, it continues to be trumpeted as a masterpiece by the very critics who can disentangle the egg noodles from the spaghetti in our pudding and even trace the motives of the chefs who introduced yoghurt into the marinara sauce.

For all the similarity in the procedures of literary detectives, classicists, and biblicists in resorting to source analysis to ease if not solve the problems of repetition and inconsistency in the masterworks that afford them a living, it must be confessed that the pretensions and accomplishments of the Homeric critics are modest, and slight in comparison to those of their blood-brother sleuths, who ply the same or similar skills in the vineyard of the Lord called Scripture. For in this area hypotheses have become dogmas; the art of literary criticism has become a science, capable of fixing the parameters of the text's historic development; and the very notion of an overarching message or pattern of messages is undermined, if not logically precluded, in a text whose developmental history has become traceable only by virtue of the irreducible inconsistencies that are its constituents.

The genetic or historic school of biblical criticism is, despite mounting dissatisfaction with its methods and conclusions, still the regnant one. My less than generous characterization of this school will therefore be bitterly contested by many who began in this school as acolytes or, like myself, entered it as converts from dogmatic traditions that could not but view as subversive of faith its reading of Scripture as an evolutionary process: a process in which one may discern a march from the superstitions of animism and the crudities of pagan concepts, a decreasingly primitive groping via henotheism and monolatry toward a monotheism that emerges in clarity and purity only in the last stage of that process. It will be argued that the source-analytic schools do not preclude a consistent overarching view of Scripture's teaching; witness the many holistic studies of biblical ideas, values, and theology by scholars who belong to the historic-genetic school, many of whom also belong to mainstream confessions of biblical religion.

While this last phenomenon is undeniable, it does not constitute a refutation of my argument that the logic of the developmental thrust of the genetic schools of Scripture rules out an affirmation of Scripture's sovereign authority. The authority lies not in Scripture itself, but in those critics who can separate out the true values and beliefs from the older outmoded ones that the latest Scriptural protagonists had outgrown. That fine minds and devout spirits can overlook this illogic, as well as the implicit substitution of their own selective authority for Scripture's pervasive one, is understandable. Religionists who have themselves come to an understanding of their faiths as the ideational and theological precipitates of an evolutionary process are so conditioned as to be unperturbed by traces of such process in the texts, which they revere for being the vessels of these precipitates. And in abstracting these precious precipitates from the ore that they have processed, they have no problem with the slag that litters the excavated slope. Not so, however, fundamentalist religionists. These, subscribing to any of several "literal" interpretations of the text (which is inerrant, revelation, word of God, etc.), often find it an insuperable difficulty to reject any part or element in a (or the) Scriptural text as a faith-fault in the authoritative (if not authoritarian) monument built for us by the agents of God's revelatory will.

While I belong to the first of the two religionist postures, my approach to Scripture is more akin to that of the second, albeit for an altogether different reason. My difficulty stems from no principle of faith, but rather from poetic considerations. I cannot conceive of any gifted author or competent editor so bound by slavishness to putative (sacred but outgrown) traditions such as would require him to remount pearls in the shells in which they were found. And even as I do not accept the notion that God addresses modern humans less often or less clearly than in the days of my biblical forerunners, so do I not pride myself or my contemporaries on a logic or rationality, a humor or imagination, a wisdom or a talent for philosophy, that exceeds those capacities in Scripture's authors (or, for that matter, in any of antiquity's compositors).

It was presumptions such as these that both contributed to and resulted from my disaffection with source-criticism as an explanation for the inconsistencies and contradictions so abundant in Scripture, and which ultimately impelled me to a poetical approach to the Bible. It was in the course of attempting to identify and classify those poetic elements common to modern and ancient literary analysis that I became aware of the difference in address to which I allude at the beginning of this preface: the disproportionately greater role in respect to the interpretation of ancient literature of genre classification and assessment of conceptual capacities. As opposed to those legitimate elements of poetics that, in *Toward a Grammar*, I classified as *foci*, I found the purely literary element of genre and the meta-literary conventions as to ancient capacities or intentions to be factors in interpretation (misleading ones more often than not), and of little use in textual explication.

As concerns genre, the most frequent and perplexing question in regard to ancient narrative is whether it was intended to present a more or less faithful reconstruction of significant events, as these had occurred in real places and times past (hence, assignable to *history*), or a largely imaginative construction of events and personae for purposes primarily of delectation or edification (hence, assignable to *fiction*). This problem, in a number of modalities, is treated in *Toward a Grammar*, in chapter 1 in respect to the historiographic constituents in the legendary Trojan War and the Histories of Herodotus; and in chapter 9 with regard to biblical "histories," a discussion which, in sketchy form, anticipates the treatment in this present volume of the stories and structures in Genesis.

It is of more than passing interest that both dogmatic fundamentalists and genetistic scientific scholars share the presumption that historiography is the intent and purpose of the biblical author(s) even in the earliest chapters of Genesis; the former accept these accounts as revealed historic truths, while the latter find themselves in resonance with the theological truths (for example, in the parallel accounts of creation) even while they are confident that (as they come from two different authors and are highly inconsistent with one another) the texts cannot be accepted as history. Although the assumption of the ubiquitous historiographic intent of Scripture's authors is increasingly questioned in recent scholarship, it remains the assumption of the majority by far of scientific biblicists, who even—indeed—extend this assumption to the editors who conflated the biblical text. In illustration of this I cite a passage that came before my eyes a few hours before I wrote these lines. It is from a review by John P. Meier, a biblicist specializing in New Testament, of Robin Lane Fox's *The Unauthorized Version: Truth and Fiction in the Bible* (New York Times Book Review, June 7, 1992, page 13). It is presented here for its testimony as to the mind-set of biblicists at large, even when they are—like Father Meier—both scientific academicians and devout divines:

> One may wonder whether Mr. Lane Fox sufficiently appreciates the great gulf between the ancient biblical mentality and our own. Especially when employing narrative as a vehicle for theology, many biblical writers do not seem to have operated with our Western sense of what constitutes an intolerable contradiction. To take but one example: as Mr. Lane Fox points out, the editor of Genesis juxtaposed two Creation accounts in Genesis 1 and 2, despite what strike us as blatant contradictions.

While the reference to Genesis makes this quotation particularly apposite to my subject matter in this volume, the following extract from the next paragraph will provide a foil for my own poetical view and formulation, which is in opposition and contrast with the Rev. Meier's but not in adversarial rebuttal:

> Mr. Lane Fox apparently attributes to any one depiction of Creation more normative-ness and exclusivity than did the biblical authors. Indeed in some cases the same author could compose contradictory narratives of the same event back to back: Luke blithely juxtaposes an Ascension on Easter evening in Luke 24 with an Ascension 40 days later in Acts 1. In short, Mr. Lane Fox, like some fundamentalists, sometimes engages in an anachronistic imposition of a Western notion of truth on authors whose thought patterns were markedly different from ours.

Implicit in "a Western notion of truth" is that the biblical authors owned an *Eastern and different notion of truth*. Implicit in "anachronistic" is that the radically different notion of truth is not just a matter of East and West but of mentalities in the biblical past and our own present. This positing of a gap (apparently unbridgeable, for it is never bridged) between our mindset and that of antiquity's authors, ours in the West and theirs in the East, would—as I have argued elsewhere—preclude any attempt on our part to decipher the meanings and relate to the communications of the ancients.[1] If, on the other hand, we are not to ignore their writings, it is my contention that we must posit continuity rather than divergence in the mindsets of yesterday and today and a sharing in a single notion of truth.

It is just such a unity and continuity in the expressions of the human mind then and today that is affirmed and, I believe, convincingly demonstrated by the poetical approach. The poetical approach exposes the similarity in the imaginative patterns of narrative and structure deployed by artists in different times and places; it reveals how parallelism in narrative and parataxis in syntax, how narrative in the frame of the prescriptive and the prescriptive imbedded in narrative, enrich or deepen the author's message; so, also, how apparently pointless repetition, inconsistencies, and contradictions are actually significant elements in a single coherent design. Drawing on graphic and musical vocabulary we may adduce the juxtaposition of the symmetrical and the asymmetrical, the succession of assonance and dissonance, for serviceable analogies for the rhetorical craft that enlists the seemingly erratic in the interest of order, and inadvertency as a strategy to win ungrudging assent.

It is a fact that the discernment of different documents or authorial hands or schools (and the subsequent chronological ordering of these strata) owes its rise to the perception of the existence in Genesis of repetitious narratives that are in various details inconsistent or contradictory. It is also a fact that one of the paramount inconsistencies, providing the chief clue to the unraveling of these strands, was the assortment of terms or names for the Deity and his numen representatives. It is a matter of autobiographical (and little other) interest that my dissatisfaction with the rationales offered for the alternation of YHWH and Elohim antedates my quest for alternatives to the source-analytic explanations of the inconsistencies in the Genesis texts. Yet it was only subsequent to the poetic analytic treatment of the narratives, and owing to that treatment, that I began to discern the literary and meta-literary clues to the deployment of these two primary names for Deity. My original plan, therefore, was to present what is now the first chapter, "The Names of God," at the end of the book. Colleagues urged me to change this plan, arguing that the change was almost dictated by the powerful grip of source-analytic methodology on the majority of today's biblicists, and particularly by the roots of that methodology in the names for Deity as deployed in the "documents" from Genesis 1 through Exodus 3 (or 6). Accepting this suggestion entailed a rearrangement of the material. Illustration of the poetic functions of one or another name had to be removed from the new introductory chapter and integrated with the exegetical discussions of the narratives in situ, and a separate recapitulation appended. What I should like to impress upon my readers in regard to the argument for the "names," divided now over the introduction, the essays on the narrative, and the recapitulation, is this: By its very nature poetics is a deductive process, which is to say that it may be characterized as essentially post hoc. One may not (or cannot) therefore proceed from even a persuasively presented post hoc to a propter hoc conclusion; a conclusion such as would enable us to predict which of the divine name options are to be expected in a narrative featuring such-and-such a theme, or such-and-such nuances. The poetic argument for the names of Deity is just that, an attempt to account in a persuasive way for an author's having chosen certain options in given stories. (It does not dictate the choice among options for anyone undertaking to rewrite these stories.) In short, it is not susceptible to proof any more than it constitutes a disproof of source-analytic explanations. Readers who find the poetic arguments for the deployment of YHWH('s angel) or Elohim('s angel) overly subtle or simply unconvincing should feel free to reject this part of the poetic analysis, while remaining open to the general thrust of the poetic explication.

Returning now to the pervasive grip of source-analytic presumptions on today's Bible scholarship, this phenomenon can perhaps be best exemplified in the work of a gifted young scholar whose research on the literary structuring of Genesis leads him to conclude that the Documentary Hypothesis (in its sundry transmogrifications) is untenable. The title of Gary A. Rendsburg's slim but dense volume—for all that not a single element in his argument is at all dependent on the assumption that Genesis is the final product of an editorial rather than an authorial hand— is *The Redaction of Genesis*. What then prompts Rendsburg to follow up his verdict that "there is much more uniformity and much less fragmentation in the book of Genesis than generally assumed" (page 105) with, "This does not mean that all of Genesis is the work of one author" (page 106)? The answer is given in the continuation of this last sentence:

For there clearly remain different sources and variant traditions. The author of 1:1–2:4a must clearly be someone different than the author of 2:4b–3:24. The tradition which makes Cain a nomad in 4:12–16 is certainly at variance with the one which depicts him building a city in 4:17

In the case of the Shakespearean dramatic corpus, the recognition of the playwright's dependence on a variety of narrative, dramatic, and "historic" sources has not led critics to attribute that corpus in part or whole to the enterprise of a compiler rather than an author. Clearly the differing verdict in regard to the book of Genesis is due to the perception that the inconsistencies and contradictions within it are considerably less explicable than similar incongruities in such works as *Hamlet, Julius Caesar,* or *Antony and Cleopatra.* (The question as to why an editorial decision to compile inconsistent narratives should be more plausible to the critical mind than the attribution of such a vagary to an author may be more rhetorical than inquisitive.)

It is therefore my expectation that Professor Rendsburg will be disposed to welcome—to the extent he finds them persuasive—my poetic arguments that the larger couplet called the Creation Stories and such smaller ones as the seemingly opposed notices of Cain as nomad and city-builder are not only mutually compatible, but indeed are fit and fitted as mortise and tenon. And so too, I suspect, will many other researchers whose studies in Bible do not reveal too heavy an investment in source-critical methodology. The larger number of veteran biblicists, however, moored to the regnant consensus, will be less charitably disposed to a methodology that points to a judgment that the genetic approach to Scripture is a century-long detour, a detour ending in a cul-de-sac. To such colleagues and companion workers I would address a reminder that detours may offer finer scenic views than a direct route, that even the road that meanders into a blind alley may have contributed to a sharpening of the explorer's sight, that—as has certainly been the case in our enterprise—the search for a Northwest Passage has recruited doughty explorers who might otherwise have stayed closer to home and the safety of overgrazed pastures.

I must confess for my own part that I should never have been drawn to the close study of biblical literature in its ancient literary ambience were it not for the excitement and romance of the path-blazing avenues opened for me by the historical source-critical school. It is highly unlikely that I should have committed myself to acquiring the philological tools requisite for the study of ancient Near Eastern culture and history but for the promise that these would provide the keys to a new and deeper understanding of the history of that ancient folk called Israel and Judah, the history that might help account for the production and preservation of that library called the Bible. I must also own my awareness of the irony that these very studies led to my dismissal of the source-critical method, and also to the conviction that "history" explains little in literature, that indeed there is hardly any other meaning to history than that which may be seen as encapsulated in literature.

While I can afford to smile at myself, I may not permit the impression that I may be jeering at those colleagues whose position I have abandoned. And yet that impression may be almost ineluctable. The polemics of the humanistic enterprises (such as art and its criticism) are remarkably similar to those of religion: yesterday's radical, who has survived the charge of heresy to become the champion of a new orthodoxy, will react to the new radical as a recrudescence of his old persecutor; while the new radical will be goaded into polemical formulations by the refusal of the establishment (as he sees it) to accord him a hearing. It is in part owing to my awareness of a polemical tone, which may be discerned in my own contesting of the source-critical approach. that wherever possible I cite E. A. Speiser for the standard position: my reverence for this beloved teacher and scholar of genius should preclude any imputation of disrespect.

I had reference a few pages back to examples of unbeauteous elements in three parallel fields of art: asymmetry in visual art, dissonance in music, and incongruity in literature. An erroneous yet widely held assumption equates esthetics (the perception of beauty) with artistry (skillful achievement). One consequence of this equation is the attempt to distinguish between craft (rude or primitive art) on the one hand, and the fine arts on the other. The borrowed beauty of illuminations (as in medieval manuscripts) or printed illustrations will be separated out as excrescences to the proper poetic considerations of the literary craft. And it is likely that the diagrammed intricacies of a floor-plan in a detective story or the descriptions of high-technology engines in science fiction are in great measure responsible for the assignment of these genres to lower levels of literary art. Perhaps analogous to this last phenomenon is the habit of the modern mind to divide prose literature into separate and complementary sections, each section implicitly assignable to a higher or lower level of the artistic. Consider: fiction and history, the former almost nonexistent in the earliest centuries in prose form, the latter read generally for its informational content, and little attention given to such artistic considerations as the stylish elegance of Herodotus and the convoluted clumsiness of Thucydides, the flights of fancy in the former and the tediously uninstructive details in the latter. Consider: fiction and non-fiction, the former inclusive of short story and novel, drama and prose epic, the latter inclusive of essay, treatise, homily and tract, diaries, epistles, orations, legal opinions, chronicles and—that most recent bestseller—the cookbook.

In the case of Scripture generally, and particularly in regard to the Pentateuch, two factors have been the main contributors to its assignment to history rather than fiction and to the overlooking or slighting of its artistry. One is the modern and widespread notion that history has the property of truth, which fiction does not (a silly notion and one which, I believe, the authors of antiquity were too sophisticated to share). The other is the presence of concrete details, such as personal and geographic names, and the incorporation of such (along with notices of moral, legal, or cultic norms) into structures such as genealogies, hierarchies, and King Lists, tables of ethnic and national origins, chronologies detailing dates of birth and death for eponymous ancestors and family lines; ancestral figures being so unmemorable and for the most part so long dead as to suggest that their preservation can owe only to the historic element in that genre of mixed fiction and historiography that goes by the name *legend*.

That family trees and political rosters are not the stuff of esthetics is a proposition beyond question. A similar universal consent can probably be won for the proposition that while such lists may be de rigueur in the craft of historiography, they cannot but represent an artistic lapse on the part of a free-spirited author of fiction. And it is the confusion of the esthetics with the artistic that is responsible for this last, and mistaken, judgment. The artistry of the author of Genesis has to be judged in terms of how he deploys genealogical charts and chronologies, cultic and artifactual niceties, in the framework of narrative to achieve his overarching poetic ends. The problem lies not with the author of Genesis but with whoever undertakes to interpret his work. If we assume that Adam and Eve were intended as historical personages, whose lives were continued in the begettings of Seth and Cain (the line of Cain to die out before the tenth generation, the line of Seth to eventuate in every human alive today), and further, that the two lives are similarly significant as historical data, it is rather obvious that the assessment of artistic intent in the narrative will be nil. Even the finest writer on history cannot overcome the tediousness of history's dates or the sloppiness of its movements. If, on the other hand, the narratives in Genesis are essentially the product of an artistic imagination, how to account for the artistic lapse represented by these unedifying structures? My argument will be that the structures are not artistic lapses at all, that for all their lack of beauty or grace they disclose the artistry of the author, an artistry that is easily discerned in his deployment of metaphor in narrative but which fails of appreciation when the kerygma of the narrative is supplemented, refined, or reinforced by the author's ingenious exploitation of *structures as metaphors*.

To treat every chapter in Genesis in the kind of detail that characterizes the exegetical essays in *Toward a Grammar* would require several volumes, an enterprise beyond my present ambition. The reader is entitled to some explanation as to the selection of some sections and the omission of others, as to why some narratives are examined with word-for-word attention and others are treated to overviews. In large part the answer lies in an initial decision to begin at the beginning and end at a point where the biblical material itself comes to a logical rest. Thus the narratives given detailed treatment fall into two roughly even sections: chapters 1–11, the Primeval History as it is termed by scholars; and chapters 12–22, the story of Israel's early beginnings in its first ancestor Abraham, husband to Sarah and by her sire to Isaac.

The brief compass of narrative chapters that I could thus afford to treat contains within it a correspondingly small amount of "structuring data" such as genealogies, eponyms, and chronologies. The interpretations that we offer for the poetical function of these data are more often than not quite novel, a novelty that might well be resisted the more for the lack of mass of the data interpreted. Hence it is that we have gone quite beyond these twenty-two chapters of Genesis, including even the book of Exodus, to include structures which—in their variety, ingenuity, and imaginative whimsy—fill out the picture and strengthen our argument that these data are integral to the poetic design of the text, and are not, as geneticists would view them, historic data preserved over centuries and included by redactors to reinforce the historicity, authenticity, and literal truth of the narrative they had received.

Cincinnati, Ohio   H.C.B.
1996

CONTENTS

PART II   STRUCTURES

SUPPLEMENTS, CONCLUSIONS, ANTICIPATIONS

INTRODUCTION

CHAPTER ONE

+⊨—⊨+

THE NAMES OF GOD

The Problem: A Preliminary Review

The problem of the names of God in the Hebrew Scriptures is so complex that movements toward the solution may be impeded, distorted, or even blocked by its formulation in the singular. It would seem advisable then to begin this review of the problem by breaking it down into the separate and sometimes separable constituents of which the problem is compounded. (And as I attempt to list these component elements in a logical order, I must warn the reader not to assign relative weightiness to these elements in respect to the order in which they are listed.)

1. There is the lexical problem of the meaning and function of the English word *name* and the Hebrew word that it most often translates, *šem*. Both words are nouns (names), and both may stand for both common and proper nouns. As common nouns, the words *name* and *šem* may be governed by the definite article (or, in Hebrew, be determined by construction); as such, the noun *name* will be governed by the indefinite article in English and the noun *šem* will appear without determination in the Hebrew language, which has no indefinite article. The connotations of both common nouns, English and Hebrew, are (a/the) name, label, epithet, title, designation, and so on.

2. A second problem is that there is in Hebrew a declinable noun, *ᵉlōhīm*, which appears both as common noun (connoting god, deity, divinity, numen, divine figurine, an ancestral spirit or ghost, and so on), and as a proper noun, an alternate name for the one-and-only-deity whose most frequently occurring name is the grapheme YHWH. As common noun this noun is treated like all other such, and is

3

indefinite, or determined by article, possessive pronoun, or construction. As proper noun, without the definite article, it is rendered into English by *God*, which is to say that the common noun *god* is rendered in writing by capitalizing the first letter and in speech by the absence of any sign of determination. Thus the question of whether any occurrence of *ᵉlōhīm* refers to the common noun or the proper noun ("name") is determined in the Hebrew only by context, in English translation only by capitalization (or lack of it) in writing, and in English speech only by the presence or absence of determination. In keeping with this is the usage in regard to (1 Kings 11:33) *kᵉmoš ᵉlōhei mōᵃb* "Chemosh the god of Moab." And by the same token *yhwh ᵉlōhei yisrāʾel* should be rendered as "Yhwh the god of Israel." This is to say that whenever *ᵉlōhīm* is definite or determined in the Hebrew, its rendering into English should feature lower-case *g*. Thus, for example, in Psalm 68:9, *ᵉlōhīm ᵉlōhei yisrāʾel* should be rendered "God, the god of Israel," and the psalmist's address in 43:4 to *ᵉlōhīm ᵉlōhāy* by "O God, my god." Yet universal usage is quite contrary. Whenever the common noun *ᵉlōhīm* refers to the object of Israel's worship, by whatever (proper) name, the *g* is capitalized. Hence: "DN, the god of Ammon" but "DN, the God of Israel" or "DN, my God."

3. Closely related to this problem, the rendering of the common noun *ᵉlōhīm* "god" by the proper noun "God," is the rendering of *hāᵉlōhīm*—the common noun with prefixed definite article—as a proper noun, as though this term, too, is indistinguishable in nuance from the proper name ʾElōhīm. Thus, for example, Deuteronomy 7:9, where *YHWH ᵉlōhē(y)kā hūʾhāᵉelōhīm* "YHWH, your god, he [alone] is god" conveys an identificatory redundancy in the usual renderings, "(YHWH) the Lord your God is God."

Here again it is a token of reverence for the one and only true god of Israel that is expressed in the capitalization. Let us note that *the deity* in English usage applies to any of the gods in a pagan pantheon, while *the Deity* is another proper name for the only deity acknowledged as such in Scripture. While the capitalizing of a common noun governed by the definite article to form a proper noun in which the article is part of that proper noun is not in keeping with accepted grammatical usage, it is not, in English itself, critical for meaning. Thus, if we come across the words "It was an insult to the president," we immediately understand that the reference is to the chief magistrate of the United States and not to the executive presiding over any corporation. In the case of translation from biblical Hebrew, however, this practice may be misleading. The definite article in Hebrew functions in two quite different ways: to express abstraction (and distance) on the one hand, and individuation (and proximity) on the other. In respect to *hāᵉlōhīm*, the former function might be rendered by Heaven, Providence, godhead, (The) Deity or Divinity; the latter, expressing some agent, representation, or vessel of the former, might refer to an angel, apparition, numen, or the like.

4. In contrast to *ᵉlōhīm*, the common noun that also functions frequently as a or the proper name of the one and only god, is the proper name represented by the four letters *YHWH*. This grapheme, bespeaking "The Divine Name" (hence the capitalization in *the Tetragrammaton*) was never, until recent times, pronounced by knowledgeable students of the Bible. Before the now widespread assumption that the etymology of the Tetragrammaton has been retrieved and is correctly reflected

in *Yahweh*, this grapheme was generally rendered by *the Lord*, a convention owing to the vocable *ªdōnay* "my lordship," which is the way the Tetragrammaton is usually rendered when the text is read aloud according to the Masoretic tradition; the phonetic signal for this *qerē* being the vowels *šewa* (*ḥatef pataḥ*), *ḥolem*, and *qameṣ* (lengthened *pataḥ*), appearing under the first three letters of the Tetragrammaton to indicate the pointing of the vocable *dny* (*ªdōnāy*). (To be noted is the lengthening in the pointing of YHWH of the final *pataḥ* of *ªdōnāy* to *qameṣ*.)[1] Thus the transcription of the pointed Tetragrammaton is *YᵉHōWāH*. This textual phenomenon is referred to as a *qere perpetuum* despite a well-known and regular exception: whenever the Tetragrammaton is immediately preceded by the vocable *ªdōnāy* "my lord(s)" (plural of majesty), the preempting of the substitution by the appearance of the noun proper results in a secondary *qere perpetuum* for the Tetragrammaton: the pointing is now that of *ᵉlōhīm*, thus in transcription *YᵉHōWīH*. Related to this convention of vocalization in respect to the lengthening of the *pataḥ* to *qameṣ* in YHWH is the same lengthening in the consonantal *dny* when the reference is to YHWH, both when the Tetragrammaton does and does not appear. Thus, for example, in Genesis 15:2, in Abram's address, *ªdōnāy YHWH*; and in Genesis 18:3, 30, 31, and 32, where Abraham is the speaker and his address to Deity is in the singular, the final vowel sign is *qameṣ*, *ªdōnāy*. By contrast, in Genesis 19:3, where Lot addresses the two angels, YHWH agents, whom he takes to be human (as indicated by verbs and possessive pronouns in the plural) the final vowel of *dny* is the [normal] *pataḥ*.

5. The foregoing points to a number of questions, some general, some specific, in regard to the two terms that together function in the Hebrew Bible—in overwhelming preponderance to others—as names of the one and only god. Which of the two names is the older, which the younger? Is there an answer to this question in terms of logical or chronological necessity? Does Scripture itself raise this question or imply an answer (if the question itself is only implicit)? And does such an answer, if it appears, comport or contrast with our own sense of logical or temporal necessity? Given the prior existence of the one, how to account for the rise of the other? And why was the one name preserved in speech while the other was preserved in writing only, its original vocalization proscribed and an epithet for sovereignty prescribed as a substitute? And for all the effectiveness of Masoretic suppression, is there reason to credit the general consensus among Bible scholars that *Yahweh* represents a successful retrieval of both sense and pronunciation of a onetime vocable reduced by tabu-tradition to a sacred but unvoiced grapheme?

6. A final line of questioning focuses on the difficulties we face when we try to imagine why, how, and when the name of Israel's god, represented by the grapheme YHWH, was lost; why, how, and when the vocables *ªdōnāy* and *ᵉlōhīm* were substituted for it. Unique in the history of religions is this loss in speech and preservation in writing of *the* name of a people's god. And it is equally remarkable that neither in rabbinic literature nor in modern scholarship do we come across surmise as to when these substitutions for YHWH were first introduced. If we ourselves begin to speculate on this question we soon find ourselves asking some other questions, of equal or greater difficulty. Such as, how was YHWH pronounced before the substitution? Or, why a substitution in the first place? And when we ask this last question

we find ourselves recalling having been taught sometime, somewhere, by someone, that the substitution for YHWH is due to its having at some remote time in antiquity come to be regarded as too holy to pronounce. Our teacher, too, seems not to have known whether that moment when the Tetragrammaton became ineffable was in the days of David or of Nehemiah. And when, in search of a clue, we seek for a written source about this tradition of holy ineffability, we find that there is none, none whatsoever. And in the absence of a tradition written or oral, we are driven to further conjecture: how it came about that an entire people accepted the notion that one of its names for God had become too holy to pronounce. Was this by common assent, or was it imposed by authorities ecclesiastical wielding powers temporal? In either case, is it conceivable that a name that had been a commonplace should be wiped from universal memory, leaving no trace behind? (No, not quite, for the consonants were preserved in writing—only the vowels were erased from memory.) In the former case, the plausibility of memory suppression is, as one of my students suggested, akin to the attempt to go into a corner and think of anything but of a white elephant. In the latter case, given the history of religious denominations' failure to achieve unanimity on even minor points of doctrine, can we conceive of the successful consummation of such a decree without trace of a struggle against it?

A META-LITERARY ADDRESS TO THE PROBLEM: SOURCE-ANALYSIS

In the preface to this volume I note that rebuttal of source criticism—while it may be seen as a consequence of my approach—is not one of my principal objectives. The deployment in Scripture of various names or terms for deity (or Deity) or its agents is everywhere a challenge to poetical analysis and synthesis.[2] How, in terms of the development of a given text's kerygma,[3] does the choice of one or more of such names and terms operate? This is to say that the question of the use of these terms is a purely literary one. By contrast, however, the discernment of "sources" that were first identified according to their featuring of one or another term for Deity offers a *meta-literary solution*[4] to a literary problem (and thereby implicitly forecloses the search for a purely literary or poetic solution). Whether a text features *YHWH* or *Elōhīm* as the name for the One Deity of Scripture has, for the source analytic approach, no significance whatsoever in terms of meaning, nuance, emotional distance, or intimacy. There was a source that assumed that the name YHWH was always known to mankind, and which therefore freely uses it wherever it wishes. This source is labeled J. Two other sources existed whose authors were tied to a tradition that the name YHWH was not introduced to humankind until the time of Israel's impending liberation from Egyptian bondage. These sources therefore never feature the name YHWH until after the historic introduction of that name by Deity to Moses and, presumably, by Moses to Israel (Exodus 3:1–15 and Exodus 6:2–8). These sources are labeled E and P, respectively.

Inasmuch as the source hypotheses (except perhaps for J) essentially foreclose a poetic approach to the names of God, and further, inasmuch as the source hypotheses still constitute the regnant position in modern biblical study, it is advisable to clear the way for my poetical approach by first stating the principal difficulties that led me to turn away from source-criticism and to search for another approach.

1. Not infrequently, source-critics—who have developed many other criteria for distinguishing one document or source from another—will decide that the term YHWH does not belong in a given place where it appears. It is a J contamination or an erroneously permitted editorial substitution for Elōhīm in a P (or E) source.[5] Once every exceptional occurrence is dismissed as error, or even seen as proof of the contradictory rule, the entire rule becomes suspect, if not indeed ludicrous.[6] Needless to say this is a literary objection. More important, however, it is one of logic, of rational methodology.

2. The assumption that a source—let us say P—believed and taught a tradition that the name YHWH was not introduced until the time of Moses would not have excluded the use of the name YHWH by the narrator of P passages.[7] This narrator, living and writing long after the time of Moses, *does* know the Name and is free to make use of it. He must only take care, however, that the name not appear in dialogue—be it on the part of human, God, or God's agent—before the time of Moses. This objection is, again, both literary and logical. Even if the literary aspect is overlooked, the failure of genetic theory to bridge the gap between P's knowledge and a compulsion to enslave himself (pointlessly) to that knowledge disrupts its chain of reasoning.

3. If source-criticism would have us suppose that the preservation of the various names of God in various documents owes to the Redactor's respect for the texts' sanctity, then the Redactor was not himself disturbed by the contradiction within the texts as to the time of the Tetragrammaton's introduction to Israel (and to humanity). And strange though this may strike us in itself, as he was not disturbed by this, he would not have anticipated disturbance on the part of any reader. He would therefore have let the texts speak for themselves without either drawing attention to the contradiction or attempting to gloss or paper over it. In that case, however, how to explain the celebrated sentence that constitutes the second part of Genesis 4:26: "Then did they (mankind) first call upon the name of YHWH." This sentence, coming immediately after the notice of the birth of Enos to Seth, has distracted scholarly attention from the real problem by raising questions about the point of this Name's introduction in the lifetime of the otherwise unremarkable Enos. The factitiousness of these questions lies in limiting the connection between the Name by which Deity was invoked to the last mentioned human, Enos, a name that—like Adam—has the sense of mankind/humankind. The point of the sentence is, however, that the Name came into use in the earliest generations of humankind, the generation of Cain and Seth and, to be sure—see 4:1—their parents, Adam and Eve.

But who penned this notice? It could not have been J himself, for he never betrays any knowledge of a tradition that is in conflict with his own, and hence would have discerned no reason to make explicit what he assumed to be the universal fact (or tradition). But neither does it make sense to attribute the notice to the Redactor, who would thereby be underscoring, by making explicit, the contradiction between this J assumption and the conflicting assumptions implicit or explicit in chapters 3 and 6 of Exodus.

4. Perhaps the most telling objection to source criticism's use of the names of God will derive from what we noted to be the implicit assumption of this approach: that is, that the problem is properly defined as between the appearances of two terms, both assumed to be proper nouns or proper names, YHWH and 'Elōhīm. This double assumption flies in the face of the following facts:

a. While YHWH is, indeed, a proper name, the same cannot be said with equal truth for *ᵉlōhīm*. Since this last term is normally rendered in translations by *God* (note, with a capitalized initial letter), such renderings may indicate the presence of a proper noun in places where no proper noun is at all present in the Hebrew.

b. Even if we eliminate from consideration every usage of *ᵉlōhīm* where it may not be a proper noun, there is still a third alternative to YHWH and 'Elōhīm, and that is the latter term with the prefixed definite article *hāᵉlōhīm*. Despite the normally improper use of the definite article with a proper noun, the normal assumption that the presence of the definite article before a term will be followed by an uncapitalized noun (i.e., *the god* and not *the God*),[8] there can be no question that in such instances as Genesis 5:24 *hāᵉlōhīm* is a proper name (as guaranteed by the singular verb) and can only be rendered by *God*. Hence in addition to YHWH always and *ᵉlōhīm* ('Elōhīm) frequently, we have a third "name" for God.

c. In addition to these three terms for God, there are other proper names for Deity, such as 'El Shaddai, 'El 'Elyon, 'El 'Olam, Shaddai, 'Elyon, *Paḥad Yiṣḥaq*, and *ᵃbīr Yaᵃkob*, as well as other rubrics for Deity's manifestation, such as angel, messenger of YHWH, or 'Elōhīm, and the common noun *'el*, both with and without the definite article.

d. It is a blatant and capricious disregard for the data in the texts before us to assign Genesis 2:4b–3:24 to an author who freely uses the Tetragrammaton as the normal term for Deity. For in this pericope nothing can be clearer than that the narrator is committed, not to YHWH, but to the strange compound *YHWH-'Elōhīm* as the name, the proper name, of Deity. This regularity, in contrast with the use of 'Elōhīm in the preceding pericope and of YHWH in the following one, is clearly marked as the intention of the author/narrator by his equally regular use of 'Elōhīm alone in the dialogue between Eve and the Serpent in 3:1–5.

In conclusion, then, any theory that would attempt a classification of phenomena on the basis of two different exemplars when eight or nine are present would appear as arbitrarily based as it is bound to be deemed shaky. The wealth of the database as concerns the terms and names for Deity in the first twenty-two chapters of Genesis, as well as hints as to possible approaches to these data, are presented for the readers' consideration in table 1-1.

AN ESSENTIALLY LITERARY ADDRESS TO THE PROBLEM: CASSUTO

The one notable and essentially poetical address to this problem is that of Umberto Cassuto, who systematically criticized the documentary hypotheses in *La Questione della Genesi* and in *The Documentary Hypothesis* (English translation of an essay in Hebrew). Rather than extrapolate his views from these works I will let him speak for himself, in citations from his sketchy remarks in the Introduction to his *Commentary on Genesis*. Referring to his earlier works he writes:

TABLE 1-1 Names of Deity in Context in Genesis 1–22

Text	Y (NAR.)	Y (DIAL.)	E (NAR.)	E (DIAL.)	E (W. ART)	YE	Y W. ANGEL	E W. ANGEL	Y W. ŠEM	Y W. BᵉŠEM	ᵉEL ŠADDAI	ᵉEL ᵉELYON	ᵉEL ᶜOLAM
1:1–2:4a			34										
2:4b–3:24	8			4		20							
4:1–24	1	1											
4:25–26					1					1			
5:1–32		1	3		2								
6:1–8	5				2								
6:9–22			3		2								
7:1–8:22	5		5										
9:1–17			6										
9:18–29		1		1	1								
10:1–32	2												
11:1–9	4												
12:1–20	7												
13:1–18	4												
14:1–24	1	1								1		4	
15:1–21	4	3										4	
16:1–21	2	1					4		1				
17:1–27	1		6	1						1	1		
18:1–33	7	3											
19:1–38	3	3	2		2								
20:1–18	1		2	2	2								
21:1–21	2		6	2				1					
21:22–34				2					1				1
22:1–24	3	3		3			2						

KEY: Y: Tetragrammaton; E: ᵉlōhîm; YE: YHWH-ᵉlōhîm; w: with; art.: definite article; NAR.: Narrator's voice; DIAL.: voice in dialogue; Numerals: number of occurrences

I have already shown . . . that the variation in the employment of the two names, YHWH and 'Elōhīm in the book of Genesis is subject to certain rules which I have been able to determine and formulate with precision. These rules are based on the difference in the nature of the two names, for they are not of the same type; the name YHWH is a proper noun that denotes specifically the God of Israel, whereas 'Elōhīm was originally a generic term and became a proper noun among the Israelites through the realization that there is only One God and that YHWH alone is 'Elōhīm ["God"].⁹

A study of this citation (which I shall resume in a moment), as well as of his running commentary on the text of Genesis, will convince many, I believe, that both in his address to the names and in his criticism of source hypotheses, Cassuto deserves a better fate than the impression that his work has made (or rather, not made) upon biblical scholarship. The reasons for this are worthy of research, if for no other reason than to attempt to isolate the factors that render a regnant hypothesis in a disciplined area of study impervious to powerful and reasoned attack. In regard to the citation that follows and to the execution of his schema in his commentary, I suspect that Cassuto has undermined his own potential to persuade by leading his readers to anticipate (see above, his "certain rules . . . formulate with precision") that a poetical problem is readily soluble on the basis, so to speak, of a precise formula. Literary artists work with metaphors, and precise as a given metaphor may be, it may express a completely different idea in a second context (though it may be formally identical), while exactly the same idea may be expressed in a second place by an altogether different metaphor.

Let us continue now with the Cassuto citation (the italics are Cassuto's):

Following are some of the rules governing the use of the two Names in the book of Genesis that emerged from my investigations:

(a) The Tetragrammaton occurs when Scripture reflects the concept of God, especially in His *ethical* aspect, that belongs *specifically to the people of Israel*; 'Elōhīm appears when the Bible refers to the abstract conception of God that was current in the international circles of the Sages, the idea of God conceived in a general sense as the Creator of the *material* world, as the Ruler of nature, and as Source of life.

(b) The name YHWH is used when Scripture wishes to express that direct and intuitive notion of God that is characteristic of the unsophisticated faith of the multitude; but 'Elōhīm is employed when it is intended to convey the concept of the philosophically minded who study the abstruse problems connected with the world and humanity.

(c) YHWH appears when the Bible presents the Deity to us in His personal character and in direct relationships to human beings or to nature; whereas 'Elōhīm occurs when Holy Writ speaks of God as a Transcendental Being, who stands entirely outside nature, and above it.

I believe that I understand the poetical distinctions that Cassuto is getting at in these three paragraphs, and furthermore I am in essential agreement with them. But there are ambiguities in the above formulations that render them vulnerable to quibble or to rebuttal. For example, in (a) "the concept of God, especially in His *ethical* aspect" may indeed be what the biblical author has in mind in many a place where he uses the Tetragrammaton (in preference to another name), but it is both gratuitous and a meta-literary assumption of debatable value to narrow this usage to a "concept of God . . . that belongs *specifically* to the people of Israel." For example, the Tetragrammaton is featured regularly and pointedly in God's relations with the non-Israelite Balaam (Numbers 22:8, 13, 18, 19, 22, 24, 31–32, 34–35), and indeed with his non-Israelite ass (22:23–28—note especially this last instance!).[10] Unambiguous, on the other hand, but equally gratuitous is "the abstract conception of God" expressed in 'Elōhīm being assigned to "the international circles of the Sages," entities whose very existence in the world of the biblical authors is comparable to the sometime existence of the unicorn. Similarly, in (b) the name YHWH may indeed be "used when Scripture wishes to express . . . [a] direct and intuitive notion of God," but why should that notion be "characteristic of the unsophisticated faith of the multitude"? A final example, vis-à-vis (c): the YHWH to whom the sphere of heaven is reserved while that of earth is allotted to humankind in Psalm 115:16 is both "a Transcendental Being, who stands entirely outside nature, and above it" (cf. also Psalm 24:1)—the denotation of 'Elōhīm for Cassuto—and "the Deity . . . in His personal character, and in direct relationship to human beings or to nature."

The weaknesses I have pointed out in Cassuto's formulations lie then in an overprecise formulation of the "rules governing the use of the two Names in the book of Genesis" and the reading of these two names as dichotomous categories when they may in many or most cases overlap in nuance, intention, and extension.[11] If we keep in mind that a similar distinction and overlap as well exist in English terms for the same noumenon, we shall—having freed ourselves of the source-critical incubus—be open to the subtle nuances of the biblical author's shift from YHWH to 'Elōhīm or vice versa, or from either of these two names to "angel of" one or the other, or to *hā'elōhīm* "the divine agent" or "Heaven," and the like. I will note also how these various terms figure differently in various voices: that of the narrator; those of humans in dialogue with humans, with God, or those of non-Israelites according to their association with the people of Israel and this people's ancestral figures, or such humans as outsiders of the Israelitic or proto-Israelitic continuum. We shall recognize the various nuances that Cassuto picked up (but not as invariables in equations and formulas) in the name YHWH as essentially personal, relating in particular intimacy with Israelite forebears or pre-Abrahamitic exemplars of His beloved, though oft erring, human creations; this in contrast with 'Elōhīm as often less than personal, sometimes almost an abstraction, the Cause of all phenomena—nature and the animate denizens of earth—and in dialogue with humans outside the Abrahamitic continuum or within that continuum, but to wives or children in roles foreshadowing lines ancillary to the chosen branch. We shall also be able to discern how these various aspects or modalities of the Divine in relation to creation and creatures can appear in a single narrative in shifts from YHWH to 'Elōhīm and vice versa. These promises we hope to fulfill in the poetical treatments of the narratives which constitute the bulk of the chapters that follow.

THE NAMES OF GOD IN NONNARRATIVE TEXTS AND
THE "EVOLUTION" OF BIBLICAL MONOTHEISM

It is historical fact that source criticism begins with the *discernment* of a dichotomous distribution or deployment of the names Elohim and YHWH in the early
chapters of Genesis; that the discernment of authors labeled Elohist and Jehovist,
later of sources labeled E and P and J and D, derived primarily from narrative texts
in the books constituting the Pentateuch or Hexateuch; that legal, prescriptive,
and chronological texts not identifiable by the criteria of divine names were assigned to one or another source based on derived criteria, these being stylistic or
thematic; that source identification was at an early stage followed by a chronological ordering of the sources. It is furthermore true that very little of source critical
research or thinking is in evidence in respect to the narrative (prose) and poetic
texts in the Writing Prophets or in the Book of Psalms.

I have earlier suggested as a criticism of the source-analytical address to the
problem of the names of God within Genesis that it restricts itself to the two most
common names when many other alternatives exist alongside them. I would now
supplement that suggestion with this further one: any address to a single problem
that limits itself to a small percentage of the text under study (i.e., the Hebrew
Scriptures) risks the question as to whether it is not *methodologically* flawed. Inasmuch as my own investigation in these chapters is largely confined to the narratives in less than half of Genesis and a few in Exodus, it behooves me to acknowledge that my own address is vulnerable to the very same strictures. In mitigation of
my own vulnerability I would plead the following: my own address claims to be no
more than a beginning, and offers only a literary or poetical hypothesis that stands
to be further tested, refined, and (possibly) rebutted as it is pursued in the great
mass of untreated texts. This, in contrast to the source-analytical address that has
been content to make of its hypotheses the sure base for methodological approach
to all of Scripture, even while it ignores the problem in the psalter or prophetic
writings.

In my own address to the deployment of other names of God in the Genesis narratives I will perforce have to have reference to such names in the psalter. I will
also have to deal (in less than exhaustive measure) with the question of the stage
of monotheistic religion reflected in the Genesis narratives. Psalm 82 is an exemplary psalm in which both these concerns are prominent. Yet this psalm falls into
an aggregate (Psalms 42–83) that in modern critical research is often referred to as
the Elohistic Psalter, or to cite a colleague who does not subscribe to source-criticism,
"the elohistic group, which as an entity is characterized by a rather late change of
most occurrences of YHWH to *Elohim*."[12] Before I go on to address Psalm 82 I have
deemed it advisable to present an excursus on the distribution of the two names in
Psalms.

EXCURSUS: ON THE NAMES OF GOD IN THE PSALTER

As is well known, the biblical psalter is divided into five books according to rabbinic tradition, a tradition whose antiquity is attested by the LXX "version."[13] In

TABLE 1-2   Distribution of YHWH and Elohim in the Psalter

Book	Psalms	YHWH	Elohim
I	1–41	272 times	14 times
II	42–72	30 times	164 times
IIIa	73–83	13 times	36 times
b	84–89	31 times	7 times
IV	90–106	exclusively	0 times
V	107–150	exclusively (108)	1 time

table 1-2, a chart of the distribution of the terms YHWH and Elohim, the division of Book Three into two sections helps show why Psalms 42–83 have been designated as *elohistic*. The contrast between this elohistic aggregation of psalms and those preceding and following it is sharpened when we consider the following: Of the fourteen occurrences of *Elohim* in Book I, only five or six can be considered as instances of the proper name, for in all the other instances the term is featured in an attributive mode. Further, of the seven instances of Elohim in IIIb., only two or three appear to be the proper noun. Hence the occurrences of the proper noun YHWH are in overwhelming preponderance in Psalms, except for Psalms 42–83, where the proper name Elohim occurs in similar preponderance as against the Tetragrammaton. Now while there is no way to demonstrate that most of the appearances of Elohim in 42–83 represent "a . . . change of *YHWH* to *Elohim*," the plausibility of such a change—or rather, substitution—is enhanced by the appearance of the two proper names in two psalmic deuterographs: Psalm 14:2, 4, 7 features YHWH, while Psalm 53:3, 5, 7 features Elohim. Psalm 40:14 features YHWH twice and verse 17 does so once, while verse 18 features consonantal *ᵃdōnāy*. In the parallel verses in Psalm 70, verse 2 features Elohim once and YHWH once; verses 5 and 6 feature Elohim (although the end of verse 6 features YHWH where the corresponding verse 40:18 features *ᵉlōhay* "my god").

That Elohim as a proper noun, a name of the one god of Scripture, is preceded in time by the name YHWH is beyond question. But the very question of when and how biblical Israel began to worship her god as the only god, and by what name (or names), is a thorny one to which I will devote a brief—and admittedly partisan—sketch.

ON THE EVOLUTION OF BIBLICAL MONOTHEISM

While not a necessary concomitant of the source critical approach in terms of logic or the history of scholarship, the chronological and evolutionary thrust of the Graf-Wellhausen Documentary Hypothesis has provided a congenial framework for various theses about the development of the God-concept in the writings that constitute the Hebrew Scriptures, from the periods of patriarchs and Judges to those of kings and prophets, and priests presiding theocratically in a shrunken Judean state. For the first few decades of our century the fashion of savants was to find animistic

concepts in the earliest stages of biblical history, and then in chronological progression unadorned polytheism, then henotheism and/or monolatry, and finally—
not until such late writings as Second Isaiah—a monotheism closely resembling
our own. Thus Yehezkel Kaufmann was the cause of some stir when word reached
scholarly circles (this in the 1940s, when few scholars could read modern Hebrew)
that in his *History of Israelite Religion* he was making bold to find the origin of biblical monotheism in the period of the exodus some seven centuries or more before
the exilic prophets. As a matter of fact, Kaufmann actually dated that phenomenon much earlier, for by the time of the exodus he finds monotheism as the general
religious heritage of the Israelite tribes that had left Egypt. And in 1964 in the Anchor Bible volume on Genesis, E.A.Speiser argued that our knowledge of Mesopotamian culture in the middle of the second millennium pointed to Abraham as
the earliest pioneer of that monotheistic surge that he calls "the biblical process."[14]
It is likely then that some biblicists will find it fitting, and others amusing, that I, a
student of Speiser, find precursors of biblical monotheism in revolutionary critiques
of polytheism in pagan Mesopotamia and Egypt.[15]

However that may be, and persuasive or not in the judgment of my readers, I
would underscore that I arrived at this conclusion on the basis of a poetical reading
of the literature of Egypt and Mesopotamia and not, as is common to all my predecessors, on the basis of an ascription of either historiographic intent or authentic
"historical memory" to the biblical authors. In this connection, it may be permissible to quote Speiser, keeping in mind that I do him less than justice by removing
this brief citation from its well-reasoned context:

> As a drastic departure from existing norms, the concept of monotheism had to break
> new ground. There had to be a first time, and place, and person or group of persons.
> . . . Furthermore, the author of the narrative about Abraham's call did not get his in-
> formation from a researcher's files. And he could not have obtained it from cuneiform
> texts since, even if his scholarship matched his literary genius, the documents from
> the pertinent period had by J's time been covered up for centuries, and were to remain
> buried for nearly three thousand years more. J could have gotten his material only
> from earlier Israelite traditions, which in turn reached back all the way to patriarchal
> times.[16]

True, "the biblical narrator could have gotten his material only from earlier Israelite traditions"—but only if his narrative were intended as historiography, that
is, a literally true revelation by a true Deity revealing His True and Unique Divine
Nature—which is never (at least, explicitly) the content of any of these revelations—to a literally true ancestor named Abram, of a yet-to-be multitudinous seed
that will be known not as Abrahamites but as Jacobites or Israelites. And, let us
note that by the cuneiform "documents from the pertinent period" that were no
longer available to J, Speiser has in mind theoretical historic documents about
Abraham, not such literary works as Gilgamesh and *Enuma elish*, which for centuries were read regularly between the two rivers in one form or another.[17]

My skepticism about the historiographic reading of biblical narrative is but a
mild stricture (deriving from my poetic methodology) compared to my quarrel with
the suppositions of progressive movements, from crude forerunners of true biblical

religion in chronologically early layers of biblical tradition to realization of a noble monotheism in late layers of that tradition. For this kind of supposition asks us to believe the following: an editor who knew how true and sophisticated were the theological teachings of a Deuteronomist or a Deutero-Isaiah, and who could not but know how fallacious and naïve were the concepts in earlier writings, which were hangovers from a pagan idolatrous past, yet so reverenced these fallacious traditions as holy that he preserved them out of a slavish filial piety, with the serendipitous result (not intent, of course) that scholars two and a half millennia later might retrace the evolution of Israelite monotheism from such beliefs as must have been held by the hero-of-faith ancestor Israel who chased after numina, whom he worshiped after besting them in night-long struggle.[18]

Perhaps it is not out of order to observe that the question of what constitutes pure or non-idolatrous monotheism has not been settled to universal satisfaction to this day: When, within one biblical tradition, the adherents of one denomination may regard the veneration of saints or trinitarian formulations of Godhead in a sister-denomination as essentially pagan; when within another biblical tradition the adherents of one denomination may regard the beliefs in angels and demons as pagan elements in the ritual-and-magic-obsessed practices of a mother-denomination, how can we come to a conclusion as to where on the polytheistic to monotheistic spectrum to place one or another layer of Scriptural text (assuming that such layers can be demonstrated to exist)? Since, therefore, all but the most abstract and philosophical of theologies include various instrumentalities of Deity as entities within the natural or supernatural realms or straddling the two, a meaningful definition of monotheism would be one that could serve for a system of belief that is roughly the same in Scripture at large as in the latest formulations of Scripture-derived religions. Such a definition would eschew the ontological question of Divinity's agencies and representations as human or superhuman, semi-divine or divine, natural, preternatural, or supernatural. It would recognize monotheism as a theology that admits of only one autonomous ultimate power and will upon whom all other powers and wills are dependent for their existence and exercise. Hardly a passage in Scripture can be read as necessarily contradictory to such a view, and the biblical expression of this view is essentially expressed in the metaphors of Psalm 82, which pointedly uses ʾel and ʾĕlōhīm for the common noun god(s) and the proper noun God, despite the confusion that such ambiguity invites, and just as pointedly uses the name ʾElyōn ("All High/Most High") rather than YHWH:

(1) God (ʾĕlōhīm) stands forward in the Council Divine (ʾel), speaks indictment (špṭ) in the body of the gods (ʾĕlōhīm):

(2) "How long yet will you exercise nefarious judgment (špṭ), showing favorable bias to malefactors?

(3) [My charge to you was,]
Take up the cause (špṭ) of the weak and the orphaned,
Uphold the right(s) of underprivileged and dispossessed!

(4) Exonerate the weak and the needy,
Deliver them from malefactors' clutch!"

(5) [Turns His back on them]

"They show no awareness, no understanding,
They proceed ever in night-darkness—
(So that) the very foundations of the world are disintegrating."

(6) [Turns back to them]
"My decree it was, *gods* (*ᵉlōhīm*) you are,
Verily, vassals of ˈElyon . . .

(7) [Alack then] like mortal man shall you die,
Yes, fall from grace like any official."

(8) [The Psalmist:]
"Proceed then, O God (*ᵉlōhīm*), Yourself give judgment for the world,
For You alone acknowledge all nations as your own." (Psalm 82)

ON TERMS FOR DIVINITY, COMMON AND PROPER

Even if this psalm were not included in that body called the Elohist Psalter, few would argue my assumption that the first use of *ᵉlōhīm* in verse 1 of the psalm and then again in verse 8 represents a studied avoidance of the name YHWH. And it is beyond the scope of our present study to take up here (as elsewhere in the Elohist Psalter) the poetic implications of deploying *Elōhīm* "God" in two instances where the name YHWH would seem most in place (verses 1 and 8). But the implicit presence of the One Divine Creator persona identifiable by name is unarguable in verse 6 in the asseveration that the *ᵉlōhīm* "gods" are the *bᵉnē ˈElyōn* "sons or vassals of ˈElyōn." Here we should not expect the Tetragrammaton, for we never have "sons" in construct with YHWH, as we do twice (Genesis 6:2, 4) with *hāᵉlōhīm* "supernal beings," and so also twice in Job (1:6; 2:1), where they come to stand in attendance upon YHWH, and once in Job 38:7 with *ᵉlōhīm*; and once with *Elḥay* (Hosea 2:1), where the countless Israelites who had formerly been repudiated by YHWH under the rubric "Not-My-People" will be spoken of as "children of the *Living God*."

The anomalous juxtaposition in Psalm 82 of *ᵉlōhīm* in the senses of both *gods* and *God* provides us, nevertheless, with a springboard into our discussion of the terms *ᵉlōhīm* and YHWH; for the linguistic phenomenon in English of *god* (and *gods*) and *God* is a function of its matrix phenomenon in biblical Hebrew. That is to say, *god* (in English) and *ᵉlōhīm* (in Hebrew) are both common nouns, that is, terms for a class of beings or for one or more members of that class. Yet *God* (in English) is always a proper noun and *ᵉlōhīm* is also—more often than not—a proper noun, which is to say a designation for a particular divine person, one who is most often represented by a different proper noun or proper name, YHWH. Now it is clear that there is only one YHWH, although there may be (in human minds at least), many gods. But it is equally clear that there is only one God (for this name no more admits a plural than does YHWH), although there may be (in human minds, at least) many gods. YHWH, however, might be (in human minds, at least) one of many gods, whereas even in my English rendering of Psalm 82, we can speak of God speaking up in *the midst of the assembly of gods* but not *in the assembly of Gods.* There is only one God, as there is only one YHWH. And this is because as YHWH in Scripture is the One and Only Transcendent member of the logical class "god," so is God another name, a proper name, for that same One and Only Transcendent member of the class of gods. The difference then between God and god is that the former is a class that has but one member, while the latter is a class with many. The gods of the latter class are superhuman or supernatural in one sense or another, but none of them is in the class of (the Transcendent) God. As intricate or simple as the foregoing may be judged to be, it all adds up to something so obvious as to go unremarked and, because unremarked, lost to our consciousness. The proper noun God is ontologically (linguistically speaking) not so much a product as it is a witness of monotheistic thinking, as in Exodus 6:2–3 YHWH is declared by (that) God to be his (only, in some sense or other, proper) name.

This brings me to reconsider and modify my earlier statement that a proper noun does not, properly speaking, admit of qualification by the definite article, or—for that matter—by an indefinite article. We do, as a matter of fact, apply grammatical articles to proper nouns; but let us note that in all such cases the proper noun is present not as an indication of the particular person, place, or thing, but as a *representation* in time or thought or art of that proper noun. Thus, for example, *a Cleopatra* who could bring *a Caesar* to his knees, *an Earth* that could become a lifeless waste, *the Richard III* of Shakespeare or of history. Analogous to this linguistic usage is *the God* of Scripture or *the God* of the Scholastics, where both proper nouns bespeak a Sole Deity, albeit differently represented, or *the God* of Aristotle, but never *the God of paganism*. And, similarly, we can imagine a modern biblicist drawing distinctions between *the YHWH of Noah's flood* and *Hosea's YHWH*.

The absence of capital letters in Hebrew makes it possible for Scripture to engage in fanciful and philosophical plays on the term *ᵉlōhīm* that must be lost in English renderings, where the translator has no choice but to opt for upper or lower case *g* or for one or another of *ᵉlōhīm's* many connotations. Thus, for example, in contrast to *ᵉlōhīm* (or *ʾElōhīm*, as I would transcribe it) as a proper name, God, is the use of *ᵉlōhīm* with the affixed definite article. On the one hand it may be a signal that the narrator, though speaking of the One and Only Deity, wants to deemphasize or distance himself from the personhood of that Deity, the definite article serving as the *he* of abstraction, and expressive of the nuance we achieve in English by such terms as Heaven, Providence, Deity, the Divinity. On the other hand, with the emphasis on *ᵉlōhīm* as a common noun, inclusive of non-mortal entities such as ghosts, numina, or angels, the article in *hāᵉlōhīm* can be the *he* of individuation and proximity—*the* (or *this*) entity representative of God (or YHWH). Thus wherever we come across *hāᵉlōhīm* we must realize that we are not faced with a stylistic variation on the name God as opposed to the name YHWH, for all that the apparition truly represents the One and Only Deity.

THE NAMES ʾELŌHĪM AND YHWH

As I suggested earlier, the explanation offered by the genetic or source approaches of the deployment of YHWH and Elohim is a meta-literary solution to a literary problem, and one that makes little sense in terms of simple logic or poetic operation. These approaches confuse literature and history, read all literature as if it is intended as historiography, and retroject into unrecorded—hence irretrievable—past traditions supposedly inherited by these separate sources, such as the moment in historic time when the name YHWH was introduced to Israel. I will soon examine the pericopes in Exodus 3 and 6 that are cited as evidence for the supposition that two of three sources (E and P) had inherited these sacrosanct traditions, hence themselves eschewed the use of the name YHWH that was admittedly known to them, while the third source (J) had inherited a conflicting tradition that ascribed knowledge of the name YHWH to the first generations of humankind. But if, for the sake of argument, we put aside our objections and ask why Scripture should have been concerned with the names of Deity at all, we shall realize a monstrous self-contradiction in source-hypothesis. Since *ᵉlōhīm* in Genesis 1:1 is not a common noun, neither "a god" nor "(the) gods" but a proper name "God," which of the two names—Elōhīm or YHWH—is the older? If P (the author of Genesis 1) avoids the name YHWH until the time of Moses, when it was first introduced, then his non-avoidance of Elohim would indicate that for P this *name* was already known before that time. But this generic term as a proper name could only have come into being at the end of that evolving process of biblical monotheism that is posited by source hypothesis! Hence we have the ludicrous logic of the youngest source, P, using the youngest *name* at the beginning of "the Primeval History" so that it may avoid the older name YHWH, and this as if oblivious to the existence of an older source (J—older by quite a few centuries) that has a conflicting tradition; an older source that must have been leading a subterranean existence until it emerged sometime after P to be set alongside it by R (the redactor). And all this is utterly unnecessary, for the P (note the definite article with a proper name!) of Exodus 6:2–3 who has YHWH declaring to Moses that he appeared to the patriarchs as ʾEl Shaddai could have used (in place of ʾElōhīm) that same proper name for the Deity, or, for that matter, almost any of the other terms or names for him (e.g., ʾEl, hāʾel, ʾEl ʾElyon, ʾElyon, Shaddai, ʾElōhᵃ) that were not first introduced to Moses.

A poetical address to the names of Scripture's Deity, granting that the books of the Hebrew Bible are the result of an editorial process that brought together the products of at least three centuries (Amos-Malachi, c. 760–460), would nevertheless assume an essentially stable and developed monotheism for that entire period. Hence, it would see in YHWH and ʾElōhīm two proper names for Israel's Deity; one, Israel's label for its national Deity, who is also the One Deity of Creation and History, nature and humankind (like Marduk and Aššur in the creation theologies of Babylon and Assyria); the other, the transformation of a common noun into a proper name expressive of the idea that, the common noun having but one member, that noun is more a particular than a genus. But language is extremely conservative, and old usages would not be erased from speech or memory for all their having become otiose from a purely philosophical point of view. As such, the various names and combinations of names for Deity would be available to authors and editors, poets and historians, to express various aspects of the One Divinity.

Even such a source critic as Speiser, who does not look for an evolutionary process distinguishing the YHWH of J from the Elohim of E or P, can reach the following essentially poetical awareness: "the term [Elohim] can also be used, by virtue of its general connotation, not only for alien gods and idols but also in the broader sense of our 'Providence, Heaven, Fate,' and is actually so attested in the J source among others."[19] A poetical distinction, too, is the ancient rabbinic suggestion that YHWH is more expressive of God's attribute of mercy, while Elōhīm is preponderantly expressive of His attribute of justice. The rabbis, of course, knew their Scripture at least as well as we do, and such egregious appearance of YHWH in quid pro quo retribution contexts (such as Exodus 32:35, Deuteronomy 28:20–68) could not have escaped their notice. The distinction, therefore, is in the terse style characteristic of the rabbis, a hint as to how we should look for different nuances in the varying expressions for God.

Let us now attempt a poetic treatment of two critical texts that feature the name YHWH and its introduction into ancient Israel's tradition.

YHWH INTRODUCES HIMSELF BY NAME

Two passages in Exodus feature a revelation of Deity to Moses, at the center of which is a declaration, implicit in one case, explicit in the other, that the Tetragrammaton is being introduced to Israel for the first time. Inasmuch as source criticism had early discerned three sources in Genesis, one deploying and two eschewing the Tetragrammaton, it would seem inevitable that these two passages in Exodus be assigned to one or the other of the latter two. As we will see, in the first of these two passages (in Exodus 3), the name YHWH appears in the voice of the narrator before this name is disclosed. Fortunately for the source-critical enterprise, it had already determined that the YHWH-eschewing source labeled E (for *ᵉlōhīm* or Elohist, let us recall) had become so inextricably intertwined with J that it was futile to attempt to untangle all the elements in a narrative that originally owed to the one or the other. Therefore, in the JE narrative in Exodus 3 the introduction of the name YHWH is E's, compounded by snippets from J (i.e., where YHWH appears but should not), and the introduction of the name YHWH in Exodus 6 is—by default—P's. (There are further claims as to different stylistic pointers to E versus P that altogether defy this reader's critical eye and ear.)[20] Aside from the critical function of these two Exodus passages in the genetic approach, these two passages are worthy of poetical study in the interest of discerning the variety of reasons a biblical author would opt to deploy *malʾak YHWH* and *hāᵉlōhīm* for representatives of Deity, and to use YHWH or Elohim as names of Deity, all in a single context.

1. At the (Non) Burning Bush: Episode A

(1) Moses, now, was shepherding the flocks of his father-in-law Jethro, priest of Midian. He drove the flocks deep into the steppe, and reached Horeb, the Mount of God. (2) YHWH's angel appeared to him as a fiery flame from the depth of a certain bush. He caught sight, yes—the bush there ablaze with fire, yet the bush intact, unconsumed. (3) Thought Moses, "I must turn aside and inspect this wondrous phenomenon! How is it the bush is not burned away?" (4) When YHWH noted that he was turning aside for a closer look, Divinity [*ᵉlōhīm*] called to him from the bush's core, "Moses!" "Yes-s-s-sir," said he. (5) "Approach no closer," He said, "Remove your shoes from your feet, for the spot upon which you are standing is holy ground." (6)[And in this address] He said, "I am the God of your father, yes the God of Abraham, the God

of Isaac and the God of Jacob." Thereupon Moses cloaked his face, fearful of gazing upon the godhead [hāᵉlōhīm].

(7) YHWH then said, "Long have I viewed the affliction of My people there in Egypt, and heard their cry against their taskmasters. Well do I know his pain. (8) And it is to deliver him from Egypt that I have come down, and to lead him up from that land to a land fertile and spacious, a land oozing milk and honey, even the place of [or, even to replace] Canaanite, and Hittite, and Amorite, Perizzite, Hivvite and Jebusite. (9) Now then, here is the plaint of the Israelites come for My audience, and I, having noted the oppression which Egyptians are imposing upon them.— (10) Now then, bestir yourself that I may dispatch you to Pharaoh; free now My people, the Israelites, from Egypt." (11) Moses said to the Divinity [hāᵉlōhīm], "Who am I to go to the Pharaoh, and to free the Israelites from Egypt?" (12) He said, "Just so! I AM [am] with you. And here's the sign for you that it is I Who have sent you: when you have brought the people free from Egypt, you will all worship the godhead [et-hāᵉlōhīm] at this very mountain." (Exodus 3:1–12)

Light and heat are qualities or attributes of fire, not metaphors for it. But fire standing for love or for power is a metaphor. The burning candle as a metaphor for self-sacrificial love, burning up its own substance to give light to others, is a deep metaphor as, in a sense, it is almost obvious. The metaphor of the flame within the burning bush has long been recognized as one of the most imaginative and profound of Scripture's metaphors. Recognized, but without elucidation of its unique poetic function in this specific context. Fire as the most powerful of God-given tools is the climactic summation in Exodus 35:3 of the prohibition of work on YHWH's Sabbath: "You shall kindle/feed no fire in any of your settlements on the Sabbath Day." Here, the fire within the bush—for whatever else it may symbolize—bespeaks the awesome transcendent Power of Deity made Immanent yet unscathing in the lowly fragile bush. But this flame here is YHWH's malʾak, a numen that, despite Moses' fear to view it, speaks reassurance that the human malʾak too can harbor YHWH's flame, and can (as such) lead the oppressed Israelites to freedom. And these Israelites are the descendants of the patriarchs to whom promise was made by Heaven. The Deity who cites himself as the ancestral god calls himself by no name. He characterizes himself first as "your father's god," as though Moses had only one "father." And this singleness of identity of all the patriarchs may operate to affirm the single identity of their god, even as the enumeration "God of Abraham, God of Isaac and God of Jacob" affirms that singleness for all the variety of each of the patriarch's experience of this One God.

The grandeur of the imagery here, the terse power of the formulation of monotheistic theology in lean and simple words, were best left to speak for themselves. Our preoccupation here, however, is with philology, with the critical discipline of poetics, and with the vindication of a poetical approach to the names of God as opposed to the non-poetical approach of source criticism. So let us note that the narrator begins in verse 2 by declaring that it was YHWH's angel who appeared to Moses in the guise of, or from within, the tongue of flame. In verse 4 this narrator has the intimate God of Israel, YHWH, noting Moses' approach, but His response to this movement of the mortal is Elohim's address to him from within the bush. Thus we have YHWH YHWH's angel/agent = *ᵉlōhīm* → the numen within the bush=the apparition (to Moses) of a self-sustaining flame.

This graphic equation, like all semiotic representations, is neither an argument in itself nor a proof of an antecedent argument. It is a graphic or semi-graphic outline of a sequence of thought(s) enlisted to clarify an argument. In terms of the elemental units for divinity and their sequence as present in the text, we should have to rewrite our equation to distinguish between what is implicit in the argument and explicit in the text. Thus, placing the implicit in brackets: [YHWH] → YHWH 's angel/agent (verse 2) = YHWH (verse 4) "noting" and God/Elohim (verse 4) "calling" = I, the dialogic first person pronoun (verse 6) = *hāᵉlōhīm*/the numen perceived by Moses in the guise of, or present within, the flaming bush. In terms of the deployment of the various terms for Deity, the omniscient narrator signals the favored and intimate status of Moses by identifying that Power/persona by the name YHWH; so in the implicit commissioning of the angel/agent, and in the explicit subject of the verb "note" in verses 4 and 7. The representation of this persona is to Moses, so the narrator informs us, in the marvel of the unconsumed bush, which—as the narrator knows, but Moses does not—is the agent of YHWH, the numen *hāᵉlōhīm*. It is only after hearing the voice from the bush that Moses recognizes the phenomenon for what it is, and so it is that he fears to gaze upon *hāᵉlōhīm* in verse 6, and thereafter in his dialogue with Deity addresses himself to that numinal presence, the *hāᵉlōhīm* in verse 11 and, as we shall yet see, in verse 13. Mediate between the caring YHWH and his numinal representation is *ᵉlōhīm*, without the article, that is, Divinity/God, who speaks from within the bush in verse 4 (and again, as we shall note, in verses 14 and 15). It is clear that in verse 4 the YHWH who "notes" and the Elohim who "calls" are one and the same entity. But note the narrator's subtlety in identifying that speaker as Elohim when he warns Moses of the dangerous ground he is treading and, in verse 7, as YHWH when his message is his concern for "my people," "that is in Egypt"—suffering its tyranny—and his plan for his people's redemption and entrance into a land of felicity.

Moses' response to the call, together with Deity's response to the mortal's in verse 12, is a masterpiece of rhetorical density. Moses apparently has gotten the point of YHWH's puissant Presence's capability to inhabit a material vessel without doing it harm. But his response to the call, while appealing to our sympathy for such seemly humility, may also be interpreted as a lack of faith in the Deity summoning him to his service. Instead of fearing the role of being God's vessel, his *malʾak* to Pharaoh, it is the power of that Pharaoh that he now seems to fear. "What am I that I might go to Pharaoh, [who am I] that I might liberate the Israelites from Egypt?"

And the answer to this fear (if it is that) or self-doubt is given in a two-part statement that concludes this synoptic episode. First, let us note that the answer, introduced by the third singular masculine verb *wayyōʾmer* "He said," is provided with no explicit subject—not YHWH, not *ʾElōhīm*, not *hāᵉlōhīm*—and it features an instance of paranomasia so delightful as to excite any rhetorician's envy. The answer features the verb "to be" in its denotative sense "I am," in which sense it is totally superfluous, for biblical Hebrew regularly omits the verb "to be" in the present tense: "I (am) with you" would normally appear as *ānōkī ʾimmāk* (cf. verse 6). The verbal form, then—*Ehyē ʾimmāk*—is "I AM (am/is) with you." And this name

I AM, which equally means *I WAS* and *I SHALL BE*, is the name of God, which will in the resumptive episode be expounded in terms of itself. But, as we shall see in a moment, at this point Moses is unaware that *I AM* is a name of God (as against the awareness of the narrator or of the reader who is reading this not for the first time); therefore, from his point of view the answer to his question is "I [the Deity] am with you."

What kind of answer is "I am with you" to the question "Who [— of what standing —] am I?" Implicitly it says, "Your point is well taken. You are indeed a nonentity, in yourself. But you are not going for yourself, alone, on your own. I, God, am with you. And that changes everything. For you are no longer you, you now are my vessel." And if Deity's answer stopped here, that would be the bottom line of the kerygma: when God calls to service, modesty is as silly as fear. But the answer of Deity does not stop there. It goes on to answer a question that Moses has not asked. Explicitly. But the question is there in the elliptical density of the second part of the answer: Deity's offering of a token by which the mortal may be reassured "that it is I Who have sent you" reveals a very basic problem of faith and revelation. Doubt about a revelation, even as it is being experienced, may bespeak no lack of faith in God as such, nor in his ability to call upon mortals in such direct and specific communication, but rather self-doubt: Can I really believe that this is happening to me, that the transcendent Lord has picked this unlikely frame for his spirit? And the answer to this doubt, this reassurance by Deity that he is indeed speaking and commissioning Moses as his prophet, is as ironic—yet existentially true—as the irony of the prophetic ear doubting its capacity to recognize its Caller. For a divinely provided sign that will set doubt to rest, that will reassure the agent of the future success of his mission (hence validation of the fact of the commissioning), must take place in the present. Yet the sign offered by Deity to Moses lies in the future, indeed in the future when the present doubt will have been cancelled by a reality that is yet to transpire. Just so. That is the kerygma: when the receiver of the prophetic call would doubt the reality of the call, would tremble to undertake an enterprise of such dubious chance of success (if the call is an illusion), there can be no reassurance. If prophetic call is questioned by prophetic self-doubt, well then, the proof of the pudding can only be in the eating. "When you will have brought the people free from Egypt, your sign that it was indeed I Who sent you will be that all of you will worship Me at this very mountain."

This last quote is faithful to the Hebrew text except in one particular. The Hebrew has no *Me*. Although Deity is speaking, he does not refer to Himself in the third person as God (Elōhīm), nor as YHWH, but as *hāᵉlōhīm*, in this context the most distant abstraction for Deity. Why? Because the introduction of the name YHWH for Elōhīm, for Elōhīm that is both genus and proper name, *Godhead*, is yet to come, in the resumptive episode.

2. Episode B: The Tetragrammaton

(13) Moses said to the godhead (*hāᵉlōhīm*), "Well and good, here I am come to the Israelites, and I say to them, 'the god of your fathers has sent me to you,' and they then say to me, 'What is his name?'—what do I say to them?" (14) God said to Moses, "*Ehyē ᵃšer Ehyē*." [That is,] he said, "Say so to the Israelites, "*Ehye* has sent me to you.""

(15) In full said God to Moses, "Say so to the Israelites, 'YHWH, god of your fathers, god of Abraham, god of Isaac and god of Jacob has sent me to you.' That is my Name for all time, and that is my Mark for ongoing generations." (Exodus 3:13–15)

As we noted earlier, *hā^elōhīm* can have two different connotations, according to what the context will allow or demand. In the one connotation the definite article is the *hē* of abstraction: "Heaven," the Godhead, Divinity (both with capitals). Only this sense is possible, as we have just seen, in verse 12, where the self-reference by that Power excludes the possibility of a lesser, derivative, representative power. In the alternative connotation, the definite article is the *hē* of concreteness, specificity; hence the connotation of a particular manifestation of Divinity/God (*'Elōhim*, without the article) is the divinity, the god, the numen, etc. In this episode B, the subject of *wayyō'mer* is Elohim/God in verses 14 and 15 (as in verse 4, the subject of "called"). In all these cases Elohim is that Power or Principal who speaks through the intermediary angel/agent (*mal'ak*) appearing to Moses in or as the tongue of flame. Moses, however, here in verse 13, as in verse 11, addresses himself to the intermediary numen, *hā^elōhīm*, upon whom, in verse 6, he was afraid to gaze. Finally, let us note that the appearance of the definite article in English with a proper name—as in "the God of the Hebrew Bible"—to express not an ontological Being but a particular delineation of that Being, is here expressed with God, but the particularity is conveyed by the construct *^elōhēy 'abōtēykem*. So much for the terms for God in this episode.

The separate kerygma about the prophet's self-doubt having been achieved in Episode A, this episode resumes with Moses' response to the bidding to return to Egypt. Before he appears before Pharaoh he must, of course, win Israelite concurrence to his making representations to the throne on their behalf. The first obstacle to be overcome in gaining their confidence is that of convincing them that he has been commissioned by Heaven. Passing strange, however, is the metaphor for that difficulty. As though Moses and his brethren of the various tribes of Israel do not have common knowledge of the name of the ancestral Deity! If the name were known to the Israelites but kept secret from outsiders, how convincing a sign of Moses' *bona fides* if he too knows the name? If the name is to be introduced now by Moses to the Israelites, it would seem that to convince them that this name is to replace an older one would add to his difficulty rather than ease it. Yet God has no problem with this question of Moses' and gives him a name, which in the context can only be a single name, yet the giving of which is narrated in three steps, each of which seems to present a variation of that name that must be one. Whatever the metaphor for credibility in the name, there can be no question that the name successfully serves its purpose, to remove all doubts. Nor can there be any question as to which of the three variations is the precise and correct one. The precise and correct one is YHWH, for a number of reasons. It is the only one of the three that will appear again, and ever thereafter, as the name of Israel's God. It is the third of the three variations, and the only one that is explicitly characterized as "the name of the God of Abraham, God of Isaac and God of Jacob." And finally, it is the name that in verse 16 (which opens Episode C) is the name that God assumes will without question be accepted by the elders of Israel. Moses, too, assumes this, for in 4:1

(which opens EpisodeD) Moses' question reveals that all doubt about the credibility of YHWH as truly the God of the Ancestors will be dissipated. The only room for doubt will be in the question as to whether Moses has indeed experienced a commanding revelation from YHWH: Moses then spoke up. He said, "And suppose they put no trust in me, will pay no heed to my bidding, saying 'YHWH did *not* appear to you'?" (4:1)

Let us note a feature common to the third variation, God said to Moses, "Say so to the Israelites, 'YHWH God of . . . sent me to you,'" and to the second variation, He said, "So say to the Israelites, 'Ehyē sent me to you.'" Both YHWH and 'Ehyē are answers to the question of Moses, "What [name] shall I say unto them?" Not so the first variation. Here the text reads, God said to Moses, "'ehyē ᵃšer 'ehyē." This Hebrew sentence then is an exposition of the name to come—'Ehye—and its meaning is, as we have previously pointed out, all of the following: "I am what I am, I am what I was, I am what I shall be, I was what I am, I was what I was, I was what I shall be, I shall be what I was, I shall be what I am, I shall be what I shall be."[21] In other words, the name 'Ehyē—appearing first in Episode A but not there recognized by Moses as a name, and now about to appear as *the* name—has the connotations in the one-word name of eternity, timelessness, without beginning or end, and in the exposition of changelessness, enduring dependability. And the difference between 'Ehyē and YHWH is that the first stands for God speaking of this unchanging timeless Being-ness in the first person, and when Moses retells this experience to the elders he will have to translate this first-person pronouncement by God to a third-person pronouncement: YHWH, standing for Yihyē "He was, He is, He shall be." (While it is true that we never have *medial waw* in the imperfect of the verb "to be" in biblical Hebrew, its attestation in the participial and imperative forms is grounds enough for seeing a clear play, if nothing else, on the third person singular imperfect; and if the *waw* in place of *yodh* is a relic of the older pronunciation, why all the more reason to attach the *patah* vowel to the afformative *yodh*, as in the older pronunciation, to yield the widely accepted *Yahweh*.)

3. From El Shaddai to YHWH

(2) God spoke to Moses, He said to him, "I am YHWH." (3) I appeared to Abraham, to Isaac, and to Jacob as El Shaddai. But My name YHWH I made not myself known to them. (Exodus 6:2–3)

This brief pericope is problematic on a number of counts: for one its setting; for another its featuring of terms or names for Deity; and for yet another its redundancy or pointlessness in the context of similar narratives.

In terms of setting it comes after Moses' complaint that God has failed to help Israel and to support Moses in his mission; on the contrary, matters have gone from bad to worse. And it comes after God's response that He would soon take action to force Pharaoh not just to release the Israelites but to expel them. What need then to begin anew with a statement of address by Deity to Moses, in which he may introduce himself as though for the first time?

As concerns the expressions for Deity, verse 2 begins with 'Elōhīm as the subject. This appears altogether natural to us in light of our own conditioning (by the

Scriptural tradition) to relate to "god/God" as both common noun and proper noun. Let us note, however, that there is no capitalization in speech, and that in spoken context "god" as a common noun must always have some qualification in terms of definiteness or indefiniteness, while "God"—without such qualification— is itself a proper name. But this is, as we have noted, a peculiarity everywhere in Scripture, as in the languages into which Scripture has been translated. What must be stressed here is that the use of Ĕlōhīm in the narrator's voice in verse 2 is not, as is often the case elsewhere, an indication of the Deity's lesser intimacy or friendliness. Inasmuch as the speaker is going to identify himself by the name YHWH (i.e., in dialogue), the narrator must use a term for "Deity" that is not quite, although it is in a sense, a proper name. But again, in terms of setting, there is something bizarre about God's introducing himself by the name YHWH when such introduction has taken place in chapter 3, and further, the name YHWH has become the commonplace term for God in the intervening narrative (cf. e.g., 5:21, at a remove of only four verses).

Problematic also is the stress on an alternative designation or proper name for Deity, in contrast to the name YHWH, El Shaddai. Not El Elyon (as in Genesis 14:18–20, 22) nor Elohim, as though that is not a proper name at all, but as El Shaddai. This name of Deity (and its more frequent occurrence as simply Shaddai) deserves a poetical investigation in itself. As Shaddai it is Job's preferred name for God and as 'El Shaddai appears three times in dialogue, in the voice of Jacob (Genesis 28:3, 43:14, 48:3). Only twice does the self-identification "I am 'El Shaddai" appear, once to Abraham (17:1) and once to Jacob (35:11). And these last two instances are clearly the back-references of Exodus 6:3, "I appeared to them as 'El Shaddai." And equally clear is the function of this usage, that is, as the counterpoise to the name YHWH, which was not disclosed to the patriarchs. And it is this additional element in this revelatory self-identification, making explicit what was only implicit in the analogous scene in Exodus 3, that poses the most challenging problem. What point is there in fixing the appearance of the name YHWH to the time of Moses, what is the point of such knowledge having been denied to the patriarchs? This question would in itself pose a thorny question for exegesis. But there is a more daunting question for anyone who, like us, posits a poetical unity for Scripture in general and for Genesis and Exodus in particular. For the denial of knowledge of the name YHWH to the patriarchs, a denial spoken by YHWH Himself, is in explicit contradiction to the notice in Genesis 4:26b—a notice the pointlessness of which we have previously discussed[22]—that in antediluvian days the name YHWH was already invoked by humankind. And if we should try to resolve this contradiction by the supposition that somewhere between Noah and Abraham the name YHWH was lost, there would still be the poetic discrepancy of the single narrator permitting (not himself, for that is no problem, but) his characters to dispose in dialogue of the name YHWH.

THE PATRIARCHS' USE OF THE NAME YHWH

The name YHWH appears in dialogue in Genesis 4:1, where Eve's acknowledgment of God's role in her bearing a child is, "I have made a person with YHWH-

['s help]." In 5:29 Lamech expresses his knowledge that the soil's fertility was interdicted by YHWH. In 9:26 Noah praises YHWH, who in prophetic vision he recognizes as Shem's god.

The name YHWH appears in a patriarch's voice for the first time in Genesis 14:22. This chapter, regarded by source critics as unique in respect to plot, diction, and syntax, is assigned to an unnamed source other than J, E, or P. Our own analysis of this chapter concludes that it is an episode in the life of Abram that is well-integrated into its narrative setting, and expressive of a kerygma in profound resonance with Scripture's theological doctrine. A sub-kerygma of this narrative is the affirmation that the Deity served by Melchizedek, priest-king of Salem, named by him *'El 'Elyon* and characterized as Creator of Heaven and Earth, is none other than the same Deity, identical with the YHWH (Creator of Heaven and Earth) of the patriarch Abram and of both his immediate and far-off progeny.

The appearance of the name YHWH in the speech of patriarchal figures or personae in patriarchal times can be checked against the listings in table 1-1. For reasons of economy I will refer only briefly to the five narratives that I will later discuss in detail.

In Genesis 15, the story of the covenant made between God and Abraham, featuring an apparition moving between the parts of several slaughtered animals, there are six explicit references to Deity, each one featuring the name YHWH. Three times the name is used by the narrator and three times—in explicit contradiction of Exodus 6:2–3—in dialogue. Deity declares "I [am] YHWH [he] that fetched you out of Ur Kasdim" or "I, YHWH [am the one] that fetched you out of Ur Kasdim." And Abram twice addresses God as "my Lord (*^adōnāy*) YHWH."

In Genesis 16, Sarai says that YHWH has kept her from giving birth (verse 2) and later calls on YHWH to judge Abram's responsibility in the matter of the disrespect shown to her by Hagar (verse 5). Four times, so the narrator tells us, the angel of YHWH addresses Hagar and tells her to name her son *Yishma'-el* "El hears," in acknowledgement, he goes on to say, "that YHWH has heeded your suffering." (verse 11)

In Chapter 18 YHWH, speaking to Abraham, refers to himself in the third person: "Is anything beyond YHWH's power to perform?"

The last instances I will cite are those in chapter 22. The perplexing call to Abraham to offer up his son features the term *hā^elōhīm* in the narrator's voice (three times) and *'Elōhīm* (without the definite article) in Abraham's. But with verse 11, the turnabout from that command is introduced by YHWH's *angel* calling upon Abraham to stay his hand (verse 11). After sacrificing the providential ram, Abraham names the sacrificial site *YHWH-yir'ē* "*YHWH-provides.*" And YHWH's angel, in his second appearance, formulates God's promise to Abraham in a solemn oath taken by Deity,"'By mine own self have I sworn,' so the word of YHWH, 'because you have done this thing.'"

We thus have eleven instances in which the biblical narrator has various personae (God himself, God's angel, Eve, Noah, Abraham, Sarah), disposing of the name YHWH. The divine personae do this in dialogue with humans, and the humans themselves in all spontaneity, and all of these instances, before the time of its first introduction to Moses. We could go on now to present our solution to this

glaring poetical difficulty. But in the interest of preparing our readers for our suggestion, it will be helpful to make something of a detour: to examine the unique
phenomenon—unique to Scripture, unknown in the world's literature or religious
traditions—of a proper name that is never pronounced, indeed unpronounceable,
because it is written in consonants with no vowels provided.

THE SOLUTION TO THE PROBLEM: A (LITERARY) HYPOTHESIS

A recapitulation of my argument so far would include the following elements:

1. A rejection of the notion that the problem of the names of God may be confined
   to a primary dichotomy represented by the names Elohim (God) and YHWH (the
   Lord or Yahweh). This, because so many other names are featured in close association with these two names.
2. A rejection of the meta-literary solution offered by source-criticism to the Elo-
   him/YHWH bifurcation, viz., a discernment of documents traceable to different
   authorial hands or sources, this in large part according to whether the narrator employs or eschews the Tetragrammaton before the moment of its introduction to Israel in the person of Moses. This rejection is based on the poetic perception that a
   narrator's use of a name for Deity does not argue that his story's personae were
   privy to that name, nor does his own eschewing of that name imply that his personae were not privy to that name.
3. The conclusion that the proper noun Elohim (God) is not so much a product as it
   is a witness of monotheistic thinking.

From this last conclusion the following may be inferred. The proper name Elohim must be a later development in the Israelitish experience than the Tetragrammaton (however it was pronounced). A specific (proper) name for a people's god
(such as El, Shaddai, YHWH), presupposing the (assumed) existence of many gods,
must be chronologically prior to the common-noun-become-proper-noun (Elohim/
God). If the foregoing is clear to us, it must have been equally clear to the authors
and editors of the texts from which we draw this conclusion. We must therefore
look for a literary explanation of the apparent contradictions, inconsistencies,
superfluities, and non-sequiturs in the information provided by our texts as to these
two names. In short, our argument has both sharpened and complicated the formulation of the questions centering on these two names. Let us recapitulate and elab-
orate these questions.

Why would a religious tradition possess and preserve several names for a single
god? True, a single god might often be referred to by an epithet, an epithet that almost becomes an alternative "name." Such may be the case with such terms as
Elyon ("Most High") and Shaddai ("Almighty"?), but except for such rare (and un-
explained) exceptions as Jove/Jupiter, the head of a pantheon will have but one
proper name (Zeus, Odin, Marduk, etc.). But why preserve such names other than
to indicate that a deity formerly, or in another tribe, known as El Elyon, is really
the same entity known among us today as, say, YHWH? That the specific proper
name that became predominant among Israel's tribes was YHWH would seem to be
unquestionable. Why then should the Scriptural tradition inform us in one place
that that name was already known to humankind tens of generations before Israel

emerged on history's stage, while in another place it should take pains to deny the knowledge of that name to the ancestors of Moses, and this last in close proximity to a chapter devoted to a perplexing midrashic exposition of that name's etymology to the Moses, who has just asked by what name he is to identify his ancestral god to his tribal contemporaries? And why, further, does *this* Scriptural tradition preserve this name in consonantal writing, defy it a pronunciation by withholding of vowel indicators, and provide substitute terms such as *ᵃdōnāy*? And why, finally, having denied knowledge of this name YHWH to the patriarchs, does Scripture again and again feature this name in the direct discourse between these patriarchal figures and the Deity who identifies himself by this name?

Our solution to this problem will involve a radical suggestion: that there never existed a pronunciation proper to the name transcribed by the letters *Y-H-W-H*. This suggestion would seem to fly in the face of two rabbinic texts that seem to be in simple attestation that the name represented by the Tetragrammaton was still uttered in public in Second Temple times. One of these is, indeed, the one written statement on which one might base speculation that the Name was regarded as too sacred for evocation, except on rare occasion by the most sanctified of human lips. The following translation is from Danby's *The Mishnah*:

> And when the priests and the people which stood in the Temple Court heard the Expressed Name come forth from the mouth of the High Priest, they used to kneel and bow themselves and fall down on their faces and say, 'Blessed be the name of the glory of his kingdom for ever and ever!' (Yoma 6:2)

The specific context of the High Priest's pronouncing of "the Expressed Name" is his citation of Leviticus 16:10, which concludes, "ye shall be clean before the Lord (i.e., YHWH)." On this last citation in Mishna Yoma 3:8, Danby—drawing on rabbinic commentaries, needless to say—has the following footnote:

> The final word 'Lord' was pronounced by the High Priest as it was written and not, as usually, by a reverential pseudonym or alternative divine name such as Adonai.

One might quarrel with Danby's formulation on a number of counts. For one thing, what does he have in mind by "a reverential pseudonym" other than "an alternative divine name," and is not *Adonai* a *substitute for* rather than an *alternative divine name*? But these are quibbles. What is not a quibble, however, is the objection to his having the High Priest pronounce the Name "as it was written." Inasmuch as the written name YHWH is without vowels, it could not be pronounced *as it was written*. These last four words (in italics) are an interpretation of the Hebrew, which in Yoma 6:2 is translated by him as "the Expressed Name." The Hebrew thus rendered is *haššem hammᵉfōrāš*,[23] a reference to the Tetragrammaton (known in later rabbinic Hebrew as *šem hawwāyā*, i.e., the name containing the Hebrew verb *hwh* "to be"). And while it is true that later rabbinic tradition understood this phrase as the consonantal YHWH pronounced according to the original vocalization, it is equally true that this understanding is eisegetical, not exegetical. For Hebrew *haššem hammᵉfōrāš* means simply *the Name Expounded* or *the Name Explicated* and not *the Name Expressed* or *the Name Pronounced* or *the Name Enunciated*.[24]

Had the Name indeed been enunciated by the High Priest on every Day of

Atonement in the hearing of the throng in the temple courtyard, we should then have to seek for the date of the forgetfulness of the vowels in the decades after the Temple's destruction by Rome. And the Mishna's intent, that *the Name Explicated* was indeed heard at large, admits of no question. For in our second citation, Mishna Tamid 3:8, a fanciful catalogue of sounds from the Temple that could be heard as far away as Jericho, we read "and there are those who say that even the voice of the High Priest [could be heard] when he uttered (*hizkīr*) the Name on the Day of Atonement." And if that Name was the *šem hammᵉfōrāš*[25] "the Explicated Name," the name expressive of God's eternality and enduring sovereignty as expounded in the *ʾEhyē* or *ʾEhyē ᵃšer ʾEhyē* of Exodus 3 (or the attributes of Exodus 34:6–7), we should have no difficulty understanding why the *tannaitic* rabbis would have wanted the Name to resound so far and wide. And we would be in a better position to understand the response of the people to the expounding of this name. For a more meaningful translation of the people's response to the expounding of this Name—*bārūk šem kᵉvōd malkūtō lᵉʿōlām wāʿed*—is "Praised be this name for His Sovereign Presence for all time."

Where does all this leave us? If the name were indeed enunciated in Second Temple times, if only once a year by the High Priest, what authoritative rabbinic body decreed its suppression, and how did it effectuate in Roman times, on the banks of the Ebro and the Rhine, the Tiber and the Euphrates, a draught of Lethe-like waters, as potent in its universality as remarkable in its specificity? If the Name were not enunciated by the High Priest in Second Temple times, then its suppression must have taken place some centuries or even a millennium earlier, without trace in Scripture of a struggle—this on the part of a people who could wrangle for centuries over whether their God wanted sacrifices brought to him in many shrines or in one alone. In either case, the fact of or the reason for such suppression is nowhere given, and the process itself so improbable as to be well-nigh inconceivable. But the process—for all its inconceivability—must have taken place. For we have the consonantal name, we have Scripture's witness to God's having pronounced it for Moses, Moses for the elders, and into some later generation when the vocalization was somehow forgotten.

Not quite. Scripture—consider its literal meaning—is a literary witness, a witness in writing. As such it may express an eloquence unsurpassed. But as a literally (*sic!*) linguistic phenomenon, speech (*loquens*), it is mute. The vocalization for YHWH need never have been forgotten if, for example, it was never known; and never known for never having existed.[26] Let us consider this possibility. But first let us review the general assumptions and conclusions about the Tetragrammaton in regard to its ontology and etymology. That the name existed as a *vocable* in the sense of utterable sounds is, as we have just suggested, a meta-literary assumption;[27] the name as we have it is a purely literary datum, a datum in writing.

The narrative in Exodus 3 on the revelation of this name clearly entails the verb "to be" *hyh* (possibly, in earlier times, *hwh*). The third radical of this form is not a consonant as such but a vocalic consonant, which is to say, a consonantal sign indicating a long vowel; in this case a vowel for the medial consonant *y* (or *w*) in compensation for the loss of an original third radical that was either the semi-consonant *y* (reducible to vowel *i*) or the semi-consonant *w* (reducible to vowel *u*).

Thus the first person imperfect 'ehyēh is constituted of three consonants: afformative *aleph* ('), and two consonants of the stem (*hē* and *yodh*, *h* and *y*); the last *hē* is a vocalic indication of the length of the second radical: 'ehyē. The third person imperfect in biblical Hebrew is, analogously, *yihyē*, afformative *yodh* and stem consonants *hē* and *yodh*. The question before us is, supposing that the word-play in Exodus 3 proceeds from God in the first person speaking of Himself as 'Ehyē to the third person form for a speaker other than God, that third person form should be *Yihyē*. Why would the narrator opt for a *Yihwē* form, and why have scholars assumed further that the vowel of the afformative *yodh* is *pataḥ* and not *ḥīreq*? No answer is offered in scholarship to the first question, because the question is never asked. The text has a *waw* as the third consonant of Tetragrammaton and that is a fact. Furthermore, this presents no great problem, for we have indications that the medial consonant of the verb "to be" may well have been *waw* at an earlier stage of the Hebrew language. And if that earlier stage is represented in *yhwh*, then so may we posit a *pataḥ* vowel for the afformative *yodh* as attested in cognate languages representing and preserving a vocalization older than that registered by the Masoretes for biblical Hebrew. And oh yes, there is another support for *Yahwē* rather than *Yihwē*: the existence of two apparently shortened versions of *Yahwē*, viz. *Yāhū* and *Yāh*.

Now it is true that YHWH is a biblical fact. But what kind of fact is it? We have stipulated that it is a literary fact, a written datum, but not necessarily a linguistic fact, a datum of speech. But of whose speech is it not necessarily a datum? Source critics would say, among others, of the speakers labeled J or P. Whether J was correct or P was on when the Tetragrammaton became the possession of the Israelitish stock as the name par excellence of their ethnic or national Deity, by the time of the Exodus, YHWH—give it whatever vowels you will—was a staple of their speech. And they (the source critics) thus make this Name not only a literary fact, and a linguistic fact—a datum of an ancient speech—but a meta-literary fact as well: YHWH existed in the speech of ancient Israel, as an ontological or historic fact.

Now let us consider the other possibility, which we raised before this review, that YHWH never existed in speech, a conclusion we reached on the basis of the inconceivability of some version of its sound not having survived if it had existed. A conclusion strengthened by the logic of proceeding in writing from 'ehyē, through hypothetical *yihyē*, to YHWH standing for hypothetical *Yihwē*; a logic making sense in writing but not in a synchronic pronunciation. This logic does not begin with YHWH but ends with it. It begins with a name, no, *the* name for Israel's tutelary deity, as broadly attested in names of people. (Names are a conservative vessel in speech, preserving elements that have long ago become semantically meaningless, including theophoric elements that may never have had a semantic content.) That name is *Yāhū*, preserved at the end of such sentence names as *Hizqī-Yāhū*, *Yišaʿ-Yāhū*, *Šᵉmaʿ-Yāhū*. When beginning sentence names, vowel reduction resulted in its being pronounced *Yᵉhō* or even *Yō*, as in *Yᵉhō-nātan/Yō-nātan*, *Yᵉhō-rām*, *Yō-rām*. (The first syllable in the name of Moses' mother, *Yō-keved*, may be the only instance of this theophoric element in a name antedating Moses.) And in the bound-form of the call to praise (*hallᵉlūyāh*), as in a few other poetic instances, the final vowel was dropped, resulting in *Yāh*.

The narrative in Exodus 3 reflects, therefore, an expansion of a two-consonantal name into a three-consonantal name, the vocalic consonant for the second consonant being transformed into fully consonantal *waw*, and the fourth letter, *hē*, added as a vocalic consonant to indicate the length of the vowel attached to that newly emerged *waw*. All in a play on the verb "to be," to give new meaning to an old name (which may have had no meaning at all), a name (the new one) unpronounceable and unpronounced. (*Yā-hū-wā* would be a pointless lengthening of *Yāhū* without the appearance at all of the verb "to be.") This name—or rather spelling—henceforward appears everywhere where the name *Yāhū* would have appeared. If the text were read aloud, how would the reader have rendered the spelling into speech? In all likelihood, either by a substitute vocable *ᵃdōnāy*, or by the old *Yāhū*.[28]

The question that would remain is, why? Why this artificial play on the verb "to be"? Why the creation of a name spelled one way and pronounced another? What would have been the point of the displacement of *Yāhū*? And the answer becomes obvious, once we rid ourselves of magical thinking and cease to ascribe such thinking to the Scriptural authors, once we rid ourselves of the notion that the formulators of monotheism were intellectually primitive, less capable than we are to work out the implications of a theology that replaces many gods with one.[29]

Simply put, monotheism has no need, possibly no room, for a name—a proper name—for Deity. Proper names are labels by which individual or particular members of a class are differentiated one from another. If Deity is a class with but one member, then the common name or noun for that class is sufficient. Or perhaps we might say that in such case the common noun is also a—no, *the*—proper noun. And that is a problem that has been plaguing me in writing this chapter, this very paragraph. For were we strict in our own monotheistic awareness we should never capitalize *deity*, we should never speak of *the* Deity, and never capitalize *god*. For our case is the case of the biblical texts where in speaking of the one and only (true and) existing god, rather than the (false and) nonexisting gods of paganism, *ᵉlōhīm* without an article is clearly a proper as well as a common noun. Our capitalization of God or Deity owes then to the respect for the concept of singleness of deity, and to an inherited convention for the differentiation of the One and Only God of Scripture from the many gods that exist(ed) only in the minds of pagans. The name *ᵉlōhīm* (as in Genesis 1) is a singular (the plural form being the plural of majesty), a common noun doing service as a proper noun also, and its disposition as such is witness to the monotheistic faith of the writer or speaker who so disposes of it. And as such we render *ᵉlōhīm* in transcription as *'Elōhīm* and in translation as God, in both cases a proper name.

But the monotheistic biblical authors could no more ignore the polytheistic ambience of Israel's neighbors, nor the backslidings of faithful Israelites into polytheistic patterns of belief, than we can deny that the popular religion of monotheistic confessions today discloses a good many elements of the polytheism out of which and in opposition to which monotheism emerged. And, for those of us who profess to be the teachers and preachers of monotheism, let us not lay unction to our souls in this regard. In our passionate devotion to the narrower formulas of our denominational faith and praxis, do we not often in effect deny that our rival sister-denominations are worshiping the one and only god? If, as a wise pagan observed, when the gods are threatened it is the priests who tremble, is this any less true of the clergy who minister to the one and only god? In the case of ancient Israel, a people and a nation having emerged from polytheism, hailing their ancestral god *Yāhū* as Creator and god of all nature and nations, how did their conduct among themselves or their stance in regard to neighboring peoples and polities differ essentially from the conduct and stance of the Assyrians who hailed Aššur, or of the Babylonians who hailed Marduk as Creator and god of all nature and nations? How did Joram ben Ahab, who declared that "YHWH had called forth" himself and his allies to make war against Moab,[30] differ from Sennacherib, who declared that his campaigns were undertaken *ina tukulti beliya Aššur* "trusting in (the help of) my lord Aššur?" Surely there can be no argument that such was the problem of the prophets, from the Amos of 3:1–2, 4:4–5, 9:5–7, to the Malachi who declares what is ontologically true (given monotheism) for all the failure of the surrounding peoples to realize to whom they are addressing their worship:

> Verily,
> From the place of sun's rising to the place of its setting,
> Great is My name among the nations,
> Everywhere is incense presented to My name, and offerings pure—
> So great [the reverence for] My name among the nations! (Malachi 1:11)[31]

The basic insights of Scripture into a One and Only god—who is Person, who is Friend to humankind, who is by essence moral and would show his friendliness to humans if they would but make that possible by their own morality—these are often obscured from our view by the idolatry of logography, by the literal reading of breathtaking metaphor. And when one examines the range of metaphor expressed in the varied appearances of "name" (*šem*) in connection with God, it will come as no wonder that in instance after instance "the name" YHWH means anything but "the name YHWH," and that YHWH "the name" should appear just where one would expect *ᵉlōhīm*, that is, the One and Only god.

Two instances of the latter phenomenon, their significance overlooked and usually masked by mistranslation, are Genesis 12:7 and 16:13. The proper name YHWH appears in both, modified by a participial phrase. In 12:7 we are told that Abraham (in the neighborhood of Shechem) "erected there an altar to YHWH *hannirē ᵉlāw.*" Every translation I have checked renders the participle by a past, or past perfect verb, "who (had) appeared to him." The Hebrew for this would have been *ᵃšer nirā ēlāw.* The force of the participle is incompleted action, hence "to YHWH who [was] appearing to him." But such a modification of a particular person, as represented by his proper name, makes little sense. For John (for example) is John whether he appears or not. The participial phrase then is elliptical, standing for "to YHWH, [the god] who was appearing." In 16:13, which we shall examine in detail later, Hagar, addressing a god whom she does not know by name, gives him a name of her own invention. Literally *wattiqrā šem YHWH haddōber ēlēhā* is "she called the name of YHWH the [one/god] speaking to her." More correctly in terms of English idiom: "YHWH, the [god] addressing her, she named."

This second instance brings up for examination the question of the appearance of the name YHWH in construct with *šem* (e.g., Genesis 4:26, 12:8, 13:4). The translation "to call upon/invoke the name of YHWH/the Lord" is unacceptable. For one does not invoke *"the name of"* a *proper name*. Speiser, sensitive to this linguistic aberration, therefore renders the Hebrew, "invoked YHWH by name." This translation is acceptable as English but it is not faithful to the Hebrew (at least as vocalized by the Masoretes). Speiser's rendering would reflect the Hebrew "(to invoke) *baššem* YHWH," that is, "by the name YHWH." What then lies behind the construct *šem* YHWH? The construct, if rendered literally, reflects bad Hebrew and is bad English, and even in Speiser's good English would appear to be a clear contradiction of the statement in Exodus 6:3 that the patriarchal ancestors were not privy to this name. One answer is to treat the term *šem* not as "name" literally, but in a metaphoric sense, as for example in the psalmist's plea: "Act, O God, *lᵉmaʿan šmēkā*" is reduced to gibberish by the English "for the sake of Thy name." The Hebrew *lishmāh*, literally "for its name," in rabbinic and modern Hebrew means "for its own sake"—not for ulterior motives. Thus the Psalmist asks God to act not for the sake of the supplicant, who has no merit, no claim on God's favor, but to act "because You are benevolent, out of Your attribute of grace." On this line of metaphoric usage, the erection of an altar to YHWH and calling (on God) *bᵉšem* YHWH need not involve knowledge of the name on the part of the mortal engaging in such activities. It is rather the narrator's way of indicating that the patriarch, by whatever name he addressed God, truly understood him in his uniqueness, his sovereignty, his eternality, his consistency in justice and benevolence. Thus, for example, in Genesis 21:33 Abraham at Beersheba calls *bᵉšem* YHWH *ʾel ʿōlām*. While the Hebrew could be rendered "in the [other] name of YHWH, God Eternal," or "in YHWH, that is, by the name Eternal God," it could also connote in "the name [of god whom we know as] YHWH, eternal deity." Similarly too, we may understand that the narrator, when he has patriarchal personages address YHWH in direct discourse, does so as a matter of free direct discourse, in the full knowledge of the apparent contradiction of the statement in Exodus 6:3. But even this explanation is not one of last recourse. Especially if we reflect that even grim sobriety or halakhic rigidity may in Scripture mask the broad understanding and patient tolerance of authors emulating those very attributes of a long-suffering deity, who but for a sense of humor would long ago have given up on both His beloved humankind and His chosen Israel.

We need not characterize as a failure the enterprise of Scripture's authors to convey to us the fundamental insight that in monotheism a proper name for Deity is in a sense blasphemous, allowing as it may for the existence of other deities by other names. That insight is conveyed by the very attempt to eliminate *the* name, even as the implicit use of *ᵉlōhīm* in a context that admits of no more than one such is already a witness to the triumph of monotheism. But beyond this, the fact is that even in a narrow sense the biblical authors were successful. For they did virtually eliminate the name of Israel's (parochial) god. Except for appearances in the proper names of people, the name Yāhū all but disappeared from Israelite consciousness; replaced by a never-pronounced YHWH, a visual reminder of the one and only god's essence: *ʾel ʿōlām*, enduring god = *yihyē ʾašer yihyē*. As for the patriarchs who are portrayed as invoking YHWH, a name not made known to them, the statement

in Exodus 6:3 applies not only to them but to all those—including ourselves—
who came after Moses. For in the sense of a name as a phenomenon of speech, an
oral or auditory phenomenon, the name reflected in the written characters YHWH
was never made known to anyone. Hebrew *šēm* means "name" and, as often indicated by close association with *qārā* "to call out, to utter," is essentially a sonic or
auricular phenomenon. The Hebrew word *zeker*, which may indeed be a synonym
for "name," has a denotation which is essentially visual, "mark, sign, trace." Only a
pedant, himself a stranger to a sense of humor, would with assurance deny the possibility of any humorous intent in the narration of Exodus 3. After going through
the near rigmarole of the first episode in which Moses' question, "Who am I that
(*kī*) I (presume to) go to Pharaoh" receives the elliptical answer, "Verily (*kī*) *'Ehyē*
(I am)(is) with you;" this followed by the granting of an unasked for *sign* (*'ōt*) that
is no sign at all, we reach the second episode: Moses asks a rather bizarre question—
what name shall he give as the name of the ancestral god—and receives the answer *'Ehyē* *ᵃšer 'Ehyē*, which is immediately reduced to the *'Ehyē* of episode A, and
then summarized or glossed as "YHWH god of the ancestors . . . sent me to you."
And this culminates in the final pronouncement, which can refer only to the
(unpronounceable) name YHWH and not to the predicate "sent me," *zē šᵉmī*
lᵉ'ōlām wᵉzē zikrī lᵉdōr dōr "That is my name for all time and that is my SIGNature
for all generations."

PART I

STORIES—
"THE PRIMEVAL HISTORY"

THE CREATION STORY IN GENESIS,
CH. 1:1—2:4A

THE BEARING OF *ENUMA ELISH* ON GENESIS I

The appreciation in modern scholarship of the biblical creation story is dependent, to a degree that can hardly be exaggerated, on our possession of the Mesopotamian creation traditions, particularly the Babylonia Creation Epic. To pick a single striking example: How does the Genesis creation pericope begin, and how and where does it end? The how of the beginning is, of course, whether the Hebrew words constitute an independent clause ("In the beginning God created") or a dependent clause ("When God began to create"). The second option, now the greatly preferred one, was still regarded as a radical translation some fifty years ago; this despite Rashi's having anticipated it almost a millennium ago. The ending of the pericope is now universally recognized in the division of 2:4 into (a) a recapitulation of the preceding narrative, and (b) a dependent clause beginning a new narrative. As to the unanimity on this division, one can only wonder that it was only so recently arrived at when one contrasts the present translations with the gobbledygook into which this verse was previously rendered, for example: "These are the generations of the heavens and of the earth when they were created, in the day that the Lord God made the earth and the heavens." The case for the division of 2:4, providing for a second narrative beginning with a dependent clause, parallel to the rendering of Genesis 1:1 as a dependent clause, could only be strengthened by the parallel syntax of the Babylonian Epic, named (as in the Jewish tradition) according to its opening words *Enuma elish*, "When up above."

For all the foregoing, it is a matter of interest that of the many questions that long troubled readers of the biblical creation story, very few owe their resolution to the many parallel features discovered in the *Enuma elish*. A review of these problems and their plausible solutions will show that at best the adducing of parallels from the Babylonia Epic merely reinforces answers suggested before the recovery of this epic. Preparatory to presenting my own translation of the biblical text and my discussion of its problems and their proposed solutions, I think it important to cite (and criticize) E. A. Speiser's argument for viewing the biblical creation narrative as a "take-over" of the Babylonian prototypes:

> Mesopotamia's canonical version of cosmic origins is found in the . . . *Enūma elish*. . . . The numerous points of contact between it and the opening section of Genesis have long been noted. There is not only a striking correspondence in various details, but— what is even more significant—the order of the events is the same, which is enough to preclude any likelihood of coincidence. The relationship is duly recognized by all informed students, no matter how orthodox their personal beliefs may be. I cite as an example the tabulation given by Heidel, *The Babylonian Genesis*, p. 129.

Enūma elish	*Genesis*
[1] Divine spirit and cosmic matter are coexistent and coeternal	Divine spirit creates matter and exists independently of it
[2] Primeval chaos; Tiamat enveloped in darkness	The earth a desolate waste, with darkness covering the deep (tehom)
[3] Light emanating from the gods	Light created
[4] The creation of the firmament	The creation of the firmament
[5] The creation of dry land	The creation of dry land
[6] The creation of luminaries	The creation of luminaries
[7] The creation of man	The creation of man
[8] The gods rest and celebrate	God rests and sanctifies the seventh day

> Except for incidental differences of opinion in regard to the exact meaning of the first entry in each column . . . the validity of the listing is not open to question.[1]

What I find remarkable, contrary to Speiser's judgments, is the extent to which, in regard to both the substance and the order of the items, Heidel's listing is open to rebuttal. Speiser himself concedes that Item [1] is questionable, if only on account of Heidel's assumption that creation in the Bible, contrary to the *Enuma elish* version, is *ex nihilo*. To correct Heidel on this point is only to make the two creations more similar. But Heidel's speaking of "divine spirit" in *Enuma elish* is utterly gratuitous. The word "spirit" appears not at all, in contrast to the specific presence of *rūᵃḥ ᵉlōhīm* in Genesis (where, too, *rūᵃḥ* is more likely "wind" than "spirit"). Item [2]: Despite his listing of darkness as enveloping Tiamat, Heidel himself concedes that "in *Enuma elish* this expression is not expressly stated, but we can deduce it from the fact that Ti'amat, according to Berossus . . . was shrouded in darkness."[2] To conflate the Babylonian Creation Epic with the account of a putative priest of Bel Marduk, published in Greek about 275 B.C., is to commit a methodological "howler," one deserving of Samuel Sandmel's stricture: *parallelomania*. Item [3]:

Heidel (p. 101) confesses that day and night, already existing at the time of Apsu's revolt, are not part of Marduk's acts of creation. As for the illumination required to have daytime, he derives "the emanation of light from the gods" from "the radiance or dazzling aureole which surrounded Apsu." This figuration of a warrior's halo blinding and terrifying his enemies is so frequent in cuneiform writings as to be a cliché. How seriously this item should be taken as analogous to the creation of light in Genesis 1 we may glean, for example, from Sennacherib's boast that his own halo caused his royal Babylonian adversary to urinate in his chariot. Item [4], the creation of the biblical firmament, would be the first correspondence to an act of creation by Marduk, wherein—presumably—both heaven and earth were created by Marduk's splitting of Tiamat like a shellfish, the former corresponding to the upper shell and the latter to the lower shell. In terms then of the order of correspondent listings, only items [6] and [7] would seem to withstand rebuttal. Yet here too, as far as substance is concerned, the correspondence is quite discrepant. The failure of Enuma elish to provide for the emergence of vegetation and of animals other than man is in such contrast to the space given them in the biblical account as to render to the correspondence of items [6] and [7] precisely what Speiser would deny them, "the likelihood" of coincidence. The final item [8] is forced, even in the formulation of Heidel's listing. God rests or desists from his labors of creation, but does not celebrate. In Enuma elish the gods do not create—except for their brick-making for their shrine in Babylon—and Marduk and Ea, who share such creative acts as there are, do not mark the cessation of their creative labors.

The foregoing criticism of the excesses to which the comparative approach is frequently carried is not to be taken as a depreciation or disparagement of this approach, nor of its corollary, the contrastive. What we would stress, however, is the need for every generation of commentators to review and reassess for itself a text's cognate literature, just as it submits the primary text to a review of its translation, signification, and evaluation. This is particularly critical when the primary text has long been held as sacred and various interpretations of it have been accorded doctrinal or dogmatic status, and on that very account fiercely attacked and fiercely defended. Bible students will recall how the decipherment and publication of cuneiform texts were first greeted as a challenge to the originality and authority of biblical accounts, then reinterpreted and defended as helpful to a reinterpretation and enhanced understanding of the sacred text; and how the Babel and Bible debate continues to reverberate in various keys in both secular and confessional circles. Our own presentation of the biblical creation story (and it is our argument that there is but one such story, Genesis 1:1–2:4a) will thus be interlaced—not, we pray, interlarded—with considerations deriving from old and new interpretations of the cuneiform epic.

THE GENESIS CREATION STORY: TRANSLATION

Day One

(1) At the beginning of God's creation of heaven and earth[3]—(2) earth, now, was an amorphous blob, with darkness over Tehom's surface, and supernatural wind sweeping

over water's surface—(3) God said, "Let there be light." There was light. (4) God approved of the light.[4] So God made the light distinct from the darkness. (5) God then named the light "day(time)" while the darkness he named "night(time)." Thus was there evening and morning, Day One. (Genesis 1.1–5)

Day Two

(6) God said, "Let there be a firmament within the water, to separate water (mass) from water (mass). (7) Thus God made the firmament, thereby separating the water which is under the firmament from the water which is above the firmament. It happened so. (8) God named the firmament Sky. Thus was there evening and morning, Day Two.[5] (Genesis 1:6–8)

Day Three

(9) God said, "Let the water under the sky be massed in one place, that dry land may appear." It happened so. (10) God named the dry land earth and the massed waters He named seas. God approved. (11) God then said, "Let the earth produce vegetation: seed-bearing grasses, fruit-trees on earth, each producing its own kind of fruit with its seed within it. It happened so. (12) Earth produced vegetation: grasses bearing each its own species of seed; and trees, each according to its species producing its seed-containing fruit. God approved. (13) Thus was there evening and morning, Day Three. (Genesis 1:9–13)

Day Four

(14) God said, "Let there be lamps on heaven's vault to distinguish day from night. And let them serve as time-markers for days and years.[6] (15) And let them serve as lamps in heaven's vault to shine down upon earth." It happened so. (16) Thus did God make the two major lamps, the greater to hold sway by day and the lesser to hold sway by night. And the stars as well. (17) God set them into heaven's vault to shine down upon earth, (18) that is to hold sway (alternately) by day and by night, to mark off light from darkness. God approved. (19) Thus was there evening and morning, Day Four. (Genesis 1:14–19)

Day Five

(20) God said, "Let the waters teem with living creatures, and let birds fly about over the earth across the spread of heaven's dome." (21) Thus did God create the great water monsters, and every living, stirring creature of all the species with which the water teems, and every species of winged bird. God approved. (22) God then addressed them with this blessing, "Be abundantly fertile and populate the ocean waters, and let the birds increase on earth." (23) Thus there was evening and morning, Day Five. (Genesis 1:20–23)

Day Six

(24) God said, "Let earth produce animal life in its species: cattle, crawlers, land beasts of every kind." It happened so. (25) Thus did God make the land beasts of every kind, the cattle of every kind, and soil-crawlers of every sort. God approved.

(26) God then said, "Let Us make mankind in Our own image, in Our very like-

ness, that they may exercise rule over fish of the sea, and over birds of heaven, and over cattle, yes—over all earth and every mobile thing that stirs on earth." (27) Thus did God create mankind in his image: in the image of God did he create it, male and female did he create them.

(28) God then blessed them. God said to them, "Be abundantly fertile, populate the earth and master it. Exercise rule over fish of sea, over birds of heaven, over every animal that stirs on land." (29) God said, "Look now, I have made you a present of every seed-bearing grass which exists anywhere on earth's surface, and of every tree which has seed-bearing fruit: yours they are for eating; (30) and for all land beasts, and for all the birds of heaven, and for every thing stirring on earth which has the life-stuff within it: every green cereal grass for food." It happened so.

(31) God reviewed all that he had done, and lo, it had his deep approval. Thus was there evening and morning, Day Six. (Genesis 1:24–31)

Day Seven

(1) Heaven and earth and all their populations were now complete. (2) When God on Day Seven brought to an end the work he had done, he desisted utterly on this Day Seven from the enterprise he had accomplished. (3) God blessed Day Seven, declared it holy, for on it he desisted from his task, the creation which God had accomplished. (4a) These are the events, as concerns their creation, of heaven and earth. (Genesis 2:1–4a)

THE GENESIS CREATION STORY: COMMENTARY ON DAYS ONE TO SIX

Day One

(1) At the beginning of God's creation of heaven and earth—(2) earth, now, was an amorphous blob, with darkness over Tehom's surface, and supernatural wind sweeping over water's surface—(3) God said, "Let there be light." There was light. (4) God approved of the light. So God made the light distinct from the darkness. (5) God then named the light "day(time)" while the darkness he named "night(time)." Thus was there evening and morning, Day One. (Genesis 1:1–5)

My translation of the opening words of the chapter as a dependent clause, a syntax paralleled in the opening of the Eden narrative (2:4b) and by the two words which, opening the Babylonian Creation narrative, give the epic its name *Enuma elish*, is no more correct than the alternative: an independent clause rendered "In the beginning God created heaven and earth." The Masoretes who vocalized the Hebrew text could have decided the case in favor of the independent clause by vocalizing the opening preposition with a *qāmeṣ*, or in favor of the alternative by vocalizing the verb as *bᵉrō*. By doing neither the one nor the other, they ambiguated and thus enriched the opening five words of Scripture, suggesting what may have been a traditional syntax for an epic's beginning, and yet permitting us to hear the far grander apodictic tones of an unqualified assertion.[7]

Whatever the case in regard to this opening clause, there is no question that verse 2—a nominal sentence in hypotactic construction[8]—is a parenthetic flash-back, in which the narrator describes how "the earth" would have appeared prior to creation to an observer looking down upon it from somewhere above if that observer's vision could have penetrated the darkness between. What he would have seen was water, watery Depth called *tehom*—a noun of feminine gender, never governed by the definite article, and very often personified as in our capitalization of it here. The surface of the far-stretching water was very likely roiled by the awesomely powerful wind sweeping over it. The verb in its (few) Hebrew and Ugaritic appearances attests to a context of lateral motion, never in the sense of "hovering." The alternative rendering of *rūaḥ ᵉlōhīm*, "the spirit of God," is unexceptionable except that no one seems to know what this means in this context. God himself is supposedly spirit, and "the spirit of God" as a metaphor for his presence is restricted to contexts of divine inspiration or revelation.

So much for questions arising from ambiguities in the Hebrew and answered implicitly in our translation. Other questions, posed not by the Hebrew but by the general context, are: 1) If, according to verse 1, God created heaven and earth on the first day, how to account for the creation of heaven on the second day in verses 6–8? 2) If He created earth alone on the first day, why are we not so told? 3) And was earth then created before or after light? 4) In regard to that light did God not know before he created it that he would approve of it, or is there something subtle that we are missing in the Hebrew that more literally reads, "when he saw that it was good" or "saw how good it was"? 5) And if light is by its very nature distinct from darkness, what was the act of his making a *distinction/separation between light and darkness*? 6) If sun, moon and stars—normally regarded as the sources of light—were not yet in existence, whence did that first light derive and why is that source no longer operative? 7) Since the sun (and the other light-sources) would not be created until the fourth day, what were the demarcations of evening and morning of Days One to Three? 8) Finally, what is the meaning of God's giving "names" to light and darkness; are these nouns not as much "names" as daytime and nighttime?

The poetic approach, presuming a competent author and hence a purposive intent in every detail (and particularly in the problematic ones), must seek a reasonable answer to all of these questions. Needless to say, not every answer will be convincing or even persuasive to every reader; but such occasional failures, while testifying perhaps to the limited perspicacity of the interpreter or to the over-subtlety of the author, need not militate against the poetic method. In respect to our passage here the answers to the first three questions are implicit in our translation. The only thing created on the first day was light. The biblical story, like the Babylonian, begins at a point in time when something existed, something that was material in nature and was to become, but had not yet been transformed into the universe as mankind experiences it. Neither in Hebrew nor in its sister tongues is there a single word that has the unambiguous denotation of our word "universe." Like our word "earth"—which may connote soil, dry land, land and water, and Earth, the third planet from the sun, the world of humans—the Hebrew *'ereṣ* has any and all of these meanings and more. In order to express the sense of "universe," both the biblical and Babylonia compositions resort to that figure of speech called a *merism*, the expression of a totality by means of two opposing and contrasting terms connected by the conjunction "and."

The merism for universe in *Enuma elish* is "up above" (heaven) and "down below" (earth). So also in Genesis, "heaven and earth." That which did exist is in *Enuma elish* a mass of primordial water, which constituted not only the stuff and place of the creation-to-be, but also the personified power of creation, personified as the ultimate gods, male and female principles commingling and begetting. Begetting, let us note, not creation as we experience it—that creation is reserved for Marduk—but other divinities. This unity of the stuff of creation and the power of creation is divided in Genesis. The power of creation is God, the stuff of creation is *'ereṣ* ("earth"), an amorphous blob or watery chaos (containing, as we shall see, "earth" or dry land in its womb), enveloped in darkness, swept on its surface by winds of supernatural force.

The remaining questions, except for the seventh, will have to wait until we have dealt with related problems in the account of the following five days of creation.[9] We may address question 7 now, the creation of a light independent of sun, moon, and stars. And if we recall two of the poetic elements discussed in my poetic *Grammar*, we may conclude that there is no question to begin with. Those two elements are first, the *literal-figurative spectrum* and second, the *meta-literary assumptions* that we often bring to bear to needlessly complicate a literary judgment. In reverse order, why attribute to the biblical author an assumption of heavenly bodies as sine qua non conditions for the existence of light? Surely there is only a negligible qualitative difference between his oil lamp and our incandescent bulb. And why assume the most literal sense of *light*, that is, the physical phenomenon, when light is, for the ancients as for us, a metaphor for knowledge and understanding, for that reassuring order of which the antithesis is the darkness of chaos? To be sure, the biblical author himself leads us on when he goes on to associate that primeval light and its antecedent darkness with the namings *day(time)* and *night(time)*. But perhaps we may thereby learn to plumb for the depths of his sophistication at just those moments when he seems most naïve.

Day Two

> (6) God said, "Let there be a firmament within the water, to separate water (mass) from water (mass). (7) Thus God made the firmament, thereby separating the water which is under the firmament from the water which is above the firmament. It happened so. (8) God named the firmament Sky. Thus was there evening and morning, Day Two. (Genesis 1:6–8)

The word firmament is a Latin invention translating the word which in the Greek renders the *răqī'*, that which God created on the second day. The Hebrew suggests a plate (something firm), pounded out of a malleable metal block. Since this partition is inserted into the water horizontally and will soon appear to function as that plane above earth that we call sky or heaven, its shape more resembles a bowl or a dome. Inasmuch as this sky is perceived by us as a depth of space reaching to the concave plane that limits our vision above us (when not itself obscured by fog or cloud), it will help us to keep the different perception of it by our biblical ancestors if—now that it has been named sky—we render *hārāqīᵃ* as sky-dome or sky-sheet. Conforming our experience to theirs, we need not ask when this sky-sheet supporting its water-load was lifted on high; we may take it as an instance of gapping or ellipsis too obvious to require comment. Two questions, however, are pertinent here as on the first day: Why must the sky-sheet be given a name? Why, or how, evening and morning—before the creation of the sun? And a third question. If separation of waters above and below is not in itself a rather awkward description of a horizontally placed sheet separating a visible watery mass from an invisible one, what is the point of the repetition of this sheet's purpose, in the fiat and in its effectuation?

Day Three

(9) God said, "Let the water under the sky be massed in one place, that dry land may appear." It happened so. (10) God named the dry land earth and the massed waters He named seas. God approved. (11) God then said, "Let the earth produce vegetation: seed-bearing grasses, fruit-trees on earth, each producing its own kind of fruit with its seed within it. It happened so. (12) Earth produced vegetation: grasses bearing each its own species of seed; and trees, each according to its species producing its seed-containing fruit. God approved. (13) Thus was there evening and morning, Day Three. (Genesis 1:9–13)

Dry land, according to the formulation in verse 9—and water, for that matter, as well—seems not to have been, properly speaking, created. Earth, "dry land," or solid matter, seems to have existed under the water's surface until shifts of these masses formed deep pools in some areas and (perhaps in a see-saw-like effect) raised continents elsewhere. Once again the assignment of names. Watery stretches are now called seas, dry land is now called earth. Earth now is called upon to produce growths of two kinds, grasses and trees. Is this to the exclusion of other growths of various sizes and characteristics, such as vines and bushes, or growths that propagate via spores rather than seeds, for example, mosses, mushrooms, and ferns? Hardly. The inclusive term for vegetation in Hebrew (*dš*) is explicated by a merism (grass and trees) expressive of growths low and high. Having created light on the first day and the sky-sheet on the second, both by the fiat "let there be," now on the third day God produced dry land by separating out this preexistent solid matter from its preexistent ambience, the water. Two considerations remain: Why the emphasis on this third day on the reproductive mechanism of the vegetation? And, as once again we have evening and morning with no sun in existence to set or to rise, we now also have the existence of vegetation without sunlight!

Day Four

(14) God said, "Let there be lamps on heaven's vault to distinguish day from night. And let them serve as time-markers for days and years. (15) And let them serve as lamps in heaven's vault to shine down upon earth." It happened so. (16) Thus did God

make the two major lamps, the greater to hold sway by day and the lesser to hold sway by night. And the stars as well. (17) God set them into heaven's vault to shine down upon earth, (18) that is to hold sway (alternately) by day and by night, to mark off light from darkness. God approved. (19) Thus was there evening and morning, Day Four. (Genesis 1:14–19)

The phenomena that God calls into being and fixes (on tracks?) in the concave surface of heaven's vault are lamps to which, in the fiat, three functions are assigned: (1) to mark off day from night; (2) to serve as time-markers for certain periods, some short, some long; and (3) to shine down upon—or illumine—earth below. In verses 16–18, where the effect of the fiat is reported, the lamps are divided into two classes, major and minor; the minor class is constituted by the stars, the major class divided into two separate entities, one greater than the other, and it is to these two that alternate sway by day or night is pointedly restricted. Inasmuch as it is our experience (as it must have been the experience of the ancients) that some nights are moonless, that clouds may for days and nights at a time veil sun, moon, and stars from sight, our author's intent cannot be that it is the sight of the celestial lamps that literally (1) marks off day from night, or must make an appearance to (2) illumine earth below. Similarly, both classes of lamps, larger and smaller, mark off day from night (sun by day and moon and stars by night), and both classes illumine earth below in varying degrees. The holding sway, restricted to sun and moon in verses 16–18, points up a kind of rivalry, as it were, between the two larger lamps, hence a limitation rather than an enhancement of their respective dominion. On the other hand, however, it is only the stars and the constellations that served the ancients in function 2, to mark the close of one year and the beginning of another, to calculate the boundaries of the seasons and the fixed days of the seasonal festivals. And it is the reservation of this function to the stars alone that is reflected in the absence of this element from the list of functions in verses 17–18: here the three functions, applicable to all the celestial bodies, are, in order: 1) to illumine earth, 2) to hold sway by day or night, and (3) to mark off light from darkness.

The last listing, that of marking off light from darkness—not, be it noted, daytime from nighttime—now provides a clue to the answer to question 5, raised in regard to the formulation of the first day's creating activity: "If light is by its very nature distinct from darkness, what was the act of his making a *distinction/separation between light and darkness?*" The answer is that the statement of this activity in the last clause of verse 4 is proleptic: Light in its metaphoric sense came into being on the first day. In the physical sense (would it be appropriate to use the modifier *literal?*) the separation between light and darkness, and their designation as daytime and nighttime (verse 5), did not take place until Day Four, after the creation of sun, moon and stars.[10]

One element in our last sentence is conspicuous for its absence from the account of the fourth day's activity: the naming activity. In contrast to the previous three days of creation, where there is almost something supererogatory or factitious about naming light and darkness *daytime* and *nighttime*, sky-sheet *heaven*, water *seas*, and dry land *earth*, here we have celestial bodies for which biblical Hebrew has several names, and not only is the assignment of names pointedly absent, but the narrator—whom we expect to hear intoning, "God named the greater light *sun* and the lesser light He named *moon*"—leaves us with anonymity or, to sharpen our question, with the pointedly pointless circumlocutions *greater light* and *lesser light*.

Day Five

(20) God said, "Let the waters teem with living creatures, and let birds fly about over the earth across the spread of heaven's dome." (21) Thus did God create the great water monsters, and every living, stirring creature of all the species with which the water teems, and every species of winged bird. God approved. (22) God then addressed them with this blessing, "Be abundantly fertile and populate the ocean waters, and let the birds increase on earth." (23) Thus there was evening and morning, Day Five. (Genesis 1:20–23)

The progression of the acts of creation is now clear. Day One: Light is created independent of any physical source. Day Two: The water is divided into upper and lower bodies by the sky-sheet partition. Day Three: Water masses, islands, and continents appear under the sky and are covered with vegetation of all kinds. Day Four: The celestial luminaries are brought into existence and fixed (in courses) on the curving plane of the sky-sheet. And now on Day Five: The animals are created, but not all of them. The creatures of water and sky are called into being, but not the denizens of land. These are reserved for creation on a separate day. Why?

This simple question masks a rather complex poetic crux. On the one hand, the author might simply have had all living creatures created on one day, reducing the days of creation to six: five working days and one day of rest. If, on the other hand, the author (for reasons yet to be discussed) felt compelled to preserve a (or *the*) seven-day week, why not have all the land creatures except the human created on the fifth day? The sixth day, now featuring the creation of humankind alone, would thus underscore the transcendent dignity accorded to this species by the introduction of God's monologue (*direct discourse*) and the content of that monologue (verse 26), the repetition of man's being the mirror image of God in the narrator's *voice* (verse 27), and then God's grant (again in *direct discourse*) of mastery to this species (verse 28). When the question then is seen in the light of these considerations, the lumping together of the creation of humanity and of non-human land creatures on one day must appear to be either a gratuitous compositional blunder, or a deliberate feature whose poetic intent remains to be divined.

Day Six

(24) God said, "Let earth produce animal life in its species: cattle, crawlers, land beasts of every kind." It happened so. (25) Thus did God make the land beasts of every kind, the cattle of every kind, and soil-crawlers of every sort. God approved.

(26) God then said, "Let Us make mankind in Our own image, in Our very likeness, that they may exercise rule over fish of the sea, and over birds of heaven, and over cattle, yes—over all earth and every mobile thing that stirs on earth." (27) Thus

did God create mankind in his image: in the image of God did he create it, male and female did he create them.

(28) God then blessed them. God said to them, "Be abundantly fertile, populate the earth and master it. Exercise rule over fish of sea, over birds of heaven, over every animal that stirs on land." (29) God said, "Look now, I have made you a present of every seed-bearing grass which exists anywhere on earth's surface, and of every tree which has seed-bearing fruit: yours they are for eating; (30) and for all land beasts, and for all the birds of heaven, and for every thing stirring on earth which has the life-stuff within it: every green cereal grass for food." It happened so.

(31) God reviewed all that he had done, and lo, it had his deep approval. Thus was there evening and morning, Day Six. (Genesis 1:24–31)

The word *ādām* for man or mankind is not independently attested in that sense in any other Semitic language. It may, therefore, be a biblical invention, a word-play on *ᵃdāmā* "earth, soil" expressive of "earthling," and with specific reference to the clod of clay from which this creature is formed in Genesis 2:7.[11] On the sixth day, after all the other land creatures have been called into being, this entity is cre-ated in a separate act. Alone of all the acts of creation, this one is preceded by *in-ternal dialogue, direct discourse* in which God proposes to no audience—implicit or explicit—to produce a creature which, made in the very image of God, will exer-cise an undefined hegemony over nature and all her creatures. This central and dominant role of humankind, referred to in verse 27 as a grammatic singular (col-lective) "him/it" and a distributive plural "them: male and female," is underscored by the repetition of this divine imagery and by the prior address to this creature in regard to the grant of food rations. The questions in regard to humankind's sharing of the divine form derive first from the question as to where on the *literal-figurative spectrum* this expression is to be placed. Does God have a body or form? Perhaps his ministering courtiers, whom he is possibly addressing in what we took to be an in-ternal monologue, are endowed with what Blake called "the human form divine." Or is the expression at the extreme figurative end of the spectrum, representative of humankind's supreme status among created phenomena, and given some defini-tion in the grant of mastery over its environment, inanimate and animate, fauna and flora? In regard to the vegetarian diet allowed both mankind and all living creatures, has the narrator forgotten the existence of carnivores, that is to say, those creatures who cannot live but by sarcophagy? Or does he mean to tell us that these too were originally created by God with a capacity to survive as herbivores?[12]

REVIEW OF DICTION IN THE SIX DAYS OF CREATION

The narratives of the six days of creation reveal, to greater or lesser degree, features of diction whose distribution may provide the close reader with clues as to the au-thor's design. The plotting of this distribution on the graph (table 2-1) should fa-cilitate our analysis and provide a focus to our discussion. I will assign alphabetic labels to these features in the order of their appearance in the account of Day One. A: God's fiat (always introduced by the verb *wayyo'mer* "he said"); B: The response to or the effectuation of the fiat; C: God's approval ("saw/concluded that it was

TABLE 2-1   Distribution of Diction in Genesis I

	Day One— Creation of Light	Day Two— Creation of the Firmament	Day Three— Appearance of Dry Land and Production of Vegetation	Day Four— Creation of Celestial Lamps	Day Five— Creation of Sea and Air Creatures	Day Six— Creation of Land Creatures
A. Fiat	X	X	X	X	X	X
B. Response to fiat	X	X	X	X	X	X
C. God's Approval	X	O	X	X	X	X
D. Demarcation	X	X	O	X	O	O
E. Naming	X	X	X	O	O	O
F. Fixity: "And it was so"	O	X	X	X	O?	XO?

KEY: X = presence in text, O = absence in text.

good"); D: notice of a demarcational activity or function (featuring the verb *hab-dīl*); E: God's naming of the phenomena brought into being; F: the expression *vayᵉhī-ken* "it was (or it became) so/established/fixed." The cipher X indicates presence and the cipher O absence of the feature.

The ubiquity of features A and B, determined by their indispensability in the logic of the creation events, serves to point up the optional nature of the other four features. Optionality, however, is not to be equated with whimsicality or arbitrariness. Hence we must examine them to discern the reason(s) why the author may have chosen (and not always necessarily after conscious deliberation) to include or eschew these features in the varying contexts.

Proceeding then to feature C, why is it absent from the account of Day Two and from this account alone? The very uniqueness of this absence makes speculation difficult, for we have no other absence with which to compare it. Speculation must therefore focus on the nature of what was created on this day and how that compares with what was created on the other five days. Since the feature missing is God's approval, could it be that the phenomenon created on this day is not as worthy of approbation as are the accomplishments of the other five days? And, indeed, there is a sense in which the creation of the firmament is the least substantial of the creational achievements. It certainly pales in comparison to the primordial light created on the first day; it is not significant for itself, as are the creations of animals on Days Five and Six; it is merely a step that is a precondition for the creation of dry land on Day Three and the celestial lamps on Day Four. Indeed, if we compare the accomplishment of Day Two with that of Day Three, when both dry land and vegetation are produced, we realize that the creation of the celestial bodies might well have been arranged on the same day as that of the firmament. Why the author might have rejected this option has already been suggested at the end of our discussion of Day Five; it was vital for him to preserve the seven-day week. And it is perhaps to distract our attention from the logic of combining the activity of Day Four with that of Day Two, the placing of the celestial bodies in the vault that has just been made for them, that the accomplishment of dry land and vegetation is made to intervene between the creation of the sky-sheet and the creation of the lamps that traverse its inner surface.

The foregoing considerations now point to the reason for D, the demarcations on Days One, Two, and Four, and the absence of this feature on the other three days. The demarcations of Days One and Four constitute, as we have seen, a single demarcation, the first one being a proleptic anticipation of the second one. Had there been no demarcation on Day Two, that day's account would have been even more striking in its hollowness than we have already seen it to be. The feature of demarcation is inappropriate to the activities on Days Three, Five, and Six.

The feature of God's naming activity (E) on the first three days and the absence of this feature on the next three days will yield some fascinating insights into the poetic construction of the six days of creation. But first let us consider (and dispose of) an oft-suggested function for the naming activity to begin with. The first two lines of *Enuma elish* seem to equate the absence of names for heaven and earth with their non-existence; hence the notion that until a thing is given a name, expressive of its essence, it does not truly exist. The power of the word, automatic and self-fulfilling, is a concept that seems to have existed in the minds of the ancients (or some of them, at least) as attested in spells, charms, and incantations, perhaps also in oaths and curses. But this need not be the impact of those first two lines. The giving of a name may reflect the arrival at a new state or rank, of power or maturity on the part of the thing or person named. Or it may betoken or symbolize the power and authority of the name-giver. None of these significations would seem to fit the distribution of the naming activity on the six days. The first is an essentially magical concept, hence out of place in the biblical Weltanschauung, which consistently eschews magic, magical practice, and magical thinking.[13] The other two significations would then be ruled out (except perhaps for Day Two, see our discussion of C) for this reason: the power of God would be relevant to all the acts of creation, and the importance of the created entity would indicate a distribution like that for C. Or is it possible that our last sentence is simply wrong? Thus, for example, as the ubiquitous distribution of A and B point to the significance of the different distributions in C, D, E, and F, so may the distribution of the namings on the first three days point to a significance or different significances for the absence of these features on Days Four, Five, and Six. Such indeed will be our argument: The question of the pointed absence of names for sun and moon on Day Four has already been raised and will soon be treated; the absence of names on Days Four and Five, related to the question previously raised about the divisions of the animal-creation activity over those two days, will appear in Chapter 3, in connection with the argument for the poetic organicity of chapters 1–3:15.[14]

In regard now to feature F, the expression *vayᵉhī-ken* "and it happened so," let us first note the question mark in table 2-1 next to the O on the fifth day. The expression is absent in the Masoretic Text (MT) but present in the Septuagint (LXX) immediately after the fiat in verse 20. There Speiser restores it in his translation. And considering its presence on every other day except the first (particularly on Day Six after the fiat calling forth the land animals, and again in confirmation of God's decree after the matter of vegetarian diet), this is a reasonable restoration. We are left now with the absence of this expression on Day One and on Day Six for humankind. The latter poses no problem at all. Given the exceptional details attendant on the creation of the human species (God's prior monologue, the feature of this species' divine image, the repetition of this attribute in the effectuation of the fiat, the dominion decreed for this species in the fiat and repeated in its effectuation), one might judge that the author would have deemed *vay^{e}hī-ken* as supererogatory. As a matter of literary fact, however, there may be no omission to explain (see in table 2-1 the question mark after the O), for the *vay^{e}hī-ken* of verse 30 may indeed refer to the entire section on the creation of humankind.[15] We are thus left with a single omission of this feature, on Day One. Here too the stark response to the fiat (without any such additional purposive details in the fiat or its effectuation as characterize every other act of creation) could hardly be the flat *vay^{e}hī-ken*: it is, rather, the dramatic *vay^{e}hī ōr*. For anyone unpersuaded by this stylistic explanation, there is always recourse to the double meaning in this created light, its metaphoric and physical senses. While the former came into being on the first day, the latter did not until Day Four.

We may close this discussion on diction with a few observations that most of our readers will have drawn for themselves. In contrast with source criticism, which consistently tries to tie single terms or compound expressions with one or another putative document or source or stratum, the poetic approach presumes for the biblical author an untrammeled freedom in regard to diction. More important, however, is the matter of the author's freedom from the constraints that would have been put upon him by indebtedness to an inherited (and already canonical) history of the events of creation. The events he pictures, their sequence, and their articulation in stylistic idiosyncrasies, will serve his metaphoric message and enhance the power of his kerygma; his is the freedom of the creative artist and not of the reality-circumscribed scholar, the freedom of the writer of fiction, not of the faithful recorder whom we call historian.

LITERALISM AND METAPHOR IN GENESIS I AND *ENUMA ELISH*

The presumptions of the poetic approach in regard to the biblical author's creative freedom and the essentially fictive nature of the narratives he spins for his kerygmatic purposes would, I daresay, be unexceptionable to most of today's readers if that author was a contemporary of ours, wielding his pen, so to speak, before our very eyes in the manner of a C. S. Lewis, mixing fabulary prose epics for children, theological science fiction for the unwary adult, and—and, there's the rub—literary criticism of Scriptural texts and unabashedly apologetic essays in defense of orthodox Christianity. Interestingly enough, and for reasons I will explore, the same cannot be said for the author of the *Enuma elish*. Yet in regard to the creation stories produced by both these authors, the overwhelming number of scholars assume that even the learned readership of these tales in antiquity would have accepted them on the literal end of the literal-figurative spectrum.

It is a staple of scholarship that both narratives contain a cosmology, that is, a graphic account of the structure of the physical universe, and a cosmogony, a description of how this structure came to be. To the extent that this characterization is true, it would be understandable if we classified the former as science and the latter as theology, and therefore, by the nature of these two categories, placed the former at the literal end and the latter at the metaphoric end of the literal-figurative spectrum. In his discussion of the biblical account of creation, which he sees as unquestionably derived from the Babylonian, Speiser writes:

> In ancient times, however, science often blended into religion; and the two could not be separated in such issues as cosmogony and the origin of man. To that extent, therefore, "scientific" conclusions were bound to be guided by underlying religious beliefs.[16]

Since *Enuma elish* is hardly a scientific tract, it must be a religious composition reflecting the scientific conclusions of the day; and if these conclusions were themselves guided by underlying religious beliefs (whatever these were) where in this epic does cosmology (the literal) and cosmogony (the metaphoric) begin or leave off? This question is not rhetorical, nor does it seek answer. It is raised rather to highlight an observation that holds for virtually all scholars committed to the study of ancient Mesopotamia: whether the literature studied is regarded as primarily historical, legendary, and mythical, or creative and fictive, the question as to the degrees of the literalness or the figurative is almost never raised. And the prevailing and ubiquitous assumption is that wherever possible the formulations are to be read on the most literal level. However silly a text may seem to us on a literal level, it was literally understood by its ancient audience and—their mindset being different than ours—did not seem silly to them. It is such assumptions, tacit for the most part, but a scholarly consensus all the same, that we shall make bold to challenge, not only in respect to the religious elements in the literature but in respect to the "scientific" elements as well. Not only in regard to the Babylonian epic but to Genesis as well; not only in regard to Genesis but to the Babylonian epic as well.

Let us consider a few of the observable natural phenomena which are or lie behind the constitutive elements in the cosmology of epic and creation story alike. Does the fact of rain require belief in a sky-sheet supporting a primordial reservoir of water? A sheet with holes in it capable of opening or closing to release or check a drizzle or a torrent? In the absence of knowledge of the cycle of evaporation and condensation on an order of magnitude that defies the imagination today, as it would have yesteryear, the ancients were yet aware that the mystery of the waters from above is related to the mystery of the waters below. In the words of Ecclesiastes 1:7:

> All the water-courses flow to the sea,
> But the sea is not full.
> To whatever place the water-courses flow,
> Thither do they go in a return flow.

The association of rain with clouds (the latter sometimes pictured as the vapors from the nostrils of the steeds pulling the storm god's chariot) is an alternate metaphor for the sluice-gates of *tᵉhom/Tiamat*. And the author of "The Hymn to the Aton" probably eschewed the metaphors in his neighbors' literature to coin yet another one for his people in a land where rain is a rarity:

All distant foreign countries, thou makest their life (also),
For thou hast set a Nile in heaven,
That it may descend for them and make waves upon the mountains,
Like the great green sea
To water their fields in their towns.[17]

To overlook the metaphor in this cosmology then is tantamount to making a travesty of the Mesopotamian science from which so much of our own ultimately derives. An analogy would be to credit to Aristotle the belief that the world is supported on Atlas's shoulders; or—as schoolchildren are taught to this very day—that mariners a scant five centuries ago, believing the earth was flat, refused to enlist in Columbus's crews for fear of sailing over the edge. But such overlooking of metaphor, veiling from us the conclusion that there is neither cosmology nor science whatsoever in the creation narratives, accounts in great measure for the misjudging of the metaphoric elements in what must now be seen as purely religious literature, and indeed to make a travesty of the religious beliefs of the poet who authored *Enuma elish*.

This brings us back to the observation made at the beginning of this section, that the Genesis account, were it penned today, could be readily accepted as a fictive composition written to embody a religious preachment, but that the same would not hold true for *Enuma elish*. Baldly put, the near absence of plot and characters in the Genesis account, making for a structure rather than a story, a largely logical structure progressing through six stages of a cosmogonic process conducted by a single Deity, would make for its credibility as a twentieth-century product. The very richness of *Enuma elish*'s plot, its many characters, and the specification of motivations, strategies, and series of alternate successes and failures, make for a concoction of grotesque personae in a welter of tortuous turns in plot, a concoction so lacking in logic or coherence as to preclude its acceptance as a serious work by a contemporary artist, even if the concoction was intended as a fairy tale, much less as a religion-oriented myth.

For the disinterested student of literature, the problem is: whatever can be the kerygma of a tale seemingly so artlessly constructed, featuring so hapless or grotesque a cast? If the preachment is the creative power and enduring lordship of Marduk, is not that very proclamation undermined by the plethora of poetic flaws? And if, like the Pentateuch in the view of modern biblical scholarship, it represents a pastiche of ancient and venerated traditions, some reworked and updated, others left in their jejune primitivity, what moral or spiritual message does it contain to account for the poetic talent lavished on its final formulation and for its faithful preservation by long lines of priests and kings? For the student of the religion of ancient Israel and the biblical literature that embodies or expresses or was produced by that religion, the question is how could the esthetics or ideology or "science" of biblical Israel be derivative of—or, for that matter, have found its counterbalance in—a composition that is so clearly by comparison *infra dignitatem*?

The poetic address to Scripture has thus forced upon us a poetic address to a significant unit of Mesopotamian literature. And this not because the comparative and contrastive approaches have historically juxtaposed *Enuma elish* and the Genesis creation story, but because such a juxtaposition is ineluctable. Regardless of the methodology employed in the study of Scripture—as it was more or less probably intended by its authors and interpreted (more or less) literally or figuratively by various levels of its ancient audience—a full picture of the intellectual capacities, the cultural achievement, and the degree of (what we are pleased to call) sophistication of Scripture's authors cannot be drawn from Scripture alone. And in regard to the assessment of these foregoing elements, we must be aware that conclusions drawn for Israel in the West are as important for the Eastern sphere as those drawn from Mesopotamia are for ancient Israel.

A POETIC READING OF *ENUMA ELISH*

It is a fact that there are literary compositions in which elegance of style accompanies a vapidity of content; and another fact, that deep and subtle ideas may be expressed in a prose singularly devoid of grace, these disproportionate qualities occurring more often in prose, rarely in verse. When the choice diction and seductive rhythms of a resourceful stylist appear in a narrative, in elevated prose, or in epic verse, a critical alarm should sound for the reader if all this talent seems put to the service of nonsensical plot and idiotic personae. Is that author, in a stance akin to the strategy of the unreliable narrator, sending two different signals in these discordant sets of canonical criteria? And if so, for one audience, or two, or for one audience made up of both dull-witted naifs and perspicacious sophisticates? In the last eventuality, the former would be reading the message as serious and straightforward (perhaps at times sober, if not tragic), the latter as tongue-in-cheek, perhaps bordering on the comic; in short, the kind of writing admitting both possibilities and which takes its name from the Latin term designating a dish containing a medley of fruits: satire. It is just this intent, the satiric, that I will divine in my sketch of the *Enuma elish*. But first, a word of caution: to read a literary work as lying in the broad vein of the satiric is not the same as proposing a thorough and poetically satisfying interpretation. For—and in particular if the literature derives from an antiquity whose conventions are themselves a matter for speculation and debate—there is the vexing question of just who and what are the targets of the jeer, the butt of the jest.

I will present, following the epic's narrative flow, the plot and the personae, and the employment of metaphor and the conceptual constructs that figure importantly. In respect to all three I will stress such poetic flaws as redundancy, inconsistency, and incongruity as they would appear to the average reader today.

The first generation of gods, though not specifically characterized by that term, are Apsu and Tiamat, respectively male and female, to be progenitors of all created things, heaven, earth, and the gods. Although the plot as it develops leads us to infer that many gods were created by the aqueous commingling of the First Pair—and it is not at all clear whether the waters are the Pair themselves or only a part of them—only four are named, probably two pairs: Lahmu and Lahamu, and Anshar and Kishar. Anshar sires Anu, who in turn sires Nudimmud (hereinafter to be also known, as the translators inform us, by the name Ea). The latter has no rival among his brothers, hence the inference that other gods were also generated. Since neither the form nor the environment of Apsu and Tiamat are indicated, it is also not clear what the ambience is, at least, of the gods whose rambunctiousness denies sleep to Apsu and disturbs the belly of Tiamat (respectively like the restiveness of a newborn at night, or the about-to-be-born kicking in the womb). Filicide is a reasonable price in the judgment of papa and a suddenly introduced vizier of his named Mummu(!) for a night's untroubled sleep, but this course is vetoed by mama's maternal scruples. When the gods receive word in stunned silence that Apsu is yet determined to destroy them, Ea overpowers Apsu by magical incantation, and upon this Apsu — who a few lines back had a lap in which Mummu might sit and a neck for him to embrace — establishes his dwelling, names that dwelling "Apsu," and assigns shrines in it. Within this holy Apsu, to Ea and his wife Damina is born the great god Marduk. Anu now for reasons unknown creates a fourfold wind to roil the currents of Tiamat and disturb the rest of another set of gods who live within her interior. Upon their instigation she prepares for war, creating serpents, dragons, and a variety of monsters, among them the Great-Lion, the Mad-Dog, the Scorpion-Man, the Dragon-Fly, and the Centaur. To the command of this army she appoints a chief named Kingu, entrusting to him the Tablets of Fate. (Tablet 1, c. 160 lines.)

It is now Ea's turn to sit in stunned silence upon learning of Tiamat's doings. Betaking himself in fear to grandfather Anshar, he repeats in even greater detail Tiamat's creation of the monsters, her elevation of Kingu to command, and her entrusting to him the Tablets of Fate. When Ea cannot respond to Anshar's bidding to go forth and slay Kingu as he had slain Apsu, his father Anu is sent in his place. He in turn recoils in terror from facing Tiamat, and reports back to his traumatized father. Anshar rouses himself from his funk to name Marduk as the new champion. Ea, who had previously been characterized as "mightier by far than his grandfather Anshar," now coaches Marduk as to how to stand up to his great-grandfather. Marduk reassures Anshar that he need not fear Tiamat, not a male — no, a mere woman — and agrees to face her in battle if Anshar will convoke an assembly of the gods (an opposition to the assembly of Tiamat's and Kingu's) to entrust to his sole keeping the determination of the fates, which power they have hitherto shared among themselves. (Tablet 2, c. 130 lines.)

Anshar sends his vizier to Lahmu and Lahamu (who, we shall soon learn, are Anshar's parents). To this vizier he entrusts (in what is the third detailed description) the account of Tiamat's hateful preparations for war against the gods, adding the details of Anu's and Ea's separate routs, and of Marduk's demand for the convocation of the assembly. We then have this tale repeated (now for a fourth time) by the vizier to Lahmu and Lahamu. These two then, together with "all the great gods who decree the fates," make their way from their undesignated places to the undesignated place where the assembly meets. After a banquet of much food and more intoxicants, with bellies full and spirits raised, the gods raise Marduk to kingship over them. (Tablet 3, c. 140 lines.)

The gods decree the fates for Marduk, give him scepter and throne and matchless weapons and, wishing him well, set him on the road to war. He arms himself with bow and arrow, the latter attached to the bowstring, as well as a mace, lightning, a blazing flame stored in his body, the four winds of the cardinal directions, a net to enfold Tiamat, and an additional seven winds (among them the Fourfold

Wind previously created by Anu); he raises the flood-storm, and mounts the storm chariot harnessed to a team of four, sharp-toothed and poison-fanged. In a confused (and confusing) confrontation, Kingu becomes befuddled, and Marduk and Tiamat taunt and challenge each other with bathetic charges, all the while reciting spells and incantations. Marduk prevails, slays Tiamat, captures Kingu, takes from him "the Tablets of Fate, not rightly his," and fastens them to his own breast. The dead and mutilated corpse of Tiamat he splits "like a shellfish into two parts: half of her he set up and ceiled it as sky, pulled down the bar and posted the guards. He bade them not to allow her waters to escape." Marduk immediately "crossed the heavens . . . squared Apsu's quarter, the abode of Nudimmud, as the lord measured the dimensions of Apsu." (Tablets 4, c. 145 lines)

In the twenty-two lines of Tablet 5 that have been preserved, Marduk constructs "stations for the great gods, fixing their astral likenesses as constellations. . . . In her (Tiamat's) belly he established the zenith. The moon he caused to shine, the night (to him) entrusting." In Tablet 6 Marduk proposes the creation of "'man'—he shall be charged with the service of the gods that they might be at ease." At Ea's suggestion Kingu, found guilty of contriving the uprising and of making Tiamat rebel, is slain, and out of his blood mankind is fashioned. Heaven and earth are apportioned among two classes of gods, and a shrine modeled after Babylon is built. This takes up about seventy lines. The remaining ninety lines of this Tablet and the 160th line of Tablet 7 are devoted to the proclamation of the fifty names of Marduk.

If the foregoing précis strikes the reader as less than edifying, perhaps even tedious, that judgment should be reconsidered for the original, which is at least thirty times as long. As for the action, the creation of the gods is more like a spawning than a birthing, the war more like maddened vipers of various species hissing and spitting venom, the space given to pointless talk greater than that to action by a factor of twenty, and the few actions mindlessly duplicated. Thus Apsu (here and elsewhere in cuneiform literature a synonym for heaven) is slain by an intrepid Ea, who makes the dead Apsu the place of his habitation. When Marduk in turn kills Tiamat, he divides her in half and ceils the upper part of her as the Apsu. Where the gods lived before the death of Apsu or of Tiamat is an enigma, as we saw in the conflicting images of the gods kicking within the womb of Tiamat and by their noise in the nursery, which keeps Apsu awake. As illogical as are the two separate battles against the two constituents of the watery chaos, personified as father and mother, and depersonified as reservoirs above and below, a poetic defense might argue that actions are often illogical. But the protean metaphors—of Tiamat as shapeless liquid mass, dragon-monster with two legs and gaping maw, human-like in maternal tenderness, black magician spewing incantations; of Apsu, also watery mass, cradling on his knees the childlike vizier Mummu, who embraces his neck, and ogre-father who would rather strangle his children than diaper them—are surely as meaningless as they are silly, an author's invention and not an inherited time-hallowed religious tradition, and if at all pointed, pointed to evoke scorn and ridicule.

If the metaphoric intent of the imagery is still open to question, let us cite the description of the newly born Marduk. A literal interpretation of the poet's intent here would be analogous to an art critic in a distant future deriving our twentieth century's standard of human beauty from some of Picasso's more adventurous paintings. Even without the broad context of the achievements of Mesopotamian civilization, the abstract concepts in this passage alone are enough to guarantee that number and size of sense organs are symbolic of faculties of unrivaled power:

> When Ea saw him, the father who begot him,
> He exulted and glowed, his heart filled with gladness.
> He rendered him perfect and endowed him with a double godhead.
> Greatly exalted was he above them, exceeding throughout.
> Perfect were his members beyond comprehension,
> Unsuited for understanding, difficult to perceive.
> Four were his eyes, four were his ears;
> When he moved his lips, fire blazed forth.
> Large were all four hearing organs,
> And the eyes in like number, scanned all things. (ANET p. 62 TAB. I, 89–98)

Our analogy to Picasso's revamping, say, of human physiognomy is relevant in another sense. For just as we search for the esthetic consideration that led to Picasso's innovations, we might search for the reasons for our poet's decision to resort to four ears and four eyes (never features of Marduk in Babylonian iconography), and lips that create fire by their friction as fitting metaphors for this god's powers. Could it be a playful and less than reverential attitude toward the gods that is responsible for the grotesquerie? It is certain that the poet was not reaching for the most appropriate or respectful of similes when he had Marduk divide dead Tiamat like a mollusk. To compare the first mother goddess to an oyster is certainly risible, and the upper half as image of the firmament ceiling is as fitting as the lower half for earth's plane is not. Ea's courage in facing Apsu is negated by his quailing before Tiamat; Marduk's male-chauvinist sneer at his adversary's femininity is as unworthy in itself for an immortal as is this deprecation of the great-grandmother of us all; the mechanical waxing and waning of the moon ordained by Marduk lends the epic a verisimilitude in regard to the heavenly scene that is offset by the absence from it of the sun; and is this last due to the remainder of Tablet V's being broken away, or to the usurpation of Shamash's orb by the god who was hailed at birth as "my son or the Sun"?

The list of absurd features in regard to plot, personae, dialogue, and characterization could be extended, but it has probably become wearisome as it is. Perhaps as perplexing as any detail is the building of Babylon (apparently on earth and not a heavenly counterpart), a city whose inhabitants knew full well that it had made its rise late in the history of lower Mesopotamia. Decreed by the gods as a shrine to be named, "Lo, a chamber for our nightly rest," this sanctuary—following upon the creation of mankind "for the service of the gods, that they might be at ease"—is reared by the gods themselves, who labor for an entire year molding its bricks. And this picture of gods in the hundreds slaving on earth to build a residence when all heaven is theirs is all the more perplexing when we consider that they are supreme in exercise of magical power and unrivaled in the decreeing of destinies. Šimtu, the word for fate or destiny, is often a synonym for that death which comes to all. Yet in *Enuma elish*, as in other myths, possession of the Tablets of Destiny no more insures dominion than magic guarantees victory. Indeed, like the stuff of magic and the elusiveness of ineluctable fate, so characterless are the gods in their collectivity and their individuation. Not until the catalogue of praise in the fifty names of Marduk do such values as love, grace, sympathy, and justice make a first appearance.

And perhaps here we have arrived at a crux for interpreting the satiric mixture, in this epic, of the serious and the humorous, the contrast of implicit standards or norms of the good and beautiful and the explicit absence of these norms or their violation. The crux is the association, perhaps the wedding, in religion of power and morality, or the converse, the dissociation or divorce of the two. But as the kerygma of the six-day creation account in the context of ancient Israel's religion requires a recourse to Mesopotamia for comparison, so does the assertion of the Babylonian creation account's kerygma require a comparison with the biblical account. It should prove helpful then to compare the metaphysics and anthropology of paganism with those of normative, biblical religion as they have been discerned in scholarship, and as these characterizations may be modified in keeping with the readings of both creation accounts at the metaphoric end of the literal-figurative spectrum.

PAGANISM AND BIBLICAL RELIGION COMPARED AND CONTRASTED

Pagan religion is polytheistic, anthropomorphic, and mythological. This is to say that pagan religion acknowledges the existence of many gods (polytheism); that it views the gods in terms of human form, function, needs, and motives (anthropomorphism); that as a consequence of this it features the gods in various adventures (mythology). Biblical religion is monotheistic, indulges in anthropomorphism only as figures of speech, and in general is scornful of mythology. God, having no divine rival, and subject to no needs, cannot have adventures. In pagan religion, gods are born and suckled, grow to maturity, contest for satisfaction of appetites and emotions, battle for prestige and power and mastery, indulge in sex, and are subject to failure, defeat, and death. Biblical religion not only removes the One God from the domain of mythology, but as often noted, it demythologizes creation itself, and this even while it echoes with the constructs of pagan mythology. Thus in Genesis, *tehom* and supernatural wind are only dimly resonant of Tiamat and the Roiling Winds of her boisterous brood. This last is true, however, in narrative or discursive prose (as in Genesis 1) and in a few passages of poetry, which I will consider in a moment. In other passages of verse the hypostasis of various aspects of nature into god-like personae (particularly participants in the clash attending creation) echoing, no—reduplicating—the gods of paganism presents a problem that has never, in my opinion, been persuasively resolved. This phenomenon is especially challenging to a poetics of Scripture such as my own, which claims a single authorial voice for all of the Hebrew Scriptures, regardless of form or category. And I will attend to this problem, but in an excursus, so as not to impede the flow of argument in regard to the creation accounts.

In Psalm 104 the biblical author pictures entities or aspects of nature (which in paganism are hypostasized) as impersonal forces doing the bidding of God. This poem also features a cunning employment of tenses (perfects, imperfects/preterites, and participles functioning as gerunds) to refer to God's—no, YHWH's—acts of creation, while at the same time representing them as taking place in an ongoing present. Verse 1 begins with a self-addressed invocation, "Give praise, O my being, to YHWH," and forthwith responds:

> YHWH, my God, how great You are!
> (2) Donning glorious majesty,
>   Draping light like a cloak,
>   Stretching heaven like tent-walls.
> (3) In the [upper] waters laying his chambers' beams,
>   His top story the clouds
>   Which rides on winged winds.
> (4) He makes winds his agents [or angels],
>   Flashing fire his servants.
> (5) He fixed earth upon her foundations,
>   Never to slip her moorings.
> (6) With Sea [*tehom*] like a blanket had you covered it [lit., him],
>   Waters overtopping the mountains.
> (7) From your reprimand they fled.
>   At your thunder's sound they panicked in flight,
> (8) Up the hills, down the valleys.
>   To the place you fixed for them.
> (9) A boundary you set for them, uncrossable.
>   Theirs never again to blanket the earth. (Psalm 104:2–9)

The psalmist then contrasts the life-enabling role of the now-tamed waters as fructifying rains and mountain freshets. Turning to the heavens, he declares:

> (19) Moon he made for the regular seasons,
>   Sun—he knows his setting. (Psalm 104:19)

The problem of this last verse—the striking discrepancies between the first stich and the second—has drawn surprisingly little comment. One would expect that as a reason is given for the moon's creation, so one would be given for the sun's creation. A review of our discussion of Genesis 1:14–18 will show, however, that the poet—having reference, let us suppose, to this prose passage—had little choice on this point. The function of marking off the seasons, shared in Genesis by moon and stars, the psalmist may ascribe to the moon alone, the sun having no role in this regard at all. But what singular function does that leave to the sun? Illumining earth and holding sway are functions he (note the pronoun) shares with the moon. Still, the poet could—if a bit lamely—have concluded with the sun holding sway by day. The choice he does make, however, seems not only not to be a balancing contrast, it is an utter non-sequitur. And non-sequitur it has to be judged unless we penetrate to the poet's intent, the same intent expressed in the pointed failure in Genesis 1 to give names to either the greater or lesser lamp. The sun-god (except for a few Mesopotamian urban centers where the moon-god Sin figures prominently) is supreme in the celestial scene. In our psalm, the moon is permitted the dignity of serving humankind in its calendrical role, but sun (Sol/Helios in classical antiquity; Shamash in Mesopotamia, perhaps ᵈMAR·UTU[K] in *Enuma elish*), even without the definite article—like *yārēᵃḥ* "moon"—is no god, no autonomous willful creature. It—not he—is a lamp, no more, no less, rising on schedule and on schedule setting.[18]

A continual and continuing problem for the practitioner of the comparative-contrastive approach, whether in ascertaining the features of different religions in antiquity or interpreting the literature from which we get our information on those religions, is the avoidance of construing parallels on flimsy grounds or overdrawing the significance of contrasting features. We have noted many of the unmistakable parallels that insightful scholars have drawn from the two creation stories, even as we have been stressing unmistakably divergent treatments of themes in the two stories, which are themselves parallels to one another. Yet given the small compass and economy of expression in the Genesis prose account, and the busy doings and talking of the far lengthier Babylonian epic, it is likely that any attempt to be exhaustive in treating the two would be more likely to fail in regard to contrast rather than to similarity.

With the foregoing in mind as a caveat (and admitting Psalm 104 to the biblical prose material for comparison) let us consider a feature that figures centrally in the one, and only incidentally in the other. Psalm 104 begins where *Enuma elish* ends: the "heavenly" palace of creation. The psalm begins, however, where the Genesis story begins: with the creation of light. Light was to the ancients, as it is for us today, not only the opposite of physical darkness, but the antithesis of that darkness which is chaos; light is the precondition (and a metaphor) for perception, intellection, and reason, indeed for order itself. And order is what creation is all about. Our own word for the universe is the Greek *cosmos*, which means order. To marvel at the wonders of creation is to stand in awe of its order. And this is why the narrator of the Genesis creation story, who is so sparse with details, so thrifty with words, stresses the concept of species and their reproduction. Vegetation is divided into growths small and large, the cereal grasses representative of the first, trees of the second, each with its own mechanism for reproduction. In the case of grasses we eat the seeds themselves; in the case of trees, we eat the fruit, which contains the seeds within it. The focus on reproduction in the case of animals is explicit in God's blessing of fertility for the animals he creates on Days Five and Six, in the rubric "according to its species" separately specified for the water creatures and for the birds on Day Five, and for the large animals and for the crawlers on Day Six, as it was on Day Three for the cereal grasses and for the fruit trees. Be the species flora or fauna, the narrator suggests, the marvel is that reproduction itself is so orderly that they do not—except on rare occasions—produce biological sports. All the species breed true, like "the fruit trees each producing its own kind of fruit with its own seed within it." Whether we can come up with a persuasive conjecture for this emphasis on order generally and specifically in regard to biology may be a test of our poetic insight. But, as we stressed earlier, neither Genesis nor *Enuma elish* purports to be a scientific lesson in cosmology (or biology). Both presume the popular science of their day. Any perceptive creature can witness to the order about him, the order of which he is a part. These compositions are concerned not so much with things as they are, not even with how they came to be, but rather with the power that brought them into being and the nature of that power. What is the nature of that power called Deity, and how does that power relate to mankind?

Power. That idea would seem to be indissociable from the idea of divinity in any language, and seems in Hebrew to underlie the root 'el in many words betokening might or divinity. Yet in the distinction between pagan religion as polytheistic (power shared among many gods) and biblical monotheism (power reserved to the one and only God), between the many and the One, between a race of superhuman beings and a unique abstraction that transcends human categories, a crucial difference is often overlooked. This difference has been worked out in laborious detail by Yehezkel Kaufmann. In the pagan scheme of *Enuma elish*, as in every polytheistic religion, the seat of ultimate power is not in the gods.[19] Ultimate power is a force beyond them, a force they may tap to achieve their ends, and which other creatures may tap for effective use against the gods themselves. We have no name for that power, nor, apparently, did the ancients. Anthropologists, borrowing a term from South Pacific islanders, call it *mana*. If we may take a conceptual term of our own that is usually thought of as technique (procedural and adjectival in sense) and treat it as a noun standing for an essence or entity, we might call it Magic. The gods themselves are identified with the stuff of nature, or separated out from it as personified beings wielding the functions of natural phenomena as tools or weapons. Thus the ambiguities of Tiamat and Apsu as the watery stuff of nature, commingling in mindless fashion and engendering within themselves the boisterous turbulent powers which are their offspring. And this water-stuff, which is the very environment of the personified offspring itself, assumes differentiation as "person" in the struggle for mastery and, indeed, survival. And the weapons which these deities deploy against one another are the stuff of magic: spells and incantations and plants to put out poison.

The break with paganism, the revolt—if you will—against it, is the revolutionary theology of biblical monotheism, expressed in the spare and austere style of Genesis 1. Whereas in paganism the ultimate power is an enveloping ocean of power—inanimate, impersonal, mindless—Scripture has that ultimate power as the infinite source of all existence; in language borrowed from metaphysics, the Ground of Being. But this power is anything but inanimate. It has the attributes that the pagans reserved for the gods and denied to their environment: the attributes of person. In Scripture this ultimate power and environment (a rabbinic name for God is *Hammaqom* "The Place"), this God, is Person. Sexless, but not without gender—a category of grammar—this Person may not, out of respect, be referred to as "it," and so becomes a he. This Power is Person, Who is conscious, Who purposes, Who wills, Who acts. Who is the source of nature, yet independent of it. Who by His will and purpose is present in nature and her creatures while remaining essentially beyond, unlimited, uncontainable and—for the most part—unfathomable.

The schematic sketch (figure 2-1) may be helpful in making graphic the contrasts between the two conceptions:

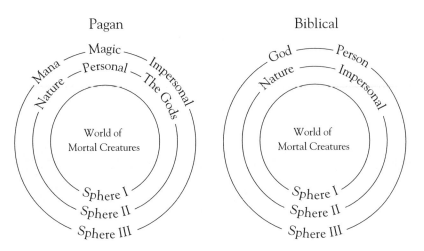

FIGURE 2-1 Theological Spheres, Pagan and Biblical

I. The inner sphere is the same in both conceptions. It is the material world, animate and inanimate, mineral, vegetable, and animal, human and nonhuman. It is
   part of, and subject to, the workings of:
II. The sphere of natural powers and laws. In the pagan conception these powers are
    personified as the gods, themselves part of the natural order, and subject to its
    powers or wielding them as the case may be. In the biblical conception these
    powers and laws are never "person." In both conceptions this sphere derives
    from:
III. The ultimate source of all power, which in the pagan conception is impersonal
     and capable of being manipulated, whereas in the biblical conception it is the Per-
     son called God, sovereign in will and purpose.

In a manner of speaking, if we focus on the sphere of deity, pagan religion is natural, while biblical religion is supernatural. The revolutionary nature of biblical
thought is that it transposes the attributes of spheres II and III. Deity, which in paganism is person, and subject to the impersonal sphere of III, becomes (in the
Bible) person as sphere III, and the impersonal sphere of magical power becomes
sphere II.

One of the crucial consequences of this shift is in regard to the very existence of
the cosmos, the ordered world. In paganism, the order of the universe—including
the existence and power of the gods—may be dissolved by a reckless tapping of the
mindless power of sphere III. In biblical religion no such danger exists, for the cosmos is there by will of God. Another consequence is in regard to the religious
stance of humankind. The praxis of magic is the coercion of power, hence incantation, charm, and spell. In paganism it is conceivable for man (or other entities) to
go over the heads of the gods, so to speak, and to coerce even deity by magical
technique. The practice of religion is appeal or prayer. Paganism allows, therefore,

for either religion or magic. Biblical religion does not admit of magic as an option over or against prayer.

PAGAN AND BIBLICAL ANTHROPOLOGY: A CONTRAST

Since theological speculation is an exclusively human activity, it would be surprising if a basic theological composition were silent on the place of mankind in the scheme of things. Neither *Enuma elish* nor Genesis offers such a surprise. Essentially centered on the nature of the divine, neither of these narratives goes into great detail on this point. Enough is said, however, to provide an interesting contrast in viewpoints.

The gods of paganism are children of nature and, as such, have natural needs. Not least among them is food. It is this problem which must have been featured at the end of Tablet V of the *Enuma elish*, the greater part of which has been lost to us. But it is clear from what follows in Tablet VI that the options available to the victorious gods were to work for themselves or to impose servitude on their defeated rivals. Marduk proposes an alternative:

> Blood I will mass and cause bones to be.
> I will establish a savage, man shall be his name.
> Verily, savage man I will create.
> He shall be charged with the service of the gods
> That they might be at ease! (ANET Tab. VI 5–8 p. 68)

And from the blood of the executed Kingu mankind is created, a race of serfs to till the fields and harvest the crops, to tend the flocks and the herds from among which sacrificial offerings are made, feasts for the gods. Throughout Mesopotamian mythology as well as polity, this is the consistent theme. The gods have a vested interest in order in human society, that their serfs may prosper, and that their offerings continue regularly and without interruption. To that end the gods even deign to mandate law and justice for their slaves, bestowing upon them the institutions of kingship and priesthood. Yet as the gods continue to vie with one another, so do various polities—or perhaps, vice versa. When Assyria conquers Babylon, it appropriates for itself the anthem *Enuma elish*, and in the Assyrian version it is its own tutelary genius, the god Aššur, who is hymned as victor over Tiamat, king of the gods and lord of creation. But victorious in war or defeated, mortals remain serfs charged with the service of the gods.

Not so in Genesis. In a few deft strokes an altogether different status is conferred on mankind. In *Enuma elish*, the prototypical god Anu begets Marduk's father, Ea, "in his own image." In Genesis, when the stage has been set for him, man appears, the culminating work of creation, made by God "in his very own image to conquer earth and hold rule over fish of the sea, birds of heaven, cattle and every crawling creature that stirs on earth." What is Scripture's intent in assigning to humankind the image of God? Does it betray a notion that in some literal sense the One God assumes shape on occasion, and that shape is, to use William Blake's phrase, "the human form divine?" Perhaps. But Genesis 9:6 gives it no literal meaning. In the context of assigning a sanctity to human life the shedding of human blood is forbidden, the reason being, "for in the image of God did he make man-kind." Elsewhere in the ancient world (and also more recently) divine parentage has been claimed for individual heroes, even for a single strain of the human race. Nowhere else but in Scripture has Deity so benevolent bestowed such royalty and sanctity on the entire human race.

But to what end, for what purpose? The Genesis account does not say. But an-other biblical author, the poet of Psalm 8, does. Here is his hymn to the God of Creation:

Psalm 8

(2) YHWH, our Lord, how majestic your name over all earth,
    Even as your glory is rehearsed across the heavens!
(3) Out of the mouth of suckling babes you founded power
    On account of your adversaries,
    To bring to naught the enemy ever-vengeful.
(4) Lo, as I view your heavens,
    The work of your fingers,
    Moon and stars you fixed in place, [I muse:]
(5) What is mere man, that you take note of him,
    Earthling, that you take notice of him?
(6) That you have him falling so little short of being a god—
    Wreathing him in dignity splendid?
(7) That you grant him lordship over the work of your hand?
    All things 'neath his feet have you subjected:
(8) Small cattle and large, all of them,
    And animals of the wild,
(9) Birds of heaven, fish of the sea—that traverse oceans' currents.
(10) YHWH, our Lord, how majestic Your name over all the earth!

Consideration of nature's grandeur—for all its vastness a trifling indication of its Creator's power—moves the poet to reflect on the greatest of marvels: the role assigned to puny mankind, to be creation's overlord. What prompted God to endow this race, in itself as weak and helpless as an infant at the breast, with this status? The answer is in verse 3, the responsible role assigned to mankind, and not—as assumed by many interpreters—Israel. This latter and clearly erroneous conclusion owes to a number of factors. For one there is the overlooking of the force of the participle normally rendered "avenger," a meaning which would inhere in the qal participle of nqm; the form here, disguised as a regular *hitpael*, is the dura-tive *hitpael* (recovered by Speiser) and so rendered by us as "ever-vengeful."[20] But when does (or did) that vengefulness begin, and for how long does (or will) it en-dure? The answer, again, is to be sought in the one identity of "your (God's) adver-saries" with the ever-vengeful enemy to the end of whose elimination God has cre-ated humankind. This enemy is the one element in the Genesis creation story not explicitly present in the psalm, but there can be no question that it is *tehom*, itself the metaphor for chaos, *tōhū wābōhū*, here personified as the enemy of God in time of yore, of both God and humanity in the ongoing present. The role of humankind as creation's overlord, explicit in Genesis 1, is here complemented in a metaphor (which may be a clichéd homily in today's synagogues and churches, but is in the original formulation one) of breathtaking boldness: humankind is God's ally, partner—so to speak—in the continuing struggle against the powers of chaos which, subdued at the time of creation, may nevertheless erupt at any time to challenge the stability of the cosmos. "Your adversaries"—God's opponents—are the "ever-vengeful enemy" that puny mankind has been given the power to oppose, even to bring to naught. The metaphor of physical chaos is thus given a moral dimension.

A moral dimension: the dimension that I find notably absent in the *Enuma elish*, either in Tiamat/chaos or Marduk/lord of creation. A dimension implicit in Genesis 1 in the (moral) dignity assigned to humanity and perhaps implicitly withheld from humanity in *Enuma elish*'s depiction of this species as a race of serfs created for the single purpose of serving the pleasure of the indolent gods. If we recall that we had initial recourse to *Enuma elish* for a comparative-contrastive foil for the interpretation of Genesis 1, ventured into a poetic reading of *Enuma elish* itself, then broke off that reading to contrast the religions of paganism and Scripture, we shall recognize that our discussion of both religious cultures as read from both religious literatures respectively remains incomplete. And we shall return to some of the questions which remain wholly or partly unresolved in an excursus devoted to Scripture's mythopoeic imagination, and the question as to whether the author of that great text on paganism, *Enuma elish*, was himself a pagan.

For the present, however, the reader whose main concern is the text of Scripture may be feeling somewhat restive over my failure to return to the seventh and last day of creation. Before I go on to this, let me plead in mitigation the clear poetic division between the six days of rest (in rabbinic tradition, the *šēšet yᵉmē hamma'ᵃśē*) and the seventh or Sabbath day, which concludes that First Week (*šibᵉᶜā yᵉmē šabbātā*). And, as a distinct pericope, these six days have their own kerygma. That kerygma is, first, the statement of Scripture's metaphysical foundation, a kerygma that cannot be appreciated except in contradistinction to that of the pagan environment in which, and to combat which, Scripture came into being. That kerygma is embodied in figure 2-1 and its accompanying explication. Not separable from that metaphysical statement in filling out the kerygma is the role assigned to mankind in Genesis 1, not fully appreciable without the contrasting role assigned to it in the pagan conception, and—again—not fully appreciable without the climactic blossoming of that role in Psalm 8. Morality as a concept is unthinkable except in terms of a set of norms for creatures who are both free and fallible, the norms themselves deriving from a source that transcends those creatures and has them as a central concern. To recapitulate then the kerygma of the six days of creation:

Creation—the order brought out of chaos—is the work of a transcendent unitary power perceived as person, called God. That chaos and disorder, which is called in another metaphor, a metaphor for evil—a moral category—the forces of darkness, is not eliminated by the creation of light, but merely held in check. Disorder, the forces of darkness, is/are dormant, yet ever-vengeful. The end, the culmination, perhaps the very purpose of creation, is the human race. Humanity's delegated sovereignty over nature (a hyperbole, if we think of storm, earthquake, volcano) is a pale dignity compared to the moral aspect of human grandeur, which—implicit everywhere in Scripture—is made explicit in Psalm 8. Humankind is God's partner in the ongoing work of creation, of sustaining the world against God's adversaries, who are, necessarily, mankind's also.

Day Seven

(1) Heaven and earth and all their populations were now complete. (2) When God on Day Seven brought to an end the work he had done, he desisted utterly on this Day Seven from the enterprise he had accomplished. (3) God blessed Day Seven, declared it holy, for on it he desisted from his task, the creation which God had accomplished. (4) These are the events, as concerns their creation, of heaven and earth. (Genesis 2:1–4a)

The varied effects made possible by the paratactic deployment of waw-conversive in narrative prose are extensively discussed in *Toward a Grammar*.[21] We saw that succeeding clauses may express a simple sequence, temporal or logical; a synoptic event followed by a resumptive expansion; a relational clause bespeaking circumstance, purpose, result, and so on; and an ambiguating double entendre allowing for the possibilities of hard and soft disjunctional function. This last pericope, for all its small compass, could occupy many pages in exploratory discussion of these possibilities. Our translation above is therefore but one of many possible translations. At each of the five appearances of the waw-conversive we were compelled to settle for a single one of several options. Repetitions of the same verb, phrase, or event alternating with different words for the same action or concept, and sudden appearances of seemingly redundant information in hypotactic syntax, make for a literary maze of Daedalian intricacy.

One semantic crux will serve to exemplify the riddle-like nature of this passage. The passage opens with a statement in the passive mood about the completion of the world ("heaven and earth") together with its contents, follows with the same action in the active mood with God as subject and referring to the world now as "his work," which he had done (how not?), and proceeds to tell us of God's desisting from "all his work" (again!) which he had done (again!); and, once more, in giving God's motive for blessing and sanctifying the seventh day it repeats the theme of desisting, "from all his work" (yet again!) which, literally, "God created to do." Thus the verb ʿsh "to do" a third time, but in conjunction with brʾ "to create." Since the latter verb never appears in Scripture with other than God as its subject, the sense of "create," that is, to bring into being out of nothingness, may stand to the "doing" or "accomplishing, completing" sense of ʿsh as the alpha to the omega: from absolute beginning to perfect ending. The semantic crux, however, lies in another repetition: the first two (of the three) appearances of Day Seven. In verse 2 God first completes (klh) His work on Day Seven, and then desists from it on that very same Day Seven. Since tradition understood the verb sbt more in the sense of "to rest" than "to desist," and further understood that rest to be absolute in contrast to the work that was performed on the first six days (this last being the plain intent of verse 1), God's completion of his work on the seventh day smacked of a contradiction. No wonder then that the Greek versions render the first part of verse 2 by God's completing his work "on the sixth day!"

This implied emendation of the Hebrew text may, however, be based on a misunderstanding of the text. Thus: the physical world and its constituencies were indeed completed on/by the sixth day (verse 1). On the seventh day, however, God brought the work He had accomplished on those six days to a fitting close by a creative act of non-action; in desisting he created the Sabbath (verse 2). This act is not so much explicated as it is defined in the act of blessing and sanctification (verse 3). If such is the intent of the Hebrew, we have before us another example of the poetic craft of the biblical narrator. The more pointless the repetitions, the clumsier the prose, the more incumbent upon the critic to search out the reasons why the presumptions in favor of a gifted artist must yield to one in favor of a hapless editor bound to the inanities of an inherited and cult-centered text.

To enhance our appreciation of the subtle ambiguities and complementary alternatives presented by the vocabulary and syntax of Hebrew, I offer a second translation—every bit as faithful as the first—and set the two in parallel columns for easier comparison, the contrasting alternatives appearing in boldface type:

1. Heaven and earth and all their populations were now **complete.**	**Completed** now were heaven and earth and all their populations.
2. **When** God on Day Seven brought to an end the **work he had done, he desisted utterly** on this Day Seven from the **enterprise** he had accomplished.	God **now** brought to a close on Day Seven the **enterprise he had completed by desisting utterly** on this Day Seven from the **work** he had accomplished.
3. God blessed Day Seven, **declared it holy** for on it he desisted from **his task, the creation which God had accomplished.**	God **thus** blessed this Day Seven, **establishing its holiness, in that** on it did he desist utterly from **this enterprise of his,** [this enterprise] **which God had created [from beginning] to perfection.**

If we may presume, in regard to this Sabbath pericope, a restored presumption in favor of its careful and meaningful design, the content of this pericope and its placement at the conclusion of the creation story raises a different kind of literary question, a question that is rarely raised because we live in the penumbra of the biblical sabbath. A mandatory day of rest on one day out of seven is a cultural fact of the Western world into which we and our children are born, and is an essential element of the time frame in which we are all reared. Mores and law, and social, political, and economic sanctions have been mustered to fix and preserve this peculiar Israelite institution for more than twenty-five hundred years. And even with the shift of "the Sabbath" for the majority of the Western world from the seventh day to the first, the seventh day has not become just another work day. Seventh day and first are merged for the most secular of us into the social and economic rhythm that is expressed in working weekdays and leisure-oriented weekends. Were this not so, were we not so culturally conditioned (not to speak of those of us who are religiously committed), many of us would be compelled to the poetical judgment that this biblical creation narrative culminates in an anticlimax.

The problems we have reviewed about the sense of various details of the creation process, their incompatibility with general surmise about the age or develop-

ment of the world we inhabit, with what we know about the causal relationship between sun and daylight, between sun and plant life, have precluded for many in our
generation an appreciative approach to this chapter of the Bible. But even for
these—if they can manage to hold in abeyance the arguments for evolution, the
findings of ecologists and paleontologists, astronomers and physicists—there may
yet be something grand in this story of creation. For all the primitiveness of its science and the myopia (if it is that) of its anthropocentricity, there is a sweep to the
progression of creation, from the wonder of a sourceless light through the emergence of heaven with its sun, moon, and stars; from oceans teeming with schools of
minnows and monster leviathans, to continents with their multifarious plants and
creatures of earth and sky, to the appearance of nature's king: humankind. But is all
of this artful construction to arrive at one cultic dogma? An omnipotent God who
needs but speak to create a universe suddenly breaks off his "labors" so that mankind
—no, not humankind at large, rather the tiny people of Israel—must come to a
mandatory rest one day out of seven!

Were the Sabbath, the seventh day, merely a cultic dogma, the culmination of
the Creation story in the notice of this day's sanctification, in four verses of multi-
layered and richly ambiguous syntax, would constitute an anticlimax. But the key
to the understanding of this peculiar biblical institution—and its place in Scripture's first chapter—was provided some twenty years ago by Matitiahu Tsevat in an
essay entitled "The Basic Meaning of the Biblical Sabbath."[22] This interpretation
has proved so seminal in my own understanding of many a biblical text that my use
of it involves a double danger. On the one hand, I may read into Tsevat's argument
elements that he never intended and for which he should not want to be held responsible. On the other hand, I may give the impression of claiming credit for ger-
minal constituents of his argument. To avoid these risks I shall essay first a recapitulation of Tsevat's argument:

> Although there are etiothetic rationales associated with the sabbath in widely scat-
> tered Scriptural texts, such as the palliation of the hard lot of bondservant or beast of
> burden (social or humanitarian legislation) and establishment of celebratory occa-
> sions (cultic enactments of weekly or seasonal days and cycles), these are not central
> to the meaning of the sabbath. That central meaning is encapsulated in an oft recur-
> ring phrase *šabbat leYHWH* "a sabbath of the Lord." The cessation of labor once every
> seven days is an obligation on the Israelite householder and not a privilege, as is the
> ban on the cultivation of the soil on every seventh year of the *šemitta* cycle. In the
> latter case (e.g., Leviticus 25:3f.), "'The land shall have a sabbath of complete absten-
> tion; it is a sabbath of the Lord.' Man in refraining at regular intervals from exploiting
> the land for his own needs, thereby places it under the lordship of God. And with the
> land he places himself, its possessor and cultivator, under divine dominion." In the
> former case (e.g., Decalogue and Leviticus 23:3), God's dominion over the land is par-
> alleled and complemented by God's dominion over time. "The Israelite is duty-bound
> once every seven days to assert by word and deed that God is the master of time . . .
> [to] phrase it more simply: Every seventh day the Israelite renounces his autonomy
> and affirms God's dominion over him."
>
> The Bible elsewhere presents us with the proposition that time is indeed God's do-
> main. Two psalm passages of identical structure speak of him, respectively, as the lord
> of space and the lord of time: "Yours is the heavens, the earth is yours also," and

"Yours is the day, the night is yours also" (Psalms 89:12 and 74:16). . . . God's dominion over space and His dominion over time are largely two aspects of the same thing: His dominion over man and especially over Israel. There is, therefore, nothing incongruous nor bold in the conclusion that every seventh day the Israelite is to renounce dominion over time, thereby renounce autonomy, and recognize God's dominion over time and thus over himself. Keeping the sabbath is acceptance of the sovereignty of God.

"All regularly recurring events in ancient Israel were bound up with the cyclical changes of nature—the seasons or the revolutions of the moon or the sun. . . . Man who structured social a time in accordance with the natural divisions of time was likely to be in harmony with nature. . . . For the sabbath, however, there is no room in this physico-human periodicity. Having no bond with nature other than the change of day and night, the sabbatical cycle, is indifferent to the harmony of the universe. . . . Since the rhythm of the sabbath is the only exception to this prevailing natural rhythm, and since the exception in no way derives from time as such nor is traceable to any aspect of time experienced in the ancient Near East, it is likely that the dichotomy between the sabbath on the one hand and nature on the other hand was not unintentional. The intention was, I suggest, to fill time with a content that is uncontaminated by, and distinct from, anything related to natural time, i.e., time as agricultural season or astronomical phase. . . . That content, displacing the various ideas and phenomena associated with natural time, is the idea of the absolute sovereignty of God, a sovereignty unqualified even by an indirect cognizance of the rule of other powers."[23]

In the years since the publication of Tsevat's essay, my appreciation of his insights into biblical texts seemingly unrelated to the sanctification of the seventh day in Genesis 2, and my admiration for the cogency of his argument, occasioned in me a sense of scandal that so seminal an interpretation of so central a biblical institution could so fail of remark—not to speak of appreciation—among biblical scholars. The sense of scandal gave way in time to a less self-indulgent reflex: an attempt to understand the cool reception of this contribution by so widely respected a student of ancient Israel and of her ancient neighbors and their cultures. *Tout comprendre, c'est tout pardoner.* The factor operating against acceptance of Tsevat's discovery was, I came to realize, a complex of metaliterary conventions, specifically: the perception of the literal/metaphoric dichotomy as one of polarity rather than spectrum; of the naivete of the ancients as against the sophistication of us moderns; and the habit of attributing to ourselves a capacity for the metaphoric and the abstract while limiting our early forerunners to the literal and the concrete. These deeply ingrained prejudices incline us to view matter and the space it occupies as concrete conceptions apprehensible by the most naïve, while time as a dimension and a potential is a concept of so high a level of abstraction as to be denied to the early or primitive mind.

Thus the physical objects or phenomena—astral entities, mineral, vegetable, and animated matter—are explicitly listed in the Genesis catalogue of creation; and the sovereignty of the creator over his creations is so obvious as to require neither formulation of the axiom nor its explicit application in this narrative context. Not so, however, as concerns the reaction of that abstraction that we call time. That word (in Hebrew, of course) is absent from the Creation catalogue. Yet it is undeniably there, mythopoeically present in the succession of days; even the first day, the second day, and the third, before the creation of sun, moon, and stars on Day Four.

The Genesis creation story is structured on the theological time-frame of the seven-day week. The authors of Scripture were well aware that the theology of paganism was chained to the natural rhythms of time, even to the celestial deities, personified as Sun, Moon, Stars, and Constellations, which lorded it over the cycles of days and nights, months and seasons and years: personified powers of nature which are demoted in Genesis to mere artifacts, lamps rising and setting on command of the One Creator.

In its conclusion on the Sabbath theme, the biblical creation story is a parallel to the Enuma elish epic, which concludes with an anthem of praise to Marduk. The proclamation of his fifty names, ascribing to him the powers and attributes of the gods, comes across to us almost as a paradoxical paroxysm: polytheism straining for a monotheistic rebirth. In vesting all power and praise in Marduk, paganism comes close to abandoning polytheism altogether. Like a number of hymns from ancient Egypt, it all but breaks through to a formulation of monotheism. But it was left to Israel to arrive at that formulation, to make deity not only one, but Ultimate and Person, the formulation already presupposed in the first words of Genesis: "In the beginning, God . . ." The Sabbath passage is the creation story's doxology: a hymn of praise that is not so much an assertion of the oneness of Deity as a call to Israel to acknowledge that oneness, to affirm the lordship of that One over ourselves, over our person and our property, over our time and activity—which is to say, the uses to which we put time. This biblical paean to the One Creator, proclaiming the seventh day as "the Lord's/YHWH's Day," is anticipated in the first day. This day, and the five that follow it, are merely rungs necessary to arrive at the seventh. Thus the very creation of the seven-day week is a poetic triumph of Israel's religious genius.

The purely poetical consideration of the parallelism between the doxological conclusion of Enuma elish in the fifty names of Marduk and the doxological conclusion of the creation story in the seventh day sabbath holds, of course, whether one accepts the former as the literal intention of a pagan poet, or (our own view) as the metaphorical message of a poet who has outgrown the polytheistic postulates of paganism. In content, however, the fifty names celebrating Marduk's sovereignty still reflect the nature-tied theology of paganism, while the new way of structuring time in Genesis—breaking with the time-and-nature-bound theology of paganism—creates, so to speak, a new concept of time, time which is meta-natural, meta-physical. And also, in contrast with that pagan sense, and with the sense soon to be introduced, the sense of historic time, that is, time as measure of events, the time of the first seven days is meta-historical. The seven-day week of creation, to be observed by mankind in historic time—now that time itself has been created—is the culminating praise of the lord of matter and spirit and time itself. Were we to remove the days, the first six and the seventh, from the Genesis prose-poem, the tapestry of the creation composition would fall apart, for we would be removing its very warp and woof. From beginning to end, in material and structure, in content and form, the Genesis creation composition is—like its Sabbath conclusion—a celebration of that Deity who transcends both time and nature

THERE ARE A NUMBER of issues of critical import for the understanding of biblical religion, and particularly in connection with the Creation, the Sabbath, and the mythopoeic imagination in and beyond Scripture whose treatment would have further convoluted this discussion. Hence I have deferred them to a concluding chapter. Their placement at the end of the volume rather than here is in the interest of moving more expeditiously to the narrative that is generally regarded as a second creation story, discordantly divergent from the one preceding it.

THREE

EDEN AND EDEN'S
AFTERMATH

The characterization of the story that begins with Genesis 2:4b as a second creation narrative is almost never challenged, questioned, or even examined in modern scholarship; not even by scholars who, disenchanted with the Documentary Hypothesis(/es), do not keep company with those who ascribe authorship of the first narrative to P and the second to J. That this second narrative involves creational themes is undeniable; whether that warrants the genre-label "creation story" is not. That it contains elements parallel to features in the first narrative is true, but such parallelism does not in itself point to it as independent of its precedent account; and such independence is both an assumption and a consequence of the genetic division. Nor is independence a necessary consequence of such dissimilarities as in the deployment of the names of God or indulgence in anthropomorphisms. The only persuasive basis then for the independence of these pericopes and their separate origins would be in such discrepant or contradictory items as the following: the creation of humankind, male and female, in a single action in the first account as against the discrete steps of that creation in the second; the creation of the animals before man in the first account, and after his creation in the second, and—no more; these two exhaust the list of discrepancies.

That these two do, indeed, constitute discrepancies and not contradictions will emerge from our poetic analysis of this second story and from its comparison with the first narrative. In a word, we shall see that Scripture begins with that narrative technique, the synoptic-resumptive, the first story constituting the former and the second the latter. My procedure in the close reading of the Eden story will be to present it in my own translation, to raise such moot questions of narrow philology as are vital for the story's poetical analysis, together with the answers I find cogent and persuasive, and then to proceed to larger questions of interpretation, which will entail a comparative study of the Gilgamesh Epic. Only then will I present my understanding of Eden's kerygma, a kerygma whose dilemma begins within the garden and finds its resolution outside it.

THE STORY OF EDEN

Man Is Placed in the Garden

(4) When YHWH-God made earth and heaven—(5) no wild shrubs having yet appeared on earth nor wild grasses having yet sprouted, since YHWH-God had made no rain to fall on earth and man there was none to till the soil; (6) yet a ground flow might well up and water an entire stretch of ground—(7) YHWH-God fashioned Man, [from] a clod of earth, and blew life-breath into his nostrils: Thus Man became a living being. (8) YHWH-God planted a garden in Eden in that time of yore,[1] placing there Man whom he had fashioned. (9) YHWH-God caused to sprout from the soil all trees, pleasing to the sight or valuable for food, including the tree of life within the garden, and the tree of knowledge—good and bad.[2] (10)—Now a waterflow spills from Eden to water the garden, branching out into four headwaters. (11) The name of the first is Pishon; that is the one which winds through Havilaland, there where the gold is; (12) (That area's gold is high-grade, there too is bdellium and lapis lazuli.) (13) The name of the second river is Gihon, this is the one that winds all through Cush territory. (14) The name of the third river is Tigris, this is the one which flows east of Asshur. And the fourth river is the Euphrates.—(15) Taking up Man, YHWH-God set him down in the garden of Eden for the task of tending it. (16) YHWH-God laid this charge upon Man, "Of all the trees of the garden you may eat freely, (17) but of the tree of knowledge—good and bad—of it you are not to eat: for when you eat of it you shall be doomed to die." (Genesis 2:4b–17)

This story begins, like the preceding creation narrative and the *Enuma elish*, with a temporal clause, followed by a parenthetical flashback and then the main clause, a stylistic feature that suggests the possibility of a common literary tradition rather than mere coincidence. All three opening sentences feature the merism "heaven and earth" for the created universe. Another merism common to the two Genesis narratives is "shrubs and grass," standing for all vegetable growth, big and small. A third merism—in verse 5—has escaped general notice: God and man. Here they are the two opposites, each of whom might have—but had not yet— made vegetation possible by providing its quintessential requirement: water. God provides water in the form of rain, and man's role in watering the soil is expressed in the rubric "irrigation."

A tiny point, this last observation. But for the literary detective the most minute point may provide a critical clue. Chesterton's Father Brown solved his most celebrated mystery by observing that it is the all-too-obvious and commonplace that becomes invisible to witnesses. In that story it was the postman. In ours it is an ecological detail so obvious that we should never have missed it had it been omitted: of course plants grow as a consequence of falling rain or irrigated fields. This "of course" in our minds is culturally determined and far from ubiquitous or universal. In Egypt, where it almost never rains, agriculture is totally dependent on irrigation, the channeling of the Nile's water to the fields under cultivation. In Canaan (or Palestine) irrigation was not the practice; the farmer prospered or went hungry in the measure that heaven's rains flowed or were withheld. This contrast between a land where man may rely on his own efforts and a land where he is altogether dependent on Providence appears in Moses' exhortation of Israel to be obedient to God:

> For the land which you are about to invade and occupy is not like the land of Egypt which you have left, where you sowed your seed and watered with your foot [on the pedal-pump] like a vegetable garden. The land you are about to cross into and occupy, however, is a land of hills and valleys, only from heaven's rains does it drink water. It is a land which has ever the attention of YHWH your God, from year's beginning to year's end. If then you obey the commandments . . . (Deuteronomy 11:10–13)

The area where crops are dependent both on rain and an extensive system of irrigation canals ("the waters of Babylon") lies between the Tigres and Euphrates. It is to this area of the world that the author of this verse and chapter (as indeed the pervasive authorial voice of Scripture) is primarily oriented. Himself situated on the land-bridge between Mesopotamia to the north and east and Egypt to the south and west, he—as Speiser once observed—sets his face to the former and his back to the latter.

The location of Eden in the vicinity of the Tigris and Euphrates rivers is explicit. The very name "Eden" we now know was the Sumerian term *edin*, "the plain" between the two rivers in the south. And the Hebrew word *'ed* (appearing only once more in the Bible and formerly translated "mist") is a Sumerian or Babylonian word for a river or for a stream that breaks through to the surface from underground. The function of this water-source spilling into Eden is to account for the luxuriance of the garden, while outside it, in the absence of rain or cultivation, everything is barren.

The realistic details of the garden of Eden's location[3] and the casual, matter-of-fact observations on the ore and minerals of the region, the setting of the stories to come, should not divert us from the focus of this narrative's opening: Man. In contrast to Genesis 1, this is not a general creation account, proceeding from one act to another. Rather, assuming the world created in the preceding account, it begins with the making of mankind in one area of that world, a mankind embodied in a single "earthling" shaped out of a lump of clay (or, more literally, a shaped lump of clay), animated by the breath of life. Placed in the garden abundant in shade trees and fruit trees, his purposed role is defined by two infinitives in verse 15, normally and correctly translated, "to till (or work) it and tend it." This literal rendering has been noted by commentators as a contradiction of what follows; namely, that man did no work in Eden but began his career as tiller of the soil only after banishment from the fruitful garden. Our own translation of the two infinitives resolves the problem of contradiction by treating the two verbs as a hendiadys. Man's role in the garden is to tend it, to be its keeper or steward. But why does the garden need a guardian at all? Who or what other creatures are there in the world? Clearly, this statement of role is anticipatory. There will yet be other protagonists. But before these are introduced, the story presses on to the principal mechanism of its plot. Among the many trees of many kinds in the garden, trees presumably known to us, the readers, in our existential world, are two trees we have never experienced, fabulous trees, one a tree of life, the other a tree of knowledge,—that knowledge characterized as "good and bad" or "good and evil." We might have expected a tree of life and a tree of death, or a tree of knowledge and a tree of ignorance. Just what are the potencies of a tree of life and a tree of knowledge? And why does God implicitly permit man to eat of the tree of life when he explicitly excludes from man's diet the fruit of the tree of knowledge?

What is the tree of knowledge, and why does God forbid its fruit to man? If, as the serpent will later suggest, man's eating of it will render him "like God"—a status that is contrary to God's will—why did God make this tree available in the first place? Apparently, as a test of man; clearly, as a test of his obedience. But a test of obedience could have involved any tree—why this one in particular? And the obedience test could have been arranged without allowing man to eat the plucked fruit. This points to the possibility that man was not so much forbidden to eat of this fruit as given a choice: Eat of this tree and die, or abstain from it and live. For how long? Forever? (How long, by the way, is forever?) Another line of questioning has to do with the potency of the fruits of the two trees. Assuming that such potency is unlimited, that is to say the power of the fruits is literal, mechanical, and ineluctable, then if man had not given in to the temptation to eat of the tree of knowledge he would never have died. By virtue of his continued obedience? No, for what need then of the tree of life! By virtue then of his access to the life-guaranteeing fruit of the tree of life. But if that be so, why could man not have eaten of the fruit of both trees, eating first of the tree of life, whose fruit had never been forbidden to him, and then of the tree of knowledge? An answer to this is either that the author wants his readers to assume that the man had just not gotten around to eating of the tree of life before he succumbed to the temptation to disobey, or that he did not learn of the power of this tree's fruit until it was too late, that is, after having eaten of the tree of knowledge. An alternative understanding, which would still assume the mechanical power of the fruit to guarantee life, would require periodic ingestion of the fruit. This would then allow for man's having indeed eaten of the tree of life, and the death-consequence of his partaking of the Tree of Knowledge constituted by the denial to him of further access to the tree of life.

Another question is how to translate the words that qualify the kind of knowledge that the fruit of this tree engenders in the eater: "good and bad," or, as the older translations render the Hebrew, "good and evil"? The difference in translation is critical for interpretation. "Good and evil" presupposes that the nature of the knowledge is moral; that is, knowledge of right and wrong, for "evil" is a moral category. To opt for this interpretation is to raise a conundrum. If man had no knowledge of right and wrong before he ate of the fruit, would he have known that disobedience was an evil? And if he did not know, how could he be blamed for an action of whose wrongness he was unaware? To opt for the interpretation "good and bad," that is, knowledge of a general rather than of a moral nature, is to raise another set of questions. Is "good and bad" a merism for all knowledge? If so, then man would have had no knowledge of any kind until he ate of the fruit, including—presumably—knowledge of God's charge. Since this is manifestly absurd, "good and bad" would have to qualify a particular area—a particularly critical area—of knowledge, which was closed off to man except for the key provided by this fruit. What area of knowledge might the author have intended?

Man Finds His Mate

(18) YHWH-God thought, "It is not good, man's remaining alone. I shall make him a suitable help." (19) Whereupon YHWH-God formed out of earth all beasts at large and all the fowl of heaven, bringing each to man to see what he would call it; and whatever man would call it—each living creature—that would be its name. (20) So man gave names to all cattle, all fowl of heaven and all beasts of the wild—yet for man no suitable help had been achieved. (21) YHWH-God then cast a stupor upon man. While he slept he took out one of his ribs and sealed the flesh at that spot. (22) YHWH-God then built up the rib which he had taken from man into a woman, and he brought her to man. (23) Man said, "This time now—bone of my bones and flesh of my flesh! This one will be called Female for from Male was she taken." (24) Hence it is that man leaves his father and mother, sticks to his wife so that they become a single flesh. (Genesis 2:18–24)

The contrasts, even contradictions, in the accounts of mankind's creation here and in Genesis 1 could hardly be more striking. In Genesis 1, each act of creation proceeds by the fiat of God, the style is spare, and anthropomorphic attributes are notably absent. God "creates"—the verb *bārā'* in Hebrew never appears with other than God as subject—mankind in his own image. The notion that God has a form, which would be anthropomorphism indeed, is not clearly present, and we concluded that this is a poetic metaphor for the supreme dignity and worth with which God endows humankind, an endowment underlined in God's granting mankind dominion over earth and all her creatures. Another argument against the image of God as a literal reference to form is that mankind is created in one act, both male and female ("God created man in his image, in the image of God created he him, male and female created he them" [1:27].) To take this literally would require the single divine form to possess both male and female sexual characteristics, a manifest absurdity.

In Genesis 2, the author indulges freely in anthropomorphisms. God fashions man out of clay (so too the animals in verse 19), the verb for "fashions" being the one that is used most characteristically of a potter, who works in the same medium. And the creation of mankind involves several stages: first the shaping of the male and his animation, then a surgical extraction of a part of his body, which is built up into a female. And whereas in Genesis 1 mankind is the culminating act of creation, following God's production of the land creatures on the sixth day, here the fashioning of the creatures of earth and sky takes place after man has come into existence. There surely is a contradiction here, but only if the intention in both accounts is a matter of chronological order. Priority and precedence are not necessarily a matter of timing. Both are also terms for ranking. Last is not least—it may even be most. Certainly that is the case in Chapter 1, where the theatre is built, the stage set, the courtiers are assigned their places, and the last to appear—man—is the cynosure, the king.

In Chapter 2, the metaphor is different but the assignment of value and dignity is identical. The creation of the macrocosm having already taken place, the focus is on man and the habitation created for him. The creation of the beasts and birds is in itself only incidental to the enterprise of getting him a mate. In the course of that enterprise, his superiority over all other creatures is revealed in the recognition that none is his match. So, too, is his majesty expressed in that God delegates to his deputy the act of naming them; naming, which we saw in Chapter 1 and in *Enuma elish* as a metonym for the creation of something or the fixing of its existence, or for the authority of the name-giver. And in the event, it turns out that the enterprise of providing man with a mate is not so much a matter of matchmaking as it is a matter of completing the creature called earthling. Half a species is none at all. Man as a species is only viable as both male and female. The creation of man as a "him" in 1:27, and then immediately thereafter as a "them," male and female, may be viewed as the synoptic version of which this section in Chapter 2 is the resumptive expansion. Thus it turns out that in both chapters even the chronological order is the same: man was not truly created until after the production of the beasts and birds. In this respect, the discrepancy (not to speak of contradiction) as between the two accounts in the order of creation is nonexistent. But it is noteworthy that another possible and likely discrepancy in the two accounts—had they indeed been independent of one another—has been avoided. We noted in our discussion of the creation story that the stress on the higher dignity of humankind would have been reinforced by having the beasts created on Day Five, leaving to Day Six the creation of man alone. But this, we can now appreciate, would have indeed been discrepant with the poetic necessity in the Eden story to have the other animals created on the same day as man, inserted between the two stages of the creation of the human species.

It is doubtful that the assumption of the priority of the male over the female—universal and ubiquitous until most recently in our own place and time—is to be equated with Scripture's prescription of such sexual inequality. But it is undeniable that the dominance of the male sex over the female has been so read, as prescription, into the ancillary role projected for her by God: "a suitable help"—as we render it—for man. In the older translation, "a help meet"—which yielded the still-heard corruption "helpmate"—the word "meet" is cognate with "mate, match, mitten," and has the sense of "fitting, following suit, corresponding to." The sense of this correspondence (the precise meaning of k*eneged*) between man and his "help" is expressed in three ways. First, God's bringing each of the species to man for naming is evocative of an intelligence test, a test that man passes. Unlike the young Tarzan, who thought of himself as a peculiarly hairless ape, man knows that none of the creatures brought to him is a match for him, of his own suit, so to speak. This recognition on his part is implicitly assumed in the names he assigns to them, and in the narrator's note that "a help corresponding to him was not achieved." The second expression of this recognition is in the Hebrew idiom uttered by man when woman is brought to him. Without necessarily knowing that surgery had been performed upon him, that a rib of his with the attached flesh was used to produce this creature, he says of her that she is "bone of my bone and flesh of my flesh." Our corresponding idiom in English, normally in reference to one's natural offspring, is "my own flesh and blood." The Hebrew idiom is a metaphor for the abstract concept of "essence." The very tale, the myth of woman's origin, may therefore have arisen from a literal phenomenon (flesh and bone) that became a metaphor for essence, which in turn suggested the myth of woman's manufacture from man's literal bone and flesh. The third expression of correspondence is in the pun of woman's "name," which balances the previous naming of the animal species. The Hebrew words 'îš and 'iššâ make for a passable pun, and pun it is, for the two words are etymologically unrelated. Translators of the Bible into English are grateful for the pairs male/female, man/woman. But what a headache for the translator into Greek who would attempt to render this pun into an idiom in which the terms are *aner/andr-* for man and *gyne* for woman!

The (literary) facts of pun and metaphor in this story of humanity's creation are clear. The question that must be addressed, however, is why they are here, and why did the author choose to indulge in such playfulness? Or, if it is silly to question a writer's penchant for whimsy, why did the editors of Scripture choose to include so whimsical a tale? If there is a moral to the story, it would seem to be that male and female share the same essence. Why, however, go to such roundabout length to affirm a moral when there is no reason to believe that its principle was ever brought into question?

The answer to these questions lies in verse 24, which concludes this episode, a verse whose meaning, purport, and function are all problematic. "Hence it is that man leaves his father and mother, sticks to his wife so that they become one flesh." This verse seems clearly to be a parenthetic remark; an afterthought, so to speak, thrown in by the author. Or, as most modern scholars are agreed, it is an editorial gloss, which is to say, an explanatory remark added by someone other than the author. The trouble is that this "explanation" seems to answer no problem, and itself raises a whole series of questions. Supposing the verse is a gloss, what does that mean: that the gloss explains the story, or that the story is an explanation of the behavior described in the gloss? Did the man in ancient Israelite society leave his parents when he married to join the family of his wife? There is not one such case in the Bible, for the Israelite family was patriarchal: the woman left her parents to join the family of her husband's father. Might there have been a time in Israelite prehistory when its social organization was matriarchal? Of which this sentence might be a trace? For all that such a theory has been advanced and accepted by many, there is not a shred of evidence for it. And even if there were, the puzzle would remain: why would the biblical editor seek to account for a practice no longer in force, and—by use of the present tense—treat it as if it were, indeed, still in force somewhere?

The entire assumption about this sentence is that it addresses itself to a sociological or anthropological phenomenon, a social organization in which the male leaves his family and joins the family of his wife. We have seen that from the point of view of ancient Israel's society such a phenomenon is unattested. Indeed, there is precious little evidence for the phenomenon of matriarchy in the ancient Near East. But there is another consideration that is more to the point, and which ex poses the absurdity of the assumption. It is that even in societies that are organized along the matriarchal principle, it is not the case that the husband abandons his family to join that of his wife. In such societies, marriage is an arrangement by which an outsider male has visiting rights in his wife's lodge. The husband returns to his own mother's family where, as maternal uncle, he plays the father-role of provider and protector for his sisters' children. The absurdity of our assumption lies then in the application to a literary text of an anthropological explanation that has no validity in anthropology. The coup de grace to the initial assumption is, however, a common-sense observation of literary logic. The story of woman's having been originally extracted from man would logically culminate in: "This is why woman leaves her father and mother." After all, it is she who is returning to her source, not he to his.

That is to say, according to the logic of the story she is returning to her source. But she is not returning to her source according to the explicit statement in this sentence. On the other hand, despite the seeming explicitness of this sentence, man cannot be returning to his source for, according to the logic of the story, she is not his source. We must conclude then that the purport of the sentence is not in either one of them returning to his or her source. (Note, for reference to our following argument, the possessive pronouns "his or hers" in this English sentence!) What alternative remains? Perhaps the forsaking of parents on the part of both, which woman clearly does in the act of marriage, in a literal sense, and which man also does in the act of marriage, in a figurative sense.

The key to the solution of our problem lies in a linguistic and literary phenomenon. If the reader will backtrack a few sentences, to the notice in parentheses, he (or she) will remark that despite the existence in English of a neuter gender, that gender is not a common gender, applicable to either a male or a female antecedent, hence the rather prosaic, if not laborious, "his or her" course. The problem of pronouns and the genders of their antecedents is somewhat more complicated in Hebrew than in English, for here there exist only two genders, masculine and feminine (there being no neuter), and gender—let us remember—is a grammatical phenomenon rather than a sexual one. All nouns, concrete or abstract, even if not persons, fall into the category of a he-it or a she-it. Whereas in dealing with a reciprocal relationship in English, be the nouns animate or not, we can say "one another," in Hebrew, even in regard to inanimate (neuter) nouns, one must say something like "the [noun] his brother" and "the [noun] her sister." When nouns of both genders are involved, Hebrew normally opts for the masculine, functioning as a common gender.

Applying this now to our verse 24 we will realize that the intent in both clauses is that both man and woman leave their (lit., *his*) parents and hold fast to *one another*. (No finely developed sense of style is required to appreciate why the author would not resort to anything so pedantic as, "That is why a man leaves his father and mother and a woman leaves her father and mother.") Our verse is not a gloss on the part of author or editor. It is the culmination and raison d'etre of the entire episode, an episode in which our author addresses in mythopoeic imagery a celebrated and ongoing phenomenon in the dynamics of the human family. On the one hand, there exists no closer and more binding relationship than the genetic or biological one of parent and child. On the other, the universal incest taboo requires that bride and groom be at least minimally removed in terms of consanguinity, of biological closeness. And yet, what heartaches have been suffered, how many parents have felt betrayed, how many marriages have been destroyed because of the psychic strains involved in the demands of the marriage act: that parents allow and children give the biologically-unrelated mate a loyalty superseding that which is owed to one's own "flesh and blood!"

Who would argue with our author's verdict? To come down on the side of the family is to give highest priority to the tie between husband and wife. And yet, in terms of flesh and blood (or, in his terms, flesh and bone) and by virtue of years of nurture and devotion, are not parents closer, more deserving of solidarity? Not really, our author replies, and tells his story. Man and woman were originally one. For reasons we have not yet gotten to in our story, it was crucial that man (he, she, they?) become two. Every marriage is a union; not a union of two strangers, but rather a reunion, a reconstitution, so to speak, of the primordial unity.[4]

Perhaps half a millennium after this story was written, Plato in *The Symposium* has Socrates at a banquet, engaged with friends in a discussion of love. Aristophanes (master of comic drama, be it recalled) attempts to account for the love-affinity in its various heterosexual and homosexual permutations. Originally, he tells us, all humans were joined pairs: male-male, female-female, and male-female (*androgynous*, from *aner/andro-* "man" and *gyne* "woman"). The riotous and heavenward vaultings and somersaults of these eight-limbed creatures led to the sundering of these pairs by Zeus. Let the ribald Aristophanes speak for himself:

> This meeting and melting into one another, this becoming one stead of two, [is] the very expression of his [man's] ancient need. And the reason is that human nature was originally one and we were a whole, and the desire and pursuit of the whole is called love. . . . Each of us when separated, having one side only, like a flat fish, is but the split-off of a man, and he is always looking for his other half.

Perhaps we need not go back to Athens twenty-three hundred years ago to argue the naturalness of the Genesis imagery. A chivalrous way of presenting one's spouse in English is still "my better half."

Man Finds His Fate

(25) The two of them, man and his wife, were naked—yet they were without sense of shame.—(1) The serpent, now, was the most wily of all the beasts of the wild which YHWH-GOD had made—He addressed the woman, "Did God really say: 'You are not to eat of any tree in the garden?'" (2) The woman replied to the serpent, "Of the fruit of the garden's trees we may eat. (3) Only of the fruit of that tree at the garden's center did God say, 'Eat not of it, touch it not, lest you die.'" (4) The serpent said to the woman, "You won't die at all! (5) Full well does God know that

when you eat of it your eyes will be opened wide, and that you will be like gods, knowing good and bad." (6) The woman concluded that the [fruit of the] tree was all right for food, indeed seductive to the eyes, and the tree so appealing for its wisdom-giving property. So she took of its fruit and ate. Along with her she gave to her husband too, and he ate. (7) Then were the eyes of both of them opened and they became aware that they were naked. So they sewed together fig leaves and made themselves loincloths. (8) When, at the breezy time of day, they heard the sound of YHWH-God moving through the garden, man and his wife hid from YHWH-God among the trees of the garden. (9) YHWH-God called out to man, the call to him: "Where are you?" (10) He replied, "I heard the sound of you in the garden, and I was afraid over being naked, so I took cover." (11) Then he said, "Who [could have] informed you that you were naked? Can it be that you ate of that tree of which I charged you not to eat?" (12) Man said, "The woman you put at my side, she it was gave me of the tree—so I ate." (13) YHWH-God then said to the woman, "How could you do so?" The woman answered, "The serpent beguiled me, and I ate." (14) YHWH-God said to the serpent,

"For having done this,
Banned are you from among all cattle and wild beasts:
On your belly shall you travel,
And dirt shall you eat
All the days of your life.
(15) And enmity do I impose
Between you and the woman, that is,
Between your offspring and hers:
He shall strike at your head,
And you shall strike at his heel."
(16) To the woman he said,
"Grievous will I make
The pangs of your childbearing:
In pain will you give birth to children
For your husband ever your lust,
So that he will lord it over you."
(17) To the man he said,
"For doing your wife's bidding,
Eating of the tree about which I expressly charged you:
'You are not to eat of it,'
Bewitched is earth 'gainst your interest,
Anguish the price for your eating of it
All the days of your life:
(18) Thorn and thistle she'll put forth for your tilling
And you shall need eat the grasses that grow wild.
(19) By the sweat of your brow
Shall you get to eat bread,
Until you return to earth:
From earth were you taken—

Yes, earth-clod you are,
And to earth-clod shall you revert."

(20) Man then named his wife Eve [*Hawwa* "life"], for she became mother of every human to live. (21) YHWH-God then made garments of skins for man and his wife, and clothed them. (Genesis 2:25–3:21)

The interpretations of this part of our story, its core, are marked by disturbing inconsistencies, be the interpreters orthodox religionists on the one hand, or hard-headed skeptics or liberal scholars on the other. Let us examine typical examples of each.

The importance of this story for doctrinal Christianity is difficult to overstate. Yet the doctrinal reading of it seems to require that the tale be taken both as literal history and as philosophical allegory. The serpent is Satan, embodiment of evil and tempter of mankind to disobedience to God. Man's failure to resist the serpent is the first fall from grace, the "original sin" that infects all generations and cannot be purged without special aid from God. Verse 15, for example, has been called the protoevangelion—the adumbration of the gospel (i.e., the good spiel), the good news of salvation: The woman who is set in inveterate enmity with Satan is (not Eve but) Mary, she who will bear the Savior, who will be the one to crush the serpent's head. He will defeat Satan; by his self-sacrifice he will become the agency by which mankind will be able to efface the stain of original sin, to achieve restoration to a state of grace and attain the salvation of eternal life, the eternal life that was lost in Eden. The characters and events are symbolic, yet somehow they must also be taken as historic fact, for a symbolic "fall" could hardly involve future generations in *the* original sin, or in the need to be saved from its effects. The specifics of the sentences pronounced on woman, man, and the serpent, it need not be stressed, are not congruent with the large and grand theological scenario of choice and sin, fall and damnation, redemption and salvation.

Among the modern critical scholars, a celebrated exemplar can characterize the tale as "an immortal classic . . . [by] a supreme artist . . . touching upon the elemental and eternal mysteries of existence." Yet in the same breath he asserts that "the story is by no means entirely the product of his [the artist's] own fertile imagination," for he included "ancient folktales, the product of the childhood period of Israel's cultural evolution." Thus, for example, the sentence of back-breaking toil on sinning Man is not so much the verdict of a judging God as the view of early Israel, "the nomad of the Arabian desert . . . [who] looks down with undisguised contempt upon the farmer . . . compelled to bend his back in servile toil." This hypothetical Israelite nomad from the Arabian desert, for all that "his food supply is monotonous and scanty . . . is more than compensated for by the perfect freedom of the desert which he enjoys."[5]

If dogmatists and scientific scholars may peddle such wares, how blame the skeptic who marvels that so childish a fairy tale should be spun at such length in what is purported to be the most profound and sacred tract of revealed truth. Whether as figurative treatment of the human condition, or literal intention, who today can take seriously a snake talking, a woman balking, and a God stalking, all in the interest of explaining why the snake has no legs and the human a horror of a snake in the grass; why living is hard and childbirth painful; why woman is subject to man, and why man cannot enjoy eternal leisure for an eternal life? And is the concluding verse of this episode an example of misplaced bathos, or of the artist's ineptitude for plot? The God who has so savagely sentenced the first human couple relents for a moment. To provide them with a consoling compensation he becomes designer and tailor, replaces their improvised fig-leaf aprons with full-length costumes of well-dressed leather!

Let us address ourselves first to the art of our storyteller. He begins with a pun — two unrelated homonyms in Hebrew — characterizing the human couple as "naked" and the serpent as "wily." The wiliness is immediately disclosed in the serpent's opening ploy. He pretends ignorance of God's true charge in respect to forbidden fruit, and asks incredulously whether all fruits have been denied to humans. The guileless woman falls for the gambit, and scornfully corrects the serpent as to the true charge. The serpent darts into this opening. The reason for God's injunction as given earlier is that eating of the forbidden fruit will result in the death of the eater. The Hebrew is ambiguous about the matter of the death; it may be immediate, or in some distant future. The serpent denies, truthfully, that death will result immediately. He then goes on to extol the virtue of the fruit, the enhanced quality of life its eating will occasion, a godlike status that humans will enjoy if they do eat of it. And in this too, as God himself will confirm in verse 22, the serpent speaks truth. The woman eats, she survives, the fruit takes effect. What sense of heightened consciousness does she experience? Whatever it is, she does not hoard the fruit, but gives it to her husband to eat "along with herself," and both are now enlightened. The enlightenment relates somehow to the implicit unconsciousness of "nakedness" with which the episode begins, and culminates in a remedy for the hitherto unrecognized consequence of being naked.

The storyteller might have proceeded directly to God's knowledge of the disobedience and to his sentence. But no, that would be rhetorically artless. One mode of divination in ancient times was the interpretation of the wind soughing through the leaves of a tree. "At the breezy time of day" they discern the sound of stirring indicative of God's presence. Man and woman hide from the Presence. This gives God the opportunity to open with a rhetorical question. The one-word Hebrew question 'ayyekka is not so much a question as to location as it is the query of a parent with mischief-prone children: "What have you been up to?" The response of man, honest as it is, betrays his sense of guilt over his real transgression, even while it attempts a plausible, if feeble, defense for his attempt at concealment. To appear naked before God is sacrilegious, hence he took cover. God overlooks the contradiction of this defense constituted by the fig-leaf loin clouts. Like a prosecuting attorney, he pounces on the indication of guilt, a consciousness that could derive from one source only, and that a forbidden one. God's response, "Can it be that you have eaten from that very tree" could be characterized as coy, were it not that it sustains the tone of chiding parent to wayward child. Man, child that he is, neither affirms nor denies the ironic question explicitly; he points to a scapegoat. "She, whom you put at my side," is responsible! The rabbis correctly note this as the first instance of ingratitude: God, in his solicitude for man's well-being, is responsible for presenting him with a temptress, as though man himself were not free to choose. And woman in turn passes the buck to the serpent who, having no defense, is subjected to no interrogation.

Now to the crux of this episode, the linked concepts of nakedness and knowledge and sexuality. The episode begins with the voice of the omniscient author: "Now the two of them were naked, man and his wife, but they felt no sense of shame."

That an author will assume the conventions of his society and culture is obvious; yet it is a factor easily overlooked, and its significance can be totally missed by a reader who is not native to the writer's culture. The issue of nakedness, not nudity, is the key to the mythos of the Eden story. While these two terms are synonyms, they cannot (in common with all synonyms) do duty for one another in every instance. Both mean bare, without clothing. Yet "nude" conveys a neutral meaning, and is nonjudgmental, while "naked" conveys an assessment of deficiency, such as defenselessness or moral impropriety. Many a prude will view the lusty nudes of a Rubens with equanimity, but recoil in distaste from the (even partly) naked woman in a magazine's centerfold.

Clearly it is our author's intention that the first human couple were without shame, despite the "fact" that they were naked. Which is to say that while the author and his readers share a sense of impropriety about the state of the couple, the personae themselves did not. God's rhetorical question, linking man's awareness of his nakedness to the eating of the fruit of the tree of knowledge, underlines that the phenomenon at issue is not lack of clothing but consciousness of "nakedness." The reader, of course, already knows this. The reader has been previously informed that the "opening of the eyes," the consequence of the eating of the fruit of the tree of knowledge, was immediately expressed in their awareness of their nakedness and in their improvisation of—what? The Hebrew word, rendered as "girdles" in the older translations, refers to any band that circles the waist; the newer translations recognize that this word is a metonym, a part standing for the whole, and that from the string there hung a covering patch. In front or in back? Clearly, in front. Why, clearly? Because the nakedness here refers not to exposure of face, torso, limbs, or buttocks but to the sexual organs proper—to the *pudenda*, a delightful word which in the original Latin means "those parts about which one should have a sense of shame."

In ancient Israel, nakedness—the exposure of the genitalia—was a powerful taboo. The expression "reveal the nakedness of" is often equivalent to "have sexual intercourse with." And the word "nakedness" alone may stand for any sexual act that is illicit. The awareness of nakedness as a consequence of eating of the tree of knowledge is equivalent to an awareness of sexuality.

Another link between knowledge and sexuality is the Hebrew verb "to know," in the meaning of "to have sexual relations with." Thus, for example, Chapter 4:1 begins, "Now Man *knew* his wife Eve, who conceived and gave birth." This verb appears again in Genesis 19:5, where the men of Sodom demand that Lot surrender his (male) guests to them, "so that we may *know* them;" hence the term *sodomy* for carnal copulation in any of certain unnatural ways. What accounts for this particular kind of "knowledge," carnal knowledge, is an underlying meaning of the Hebrew verb: "to come to know, to have experience of."[6] The tree of knowledge, therefore, would seem to be more than one whose fruit imparts sexual awareness; it is the tree of *experience*, the experience of sexuality, to be precise. And it is likely that an intuitive grasp of this imagery in Genesis lies behind the English metonym for sexual experience: "forbidden fruit."

Let us recall that "tree of knowledge" is an abbreviation of this tree's name; it is the tree of knowing (or experiencing) of good and *bad*. What is the intent of this merism? *Knowledge of all things* must be ruled out, for Man knew many things before eating of the tree and remains ignorant of many things after the eating. The same is true for *experience of all things*. It is a tree whose fruit makes for an experience of everything that—in some ultimate sense—counts. With it one has illumination; the eyes are opened, one becomes "like God." Without it there is no enlightenment, no being "like God." In what way is one like or unlike God? And what does this have to do with sexuality? There would appear to be something in the mindset of the biblical author so removed from our own that it cannot but elude us. For the key to this mindset, and indeed to the puzzles of God's sentences on the various protagonists and on his venture into suede couture we shall have to explore a Mesopotamian epic. For the moment let us go on to the next episode.

Expulsion from Eden

> (22) YHWH-God mused, "How now, man has become like one of us in awareness [knowledge] of good and bad, how prevent him from reaching out to take of the tree of life as well—to eat and to live forever! (23) So YHWH-God expelled him from the Garden of Eden, to till the soil from which he had been taken. (24) When he had driven man out he stationed on the approach[7] to Eden the cherubim, equipped with ever-turning flashing sword blade, to guard the path to the tree of life. (Genesis 3:22–24)

This conclusion, with its sense of timelessness—a forbidden garden eternally existing, containing within it a tree of life, its approaches guarded by fantastic creatures wielding fabulous weapons—is artistically satisfying, for a fairy tale. Is this all we have here? Does God really fear an assault on his garden? Is he so jealous of humankind that he cannot bear the thought of its achieving parity with the divine beings, sharing eternal life with them and, as well, possessed of that enigmatic knowledge of good and bad? And if God is indeed to be so pictured, why has he no other recourse? Why not destroy the tree, or the garden, or the human race?

And if the source-critical dating is correct, if the abstract conceptions of Genesis 1 reflect a relatively late, philosophically sophisticated theology, while the Garden of Eden tale reveals in its anthropomorphisms a naïveté that is centuries older, why did the editors include this second story in the sacred canon? What does it add to our understanding of God and his ways?

We have reached a point in our discussion where we must draw on literary texts from Mesopotamia for metaphors and symbolism analogous to those that must surely be present in the Eden story; if, that is to say, we are to offer an explication of the text as an artistic product of a sophisticated thinker, as a composition worthy of placement at the beginning of antiquity's most serious (and successful) venture into the questions that lie at the heart of the religious enterprise. The specific text to which we will have reference is the Gilgamesh Epic, itself the supreme literary creation of the cuneiform culture, and perhaps the only one of that provenance meriting a place alongside the literary achievements of Israel and Hellas. Before I proceed to this step, I think it will be of use to formulate or reformulate questions on plot elements that have been raised explicitly or implicitly in my discussion hitherto.

In contrast to such trees common to our own experience and that of Eden's tenants as the fig tree, which produces so luscious a fruit and leaves of a breadth suitable for the first apron-coverings, are the two fantasy trees. Why particularly these two, and what or wherein is the implied antithesis between a life-ensuring tree, whose fruit (although never explicitly brought to human attention) is licit, and of a knowledge-inducing tree whose fruit is explicitly forbidden?

The creation of all animals other than the human is in both stories noted without reference to sexual differentiation. Why in the Creation story is the human species singled out for such differentiation, this new entity *ādām* or *hā'ādām* awkwardly (hence pointedly) characterized as a unit, single or collective—a *him*, and hard upon as male and female—a *them*? And why, in the Eden story, is this seemingly single act of creation divided into two phases, the creation of the male and then the extraction from him of the stuff from which the female is formed? And, let us note, the separation of these phases (as plot) is impressed upon the reader by the insertion (as a narrative strategy) between the two phases: first, of God's charge to *hā'ādām* not to eat of the forbidden tree; and then—as if it were an afterthought—his rumination on the unsatisfactory condition of *hā'ādām's* being alone, and his consequent decision to rectify this situation.

In our discussion of the giving of names in the creation story we noted that this activity may express two metaphors, the calling into existence or fixing into existence of the thing named, and the subordination of that which is named to him who does the naming. It seems unlikely that the former is the intended metaphor in *hā'ādām's* assignment of names to the creatures of earth and sky. Can we be confident then that human dominance over the nonhuman is the implicit intent here, as it is explicitly formulated in the creation story? And what then is the point of the narrator's assurance to the reader that "and [indeed] whatever man would call it—each living creature—that would be its name?"

In connection with this last question is it possible or likely that man's naming activity is here a metaphor for sagacity, informing us that man had intelligence even before he ate of the tree of knowledge? And furthermore, is there any connection between the choice of the serpent (alone of all the creatures) for the role of tempter and man's happy facility for hitting upon an appropriate name for each creature? It is a fact that the term *nḥš* in Hebrew is not only the generic name for reptile, but also in the piel conjugation a verb for divination.

In the matter of the punishments peculiar respectively to snake, woman, and man, are these ad hoc improvisations by the author, or are they particularly appropriate to an overarching symbolism in keeping with a kerygmatic proposition? In a similar vein we may ask, why the banishment from a garden that remains intact, when God's objective could have been realized by his destruction of the tree of life or of the garden itself? Why, between the pronouncements against the three culprits and the banishment from the garden, the notice of God's manufacture of leather breech-clouts and of his clothing his creatures in them in place of the fig leaf clouts they had made for themselves?

And finally, what is the nexus of sapience and sexuality and the withdrawal of immortality?

SEXUALITY, SAPIENCE, AND CIVILIZATION

The puzzling complex of knowledge, sexuality, and humanity's becoming in some manner godlike, which lies at the core of the Eden story, appears as a crux in the Gilgamesh Epic also. Gilgamesh, the demigod king of Uruk, is so endowed with unbridled appetites and the power to satisfy them as to become a burdensome problem for the nobles of his city. To the end of distracting his attention from them (or more properly, from their wives and sons and daughters) his goddess mother Aruru is entreated to create a countervailing force. This she does in the person of Enkidu. Conceived as a double of the god Anu, he is fashioned in fully-formed adulthood from a clod of earth. On his native steppe this child of nature consorts with gazelles and, like Kipling's Mowgli or Tarzan of the Apes, rubs shoulders with wild beasts at the watering-place. The plot requires that Enkidu be brought to a confrontation with Gilgamesh; the stratagem to achieve this calls for his coupling with a harlot. Lest his audience overlook the critical significance of this device, the author repeats its essential features (three times in the space of seventy lines), twice in anticipation of the action and once in its fulfillment. We shall cite the last one, in E. A. Speiser's translation:

> The creeping creatures came, their heart delighting in water.
> But as for him, Enkidu, born in the hills —
> With the gazelles he feeds on grass,
> With the wild beasts he drinks at the water-place,
> With the creeping creatures his heart delights in water —
> The lass beheld him, the savage man,
> The barbarous fellow from the depths of the steppe:
> "There he is, O lass! Free thy breasts,
> Bare thy bosom that he may possess thy ripeness!
> Be not bashful! Welcome his ardor!
> As soon as he sees thee, he will draw near to thee.
> Lay aside thy cloth that he may rest upon thee.
> Treat him, the savage, to a woman's task!
> Reject him will his wild beasts that grew up on his steppe,
> As his love is drawn unto thee."
> The lass freed her breasts, bared her bosom,
> And he possessed her ripeness.
> She was not bashful as she welcomed his ardor.
> She laid aside her cloth and he rested upon her.
> She treated him, the savage, to a woman's task,
> As his love was drawn unto her.

For six days and seven nights Enkidu comes forth,
Mating with the lass.
After he had had his fill of her charms,
He set his face toward his wild beasts.
On seeing him, Enkidu, the gazelles ran off,
The wild beasts of the steppe drew away from his body.
Startled was Enkidu, as his body became taut,
His knees were motionless—for his wild beasts had gone.
Enkidu had to slacken his pace—it was not as before;
But he now had wisdom, broader understanding.
Returning, he sits at the feet of the harlot.
He looks up at the face of the harlot,
His ears attentive, as the harlot speaks;
The harlot says to him, to Enkidu:
"Thou art wise, Enkidu, art become like a god!
Why with the wild creatures dost thou roam over the steppe?

Come, let me lead thee to ramparted Uruk,
To the holy temple, abode of Anu and Ishtar,
Where lives Gilgamesh" (ANET p.75 iv 1–38)

Enkidu is thus neither beast nor quite human. He is a throwback, as it were, to what man was when he was first created—wild, uncouth, uncivilized—a species only somewhat higher than the beasts and far lower than the gods. His affinity with the beasts is expressed in their acceptance of him as one of themselves. And so (unlike man in Genesis) does Enkidu regard himself—as one of them. How is Enkidu to be raised from the status of *homo ferus*, man-beast, to the human? Through the experience of sexual intercourse. That the transformation of Enkidu is just that, a radical transformation, and not merely a raising of his consciousness of himself as human, is assured by the reaction of his erstwhile fellows. The gazelles and the wild beasts now know—as Enkidu does not yet—that he is no longer what he was. "Enkidu had to slacken his pace—it was not as before." This may just reflect Enkidu's consternation at his rejection by his companions. Or it may be that there was a notion in Mesopotamia—as it is attested elsewhere—that in the act of copulation a considerable amount of his strength and vitality is drained from the male. In either case, the narrator's voice tells us what Enkidu will not know until the harlot informs him. He has been compensated for his loss, "but he now had wisdom, broader understanding."

Could we ask for a clearer correspondence between our two stories? Eden: tree of knowledge/sexual experience results in enlightenment, the opening of the eyes. Gilgamesh: sexual experience results in wisdom, broader understanding. But we have more than this parallel, we have an identical expression in both stories. The harlot says to Enkidu, "Thou art wise, Enkidu, art become like a god." The serpent says to Eve, "God knows full well that you will be like God [or gods];" a judgment confirmed by God himself in 3:22, "Man has become like one of us." We shall have to explore further this remarkable chain: knowledge/enlightenment, sexual experience, becoming like a god in wisdom, or in knowing good and bad. For the present, let us note where we have arrived. The Gilgamesh Epic attests to the notion that seems present in the Eden story. The sexual experience is the crucial one that marks off civilized humanity from its not-quite-human or not-altogether-human primeval predecessors. The animals also meet in sexual congress, but for them sexuality has no critical significance. This, in all likelihood, also explains why in both the creation story and the Eden story the differentiation into sexes is noted for humanity and humanity alone.

SEXUALITY AND DEATH: THEIR NEXUS

God, in inquiring about the eating of the forbidden fruit, addresses man first, the woman next, and in eloquent silence ignores the third protagonist, the serpent. In a chiasmic reversal of that order, he pronounces sentence on each of the three in turn: serpent, woman, and man. It is generally assumed that these pronouncements reflect the naïveté of folkloristic traditions, accounting for such interesting phenomena as the necessity for man to toil, for woman to suffer in childbirth, the fact of male supremacy, and the serpent's deprivation of limbs on which to move. The fallacy of genre-assignment as a tool for literary analysis, particularly in regard to the etiological genre, discussed in *Toward a Grammar*, need not detain us here.[8] The data provided by the Gilgamesh Epic, among other literary creations from the ancient Near East, provide us with a better perspective on the elements that our biblical author inherited from the literary tradition of his time and place, and thereby leave us better equipped to appreciate the way he adapted them for his larger purpose and integrated them so fittingly into his composition that not a single detail will prove to be arbitrary or whimsical.

Let us recall God's warning to man not to eat of the tree of knowledge. The Hebrew term that introduces a temporal clause, "when," is literally, "on (the) day of." Thus God said literally: "On the day of your eating of it you will die." The rabbis, who knew the ambiguity of the conjunction and of the context, which make it possible for the serpent to deny truthfully that death in its literal sense will follow immediately upon the eating, playfully suggested that the warning may have been fulfilled even in a literal sense. Man was born on a Friday (the sixth day of creation) and it was on a Friday that he breathed his last breath. God's meaning, as the rabbis also tell us, is clear: eating of the fruit will set man on a course for death. Was deathlessness otherwise automatic? The answer, which lies in verses 22–24 of Chapter 3, is confirmed by the witness of the Gilgamesh Epic. Deathlessness would not have been automatic. Life would have been indefinitely sustained by repeated eating of the fruit of the tree of life, the tree from which man and his mate are barred in their expulsion from Eden. The nature of this, and no other potency of the tree of life, may be adduced from the plant that Gilgamesh won and lost. It was not a once-and-for-all potion of an elixir of life, but rather an antidote to the debilitation that attends old age and heralds the coming of death. The plant named "Man Shall Become Young in Old Age" by Gilgamesh is a tonic of rejuvenation. The distance of almost four thousand years that separates us from Gilgamesh shrinks somewhat when we consider that only a tenth of that time lies between us and Ponce de Leon, who, we are told, sought the Fountain of Youth in Florida some four or five centuries ago. Is sophistication a property of intellect or culture

that increases as a rule with the passage of time? Is it likely that only so few centuries ago that grandee of imperial Spain was as literal-minded in his quest for the
Fountain of Youth as he was in his search for the fabulous hoard of El Dorado?
While the authors of the Epic and of Genesis millennia earlier were exploiting the
poetic imagery of the folk imagination to spin philosophical fables?

The literal-mindedness of Ponce de Leon we may leave as moot. The free use of
metaphor and of symbolism by the ancient authors is beyond debate. Why, of all
creatures, is it a snake that deprives Gilgamesh of his life-renewing prize, a snake
who—apparently out of motiveless malice—sets man on a course that will lead to
his loss of the tree of life? The answers lie in the ancient texts themselves. It lies in
the symbolism of the snake as it functions in the ancient imagination, and not in a
Freudian-inspired paradigm that dogmatically posits a universal phallic-symbolism
for the snake, functioning as such in hypothetical fertility cults, which were hypothetically rampant in the ancient world. In the ancient near East, in biblical and
extra-biblical texts, the serpent is a canny creature endowed with uncanny knowledge of powerful charms, particularly for the promotion of life and healing. Even
the Greek tradition, which associates the serpent with divination, (e.g., Apollo's
Python) may owe to this near-Eastern symbolism. So also the physician's symbol
(conventionalized to this day in the barbershop's pole): the caduceus, which derives from the staff of Hermes—god of healing and messenger of the gods—
consists of two serpents intertwined on a pole.

The very symbolism of life-renewal inheres in the snake. Like the molting of
birds, which gave rise to the myth of the phoenix arising reborn from the ashes of
its pyre; like the bird invoked by the poet in Psalm 103—may God forgive your
sins and heal you "so that you may renew your youthfulness like the eagle"—so the
serpent's casting off of its slough. The serpent gained by theft from Gilgamesh, and
apparently held on to the rejuvenating plant that Gilgamesh tasted but once. The
serpent in Eden is a reflex of the serpent in the Epic. The serpent is to man as
Prometheus is to Zeus. And our author in Genesis, to God's punishment of the
thief of life, adds a decree that extends the symbolism of the Man-Serpent conflict
to all future time: the contest between man striving for immortality and the dark
and potent forces that deny it to him is never-ending. To this Eden text and to this
one alone is traceable the equation of the serpent with evil or with humankind's
inveterate adversary in general, and with Satan in particular.

Now to the woman who is twice named by her mate. The first time he does not
give her a name proper or a proper name. The 'iš-'iššā, the male-female couplet, expressing the correspondence of man and his mate, endows her with the generic
label: woman. After the sentences have been pronounced, we are told, "Man
named his woman [wife] Eve, for she was [to become] mother of all [human] life."
At this point in the story this proper name is appropriate—as it would have been
inappropriate before the eating of the tree of knowledge—because, like the pronouncement of sentence upon her, it anticipates a consequence of the eating. With
the eating man-woman becomes sexually activated. And such activity results in
propagation.

It is on this vital function that God focuses in the sentence of woman: childbearing. No joy exceeds that attending the birth of a child. What then, other than

punishment, can account for the painful price the mother must pay for such a blessing? And to become a mother, woman needs a man. The sentencing of woman continues, however, with a puzzling twist: woman's need for man is what accounts for the existential fact of male domination: "For your husband shall you ever lust, so that he shall lord it over you." The incongruity for us in these last words is due to their constituting a reversal of our own psychology. For us, in our still male-centered age, the male is the stronger by nature and by nature the more driven by sexual lust; woman is by nature the weaker and far less victim of her sexual need. Indeed, it is by reason of a woman's allure and ability to capitalize on man's desire that the prototypical femme fatale reverses the roles of master and subject. (Ironically enough, the dominance of the paramour over her lover is still reflected in the use of "mistress" for a kept woman.) For all its incongruity with our own perceptions, it is possible that the ancients viewed woman as drawn to man by his allure, as was Ishtar by the virile beauty of Gilgamesh. More likely, however, the basic idea here is that woman's desire, which renders her dependent, is traceable to her need to fulfill her maternal instinct. In either case, since allure can and does work both ways, the author's deployment of one vector of this desire is in keeping with his manipulation of facets of the human condition. Male dominance is an existential fact, and this fact our author traces to an existential principle expressed by God in a metaphor. We shall soon see how the metaphor here prepares us for the deployment of the identical metaphor in a more trenchant context. For now let us recall what sociologists have called the principle of lesser or least interest: In a relationship involving two partners, the one with the greater need of the other is the more vulnerable, while the one with the lesser interest in the relationship is in a position of dominance.

Last comes the sentencing of man. The infinite leisure in an opulent garden is withdrawn. In its place is unremitting and frequently unproductive toil. Man will plough the earth, sow it with edible grains, and all too often the soil will produce thorns and thistles, so that man will again become a food-gatherer seeking out the cereal-grasses that grow wild. Until the day of his death, man must toil for bread, for himself, and now, for wife and children as well. This is the poetic pronouncement. But in the prose of verse 21, God replaces the loincloths of fig-leaves that the couple had improvised for themselves with full dress made of animal hides.[9] Symbolic of what? Of man's new status, perhaps. Man, no longer one of the animals, ousted from paradise where—like Enkidu—he had fraternized with them, is about to begin his civilized career. And animals now are no longer companions, but commodities to be exploited.

Death has entered the world: death of animals, and death of man. Man, says God, has already become like the gods "in knowing good and bad." He may not possess both this attribute and eternal life as well. The power of creativity, certainly a divine attribute, is now man's in sexual activity and procreation. The other attribute of divinity—immortality—is now denied to him. He was permitted one or the other. Both he may not have. Why?

WHY MUST MAN DIE?

With the help of some striking parallels from the Epic of Gilgamesh we have been able to answer a few of the puzzles raised by the story of the Garden of Eden. We have been able to come to an appreciation of the author's gifts of rhetoric and talent for metaphor. We have traced the consistency of the plot, the relevance of the parenthetical asides, and the depth of insight into several aspects of the human condition. Yet our last paragraph ends with a question, a question that may be amplified and to which others may be added. Essentially the questions are: What is the central message of the story, and why was it placed alongside the theological statement of the creation narrative?

As *Enuma elish* proved a productive foil for fixing the central concern of the Genesis creation narrative, so will Gilgamesh prove for the Eden story. What is the central theme developed in the Epic of Gilgamesh? The answer is as clear as it is simple. The theme is a question: Why must man die? In raising this question for Gilgamesh—bravest, strongest, most heroic of men—it is raised for all people. For Gilgamesh, at the height of his powers, with his newly won bosom companion at his side, ready to challenge the most formidable of foes, death holds no terrors. Perhaps because, like all the truly young, he does not really believe that he will ever die. When even valiant Enkidu questions the wisdom of looking for trouble, of seeking to engage the fearsome Huwawa in "unequal struggle," Gilgamesh in his answer recalls to us the choice made by young Achilles between a long and uneventful life or a short but heroic career:

> Who my friend can scale heaven?
> Only the gods live forever under the sun.
> As for mankind, numbered are their days;
> Whatever they achieve is but the wind!
> Even here thou art afraid of death.
> What of thy heroic might?
> Let me go then before thee,
> Let thy mouth call to me, "Advance, fear not!"
> Should I fall, I shall have made me a name:
> "Gilgamesh"—they will say—"against fierce Huwawa
> Has fallen!" [Long] after
> My offspring has been born in my house . . .
> . . . [several lines mutilated]
> My hand I will poise
> And will fell the cedars.
> A name that endures I will make for me! (ANET p. 79 Tab. III (iv) 5–25)

Not so Enkidu. Perhaps because unlike Gilgamesh, who was born fully human, Enkidu has known another state, another condition. The contrast of Enkidu before and after his sexual experience is sharpened in the following passage. He who was wont to suck the milk of wild creatures must learn to partake of human diet. After a banquet and the good cheer that comes out of a cup (seven cups, to be exact), "his heart exulted and his face glowed. He rubbed the shaggy growth, the hair of his body; anointed himself with oil, *became human. He put on clothing,* he is like a groom!" The former protector of the creatures of the wild now "took his weapon to chase the lions, that shepherds might rest at night. He caught wolves, he captured lions, the chief cattlemen could lie down; Enkidu is their watchman, the bold man, the unique hero."

Perhaps, as in the animal state there is no conception of the significance of sexuality, so in that state is there no real conception of death. Perhaps Enkidu, who has made the transition from one state to the other, has a more realistic dread of death than brash Gilgamesh. Certain it is that when Enkidu lies on his deathbed he reviews the succession of events that led him to this pass. And as though he thinks that, left in his former state, he either would not have had to die or consciously face death, he bitterly curses the hunter and the harlot who had engineered his becoming human. The god Shamash calls down to Enkidu from heaven. He points out the injustice of cursing the harlot who, after all, brought him to human state, a state of royalty, almost of divinity: companionship with the lordly Gilgamesh. And he consoles Enkidu with the prophecy of how Gilgamesh will mourn for him:

> He will make Uruk's people weep over thee and lament,
> Will fill joyful people with woe over thee.
> And when thou art gone, he will his body with uncut hair invest,
> Will don a lion skin and roam over the steppe.[10] (ANET p. 86 Tab. VII (iv) 45–49)

And roam over the steppe Gilgamesh will, in his search for Utnapishtim and the secret of eternal life.

Like Enkidu, whose career falls into two phases, so Gilgamesh. In his first phase, in defiance of all warnings, he will roam afar to risk his life in unequal battle that he may "cause the lands to hear, how strong is the offspring of Uruk: A name that endures will I make for me." That this is the phase of immaturity is to be gleaned from the reply of Uruk's elders to the hero:

> Thou art yet young, Gilgamesh, thy heart has carried thee away.
> That which thou would achieve thou knowest not. (ANET p. 80 TAB. III (v) 10–11)

The turning point for Gilgamesh is the death of Enkidu, of a wasting disease, not the death he would have preferred. Enkidu laments to Gilgamesh:

> Not like one fallen in battle shall I die,
> For I feared the battle [. . .].
> My friend, he who is slain in battle is blessed,
> But as for me, [. . .]. (ANET p. 87 TAB. VII (iv) 17–20)

The second quest of Gilgamesh is attended by warnings also, this time not of the dangers—great though they are—but of the futility of his enterprise. Shamash warns him:

> Gilgamesh, whither rovest thou?
> The life thou pursuest thou shalt not find. (ANET p.89 TAB X (i) 7–8)

The same warning opens the speech of Siduri, the alewife:

> Gilgamesh, whither rovest thou?
> The life thou pursuest thou shalt not find.

When the gods created mankind,
Death for mankind they set aside,
Life in their own hands retaining.
Thou, Gilgamesh, let full be thy belly,
Make thou merry by day and by night.
Of each day make thou a feast of rejoicing,
Day and night dance thou and play!
Let thy garments be sparkling fresh,
They head be washed; bathe thou in water.
Pay heed to the little one that holds onto thy hand,
Let thy spouse delight in thy bosom!
For this is the task of mankind! (ANET p. 90 TAB. X (iii) 1–14

Here is the answer of the Epic of Gilgamesh to the question, "Why must man die?" Immortality is a boon the gods selfishly reserve for themselves. Mortal man has no alternative but to resign himself to his lot. The course of wisdom for man is to make the most of his brief days under the sun, to extract from them what pleasure he can. In common English idiom: You only live once. But the advice concludes on a note of consolation, meager though it is. Man does have a kind of immortality through his children. Lie in your wife's embrace and beget the only kind of immortality that lies in the enterprise of man.

The pervasive and enduring influence of the Epic of Gilgamesh in the ancient world has previously been noted. Almost since the discovery and decipherment of this epic, a passage in one of the Bible's latest books has been recognized as at least a paraphrase of the preceding advice:

Come now, eat your bread in joy,
And drink your wine in good cheer—
So of yore did God will your enterprise.
At all times, be your garments sparkling white
And pomade on your head, let it not be skimpy.
Find fulfillment in life with the wife of your choice
All the days of your life so evanescent,
Days allotted you under the sun,
All your days so evanescent.
That is your lot in life,
In the career you pursue under the sun.
Whatever you find in your power's scope,
Pursue its accomplishment with all vigor.
For there is no purposeful work
Nor meaningful experience [lit., knowledge, consciousness]
In [nether-world] Sheol
Where you are destiny-bound. (Ecclesiastes 9:7–10)

Why must man die? That is the central theme of the Epic of Gilgamesh, and the central theme of the story of Eden. Because—answers the Epic—the gods have willed it so. Because—echoes Ecclesiastes—Divinity has willed it so. But not the author of the story of Eden. Why does he not, why perhaps can he not, give the same answer? Because his enterprise is theology; a new theology which breaks with that of paganism. We discussed in the preceding chapter the nature of the divine in pagan polytheism and in biblical monotheism. We discussed there the different role and dignity assigned to mankind in these rival systems. The gods of paganism create humankind to exploit it for their own indolent purpose; in their relations with mankind they are—variably—condescendingly paternalistic, hostile, or indifferent, capricious, and inconsistent. In the biblical scheme, God created man as the crown of creation; in His relations with mankind God is benign and benevolent. Death and dissolution are, however, unquestionably evil. How then to postulate death as God's will without attributing malevolence to him? Or is it possible that death is not God's responsibility? If so, whose is the responsibility for this ineluctable fact? Why must man die?

THE EDEN MYTHOS: ITS KERYGMA

"Why must man die?" Who is asking the question? You, and I, and the author of the Eden story. And to answer your question and mine, and to answer the question the author asks of himself, the author constructs a mythos.[11] The mythos is our story, set in Eden, envisaging two possible worlds, one with death and one without it.

The world without death is pictured as a historical or prehistorical fact or age. Humankind, in the persons of First Man and his Woman, live an idyllic and toilless existence. The climate is ideal, so neither clothing nor shelter is required. Fruit of every kind provides a nutritious and varied diet, obviating the need for cereal grains, which require processing and preparation before they can be eaten. And a tree of life, whose fruit is a specific against disease and debilitation, guarantees eternal life. For humankind is supreme in the garden, where no enemy or rival exists. There is in the garden another tree whose fruit mankind never touches; this fruit imparts knowledge, experience, sexuality. Hence mankind is naïve rather than knowledgeable. Or, to use a word whose Latin origin means "harmless" and which is by association synonymous with "naïve," man is *innocent*, endowed with no cunning (from the same root as "ken," awareness or knowledge). Innocent of experience, unconscious of sexuality. In the absence of sexuality there is, of course, no propagation. No propagation, no children. A world in enduring stasis.

Let us call this world of possibility the Age of Innocence. And the alternatively possible world we shall call—borrowing from William Blake, who juxtaposed the two terms—the Age of Experience. In this world nothing differs from that of Innocence except that man does eat of the tree of knowledge, after which everything is different. For the eating entails a chain of consequences: First and directly, awareness and sexual experience, which will, of course, eventuate in procreation. Second and incidentally, banishment from Eden and barred access to the tree of life, which spells toil and death, the latter by natural causes or—as suggested by the sentence on the serpent—hostile action.

The Age of Experience is ushered in—or rather, precipitated—by the eating of the forbidden fruit. Why, however, did our benevolent Deity deny the tree of life to those favorites of his who had eaten of the tree of knowledge? Why could he not have allowed them both? The answer is now fairly obvious: Because the nature of things does not allow for a world in which both deathlessness and procreation obtain. Such a world would quickly realize the Malthusian nightmare: overpopulation, starvation, and chaos. Any doubts that the nineteenth-century parson could have been anticipated four millennia before his time—and let us remember that the Rev. Malthus assumed that people were going to continue to die—are set to rest by Ishtar's threat to her father, Anu, when he is disinclined to support her designs against Gilgamesh:

> If thou does not make me the Bull of Heaven,
> I will smash the doors of the nether world . . .
> I will raise up the dead eating and alive,
> So that the dead shall outnumber the living. (ANET p. 84 TAB. VI pp. 96–100)

There is another crucial factor or dimension of the Age of Experience that does not obtain in the Age of Innocence: time. We asked the question: Why had man not eaten of the tree of life, the fruit of which had not been forbidden? Our recognition of the tree of life as a means of renewing life periodically rather than of guaranteeing it forever by a single taste makes our question academic. Our human couple may indeed have eaten of it. But how often? The answer to this is another line of questions: What difference would it make? How much time lapsed between the creation of humanity and the eating of the forbidden fruit? How long did the Age of Innocence last? Obviously it could have been a moment or an eternity, for time has no meaning in the static Age of Innocence. Time, as humans experience it, is a measure of events. Where there are no events there is no time. Events are the stuff of history, and the Age of Innocence has no history.

Our author has achieved a supreme philosophical mythos. Genesis 1 affirms the existence of one all-powerful, purposive God, which is good, from man's point of view, for God is benevolent to man, the center of creation and his chief concern. Life is the ultimate good, death the ultimate evil. In tackling the question of why man must die, our author has set himself no less a task than theodicy: to justify the ways of God to man. How, without denying him omnipotence, to affirm both his existence and the existence of evil? How to affirm his friendliness to man and, at the same time, affirm him as the author of man's death?

Well—the author proposes—let us consider two possible alternatives. One is a world in which there is no death, where man lives in the archetypes of the species —male and female—suffering no pain or grief or need unfulfilled, ignorant of sex and procreation: The Age of Innocence. And innocent it can afford to be, for what need of sex and procreation has a species which, living endlessly, needs take no precaution against the scythe of time?

The alternative to this static, timeless world is the Age of Experience, which contains knowledge, sex, procreation, and death. Here is the nexus of Sex and Death. Sex, the reproductive power, is the answer to death. The limitations of space and the endlessness of time render inconceivable the coexistence of procreation and deathlessness. We are faced with a hard disjunction, an either/or, but not both. The species can exist as the deathless universal in the realm of perfection— Plato's World of the Ideas—or it can live in the chain of particulars: the generations which, succeeding each other in time, make history: history which, for man, is the only measure of time.

And the choice is left up to man. He is born into the Age of Innocence. It is for him to choose whether there ever will be an Age of Experience. A precondition for the existence of this choice, however, is that all the potentials must exist. Hence from the moment of creation man—he/she/they—is endowed with the organs of sex and reproduction. Was the choice to activate these capacities an act of disobedience to God? That depends on whether God's declaration concerning the tree of knowledge was a command or a warning. And the Hebrew is ambiguous; it can be read either way, or both: "But of the Tree of Knowledge *you are forbidden to eat,*" or "But of the Tree of Knowledge *you dare not eat.*" Was the choice that man made evil? Perhaps the question itself is too restricting: Was there evil in the choice?

Yes, there is evil in the choice. For until the choice is made—in favor of experience—there is no evil. But in the absence of evil, or of its possibility, there is nothing for goodness to overcome, there is no possibility of moral choice. Without the possibility of evil, the problems, the hurdles—which are the stuff of history— there is no history. The choice is left to man, and the question of death and evil is shifted back from God to man. And the choice was made by man. Indeed, the mythos suggests, man would not be man but for having made the choice he made. And if you ask, but man was not man until he had made the choice—well, that is why we must have a mythos. If categorical propositions were adequate to deliver the message there would be no need for a mythos. Nor, in putting forward our interpretation of the mythos, do we pretend to have exhausted its meaning.

Let us, for example, consider again the Christian interpretation of man's eating of the tree of knowledge as his Fall, with the associated doctrine of original sin: "In Adam's Fall we sinned all." Our implication in our first ancestors' sin suggests that we were all present in the original Adam and participated in the choice. Anyone who, accepting the mythos, would yet reject his share in the decision, would have to face the paradox implicit in the choice: Were you to choose the Age of Timeless Innocence, you would not be here to raise the question in the first place.

Is this last bit of sophistry more than a little absurd? To be sure. One can reject the mythos and the purposive, benevolent God as well. One can deny freedom of will to man and all the dignity that goes with that attribute. One can deny absolute values and be prepared to die or to kill to maintain the values we hold—relative. And perhaps such positions are less absurd.

But the author of the mythos accepts the theology we have described. And the question of death, of evil, of theodicy, is crucial for him. And so he builds his mythos, which points to one truth that no one would care to deny: The world we know, the kind of world we know, is not the best, nor is it the worst of all possible worlds. It is the only kind of world we can imagine. A world of life and death, of birth and dissolution and birth again. It is the world of time and events, the world of history. History is made possible by the expulsion from Eden. Let us see how our author sees the beginning of history.

AFTERMATH OF EDEN: SECOND GENERATION,
SECOND BANISHMENT

(1) Now Man having had relations with [*lit.*, knowledge, experience of] his wife, she conceived and gave birth to Cain, her thought [in naming him, being], "I have produced a person with YHWH's help." (2) She gave birth again, to his brother, Abel. Abel was a shepherd, Cain was a farmer. (3) In the course of time, Cain brought an offering to YHWH of the earth's produce; (4) while Abel, for his part, also brought one, from among the firstlings of his flock, that is, of their choice fat parts. YHWH showed regard for Abel and his offering. (5) But for Cain and his offering he showed no regard. Quite upset by this, Cain was downcast. (6) YHWH said to Cain,

"Why are you upset,
Why so downcast?
(7) Surely, if you do right,
Favor will be [yours].
Should you not do right—
Sin at your door lurks demon-like:
For you he lusts,
Yet you can be his master."

(8) Cain's thought, however, was [fixed] on—his brother, Abel.[12] And so when they were far afield, Cain set upon his brother Abel and killed him. (9) YHWH asked Cain, "Where is your brother Abel?" "I don't know," he replied. "Am I my brother's keeper?" (10) "What have you done!" He said. "Listen . . . your brother's blood—crying out to me from the soil . . . (11) Now, therefore: Banned you are from the soil whose mouth gaped to receive from your hand your brother's blood. (12) If you till the soil, it will no longer yield its strength to you. A wanderer ever on the move shall you be on earth." (13) Cain said to YHWH, "My punishment is too great to bear. (14) Just now have you banished me from earth's expanse, and your presence am I denied. When I am a wanderer over earth, ever on the go—why, anyone coming upon me will [feel free to] kill me." (15) "Therefore," said YHWH, "[I hereby decree:] Whoever kills Cain will suffer vengeance sevenfold." Whereupon YHWH imposed a sign upon Cain, that no one coming upon him might kill him. (16) Then Cain withdrew from YHWH's presence. He settled in the land of Nod [i.e., Wandering], facing Eden. (Genesis 4:1–16)

The first verb in verse 1 is a pluperfect,[13] a point missed by all the standard translations: Man's first sexual experience of his wife took place in Eden, following their eating of the fruit of the tree of knowledge. The birth took place outside of Eden. The pun on the name that Eve gives her firstborn involves the two consonants QN in his name, and in the verb, which means "to acquire, to be or become owner of, to create." The significant point in the thought behind the naming is the credit she gives to YHWH. It is not that she is unaware of her husband's role in her conception; but the birth of a child, especially of a male child—who can continue the ancestral line and thereby assure its felicity in the afterlife—is a gift from God, for mating does not necessarily eventuate in conception, nor conception in successful birthing. No pun is made on the name of the second son, for the name itself is a metaphor. Abel, Hebrew *hebel*, means "a puff of wind," a common figure of speech for the insubstantial, transitory, evanescent. This name, symbolic of the fate of its owner, is provided by the author; the mother, who could not know his fate, could not have so named him; so we have here the first clue that this entire episode is likely to be of the nature of an allegory.

Not a single detail intervenes between the notice of the birth of the sons and the plot action, which begins with the sacrificial offerings that the two present to YHWH. The occupations of the brothers determine the nature of the offerings. Cain, the farmer, brings a grain offering as his tribute; Abel, the shepherd, brings an animal offering as his tribute. Inasmuch as meat offerings are more costly than those of grain or fruit, the latter might represent the more generous gift. The biblical assessment of the value of an offering to God is, however, more in terms of what the worshiper can afford than in the objective value of what is presented. The farmer's choicest offering is *bikkūrīm* "the first (choice) fruits or produce," as the choicest of animal stock is *bekōrōt* "(choice) firstlings." Cain's offering, uncharacterized as to its quality (no *bikkūrīm*), must be understood as a middling one; this in contrast to the generosity of Abel, who presented the choice fat parts of his choicest firstlings (*bekōrōt*).

The word for the offering brought to God here, *minḥā* "tribute," is used also for the tribute brought by a subject to his lord for the purpose of winning favor. The brothers are pictured then as courtiers seeking to ingratiate themselves with their divine sovereign. The two are not necessarily rivals: there is room at court for both of them. The details as to how the Sovereign indicated the acceptability of one gift and his rejection of the other are not given. What is crucial is that the chagrined and crestfallen courtier is immediately apprised that the verdict in his case is not final. The rejection owes to his own behavior; he is free to make amends and win restoration to favor. God's address to Cain thus makes explicit man's freedom of will, even as this is implicit in man's choice to eat or refrain from the forbidden fruit. This address is formulated in two parts, the positive and negative alternatives. The formulation of the negative alternative is richly dense with imagery and meaning: "If, however, you are not inclined to behave, sin is a demon lurking by your door." The Hebrew word for "demon" is a borrowing from Akkadian, Hebrew's sister-language in Babylonia and Assyria; in Mesopotamia demons abound, and physical images were placed at the entrance to homes to welcome benevolent demons and repulse wicked ones.[14] Then comes the notice, "His lust is for you, hence you may dominate him." Let us compare this with God's words to woman in Eden:

TO WOMAN	TO CAIN
Your desire will be for your husband, So that he will dominate you. (Genesis 3:16)	His [Demon Sin's] desire will be for you, Yet you may dominate him. (Genesis 4:7)

What is not crystal clear in either formulation alone becomes clear when they are set side by side. In both we have, as we suggested earlier, the principle of least interest: in a two-person relationship the one who has the least to gain—or feels that he has less at stake—is in the dominant position. Hence, in God's words to Cain, temptation to wrong is personified in a demon, and—the metaphor continues—he needs you, you do not need him; without you he can do nothing. Shades of Pandora! She opened the box and let evil out; Cain must open the door to let evil in. Pandora opens the box and releases the (external) misfortunes that afflict mankind.[15] Genesis says that it is man who opens the door, for the evil that he himself commits.

Cain has been given a choice and a warning. Instead of accepting the clear word of God that his standing with his lord is a matter between himself and his master, he searches outside himself for the reason for his disgruntlement. It is Abel who is somehow responsible for his discomfiture, for he has shown him up. The world is not big enough for both of them: Abel must die. And the act of violence that takes place "in the field" is to make it explicit that the murder was premeditated. "In the field," equivalent to our "out in the wild," is a biblical expression for an unfrequented place, a place where intervention by a third party is ruled out, or at least unlikely.[16] In this clear assertion (by the narrator) of premeditation, the psychology of the murderer is simply and tellingly sketched. As it is in the murderer's assumption that, there being no witnesses he will get away with it. And most profoundly in the paradigmatic retort of every killer, "Am I my brother's keeper?" No one asked him to guard his brother; he was expected only to leave his brother alone! But the path to murder is prepared by the denial of responsibility.

God's reply, that Cain himself can hear his brother's blood crying for justice, is a metaphor for "murder will out." But with the additional element of biblical theology: murder will indeed out, because however helpless or indifferent society may be, God is the ultimate guarantor of justice. And God continues with his pronouncement of sentence.

To appreciate the sentence and Cain's response to it, we must understand the conventions of Israelite society in the matter of crime and punishment, conventions that remained in force in regard to crimes against the person long after the establishment of a strong central government. These conventions, in brief, are as follows: A crime against an individual was a crime against the kinship group to which that individual belonged. Punishment was exacted by the group to which the victim belonged, normally by the agency of a member of that family or clan called "the redeemer of the blood," (analogous in some ways to "the hatchet man" of the Chinese tongs). If the offender's group refused to deliver him for punishment, all members of that group became "fair game" and the result might be vendetta or war. In other words, justice was vengeance, and the certainty that vengeance would be pursued was the chief, if not the only, deterrent to murder. A member of the group who committed a serious breach of the group's standards was normally punished not by execution but by being declared 'arur, "banned, banished, anathema, outlaw, outcast."[17] Shorn thus of the protection of deterrence, the outcast was often considered to be "as good as dead."

This exactly is the meaning of Cain's response to God's pronouncement of sentence. The sentence is banishment. No, says Cain, it might as well be death. He then employs a merism for being shorn of any protection, human or divine. The first, "You have just banished me from earth's expanse," means "I have no place on earth to call home, no one to call kin." The second, literally "from Your presence I am hid," means "I cannot count on you to protect me." Anyone coming across Cain may kill him with impunity, undeterred by fear of man or God.

But God does not want Cain's career ended. And so he puts a mark upon him, a mark clearly visible at all times—probably, therefore, on his forehead[10]—a mark that anyone will recognize as signifying that Cain is under God's protection, that God is Cain's "redeemer of the blood." This raises a number of questions. First, why should God want to keep Cain alive? Cain is, after all, a murderer. His victim had done him no harm, the murder was premeditated, and everywhere in the Bible justice requires capital punishment for such a crime. Why not here? A second question—and a prior one, at that—is, who was there in existence who might, but for God's intervention, have killed Cain?

The answer to the second question is: no one. Is that not absurd? No. Not any more than the absence of women from the genealogical tables, no more than the absence of Adam and Eve from the tale of Cain and Abel, no more than the retrojection to the second generation of mankind of the conventions of Israel's sacrificial cult or of its tribal system of criminal justice. The story is an allegory, like the preceding story of the Garden of Eden, of which this is the culmination.

From the very first verse, which begins with the flashback to the hitherto implicit sexual congress that followed the eating from the tree of knowledge, the Cain and Abel tale continues that story. That parenthetic pluperfect is not concerned with the historic question (extensively debated by scholars since the time of St. Augustine) whether the first copulation took place before or after the expulsion, in Eden or outside of it. Rather, it underlines that the eating of the fruit is a metaphor for the sexual experience itself. The experience in the garden culminated in propagation. Cain was born, then the short-lived descendantless Abel who, himself innocent and victim, exists only to bring out the character of Cain. And Cain is egotistic, selfish, jealous, disobedient, obstinately and sinfully blind, and a murderer. Given freedom of will by God, instructed as to the consequences of the way that he uses that freedom, Cain exercises that freedom in defiance of his Creator. Sexuality and reproduction mark the beginning of time, the beginning of history; and history begins with atrocity. History begins with murder, history begins with fratricide; every murder is fratricide, because all men are brothers. And Cain had to live, in this allegory, to father the human race. So that the moral be not lost: Cain, ancestor of all mankind, is your father and mine.[19]

POETICAL REVIEW OF EDEN VIS-À-VIS THE CREATION STORY

The creation story (Genesis 1:1–2:4a) and the Eden story (Genesis 2:4b–4:16) are parallel and different: parallel in that both deal with the beginning of the world; different in that their themes, though complementary to one another, are separable and independent. The creation story as we discerned it is essentially God-centered, almost without plot, and owning only one persona, more a structure than a story. The Garden of Eden has four personae (six, if we count the serpent and God), and a plot as intricate as it is intriguing; and it is unquestionably man-centered. The two narratives converge in but one respect: the creation of man by God. And it is only in respect to this one element that a difference between the two stories may actually be viewed as a contradiction: the apparently chronological ordering of creation in Genesis 1, which has man created after the land animals, and the logic of narrative flow in Genesis 3, which has man created first, then the animals.

We raised the possibility that even chronological order might serve as a metaphor for rank, dignity, value. (Thus for example, in the U.S. military, officers enter a passenger vehicle in ascending order of rank and come out of it in the reverse order.) And first in one context, last in another context, may both be emblematic of supreme dignity, as is surely the case with mankind among the animals in both creation and Eden stories. There is actually a clue to the poetical harmony of the two stories in an option available and not elected in the creation story. Creatures of sea and sky are created on Day Five, creatures of land on Day Six. It would certainly have been more in keeping with the unique dignity explicitly assigned to humankind to have the other land animals created on Day Five, leaving Day Six for the creation of Man. Why did the author reject this option?

Because in that case, he would have created a narrative contradiction between the stories of creation and of Eden. For as it is, in both stories man and the animals are created on the same day! And according to our interpretation, there is no contradiction as between the two accounts on the order of creation of beasts and humans. In both accounts man is the last of the creatures created. As far as theology is concerned in the Creation story, the bottom line is the praise of the Creator in the Sabbath pericope. But as far as anthropology is concerned in this story, the bottom line—after the dignity of man's being patterned on the divine image—is the creation of man as a singular collective, a *him*, immediately reformulated as a creation of man as a distributive plural, a *them*. Verse 27: "God then created *ha'adam* 'the man/mankind' in His image; in the image of God did He create *ōtō* 'him'; male and female created He *ōtām* 'them'."

This last verse then is the bottom line of a synoptic episode.[20] And the resumptive episode begins with 4b. The Eden story tells how man was created, how man became man, which is to say, that regal line among the created species in which so much depends on its differentiation into two opposing and complementary sexes. If we go back to 1:20 ff. we note that God *created* water and sky creatures by fiat: "God said: Let the water teem . . . let fowl fly about." God *made* the land creatures by fiat: "God said: Let earth produce living creatures." Only in the case of man is there no report of such a fiat. And this too is in poetical harmony with the resumptive episode in which YHWH-God creates mankind in two stages: first, by shaping clay and animating it—a male form—and then, after *fashioning* all the creatures of earth, extracting from the male form a rib-cut and building it into a female form. Thus, as in the creation story, man is created after the animals, for half a species is none at all, and man (the *them*, male and female, of 1:27) is only created when both halves exist. But why, then, this seeming whimsy in this resumptive episode?

The answer to this will emerge from a poetical review of the entire Eden narrative. It starts with verse 4b and continues with verse 7, with God fashioning man at the beginning of creation. Verses 5 and 6, like verse 2 of Chapter 1, are a parenthetic aside, and like it describe a barren world. But whereas 1:2 describes the total chaos before anything existed but Tehom's all-enveloping water, Chapter 2 assumes creation of light, sky, dry land, and celestial bodies. It even assumes the existence of vegetation—high growth and low—but indicates that except for an exceptional place watered by the spill of spring-fed stream(s), vegetation was not the general rule. This barrenness makes for the contrast with the lush vegetation of the garden in Eden, where YHWH-God provides His human creation with shade and fruit trees. It is into that barrenness that man will soon be thrust to toil for his living, a banishment repeated a generation later when Cain too will have to scrounge *qidmat Eden* "facing Eden," that is, the lush paradise lost.

The location of the paradisiacal park serves a number of purposes. For one thing, this is the first of many identifications in Genesis 1–11 of Mesopotamia as the geographical place of origins; this phenomenon itself owing to the biblical author's consciousness of indebtedness to the cultural—particularly the literary—traditions of what we may metonymically term the cuneiform world. For another, the four rivers—two famous and historic, two fantasy-like and never heard of again—provide a legendary setting for a story so magical as to call for a place in the near and familiar even as it is beyond reach or ken.[21]

The creation of man in two stages is, like a number of attendant particulars, proleptic of the sex-procreation-family-civilization-history theme. Thus the creation first of the male constituent, then of the female; the awareness of the former that the latter is of his own substance and essence; the pun on man-woman, male-female; and the "cleaving" of the two sexes to one another, adumbrating the drive to copulative union of husband and wife, which is from their perspective a centripetal force (while from the perspective of the parents of bride and groom it is a centrifugal one). Proleptic, because all this precedes any awareness of sexuality and its consequences on the part of the man and the woman, the one and only "generation" that is and has been. The woman's dialogic exchange with the serpent shows that her consciousness of God's admonition on the eating of various fruits was hers directly, she having been there "in man" all along, even before her extraction and upbuilding. So too, the gapping in regard to the sexual congress—nuanced as sexual awareness—and bridged by the pluperfect verb in 4:1, and the adumbrations of biological generation, the family as biological chain and the ongoing quest in history for the immortality which, lost way back then, is never nor finally despaired of. Thus the punishment of the serpent anticipates the posterity of the serpent and the posterity of the woman he beguiled; so too the punishment of the woman features her central function in history, the propagation of her race; and the punishment of the man features him as breadwinner for the families that he will sire and for whom he must provide. And, finally, the first expression on the part of man of his awareness that the sex act he experienced was not mere indulgence either for him or for his mate. He now names her properly, for the first time, *Hawwa* "Life-Giving," "in recognition that [*ki*] she *had [now] become ancestress of every one who would ever live.*"

Have we overlooked anything in this review, any discrepancy that might constitute a weak link in our argument that, as the separate stories of Creation and Eden are in themselves poetically consistent and of consummate artistry, so are the two poetically congruent and complementary? Yes, there is: the use of the term *Elohim* for God in the Creation story and the consistent use in the Eden story of *YHWH-Elohim*. This item, which has been the nodal factor in the rise of the source-critical school of biblical scholarship, I will treat soon in a separate poetical review centering on the names of God. For the present I draw the reader's attention to the excursus at this volume's end on the kinds of presuppositions with which modern scholarship has addressed the Cain and Abel story, preparatory to our address to the structures, the lists and *obiter dicta* that intervene between the narrative of Eden's aftermath and the narrative of the flood.

POETICAL REVIEW OF THE NAMES OF GOD

Source-critical scholarship ascribes Genesis 1:1–2:4a to P, a key clue to its authorship being the exclusive use of Elohim for Deity. The next large block of text (which we call the Eden story and its aftermath), 2:4b–4:26, is assigned to J, the key clue here being the use of YHWH for the Deity. And Chapter 5 resumes the use of Elohim, once again revealing the hand of P. The most glaring difficulty is that posed by the observation that, useful as this dichotomy in the divine-names usage may be elsewhere, it simply does not exist. For the contrast in usage is not as between Elohim and YHWH, but as between Elohim and an anomalous compound name: YHWH-Elohim. No satisfactory explanation of this anomaly has ever been presented, but the problem would appear to be particularly critical for the source-critics who have so much riding on the dichotomous usage. Perhaps the poetical address may produce a solution more persuasive that any hitherto offered.

Let us recapitulate the contextual contrasts for the biblical usages of YHWH and Elohim that we adapted (and adopted) from Cassuto's characterization:

A. YHWH appears particularly in connection with Israel or its forebears as against aliens and non-Israelite offshoots of the stock of Shem and Israel's patriarchs.

A' The one and only God in the context of dealings with humans other than Israelitish (and predecessors) will normally be rendered by Elohim (note, without the definite article).

B. The preceding (A), reflecting a time when YHWH was seen exclusively as Israel's tutelary genius, and—possibly—before the transformation of *ᵉlōhīm* into a proper name, is to be expected in the speech of ordinary Israelites, but not in the speech of other peoples as a generic name for God.

B' Non-Israelites will normally refer to their revered gods by name and refer to YHWH only in invidious contrast. For the Power that rules all the world, non-Israelites and Israelites as well will normally use Elohim, both with and without the definite article.

C. In contexts where the distinction between Israelite and non-Israelite is irrelevant (as, for example, for the existence of the Shemitic line destined to eventuate in Israel) YHWH may be expressive of the one Deity in a direct, personal, intimate relationship with people.

C' In contexts where the distinction between Israelite and non-Israelite is irrelevant (as, for example, before the existence of the Shemitic line defined, to eventuate in Israel) humans may be associated or associate themselves with the one God as Elohim, expressive of greater distance or greater impersonality in the sense inhering today in such expressions as Heaven, Providence, etc.

The one narrator (whom we posit) of all five chapters uses Elohim, in his own narratorial voice throughout 1:1–2:4a in consonance with A' and C'; the context is expressive of Deity, for all the dialogic activity ascribed to him, as impersonal, abstract, creative force relating to nature as cosmos. In 2:4b–4:24, where the focus is on Deity's personal and intimate relations with the first generations of humankind, he feels free to deploy the name YHWH in his own voice. In the dialogue of the woman and serpent, the name Elohim alone appears, twice in speech by her, twice by him. The poetic distinction of "voice" is what renders this exception unexceptionable. The distinctive nuances of the two names (YHWH and Elohim) are ever in the consciousness of the narrator, as is his consciousness of that consciousness. The narrator is conscious that he has not (yet) ascribed knowledge of the name YHWH to these creatures; and has further determined that Elohim as the creative power that has permitted or forbidden (in a seemingly capricious way) fruits necessary and fruits desirable is more appropriate than the personal, paternal, even loving YHWH. So too "becoming like gods/God" in 3:5 (the serpent speaking) and "has become like *one of us*" in 3:22 (YHWH-God speaking) are unthinkable with YHWH replacing Elohim (explicit or implicit).

Beginning with 4:1, the story of the post-Edenic first couple, the narrator drops the compound name YHWH-Elohim and uses YHWH alone, regularly in his own voice and once in the speech of the woman in 4:1, where her collaborator (so to speak) in the achieving of her first (male-)child is (pointedly, not her husband, but) YHWH himself. Now this first acknowledgement of Deity's part in human procreation is balanced by a second such acknowledgment, in 4:25. But here the role of Deity is designated by the name expressive of greater distance: not YHWH, but Elohim. And hard upon this parallel and contrasting notice comes the narratorial notice: "Back then it was that invocation first was made in YHWH-name."

In discussing this last notice of this volume, chapter 1,[22] I observed that it could not in any reasonable way be attributed to the *authorship* of any of source criticism's candidates for that role. It cannot be P (or E), for it contradicts the thesis imputed to him as fingerprint. It cannot be J because he, having no knowledge of a tradition in conflict with his own, would see no reason to make explicit that which no one questioned. It cannot be the redactor, for his role is to harmonize his sources where possible, and to leave well enough alone when it is not; were he the author of the notice he would be underscoring the flat statement of J, and the equally flat statements of E and P (Chapters 3 and 6) as to when the name YHWH was first disclosed. In this last sentence we have, however, another bit of evidence for our poetic explanation of all three "sources" and their congruent stance in regard to the common noun that became a proper name (*'elohim* → 'Elohim) and to the proper name YHWH, which is twice "disclosed" in Exodus. Properly speaking, the name YHWH was never disclosed. In Genesis 4:26 there is no mention of disclosure at all, merely a notice as to how early in history recourse was had by humans to the Tetragrammaton. In Exodus 3 and 4, where the Tetragrammaton figures as if for the first time, there is the implicit denial (Chapter 3) and the explicit denial (Chapter 6) that YHWH had revealed himself to Israel's patriarchs by that name. But, as we argued in our discussion there and now reiterate, true though that denial may be, it does not contradict (a passage in a document called J which makes) an affirmation that "the name YHWH" was ever "revealed" to anyone. For YHWH is a written sign, never pronounced, and in the absence of vowels quite unpronounceable; it is the true *mark* of the one God as properly conceived, no matter by what vocable identified. And so here in Genesis 4:26, the one authorial voice of Scripture, the single narratorial voice, self-consistent despite his many metamorphoses and obtrusions, transformations, and transmogrifications, having started the chapter with the first mother invoking YHWH as she names a son, and having concluded the chapter with her invoking Elohim as she names another, informs us in this concluding notice that—what? That antediluvian mankind spoke Hebrew, pronounced the Tetragrammaton, had information never transmitted to Abraham, or—for that matter—to Shem and Eber? No. Rather that the conception of divinity, which we call monotheism, was already the common property of humankind's first generations, and that whatever their speech or utterance, whatever their names for that monism which holds a monopoly of power and evinces the personhood expressed in the delegation of power and the revelation of will, those first generations knew what the one God wanted of them, and in obedience or disobedience knew what their responses constituted.

It is this last characterization of the stance of Genesis in regard to the origins of monotheism that is likely to be most troublesome to students of Scripture. Standard scholarship, oriented to trace history *wie es eigentlich gewesen war* in the literary sources and to ascribe monotheism to a sophisticated mentality unthinkable in the ancients, must by its postulates be closed to this possibility. And these tenets of a scholarly dogma will be supported and reinforced by a prejudice common to scientific researchers and loyal religionists alike: that biblical monotheism did not so much evolve from, but rather with thunderclap suddenness broke with, the "paganism" of its neighbors; that monotheism was the invention of our spiritual ancestors whom we are pleased to call, variously according to our narrower pieties, Jews, 'ābōt "fathers" (patriarchs), ideal Israel; that to deny to these latter this distinction is to be disloyal to them and their unique spiritual genius. What all this overlooks, however, is that to ascribe authorship, invention, or discovery of monotheism to any generation of humans, is to deny it to God; either this, or else another absurdity: to affirm that Deity capriciously withheld this revelation from earlier generations of humanity.

THE COMPOUND NAME: YHWH-ELOHIM

It remains now to address the feature of this compound name that is unique to the Eden Story, Genesis 2:4b–3:24. The uniqueness lies not in the *collocation* of the two names YHWH and Elohim, for such collocation is frequent. What is unique is the welding of the two into a single name. This is to say that YHWH and Elohim frequently appear together with Elohim serving as adjective (attributive or predicative) for YHWH; what never appears elsewhere is the use of YHWH-Elohim as the subject of a sentence. Correction: *almost* never! There is one (and only one) other instance where this compound name YHWH-Elohim appears as the subject of a sentence. And it is this appearance which provides a clue as to the poetical function of the compound name in the Eden story. For this name appears in the *transitional* passage intervening in a single episode between sentences featuring the subject as YHWH, Elohim, and a third alternative, *hā-ᵉlōhīm*. This appearance is in the Book of Jonah. I refer the reader to my discussion of this entire book in *Toward a Grammar*, with special reference to the punctilious usage of YHWH, ᵉl, and ᵉlohim (either alone or with definite article or possessive suffixes), and to the concordance of these various occurrences with our description of the poetical functions of these terms.[23] Here we must limit ourselves to Jonah 3:10 and Chapter 4, where the compound name appears. The last verse of Chapter 4 is the synoptic conclusion of an episode relating the repentance of Nineveh's inhabitants:

> The Deity [*hāᵉlōhīm*] took note of their deeds: they had indeed turned away [/repented of] their *evil course*; so the Deity [*hāᵉlōhīm*] reversed himself on the matter of the *evil* [i.e., the punishment] he had proposed to execute upon them: He did not so execute [it]. (Jonah 3:10)

Chapter 4 begins a resumptive episode with Jonah's reaction to the Deity's change of heart:

> (1) This seemed to Jonah a great *evil*. He was quite upset. (2) He prayed to *YHWH*, "Now then, O *YHWH*, was this not my very word [/consideration] while I was yet on my native soil—the reason I faced about to flee to Tarshish—knowing as I did full well that you are a God [*el*] gracious and compassionate, slow to anger, abounding in love, and reversing yourself in the matter of *the evil* [/punishment, condemnation]? (3) Now then, O *YHWH*, take my life from me. I prefer death to life. (4) *YHWH* said, "Are you really all that upset?" (Jonah 4:1–4)

My translation, for all its defensibility, fails to convey the ironic play of the Hebrew in using the simple term *rᵉ* "bad, be bad, badness" for a variety of connotations. The *evil course* of which the Ninevites repent in 3:10 is literally "their bad way." In that same verse and in 4:3 the condemnation or decree that is reversed is literally "the badness." And in 4:1, for my "seemed a great evil" or the equally acceptable "was a source of great displeasure," the Hebrew literally reads "It was bad to Jonah a big badness." Thus Jonah judges as bad or disastrous the (benevolent) decision of Heaven to annul the bad or condemnatory sentence as a consequence of the perpetrators of badness, having achieved a change of heart and change in conduct from bad to good.

Throughout the second pericope (Jonah 4:1–4) the intimate relationship between Jonah and his personal God, between God and his chosen servitor, is expressed in the exclusive use of YHWH, in the voice of both narrator and character; even the reproof implicit in the gentle jeer at Jonah comes from YHWH, and it is to this YHWH that the foolish prophet appeals for death in preference to living in a world where penitents are spared. This usage is in clear contrast to that in the preceding pericope (3:4–10), where the royal decree calls upon the populace (humans and cattle) to invoke Elohim (verse 8) where we might have expected *ᵉlōhaynū* "our gods"; where the narrator informs us that the Ninevites had faith in

Elohim (verse 5); where "in Jonah" would have sidestepped the problem of a poly-theistic people invoking a single Deity. YHWH in place of Elohim here is, of course, unthinkable. (Unlike the pagan sailors in Chapter 1, these Ninevites have not had that YHWH introduced to them.) Yet while this usage expresses, so to speak, the greater distance of God from these pagans, this deployment of Elohim as a/the name for Deity suggests that these pagans have in their repentance come closer to an appreciation of Deity's oneness. Nevertheless, both Deity's greater dis-tance from pagans (than from Israelites) and the distance separating pagan Nine-vites from Israel's monotheistic theology are expressed in the Ninevites hope in verse 9 that *hā'lōhīm* "the powers that be, the Power Above" may yet change their/its angry course; and in the narrator's assurance that *hā'lōhīm* "the (one) Deity" did indeed reverse Himself.

As 4:1–4 resumes the thread of 3:10, giving us Jonah's response to the accep-tance of Nineveh's repentance, and YHWH's response to Jonah's response, so 4:5 resumes an earlier thread of the narrative (ending with 3:4, Jonah's proclamation in Nineveh). Jonah does not yet know of Nineveh's acceptance of his message, nor, a fortiori, of God's reversing the decree. Jonah, we are told, leaves the city to await outside its walls the outcome of his preaching. And it is to further insulate Jonah in the shade of the lean-to, which the prophet has improvised against the heat of the sun, that Deity commissions a bushy growth that sprouts from soil to ceiling in a matter of hours or minutes. But note the designation here of this Deity:

> YHWH-*Elohim* commissioned a vine-covering, it climbed over Jonah['s trellis] to pro-vide him shade from above, to deliver him from his suffering [lit., "his badness"]. (Jonah 4:6)

Not the distant *hā'lōhīm* of 3:9–10, nor the transcendent author of nature *and* the immanent father of humanity, deploying nature's flora for the benefit of his favored fauna—here, rather as in Genesis 2–3, shades and echoes of Eden's garden—the One who is both in one and one in both: YHWH-*Elohim*.

The narrative does not end here. For as we indicated, this verse is transitional, as is the function of the compound name. It is again the distant and impersonal *hā'lōhīm* which/who/that commissions the vicious worm-pest that will deprive the vine of its life and the prophet of his overhead cover. Oppressive, but far less de-structive, is the numbing east wind, which in verse 8 is commissioned by Elohim. Now, overcome by the intolerable heat and atmospheric pressure, Jonah again ex-presses his preference for death, but does not—as he did before—address Deity. (Like Elijah in I Kings 19:4, he says to himself, "Die already!": lit., "he asked his life-spark to die.") This time it is the pointedly ignored Deity, 'Elōhīm, who repeats the jeer of the preceding episode, "Are you really all that upset?" And, finally, after the obtuse response of Jonah, it is YHWH who pronounces the kerygma of his pa-tient and forebearing love for all his—alas, so bovinely insensitive—creatures.

EXCURSUS: THE NONLITERARY APPROACH TO CAIN AND ABEL

A significant characteristic that distinguishes the poetical approach to a narrative text (or other than narrative text, for that matter) from the source-critical approach (which has long held sway under the utterly inappropriate label "literary-critical") is the former's unconcern with the factuality or historicity (or literalness) of character, event, and ancillary data in the text. This unconcern, though it need not serve so as a matter of logic, will probably be as disturbing to fundamentalists committed to the literal historicity of Adam and Eve, Cain and Abel as to scientific scholars who assume, for the most part, that an essentially literal historic intent governed the mind and hand of the biblical writer. Neither fundamentalist nor scientific scholar, for all the differing reasons for their insistence on historicity and literal intent, will be prevented from an appreciation of the symbolic meanings, the moral lessons, of these narratives. But for some reason or other—I suspect that it is an unconscious assumption that historical research is more *scientific* than literary analysis—modern scholars seem driven, although they recognize the essentially metaphoric or allegorical nature of such stories, to extract or recover as much as is possible of the historic core or setting behind the story itself or of the literary and historic traditions to which it owes. In the case of our story of Cain and Abel, this leads to the assumption that at its heart lies a theme that is a subject for social anthropology: the age-old conflict between two ways of life, the pastoral and the agricultural. This assumption asks us to impute to the author of the story a set of assumptions that, to the literary analyst, appear unfounded, inconsistent with one another, and even patently absurd.

Since Adam was fated to be a farmer—so scholars who assume a literal-historic intent read God's curse in 3:17–19—Cain followed his father's occupation, while Abel launched into a new way of life as shepherd and herdsman. God—for some capricious reason, perhaps a dietary preference for meat over vegetables—favors the pastoral way of life over that of the farmer. The assumption by the author of this preference on the part of God reflects the early history of Israel, that is, the pastoral occupation of Israel's nomadic patriarchs. Never mind that one of these patriarchs, Isaac, is a farmer as well as a cattleman. Never mind that the promised destiny of Israel is to possess a land where it may farm the soil and build villages and cities. Never mind that at the time the author was writing, Israel had already achieved this destiny and interpreted the fulfillment of the promise as a sign of God's satisfaction with His people. And never mind that while the first patriarch emigrated from his native land and both he and his children migrated within a restricted territory, they are never pictured as nomads!

Furthermore, the author, who is trying to tell us something about an anthropological phenomenon with which he is acquainted, reverses the roles of aggressor and defender, attacker and victim. The half-savage keeper of herds and flocks who raids the cultivated fields becomes the victim Abel, while the peaceful and prosperous farmer becomes the jealous aggressor. God, for his part, permits his favorite—the shepherd—to be killed by the ill-regarded farmer, and then forces the farmer off his land to become a nomad. Result: both ways of life are destroyed. Yet mankind manages to survive, with the murderer Cain as ancestor of all future humans, be they pastoral or agricultural.

Aside from attributing such absurdities to our defenseless author, this anthropological interpretation is based on very poor anthropology. The history of ancient

Near Eastern warfare is overwhelmingly between communities that share the same economic base. To the extent that clashes took place between groups resting on different economic bases, they were not between pastoral and agricultural societies; they were between the sedentary, urbanized societies in the rich river valleys on the one hand, and the less "civilized" hill people or steppe-nomads on the other. Every urban-agricultural society reckoned a good part of its wealth in the form of livestock, and even hill people and keepers of cattle engaged in cultivation of the soil.

POETICAL REVIEW OF GENESIS 1–5

The general convention in biblical scholarship that Genesis 1:1–2:4a and the Eden story that follows it are both "creation narratives" exemplifies the uselessness as a literary tool of classification as to genre. Indeed when, as so often happens, a theme (such as "creation") is used as a genre label, such resort to an arbitrary categorization may be treacherously misleading. The innocent-appearing genre label operates to create a presumption as to the narrative's kerygma, which—as we argued in *Toward a Grammar*—must emerge from the analysis, and hence can never precede it.

In the case of our two adjoining narratives, the two separate kerygmas (one centering on Deity, the other on humanity) are achieved by means of the uniquely Scriptural narrative technique, the synoptic-resumptive. These are the two longest episodes exemplary of the technique, particularly illustrative of the thesis that in Scripture "parallel and independent" as narrative attributes do not bespeak repetition and inconsistency.

The subtle nuances inhering in the original language of a text and the traduction of that text's meaning in translation are exemplified in the correct rendering of the verb 'bd "to till" in 2:5 and 4:12 and its incorrect rendering as "till" in 2:15, where the force of the verb is significantly affected by its function in a merism and as determined by its narrative context. It is interesting to note how few commentators will recognize that to render the term as "till" in this last context is to create a contradiction with the sentence on the man in 3:17–19. Scholars who are conditioned to inconsistency as a normal phenomenon in a multi-authored, heavily edited, clumsily-transmitted, scissors-and-paste product will not draw the line at the unlikelihood of a single author (such as J) contradicting himself in the scope of a narrative where the contradictory notices are only twenty-six verses apart. As against such sloppiness attributed to a poet, like Homer given to nodding, consider the artistry and precision in diction of the author of the Eden story. He employs the term 'bd as "till" in 4:12 in respect to Brother Cain, whom he has identified in 4:2 as "a tiller of the soil." In respect to the career of post-Edenic man, he eschews the term 'bd—although he clearly alludes to husbandry—for this First Man, who as *type character*, symbolic of the race he will engender, will indeed suffer the unremitting toil ordained for him, but as individual(-ized) character he is not (as Cain was and Abel was not) a farmer.

It is remarkable how much of the Creation Story—which is, as we noted, almost more structure than story—consists of dialogue (which is to say, direct discourse), the fiats of the one persona, God. The narration of the fiat in the Deity's speech and then of the fiat's fulfillment in the voice of the narrator makes for a repetition that emphasizes the unqualified command of God in regard to the created things, which are inanimate; and the absence of the narrator's voice in regard to the animate creatures suggests the qualification of the blessing, for the blessings' fulfillment is contingent on the response to come of these living entities. To be noted also is the feature of free direct discourse in the inclusion of purpose and function in the various instances of God's creative fiat.

In the Eden story, the dialogic feature brings a roundedness, the vividness of personhood to the Snake, the Man, and the Woman, who would otherwise retain the flatness of character that is normal to the type. We need not dwell on the details of how the provision of dialogue to God, the snake, the woman, and the man engage the reader's interest, allowing for what Meir Sternberg calls "the drama of reading," empowering—or rather, compelling—the reader to compare the discourse of the personae and make judgments for himself on the attributes of the persona. But one aspect of dialogue in this Eden story, as in stories to follow, is the telling appearances of Elohim or YHWH in the voices of narrator and personae.

FOUR

THE FLOODS OF NOAH
AND UTNAPISHTIM

Theology Straight and Theology Satiric

Archaeology and history, anthropology and sociology, mythology and folklore, and comparative literature and literary criticism are among the many academic disciplines whose findings and methodologies have been mustered in modern times for the study of the Bible in general and in particular for Genesis 1–11, often referred to as the Primeval History. The narrative centering on Noah, Genesis 6–9, will probably remain one of the last testing grounds for the relevance of these sundry approaches. For example, in respect to the genetic literary approach, many scholars who have abandoned the J and P division of other pericopes in Genesis will remain confident that this narrative block is proof against a poetically-based assault on source-analytic method. Parallel episodes and notices expressive of either redundant or contradictory repetition; alternative introductions and conclusions; thematic discordance in identical or nearly identical contexts; the deployment of the names YHWH and Elohim in conjunction with other separable and respectively assignable stylistic features; such criteria seem to abound, and with such consistency as to persuade most biblicists that this bastion of genetic analysis will yet stand when and if all the others have fallen.

The retrieval of the flood narrative in Tablet XI of the Gilgamesh Epic and the recovery of other cuneiform texts testifying to a long and developing tradition of flood stories that culminated in Tablet XI has added grist to the biblicists' mill. These texts have provided literary critics of the genre-oriented and source-history schools with analogical arguments and inexhaustible lodes for the comparative studies of the developmental modalities of mythology and religion. The academic impetus to study literary texts for their chronological development—which is to say, for their *history* (as over and against their meaning or as clues to their meaning)—is reinforced many times when several versions of a narrative text can be cited in support of conjecture. In my introductory chapter to *Toward a Grammar* I raised serious questions relating to methodologies employed in the study of ancient literary texts, among them: the classification of texts according to *genres*, the parameters of which remain undefined; the division of narrative as between the historical/historiographic (and, therefore, true) and the fictive (and, therefore, untrue); and the predisposition to determine ancient authors' metaphoric or literal intent on the assumption that their conceptual faculties were considerably weaker than our own, be those ancients pilloried pagans or Scripture's sainted seers. These questions are of particular weight for the contesting analyses, assessments, and interpretations of the various flood narratives from Mesopotamia in Genesis, both separately and vis-à-vis one another.

Our address to other biblical narrative entails a challenge to the methodologies (and the assumptions lying behind them) that inform the modern studies of both cuneiform and biblical flood traditions. This, in turn, requires a presentation and a new interpretation of Tablet XI of Gilgamesh before we address the biblical narrative. The risk in this procedure is that we may seem to lose sight of our main focus, the biblical material. In the hope of mitigating this risk, I will first select one or two features common to both flood traditions to illustrate the difference between the two addresses to these narratives: the conventional one, which may be fairly characterized as diachronic, developmental, historical, evolutionary, and oriented to folklore and literary source analysis; and my own, which by contrast is synchronic, ahistorical, oriented to the modalities of fiction and metaphor, and founded on the assumption that the mental and artistic sets of Mesopotamian and biblical authors are contrasted best with those sets of our own modern Western traditions when predicated on intellectual capacities and philosophical concerns common to both.

ON FLOODS AND BIRDS; ON LITERALNESS AND SOURCE ANALYSIS

The stories of a Great Deluge in Genesis and on Tablet XI of the Gilgamesh Epic feature so many and detailed parallels that no one would ever argue that the two narratives could be unrelated. On the other hand, it is certainly hyperbolic to claim—as some do—that a great flood, from which one human pair escaped to propagate their race, is a universal motif in mythology. The myth of Deucalion bears little resemblance to the two tales we shall discuss, and its flood element, like so many Greek motifs, may well derive from Mesopotamia; the tales reported from widely separated societies by anthropologists may be the fruit of earlier contacts between natives and missionaries. Ecology is certainly a limiting factor in the origin of myths; no one would credit an independent flood story to the inhabitants of the Arabian or Gobi deserts. The ecology of lower Mesopotamia, to be sure, qualifies admirably as a setting for such a story. Yet one can only wonder at the naiveté of a

Sir Leonard Wooley, who applied the tools of archaeology to ancient silt levels in the hope of finding traces of the specific inundation that inspired the first Sumerian version of the Deluge.[1]

Such is the spell of literal-mindedness. It is a phenomenon that deserves further exploration. It begins with an assumption that a literal-mindedness of a nature we should judge absurd in a twelve-year-old of our own twentieth century was characteristic and pervasive in the poets and scientists who were the culminations of civilization's first blossoming some four or five thousand years ago. Then, some twenty-five hundred years ago, probably in Greece, some of mankind's finest minds suddenly ceased to be literal-minded. They then proceeded to give allegorical interpretations to earlier human expressions, which had originally been intended, and were still understood by the common herd, literally.

Now while these foregoing assumptions may be contemptuous of the ancient mind, and perhaps even wrong, our appreciation of the civilization of ancient Greece, and of its literary heritage in particular, has not thereby sustained serious injury. We may delight in the exquisitely sculpted lineaments of an Apollo, whether the sculptor worshiped him literally or not. We may be inspired by the metaphors we find in myths even if we cannot prove that they were ever intended as such. And, in any case, the adventures of Achilles and Ulysses are at the least rousing good stories. But the case is different in regard to the Bible, or to any literature falling within its penumbra.

The Bible is understood literally by millions today. And by many millions it is accepted as literally true, this on the strength of its truths having been revealed by God, which guarantees as true what in another source would be judged as implausible. On the other side, anyone inclined to doubt the divinely revealed nature of the Bible or its truth-claims finds welcome reinforcement of his inclination in the discovery that some of the Bible's stories are borrowings from Babylonian fairy tales, which is to say, they are what we recognize as fairy tales, but which were understood and accepted as literally true by the ancient Babylonians. Yet such is the reverence accorded to the Bible that the archaeologist will find it easier to attract funds for his project if he digs in that place where he may find evidence of the natural disaster that inspired the story of Utnapishtim, which in turn inspired the biblical story of Noah. The scholar who would sneer at the thought of searching for Noah's ark atop Mount Ararat will dig for evidence of the flood, the biblical version of which he does not accept.[2]

That is to say, he does not accept the biblical story as an account of what actually occurred. Nor does he accept the Babylonian story as such an account. Yet he assumes that the ancient writers in Israel and Mesopotamia themselves either literally believed the stories they were telling, or at least intended that their audiences so receive them. And since we have a tradition in cuneiform of the development of the flood story over a period of a thousand years at the least, and evidence both internal and external of the biblical story's indebtedness to Mesopotamian versions, it is not surprising that scholars investigating the story in Genesis should trace elements of it to this or that known or hypothesized Mesopotamian version, even while they pursue the different and often contradictory strains of the indigenous Israelite account. But when literary criticism of the Bible is virtually synonymous

with source-criticism, and when source-criticism goes hand-in-hand with the assumption or presumption that the stories were meant to be taken literally (i.e., as
history, and not as fiction or metaphor), this combination of approaches induces
rather strange twists and turns in the scholarly mind. To illustrate such aberrations
we have elected to examine one incident in the Babylonian and biblical flood stories and its treatment by two pioneering students of Genesis narrative.

In Tablet XI of the Epic of Gilgamesh, Utnapishtim tells how the world was ravaged by the flood waters, which had raged for six days:

> When the seventh day arrived,
> I sent forth and set free a dove.
> The dove went forth, but came back;
> Since no resting place for it was visible, she turned round.
> Then I sent forth and set free a swallow.
> The swallow went forth, but came back;
> Since no resting place for it appeared, she turned round.
> Then I sent forth and set free a raven.
> The raven went forth and, seeing that the waters had diminished,
> He eats, circles, caws, and turns not round. (ANET p. 95 TAB. XI pp. 146–154)

In Genesis we read:

> (6) After forty days, Noah opened the hatch which he had made in the ark. (7) He re-
> leased a raven, which took off, flying thither and back until the water dried up from
> the earth. (8) He then dispatched a dove, to ascertain whether the water's weight had
> eased up on earth's surface. (9) But the dove could find no perch for its foot and re-
> turned to him to the ark—the water so far-reaching over all earth's surface. He
> reached out and fetched it back into the ark. (10) After a wait of yet another seven
> days, he again released the dove from the ark. (11) Toward evening the dove returned
> to him, in its mouth a freshly plucked olive leaf. Noah then knew that the water had
> eased from earth. (12) Yet another seven days' wait, and he released the dove; it re-
> turned to him no more. (Genesis 8:6–12)

Hermann Gunkel is the most celebrated twentieth-century pioneer in the study
of biblical narrative, and particularly of the narratives in Genesis. For him, Deluge
story is one of the tales, akin to a myth, that comes "from a period of Israel's history
when the childlike belief of the people had not yet fully arrived at the conception
of a divinity whose operations are shrouded in mystery." He finds, however, that
these tales suffer because "the art of story-telling, which in olden times was in such
high perfection, degenerated in later times." In a number of "instances we can see
that the stories, or particular portions of them, have lost their connexion and were
accordingly no longer rightly understood." The first of a half-dozen examples of this
is that, "The narrators do not know why Noah's dove brought precisely an olive
leaf."[3]

Is it possible that "the narrators" not only knew why, but also assumed that even
the simplest in their audience would understand why, without having to have it
spelled out? A comparison of the biblical account with that given by Utnapishtim

reveals that the plucked olive leaf is the very opposite of a "lost connexion;" it is a detail absent in Utnapishtim's account, an addition or innovation by the hand of the biblical author. Julian Morgenstern, celebrated biblicist himself, believes that he understands the "why" of the olive leaf:

> The freshly plucked olive leaf showed that the waters had abated sufficiently for the olive trees, which do not reach a great height, and do not flourish in high altitudes, to be above water, and to be fresh and green once more.[4]

Now while one might quibble about the height attained by olive trees or the height of the altitudes in which they flourish, Morgenstern's conjecture shows a perceptivity to the kind of gapping that an original author might arrange as a challenge to his reader's imagination. Now contrast this literary insight with his immediately preceding comment:

> The statement that the raven was sent forth and did not return is probably not an integral part of the story proper, but must have come from some other version of the myth. For if the raven did not return, Noah would presumably have at once inferred that the waters had already abated, just as he did later when the dove did not return.

The implicit question as to the logic of the raven's release and its failure to return is a fine example of literary reasoning. Not so, however, is the answer (which in good dogmatic fashion he gives before he poses the question). When he postulates "some other version of the myth" from which the biblical "story proper" borrowed this detail, Professor Morgenstern reveals his knowledge of the version we do have, in which the raven appears, is dispatched by Utnapishtim, and fails, as here in the Bible story, to return. Why, for one thing, would the storyteller in Genesis commit such a pointless act of borrowing? For another, if the initial release of a raven that does not return makes no sense here, what sense would it have made in the hypothetical "other version"? Perhaps Morgenstern would have been better advised to have asked a different question: Why is it that the raven, which does not return in either story, is the first bird to be released by Noah and the last bird to be released by Utnapishtim?

The reason I dwell on this small detail at such length is that it so tellingly and typically exposes what is responsible for the vagaries of such fine academicians as Professors Gunkel and Morgenstern alike. What is responsible is a mindset consisting of four assumptions: that the stories under study proceed from primitive, if not infantile, authors; that expressions which to us are absurd if taken literally were, nevertheless, intended literally by the authors; that details incomprehensible to us are indications of imperfect transmission or botched additions on the part of incompetent redactors; and that our failure to understand any aspect of the narrative may be confidently ascribed to the ignorance or ineptness, the naïveté or illogic of an author or editor, rather than to a deficiency in our own critical acumen.

Let us start with a different set of assumptions. Let us assume that storytelling— as Professor Gunkel points out—is an art, and that a great storyteller must be presumed a great artist; that apparent flaws in an artistic work may not be flaws at all, neither in an original source, nor occasioned in the work before us in the process of transmission; that unless we share with the ancients a universe of discourse (cate-

gories of logic and experience, humor, irony, metaphor, and other rhetorical devices, etc.) it is futile to study their works for meaning; and, finally, that when we
have two versions of one traditional narrative—especially when we can set them
in chronological order—the study of their similarities and differences may reveal
different and similar perspectives, without disparagement to the artistic integrity of
either or both. And now, so equipped, let us go on to the birds.

Neither Noah nor Utnapishtim wittingly released a first or a last bird. Neither
knew, at the time of dispatch, that the first bird would not be the last, or that the last
bird would be the last. In Utnapishtim's case, there are three releases of a different
bird each time, in the order of dove, swallow, and raven. In the case of Noah there
are four releases, but only two birds: first the raven, then, three times, the dove.

In Utnapishtim's case, the first two birds return because the flood waters deny
them a perch. The last, the raven, does not return because the waters have receded. In Noah's case, the first bird—the raven—seems not to return, despite the
prevalence of the flood waters. The dove returns twice, once empty-billed, the second time with the olive leaf; the third time it stays away.

Why does the poet-author of the Utnapishtim story arrange the birds in the
order that he does? A likely answer may lie in the flying range that he attributes to
them.[5] The dove and the swallow (if we can be sure of this second bird's identity)
travel long distances: the dove, kin of the carrier and homing pigeons, flies afar and
is trusted to return; and the migratory swallow is one of the first species to return in
the spring. The raven (like its kin, the crow) does not, for good reason, and reason
apposite to our story, migrate or stray very far; it remains quite close to home. Utnapishtim knows that the waters must be receding; the question is how far away (or
rather, how far down the mountain slope) have the waters retreated; for Utnapishtim is perched on a barren peak far above the timberline. Somewhere below the
waters stretch: above or below the timberline? And since doves coo and swallows
chirp or twitter, whose but the raven's croak could so fittingly supply the grimly
raucous note of this episode's closing line: "He eats, circles [looking for more food?],
caws, and turns not back!"

In the Genesis story, the same basic elements are present; the metaphor, however, is differently deployed. The range of the dove, as in the Utnapishtim tale, is
wide. The height of the water level is here expressed, however, in this one bird's
three responses to its release: returning empty-billed the first time, with the olive
leaf the second, and not at all the third. But what of the raven, which was dispatched first? The standard translations render the verbs describing the raven's activity along the lines of "went to and fro." Only a rendering along the lines of our
own is faithful to the Hebrew, which literally reads, "it left, leaving and returning,"
the normal Hebrew way for expressing the repetition or continuance of an action.
The raven kept coming back to the ark and leaving it.

Why do all the translations misrepresent the Hebrew? Obviously because—in
an inversion of Morgenstern's argument—the raven cannot return according to
the story's logic! If the raven returned, Noah could have dispatched the same bird a
second time. Furthermore, it is not told of the raven as it is of the dove that Noah
reached out and pulled it back into the ark. Thus do translators, missing the point,
conceal the clue from the readers who depend on them for faithful rendering. In

both narratives there is clearly dry ground; if not in the vicinity of the ark, atop the ark itself, for the birds to alight upon. The perching-place, the "resting-place for its foot," is therefore a metaphor for a condition making for survival: until edible vegetation is uncovered, the dove must return to the ark for food. But the raven? Ha! says the Genesis storyteller: the raven proves an undependable harbinger indeed! Neither his return to perch atop the ark nor his ability to do without the food in the ark signifies anything about the retreat of the water. The raven (from whom derives our adjective "ravenous," hungry to the point of omnivorousness) gluts on carrion. And so, in the aftermath of the deluge, the appearance of the world as the waters begin to subside is captured in the same image, in Utnapishtim's last, and Noah's first, bird dispatched: a watery waste, bloated corpses floating here and there, in invitation to nature's few surviving scavengers.

Before we proceed to a poetical analysis of Tablet XI of the Gilgamesh Epic, let us examine one more example of scholarly literal-mindedness and the absurdity of the absurdity it imputes to the biblical text. The dimensions of the biblical ark are 300 cubits in length, 50 cubits in width, and 30 cubits in height. Professor Morgenstern correctly notes, "The Hebrew word *tebah*, generally translated ark, really means a kind of box. The same word is used for the little basket or box in which the babe Moses was placed." He then adds, "The use of the word here shows how altogether deficient was our ancestors' knowledge of seafaring. The ark is here represented as a rectangular shaped box, divided into three stories, which floated with exactly half its volume in the water and half above."[6] A fully loaded craft might well sit so low in the water, although propelling it might present its captain with a serious problem. The Israelites, whose King Solomon built a far-ranging maritime fleet, would have known that houseboats had not yet been invented, and—without question—that the word *tebah* means box or chest. And knowing all this, would they have missed the point? Noah's ark, a rectangular box without keel or rudder built, according to divinely revealed specifications, without bow, stern, or helm, was designed to go nowhere, except where it would be carried by currents dictated by Providence.

But such a metaphor can hardly account for the specifications dictated by divinity for Utnapishtim's craft. Except for its roof, which was curved "like the sky"—to shed the rain, of course—Utnapishtim's vessel, which is called a *ship*, measured 120 cubits in each direction, a perfect cube! And this addressed to a people whose marine technology has inspired numerous scholarly articles and at least one monograph!

THE BABYLONIAN FLOOD STORY

A ship in the shape of a cube: this absurdity of nautical design is the clue to the larger design of our narrator. From beginning to end the tale of Utnapishtim is a concatenation of absurdities. And when the absurdities are seen as intentional, everyone will bear witness that in this section of the Gilgamesh Epic the poet's inspiration is the muse of comedy. Our author is, as before, a master rhetorician, but here the tones of his rhetoric are those of sarcasm and irony, the subtlety of bathos and the ribaldry of lampoon.

The note is struck in the first line of Tablet XI in the address of Gilgamesh to "Utnapishtim the Faraway." In the colloquial idiom of America today, the sense of Utnapishtim's epithet is—as we shall see—more felicitously conveyed by "Utnapishtim the Far-out." Gilgamesh's words:

> Gilgamesh said to him, to Utnapishtim the Faraway:
> "As I look upon thee, Utnapishtim,
> Thy features are not strange; even as I art thou.
> Thou art not strange at all; even as I art thou.
> My heart had regarded thee as resolved to do battle,
> [Yet] thou liest indolent upon thy back!
> [Tell me,] how joindest thou the Assembly of the gods
> In thy quest for life?" (ANET p. 93 TAB. XI 1–8)

More recent research into the Akkadian formulation seems to indicate a somewhat different translation: one that would have Gilgamesh himself charging into Utnapishtim's presence resolved to do battle, and suddenly finding his own sword-arm gone slack, his resolve drained by the unexpectedly unformidable appearance of this mortal who has joined the Assembly of the gods. Gilgamesh, who in titanic struggle had overcome the monstrous Huwawa, guardian of the Cedar Forest, had expected no less a contest before he might wrest from a vanquished Utnapishtim the secret of immortality.[7] Yet all the fight is drained out of him now that he faces this immortal, oh so human and oh so meek. His question then rings with incredulity: How came you, of all people, to win such a prize? Utnapishtim's reply:

> I will reveal to thee, Gilgamesh, a hidden matter
> And a secret of the gods will I tell thee:
> Shurippak—a city which thou knowest,
> [And] which on Euphrates' [banks] is situate —
> That city was ancient, the gods within it,
> When their heart led the great gods to produce the flood. (ANET p. 93 TAB. XI 10–15)

The first question that must be asked is what is the "hidden matter, secret of the gods" that Utnapishtim is about to disclose? It cannot be the story of the flood itself, for the author knows that various versions of the flood story are current. (We, who do not have any of these versions intact and cannot compare them to ascertain what novelty Utnapishtim is revealing for the first time, will only be able to guess at the answer.) In general, however, a number of things about this narrative call for notice. Of all the myths and tales relating activities of the gods, this one stands out in that the teller of the myth is in a position to know, for he was himself a participant. This itself would seem to lend the speaker's tale a measure of credibility; yet the bard will not hesitate to let Utnapishtim's voice merge, at times, with his own, the voice of the omniscient narrator, when he describes events to which Utnapishtim could not possibly have been a witness (the scene of the gods on their mountain retreat, for example, at a time when Utnapishtim is locked in his box bobbing on the flood waters). By making Utnapishtim the participant-teller of the tale to Gilgamesh, the author manages to manipulate several levels of time, thus: Level I, the present time of the author and reader, that is, when the author of the entire Epic is addressing his audience; Level II, the present time of the narrative, when Utnapishtim is addressing Gilgamesh; Level III, the past time of the narrator, that is, after Gilgamesh has heard the story; and Level IV, the remoter past, that is, the past time of Utnapishtim's narrative, the time of the Deluge.

The site of ancient Shurippak, identified by archaeologists, lies today more than twenty miles distant from the Euphrates. The Euphrates has changed its course several times in the past several millennia, and so we cannot know whether there is an incongruity in Utnapishtim's locating it on the river. If it did indeed lie on the river in the times of Levels I and II, there would appear to be something prolix in Utnapishtim's assured aside that Gilgamesh must know of this famous city, but at the same time locating it for him as though there may have been another town by the same (improbable?) name. (Compare, for example, "Washington, D.C. on the Potomac" or "New York City on the Hudson.") But there is a tongue-in-cheek quality that is unquestionable in the words "a city which thou knowest;" for how could Gilgamesh possibly know Utnapishtim's city of yore, Shuruppak-on-the-Euphrates, when the all-destroying flood had intervened between Levels II and IV?

Utnapishtim talks of Shurippak as though it were not the first but the only city on earth (what need then for a name?), itself the ancient home of the great gods Anu, Enlil, Ninurta, and Ea, until they determined to lay world and mankind waste. From fragments of other versions of the deluge story the motive for this decision appears as mankind's noisy rambunctiousness (in *Enuma elish* the motive for Apsu's hostility to the younger gods) or earth's overpopulation by humanity. Here, Utnapishtim mentions the decision without a word as to motive, as though a capricious decision on the part of the gods to doom humankind, together with the implicit doom of the rest of earth's fauna, is nothing to occasion surprise. Similarly, without any reason given, the god Ea determines to save Utnapishtim, and to that end reveals the danger to him. Ea conveys the decision of the gods in these words:

> Reed-hut, reed-hut! Wall, wall!
> Reed-hut, hearken! Wall reflect!
> Man of Shuruppak, son of Ubar-Tutu,
> Tear down [this] home, build a ship!
> Give up possessions, seek thou life.
> Forswear [worldly] goods and keep the soul alive!
> Aboard the ship take thou the seed of all living things.
> Her dimensions shall be to measure.
> Equal shall be her width and her length
> Like the Apsu thou shalt ceil her. (ANET p. 93 TAB. XI 21–31)

The reed-hut here evokes an association with the most ancient form of lower Mesopotamian temple architecture. The context of disclosure, therefore, can only be a widely attested divinatory phenomenon known as the "incubation dream." That is, a divine revelation which is granted a person who spends the night in a sanctuary, sometimes to one who has entered it in the hope of receiving such a message. (Biblical examples are the revelation to Samuel in I Samuel 3 and to Solomon in I Kings 3:3–15.) But why should Ea first address the wall of the reed-hut and then Utnapishtim himself? The ship which is to be built, so we are compelled to infer, is to be made of the materials of the house which the man (i.e. lord) of Shurippak is to tear down. But ships are made of wood while houses are made of clay brick! Utnapishtim, oblivious to such nonsense, continues:

> "I understood, and I said to Ea, my lord:
> '[Behold], my lord, what thou hast ordered,
> I will be honored to carry out.
> [But what] shall I answer the city,
> the people and elders?'"

Not a word has been said about an impending catastrophe. But Utnapishtim, by a master-stroke of deduction divines, so to speak, that a lead-encased subterranean shelter can only be intended as a precaution against an assault by nuclear bombs. He also understands the "honor" Ea has bestowed upon him, and that the real reason for the ship must be kept secret from the senate and populus of Shurippak who might divine the reason for the shelter and be miffed by their own exclusion from such honor. How achieve this?

> Ea opened his mouth to speak,
> Saying to me, his servant:
> 'Thou shalt then thus speak unto them:
> "I have learned that Enlil is hostile to me,
> So that I cannot reside in your city,
> Nor set my foot in Enlil's territory.
> To the Deep I will therefore go down, To dwell with my lord Ea.
> [But upon] you he will shower abundance,
> [The choicest] birds, the rarest fishes.
> [The land shall have its fill] of harvest riches.
> [He who at dusk orders] the husk-greens,
> Will shower down upon you a rain of wheat."

Ea's advice features a mixture of sense and nonsense. Enlil is a cosmic god—not a local Shurippakian deity—and Ea is not (like Neptune) a sea-god, so this explanation of flight from the security of shore to the hazards of sea is not likely to satisfy the apparently sensible questioners. The text of the last two lines, as our translator (Speiser) informs us, "features word-plays in that both *kukku* and *kibati* may designate either food or misfortune . . . Wily Ea plays on this ambiguity: To the populace the statement would be a promise of prosperity; to Utnapishtim it would signalize the impending deluge." Some forty-odd lines later, he translates the same words, where they serve as the signal to Utnapishtim that the impending deluge is about to begin, in only one sense of the double entendre:

> He who orders unease at night,
> Will shower down a rain of blight. (ANET p. 94 TAB XI 86–87)

The fun at the expense of unsuspecting mankind is close to the humor of the gallows variety. There is something macabre about the reversal of metaphor: "shower," a metaphor for the blessing of fructifying rains, becomes a "shower of abundance," in the sense of unexpected torrents of rain. The scene conjured up for us, of mankind being pelted—literally—by a rain of birds and fish, has a comic-strip vividness. It resonates also with our own (incongruous) metaphor: "raining cats and dogs."

There follows a description of the building of the vessel and its provisioning:

One [whole] acre was her floor space,
Ten dozen cubits the height of each of her walls,
Ten dozen cubits each edge of the square deck.
I laid out the contours (and) joined her together.
I provided her with six decks,
Dividing her thus into seven parts . . .
I saw to the punting-poles and laid in supplies. (ANET p. 93 TAB XI 56–62, 64)

A cubit equals approximately a foot and a half. Thus, when it comes to the launching of the vessel, 180 feet high—roughly the height of a fifteen-story apartment building—and of equal dimension in length and breadth, Utnapishtim's work is laid out for him. And as if this were not ludicrous enough, our hero sees "to the punting-poles" as though the vessel to be propelled were a raft! Where did he get these poles, which would have had to be at least one hundred fifty feet in length if, as we are soon told, two-thirds of the superstructure went into the water? Who could have plied such monstrous beams, and where did the punters stand? And which of the world's mighty rivers, let alone the Euphrates, could accommodate a ship that extends 120 feet below the water line?

We shall skip the details of the ship's provisioning, its lading with gold and silver and some 16,000 gallons of oil (the caulking consumed 48,000 gallons of bitumen, 24,000 gallons of asphalt, and 24,000 to 32,000 gallons of oil); the embarkation of family, kin, retainers, craftsmen, beasts of the field, and creatures of the wild. So also shall we skip the vivid description of the onset of the deluge. We resume with citation of one of the poem's most oft-quoted passages:

The gods were frightened by the deluge,
And shrinking back, they ascended to the heaven of Anu.
The gods cowered like dogs
Crouched against the outer wall.
Ishtar cried out like a woman in travail,
The sweet-voiced mistress of the gods moans aloud:
"The olden days are alas turned to clay,
Because I bespoke evil in the Assembly of the gods.
How could I bespeak evil in the Assembly of the gods,
Ordering battle for the destruction of my people,
When it is I myself who gave birth to my people!
Like the spawn of the fishes they fill the sea!" (ANET p. 94 TAB. XI 113–123)

The fortress-like castle of the gods is visualized as sited on the top of a cosmic mountain, its battlements reaching into the cloud-enshrouded "heaven of Anu." The flood waters have mounted that high and are now beating against the outer walls. On the other side of the wall the gods cower, fearful that the wall will collapse or the water rise higher and come spilling over the top. They cower like dogs. This less than reverent stance toward the gods on the part of the Epic's author has long been recognized, its implications, however, never worked out for the story as a whole. Similarly unremarked is the significance of the picture the author gives here of the "sweet-voiced mistress of the gods." (Contrast this epithet with her strident threats against Enkidu, Gilgamesh, and Anu when Gilgamesh, according to Ishtar, "has recounted my stinking deeds, my stench and my foulness.") Ishtar's heartless-ness toward the human race, the children to whom she herself has given birth, is self admitted. That she is brought to a sense of remorse only by the threat to her own survival is another giveaway of the poet's estimate of her character. The poet's genius for sardonic comedy is most fully realized in the bathetic climax of the last line, a simile expressive of Ishtar's grotesque psychology: "Like the spawn of fishes they fill the sea." For the teeming schools of fish, water is their natural element, their life-sustaining environment. But for gill-less mankind? It is as though a mother today, bereaved of her entire brood by a sinking at sea, were to bring her tale of grief to a climactic wail: "O, in the briny broth they lie, like herring salted in a bar-rel!" Such a simile, in a modern short story, would be likely to evoke a smile if not a laugh. But in poetry, and coming from the mouth of the goddess of love and pro-creation, only its grotesqueness might preclude hilarity.

The cube-shaped vessel is completed on the seventh day; the flood-storm sub-sides on the seventh day; the ship grounds on Mount Nisir and is held fast for six days, and on the seventh day the birds are released. If, as we suggested, the order in which Utnapishtim releases the birds reflects his perception of their ranges of flight, then his reasoning is absurd. What connection can be inferred from the jux-taposition of the level of the waters as they progressively recede and the differing distances various birds might travel?[28] Whichever bird failed to come back would indicate that somewhere below vegetation had been uncovered. Except, of course, for the last bird, the raven whose failure to return at high tide or low would, given its omnivorous diet, prove (as Noah learned) nothing. Following the notice of the crow's release ("the raven went forth and, seeing that the waters had diminished, he eats, circles, caws, and turns not round") we read:

Then I let out [all] to the four winds and offered a sacrifice.
I poured out a libation on the top of the mountain.
Seven and seven cult-vessels I set up,
Upon their pot-stands I heaped cane, cedarwood and myrtle.
The gods smelled the savor,
The gods smelled the sweet savor,
The gods crowded like flies about the sacrificer.
When at length as the great goddess arrived,
She lifted up the great jewels which Anu had fashioned to her liking:
"Ye gods here, as surely as this lapis upon my neck I shall not forget,
I shall be mindful of these days, forgetting [them] never.
Let the gods come to the offering
[But] let not Enlil come to the offering,
For he, unreasoning, brought on the deluge
And my people consigned to destruction." (ANET p. 95 TAB. XI 155–169)

Here, too, it has long been recognized that the comparison of the gods (who have gone unfed for two weeks or more) to flies swarming greedily over honey is a simile scarcely designed to flatter them. But again it is Ishtar who, making a dra-matic appearance, is made to utter a vow that is a masterpiece of bathos. To revert to our analogy of a mother today suddenly bereft of her entire brood, she would as soon forget the cataclysm that took them from her (in this case, a cataclysm to which she has confessed herself a consenting accomplice) as she is likely to lose or misplace her favorite necklace! Lapis was then, as it is today, a semiprecious stone. The necklace therefore is a trinket made for his child by Daddy Anu. And, as if this betrayal of her ludicrous scale of values—an entire race rendered comparable to a string of stones—were not comedy enough, she continues with a petulant addition. It is she who is the hostess at the banquet spread by Utnapishtim; the lost children were, after all, hers. That rascal Enlil is not invited to the wake—no share for him in the funeral meats! Utnapishtim continues his story:

> When at length as Enlil arrived,
> And saw the ship, Enlil was wroth,
> He was filled with wrath over the Igigi gods:
> "Has some living soul escaped?
> No man was to survive the destruction!" (ANET p. 95 TAB. XV 170–173)

Enlil's anger upon seeing the ship owes to the thwarting of the decree that he pushed through the assembly of the gods. Not a single human was to survive. The presence of the ship, he reasons, is evidence that the divine will has been frustrated. Someone must have escaped. His reasoning is faultless, as far as it goes. But it never occurs to Enlil to ask why it was necessary, in order to harbor one human couple, to construct a craft with a volume of some six million cubic feet and almost a quarter-million square feet of deck space. One wonders what intuition led him to recognize a ship at all in a cube seven stories high, containing sixty-three compartments, into each of which could have fitted three temples the size of King Solomon's! In any case, Enlil was bemused in some other important business at the time that the seven-story floating hotel had opened its doors to disembark its passengers, that they might begin the business of repopulating the world.

The god Ninurta suggests that only Ea could have had the wit to thwart the decree of the gods. Ea speaks up: first, addressing Enlil as "thou wisest of gods, thou hero," he upbraids Enlil for his unreasoning bringing on of the deluge, with its indiscriminate destruction of sinner and innocent alike, when other means would have provided punishment to fit the crime. (As noted earlier, there was no motive for the flood decree, hence no crime to speak of.) He then goes on to disclaim responsibility for the disclosure of the secret:

> It was not I who disclosed the secret of the great gods,
> I let Atrahasis [Utnapishtim] see a dream.[9]
> And he perceived the secret of the gods.[10]
> Now then take counsel in regard to him. (ANET p. 95 TAB. XI, 186–188)

Is it only the obtuse Enlil who is being ridiculed, or does the author also target the slippery wiliness of Ea? For Ea first challenges Enlil on the score of a decision that he did not himself, apparently, challenge in the Assembly. He then disavows responsibility for disclosing the secret of the gods, but not totally. He did let the cat out of the bag by letting Utnapishtim "see a dream," from which the mortal deduced everything. We now can understand why the incubation-dream is introduced by an address to the reed-hut and its walls, rather than to Utnapishtim. But

the detailed instructions that Utnapishtim received about the building and stock-
ing of the vessel, the answer with which to put off the populace, the clever code
announcing the flood's onset—all these would lead us to conclude that Ea is, at
the least, disingenuous. This polite word for *liar* is appropriate, however. Ea is not
so much concerned with exculpating himself as he is with baiting Enlil, with ex-
posing his imbecility. A fair analogy would be Aeschylus picturing Prometheus
pleading—and Zeus swallowing the plea—that he gave no knowledge to mankind; he was merely talking in his sleep, reviewing the logarithm and periodic tables, in the fortuitous presence of an overnight guest!

Enlil does not disappoint. In response to Ea's closing challenge—in effect,
"Now what are you going to do about it?"—what does Enlil actually do? He sees to
it that the will of the gods will not, after all, have been successfully defied. No man
was to survive the destruction? Utnapishtim, a mortal man, has survived? Well,
that too can be fixed. Utnapishtim continues:

> Thereupon Enlil went aboard the ship.
> Holding me by the hand, he took me aboard.
> He took my wife aboard and made [her] kneel by my side.
> Standing between us, he touched our foreheads to bless us:
> "Hitherto Utnapishtim has been but human.
> Henceforth Utnapishtim and his wife shall be like unto us gods.
> Utnapishtim shall reside far away, at the mouth of the rivers."
> Thus they took me and made me reside far away,
>   At the mouth of the rivers.
> But now, who will for thy sake call the gods to Assembly
> That the life thou seekest thou mayest find? (ANET p. 95 TAB. XI 189–198)

Since humans have survived contrary to the will of the gods, Mr. Fixit Enlil will
negate this frustration by eliminating the surviving humans. The comic scene here
is a parody of solemnity. Enlil leads Utnapishtim and wife back on to the ship,
which he will presumably waft through the air from Mount Nisir to the faraway
"mouth of the rivers." The lines of his benediction recall the joke of some decades
ago when Roman Catholics were expected to abstain from meat on Fridays. A fresh
convert to Catholicism, surprised by his priest on a Friday over a beefsteak dinner,
is asked how he could so quickly forget his instruction and eat meat on a fast day.
He replies, "Father, you sprinkled me with holy water and said, 'You were a Jew,
you are now a Christian.' So I sprinkled the steak and said, 'You were a beefsteak,
you are now a fish.'" It is the sophomoric humor in the joke that provides the analogue with Enlil's solution of his problem. But the joke can be read two ways: the
sly convert teasing his new mentor, or the foolish convert who thinks reality can
be changed by a pronouncement. In the case of Enlil there can be no question as to
who is being lampooned. For Enlil's fatuousness is boundless. He does not really
make Utnapishtim into a god, does not admit him to the pantheon as even a minor
deity. He merely removes him from time and history, to the never-never-land "at
the mouth of the rivers"—the garden of Eden?—where he can live in meaningless
eternity: a condition reflected at the very beginning of Tablet XI, where Gilgamesh
was struck by Utnapishtim's appearance: ungodlike, human—oh, so human—and,
at that, a humanity featured by an eerily unhuman impassive passivity.

THE BABYLONIAN FLOOD STORY AS A CRITIQUE OF PAGANISM

Violence is the life of nature. Conflict is the stuff of history. This is as true for us as it was for our pagan ancestors, but with a difference. For us there is a discontinuity between the two realms. Nature's violence is, for us, either the eruption of impersonal forces in haphazard purposelessness, or abstract principles operating in iron necessity determined by the law of cause and effect. History's conflicts are events precipitated by human needs and passions. Nature's events are, for us, either random and inscrutable, or so rigidly patterned as to be ultimately reducible to the mathematical formulae of science; whether random or regulated, they are infinitely repeatable. History's events are discrete and unique, for history is story: persons and their actions, character and plot. Needs and passions may be repeated and plot lines fall in congruent patterns, but characters are unique, so even "the same old story" is never quite the same. You cannot step into the same river twice, for even if the river is the same, you are not the person you were.

For the pagan, nature and history are much more a continuum. Natural forces are personified, their actions the result of purposing characters who create plots— story lines—as they work out their needs and passions. As the gods are superhumans, humans are somewhat deficient gods. And so it is that in paganism history and science blend. Everything is story: myth, in which the adventures of the gods predominate although human characters may appear; and legend, the historic adventures of human beings, in which the gods may act a role.

The line between myth and legend is, therefore, not always easy to draw. The *Enuma elish* is clearly a myth, as is the Story of Utnapishtim. The Epic of Gilgamesh, in which the gods play minor roles, is a mythopoeic legend incorporating within it such totally mythic elements as Ishtar and the Bull of Heaven, the creation of Enkidu, and the independent Utnapishtim story, all of which are integrated by the author into his plot. The mythic Ishtar, who is the insatiable seductress of fabulous beasts and legendary humans, is quite different from the mentally incompetent mother of humanity in the flood story. The author made use of traditional material in drawing the various lineaments of the two Ishtars, and there can be little question that the stamp of his own philosophic and comic genius has left its impress on both the essence and form of the goddess, which he received from tradition. It is likely that a significant proportion of the audience accepted the story literally. But the widespread and enduring popularity of the epic, the intuitive sense of even the literalists that there was some important message in the deluge story, and the sophistication of the non-literalists in the audience, all combined, suggest this: As the story of Gilgamesh rang with existential truth for the ancient audience in terms of its experience of man's lusts for love and power, anxiety over illness, and dread of death, so did the mythic metaphors largely accord with the audience's theological heritage.

And the picture of the ruling class of the world, the invisible gods who are manifest in what they do and have done, rather than in their personal presence, is what? A close analogy is provided by a theme frequently exploited in science fiction: A race of incredibly long-lived creatures who have inherited from their remote ancestors an unbelievably advanced technology whose scientific base has long been lost to them. These surviving heirs of powers they never earned are a mixed bag in terms of intellect, maturity, and decency. And theirs are the fingers on the buttons! A difficult lot to love, these lords of creation, but impossible not to fear. One can be grateful for those of them who support the rational and life-enhancing principles and institutions of mankind. One can only hope to enlist their aid through worship in warding off their baser, or more capricious, or moronic, colleagues. And as for poking ridicule at them by portraying them as they are, perhaps being no brighter than so many in the human audience, they will follow the plot literally and, forgetting what gods should really be like, will take no offense.

This last sentence is, of course, written with tongue in cheek. It points, however, to a weighty conclusion that must be drawn from our poet's satiric stance. One does not jeer at those one fears. And our poet's fearlessness bespeaks his disbelief in the gods whom he lampoons. In the section to follow, in our comparison of the two flood narratives, we shall see that the biblical author eliminated the jokes and mitigated the absurdities, for to him the attributes of divinity are not a laughing matter. But neither were they a laughing matter for the author of the Gilgamesh Epic. The mythic Utnapishtim can be and is lampooned. But Gilgamesh, in his rejection of death and in his quest for eternal life, is every one of us. He, like us, may be defeated. But can his creator accept the theology he has inherited? Can he make his peace with a theology that posits a race of capricious supermen-by-chance, who mock the canons of reason and jeer at the demands of the human heart?

Biblical monotheism, of which Abraham seems to be the first champion, seems to have sprouted from the inhospitable soil of paganism as if a spore wafted to earth from outer space. The text of the Gilgamesh Epic that has come down to us is a late Assyrian version. What we are suggesting is that perhaps a millennium earlier, in Babylon, a genius weaned himself from the outworn pagan creed in which he had been suckled. He provided the critique. An alternative creed was perhaps beyond him. The alternative creed was formulated in Israel, and is present for us in Genesis.[11]

THE BIBLICAL FLOOD STORY: THE TEXT

As I indicated at the very beginning of this chapter, no single narrative in Genesis can rival the Noah flood story for the number and clarity of those features that led to the discernment of two different authorial hands, or—as they are termed in genetic scholarship—sources or documents. As a matter of (literary) fact this is the one and only continuous narrative that is seen to consist of a conflation of pericopes or episodes from the two main sources, J and P. My own literary analysis, positing a single author and rebutting the evidence for conflation, is more likely to be granted a hearing (or, less metaphorically, a *reading*) if the text of the narrative is presented in a way that fully displays the source-critical divisions. To that end I will, in the translation that follows, crowd the passages assigned to J against the page's left-hand margin and those assigned to P against the right-hand margin, providing each passage with a caption that will highlight repetition and/or contrast as discerned in source-analysis. I will identify the columns as J and P, but in fairness to my own position, refer to then as *strands* rather than sources. Documentary theory posits that the sources have on occasion been contaminated so that an element characteristic of J, for example, will appear in a pericope that is essentially P, or vice versa. When an element in these passages is seen as an intrusion from the other source I will place that element in italics; thus italics in J point to intrusion from P, and italics in P point up intrusions from J.

STRAND J   STRAND P

A. *Introduction (I)*

(1) With mankind's first increase on earth—and the birth to them of girls—(2) divinities remarked how beauteous were these human maidens, and freely as they chose took themselves wives from among them. (3) YHWH then decided, "My spirit shall not enduringly abide in man—flesh[-creature] that he is—a hundred years and twenty shall [the limit of] his lifetime be"—(4) the Nephilim were in existence on earth in those days, (and also thereafter), following on the divinities' mating with human womenfolk who gave birth by them: these [offspring] those "heroes" of old, famed afar.

(5) YHWH took note of man's wickedness on earth so great, that the very bent of his imaginings was ever contrarily wicked. (6) YHWH came to regret that He had ever made mankind on earth, He was pained to the quick. (7) YHWH decided, "I must blot out from earth's surface this mankind I created—beginning with man, and inclusive of beasts, of crawlers, and of birds of the sky—such is my regret that ever I made them!" (8) Noah, however, had earned the favor of YHWH. (Genesis 6:1–8)

B. *Introduction (II)*

(9) This, now, is the story of Noah—Noah alone wholly righteous in his age; obedient to the Deity was Noah ever—(10) Noah sired three sons: Shem, Ham, and Japheth.

(11) The earth, in the Deity's judgment, was corrupt, earth being rife with lawlessness, (12) so that when God passed earth in review: lo, corrupt indeed it was—every species of

flesh had perverted its course on earth. (Genesis 6:9–12)

C. Noah Is Informed (I)

(13) God then addressed Noah: "Finis to all flesh—is the verdict I have reached. So rife is earth with lawlessness theirs. So must I lay them waste together with earth. (14) Make yourself, then, an ark of gopher-wood; of compartments make the ark; caulk it with pitch, inside and out. (15) And here is how you are to construct it: 300 cubits, the length of the ark; 50 cubits, its width; and 30 cubits, its height. (16) Light-openings provide in the ark, bring the lintels to a cubit from [the deck] above; an entrance from the side of the ark provide; with a bottom deck, a second deck, and a third deck make it.

(17) I, for my part, am about to bring on the Deluge—waters upon the earth—to waste from under heaven all flesh in which there is breath of life; everything on earth shall expire. (18) But I will establish my covenant with you, that you may enter the ark—you, your sons, your wife, and your sons' wives with you. (19) And of everything alive, of all flesh, a pair of each shall you bring into the ark to survive along with you—male and female shall they be. (20) Of the birds of every species, of the beasts of every species, of land crawlers of every species a pair of each will come to you for survival. (21) You, for your part, fetch some of every permissible edible and store it away, to provide yourself and them with food." (22) Noah did so—just as God had bidden him, just so did he do. (Genesis 6:13–22)

D. Noah Is Informed (II)

(1) YHWH said to Noah, "Go into the ark, you and all your family. Yes, you alone in this generation have I in my judgment found righteous. (2) Of every clean animal admit with you seven pair, male and mate; and of the animals which unclean are, one pair, male and mate. (3) Of the birds of the sky, seven pair, male

and female, to perpetuate live seed on earth's surface. (4) For in but seven days from now I shall make rain fall upon earth, for forty days and forty nights; and so will I blot out from everywhere on earth that which I have brought into being." (5) And Noah did just as YHWH had bidden him. (Genesis 7:1–5)

E. Entering the Ark

(6) (Noah, now, was six hundred years old when the Deluge took place,—water—on earth.) (7) *Noah went into the ark, his sons and his wife and his sons' wives with him, for shelter from the water of the Deluge.* (8) *Of the animals clean and the animals unclean, of the birds and every species astir on the ground,* (9) pairs came to Noah to the ark, *male and female*, as God had instructed Noah. (10) *In seven days time the waters of the Deluge came upon earth.* (11) In the year 600 of Noah's lifetime, in Month 2, on Day 17 of the month—on this day precisely—did the wellsprings of Great Deep crack apart and the sluice gates of heaven spring open.) (12) *And the rain continued on earth forty days and forty nights.*) (13) On that very day did Noah enter—and Shem and Ham and Japheth, and Noah's wife and the three wives of his sons with them—into the ark; (14) they and every life-form of every species, all the fowl of every species, every bird, every winged thing.

(15) They came to Noah, to the ark, pair by pair of all flesh in which abides the breath of life. (16) Those arriving were male and female, of all flesh did they arrive in accordance with God's instructions to him. *And YHWH battened him in.* (Genesis 7:6–16)

F. Deluge and Destruction

(17) The Deluge continued on earth *for forty days. As the waters swelled they buoyed up the ark and it lifted free from earth.* (18) As the water intensified, increasing in volume upon earth, the ark floated around on the water's surface. (19) The waters ever increasing in intensity on earth, they blanketed even the

highest mountains everywhere under heaven —(20) fifteen cubits above [them] the waters prevailed.) With the blanketing of the mountains, (21) all flesh astir on earth expired— fowl, cattle, beasts, all the swarms that teem on earth, and all mankind. (22) *Every last thing with nostrils inhaling lifebreath on earth, every last thing on shore died.* (23) *Thus did he blot out all existence on earth's surface, ranging from man through animals, crawlers, and birds of the sky. With these blotted out from earth there remained only Noah, and whatever was with him in the ark.* (Genesis 7:17–23)

G. The Deluge Is Checked

(24) The waters prevailed in intensity on earth for 150 days. (1) God was mindful of Noah and all the beasts and cattle that were with him in the ark. God then swept a wind over earth and the waves subsided. (2) The wellsprings of Great Deep and the sluice gates of heaven bolted closed, *and the rain from heaven held in check,* (3) *the waters began to retreat from earth, a steady retreat;* the waters beginning to abate on about Day 150. (4) So did the ark ground in Month 7, Day 17 of the month, on the mountain-range of Ararat. (5) The waters, now, continued to abate steadily until Month 10; in Month 10, on the first of the month, the mountain peaks showed through.) (Genesis 7:24–8:5)

H. Episode of the Birds

(6) After forty days, Noah opened the hatch which he had made in the ark. (7) He released a raven, which took off, flying thither and back until the water dried up from the earth. (8) He then dispatched a dove, to ascertain whether the waters had eased up on earth's surface. (9) But the dove could find no perch for its foot—the water so far-reaching over all earth's surface—and so returned to him, to the ark. He reached out and fetched it back into the ark. (10) After a wait of yet another seven days, he again released the dove from the ark. (11) Towards evening the dove re-

turned to him, in its bill a freshly plucked olive leaf! Noah then knew that the water had eased from earth. (12) Yet another wait of seven days more, and he released the dove. It returned to him no more. (Genesis 8:6–12)

I. The Disembarking

(13) In the year 601, in Month 1, on the first of the month, the waters had drained off from earth. *When Noah raised the hatch-cover, lo he saw that the earth's surface was drained.* (14) And in Month 2, on Day 17 of the month, the earth had become dry.)

(15) God addressed Noah, (16) "Come out of the ark, you, your wife, your sons, and your sons' wives with you; (17) every living creature which is with you, of all flesh—fowl, animals, and everything that crawls on earth—bring out with you, that they may teem on earth, abundantly reproduce on earth." (18) So Noah came out, his sons, his wife, and sons' wives with him; (19) every living creature, every crawler, every bird, everything which stirs on earth came out of the ark, species by species. (Genesis 8:13–19)

J. Sacrifice and Promise

(20) Noah then built an altar to YHWH. Taking from among all the clean cattle and clean fowl, he offered burnt offerings on the altar. (21) YHWH sniffed the pleasing odor. YHWH said to himself, "Never again will I abuse the earth on man's account—[seeing that] the bent of man's mind is evil from his youth—nor will I ever again strike down every living creature, as I have done. (22) So long as earth endures, seedtime and harvest, cold and heat, summer and winter, day and night will not cease." (Genesis 8:20–22)

K. Blessing and Meat for Man's Table

(1) God blessed Noah and his sons, saying to them, "Increase abundantly and populate the earth. (2) The dread fear of you shall descend upon all living creatures of earth and upon the fowl of the sky, upon every thing with

which the earth is astir, and all fish of the sea: into your power are they delivered. (3) Every stirring thing that lives shall be yours for the eating, like the grass greens do I give them all to you. (4) Only flesh with its life-blood in it you are not to eat. (5) And also—for your own life-blood will I exact retribution: of every beast will I exact it and of humankind; of every man for his brother will I exact retribution for a human life. (6) Whoever sheds the blood of man, by man shall his blood be shed. This is the meaning of: 'In the image of God made He man.' (7) You, then, for your part, increase abundantly, teem on earth and be fertile upon it." (Genesis 9:1–7)

L. The Promise of the Rainbow

(8) God then said to Noah and to his sons with him, (9) "I hereby make this covenant of mine with you and your offspring to come, (10) and also with every living creature that is with you—of birds, cattle, and beasts of earth along with you—all that have come out of the ark, of every creature on earth. (11) This covenant of mine I will fulfill: never again shall all flesh be cut off by Deluge waters, never again shall there Deluge be to waste the earth."

(12) God said, "This, now, is the sign of the covenant I grant as between me and you and every living creature that is with you, for all ages to come: (13) My bow have I set in the clouds, to serve as a sign of the covenant between me and earth. (14) So shall it be, when I mass clouds over earth—and the bow appears in the clouds— (15) I shall be mindful of this covenant of mine which exists between me and you and every living creature among all flesh. (16) The bow will be in the clouds, by my providence, to mark an enduring covenant between God and every living creature of all flesh that is on earth." (17) God pointed out to Noah, "There now is the sign of the covenant that I have established between myself and all flesh that is on earth!" (Genesis 9:8–17)

ON THE SOURCES OR STRANDS IN THE FLOOD STORY:
A PRELIMINARY DISCUSSION

Before we proceed to a synoptic review of the twelve pericopes (§§A–L) that make up the flood story, we shall first note and criticize the distinctive features of repetition and contrast that source-criticism has found significant for the identification and isolation of the J and P documents.

1. *Source-criticism:* J regularly features YHWH, while P with equal regularity features God (Elohim) as the name for Deity. On the basis of this feature alone we then have a P narrative of eight pericopes, complete from introduction through body to conclusion, and virtually if not altogether without gap. This complete narrative has been supplemented (from a presumably parallel narrative) with an alternative introduction (§A), conclusion (§J), a pericope (§D) without the addition of which the alternate conclusion (§J) is incongruous, and a fourth pericope (§H), the episode of the birds.

Poetical comment: The regular appearance of YHWH and God in the J and P strands is stipulated (with the exceptional contamination, so source-criticism, of YHWH appearing in 7:16, [P]). Noted, however, is the absence of YHWH as an identifying mark in §H, an episode that—borrowed from the Utnapishtim story— might just as well come from P's narrative. That would leave only three pericopes from J. Of these the sacrifice theme in §J, and the seven pairs of clean animals required for §J in §D—like the birds episode borrowed from the Utnapishtim story—would have been available to P as it clearly was to J. Why would P have omitted it from his narrative? If, because it is discrepant with other elements in the P narrative, why did the presumably perceptive editor restore what to P had become excrescence? And, in respect now to the remaining interpolation from the original J narrative, is there any basis for viewing §A as a (repetitious) introduction alongside the original P introduction in §B? There is not a single element in the two "introductions" that is repetitious, except for the notice of Noah's having earned Deity's favor in a world that had signally failed to do so. And finally, the arguments in this volume's chapter 1 for a poetical contextual reading of the names YHWH and Elohim, which—if borne out in our further discussion—renders all the previous poetic comments supererogatory.

2. *Source-criticism:* Additional hallmarks testifying to the authorial hands of P or J are to be discerned in proclivities in respect to numbers in general and chronology in particular: J is inordinately fond of round numbers, particularly seven and forty, and is otherwise totally uninterested in chronology. By contrast, P evinces a preference for precision in numerical detail, and for exactitude in respect to chronology. Examples are the seven and forty days in §D and §H (both J) and in the J contaminations of P in §E and §F.

Poetical comment: First of all, the numbers seven and forty in regard to days are totally unrelated to the numbers of 150 days or the day-of-the-month in the calendrical tally. The two systems exist side by side, the first as matters of narrative detail, the second as independent calendrical markers whose poetical purposes must be searched for. But even the very contrast between J and P as to round or precise numbers is one that will not bear up under scrutiny. While the 3:5:30 ratio of the ark's height, width, and length compares favorably with the 1:1:1 ratio of Ut-napishtim's cubic craft, the numbers in cubits (30, 50, 300) are suspiciously round. So too Noah's age, 600, in the year of the flood, and the 150 days of the rising waters to a level fifteen cubits above the highest mountain top.

3. *Source-criticism:* The J source presupposes the legitimacy of animal sacrifice and of the eating of flesh in the offering brought by Abel in Genesis 4:4. This source could therefore borrow the post-deluge sacrifice theme from the Utnapishtim story (§J) so long as it provided for more than a single pair of these edible animals entering the ark; otherwise these sacrifices would have spelled extinction for the edible species. This provision is supplied in §D, which—needless to say—is discrepant with the single pair of all species in §C. P, on the other hand, which has God mandating an exclusively vegetarian diet for all creatures in Genesis 1:29–30, must therefore pass up on the sacrificial theme. P does, however, signal God's reconciliation with humankind in §K, wherein the ban on human consumption of animal flesh (of Genesis 1:29–30) is formally withdrawn.

Poetical comment: If pericopes §C and §E are not by definition assigned to one source while §D is assigned to another, the presence of seven pairs of clean animals as opposed to the single pairs of unclean ones in §D is merely an expansion and clarification of the general heading of pairs in §C. Thus, for example, in §E—a pericope assigned mostly to P but with inexplicable intrusions from J—we are asked to believe that an intrusion from P is present in the J intrusion. Let us duplicate this passage, P except for italicized J:

(8) *Of the animals clean and the animals unclean, of the birds and every species astir on the ground,* (9) pairs came to Noah to the ark, *male and female,* as God had instructed Noah. (7:8–9)

It is clear that the only reason for assigning this verse to J is the distinction between clean and unclean supposedly known only to J. P supposedly has a single pair of each species, whether clean or unclean. But then the non-italicized words at the beginning of verse 9, translated by Speiser (for example) as *two of each* is seen as expressive of this P notion. My translation of *šᵉnayīm šᵉnayīm* "pairs of each" is equally in place in a supposed J, for the animals came to Noah in pairs of every species; single pairs in the case of the unclean, seven pairs in the case of the clean. Let us note further that the vocabulary of this supposedly J insertion is in every respect that of the P vocabulary in Section C: *bᵉhēmā, ʿôf, rōmeś,* and male and female (*zākār unᵉqēbā*) rather than male and mate (*ʾīš wᵉʾištō*).

IN REGARD TO THIS preliminary discussion of the considerations that might yet dispose us to distinguish between the text passages crowded against the left-hand or right-hand margins, let us note that neither singly nor collectively do these considerations compel a conclusion that these columns represent separate sources, sources patched together by an incompetent redactor, or one made to seem so by the imposition of a slavish compulsion to include discrepant details from two traditions, both of which had (inexplicably) become sacrosanct. Let us note that differences are not necessarily discrepancies, that inconsistencies are not necessarily incon-

gruities, and that neither differences nor inconsistences nor discrepancies are necessarily contradictions. And, further, that even seemingly clear contradictions
(such as the chronological order of the creation of man and animals in Genesis 1
and 3, or the line of humanity in the Cainite and Sethite genealogies) may represent strategies of metaphor in a single work by a single author.

POETICAL REVIEW OF THE FLOOD STORY

Episode A. Prelude (Introduction I)

(1) With mankind's first increase on earth—and the birth to them of girls—(2) divinities remarked how beauteous were these human maidens, and freely as they chose
took themselves wives from among them. (3) YHWH then decided, "my spirit shall
not enduringly abide in man—flesh[-creature] that he is—a hundred years and
twenty shall [the limit of] his lifetime be"—(4) the Nephilim were in existence on
earth in those days, (and also thereafter) following on the divinities' mating with
human womenfolk who gave birth by them: these [offspring] those "heroes" of old,
famed afar.

(5) YHWH took note of man's wickedness on earth so great, that the very bent of
his imaginings was ever contrarily wicked. (6) YHWH came to regret that He had
ever made mankind on earth, He was pained to the quick. (7) YHWH decided, "I
must blot out from earth's surface this mankind I created—beginning with man, and
inclusive of beasts, of crawlers, and of birds of the sky—such is my regret that ever I
made them!" (8) Noah, however, had earned the favor of YHWH. (Genesis 6:1–8)

The integral connection between the first verse of our text here and the begettings in the line of Seth that precede it in Chapter 5 could be lost only on a devo-
tee of source-criticism, which assigns the pericope here to J and the preceding genealogy to P. That genealogy presents a single family line, tracing a male heir from
Adam/hā'ādām to Noah in the tenth generation, with Noah's siring of an eleventh
generation of three sons. This, we know, is the line of humankind. But what is crucial for our understanding of this pericope in Chapter 6 is the refrain-like notice
that each of Noah's nine ancestors sired not only the one son named but additional
unnamed sons and daughters. And, indeed, why bother with names, since all these
lines ended with the flood! But why then the notice of daughters (whose descendants would also have perished in the flood), whose lines are supererogatory in a
patrilineal tradition (such as Scripture consistently represents)?

The answer to this last question is provided by the first half of our passage,
verses 1–4, which constitute a pericope in themselves. The comely women of humankind's first generations also mothered a descendent line of humans, sired upon
them by a race of divinities. These descendants, the narrator permits us to presume,
might well have succeeded to their paternal heritage of immortality (or a longevity
of near-equivalence in the eyes of mayfly mortals) but for YHWH's decree limiting
them to a maximum of 120 years. This limitation is striking on a number of counts.
If applied to the centuries before the flood, this mixed breed of semi-divine mortals
lived ephemeral lives compared to the humans in the line of Adam through Seth,

Methuselah attaining the high water mark of 969 years, while his father Enoch is the shortest lived, fetched by God in mid-career at the age of 365. If applied to the centuries after the flood, the limitation could apply only to purebred mortals in the line of Noah (the mixed breed having perished in the flood), but the shortest-lived in this register is Nahor at 148 years, and the first to whom this number 120 applies is Moses. Or is it possible that this limitation to a maximum of 120 years is to be understood as applying to a separate class of post-diluvian mortals, humans (*bā'ādām*, verse 3) on their maternal side, and this despite their paternal genes (*bᵉšaggām hū' bāsār*, "flesh creature nonetheless")? We should then have to conclude that this line somehow managed to survive the flood!

As unwarranted as such a conclusion would seem to be according to the biblical account, it is just such a presupposition that must be behind the midrashic story that the Og king of Bashan, who was annihilated by the Israelites (Numbers 21), lived as a titanic figure at the time of the flood, and managed to ride out (literally!) that cataclysm by hitching his mount to Noah's ark. Fanciful as is the free play of the rabbinic imagination, it is not without some basis in a close reading of a biblical narrative that the rabbis will permit themselves an embroidery that seems starkly to contradict the hallowed text. And the pointer to the existence of a mortal breed existing both before and after the flood is in verse 4, a hypotactic sentence, a concluding parenthetic notice that bridges the gap between verse 2 and verse 3; between the supernals' wiving of human women and YHWH's decree limiting the lifetimes of "the humanity which is also flesh," namely, the offspring of these unions. The hypotactic construction serves, among other effects, to highlight the temporal contrast between "in the days" and "as well as thereafter." And the hitherto unmentioned-as-such offspring are associated with—if not explicitly identified with—the Nephilim, with the progeny born by "the daughters of hā'ādām" as a consequence of their congress with "the sons of the *ᵉlōhīm*."

These Nephilim, spawned (as we are now reminded) in antediluvian times, are present in their descendants—also known as titans (*bᵉnē ᵃnāq/hāᵃanāq*) or Rephaites—as late as the time of David and as early as the time of Moses. Of all these populations, one individual alone is singled out for this mention: "Verily, only Og king of Bashan, remained of the *rest* of the Rephaites" (Deuteronomy 3:11). But for these four verses in Genesis 6 we would have no idea of the provenience of these "mighty ones reputed of yore." On the other hand, where but in the narrative immediately preceding the story of the flood should Scripture's authors have informed us of this miscegenate race, which somehow survived the flood and lived into the early centuries of Israelite history? Yes, these verses belong here in Genesis, and the rabbis correctly read the message of "in those days—and also thereafter." The question we must ask, however, is what function do these titanic creatures serve in the ideational literature we call Scripture, and specifically for the introduction of the flood story? How much wiser are we for knowing that among the aborigines conquered by Moses and David were the titanic Og of Bashan and Goliath of Gath? And how does this race figure in YHWH's motivation for bringing on the flood?

The mating of the male divinities with the human females does not in itself constitute motivation for the flood. The human parties are victims of force majeure and thus absolved of any responsibility; the aggressor males are punished—not to perish in the flood—but by the truncated life-span. The punishment of the truly and fully human race is the burden of the second part of our pericope, the death of this race in the flood, except for the line of Noah. And the crime is a wickedness of such magnitude that no details or specifics need be provided; suffice it to say that it can be gauged, not by any act, but rather by the human mental condition: a perverse and stubbornly wicked imagination. Given the context, that of the preceding four verses, one can see what led Speiser to read the "facts" of those four verses as the figment of the imagination that produced them: the mythological world of paganism in which rapacious and miscegenating gods (of both sexes) bed human partners to produce such mighty heroes of renown as Gilgamesh and Achilles. The sinfulness of such fancies lies, of course, in the misrepresentation of the non-human nature of God and the non-godly nature of man.

The failure of Speiser's suggestion to command attention is due, we would suggest, to a lack of a poetic framework or underpinning. Consider Speiser's own opening comment on verses 1–4, in keeping with his own essentially source-critical presuppositions (the italics are mine):

> The *undisguised mythology* of this *isolated fragment* makes it not only *atypical of the Bible as a whole* but also puzzling and controversial in the extreme. Its problems are legion: Is what we have here an *excerpt* from a fuller account? Why was such a stark piece included altogether? Does its present place in the book imply a specific connection with the Flood?[12]

My own discussion of the miscegenate race is in rebuttal of such characterizations as isolated and atypicality. And the predisposition to be shocked by *undisguised mythology* in the Bible is, as we discussed in chapter 2, based on a misunderstanding and misrepresentation of how Scripture's authors freely allude to or cite and exploit mythological elements.

What is it in Speiser's suggestion as to the relationship of verses 5–8 to verses 1–4 that will cause most scholars to judge that he is making a huge leap, and an unwarranted one at that, in bridging the narrational gap between the two pericopes? For one, the failure to recognize that gapping is an intriguing poetic strategy, frequently most effective when it demands that the reader search for the bridge. For another, how can verses 1–4 possibly be intended as the product of a pathological imagination when the formulation of these verses is unquestionably one of narrational fact? Specifically: how could a pagan imagination picture YHWH himself decreeing the punishment of this semi-divine race? (This last question is oblivious to its obverse: How could a Scriptural imagination picture YHWH tolerating a class of divinities mating with humans and producing a hybrid species?) In general these questions raised by philologians fail to distinguish between the narrational facticity of the historian and the narrational facticity of the writer of fiction. And a vital strategy in the latter is unthinkable in the former: the unreliable or the less-than-reliable narrator.

In respect to this strategy of the art of fiction, we should note that for all its late recognition, identification or categorization in literary criticism, it is present—and must have been intuited by at least part of the audience—in the earliest of literary productions. (And, let us note in passing, the more subtle, the more verisimilitudi-nous, that is, the more artistic a caricature or a lampoon, the more likely that many will interpret it as a realistically intended portrait, faithfully or falsely representing its subject.) Whenever a writer refuses to signal to the least perceptive of his audi-ence that he is engaging in satire or parody, in fanciful figuration of praise or criti-cism, in parable or allegory—rather than in straightforward narration—that writer is, for that part of his audience, playing the role of the unreliable narrator. And in the ideological or ideational fiction of Scripture, that is how we must view the nar-rator of story/history. Whether in Eden in respect to the historicity of an Adam mated to an Eve built up from his rib, of a Noah punching the tickets of every pair of every species that is to travel with him, of a David conquering Goliath or seduc-ing his loyal colonel's wife, the narrator who permits his reader to read him as reli-able (and omniscient) historiographer is indeed an unreliable narrator.

Writing as they did for audiences whose members differed greatly in their levels or capacities for understanding, Scripture's authors must have reconciled themselves to the likelihood of being misunderstood more often than not by the larger number of their readers. But in the case of a passage such as the one before us, seemingly so raw in the acceptance of the mythological staple that the two races, human and di-vine, could not only mate but produce fertile offspring, the biblical author/narrator could signal his exploitation of the unreliable narrator strategy by means of a num-ber of exceptional deployments of diction, syntax, and literary style.

In terms of diction: The use of the adjective "good" for human women as per-ceived by the divine beings is ambiguous: good looking, well-mannered, eugenic, or morally correct? The singular appearance of the verb *yādōn* in YHWH's solilo-quy, the stem suggesting "judgment," but that sense altogether inappropriate in the context and the meaning of the term not terribly relevant since the context itself forces us to read *endurance* into it. The apparent contraction of the conjunction *ªšer* to *šᵉ* (rare in early biblical Hebrew) and its joining with the adverb *gam* "also" and followed by *hūʾ bāsār* "he (is) flesh;" yielding the sense "for he also is flesh" (as compared to the fully human breed of *hāʾādām*) rather than—as in our own render-ing—"in that he is also flesh." The use of the term *hāʾādām* "humankind" for the purebred human race in verses 1, 2, and 4, and, in verse 3—with the preposition *bā*—for the half-human and half-divine breed; a breed of whose existence we do not become aware until verse 4.

In terms of style and syntax: The formal paratactic construction of verses 1, 2, and 3, in contrast with the hypotactic construction of verse 4. The recognition that this requires verse 4 to be read as a parenthesis, a parenthesis that anomalously ends the pericope, and forces the reader to search for the place where it semanti-cally belongs. Only then does the reader realize that the parenthesis must be read between verses 2 and 3, that only so can sense be made of the divine decree in verse 3. All this syntactic complication is in the interest of the gapping and bridg-ing strategy. But why the recourse to such a strategy at all? Why not formulate verse 4 hypotactically and place it between verses 2 and 3?

Part of the answer is of course, that by introducing the Nephilim—who by the logic of the larger narrative could not have survived the flood, yet somehow man-aged to do so—at the end of the pericope it ties their existence, or rather their re-

puted existence, into the judgment of YHWH in the very next verse on the perse-
vering perversity of the human imagination. So, the deployment of anomalous diction and tricky syntactical construction in verses 1–4, which constitutes a pericope
of sorts, presents the reader with a puzzle, a challenge to our poetic wit; a challenge
we shall never meet unless we adduce the relevant allusions elsewhere in Scripture
and then return to Genesis to realize that the pericope of sorts, verses 1–4, can
only make sense when tied to the continuing pericope in verses 5–8, the role or
function of a misguided sense of the world, natural and supernatural, in the disasters ensuing from the diseased imagination, or possibly from the kinds of conduct
that will characterize a humanity which owns a distorted view of reality. These
last two alternative understandings of Scripture's teaching (kerygma) in regard to
the relationship between theory and practice, ideology and praxis are both present
in verse 5. Questions of parataxis and hypotaxis in form and meaning leave moot
the question of this verse's correct translation. Our translation, subordinating the
conjunction *waw* to the preceding *kī*, renders the perverse human imagination as
identical with "humankind's great wickedness." The sentence may be read, however, as pointing to two separate (though not necessarily unrelated) aspects of
human deficiency: "YHWH took note that great indeed was the wickedness of humankind on earth, and also that the shape of his deepest thoughts was ever and
yet evil."

Two additional stylistic peculiarities must be noted in the second half of our
pericope. One is the pleonastic appearance of *hā'āreṣ* "the earth / the world" in
verses 5 and 6, and of *hā'dāmā* "the earth / the ground" in verse 7. Doubt that these
are redundancies will be dispelled, even in the translation, by omitting of these
words and asking if anything is lost thereby. The other peculiarity is in verse 7,
where the mankind (*hā'dām*) to be blotted out in YHWH's soliloquy is glossed as
an entity constituted of man (*ādām*) plus the whole range of animals of land and
sky. That this gloss is *free direct discourse* goes without saying. A definition of humankind is superfluous in itself, and particularly so in the mental processes of the
Deity engaged in internal dialogue. But the perplexity of superfluity is compounded
with that of incongruity. And together with the redundancies of the world, the
earth, and the ground finds its solution in a metaphor rich with meaning. On the
one hand, the repetitions of earth and world and soil emphasize the distance between the incomparability of this realm of human beings and the realm of the creator who observes them from on high. The image is reminiscent of an infinitely resourceful scientist in his laboratory, creating and testing life forms in a microcosmic
culture. One life form in particular he has provided with so rich an ecology and endowed with such potentiality and freedom as to warrant from it the highest of expectations. Indeed, so central is this life form to its creator that all the other life
forms were created only in conjunction with and subordination to it, even to such
a degree that they can be viewed as constituents of, rather than entities separate
from, that life form so replete with capacities and freedom. And such is the disap-
pointment of the creator of this experiment that he cannot but choose to utterly
destroy the disappointing creature and his so painstakingly fashioned environment.
Utterly, except for one exceptional strain of that species, exceptional in a way yet
to be made clear.

Episode B. Introduction (II)

> (9) This, now, is the story of Noah—Noah alone wholly righteous in his age; obedi-
> ent to the Deity was Noah ever—(10) Noah sired three sons: Shem, Ham, and
> Japheth. (11) The earth, in The Deity's judgment, was corrupt, earth being rife with
> lawlessness, (12) so that when God passed earth in review: lo, corrupt indeed it was—
> every species of flesh had perverted its course on earth. (6:9–12)

The careful reader will have noted that the heading of §A of the pericope,
6:1–8, has been changed from *Introduction (I)* to *Prelude*, and now section §B is
headed *Introduction*. The change requires no justification. The intricately composed and many-faceted concatenation of metaphors that constitutes §A has but
one item in common with §B: Deity's recognition of the world's evil. Noah figures
not at all in the Prelude until the last verse, and then only as the one exception to
the ubiquitous malfeasance. The introduction proper to the story of Noah ties in
then with the mention of Noah in verse 8, and begins his story by stressing the reason for his having found favor. Keeping in mind that both YHWH and Elohim are
proper names for the Deity, it is readily apparent why the narrator would want to
distance the *Deity* from the *bᵉnē hāᵉlōhīm* who figure so importantly in §A. This he
does by opting consistently for YHWH in this pericope. Beginning now with
Noah's righteousness and obedience, these qualities are defined not in relation to
the Creator as person, but as that impersonal abstraction of all-encompassing power
and morality in both verses 9 and 11, *hāᵉlōhīm*. God as person, Elohim, appears first
as the reviewing magistrate in verse 12, and will continue to be featured as such in
pericope §C (verses 13 and 17). If affinity, rather than discrepancy, is to be looked
for in pericopes §A and §B, what better evidence than the conspicuous predilection in §B for the term *hā ʾāreṣ*, which in its two appearances in §A seemed quite redundant. In §B now the term appears three times; the first occasion in the omniscient narrator's voice featuring the corruption of the world by Heaven's standards,
namely the breach of morality; the second confirming the narrator's statement by
picturing God's personal confrontation of that corruption of the world and then
underlining the extent of that corruption, hitherto expressed by the earth as subject of the passive (niphal) verb, by the same verb in the active (hiphil) conjunction with "all flesh" as its subject, and again "on earth." Despite this repetitiveness,
the nature of this perverse conduct, apposite apparently both to ratiocinative
human and to dumb beast as well, remains unspecified. The possibility that this
represents a gapping strategy will alert us to possible clues in episodes to come for
the bridging of such a gap.

Episode C. Noah Is Informed

> (13) God then addressed Noah: "Finis to all flesh—is the verdict I have reached. So
> rife is earth with lawlessness theirs. So must I lay them waste together with earth. (14)
> Make yourself, then, an ark of gopher-wood; of compartments make the ark; caulk it
> with pitch, inside and out. (15) And here is how you are to construct it: 300 cubits, the
> length of the ark; 50 cubits, its width; and 30 cubits, its height. (16) Light-openings

provide in the ark, bring the lintels to a cubit from [the deck] above; an entrance from the side of the ark provide; with a bottom deck, a second deck, and a third deck make it. (17) I, for my part, am about to bring on the Deluge—waters upon the earth—to waste from under heaven all flesh in which there is breath of life; everything on earth shall expire. (18) But I will establish my covenant with you, that you may enter the ark—you, your sons, your wife, and your sons' wives with you. (19) And of everything alive, of all flesh, a pair of each shall you bring into the ark to survive along with you—male and female shall they be. (20) Of the birds of every species, of the beasts of every species, of land crawlers of every species a pair of each will come to you for survival. (21) You, for your part, fetch some of every permissible edible and store it away, to provide yourself and them with food." (22) Noah did so—just as God had bidden him, just so did he do. (Genesis 6:13–22)

The logic of our narrative requires, to be sure, that Noah be informed of the impending deluge and advised as to God's plan for the survival of Noah's line. Two elements in God's address to Noah are worthy of brief notice here for their contrast with the Utnapishtim story (in anticipation of a more detailed comparison that will follow). One is the differing shape and dimensions of the vessels that will ride out the storm; the other is the imparting to the mortal of Deity's motive in bringing on the cataclysm. This latter may strike the reader as repetitive, in that it is the third time that it is expressed. The significance of the repetition, however, must be gauged by the total absence of motivation for the flood unleashed against mankind in the Utnapishtim story. Noteworthy also is that the information as to the flood is given in direct discourse of remarkable length: a full nine verses. Another feature of the dialogue that the narrator puts into the mouth of God discloses an artistry that has escaped both observation and comment. The doom impending over humanity is not revealed to Noah in a continuous flow, but is divided into two parts. First, the verdict of guilt and the sentence of doom: "all flesh together with the earth" will be laid waste; the manner of the sentence's execution is not mentioned. Then comes the instruction to build the three-storied wooden vessel. The casual reader—and most of us are such most of the time—knowing the plot in advance, forgets that Noah has no idea of what is coming, and so misses the astonishment with which Noah must have attended the details of the huge building project, and misses as well the significance of the label for the object-to-be constructed; it is not called a ship (for which Hebrew has a word) but a "box/chest/ark." Only after this comes the disclosure that the devastation is to be wreaked by water. This deployment of God's monologue makes possible a fourth declaration of creature doom, to be immediately followed by the gracious promise (*bᵉrīt* "covenant," by synecdoche of whole for the part) that the vessel to be built will spell salvation for humanity and all living species as well.

Two additional features of diction require comment (both of weight for—or rather, against—source-division). The name for the destructive phenomenon to be activated by God is *mabbūl*, glossed by God himself as "water upon the earth." This term, which appears only here and once again in Scripture, means neither flood, for which biblical Hebrew has a word, nor storm, for which it has a plethora of terms. The second feature is the characterization of the food that Noah is to store as—in our translation—permissible edibles. The Hebrew *mā͏ᵃakāl ᵃšer yēᵓakel*, literally "eatable edible," points to permissible rather than to palatable or digestible. What foods, then, are not permissible? What, furthermore, in this connection is the point of the seemingly redundant addition that the food store is *to provide yourself and them with food*?

Episode D. Noah Is Informed (II), or Noah Alerted: The Rain Is Imminent

(1) YHWH said to Noah, "Go into the ark, you and all your family. Yes, you alone in this generation have I in my judgment found righteous. (2) Of every clean animal admit with you seven pair, male and mate; and of the animals which unclean are, one pair, male and mate. (3) Of the birds of the sky, seven pair, male and female, to perpetuate live seed on earth's surface. (4) For in but seven days from now I shall make rain fall upon earth, for forty days and forty nights; and so will I blot out from everywhere on earth that which I have brought into being." (5) And Noah did just as YHWH had bidden him. (Genesis 7:1–5)

Once again we have changed the headings of our pericopes, §C and §D, so as not to concede the pointless redundancy of the two passages that, in the view of source-criticism, underlines the difference in source-provenance already betrayed by the use of God (Elohim) in §C and of YHWH here in §D. We do not concede *pointless* redundancy, but neither do we deny the *appearance* of redundancy. Our (self-imposed) task of poetic analysis requires us to compare the two pericopes in respect to similarities and differences, with a view to demonstrating the purposeful intent of a single author of both pericopes.

The two pericopes are certainly parallel in many ways. Both begin with Deity addressing Noah, and both consist entirely of monologue, except for the concluding notice in both that Noah did exactly as Deity had bidden him. One clear difference is the appearance of the two names for Deity. As we have repeatedly stressed, most recently in our discussion of §B, the availability of both YHWH and Elohim as proper names for the Deity does not require that the choice of one or the other be justifiable in every case in terms of the subtleties of a passage's content and context. In the case of our two passages we would be hard-pressed to argue that the nuance of greater intimacy or personhood or benevolence is such as to determine the choice of YHWH in §D as against that of Elohim in §C. Interesting, for the source-critical claim that J and P passages (marked as such by their respective hallmarks YHWH and Elohim) are also distinguished by parallel distinctions in diction, are the opening verses of §B and §D. The former (6:9) has Noah a righteous man (*ṣaddīq*) in his generations (*dōrōtāw*) obedient to Deity (*hāᵉlōhīm* here, and also in verse 11, but Elohim "God" in verse 12); the latter (7:1) has YHWH declaring that he has found Noah alone righteous (*ṣaddīq*) in his generation (*dōr*).

Similarities in §C and §D, read as redundancies and pointing to different sources, are: 1) the announcements of the flood to Noah; 2) the intent to blot out all living things; and 3) the destruction traced to the lawlessness of these creatures. In respect to these similarities we would point to the following differences. Whereas the announcement in §C is made long before the flood, calls for Noah to build the ark, and gives no indication how long it will (or actually did) take to build, the announcement in §D follows the completion of the ark, and calls for boarding it due to the imminence of the rain. As for the righteousness of Noah and the wickedness of all other men and species, §C specifies the latter and implies the former, while §D makes the former explicit and implies the later. And, indeed, in regard to the similarity in diction pointed out above in 6:9 and 7:1, a famous ambiguity expounded by the rabbis in 6:9 finds its resolution in 7:1. Noah's "righteousness in his generations" (note the plural, which prompted our translation "age") can mean that he was righteous compared to the pervasive wickedness of his age, or that his righteousness was even more remarkable for the example of his contemporaries. Noah in 7:1 is judged by YHWH as "alone righteous in his generation" (note the singular). There is only one standard of righteousness—God's—for all generations, and Noah met that standard: no one else did.

The chief difference between the two pericopes, the specification of a single pair of each species in §C and of a single pair of unclean species as against seven pair of the clean, as has been discussed above, need not be read as discrepant. The instruction as to the animals in §C is synoptic—a pair of each species—minimally, and refined in the resumptive §D into two orders of pairing: single pairs for the unclean, seven pairs for the clean. We have thus argued that neither discrepancies nor pointless redundancy can be upheld as evidence for a conflation here of those different sources. For all that, our poetic analysis requires us to seek for the purpose of the tricky deployment here of the synoptic-resumptive and as well for the unquestionable redundancies that are a feature of the entire narrative. Thus, we cannot overlook that this last pericope constitutes the fifth time that the living creatures are mentioned as slated for destruction (this time by "erasure, blotting out," which as Speiser pointed out evokes the imagery of the inscription on a clay tablet destroyed by immersion in water). The difference between §D and §C lies in the order of destruction and refuge. The latter begins with the doom in 6:13, resumes that motif in 6:17, and then proceeds to the ark as refuge for Noah and his company; in §D the entry into the ark for the righteous Noah comes first (7:1) and the doom of all others constitute the Deity's closing words (7:4). And, yet again, as in the three pericopes that precede it, the earth (hā ʾāreṣ), the habitat created by God for humans, beasts, and birds is mentioned three times.

Episode E. Entering the Ark

(6) Noah **now** was 600 years old when the Deluge took place—waters on earth. (7) Noah entered—and his sons and his wife and his son's wives with him—into the ark, [for shelter] from the waters of the Deluge. (8) Of all the clean beasts **now**, and of the beasts which unclean are, and of the fowl and everything which scurries on the ground, (9) pairs of each came to Noah to the ark, male and female, even as God had charged Noah. (10) It was in the seven-days time [earlier mentioned] that the waters of the Deluge occurred on earth.

(11) **Now** in the 600th year of Noah's lifetime, in Month 2 on Day 17 of the month—on this day precisely—did all the wellsprings of Great Deep crack open and the sluice gates of heaven spring open. (12) The rains continued on earth for forty days

and forty nights.) (13) **[Yes,]** on this very day did Noah enter—and Shem, Ham and Japheth (Noah's sons), and Noah's wife, and the trio of his son's wives with them—into the ark. (14) **[Yes]** they and all wild beasts according to their species, and all grazing beasts according to their species, and all beasties which scurry on earth according to their species, and all fowl according to their species: every bird, every winged thing.

(15) Thus they came to Noah to the ark, pairs of all flesh creatures in which abides the breath of life. (16a) And those arriving **now**—male and female of every creature came, even as God had charged him. (7:6–16a)

The above translation differs in minor respects from my earlier translation, which was designed primarily to highlight the separate source elements read into this pericope. In my preliminary discussion of these elements I disposed of the criteria by which scholarship has assigned the contents of this pericope to P and J, and so have been been able to dispense here with the italics. In the interest of a poetical analysis I have used paragraph indentations, parentheses, and rubrics in boldface type, so that the reader may review this pericope with an eye to the disposition of paratactic or hypotactic syntax in the original Hebrew. Thus, for example, the rubrics **now** and **Yes** in boldface, signaling hypotactic syntax (verses 6, 8–9, 11, 13–14, and 16), and the absence of these (verses 7, 10, 12, and 15) indicating paratactic syntax. Let us recall that the normal usage in narrative is paratactic syntax (verbal clauses, introduced by waw-conversive construction), while hypotactic syntax (nominal clauses with following verbs in the normal sense-functions of perfect and imperfect) expresses a subordination, often a parenthetical or flashback aside. Consider, then, how anomalous is this pericope. Of a total of eleven verses, seven are hypotactic in structure, only four are paratactic; the narrative brunt is carried by the former. Not only that, however: Of the four verses in paratactic syntax, two—verses 10 and 12—are parenthetic in function, hence subordinate in this respect to the hypotactic verses, which are normally subordinate in function. That leaves us with only two paratactic verses out of eleven, and of these two, verse 15 is a kind of resumptive coda, supererogatory in respect to information and semantically as gratuitous as the final verse that is attached to it (in hypotactic construction). What can be the point of these so consistent departures from standard style?

Another problem: What significance did our narrator attach to numerical tidbits as to twice inform us that the Deluge took place in the 600th year of Noah's lifetime? And this without telling us whether it was possibly the day after his 600th birthday or the day before his 601st. Which, of course, raises the question as to why precision matters in regard to the onset of the deluge on Day 17 of Month 2, a precision that is twice commended to our attention by the formulation "on this day" for the onset of the waters (verse 11) and "on that very day" for the entry into the ark (verse 13). In respect to this last notice which, tied in with verse 14, states baldly that all the humans and all the animals filed over the one gangplank and through the one door in the ark's side in a single day, is it idle to ask whether this does not run counter to the logic of 7:1–5? There, the seven days notice of the flood's advent, following upon the bidding to begin the boarding of the ark, seems to be in recognition of the many days it would require to settle the multitudinous species into the ark. To be sure, the intent behind verse 13 may be that the animals took six days and part of the seventh to go aboard, and that only the last of these, together with the humans, boarded the ark minutes before the waters began to pour. But if this was the intent, why so blurred, why in such contrast to the time of the waters' onset, the time of the boarding, both of these on that fateful day in the second month of Noah's 600th year?

The problem of narrative redundancy, noted in respect to previous pericopes, is so remarkable a feature of this pericope that it warrants a repetition of the text, arranged so as to facilitate our grasp of its extent:

(6) Noah **now** was 600 years old when

the Deluge took place — waters on earth.

(7) Noah entered — and his sons, and his wife and his sons' wives with him — into the ark, [for shelter] from the water of the Deluge.

(8) Of all the clean beasts **now** and of the beasts which unclean are, and of the fowl and everything which scurries on the ground

(9) pairs of each came to Noah to the ark,

male and female, even as God had charged Noah.
(10) It was in the seven days time [earlier mentioned] that the waters of the Deluge occurred on earth.

(11) **Now** in the 600th year of Noah's lifetime, in Month 2 on Day 17 of the month — on this day precisely — did all the wellsprings of Great Deluge crack open and the sluice gates of heaven spring open.
(12) The rains continued on earth for forty days and forty nights.
(13) **[Yes]** on this very day did Noah enter — and Shem, Ham and Japheth Noah's sons, and Noah's wife and the trio of his sons wives with them — into the ark.
(14) **[Yes]** they and all wild beasts according to their species, and all [grazing] beasts according to their species, and all beasties which scurry on earth according to their species, and all fowl according to their species: every bird, every winged thing.
(15) Thus they came to Noah to the ark, pairs of all flesh creatures in which abides the breath of life. And those arriving **now** — male and female of every flesh creature came, even as God had charged him.

It is a telling commentary on source-criticism that the above arrangement of pericope §E yields what J- and-P-based analysis has never produced: two self-standing

complete versions of a narrative episode, virtually identical in content, and arranged in consecution such that either the first sequence (verses 6–10) or the second (verses 11–16) could be omitted without any loss whatever to the narrative
flow. This episode is a marvel of pointlessly redundant repetition: (1) Twice (in
verses 6 and 11) is the onset of the waters dated to Noah's 600th year; (2); Twice
(in verses 7 and 13) do Noah, sons, wife, and sons' wives—in that identical male-
chauvinist order—enter the ark; (3) Twice (in verses 8–9 and 14–16) do all the
animals come to the ark, in pairs, male and female; (4) Twice (in verses 9 and 16)
the arrival of the animals is characterized by a strange formulation (in almost identical diction): they come, these multitudinous species—not in keeping with God's
prediction or promise to Noah, but—according to what he had *charged* or commanded him.

I will defer conjecture as to the poetic design behind such redundancy, for it will
continue to characterize this narrative. (That it is indeed by design must be the
premise and conclusion of a poetic address to a literature that is everywhere else
noted for its economy and density.) I will, however, focus on the last redundancy, a
redundancy not only pointless in itself (else it would not be a redundancy) but
contextually nonsensical. And, the poetical purpose of the ubiquitous redundancies will be foreshadowed in our argument for the poetical purposefulness of this
contrived absurdity.

As in this pericope we have two tellings of the coming of the animals to the ark,
so do we have earlier in our narrative two anticipations (in the words of the Deity)
of that event. In §C, in 6:19 the verb used is *tābī*, the imperfect tense. In my first
translation (so my manuscript bears witness) I rendered this verb "take (into the
ark)." In my revised translation the word is "bring." This revision followed a prior
revision of the rendering of Deity's word in §D, 7:2. Here the verb (again in the
imperfect tense but imperative modality) is *tiqqaḥ-leka*, which I had first rendered
"fetch yourself," but which now reads, "admit with you." The reason for this revision was the realization that "fetch (for) yourself" implied that Deity was charging
Noah with responsibility for rounding up the pairs of every species. Since such a
charge would have constituted an existential absurdity, the newer (and altogether
legitimate) rendering suggested itself. I then backtracked to 6:19 and changed the
innocent enough "take (into the ark)" to "bring," so as to conform the verbal usage
with that in the following verse 20. Here the qal of the verb is featured in a seemingly redundant addition that "a pair of each will come (*yābō'ū*) to you for survival." The redundancy is thus resolved by the need to clarify God's declaration as
constituting a prediction and not a command. This should not obscure from our
consciousness that the ambiguity in the sense of the verse is a function of our overlooking that one of the two senses is, in context, absurd. In any case this *prediction*
by Deity in §C and in §D is fulfilled in the two notices in §E (7:9 and 15) that the
pairs did indeed *come to Noah*. In both notices, however, the incongruous addition
as God had charged him is a back-reference to the silly ambiguity in 6:19 and 7:2.

Let us see now how the author (or should we speak rather of the unreliable narrator) expands this initial bit of silliness in pericope §E. The first notice of the animals' arrival in verses 8–9 is in hypotactic construction, here in unjustifiable departure from the normal paratactic construction, as indeed in the preceding verse

7. This anomaly, however, is only part of a masterpiece of befuddling redundance, for verse 13 tells us in (formally and justifiable) hypotactic construction that the humans entered the ark. (Note the utter gratuitousness of the identification of Shem, Ham, and Japheth as "Noah's sons.") Verse 14 adds: *They (the humans) as well as the animals*, and the latter are, in an excess of pleonastic ontology and taxonomy, glossed by four terms for four categories, each specified by *according to their species* and the last reiterated as *every bird, every winged thing*, as if to remind us that such ratites as the ostrich are for all their flightlessness fowl nonetheless. Then verse 15 tells us in normal paratactic construction that they—all flesh endowed with animating spirit—came in pairs "to Noah, to the ark." This is followed by verse 16 in hypotactic construction, a parenthetic assurance to the reader, that "now as for those *coming*, male and female of all flesh came." And this with the addition, "as God had charged him."

Pity the poor translator! Or rather, pity the good translator! Pity the poor reader, victim alike, alas, of good translator and wily author. And pity the scientific Bible scholar. It is with no thought of avenging himself on Scripture's authors or editors that he labors with dissecting scalped to sunder into historically meaningful snippets what they created and joined in tautological wedlock.

Episode F. Deluge and Destruction

(16b) YHWH battened him in. (17a) The Deluge continued forty days on the earth. (17b) As the waters increased greatly on earth, they buoyed up the ark and it lifted free from the earth. (18) As the water intensified and increased greatly on the earth the ark moved on the water's surface.

(19) **Now** the waters intensifying very greatly on earth, they blanketed even the highest mountains that are under the sky everywhere: (20a) 15 cubits above [them] did the waters prevail [lit., "intensify"].

(20b) With the blanketing of the mountains, (21) all flesh creatures that scurry on earth expired—in the category of fowl, of cattle, of wild beasts, of every swarm-breed that teems on earth—and all humankind as well. (22) **Yes**, everything that [has] the breath of life-spirit in its nostrils, of every [category] that is on dry land, died.

(23) Thus did he blot out all existing things that are on the surface of the ground, inclusive of humankind [and extending] to herbivores, to beasties and to sky-birds. With them erased from earth, there remained only Noah and that with him in the ark.

(24) The waters intensified on earth for 150 days. (7:16b–24)

Except for the number forty (days), supposedly a round number, in verse 16, and the number 150 days, supposedly not a round number, in verse 24, there is no good reason, even by the dubious criteria of source-criticism, to assign any part of this pericope to one source rather than another. (Speiser for example, makes no attempt to justify the division—which he accepts—according to sources.) The only pressure for division at all is the presumption that the many redundancies are explainable only as the sewing together of pieces from two original and parallel narratives. Why an editor should choose to piece together such repetitious snippets is a question altogether ignored. Interestingly enough, one example of striking redundancy in two verses universally recognized as assignable to J and P respectively need not be redundancy at all. As our translation reveals, the increase or swelling of the waters in verse 17 explicitly accounts for the ark's lift-off from the ground, while in verse 18 the intensification of the waters' swell results in the ark's move- ment, headed for the mountain top in respect to which the blanketing waters of verse 19 are a proleptic hint.

But redundancy there is in this passage of seven verses, enough perhaps to jus- tify three or four hypothetical sources. The *intensification* of the water's rise is men- tioned five times, featuring the verb *gbr* "to be strong" and the verb *rb'* "to be nu- merous, much." The expression "the earth" *hā'āreṣ*, ever so supererogatory (as we noted) in preceding pericopes, appears eight times, and twice more in the synony- mous *ᵃdāmā* "ground" or *ḥorābā* "dry ground." In the space of three verses (21–23) three verbs appear betokening the extinction of animal life (*gw'*, *mūt*, *mḥh*).

In respect to these last verses, the careful reader of the Hebrew text will note at least three anomalies in the expressions for the animal life extinguished:

1. In verse 3, the generic term for animal life is *bāśār* "flesh." This term appears six times earlier in our narrative, but never modified as it is here by an adjective. The adjective is the active participle of the verb *rmś*, normally rendered into Eng- lish by "creep, crawl," or the like; this participial adjective appears with a noun form of the same stem: *remeś*. Since this noun often appears in a context with other terms in series betokening wild and domestic animals and birds, we have rendered the noun by "beasties," that is, small or tiny creatures and the participle by "scurry- ing." This participle appears twice in Genesis 1. In 1:21 it appears as adjective with *kol nefeš ḥāyā* "every living animal" and rendered by us "that stirs." Inasmuch as these creatures derive from the water along with other *teeming* life such as great amphibians and crocodiles and the like, we assume that this reference is to such small land-and-water creatures as frogs and snakes and otters. In 1:30 the participle as noun, appearing in series with wild beasts (*ḥayyat hā'āreṣ*) and birds of the sky, can only be a catchall term, and so *kol hārōmeś 'al hā'āreṣ* can only be rendered along the lines of "and everything astir on earth." (Interestingly, this phrase is fur- ther modified by the clause *ᵃšer bō nefeš ḥayyā* "which has within it the life- essence.") Only here, in 7:21, does the participial adjective appear with the noun *bāśār*, to wit, "all flesh that stirs upon the earth (expired)." Since *flesh* in itself (without animating spirit) is both metonymy (part for the whole) and metaphor, the addition of the adjective "stirring" makes for an extended—and incongruous— metaphor. This incongruity, in a text replete with repetitive figurations, might have gone unobserved but for the series of particulars that is in apposition to the generic "stirring flesh," and which is given an anomalous and incongruous formulation. The series of fowl, herbivores, wild beasts, and teeming things is unexceptionable in it- self (except for the order). But it is rendered incongruous by the preposition *bᵉ* "in, among," which governs each of these—note the gap-bridging interpolation in our translation—four *categories*. The narrator's subtlety is also expressed by the absence of this governing preposition in respect to "all humankind." Thus there are two sub- jects for the verb *expire*, one at the beginning of the verse, "all stirring flesh"— glossed as four categories of creatures—and one at the end, "all humankind," which is thus excluded from the generic subject at the beginning!

2. In the foregoing instance, the application of the preposition to the four sub-categories, instead of to the generic category to which it belongs, is already a case of hypallage. This trope (like *histeron proteron*, for example) appears always in (often, slyly) humorous contexts, a fact that is neglected in the teaching of classical rhetoric. Witness our dictionary's definition of hypallage: "A figure consisting of an interchange in the syntactic relationship between two terms; as, 'to apply the wound to water' in place of 'to apply water to the wound.'" Our second instance also features hypallage, this time featuring the preposition *mᵉ* "of, from, among." The subject of verse 22 is, literally, "everything that (has) the breath of the spirit of life in its nostrils." This is a triply redundant expression, inasmuch as breath (*nᵉšāmā*) and spirit (*rūᵃh*) are synonyms, and both are metaphoric expressions for life (*ḥayyīm*). This redundant redundancy is then compounded in another redundancy "*in its nostrils.*" This last, if not redundant, is at least superfluous in that Genesis 2:7 tells us that God, to animate the human earth-child, "blew *into* his nostrils the breath of life (*nišmat ḥayyim*)." But even a non-biblicist, oblivious to the intertextual allusion, might ask, where but in the nostrils would the life-breath be? And the humorless rhetorician—or rather, the rhetorician who cannot cede a sense of humor to a biblical author—would snort in response, "Why, in the mouth, of course—or in the throat or lungs!" The humor that we, then, see or read into the quadruple redundancy is reinforced by the humor in the hypallage; the compounded subject of the sentence is then glossed "*of* everything [*mikkol*] that [was] on dry land." Thus instead of: *Of everything existing on dry land, every animal life-form died*, we have: "Every[thing] that [has] the breath of the spirit of life in its nostrils of everything that [was] on dry land died." What else on dry land that could have died did not die?

3. The third instance features two prepositions expressive of a range or gamut *mᵉ . . . ʿad* "from . . . to." This verse (7:22) is anticipated by 6:4, almost identical in diction, with which it must be compared.

GENESIS 6:7	GENESIS 7:23
YHWH said: I will blot out *the humankind* I created from the ground's surface, from mankind [*ādam*, no article] to cattle to beasties and to sky-fowl. So great [is] my regret at having made them.	He blotted out everything extant [*yᵉqūm*, cf. 7:4] which [is] on the ground's surface, from mankind [*ādām*, no article] to cattle to beasties and to sky-fowl.

As we pointed out earlier, the formulation in 6:7, literally (i.e., with literary intent) identifies the human species with the totality of God's (created) creatures, by making the gamut of the *humankind*, that range of animals from human, through cattle large and small, to sky-fowl. But whereas the first underlines the dignity of the human race by rendering all other creatures as virtual constituents of human existence, having hardly any independent ontology, the second achieves the opposite effect. In specifying the gamut of *everything extant* in an apparently descending *rank* (cognate with *range*) from human to birds, the context of God's malefic attention makes for a bathos (from the sublime to the ridiculous) whose humor can only be at mankind's expense: God erased all living things, from human to roach.

Our discussion of the humorous and human-deprecating effects of our narrator's diction, in all its redundantly repetitious and perversely convoluted syntax, is not to assess the narrative as a joke, in glorification of a divine monarch's capricious power to destroy a contemptibly sinful humanity together with its brutish and insect adjuncts. Even as our rhetorical analysis reveals the meanings of the subtext in the contrast between the power, morality, and dignity of Creator on the one hand, and his creatures on the other, so also is it not in denial of another kerygma. The repetitions of God's frustrated hopes, of his intent to erase what he cannot correct, of that teeming world of multifarious life, throbbing—from greatest to least and from least to greatest—with vitality, all these build to the emotional climax of death, death, death everywhere, except for those snug in the ark with Noah. The God of Creation, our narrator conveys to us, was fully aware of the atrociousness of the cataclysm he was about to perpetrate, and nevertheless he did what he had to do. From the standard translations of the last four words of 6:7, "for I regret that I made them," one would never guess the pain that YHWH's own confession expresses. And as there in the story's introduction, the final verse, 6:8, reads, "Noah, however, found favor in YHWH's eyes," so our pericope concludes that, for all the savage waste of a single generation, not a single one of the many species became extinct. Within the ark, every seed of every life-form was preserved to give the world another chance.

Episodes G and I. The Deluge Is Checked and The Disembarking

(24) The waters intensified on earth for 150 days.

(1) God bethought himself of Noah and all the wild beasts and all the cattle that were with him in the ark. God then swept a wind over the earth and the waters were calmed.

(2a) Both the wellsprings of the Deep and the sluice gates of heaven were bolted closed. (2b) With the rain from heaven restrained, (3a) the waters began to recede from earth, a steady recession. (3b) The waters began to abate from [i.e., beginning with] Day 150. (4) The ark thus grounded in Month 7, Day 17 of the month, on the mountain range of Ararat.

(5) **Now** the waters were [in a state of] continuous recession until Month 10. On the tenth, on the first day of the month, the mountain peaks showed through. (7:24–8:5)

[Here follows the Episode of the Birds, 8:6–12]

(13) It came to pass in the Year 601 [of Noah's lifetime] on the first [month] on Day 1 of the month—did the waters dry up from on the earth—Noah removed the [hatch-] cover of the ark and beheld, lo the ground's surface was dry.

(14) [But **now**] in Month 2 on Day 7 of the month the earth became [bone] dry.

(15) God addressed Noah, (16) "Come out of the ark: you and your wife and your sons and your sons' wives with you; (17) every living thing that is with you, of all flesh, in [the categories of] fowl, of cattle, and of all the beasties that scurry on the earth bring forth with you, so that they may teem on the earth and abundantly repro-

duce on the earth. (18) So Noah came out, and his sons and his wife and his sons' wives with him. (19) All the beasts, **now,** all the beasties and all the fowl, everything that stirs on the earth—according to their species [*lit.*: families) came forth from the ark. (8:13–19)

A review of the passages in our first translation will reveal that both are assigned to P, with the exception of a few sentences (amounting to about three verses out of a total of thirteen). Aside from the matter of various numbers and dates, which I will discuss separately, the rationale for these source-assignments is redundancy. The extent of the redundancy, however, is such that the source-division falls far short of accounting for it. How far short may be gauged from the following. As far as concerns the bare plot of the narrative, the content of these thirteen verses could be reduced to the length of a single average verse, to wit:

> After 150 days, the wellsprings of the Deep were closed and the water began a steady retreat. When earth dried up God called Noah to come forth from the ark. He did so, with all that were with him.

Such prolixity in a body of narrative noted for its economy must be considered together with other anomalous stylistic features in the passages under consideration: features of plot, character, grammar, and syntax.

God, we are told in verse 1, remembered Noah. How the narrator came by this knowledge and why he chooses to pass it on to us are not frivolous poetic questions. Could this God, who is elsewhere characterized as a guardian who never sleeps or even dozes, have forgotten the one and only world (so our narrative permits us to infer) that he created, the world that he is now engaged in destroying, except for the one vessel that he has ordained for the preservation of that world? And if the verb for memory *zākar* has the connotation of care, concern, and cherish, rather than recovery from a mental lapse, is the dignity thus conferred on Noah—best representative of the human race—not compromised by the addition that that concern extended also to animals wild and tame? This notice, reeking of bathos (cf. the last verse of the Book of Jonah) is then followed not by his turning off of the destructive spates, by a calming of the waters. And this is expressed in another incongruous image. The wind, which normally whips the waves to life-threatening heights, is used here to flatten—as a scythe the high and full-eared grainstalks—the crests of the presumptuous swells. Only then are we told that the waters rushing from below and above were suddenly dammed. Both sources, at the same time? Why, then, is the water's recession in verse 3a related only to the cessation of one of the flows, the rain, in 2b? (A question far more perplexing in view of the notice in 7:12 that the rain only endured forty days, hence ceasing 110 days before the damming of the flow from Deep's fountains!)

With the grounding of the ark and the recession of the waters, there follows §H, the episode of the birds, which we discussed earlier. In comparing that episode with its counterpart in the Utnapishtim story, we saw that Utnapishtim in his choice of birds is portrayed as something of an ass, while Noah's choice of the raven could be attributed to a momentary mental lapse. We also saw that Noah's raven did return to the ark's vicinity, but not for food. Why then did he return at all? To be closer to his mate, still pent in the ark? The reason for our question is, of course, that at the moment the raven was set free there must have been thousands of dry acres around the ark. For Noah would have sent out no avian scouts unless he could spy no water from the window in the side of the ark through which he released the birds. What then can be the meaning of the second half of 8:13, that Noah, lifting the hatch cover, suddenly beheld the dry surface of ground all about him? The first half of this verse, giving the date for the water's drainage, is unquestionably a parenthesis, in the narrator's voice, for all its anomalous formally paratactic syntax. Noah's realization follows then the conclusion of the birds episode; that is, it comes immediately after the failure of the dove to return from its third flight.

This suggests some further questions. If the raven returned to the ark's vicinity to be near its mate (the only motive we could come up with), why would not the dove have returned for the same reason? Furthermore, there is the perplexing matter of the avenues of ingress and egress to and from the ark. In the description of the ark, 6:14–16, only one such avenue is specified, "the entrance in the side of the ark." This detail, which evokes no comment from critics, shows what careful consideration has been given to this matter. The largest ships in antiquity were onboarded or off-boarded (note this denominative verb from a term synonymous with *plank*) via a gangplank extending from land to the ship at its lowest deck. The thirty-foot height of the ark would have required an unrealistically long or steep ramp to its rooftop, which was also its only exterior deck. Hence the provision of a side entrance (perhaps the first such maritime design in antiquity) in the ark. The second mention of an opening in the ark is the window through which Noah releases the birds; here, too, the narrator signals his attention to detail, for with this first mention he casually adds, "that he had made." In view of this, the third opening (in our verse 13) is both unnecessary and comically absurd. Noah removes the *miksē* "cover, lid" of the ark. Since he could not have removed the entire roof we render it "hatch-cover," presuming metonymy of whole for the part. The comic absurdity, however, lies in this. Had Noah stuck his head out of the hatch he would have seen nothing but sky in all directions; had he climbed onto the ark's (flat) roof and walked to its edge, he still would have seen nothing more than he had when he had first looked out of the window before releasing the raven. Needless to say, these features of narrative details both realistic and incongruous at the same time are, along with the remarkable redundancy, poetic problems that we must try to resolve. A third such riddle-element is that series of numbers and dates that concludes in §I.

Let us first dispose of those numbers that, regarded as contradictions, are apportioned to J or P. The forty days and nights for the duration of the rain appears three times: in 7:4, in God's prediction; in 7:12, as an accomplished fact; and in 7:17, where the forty days duration has as its subject not the rain (*gešem*), but the word we rendered deluge, *mabbūl*. This word, first appearing in 6:17 as the cataclysm to be brought on by God, is glossed there by "waters upon earth." This notice contributes to the source-critical assumption of contradiction, for the general failure to recognize that this word *mabbūl* refers only to the combination of flow from the sluice gates of heaven and from the wellsprings of the great deep.[13] The *mabbūl* proper begins in 7:11, and endures as long as the forty days of rain in 7:12, but no longer. The waters of the deep, however, continue their flow—though unperceived by human eye—and their volume on earth increases for another 110 days (thus equal to the 150 days explicitly in 7:24 and 8:3 and implicit in 7:20).

On the 150th day the water crests at fifteen cubits higher than the highest peak of Ararat (7:20); on this same day the waters begin to abate (8:3). Hence, the grounding of the ark—which, being thirty cubits high, floated half in and half out of the water—by marvelous coincidence or providential whim on that peak occurred on that 150th day. But the date of that grounding is given in 8:4 as the 17th day of Month 7 (8:4), and the onset of the waters is dated the 17th of Month 2 (7:11). The lunar month being 29 days plus a fraction, it must be clear that the 150 days corresponding to exactly five months must be a round number. The waters abate until Day 1 of Month 10 (8:5)—seventy days later—on which day the mountain peaks(!) showed through (8:5), not, however, to the ken of Noah, who was sitting atop that peak in his shelter. Forty days later (8:6) the waters have receded beyond Noah's sight, whereupon he sends out the dove, and twice more at seven-day intervals. This would bring us close to the beginning of Month 12.[14] Noah, however, remains in the ark another month until (probably on Month 1, Day 1), the waters having drained off from earth (8:13), he receives God's call to come out.[15] In between the notice of the water-drainage and God's call to Noah comes the parenthetic notice (8:14) in hypotactic construction that the water did not dry up until Day 27 of Month 2, exactly one year and ten days from the flood's onset. There is no contradiction between the two notices. Our narrator has arranged the schedule so that God's call to Noah and his animal company to come out and begin the rebirth of the world should fall appropriately on New Year's Day. (According to an erroneous rendering of a rabbinic tradition, Rosh Hashana—the first day of the seventh month, Tishri—is hailed as the birthday of the world. The tradition, however, hails it as yōm harat 'ōlām "the day the world was conceived." Almost certainly, then, the tradition relates not to the creation of Genesis 1 but to Genesis 8:13, when the ancestor pairs of all species, issuing from the ark, could resume the cycle of gestation precluded by the confined quarters of the ark.) The appropriateness of this symbolism is beyond debate. But our narrator does not stop there. He arranges for another coincidental date, one so bereft of meaningful symbolism as to be bathetic in comparison to this one. Day 1 of Month 1 marked the recession of the seas to the normal level ordained for them by God. But everyone knows that after a flood of such proportion the recession of water to pre-flood level would still leave many low-lying areas awash in stagnant pool. It required, he informs us, another two months for the last of these pools to dry up. This happens on Day 27 of Month 2, a full year and ten days after the mabbūl had begun. Why not Day 17 of Month 2, precisely a year from the onset of the waters?

In connection with this last bit of intentional bathos, we must now confess that our translation of the verb ḥārᵉbū in 8:13 by "was drained," and of the verb yābᵉša in 8:14 by "had become dry," is wrong, and unforgivably so. It is typical of any number of instances where translator-critics who know better than the Scriptural author what he intended implicitly emend the Hebrew by departing from literal meanings of the Hebrew in their translations. In our instance, the translation we present permits a logical progression from an earlier completion of drainage to a later completion of evaporation. The Hebrew diction, however, reverses the logic of meaningful sequence, so as to render the two statements as not only bathetic, but semantically absurd. The verb *ybš* for the last stage means "to be (relatively) dry," while the term *ḥrb* for the preceding stage means "to be bone-dry!"

Episode J. Sacrifice and Promise

(20) Noah then built an altar to YHWH. Taking of every clean cattle[-species] and of every clean fowl[-species] he offered up holocausts at the altar. (21) YHWH sniffed the pleasing odor. YHWH promised himself, "Never never again will I so abuse the earth on account of mankind—[seeing that] the bent of man's mind is evil from his youth—nor ever ever again will I strike down every life-form, as I have done. (22) So long as earth endures, seedtime and harvest and cold and heat and summer and winter and day and night will not ever cease. (Genesis 8:20–22)

Of the three pericopes assigned by source-critics to J we saw that §H, the Episode of the Birds, could have as readily and arguably been assigned to P. That leaves, however, §D and this pericope §J left to J. The affinities between the two passages are: first, the appearance of YHWH in both; and second, the seven pairs of clean animals specified in §D as against a single pair of the unclean animals. The argument—and it is a persuasive one—is that but for this greater number of pairs of the edible species, the sacrifice in this passage would have resulted in their extinction. Furthermore, the permissibility of flesh-eating granted in the following Episode §K—a P passage—indicates why the same source in §C, consistent with the divine mandate for vegetarian diets in Genesis 1:29–30, needed to make no distinction as between clean and unclean animals. We accept this argument in principle, and will add reinforcing elements for it without, however, conceding the existence of "sources." There are narrative strands in these early chapters of Genesis and I will discuss them shortly in terms of their thematic elements and their diction as well as their integration into a single narrative by a single narrator. For the present, let us note that although in Scripture "cleanness" in animals is criterion for edibility and sacrificeability alike, there is no contradiction between our episode §J and the first grant of legitimacy to a meat diet in §K. For the sacrifices offered by Noah are all, and explicitly, holocausts (*ʿōlōt*), completely burnt on the altar; this to the exclusion of *zebaḥ* or (*zibḥē-*)*šᵉlāmīm*, of which the humans may partake.

It is clear that YHWH's promise in this pericope constitutes a climax of the Noah narrative (*a* climax, for there are others). The power of the four-fold merism in verse 22 testifies to that. So also does the role played in YHWH's self-confessed motivation for his resolve. Echoing the diction in §A in connection with the proclivity of the human imagination YHWH declares that the *yēṣer* "fashion(ing), form, shape, tendency" of the human mind is evil from youth, the last word ambiguous as to reference; is it to each individual or to the first generations of the species? But this declaration, which might almost be taken as a formulation of "original sin," is not the reason for YHWH's promise; it is despite this unfortunate trait, whose eluctability he seems to be conceding, that the promise is made. Hence, a statement as to human sinfulness and God's grace, but also by inference, a judgment on the flood: given what God must have known before, the flood should never have taken place.

There are further elements of rhetorical playfulness, of, if you will, tongue in cheek. Taken literally, verse 20 has Noah offering at least one sacrificial victim of every clean species of beast and fowl. For all that cloven-hoofed ruminants and edible fowl are greatly outnumbered by unclean species, the number of those qualified for sacrifice would have required many days and many altars for cremation. The narrator may be signaling this awareness in the choice of preposition to govern the altar. Sacrificial meats are burned *upon* (*'al*) the altar, and the same preposition is used when the blood is sprinkled on the surfaces of the altar's sides or on the hangings of the tabernacle. The employment here of *b^e*, which can mean *in*, *by*, *at*, *for*, or *against*, but never *upon*, can only be intentional. So too the word describing how YHWH related to the aroma (or is it *stench?*) of the sizzling flesh. He does not *show regard* for it (*šh* as in respect to the offerings of Cain and Abel) nor is his acceptance expressed by the normal term *rṣh*. He sniffs it. This expression for God's receipt of an offering appears only once again, and that one in a context of denigration. In 1 Samuel 26:19, David remonstrates with the king, who is persecuting him. His argument to Saul is that he is being instigated by God (who, for one reason or another, must want David punished) or malevolent humans. He expresses his disdain at the likelihood of the first alternative in the words, "If it is YHWH who is egging you on against me, let him sniff an offering." In a similar vein then, YHWH's reaction to the holocausts of the victims he has ordained for preservation from extinction may well be one more expression of the narrator's awareness of the silliness of the story he is reshaping; it is silly in respect to plot and in respect to its human protagonists. In this particular episode, the amused tolerance of God evokes the image of a parent viewing the compensatory offering in the outstretched hand of a repentant child, a selection of candies from its treasured hoard.

Episode K. Blessing and Meat for Man's Table

> (1) God blessed Noah and his sons, saying to them, "Increase abundantly and populate the earth. (2) The dread fear of you shall descend upon all living creatures of earth and upon the fowl of the sky, upon every thing with which the earth is astir, and all fish of the sea: into your power are they delivered. (3) Every stirring thing that lives shall be yours for the eating; like the grass greens do I give them all to you. (4) Only flesh with its life-blood in it you are not to eat. (5) And also—for your own life-blood will I exact retribution: of every beast will I exact it and of humankind; of every man for his brother will I exact retribution for a human life. (6) Whoever sheds the blood of man, by man shall his blood be shed. This is the meaning of: "In the image of God made He man." (7) You, then, for your part, increase abundantly, teem on earth and be fertile upon it. (Genesis 9:1–7)

This pericope begins with God's blessing in terms of propagation. But unlike that implied blessing in §I and its explicit forerunner in 1:22, this one is confined to the human species alone, and with good reason. For the anticipation of mankind's increase in number is in contrast to a concomitant fear of man to befall

all living creatures of earth, sky, and water. Why will they fear man? Because God has declared them fair game for mankind. This now is something new. The wording in Genesis 1:29–30, God's grant to man and beast alike, a diet deriving from "all seed-bearing grasses, all trees bearing seed-bearing fruit . . . every green herbage," is evoked now by those same words, permitting animal flesh to mankind "just like the green herbage." Meat-eating presupposes taking the life of the animal to be eaten. Humans may now take animal life. Human life, however, is sacred, in keeping with the explicit reference to 1:26–28, man's dignity as symbolized in man's creation in God's image. Neither beast nor man may take human life with impunity. In the introduction to this J (or P document) we noted that the offense was an indeterminate *ḥāmās* "lawlessness" perpetrated by both man and beast. In view of this strand's conclusion—permitting one vector of the previous prohibition (man's taking animal life for food)—it is a reasonable conjecture that the lawlessness of all the species, which precipitated the flood, was the taking of life—for food—without the permission, contrary indeed to the prohibition, of the Creator of all life.[16]

Episode L. The Promise of the Rainbow

(8) God then said to Noah and to his sons with him, (9) "I hereby make this covenant of mine with you and your offspring to come, (10) and also with every living creature that is with you—of birds, cattle, and all other beasts of earth along with you—all that have come out of the ark, of every creature on earth. (11) This covenant of mine with you I will fulfill: never again shall all flesh be cut off by Deluge waters, never again shall there Deluge be to waste the earth."

(12) God said further, "This, now, is the sign of the covenant I grant as between me and you and every living creature that is with you, for all ages to come: (13) My bow have I set in the clouds, to serve as a sign of the covenant between me and earth. (14) So shall it be, when I mass clouds over earth—and the bow appears in the clouds—

(15) I shall be mindful of this covenant of mine which exists between me and you and every living creature among all flesh that the waters will not function as Deluge to waste all flesh. (16) The bow will be in the clouds, by my providence, to mark an enduring covenant between God and every living creature of all flesh that is on earth." (17) God pointed out to Noah, "There now is the sign of the covenant that I have established between myself and all flesh that is on earth!" (Genesis 9:8–17)

Thematically, this pericope is parallel to and a variation of pericope §J. The theme, *promise*, is somewhat clouded here by the Hebrew term standing for that concept, *berīt*. This Hebrew term has the denotation of *pact, compact, covenant*, words that in English betoken formal or serious agreement, which is to say, agreements on grave matters; as reflected in another synonym *treaty*, for agreements between peoples and polities. The very word *berit*, as Martin Noth has suggested, probably derives from the Akkadian preposition *bēri* "between," and has the connotation of "between-ness." An agreement, by definition, requires a minimum of two parties, but *pact* and its synonyms also imply assent by all parties to it; thus even in a vassal treaty where a victorious suzerain may be dictating the terms to a reluctant foe, *treaty* or *covenant* may still be appropriate renderings of b⁽ᵉ⁾rīt if the defeated party's alternatives are less attractive than the terms dictated. In the case of a *will*, however, or any unqualified gift, such as in the instance before us where the grant of favor is unconditional, the term b⁽ᵉ⁾rīt is more faithfully rendered by *promise*; as we earlier suggested, by synecdoche of the whole for the part.

This lengthy dwelling on a single detail, a single word, in our pericope is dictated by its importance for the comparing and contrasting of this pericope §L with §J. In this episode, the idea of promise is certainly central, although no verb or noun with that specific denotation is present. The word 'āmar "say, think," with an enormous range of connotations, is nevertheless correctly rendered here by *promise*.

Source-criticism has identified a number of elements that support the assignment of these pericopes to J and P, with which we concur, except for our substitution of (narrative) *strands* for *sources*. In respect to the J strand, both §J and §A feature the name YHWH; both feature the evil or perversity of the human imagination; and in both the responsibility for YHWH's decision is humankind's, a shortcoming on the part of humans that the animals do not share, implicit in YHWH's promise not to destroy the world on humankind's account. In respect to the P strand, §L shares these features with features in nine of the other twelve pericopes: the name Elohim "God;" the responsibility for the cataclysm is shared by both humans and animals; the promise not to repeat the deluge is made to both humans and animals; and the featuring of the noun b⁽ᵉ⁾rīt in God's promises to humankind (here in §L and in §C, 6:19). To these I would add the feature of redundant diction, particularly with regard to the terms for all animals, in 9:10 and 15–17.

There are, nevertheless, some perceptions of redundancy within pericope §L that I would disallow. Thus, for example, the making of the "covenant" twice, in verses 9 and 11, features the verb hēqīm "establish." That sense is appropriate in verse 9, where God "is establishing" (Heb. active participle mēqīm), but in the future time in verse 11, the promise (/covenant) thus made in verse 9 *will be fulfilled*, a frequently attested meaning for the same verb. Similarly, the standard translation of verse 16—"When the bow appears in the clouds I will see it and remember"—is identical in meaning to verses 14–15. In addition to making for a pointless tautology, this rendering construes God's memory as dependent upon the rainbow: only when he sees it will he recall his promise not to repeat the flood. While the author of the Utnapishtim story might poke fun at Enlil by having him tie a string around his finger to remind himself not to reach for his war-bow, God is never the object of ridicule in the biblical story. Such a mnemonic function is absurd in any case, for the rainbow appears after the rain, not before it; thus the rainbow would function as a signal to lock the barn door after the horse has left! No, the sign is for man, not for God. And, like the promises in both §J and §L addressed to Noah, the assurance in the rainbow sign is for the comfort of later generations. The reversion of the world to chaos, the reemergence of Tiamat to dominance, mingling her waters once more with Apsu's; this cataclysm called mabbūl in Scripture, which occurred in Noah's time, will never again be unleashed by God. For God—the God of Scripture—is benevolent.

Our novel (yet not bold) translation of verse 16 is noteworthy for its enhancement of our appreciation of the author's artistry. A more transparent translation: "The bow will appear in the clouds—yes [the deictic *waw*], I shall provide it to mark [the denotation of *zkr*] an enduring promise as between God [on the one hand] and [on the other] every living essence [abiding] in any flesh that is on earth." Another seeming redundancy is seen in the words of verse 12 repeated in verse 14, "This is the sign of the promise." In its first appearance, the demonstrative pronoun *this* refers to the description of the sign that follows. In its second appearance, the pronoun *this*—as Rashi takes pains to explain—is a finger pointing to that breathtaking arc across the sky: "This—there now—is the sign of the promise!"

Perhaps worthy of note is the similarity and variations of a metaphor in three cultures: that of Babylon, of Scripture, and our own. The bow as the archer's weapon and its retirement as sign of a pledged peace is a natural symbolism, updated perhaps in our own metaphors "hanging up the gunbelt" or "burying the hatchet." In the *Enuma elish*, after Marduk conquers Tiamat, creates the cosmos, and builds the gods' palaces, the war-bow of Enlil is hung in the sky by Anu in the form of an astral constellation. Our biblical author, who, we have seen, must have availed himself of both *Enuma elish* and the Gilgamesh Epic, may well have borrowed the image from the former and adapted it to the flood context from the latter, but with how much more power and meaning for its appearance in the day-sky and the sunny promise for a humankind so often menaced by nature's awesome violence.

We began our discussion of this pericope by noting that it is parallel to and a variation of §J. We also noted that §J falls into strand J, while §L falls into strand P. It is therefore instructive as to the how and why of our narrator's deployment of parallel episodes and integration of them in his narrative, which remains both consistent and unredundant in respect to plot, that §J and §L are neither inconsistent with one another nor redundantly repetitive. In §J the promise of YHWH seems, at first blush, to be in pleased acceptance of and reward for Noah's generous offerings.[17] The promise, furthermore, is presented as internal dialogue, is addressed to Deity by himself and—as far as this pericope is concerned—was never communicated to humankind for its information or comfort. Having thus exploited in §J the theme of Introduction §A, the narrator continues in §L with the promise communicated to Noah and his sons—but addressed as well to the animals, pointedly and repeatedly; to the animals who have no imagination, but who are capable of the violence that is a precondition for carnivorousness. And, for all that animals presumably do not have the imagination to understand the symbolism of the rainbow in the clouds, the upbeat conclusion of the concluding verse 17—like the preceding verses 10, 13, 15, and 16—emphasizes again that the promise extends to "all flesh upon the earth."

One concluding note on the narrator's care with diction: In verse 10 the prepositions governing various classes or aspects of animal kind (b^e, $mi(n)$, l^e) are as precise and fitting as the corresponding prepositions in §F are incorrect, even incongruous. It is almost as if the narrator were reassuring us with a wink that he can, when he wants to, write Hebrew. But the anomaly in this verse is in respect to a specification of the animals whose species are to be preserved that appears only this one time in the entire narrative. The promise is made to humankind in verse 9 and extended in verse 10, "and with every living creature that is with you, in the category of fowl, of cattle, and of any of earth's fauna with you—*inclusive of all those coming out of the ark*—whatever of earth's fauna they belong to." The words in italics are an intrusion, whose deliberateness is drawn to our attention by the repetition after it of the words preceding it. What is the purpose of this pleonasm (as of the same seemingly pleonastic participle in 9:18, *hayyōṣᵉʾîm* "those coming out of the ark")? Were there any species which failed to come out of the ark and were therefore excluded from the promise? It is unlikely. The alternative: a species that survived the flood, but which never came out from the ark, because it never entered it: a cross-source or cross-strand reference to the semi-divine, semi-human breed of Introduction §A. Taking the word *mabbūl* in its minimal meaning "cataclysm," the promise in respect to the watery cataclysm we call the Deluge is a metaphor for a species-extinguishing disaster, And God's promise did not include the species of titans (*nephīlīm*) who "were on earth in those days and also afterwards" but had by the time of the narrator become extinct.

A NOTE ON THE STRANDS

In our pursuit of that literary critical approach to Scripture we call poetics, I have found it necessary (and will continue to do so) to confront in an adversarial way that literary critical approach to Scripture that we call source-criticism. The reasons for this, given in the preface to this volume and its predecessor, *Toward a Grammar*, need not detain us. I do feel it incumbent upon me, out of respect to my biblicist colleagues (of this generation and past ones) and honesty to my own methodology, to clarify as far as I am able my position on the two strands I discern in Genesis 1–9. Having been myself trained in—and for a good may years won over to—source-criticism, I cannot judge the extent (certainly considerable) to which my perception of the strands owes to it. But that perception as a poetical-critical phenomenon is independent of any method to which it may stand in debt.

My approach is based on the hypothesis that the text before us represents a harmonious whole, regardless of what borrowing from preexistent traditions or literary corpora may have contributed to the form in which we have it now. Source-analysis got its start to begin with in the perception, in the Pentateuch and particularly in Genesis, of clauses and sentences repetitious to the point of redundancy, or inconsistent with, even in contradiction of, one another. To the extent that I can show how these clauses and sentences are not at all redundant, inconsistent, or contradictory, I bolster the argument for poetical harmony, but at the same time cut the ground out from under source-analysis. But to do this is to risk leaving the impression that I am, by my opposition, positing a single author. Such an impression is not my intent. I have spoken of "the single authorial voice" in Scripture as a whole; and I would not look for more than a single author's pen in any given pericope—be it a chapter or several chapters in Genesis, or in the Book of Isaiah—unless I have good reason to posit several authors (or author and editor) who are not mutually aware of each other's contributions. But this is certainly not to rule out the possibility, or even the likelihood, that some of Scripture's narratives may be the result of a collaborative effort. Thus, for example, in regard to the narrative of the flood. One can imagine an Israelite professor of theology (I suspect we should identify him as a prophet) reviewing the Utnapishtim story, analyzing it—as I have done—as a satiric critique of polytheism, and assigning to two students an exercise: "Drawing as freely as you like upon this Babylonian satire, tell essentially the same story, not as a satire, to portray man and divinity so as to bring out the essential attributes of both—and vis-à-vis one another—in keeping with our Israelite view of the One God and His creatures." He might then have been so pleased with the inventions of both his pupils as to draw on the products of both his pupils to present a narrative, weaving elements of both together, but preserving a harmonious whole. This despite his incorporation of two different (but not contradictory) introductions and two different (but not contradictory) conclusions. And in the process, in drawing upon the two narrative exercises, he might even have left us a clue as to the devolution of his narrative by incorporating the terms his students used for Deity, one having preferred YHWH and the other Elohim "God."

As a matter of fact, however, such an imaginative feat of literary detection would be open to serious criticism on at least one score: the elements in the flood story that may be assigned to one or another of two original authors are not confined to the flood story. They go back to include chapters 1 to 5, and, possibly, ahead to chapters 9:18–11:32. To help the readers follow in a sketch of the compatibility of my literary analysis with standard source-criticism, I have drawn up table 4-1, limited to the Genesis text I have thus far treated.

In respect to the deployment of YHWH or Elohim as the name for Deity, I have stressed before that the most painstaking care with diction on an author's part does not constitute writing-by-formula, nor is it a legitimate demand of a literary critic that he try to hold his author to such a near-scientific exactitude. (The poetic approach need not falsify the source-critical explanation; it need only provide an equally plausible reason for choice of diction.) The two first-person personal pronouns in biblical Hebrew may serve as analogy to the two proper names of God, YHWH and Elohim. As often as these synonyms $^a n \bar{\imath}$/(pausal) $\bar{a}n \bar{\imath}$ and $\bar{a}n \bar{o}k \bar{\imath}$ appear, as richly meaningful as are the contexts of their respective appearance, yet do they elude such attempts at differentiating nuances as might allow us to predict which would appear in one or another context. Despite this, and for all our (genetic) speculation about the preference of one or another writer for one or the other name, it remains my conviction that even in and across the strands, YHWH will appear in a context in which God is more personalized, individuated, and more intimate with his creatures (with Noah as against humankind, with humans as against the animal kingdom and the like), and more likely to appear in anthropomorphisms, while God is more abstract, more concept than person, less intimate, certainly never cozy. Consider such usages as yad YHWH "hand of YHWH" and rūah 'elōhīm "spirit of God," and never the reverse.

In table 4-1, features in the P strand are identified by Arabic numerals, and in the J strand by Roman numerals. "Terms for Fauna" (2) has reference to the emphasis on the animals by classes or species, and is associated in the Deluge context with animal behavior contributing to that punishment (5), šht (trans. or intrans. with bśr). "Sexuality" (V) may point to the theme generally, or such deprecated ac-

TABLE 4-1   Strands in Genesis 1:1–9:29

P Strand			J Strand		
1:1–2:4a	1.	Elohim	2:4b–4:11	I.	YHWH
	2.	Terms for fauna		II.	*ārūr* "ban"
	3.	Dietary restriction		III.	*ṣb/ʿṣbn* "pain"
	4.	Mankind as image of God		IV.	Sacrifice
				V.	Sexuality
5:1–3	1.	Elohim	5:29	I.	YHWH
	4.	Mankind as image of God		II.	*ārūr*
				III.	*ṣb/ṣbn*
6:9–22	1.	Elohim	6:1–8	I.	YHWH
	2.	Terms for fauna		V.	Sexuality
	3.	Dietary restriction: VII. (vs. 6:21)		VI.	*yṣr lb*
	5.	*šht* with *bśr* (waste/corrupt w. flesh)		VII.	Clean and unclean
7:13–8:5	1.	Elohim	7:1–5	I.	YHWH
	2.	Terms for fauna		VII.	Clean and unclean
8:15–19	1.	Elohim	8:20–22	I.	YHWH
	2.	Terms for fauna		IV.	Sacrifice
				VI.	*yṣr lb*
				VII.	Clean and unclean
9:1–17	1.	Elohim	9:18–29	I.	YHWH
	2.	Terms for fauna		II.	*ārūr*
	3.	Dietary restriction		V.	Sexuality
	4.	Mankind as image of God			
	5.	*šht* (with *ʾrṣ*)			
	V.	"those who left the ark"			

tivities as cross-species miscegenation or violation of taboos. The distinction of animals clean (*ṭhr*) and unclean (*ṭmʾ*) may be associated with edibility of meat (3), or sacrifice (IV), or both; hence our cross-strand listing of VII with (3) in 6:21. Similarly, the cross-strand listing of the (miscegenated) survivors V in 9:10 must be considered—assuming their separate authorship or provenance—in divining the editor's hand in the final composition.

NOAH'S DELUGE AND UTNAPISHTIM'S: A COMPARISON

Did the author of the biblical flood story recognize—as modern scholarship has not hitherto done—that Utnapishtim's story in Tablet XI is a satire on the gods of paganism? Our guess would be unquestionably yes. Fine artists in a given medium will usually understand, if not approve, the work of one another. Would our biblical author have approved the achievement of his Babylonian predecessor? Again, yes. For the Babylonian's critique of polytheistic paganism is a major step toward his own (biblical) monotheism. Would our biblical author have been disturbed by a pagan's anticipation, so to speak, of biblical theology? Not at all. And in this he would differ from most modern biblical scholars. For most of us, Israel's "contribution" to religion is impressive in the degree that it is original, that it breaks utterly with all that precedes it in "pagan" thinking. The Bible itself, however, is not in the least concerned with being original; it never lays claim to originality. To the contrary, the early chapters of Genesis picture the relationship between deity and antediluvian man in the framework of a presumed monotheism. The name YHWH was already known and God invoked by that name by some, at least, of pre-flood humanity (4:26, "Back then the name YHWH was first invoked"). It is the one God who addresses Adam and Eve and their son Cain. It is he who is worshiped by both Cain and Abel, and to whom both Enoch (5:24) and Noah are faithful. Paganism, then, is for Scripture, not mankind's original estate; it represents, rather, as in 6:1–8, a falling away from true understanding of the divine.

Let us reconsider a question discussed in chapter 1, the nature of biblical monotheism. It is not a matter of numbers. YHWH is not the only member of the class called *'elōhīm*, which, while it is used for God, also connotes gods, angels, numens, ancestral spirits, the metaphor Heaven for the Power or Powers above, the supernatural, and so on. Biblical monotheism's theological dogma centers on YHWH-God as the one and only autonomous Creator of all that is, including such supernal entities as the various numina worshiped by Israel's neighbors and the primordial forces personified in Great Deep, Sea, Leviathan, and the like. Psalm 82 begins with God (elohim) rising in the divine assembly, in the midst of the gods (elohim) to present his indictment of them. His indictment expresses the frustration of his command to them that they execute justice, bring relief to the oppressed. Their failure to do so causes the very foundations of the earth (which is established on justice) to totter. God's address ends with his sentencing them, "Verily, then, like man shall you die and like one of those hero-chieftains will you fall!" Here then is a link to the divinities, supernal ones, "sons of *'elōhīm*," who in J's introduction mate with humanity to the moral degradation of both species. It is not the ontology of polytheism that Scripture condemns; it is its operation to the detriment of morality that is polytheism's most damning feature.

Assuming then the Genesis author's understanding and approval of the Utnapishtim story's critique of paganism, what motivated him to rework it as he did in order to include it in Scripture? The ultimate answer must wait upon our conclusion of the literary unit, chapters 1–11, known to Bible scholars as the Primeval History. A partial answer, on the possibility of which we speculated earlier, is the challenge presented by the universal cataclysm theme to an author whose theology predicates a single and benevolent God in place of the many and capricious gods of paganism. But even for such an author, who considered his inventiveness equal to that challenge, there is something about the flood story that makes it suitable for such a lampooning enterprise as the Utnapishtim tale, but would seem to rule it out in a "straight," didactic, non-satiric narrative. And that "something" is this: the plot depends on the silliest presumption in all of antiquity's fantasy literature, mythological or fairy tale; namely, the presumption that the entire biotic animal range might be preserved from a cosmic disaster by means of a human-built shelter capable of admitting a single adult pair of each and every species. As against this presumption, Jack's beanstalk or the goose that laid golden eggs would seem like sports of nature, rare yet conceivable. Even if the ancients presumed the number of species of birds and insects to number but a tenth of what modern science estimates, the dimensions of Utnapishtim's cubic monstrosity would be more appropriate than those of Noah's craft, its square footage only an eighth that of the cube, and its cubic footage only one-sixteenth. Scripture's author, like his Babylonian predecessor, provides for sustenance for all. Here too the Babylonian tale would seem more realistic, in that its flood lasted a single week as against the full year of the biblical flood. And while we are on the subject of logistics, what about the sanitation problem? Presuming an adequacy of water (how not?) and a system of drain spouts and even hoses, who manned the pumps? One could go on and on, but why labor the point. The remarkable fact is that scholars who indulge in the Augean stables as a prototypical metaphor and the Herculean solution of that task as a legendary hyperbole do not dream of raising such questions when assessing the literal intent of the authors of either flood story. Another fact, almost equally remarkable, is that many a denomination hewing to a slavishly literal intent for every narrative in Scripture will harbor in its midst humorous treatments of its stories. I recall, still with wonderment, the campfire occasion at a summer camp under such devout auspices, and the children who chanted:

Noah was a carpenter; he walked in the dark.
Tripped over a hammer and built himself an ark.
Along came the animals, two by two:
the lion, tiger, elephant and the key-kangaroo.

How does the biblical author meet this problem of silliness? In a number of ways. First, he ignores it overtly; second, he affirms and reinforces it covertly. The literalists will swallow anything, no matter how patent the ridicule; the sophisticates will chuckle at the humor even as they seek out the kerygmas. Where the pagan author—have we a right to label him so?—in his lampooning enterprise heightens the ridiculous everywhere he can, the biblical author excludes it where it is inappropriate, mitigates it when it is too obtrusive, and gives it subtle twists where one least expects them. Thus, for example, the Babylonian author twits alike the gods (Enlil and Ishtar), the demi-gods (Gilgamesh and Enkidu), and the altogether human hero (Utnapishtim). The biblical author may show God to be humorous, but never treat him humorously; while the human is always a legitimate target for humor, gentle, as in the case of Noah releasing the raven over a carcass-filled flood, or savage, as in the case of humanity in its mytholatrous propensities.

The ark—not in itself the laughing matter that it is in Tablet XI—is no longer a cube; it is provided with a high bank of transparent windows to let in light (to the upper and middle decks, the hold being completely submerged). One normally climbs aboard a ship from above, but with a roof (top-deck) at some twenty feet above the dock level, an entrance is provided in its side for the sake of the huge land creatures. So much for seacraft realism. But when Noah releases the birds it is from a previously unmentioned window-opening (*hallōn*); and when Noah emerges to view the surrounding ground, it is via a previously unmentioned (hatch-)cover, from which vantage point on the world's highest peak he would have seen nothing but a hemisphere of sky. So also, when the Deity (in the name for his caring modality, YHWH) tucks Noah in for the long night of rain, the verb is *sgr* "to lock (up), shut (in)" correctly rendered by us as "batten in," which is to say, *from the outside*.

Hence, we must understand that when God invites Noah (and all the ark's living cargo) to leave the ark, it is in the cajoling tone addressed to a long pent-up prisoner fearing to leave his cell, and only after the jailer has removed the bars.

It was pointed out earlier that Noah's dispatch of the birds, four dispatches and two birds, makes sense in every way, while Utnapishtim's makes sense in none. But then again, the failure of the dove to return from its third mission (itself something of a problem as we noted) should have given Noah the information he was seeking and made it unnecessary for God to coax him out of the ark. Another instance of seemingly realistic detail with overtones of historiography and undertones of humor is the matter of chronology. Table 7-1 in our Structures section will show that the Genesis author had worked out a calendar beginning with the year of creation, with the birth years and death years of first-born patriarchs serving as significant markers. What a joy then for the historiographer, for whom dates constitute the most critical data, to know just how many years elapsed between the Deity's conquest of *mabbūl*-chaos, which marked history's first beginning, and the onset and cessation of the *mabbūl*-chaos that marked history's second beginning! And to know not only the year but the very day of the month! Such data would have had to have been retrieved from an archival source that could not possibly have existed (like the apocryphal Roman coin, unearthed bearing the date 13 B.C.). Can it be that our author, in his provision of that data, was not only signaling the fictive nature of his literary enterprise, but mocking the very priority of history over fiction, of physical data over moral norms, indeed, of science over theology?

The answer given to this speculation, a literary judgment, will depend on a *meta-literary* consideration. Was the biblical author privy to the knowledge that the calendar as a historical measuring tool was a human invention? That the names he knew for some of the months, which he normally called by the ordinals from 1 to 12, derived from Mesopotamia, and that virtually every city-state there had its own calendar? Scripture again and again witnesses that such knowledge on his part is certain in some respects, likely in others. And in that case he knew also that in Noah's century (millennium) no calendar existed on which there could have been recorded the seventeenth day of the second month of any year whatsoever.

So much for the matter of silliness. Silliness that posed no problem for an author in Babylon as he crafted his satirical masterpiece, and which seems to have posed no problem for scholars who routinely assume that the satire was lost on the ancient audience. Which must have posed a problem to the biblical author, compelled by his own theological enterprise to straighten out much of the satire in the model he was adapting. And, judging by the reception of the biblical flood story by generations of audiences—with the exceptions of a few village atheists and source-critical scholars—a problem that the biblical storyteller solved admirably. He solved it by deploying for childlike literalists and sophisticated connoisseurs alike a remarkable array of seriocomic strategies, straight and ludicrous rhetoric, metaphors low and sublime, for each to read according as his wit might construe.

In terms of the larger metaphors: The theme of *Enuma elish* is the taming by the gods of the awesome cosmic energies, eventuating in the creation of the world. The Deluge in the time of Utnapishtim is the sequel to that myth. By the capricious will of the gods, the world that Marduk created is to be destroyed. The means to that end are the very same water-storm powers that had been subdued by Marduk. But once unleashed, these powers are beyond the control of the gods, who are terror-stricken when the flood threatens to inundate the cosmic mountain atop which they live. And even when the storm abates—by no action of the gods, be it noted—the dependency of this otiose breed of supermen upon their human peons is underlined in their ravenous descent upon Utnapishtim's sacrifice. Of course the human race must continue. For one thing, the gods will not again risk their own survival by pushing those red buttons. For another, they must have mankind if they want to eat. But the ultimate reality of blind, deaf, and dumb oceanic power remains, and the less-than-ultimate gods are no reliable assurance that its destructive potential will never again be activated to dissolve the fragile order of the cosmos.

In like manner, the biblical author acknowledges that the awesome powers that were activated for creation can be deployed for dissolution. And the widespread tradition of a primordial time when history was interrupted, almost ended, by such a cataclysm is shaped by this author in keeping with the theology of Genesis 1. If such a dissolution is ever to take place, it will be by no mindless eruption of soulless energy, nor by acts of a race of arrested superhumans playing with matches. It can only happen by the Will which is that Power. And that Will, called God, whose proper name is YHWH, has resolved never to will such dissolution. Not because he needs man, and not because man is deserving, but because he so graciously wills to give his favorite creature ever and ever another chance. In 8:21, YHWH's rumination is not put forward as a revelation to the author of what went on in God's mind. The decision not to repeat the Deluge is not because of, but despite, mankind's continuing evil bent. The decision then constitutes a judgment on the part of the author. Mankind's endurance since the Deluge is testimony, not to mankind's moral improvement since that generation, but rather to God's gracious tolerance. Similarly, just as the repeated and detailed description of the death of all creatures in the flood testifies to the power of God's anger, so the repeated details of all the species coming to the ark, entering it, and leaving it, along with Noah and his family, testifies to God's consistency and grace: not a single species of the original creation was permitted to become extinct by reason of the flood.

The concern of this ultimate Person for man is an aspect or an attribute of his which is as dogmatically affirmed in biblical theology as it is characteristically absent in the gods of Utnapishtim's tale: morality. As in the Cain and Abel episode, where morality is the very heart of the mythos, so in the Deluge story—but here as attribute of God—morality is everywhere present, in dramatic contrast to its pagan Babylonian counterpart.

Utnapishtim, as we have seen, has no idea why the gods have decided to destroy mankind. In the biblical account two different introductions each stress that evil was the reason for God's decision. Utnapishtim is not one to look a gift horse in the mouth (the reader will forgive this metaphor in disrespect of Ea), and never thinks to question why he alone has been chosen for survival. Noah's righteousness is twice underscored by the narrator (6:8,9), and in 8:1 YHWH Himself informs Noah that he alone has been vindicated in the judgment. For such a good and righteous man God is an ever present, ever doting parent. He Himself tucks Noah into his shelter for the long night. "YHWH battened him in." (7:16) "YHWH was mindful of Noah and of the beasts and cattle with him in the ark. God swept a wind over earth and the waves subsided." (8:1) God tells Noah when it is safe to leave the ark; and in conjunction with this he renews the blessing of 1:22, decreeing renewed fertility for the earth to be repopulated. (8:15–17).

And, as we have seen, as man's transcendence over animal status in 9:1–7 is a reaffirmation of his dignity, the image of God, a status unearned, so God's favor to future generations is explicitly not contingent upon the future righteousness of his creatures. Sinfulness there will be, and punishment too, but no cataclysmic end to the human experiment. God has hung up his war-bow. There it is, seven-hued, in the sky. And when it appears against the menacing mass of gathered clouds, our hearts leap up, not at its shimmering beauty alone, but over its Author, assurance and promise.

FROM NOAH TO ABRAM

Two stories complete the narratives of chapters 1–11, which in modern scholarship is often labeled the Primeval History. Chapter 12, beginning the story of the patriarch Abram, first ancestor of the people of Israel, begins the History of Israel; and the setting for this history is thus provided by the Primeval History. This setting consists then of the genealogies, which we treat under chapter 7, "Structures," and five narratives. The first three (Creation, Eden, Flood) have each required a separate chapter. The last two are treated in this one. The first, 9:18–27, features Noah, three sons, and one grandson in a story somehow portentous for later history, but strangely murky as to plot and character motivation, and ambiguous as to the very identities of the personae. The second, 11:1–9, tells how the unity of Noah's descendants came to be disrupted.

THE DRUNKENNESS OF NOAH

(18) The sons of Noah, those who came out of the ark, were Shem, Ham, and Japheth, (Ham being the father of Canaan). (19) These three the Sons of Noah, from these all earth['s population] branched out. (20) Noah, tiller of the soil, was the first to plant a vineyard. (21) Drinking of the wine, he fell drunk, and lay exposed in his tent. (22) Ham—Canaan's father—beheld his father's nakedness, and told his two brothers outside. (23) Shem and Japheth took a robe, held it extended from both their shoulders, and—walking in backward—they covered up their father's nakedness; with their faces

turned away, they caught no glimpse of their father's nakedness. (24) When Noah woke up from his wine[-stupor], and learned how his smallest son had treated him, (25) he declared:

"Damned be Canaan.
Most abject of slaves may he be to his brothers!"
(26) [What] he said, [in full];
"Praised be YHWH, god of Shem!
And slave to them may Canaan be!
(27) Broad scope may God to Japheth grant!
May he reside in the tents of Shem!
And slave to them may Canaan be!" (Genesis 9:18–27)

The tragedies that often attend an overlarge intake of alcoholic liquors have resulted, in some segments of society, in a stance that regards all such spirits as an absolute evil. Scripture, in common with virtually all ancient societies, would have found such a stance comparable to prohibition of food as a remedy for the vice of overeating. The ancients generally appreciated the spirit-lifting beverages as a boon, and Israel was no exception. The preciousness of wine is reflected in the libations that accompanied sacrificial offerings. The biblical idiom for the good cheer induced by wine is, "the heart is good (i.e., cheerful) in (or through) the wine;" and the superiority of the glow that comes from within over that which is painted on the outside is celebrated in Psalm 104. God is praised for the blessing of rain:

Which makes grass to sprout for cattle,
Cereal grains [in response] to the tilling of man,
To produce food from the earth,
And wine to bring joy to the heart of man—
Exceeding cosmetics in bringing the face to a glow. (Psalm 104:14–15)

"Culture heroes" is the term used for the mythical or legendary innovators of skills, arts, trades, and professions. As in Genesis 4 Jubal Lamechson corresponds to Orpheus, and Tubal-Cain Lamechson to the smiths Hephaestus or Vulcan, so is Noah the father of viticulture. In the genealogical list in Chapter 5, Noah's father, Lamech,[1] makes a pun on his son's name, a pun on the two consonants appearing in N°aH "ease, pleasant" and NaHem "to console or comfort." Lamech refers back to God's sentence of infertility upon the soil in 3:17–19, and looks ahead with prophetic sight to what this child will one day accomplish: "This one, now, will bring us relief from (or consolation for) the painful toil of our hands, out of the very soil which YHWH has placed under a spell" (verse 29). Be it today's high-pressure executive with his martini, hard-hat with his beer, or peasant with his vino—all are in debt to Father Noah.

Unlike Dionysos or Bacchus, who apparently knew what they were doing, Noah's pioneering efforts in grape cultivation were carried out in ignorance of the natural process of fermentation. Depending on whether one regards alcoholic spirits as boon or curse, Noah's discovery is serendipity or misfortune. For Noah himself, his inexperience made for history's first case of inebriation, one that engendered a train of events with apparently disastrous consequences. The one thing clear in this story is that Noah's drunken loss of self-control is responsible for the exposure of his genitalia, which somehow renders him vulnerable to mistreatment. For the rest, the story presents us with a host of problems.

The first problem is why the introduction, listing the three sons of Noah, characterizes them as "those who came out of the ark," a seemingly obvious and therefore unnecessary detail. This is the easiest question to answer, for it is not an unnecessary detail. If we turn back to Genesis 5, where the genealogy of Adam is given ending in Noah in the tenth generation, we will note that in the case of every person we are told that in addition to the male son, through whom the line descends, each of these also sired additional sons, as well as daughters.[2] Why are none of these named? The answer is obvious: all the descendants of Adam perished in the Deluge, and only that line which culminated in Noah was preserved. Only in the case of Noah are we told of more than one son, the three who were already grown and married at the time of the Deluge. These three are identified in our verse 19 as the ancestors of the three branches of mankind. The implication is clear. Noah, too, may have "sired additional sons and daughters" after the flood; he did, after all, live for another 350 years. Such additional children as Noah may have had were assimilated to one or another of the lines of Shem, Ham, and Japheth. (Just such a pattern is made explicit in Genesis 48. Jacob, by adopting Joseph's sons Ephraim and Manasseh as his own, in effect makes Joseph the ancestor of two of Israel's tribes. As for any sons that might be sired by Joseph in the future, Jacob in verse 6 says that they shall be assimilated into the two tribes he has created out of Joseph, and are to receive their family estates within the allotments made to these two tribes.)

This latest reminder that the biblical storyteller wastes no words and includes no detail without a purpose, makes even more perplexing the point of the notice in verse 19 that Ham was the father of Canaan. For according to 10:6, he was also the father of Cush (Ethiopia and the Sudan), Egypt, and Put (Libya), Canaan being the youngest of the four. Again in verse 22, where Ham looks upon Noah's nakedness and tells his brothers, he is pointedly but unexplainedly identified as the father of Canaan. And finally in the curse of Noah, it is this youngest son of Ham, and not Ham himself—as we would have expected—who is condemned. And Ham, listed between his brothers, would have had to be the middle son, whether Shem or Japheth was the firstborn. Yet when Noah learns of how he was treated (not necessarily as the translations have it, *what was done to him*) the text has him identifying the person who committed the outrage as his *smallest*, or—as the adjective can also mean and is universally rendered here—his *youngest* son.

All the scholarly attempts to resolve these problems presuppose that there were several different traditions about Noah's family or about this incident, and that the text before us must be a garbled version of these traditions. Thus, one suggestion is that in another tradition it was indeed Ham who was the youngest of Noah's sons. Why, then, was it not Ham who was cursed? A bolder hypothesis overcomes this problem: there was another tradition in which the three sons of Noah were Shem, Japheth, and Canaan, and that it was indeed Canaan, the youngest son, who committed the offense. Yet a third hypothesis would have a story in which not Noah, but Ham, was the victim, and the perpetrator his youngest son Canaan.[3]

We dwell on these solutions as typical of the approach that solves the Gordian knot by destroying it. Satisfying as this procedure may be for a soldier on his way to conquest, for the critic it is analogous to shredding a canvas because he cannot see the pattern in its painted forms and colors. The text before us is explicit and clear in so many respects: In the details of genealogy, the order of births, the person offended, the person offending, the person cursed. If there were several traditions, why was not one consistent one preserved? If a redactor had indeed inherited a garbled tradition, why would he not simply have omitted details that are as minor as they are inconsistent? For example, instead of referring to the deed of Noah's "youngest son," why did he not just say, the deed of Ham?

These problems—of Ham's seemingly pointless (and repeated) identification as the father of Canaan, of the apparently mistaken curse of Canaan by Noah, who meant to curse his son Ham and not this son's youngest son, and then of Noah, who does not seem to know that this son is his middle one and not his youngest— these problems must be considered in the light of the problems with the utterance of Noah. Let us look at this text in the JPS translation:

> (24) When Noah woke up . . . (25) he said,
> "Cursed be Canaan;
> The lowest of slaves
> Shall he be to his brothers."
> (26) And he said,
> "Blessed be the Lord,
> The God of Shem;
> Let Canaan be a slave to them.
> (27) May God enlarge Japheth,
> And let him dwell in the tents of Shem;
> And let Canaan be a slave to them." (Genesis 9:24-27)

The first question is that of the repetition on the part of the narrator in verses 25 and 26. Twice he tells us that "Noah said" something. The something that "he said" is dialogue in two versions. Although the two versions are similar in content they are far from the same. The first one is shorter, is confined to a curse of Canaan, does not specify the name of the Power who is to effectuate the curse, and makes no mention of Shem and Japheth, although it does seem to refer to them as the brothers of Canaan, to whom he will be a lowly slave. In the second and considerably larger version, blessing is added and indeed precedes curse, but interestingly enough the first blessing is not of humans but of God, and not of God in general but specifically by his proper name YHWH ("the Lord" in JPS), and with further specificity identified as "the God of Shem." God is indeed invoked in this second version but not until verse 27, where his blessing is invoked on behalf of Japheth ("May God enlarge Japheth"), and in addition to being invoked as *God* and not as YHWH, there does not seem to be a corresponding blessing on behalf of Shem. That Shem is implicitly blessed would seem to be the sense of the curse of Canaan in the last clause of verse 27, for Canaan will presumably serve two lords, Japheth and Shem. But let us note that this four-word curse (in the Hebrew), which makes sense here, is an exact repetition of the curse in the last clause of verse 26, where it makes no sense at all, since Shem and Japheth have not been mentioned and cannot therefore be the antecedents to whom the "them" of the curse refers. And to add to these perplexities, there is a further problem. The blessing of enlargement for Japheth—a pun on the three consonants of his name Y-P-T and the imperfect hiphil of P-T-(H), again Y-P-T—is followed up by wishing him the boon of residing in his older brother's tents. Now the roomiest of a brother's tents may provide pleasant guest quarters for one who has just been promised enlargement, but is it not a greater blessing to be host than guest, and who would not normally prefer to be at home in one's own small tent than a guest in another's large one?

The problem of the first and out-of-place curse of Canaan, the last clause of verse 26, scholars find easiest to solve. It is a readily understood scribal error called dittography. In copying the manuscript before him, the scribe's hand having just written "(God of) *Shem*," his eye skipped to the next *Shem* in the following verse ("tents of) *Shem*" and so we have a superfluous clause. Strike it out!⁴

The "blessing of YHWH" in verse 26 is problematic on two scores. First, as Speiser says, "One expects this blessing to be aimed at Shem rather than YHWH," which is hardly arguable.⁵ Secondly, the One God of Scripture, himself the source of all blessings, is by definition not capable of being blessed; for what needs does he have and who could supply them if he had any? This second problem can be solved everywhere that Deity appears as the object of *bērek* or the subject of the predicate *bārūk* by rendering the Hebrew as "praise" and "praised." But to render *bārūk* as "praised" in verse 26 (as we have done) is to raise the objection that there is no context here for praising God, and—furthermore—no ground for the assumption that his proper name YHWH is acknowledged by Shem alone of his brothers. This problem too has led scholars to suggest an emendation of the text. One such suggestion does not even constitute a textual emendation for it merely changes two of the masoretically supplied vowels. Read *bᵉrūk* instead of *bārūk* and *ᵉlōhay* instead of *ᵉlōhey* and you have an altogether appropriate blessing of Shem and an invocation by Noah of the god to whom he is faithful, YHWH: "Blessed of my god YHWH may Shem be." Speiser alludes to such suggestions for change but does not endorse them, noting, "Nevertheless, the ancient versions support the received text, which does not lack champions among modern critics" (cf. von Rad, p. 114).

On the perplexing prayer (or promise) that Japheth (will) dwell in the tents of Shem, Speiser recognizes that this prayer or promise is a metaphor and suggests a historic moment to which the metaphor is apposite.

> This must allude to some form of co-operation between the two groups, with Canaan condemned to enslavement by both. What, then, is the historical background of the verse in question? The most likely period that would seem to fit the conditions here reflected is the turn of the twelfth century B.C., when the Israelites were struggling against the entrenched Canaanites at the same time that the recently arrived Philistines were trying to consolidate their hold on the coastal strip . . . however, the Japhethites of the present account would differ considerably from their namesakes in the Table of Nations (X 2–5:P). For by then, the Philistines too had ceased to be a politically significant group; and they had been settled long enough to be classed with the Hamites. (X 14)⁶

This ingenious speculation, like all the other attempts to understand the metaphor of Japheth, one of three brothers, dwelling in the tents of one of them, Shem, to the discomfiture of the other, Ham, runs afoul of the separate problem that Ham is not present here except as represented by his son Canaan. And for Canaan who in verse 25 is condemned to be "slave to his brothers" and again supposedly to these same siblings in verses 26 and 27 (the antecedents of "them" in these verses), Shem and Japheth are not brothers, they are uncles! Canaan's brothers, as we pointed out earlier, are (see 10:6) Cush (Ethiopia or Sudan), Mizraim (Egypt), and Put (Libya)!

Let us now attempt a poetical approach to our text, one which starts with the assumption that the text is a harmonious whole, faithfully transmitted to us, requiring no deletions nor corrections, possibly not even of the vocalization transmitted to us by the Masoretes; that, indeed, if these rabbinic transmitters of the tradition chose a questionable reading over a clearly sensible one, their choice must be given an initial preference on the basis of *lectio difficilior praestat*.[7] Here I reproduce my translation of verses 24–27:

> (24) When Noah woke up from his wine[-stupor], and learned how his smallest son had treated him, (25) he declared:
> "Damned be Canaan.
> Most abject of slaves may he be to his brothers!"
> (26) [What] he said, [in full];
> "Praised be YHWH, god of Shem!
> And slave to them may Canaan be!
> (27) Broad scope may God to Japheth grant!
> May he reside in the tents of Shem!
> And slave to them may Canaan be!"

The problem of the narrator's transmission of Noah's verbal reaction to his (learning of his) treatment at the hands of Ham in two separate sections of dialogue, each introduced by "he said" (*wayyoʾ mer . . . wayyoʾ mer* in paratactic sequence) is resolved by recognition of the synoptic-resumptive narrative technique. The first section (verses 24–25) provides the bottom line, a dramatically apposite reaction (for the most part) to the outrage he has just learned of. Not so apposite is his substitution of Ham's son, Canaan, as object of the wrath kindled by Ham. But this lack of appositeness is equally present in the second dialogic section, the resumptive one. In the second section we have a fuller account of Noah's reaction, perhaps one reformulated some time after word of the outrage had been communicated to him; perhaps providing a clue as to the substitution of Canaan to suffer for his father's sin. And as for the problem of the narrator's referring to Ham as—in Noah's consciousness—"the youngest of his sons," the answer is simply: he does not. The Hebrew reads literally "his smallest son," which may also stand for "youngest son." Big and small in Hebrew, however, (as in English) may also stand for high rank and low, moral worth and moral baseness. As in II Kings 2:23,[8] *small* here is *base* or *mean-spirited*. Noah, our narrator tells us, learned of the meanness of spirit revealed by his son Ham when he found his father lying exposed.

The recognition of this metonymic use of "small" points to the solution of a problem in regard to the three brothers in the following chapter. In the genealogy of Noah's sons, Shem in 10:21 is identified as the "bigger," that is, "elder" brother of Japheth. But this seems to be a pointed exclusion of Ham, to whom he was also older brother. What is the meaning of this? The answer lies once again in the recognition of a metaphor, this time in the word "brother." The word "brother" here is not a reference to the genetic relationship, which Ham also shared, but to similarity. As shown by their respectful treatment of their father, Shem and Japheth were two of a kind. Ham, on the other hand, as our story makes equally clear, was odd man out.

But to recognize this is merely to scratch the surface, so to speak, of the metaphor. Another text celebrated for its knottiness, featuring this metaphoric use of "brother," appears in Genesis 49. Jacob is addressing his last words to his twelve sons. He speaks prophetically, as if his voice were the voice of God, and expresses or implies divine judgment in characterizing them:

> Simeon and Levi are brothers—
> Lawless weapons their mᵉkērōt (Genesis 49:5)

Inasmuch as all his sons are brothers to one another, the first clause can only mean—as Speiser indicates—"a pair, two of a kind." But with solution in hand, he fails to see the related answer to the "old and stubborn puzzle" of mᵉkērōt, normally and without support rendered as "weapons." He notes that "Syr. and many moderns adduce the consonantally identical noun in Ezekiel xvi 3 and xxi 35, meaning 'origins.'" *Origins* is a metonym for the noun in question. Its verbal stem *krh* "to dig, carve out, quarry" is common enough, particularly in regard to cisterns or wells. Thus the associations with earth, "motherland" in the Ezekiel passages in connection with birth or birthplace, share the imagery of Isaiah 51 (where *ḥṣb* and *nqr* are synonyms of *krh*):

> (1) . . . Look to the rock whence you were hewn,
> To the quarry whence you were chiseled.
> (2) Look back to Abraham, your father,
> And to Sarah, who gave you birth. (Isaiah 51:1–2)

The metaphor is one of affinity (cf. Eng. "chip off the old block"), the kind of affinity often associated with common origin, an affinity we associate today with genetic heredity. In our metaphor, sharing a gene pool in common, inheriting the same genetic traits from a set of parents, we sense the force of the second clause, the specific trait that makes Simon and Levi alike, two out of twelve brothers: it is their proclivity (apparently inherited) for the unlawful use of weapons. We shall soon see how this metaphor bears upon our passage.

One more metaphor remains before we may proceed with our poetical review: the residence in the tents of Shem. Rabbinic tradition holds that the *Shekina*, the Immanent Presence on Earth, graced Solomon's temple, but never returned to reside in its successor sanctuary, the temple "rebuilt" in Jerusalem by YHWH's Persian servant, Cyrus the Great. YHWH's residence in or occupancy of a sanctuary is a privilege granted to or withheld from its builders.[9] Thus Rashi on the meaning of "he shall dwell in the tents of Shem:" Although YHWH was gracious to Japheth (i.e., Cyrus, allowing him to rebuild the temple), He resided only in the "tent" built by Shem (i.e., Solomon's temple).

Thus, as Speiser can see in Japhetites a metonym for one (supposed) branch of that family, the Philistines, as Rashi can see Shem as a metonym for his descendants Israel or Solomon, and Japheth as metonym for his descendants, Medea or Cyrus, so may we read the Canaanites of verse 26 ("Cursed be Canaan, most abject of slaves may he be to his brothers") as a metonym for one particular branch of this family. And the brothers of this Canaanite branch need not necessarily be limited to Semites or Aryans, or to Hamites, but could be members of any or all of these groupings. "Praised be YHWH, the God of Shem." If Shem, now, is a metonym for Israel, as recognized by Rashi, then there is no problem in hailing YHWH as this people's God, nor is there a problem in the opening praise, for Noah is about to make a petition, and praise often serves to invoke God in anticipation of the petition. "And may Canaan be a slave to them." The antecedents of "them" cannot be "his brothers" of verse 25, for that sentence belongs to the synoptic episode. The antecedents can only be those in verse 26, namely YHWH, God of Shem (Israel) and His people, Israel. "May God"—not YHWH, who is Israel's covenanted God—"give broad scope to Japheth," the various peoples on the peripheries of the ancient world (from Israel's point of view). "But may he (God) reside in the tents of Shem," namely, grace Israel with his presence among them. "And"—again—"may Canaan be a slave to them." To whom? To YHWH and to Israel. But why to both people and its God, and which Canaanite branch in what historic context? Our bill of particulars could not be better filled than by the Gibeonites, those Canaanites (cf. Joshua 9:1) of Israel's heartland who saved themselves from extermination by a ruse, inducing Israel to accept them as "slaves" and became a caste within the people of Israel, fated for all time to provide "hewers of wood and drawers of water for," in Joshua's words, "the house of my God."[10]

Every textual problem in Noah's utterance of blessing and curse has been solved. Not a word nor a letter is superfluous, missing, or out of place. The poetic integrity of this narrative has been vindicated, and so has—in the process—the poetic unity of Genesis with Ezekiel and Isaiah and Joshua and Exodus, at least as far as their sharing of metaphors and psychology and historical overviews. The strongest elements in our analysis are those dealing with lexical, syntactic, and rhetorical questions. The weakest, perhaps, is the element of historic intent. That is, the pinpointing of the Gibeonites' service to YHWH's temple as the fulfillment of Noah's curse upon Canaan. And, convinced though we are on this point, we would stress that a rejection of this point in no way weakens the poetic understanding of this pericope. The question of history—what really happened and how events came to be interpreted—is not a central concern of poetics. Whether, for example, Noah—as fundamental religionists would have it—foresaw that reality by prophetic gift or invoked it by the power of his prayer; or whether the author invented the curse to fit an event or situation in a later generation, the implication of the curse-narrative is that before—and perhaps continuing into—the author's time, Canaanites were subjected to menial servitude by neighbors ("brothers"), be these traceable to Shem, Ham, or Japheth as eponymous ancestor. The specific subjection that the author had in mind is not a crucial consideration. What is crucial is the awareness on our part of the awareness on the author's part that, as in genetics, a trait is not passed on to all descendants, so a character virtue or defect—or reward or punishment for ancestral deeds—need not be carried over or down through all the branches of a family tree. The flaw in Ham's character, which is expressed in or which brought him to commit his misdeed, was foreseen by Noah to be continued in the line of Canaan—so, at least, the author asks us to believe—and Canaan would in time come to suffer for this shortcoming of his ancestor's and of his own.

We may now turn to one last remaining problem in this episode as a whole: the nature of Ham's offense against Noah. The literal translation of verse 24, "Noah . . . learned what his unworthy son had done to him," suggests some kind of physical mistreatment; and among the speculations as to what Ham did to his father, two are of old rabbinic tradition: sodomy and castration. We have seen that nakedness is, in the Eden story, a metaphor for sexuality. We have also encountered sexuality in the form of miscegenation between demigods and humans, or the idea of such couplings resulting in a hybrid race of heroes, which features in one introduction to the flood story. It is not surprising therefore that scholars steeped in the biblical text should read an act of sexual outrage into Ham's abuse of Noah. One rabbinic interpretation of the perversity of all living creatures that brought on the Deluge is interspecies copulation. A story in which Ham, after the Flood, committed the kind of perverse act that had occasioned it would provide an ironic balance of prologue and epilogue. *Plus ça change, plus c'est la même chose.* Man remains man.

Further support for the possibility that the offense of Ham involved an illicit sexual act may be found in Leviticus 18. In this chapter, sexual relations between people who are variously related by blood or marriage are forbidden to the Israelites. Among the forbidden sexual relations are those with a woman to whom one's father had been married. To have relations with her is "to uncover his nakedness." Suggestive as this expression may be in itself, the most telling connection may lie in something here which has not been generally recognized. The sexual practices forbidden in this chapter are, for the most part, of a kind that were almost certainly congenial to ancient Israel's mores, and explicitly so to those of their neighbors. In introducing the now-to-be interdicted practices, YHWH says:

> The practices of the land of Egypt, where you have dwelt, you shall not practice. The practices of the land of Canaan, whither I am bringing you, you shall not practice. It is my norms you are to practice and my standards you are to follow with care. (Leviticus 18:3–4)

The norms and standards of the sexual practices of Egypt and Canaan, both of them descendants of Ham!

Despite the foregoing, I stand by my translation: not "what his unworthy son had done to him," but "how his unworthy son had treated him."[11] Ham need not have done anything at all to Noah. That is to say, nothing more than we are told he did. He stumbled upon his father in his nakedness by accident. He could have acted with the respect the situation called for, but he saw, and he told. His brothers refused to look, and managed to provide their father with cover. Given the power of the biblical taboo against the exposure of genitalia, of gazing upon the genitalia of those with whom one has close blood ties; given also the allegorical thrust of the story, the contrast in the behavior of Ham and his brothers in a matter of filial piety, the offense of Ham requires no further sharpening or elaboration. The clock of history had been turned back by the Deluge and its hands stopped. It has hardly begun to tick again when Ham's conduct reveals how barbarous a civilized son and a civilized sex ethos can be. Ham, the perpetrator of the act, is not punished in his person. His act is symbolic: a judgment has been made on the values of one of mankind's civilized branches, and the historic fact of one family reduced to subjection has been traced back to an ancestral transgression, to an inherited character defect, and to a father's curse.

THE TOWER OF BABEL: TEXT AND PREFACE

(1) The whole world shared a single language and common enterprise. (2) In the course of their migration in that time of yore they came upon a valley in the land of Shinar, where they settled down. (3) They said to one another, "Come now, let us make bricks and fire them hard." Bricks served them for stone and bitumen for cement. (4) "Come," they said, "let us build ourselves a city with a tower with its peak in the sky. So shall we make ourselves a name, against the prospect that we become scattered all over the world."

(5) YHWH came down to view the city and the tower that mankind was building. (6) YHWH thought, "Here now is one people, all with a single language, and this is only the first of their achievements; no bounds, henceforth, will confine their undertakings. (7) Come now, let us go down there and scramble their language so that they are no longer able to understand one another's speech." (8) And so YHWH did scatter them from there over all the world; and so they broke off the building of their city. (9) Hence was it named Babel, for there did YHWH make a babble of the world's [one] tongue; and from there did YHWH scatter them over the reaches of earth. (Genesis 11:1–9)

This narrative could hardly be more straightforward and cohesive. Yet scholars have found grounds to question the unity of even this tale; pointing out, for example, that in verse 5 YHWH has descended to earth to view the city, whereas in verse 7 he proposes to go down to earth to destroy it. And defenders of this tale's unity have shown themselves as literal-minded as its challengers; arguing that YHWH first came down to gather the facts for himself and then went back up to heaven, where he proceeded to pass judgment and sentence. Were the commentators consistent in ignoring the author's figurative use of language, they might raise a slew of additional questions, such as: Why does the story tell us that YHWH did indeed "come down" to scramble their language? And if he did not really need to "come down" to do so, why did he propose to "come down" to do so in the first place? And why did he have to "come down" to examine the city? Could he not see it just as well from his heavenly perch? For that matter, how did the author know what was going on in the mind of God? Did he receive this information in a revelation? If so, why does he not so reassure us?

The story line is simple enough. All mankind, descendants of Shem, Ham, and

Japheth, were at the time when this story begins a single kinship unit, speaking one language and determined on maintaining their solidarity. The setting of the story, the genealogy that precedes it in Chapter 10, and the genealogy that follows it in Chapter 11, makes this clear. (A comparison of the two genealogies in Chapter 7 of this volume reveals the story's framework.) In Chapter 10, the entire line of descendants of Noah is given except for one branch, that branch of Shem which continues through his middle son, Arpachshad. This line stops at Peleg ("Division"), for it was in his lifetime that the division of mankind and its dispersion began (10:25). After the manner of the division and dispersion is told in the Tower of Babel story, Chapter 11 resumes the line of Arpachshad and carries it down to the generation of Abram.

All the translations have this homogeneous humanity moving "from the east;" my own translation is more in keeping with the flavor of the story.[12] Arrived at this valley in Shinar, humanity foresees the centrifugal force of future propagations. As their numbers grow in future generations, no one place will hold them. Against that contingency they propose the tower-topped city as an expedient to "make themselves a name," an expression that—whatever else it may mean—must be related to preserving their unity, perhaps by marking for all future time this locus of their common origin. For a reason that is not given (explicitly, at least), YHWH is impressed enough by this human accomplishment to act now to prevent even greater accomplishments in the future. He therefore acts to disrupt their unity, which he achieves by making their one language into many. No longer able to understand one another, no longer able to pursue a common purpose, they leave their building project uncompleted. They disperse far and wide, to make up the separate groupings of the human race that are thrice characterized in the genealogies of Chapter 10, "according to their linguistic families in their national territories." There is thus an ironic symmetry between the purpose of the builders and the result of their efforts. They bring about the dreaded eventuality that they had aimed to forestall. Their single language becomes many, their one purpose is divided, their monument is left unfinished, the "name" they wished to make for themselves eventuates in their many and different names, and the dispersion they feared is brought to pass. Not by accident do we arrive at this moral-in-a-metaphor: "Man proposes, God disposes." Man rears his city heavenward; God—before He takes a hand in the matter—descends earthward. Twice, man's purpose is introduced in the cohortative of dialogue, "Come let us . . ." Only once does the same expression appear in the mouth of YHWH: "Come let us . . ." For man, there's many a slip betwixt cup and lip; for God, to propose is to do, or, to make metaphor literal, "no sooner said than done."

The most commonly accepted interpretation of this story as a whole is that it constitutes an etiology. I have discussed Gunkel's label in *Toward a Grammar* with particular reference to this story.[13] There I expressed my reasons for concluding that this particular example of literary explanation by means of a genre-label is inappropriate to the aims and competence of the biblical authors. If we knew nothing more of ancient Mesopotamia than what can be gleaned from the biblical references to its cities and cultures, we might never come close to guessing what it was that the author had in mind when he pictured man's ancient building enterprise as a city with a tower reaching heavenward, or why of all the possible cities that might be candidates for humanity's center of origin he picked Babylon. Fortunately, thanks to scholarly research, we may today draw on much information that was available to the Scriptural author who crafted this narrative.

MESOPOTAMIAN CONNECTIONS

Except for the placement of the garden of Eden between the Tigris and the Euphrates, nothing in chapters 1–11 is so explicitly Mesopotamian as the story of the Tower of Babel. No single narrative is more closely tied to so important a historic locus there, and none is so dense with authentic detail. First a review of the details.

Shinar is the biblical Hebrew rendering of the name that the non-Semitic forerunners of the Babylonians gave to the lower part of the plain between the two great rivers. *Shinar* is a closer approximation to that original name, which the Babylonians called *Shumer*, and which we pronounce *Sumer*. From the Sumerians the Semites of Babylonia and Assyria received the art of writing, and with it a considerable amount of Sumerian culture, including language, literature, and religious and political lore.

The name of the city that was built by Semites into an imperial capital, *Babil*, is almost certainly not Semitic. (We do well to remember that Semitic is a linguistic category only, referring to a family of languages or to people speaking one of these.) But *bab* in Akkadian means "gate" and *il* means "god." This happy coincidence was made to order for the prideful inhabitants of this ancient metropolis. Their city was indeed the center of the world, it was *Bab-ili* "Gate of the Gods," and in their writings they claimed the same meaning in the language of their Sumerian predecessors: KA·DINĜIR·RA.

Perhaps to evoke associations with sacred antiquity, a convention developed to name temple precincts and their lofty temple towers, the *ziqqurats*, in Sumerian; a convention that continued more than a thousand years after Sumerian had ceased to be a living language. (The Sumerian name for Marduk's sanctuary in Babylon was, for example, EN·TEMEN·AN·KI "Lordly Foundation of Heaven and Earth," the meeting-place, so to speak, of the realm of the gods and the world of mortal man.) Our biblical author, addressing an Israelite audience in its stone-rich land, must provide it with an explanatory aside (verse 3) when he faithfully reflects the fired-brick building materials of Mesopotamia's temples. This item appears in *Enuma elish*, which, as its translator E. A. Speiser has pointed out, must have been part of the inspiration of the author of the Tower of Babel story, the idea we find in *Enuma elish*. For though, as a matter of recorded chronicle, the building of Babylon's ziggurat was interrupted by an attack on the city, it is not the specific Ziggurat of Babylon, but rather the idea of it, that is reflected in the biblical story. When the gods propose to build a temple for Marduk in gratitude for his triumph, Marduk invokes as the model for his heavenly abode the Babylon whose very existence is only in the proposal stage:

> "Like that of *lofty* Babylon, whose building you have requested,
> Let its brickwork be fashioned. You shall name it 'The Sanctuary.' "

The Anunnakki applied the implement;
For one whole year they molded bricks.
When the second year arrived,
They raised high the head of Esagila equaling Apsu. (ANET p. 68 TAB.VI 57–62)

The Akkadian words, "they raised high the head of [the ziggurat] equaling Apsu," namely, "high up to the sky," is what yields the Sumerian name É·SAĞ·IL·A "the house with head raised high," and is behind the Hebrew in verse 4, "with a tower with its head in the sky."

Implicit in this Babylonian creation story—creation by Marduk, the tutelary god of Babylon—is the mythopoeic claim that Babylon is the senior, the chief if not the oldest of mankind's cities, its building already decreed by the gods at Creation's beginning. We say "mythopoeic claim," for our sources inform us that the Babylonians knew that theirs was not the most ancient of cities, as surely as the citizens of Rome knew that their Eternal City was not even a village when Troy fell to the Greeks. Let us recall Utnapishtim's words to Gilgamesh about his native city:

Shurippak—*a city which thou knowest* [italics mine]—
That city was ancient, the gods within it,
When their hearts led the great gods to produce the flood. (ANET p. 93 TAB. XI 11–14)

No, Babylon can claim no such comparable antiquity. But Babylon was old when some of the cities that served as royal capitals of imperial Assyria were having their foundations laid. Heir to the legendary first Semitic conqueror, Sargon of Akkad, Babylon was the cosmopolitan city of antiquity. Ruled in turn by Semitic Amurru (the great Hammurabi, for instance), non-Semitic Kassites (for more than five centuries), conquered by Semitic Assyria, reclaimed by a Chaldean dynasty, its fiercely independent priests still preserving the classic language and traditions of most ancient Shinar/Sumer, Babylon must indeed have been polyglot. What a babble of tongues must have resounded in the bazaars of this world trade-center!

This picture of Babylon—its name, Babil, lending itself to a pretentious claim to divine favor; its Hebrew name, Babel, lending itself to a pun featuring the Hebrew root B-L-L "to mix, confuse, scramble, confound"—seems to have been made to order for a storyteller in search of a center where mankind's one original language became many. And whereas Babel's polyglot population owed historically to varied-tongued rulers, the author of our story seems to take at face value the claim that this city was indeed mankind's point of origin, its first and—for a time—only city. Yet a perplexity remains. The explicit judgment of God on Babel and its builders is a denigration of this center; Babel is the target for scorn. But for the larger part of ancient Israel's history it was Assyria, not Babylon, that was Israel's most formidable enemy and tormentor. Babylon did not throw off Assyrian domination until the beginning of the sixth century. Until then (under the Chaldeans, or, as they are called, the neo-Babylonians), Babylon never figured as rival, adversary, or threat to Israel. Why would an Israelite author pick on Babylon several centuries (in all likelihood) before she replaced Assyria as imperialist conqueror; long, long centuries before she became the Great Whore of the Book of Revelation?

E. A. Speiser, the leading interpreter of Mesopotamian-Biblical connections, has suggested that behind the Tower of Babel story there may lie a lost Assyrian original.[14] In support of this conjecture we may invoke a historical analogue. Like the Roman conquerors to the Athenians and their brethren of Hellas, so were the Assyrian conquerors to the Babylonians whom they subjected: uncouth and uncultured, hillbilly Johnnies-come-lately, barbarian bullies presuming to hold sway over their elders and betters. Virgil's Aeneid betrays in its propaganda-plot the inferiority complex of a Rome which had taken its artistic and literary models from the Greece it had subjugated. Rome — so runs the argument of the Aeneid — was no upstart, its origins are ancient, its civilized heritage noble. Aeneas, ancestor of Rome and of its Augustus Caesar, was a refugee from Troy, a noble of ancient Ilium, whose topless towers were toppled by a horde of half-savage Greeks . . . Talk of cultural antiquity and poetic justice in history! Is there a clay tablet lying in the earth of northern Iraq, waiting the turn of archaeologist's spade, waiting deciphering to take its place in our consciousness alongside *Enuma elish* and Gilgamesh? A tablet in which an Assyrian poet tells a story? An Assyrian poet who knows that more than one Assyrian king was condemned in Assyria and was brought to grief by the gods of Assyria for becoming too cozy with the god of the Babylon he had conquered, and a story that ends in a pun and a sneer: *Bab-ili* "Gate of the Gods," indeed! No, not so, confounded by the gods: not Babel, but Babble!

BABEL IN ITS BIBLICAL SETTING

Speiser's hypothesis of a missing link is an example of imaginative scholarship that, while it must remain moot, does no violence to the text on which it seeks to shed light. And even were it open to refutation (which it is not, for how can one prove that something never existed) it would still be of value for sharpening our consciousness of the social and political issues that may be reflected in literary compositions, which thereby have a bearing on the history of a composition without affecting the question of its esthetic integrity. For whether there was or was not a Mesopotamian composition closer in theme to the Babel story than any of the traditions that have been preserved, and whatever the theme or function of such a composition, one thing is clear: The biblical author used Mesopotamian literary traditions freely, always adapting and deploying them in consonance with his overview of "Primeval History."

There are two other items featuring biblical texts and conjoining the names Babylon and Assyria. One is the (apparent) intrusion into the genealogy of Ham in Genesis 10 of quite a few names that belong with the Asshur, son of Shem, in verse 22. Although I will revert to the passage in connection with my discussion of the genealogies in this chapter, it is worth citing here:

> (8) Now Cush begot Nimrod, the first man-of-might on earth. (9) He was mighty in the hunt, by grace of YHWH, hence the saying, "Like Nimrod, by grace of YHWH a mighty hunter." (10) The chief cities of his realm were Babylon, Erech and Akkad, all of them in the land of Shinar. (11) From that land sprang Asshur. He built Nineveh,

Rehoboth-ir, Calah and Resen, between Nineveh and Calah, the latter being the major capital. (Genesis 10:8–11)

As we noted in regard to the Cush of Genesis 2:13, Speiser distinguishes between the Hebrew homonym for the people of Ethiopia and the Kassite (cuneiform *Kaššiu/Kuššū*; classical Greek *Kossaios*) dynasty, which held sway in Babylon from the seventeenth to the twelfth century. Of immediate interest to us is the mention of Babylon in the land of Shinar and the following observation, "from that land sprang Asshur," Asshur being a person identified as the builder of the known Assyrian capitals of Nineveh and Calah. Now the Babylon of the land of Shinar is, with Erech and Akkad, a chief city of the mighty hunter Nimrod. Briefly in his Genesis commentary (p. 72) and at greater length in "In Search of Nimrod,"[15] Speiser makes a case for identifying this Nimrod with Tukulti-Ninurta I, "certainly the first conqueror of Babylonia" and, like "the biblical Nimrod [who] is said to have combined effective authority over both Babylonia and Assyria . . . [is] the first Mesopotamian ruler to do so on a solid basis." Of especial interest to us is that for all his legendary conquests and "his celebrated building activities . . . [giving rise to] an epic extolling his exploits [which] is one of the literary legacies of Assyria," Tukulti-Ninurta I lost throne and life in an Assyrian insurrection. A chief cause of that uprising, or a principal factor cited by his kindred rebels, may well have been his over-favoring of the city he had conquered and of its god Marduk.

In a similar vein, the king who is taunted by the prophet Isaiah in Chapter 14 and who is identified only as the King of Babylon is no Babylonian at all, but the Assyrian master of Babylon, Sargon II. This great king, taking a throne-name that evokes the first Semitic conqueror, Sargon of Akkad, lost his life on a battlefield from which his troops were routed and his body never recovered. It is this disastrous fate, denial of burial and the dire consequences of such exposure for the shade of the unburied, to which Isaiah refers in his mocking of the conqueror.[16] And we know all this thanks to a cuneiform tablet in which Sargon's son, Sennacherib, inquires of Assyria's gods as to the nature of his father's sin, which led them to abandon him to such a fate. Once again, an Assyrian monarch judged as deficient in respect to Assyria's gods because he was overly attentive to the cosmopolitan city of Marduk.

For all the interest of the foregoing, with all its authenticated and nearly authenticated historic detail, it does not bear significantly on the interpretation of the Tower of Babel story. What is crucial for interpretation is the manner in which the biblical author deployed his material to achieve his mythopoeic expression of a crucial event in his fictive Primeval History.

No Assyrians appear in the story, nor, for that matter, do any Babylonians. Despite the tale's focus on the city of Babylon and its ziggurat, its echoes of that city's pride or vainglory, the personae of the tale are not Babylonians, not even Semites. They are, as we have seen, mankind as a whole, all the descendants of Noah in the three-branch line of his sons. They are still an extended family, at the most only five generations removed from Father Noah, sharing one language and—if our rendering in verse 1 of the Hebrew, which literally reads "single words, single things, single matter," is correct—a common purpose. That purpose is to take precaution

against the negative, divisive, disuniting consequences of humanity's spreading out
as it continues to propagate. That purpose is to be achieved by building a city with
a sky-scraping tower, an achievement that will somehow "make ourselves a name."
One meaning of this phrase is, as in English, "to establish a reputation." Another
sense of "name" is, by metonymy, a stele or monument, which is raised to keep a
name alive or in remembrance. And in a related and extended context, "to keep a
name going" is an expression for the continuing of a family line so that the ancestors may enjoy felicity in the afterlife, may thereby—in a manner of speaking—
gain immortality.

The crucial question is, however, what was the objection of YHWH to mankind's ambition in building the tower-topped city? Is it to man's longing for continuity that God objects, or is it to the means by which he seeks to achieve that
goal? Is it likely, for example, that in mythopoeic fashion we have here another attack on pagan religion, symbolized in the temple-architecture of the ziggurat? Our
answer is no: it is not very likely. For as the critique is of mankind and its ambition,
rather than of Babylonians and their ambition, so is the distinctive cultic element
notably absent here. The function of the tower as a ziggurat, a temple for worship,
is masked here to the point of unrecognizability. Hence it is unlikely that the critique is pointed at the cult system of Babylon in specific, or of Mesopotamia in general. (And nothing in the formulation of the narrative bears out the traditional interpretation, that the tower's builders were intent on a stairway to heaven, a
siege-tower from which they might launch an attack on God in his fortress.)

Imagery, however, lends itself to many uses. And what serves in an original context as emblematic of reverence and piety may be distorted to express an opposite
set of values. (Even as, by a reverse process, a name given in scornful derision—
Protestant, Quaker—may come to be worn as a badge of honor.) The Mesopotamian
ziggurat was no more an expression of human pride than the Temple of Solomon or
the vaulting Gothic cathedrals of Christendom. Both of these latter were expressions of awe before divine majesty and of a hope that Deity would grace such
earthly palaces with his presence. Similarly did the ziggurat, based on earth and
reaching heavenward, express the human aspiration to the gods and a prayer for
the gods' condescension to humankind. But the ziggurat did reach for the sky, and
such a symbol of humility could easily lend itself to interpretation as a sign of pride.
Perhaps a hint as to what was in our author's mind may be gleaned from Gilgamesh's address to Enkidu, as he seeks to overcome Enkidu's fear of confronting
Huwawa, the god-appointed guardian of the mountain-peak Cedar Forest:

> Who, my friend, can scale heaven?
> Only the gods live forever under the sun.
> As for mankind, numbered are their days;
> Whatever they achieve is but the wind! (ANET p. 79 TAB. III (iv) 5–8)

In this affirmation that permanence is an attribute of the divine, while the greatest
of man's achievements is as substantive and as stable as the wind; that since death
is inevitable, it makes no sense not to risk life for a heroic triumph; and in the
characterization of man's aspiration for permanence and immortality as an ambition "to scale heaven," we have a clue to our ancient author's vision of the ambi-

tion of the Tower's builders, and of why it was condemned and frustrated by God. The ambition to be one and not many, concentrated and not scattered, to secure some kind of permanence for human achievement—all this without recourse to God—is the biblical sin of Pride, what the Greeks called *hybris*.

"THE PRIMEVAL HISTORY": AN OVERVIEW

The biblical authors can be as specific and explicit as anyone else. Often they choose to be hyperbolic, especially in denouncing Israelite cultic practices they disapprove of in terms of apostasy and idolatry, or in characterizing moral lapses as willful rebellion against the God of Israel. In the eleven chapters of Genesis, in sketching the Primeval History of mankind, the shortcomings of humanity are, and deliberately so, broadly allusive. The names of cities and countries become ancestral figures in genealogical tables, the tables themselves become the framework for story plots that are as symbolic as the actors who figure in them. The genealogies in chapters 10 and 11 are totally consonant with one another, and serve the meat of the Tower of Babel story as slices of bread do in a sandwich. First comes the line of man until the time of the Tower. This line details the branchings of the lines of Shem, Ham, and Japheth even in the generations after the Great Dispersion symbolized in the frustration of the Tower's builders. This, except for the one line of Shem that ends in Peleg, he of the generation of the Great Dispersion. After the Babel story the second genealogy picks up again this one line of Shem, descending from one of Eber's two sons, Peleg, the line that ends with Abram. With Abram "the friend or lover of God" as he is called (Isaiah 41:8), the Primeval History ends and Israel's emergence into history begins. Abram, the intimate of God, will begin the religious family tradition of fidelity to the one God of Genesis 1 and to his will. Abram, as Genesis 12 shows God proclaiming, is the one through whom all mankind is to achieve blessing. Perhaps including the blessing of unity (under God), which was in the Primeval History disrupted by God because it was attempted without reference to or reckoning with that God. The symbolic force of the Babel story—like the reasons for the Bible's inclusion of the flood story or of Noah's nakedness—will stand out more clearly, and for all its allusiveness richer in dimension, if we consider it in terms of the form into which it fits, the pattern and context of the material preceding it. The first eleven chapters of Genesis can be outlined in a three-unit synopsis:

I. FOUNDATIONS OF THEOLOGY

A. The Creation Story—Focus on God: The Nature of Deity and Ultimate Reality: (Ch. 1:1–2:4a)
B. The Eden Story—Focus on Man: Death in a World Made for Man (Ch. 2:4a–4:16)
   History begins with Expulsion from Eden and the Atrocity of Fratricide

II. GOD INTERRUPTS HISTORY

A. Man's Genealogy Culminating in Noah (Ch. 4:17–5:32)
B. The Deluge—Its Causes and Aftermath (Ch. 6:1–9:29)
    History resumes with God's Tolerance and the Atrocity of Ham

III. PRIMEVAL HISTORY ENDS

A. Noah's Genealogy Culminating in the Generation of the Dispersion (Ch. 10:1–32)
B. The Tower of Babel and the Dispersion of Man (Ch. 11:1–9)
C. Noah's Genealogy through Shem Culminating in Abram (Ch. 11:10–32)
    Israelite History begins with God's Servant and His Promise

The pattern in this outline is as linear as an arrow: chapters 1–11 constitute an introduction to Chapter 12. The overall focus is on universal man in three successive phases of relationship to the source of Creation, the God of nature and history. Each of the phases begins on a note of high promise for humankind and ends on a note of humankind's failure:

I.   Mankind as the crown of creation, with its potential for majesty under God, chooses to be historic man and begins history with murder.
II. Mankind's second chance, in the line of Cain or Seth, fails of morality and is doomed by the Deluge, save for a third chance in the person of Noah.
III. Mankind's third chance, in the line of Noah, culminates in universal man's failure, the failure adumbrated in the licentiousness of the Hamite line and symbolized in the building of the Tower and God's sentence of dispersion. A fourth chance is implicit in the narrowing of the focus on the one line of Shem, through Eber, then Peleg, culminating in Abram, first of Israel's patriarchs.

It is as though God, having tried once, twice, and a third time with humankind as a whole, concludes that his hopes were too ambitious. He will start again, this time with one man and his family, one people, slowly emerging into history, perhaps to succeed where mankind as a whole has failed. Abram will have many descendants, but his chosen role as God's destined vessel, as the one line among so many, which may be an exemplar for all mankind's branches, will go from Isaac to Jacob, who becomes Israel.

Let all who will take this literally. The evidence is abundant in Scripture that there were many in the generations of Israel who took much of this literally, especially the pride and the privilege to the exclusion of the humility which becomes the servant, and its concomitant sense of noblesse oblige. And spokesmen of Scripture—be they fulminating prophet, legislating moralist, masterful storyteller, or architectonic editor—are nothing loathe to give this phenomenon its proper name: failure before God. The notion of man's creation in the divine image, perhaps even his descent from a common ancestor, can be traced to Mesopotamian myth.[17] Only in Scripture do we have this notion so underlined as to constitute one of its few universal dogmas. Mankind is one through Adam, Seth and Cain, and Noah. Through the seed of Abraham in the line of Israel it can realize its oneness once again. The Hebrew Bible sees the past as a chain of failures; it judges its continuing present in terms of the failures so ironic in the chosen line; and for all the many failures and the paucity of triumphs it does not—in the last analysis—ever give up on Israel, or the humanity whose protagonist Israel can yet, and ought to, be. The Hebrew Bible is the expression of Israel's self-consciousness of its place and role in the economy of the universe. This is to say, it is the expression of that self-consciousness on the part of Israel's best minds and best hearts. The heirs of that self-consciousness are those who make it their own. If this last has the ring of preachment, well, the Bible is a literature of preachment. The only question is whether the interpretation which rings of preachment resonates recognizably with the ring of Scripture's voice.

SIX

EVENTS IN THE LIFE
OF ABRAHAM

ABRAM THE NOBLE WARRIOR

Biblical discourse is discursive (and it is so to a remarkable degree). What keeps the first clause of this sentence from constituting a tautology is the odd difference in the nuances of the noun and adjective. Whereas the *running to and fro* (of the original and literal Latin) conveys in the noun the sense of logical and consecutive speech or thought, in the adjective there is a strong sense of discontinuity or digression. One exemplary aspect of the discursiveness of biblical discourse is reflected in the "stories and structures" in this volume's subtitle. There are many other aspects of this (literary) phenomenon in addition to alternation of forms and genres, such as perspectival shifts in consecutive narratives hingeing on changes in identities of implied author, more-or-less reliable or omniscient narrator, and variably sophisticated implied audience.

Genesis 12–15, the first four chapters centered on the patriarch Abram, present several examples of thematic continuity interrupted by generally inapposite narratives, which could with artistic benefit have been inserted elsewhere in the chronicle of the patriarch's career. One can readily see, therefore, how inviting this would be to source criticism (or any genetic approach to the text that is undisturbed by the intervention of the incompetent editor), and—at the opposite pole—how challenging to a poetic reading (which cannot by its nature concede incapacity or inadvertence on the part of either editor or author). The way of the critic is not, however, the way of the artist, nor that of the commentator. We shall therefore in our treatment of the material in these four chapters reserve the adventures of Sarah and Abram in Egypt for treatment later in connection with other romances of the triangular modality, defer the consideration of the opening revelation in Chapter 12 so as to treat it together with the other narratives featuring divine revelations and promises, and begin Abram's career in media res with the egregious Chapter 14.

The characterization of this chapter as egregious owes to the antonymous connotations of the word, *standing out from the herd*, in the sense of "distinguished" in the original Latin, and in English, "like a sore thumb." The following citation from Speiser is a fair summation of the view of critical scholarship:

> Genesis xiv stands alone among all the accounts in the Pentateuch, if not indeed in the Bible as a whole. The setting is international, the approach impersonal, and the narration notable for its unusual style and vocabulary. . . . On one point the critics are virtually unanimous: the familiar touches of the established sources of Genesis are absent in this instance. For all these reasons the chapter has to be ascribed to an isolated source . . . it is [the successful] exploit by Abraham, in the otherwise unfamiliar role of a warrior, that evidently led to the inclusion of the chapter with the regular patriarchal material in Genesis. . . . The date of the narrative has been variously estimated. . . . A fresh re-examination of all the available scraps of evidence, both internal and external, favors an early date, scarcely later in fact than the middle of the second millennium.[1]

Speiser's well-earned repute as philologian, linguist, Semitist, and cultural historian has not lost luster in the three decades since his demise. It is the more remarkable then that his fine-tuned ear and perceptive sight and insight could be so dulled by the blandishments of source-critical literary science. Except for a single syntactic and idiomatic anomaly in the opening clause of this *account* (to use Speiser's telltale word for narrative) there is not a single item of style or vocabulary that is unusual; if anything, the style is classic biblical Hebrew. The inability of documentarists to discern traces of J, E or P in this passage entitles it to status as a unique "document" (labeled X by Speiser); a document in which we can read the translation into Hebrew (bad Hebrew, to be sure) of an Akkadian text that was incorporated into Genesis because the editor, presumably, was so thrilled to find attestation in a foreign source of the historicity of an ancestor of whose career he is himself the historian. As for the dating of a literary text (rather, snippet of a literary text) to a half-millennium earlier than the earliest of its documentary companions, why this is just further indication of that measurability that is a critical hallmark of science!

Let us proceed to the examination of the text:

> (1) In the time of Amraphel king of Shinar, Arioch king of Ellasar, Chedorlaomer king of Elam and Tidal king of Goiim—(2) they waged war with Bera king of Sodom, and Birsha king of Gomorrah, Shinab king of Admah and Shemeber king of Zeboim and the king of Bela (that is Zoar). (3) All these gathered in alliance in the Vale of Siddim (that is the Salt Sea). (4) Twelve years had they been subject to Chedarlaomer, and in the thirteenth year rose in rebellion. (5) And in the fourteenth year Chedarlaomer arrived and the kings his allies. They defeated the Rephaites in

Ashteroth-qarnaim, and the Zuzites in Ham, and the Emim in Shaveh-Qirytaim (6) and the Horites in their hill-country Seir—as far as El-paran which is at the steppe border. (7) Turning about they came to En-mishpat (that is, Qadesh) and battered the Amalekite steppe-land as well as the Amorites settled around Hazazon-tamar.

(8) The king of Sodom sallied forth, and the king of Gomorrah, and the king of Admah, and the king of Zeboim, and the king of Bela (that is, Zoar) and arranged for battle with them in the vale of Siddim, (9) namely, with Chedarlaomer king of Elam, and Tidal king of Goiim, and Amraphel king of Shinar, and Arioch king of Ellasar, four kings against the five. (10) (The Vale of Siddim **now** was pocked with bitumen pits.) They—the king of Sodom and Gomorrah—were routed. There fell there [many] casualties, while the survivors fled to the hill country. (11) They [the invaders] took all the wealth of Sodom and Gomorrah, all their food store, and departed. (12) They took Lot and his wealth, the son of Abram's brother and departed, he **now** living in Sodom.

(13) There came an escapee and told Abram the Hebrew—he **then** abiding at the Oaks of Mamre the Amorite, kinsman of Eshkol and kinsman of Aner, they being Abram's confederates. (14) When Abram heard that his kinsman had been taken captive he unsheathed his shock troops, his home-born slaves eighteen and three hundred [in number], and made pursuit all the way to Dan. (15) Separating into two forces against them at night, he and his slaves, he attacked them and pursued them all the way to Hobah which is north of Damascus. (16) He recovered all the property—and also his kinsman Lot and his property did he recover—and the women and the [rest of the] people as well.

(17) The king of Sodom came out to meet him, upon his return from defeating Chedarlaomer and his allied kings, to the Vale of Shaveh (that is, the King's Vale).

(18) **Now** Melchizedek king of Salem brought out bread and wine—he, that is, priest to El Elyon—(19) He greeted him as follows, "Blessed be Abram by El Elyon, creator of heaven and earth. (20) And praised be El Elyon [the god] that has delivered your enemies into your power." To him he gave a tenth-part of everything.)

(21) The king of Sodom said to Abram, "Let me have the humans, the material property keep for yourself." (22) Said Abram to the king of Sodom, "My hand have I raised [in oath] to YHWH-El Elyon, creator of heaven and earth. (23) That not thread nor shoelace, nothing whatsoever of your belongings will I keep, lest you ever think, It is I that made Abram rich: (24) Nothing for me except for my lads' expenses . . . and the shares owing to those who campaigned at my side, Aner, Eshkol and Mamre—they are to keep their shares." (Genesis 14:1–24)

More than any other factor—perhaps more than all other factors combined—making for difficulty and perplexity to the modern Bible scholar is the presumption of historiographic intent on the part of the biblical author. Once we grant Scripture's authors the same freedom we do to today's writers of historical romances, the freedom to blend documented persons and events with legendary motifs in a mélange in which the predominating element is pure invention, it is wondrous how so many problems simply fall away.[2]

More than a case in point, a parade example rather, is this Chapter 14. Long before Speiser, scholars were impressed by the authenticity of the names of kings and places from Mesopotamia on the one hand and, on the other, the indicators that the collocation of these names and their collaboration in an expedition on southern Palestine presents a historical absurdity. Speiser himself confessed to his students that his speculation that copper was the tribute so needed in Mesopotamia was a desperate way to account for what looked like the resources of a mighty empire being mustered to reduce a few barns in a hardscrabble farmland. As incongruous as the image invoked in this simile is, and fittingly so, its appositeness holds only for the Dead Sea landscape that meets our eyes today (and so met the eyes of the biblical author's contemporaries). But this landscape was not the one seen and chosen for himself by Lot when, as told in the preceding Chapter 13, he parted with Uncle Abram, "Lifting his eyes (to the horizons) Lot beheld the stretch of the Jordan's valley, so very richly watered—'twas [remember] before YHWH's devastation of Sodom and of Gomorrah—like YHWH's own garden, like the land of Egypt, from Zoar onwards." And the cities of that lush legendary plain must have been rich, populous and walled, like all those which, over some five centuries, fell to one or another imperial conqueror from Mesopotamia until that tide swept over Egypt itself in the reign of the Chaldean king of Babylon, Ashurbanipal.

All the five cities of the plain are legendary; two of them, Admah and Zeboim, are proverbial elsewhere in Scripture for sharing the fate of Sodom and Gomorrah. The fifth exists as a place name in the time of monarchical Israel, on the fringe of the Negeb steppe. And it is another aspect of the whimsy the biblical author permits himself that in Chapter 14 he pictures Zoar under the name Bela as one of the five cities facing up under its own (unnamed) king to the Empire in the East; while in Chapter 19, Lot, in escaping the fate of Sodom, asks that he be permitted safe haven in Zoar, punning on the stem *ẓr* "small, tiny." Presumably in asking that a spot scheduled for overthrow be spared—"after all, it is such an insignificant place"—he is referring to a settlement rather than a spot within a hypothetical boundary. And this settlement, if settlement it is, survives into centuries later. Perhaps its population turned over a new leaf some time after the sulfurous tide lapped almost to its borders, but not immediately, for Lot, "fearing to remain in Zoar," takes to a cave in the hill country with his two daughters. The possibility that Zoar had no population in Lot's time would seem to be supported by the rationalization of Lot's daughters for cohabiting with him, "there being nary a one on earth to come upon us in the normal way of the world" (19:31). But if there were no men to fear in little Zoar then why did Lot withdraw into the highlands? Did he fear that the Deity who had saved his family alone might yet relent of his gracious resolve, might yet extend the rising waters of the Salt Sea? That sea which in 14:3, our narrator informs us, is identical with what was, in those Edenic days, the Vale of Siddim, that is, "Vale of Pits." Here too we are treated to an anachronistic reversal that could only be intentional. The Salt Sea area known today for its minerals might today lay claim to the name Valley of Lime(-deposits), in Hebrew *Emeq Hassiddim*, which name it bore in pre- fire-and-brimstone days. But in those days some part of that plain was pocked with pits of bitumen, a relative of the petroleum so absent from the area, to the chagrin of the polities that are its newest owners. Just what role, if any, these pits played in connection with the battle is a question as yet unanswered. The notion, advanced by Speiser and accepted by the New Jewish

Publication Society (NJPS), that the defeated kings flung themselves into tar pits to hide from their pursuers, evokes an image so ludicrous as to warrant more support than the text provides for the possibility that this too is a result of the author's whimsy.

But whimsy is clearly at play in the names of the five kings. Most notably in the absence of any name whatsoever for the king of (Zoar = Insignificance =) *Bela'* "swallow up, destroy." But also in the long-recognized stems for "evil" (*r'*) and "wicked" (*rš'*) in the names of the kings of Sodom and Gomorrah. The authenticity of the names in the Mesopotamian coalition serving to reinforce the philologian's concern for historicity, it is only to be expected that such scholars would hardly allow that a creative author's whimsy might account for the following anomalies in respect to these items: 1) the dating of a historic event to the lifetime of four kings rather than one; 2) the heading of that list by Amraphel of Shinar (= Babylonia) in verse 1, while in verses 4–5 it is twice asserted that it is Chedarlaomer who is the liege-lord and the other kings his vassals; 3) the feature of the introductory *biymē* "in the days of" or "when," which Speiser finds "unacceptable by normal Heb. [syntactic] standards." (His solution of this last problem by recourse to a hypothetical translation of an Akkadian conjunction is linguistically unnecessary and improbable.)[3]

In the supposed strangeness of this Chapter 14 which, untraceable to the canonical sources J, E, and P, must constitute a source in itself because, being historiographic or legendary, it cannot be the work of the biblical author; in the unique status assigned to it by source-biblical criticism, there are overlooked a number of congruities and concordances with the Pentateuchal picture of the patriarchal age, and with the conventions of warfare obtaining during the centuries of Scripture's composition, beginning with the Assyrian irruption into Aram-Syria, and continuing through the Neo-Babylonian conquest of Egypt and the Persian succession to that imperialist tradition of Mesopotamia.

Of the population stocks in the area over which Israel later claimed sovereignty or vital influence, the oldest stratum, superseded by the Israelites under Moses or even earlier by Israel's kinsmen, included the legendary Rephaites (sometimes associated with the Anak titans), a few of their descendants surviving in Philistia into Davidic times. In this stratum too belonged Amorites, who founded kingdoms such as those of Og in Bashan and Sihon of Heshbon in trans-Jordan; the Emim, predecessors of the Moabites (related to the gigantic Anakites and Rephaites in Deuteronomy 2:10–11); the Zamzummim, a name given to their Rephaite predecessors by their Ammonite conquerors (Deuteronomy 2:20); the Avvim, displaced by the Philistines; and the Horites ("cave dwellers") in the hill country of Seir before the arrival of the Edomites. All of these, except for the Avvim on the Gaza coastland, are situated in the trans-Jordanian area from the northern highlands to the southern terminus, the Dead Sea and south-southwest of that terminus. All of these peoples (equating the *zzm* with the *zmzmm*) are victims of the Mesopotamian sweep, that is, Emim, Zuzim, Hori, Rephaites, and Amorites. Three other Amorite kinsmen are chieftains in the vicinity of Hebron, and allied with Abram (the *Hebrew*; what other gentilic might have been applied to Abram, given the gentilic company he was keeping?). The kings of the five Cities of the Plain are not identified as to stock, as the Mesopotamian kings are not, and while we are welcome to speculate on this question it is of no particular importance for the narrator.

The campaign conducted by the invaders is in keeping with the imperial strategy of the period of Israelite monarchy. The warfare carried on by Israel in the time of Joshua and the Shofetim (as also, implicitly, by her agnate tribesmen of Ammon, Moab, and Edom) is pictured as one for Lebensraum, requiring the supplanting of an indigenous population. The imperial wars of the Mesopotamians, by contrast, was to expand dominion over territories which might be milked of yearly tribute as economically as possible. Thus in the first stages of invasion the farm and timber lands, mines and trade-routes, and unwalled settlements were ravaged and pillaged with the aim of persuading the ruler of the city-state to accept a vassalage that left his city's walls intact. Recalcitrant polities might resist such depredations for several years, until their cities were laid under siege. When a polity had been so reduced to vassalage, rebellion was constituted by the withholding of tribute. So in the case of the Cities of the Plain, which withheld tribute in the thirteenth year of subjection and were forced to meet retaliation in the fourteenth.

Our biblical narrator, unconcerned as ever with historiographic detail, leaves us to speculate on the decision of the five kings to hazard field-warfare against their erstwhile overlord. (Here too whimsy may be in play in the choice of an Elamite king to head the Mesopotamian coalition, for Elam—for many centuries foe of Babylon—never figured as threat to any other hegemony, let alone the Syro-Palestinian territories.) Perhaps it was the small size of the force from the east that emboldened the kings of the Plain. In any case they were trounced, the survivors fleeing to the hill country. And the victors would have been free to deal with the cities, their walls now so thinly defended. There is no mention of siege or parley, nor is Sodom taken by storm. Yet the ability of the victors to abscond with "all the wealth and food stores of Sodom and Gomorrah" would seem to indicate that the invaders were able to exact from the cities' defenders, if not a reinstitution of allegiance and the yearly tribute, at least a considerable prize of valuables, and enough rations to see them safely back to home base. Among the prizes yielded to the invaders were humans, for enslavement or ransom. And among the latter it is not surprising that the Sodomites would include the alien Lot and his family among those surrendered.

This first episode is, on the whole, syntactically and stylistically unexceptionable by the canons of biblical narrative even to the element of *gapping*; for example, the omission of military details of the war. In part this omission can be remedied by the imagination of any reader who is conversant with the nature of warfare in the biblical world. To that extent then, it is exemplary of the Bible's *narrative economy or thrift*.[4] In part, however, it reflects the biblical author's mastery of perspectival leverage. Like ninety-nine percent of biblical narrative, related in that matter-of-fact manner that bespeaks the modality of history—real people caught up in real events in a real past—the "account" in Chapter 14 requires the realistic elements that will command the attention of the serious reader. (Needless to say, serious readers in antiquity, as today, would not consider fictive art worthy of their study.) To that end therefore, the author of Chapter 14 begins his narrative as an independent chronicle: "Now it happened in the [regnal] time of . . ." This without any transition from the history of its one hero Abram, who in the immediately preceding verse was engaged in building yet another altar to the God named YHWH, under whose protection he moves through a historic landscape as though it were an unpeopled continent. (Little wonder that geneticists find no room for this chapter in their register of sources, strata, or documents.) The concern for historicity or a facsimile thereof is, of course, present in the place names of the east-of-Jordan plain and the Negev-Sinai area to the south and west of the Dead Sea. So also in the verisimilitudinous names from Mesopotamia and the repetition of the royal names on both sides in verses 8–9, "four kings against the five" (although proper syntax calls for the unartistic "five kings against the four"). Realism and historicity are at one end of the seesaw, while at the other end are the countervailing elements of fantasy that we have noted: the whimsy in the names of the kings of Sodom and Gomorrah and of the anonymous king of a settlement, which in the narrator's time is called *Insignificance* but was then known as *Gulp*; in the legendary autochthonous titans (the Rephaim) who are so surprisingly vulnerable to Lilliputian invaders; in assigning command of the imperial forces to the farthermost eastern power which, never itself an intrusive force in the west, was powerful and aggressive enough to periodically distract the rulers of Assyria and Babylonia from their imperial preoccupations with the western lands.

The second episode, beginning with Abram's learning of his nephew's capture by a marauding host of the Empire in the East, also displays the badly balanced elements of historiographic realism and historically incongruous plotting. The fugitive from the war on the Plain who tells the tale of the war to Abram arrived from where? The term for him *pāliṭ* denotes a person escaped from a general disaster, hence the impression that he was one of the defeated army who escaped to the hill-country in the north, making his way ultimately to Hebron. But were that the case he would have had no knowledge of the negotiations between the victorious generals and the defenders of Sodom's walls, and—crucially—the information that Lot, Abram's kinsman, had been handed over to the withdrawing army. Nor would he have known when that withdrawal began, nor the route of the retreating army. The important thing of course is that Abram learn of his kinsman's capture; the rest he can figure out for himself. It must be presumed that Abram knew of the twelve-year subjection of the plain cities to the Empire in the East; nor would it appear strange to him that that lush country and its opulent cities (chosen for himself by the ungenerous Lot) would draw the loot-hungry empire to the neglect of the much poorer hill country west of the Jordan. So too would he have known that the invasion route would have been the King's Highway east of the Jordan, and so also the route of the withdrawal. He himself would have made a forced march through the central highlands, cutting across at some point to head off the imperial force near the Jordan's headwaters in the northernmost of later Israel's tribal land, Dan. Here too the route of the invaders and the pursuit from Damascus to Hobah supposes that this area could be made into a no-man's-land without inviting the intervention of its powerful city-states. The most factitious event in this second episode is the seemingly inapposite appearance of Melchizedek, king of [Jeru]salem. How and why would this king have climbed down to the Jordan and crossed it at one of its fords to greet Abram at King's Vale (which every one knows, though not by its former name, *Level Valley*)?

The stylistic normality of our narrative breaks down at the transition point between the two episodes. Two verses tell of the taking of booty from Sodom and the taking of Lot as part of that booty. Instead of one sentence with a hypotactic clause following the main one, we have two remarkably and awkwardly similar paratactic sentences:

VERSE 11	VERSE 12
They took all the property of Sodom and Gomorrah and all their victuals and went off. (Genesis 14:11)	They took Lot and his property the nephew of Abram, and went off. (He **now** was residing in Sodom) (Genesis 14:12)

There can be no doubt that the repetitive parataxis is deliberate, designed in part at least to draw our attention to two clumsy constructions in verse 12, first the unnecessary interposition of "his property" between Lot and the appositional phrase "the nephew of Abram," and then the hypotactic clause on Lot's residence in Sodom coming after, rather than where it belongs, before the verb whose subject is the invaders: "and they went off." A comparison with the normal and proper syntax of verse 16 will reveal that verse 12 would normally have read as follows: wᵉgam 'et lōṭ ben-ᵃḥī 'abrām urᵉkūšō lākāḥū wᵉhū' yōšeb bisdōm "also Lot, Abram's nephew, and his property did they capture—he (at that time) being resident in Sodom."

What does the narrator achieve by his departure from normative style and syntax? For one thing he suggests the avaricious character of Lot, and this by Lot's self-perception in what Meir Steinberg terms *implied free indirect discourse*. Abram's nephew is not Lot the man, nor Lot and his family, but Lot with his possessions; without his wealth he is nothing. So too with the parenthetic note of his residence, placed where it will occasion remark. It is not that without this explicit information we would be at a loss to bridge the gap for ourselves. But Lot, the wealthy cattleman, his herd and flocks tended by servants on the rich ranges of the Plain, himself with family and coffers enjoys the security of the walls of Sodom, that plutocratic city where even hospitality may be had for a price. All the more ironic that his secure haven became the trap and that together with the wealth that won him guest-status he be among those surrendered by his hosts to force majeure. Note, too, how artfully in verse 16 Lot and his property are sandwiched in between the booty belonging to Sodom proper, and in a list that reflects Sodom's values, beginning with material wealth, continuing with wives and daughters, and ending with the male rabble destined for enslavement: "He recovered all the property—and also his kinsman, Lot and his property did he recover—and the women and the rest of the people as well."

All these are fine touches. But the function of the two paratactic sentences in verses 11 and 12 are revealing in respect to the author's artistic control. It was remarked earlier that Chapter 14 begins with an abrupt turning away from the story of Abram. And so the independent, historic, and essentially neutral account of a campaign in which sympathy of neither narrator nor reader is engaged continues until its end in verse 11. This now is followed by an alternative ending in verse 12, not so much an ending as a prolepsis of the action in the next verse 13; a sentence that says in effect, everything that has been told up to this point is of no moment to us. We should never have reproduced it here but for one tiny matter, trivial alike to kings of the Plain and imperial earth-shakers: among the booty there was included a fateful victim, but for whom the withdrawing legions would have returned home unscathed. That victim the nephew of Abram, generous as his nephew is greedy, loyal to kith and kin as his nephew is opportunist and unconcerned deracinate.

An escapee came and told Abram. What he told Abram is not stated. The time factor is nowhere present in the narrative: how long the sweep through the Rephaite plains took, how long the battle in the field, how long the haggling between the invaders threatening siege and Sodom's defenders weighing that prospect and the cost of buying off the predators. An army laden with booty, textiles and precious metals, cattle and humans, with no reason to suspect the possibility of pursuit, will travel at a leisurely pace. Perhaps Abram learned from runners dispatched to Sodom that the invaders had broken camp, departing with tribute wrested from the city; that report included the one bit of information of interest to Abram. "When Abram heard that his *kinsman* (*āḥiw* "his brother"), not his *nephew* (*ben 'āḥiw* "his brother's son") had been taken captive, he unsheathed the weapon he drew so rarely, his *ḥᵃnīkīm*. The root of this noun, appearing only here, informs on its meaning. It is the root of the name of the exemplary antediluvian Enoch, appears in Scripture with the sense of "dedicate, train, or educate," and far more frequently in later Hebrew with these meanings. The number of these home-born slaves, drilled for battle and passionate in their master's service, was a formidable force in those days (compare Gideon's 300). Were such a contingent less than credible, as against the host from Mesopotamia, the author-narrator who might, as in so many other instances in Scripture, have had recourse to God working on the patriarch's side, opts instead for a more "realistic" factor, the armed might of Abram's three allied Amorite chieftains. The way in which the participation of these three allies is first anticipated, then, omitted, and finally confessed, is instructive as an example of the gapping strategy, and particularly in relation to the play of perspective.

The identification of Lot as "son of Abram's brother" in verse 12 was earlier characterized as proleptic of the introduction of that Abram in verse 13. A few sentences back we stressed the reference in verse 13 to Lot as Abram's kinsman, rather than his nephew. To this we now add the observation that this *reference* is an allusion, not an identification; for the name Lot is pointedly absent in this verse. What makes this doubly interesting is that the explicit featuring of the name in this context would have a caritative effect. Yet this opportunity for stressing the sense of endearment by the insertion of the three-letter name is passed up, even as the allusion to Lot by means of the term *brother/kinsman* is more resonant of endearment than the more specific yet one-degree-removed "brother's son/kinsman's son." Perspective is what is at play here, as it was in "Lot and his property, the nephew of Abram" in verse 12. There the perspective is that of the narrator, overlain, so to speak, or better perhaps read by the narrator onto the self-image of Lot by the device of free indirect discourse. Here in verse 13, the narrator's perspective is read onto Abram's self-consciousness in reference to the unnamed Lot. Unnamed because Abram has no particular reason to cherish or esteem this nephew, who could not or would not restrain his cattle-hands in their quarrels with Abram's hands, this despite the danger of divisiveness in the face of the far more numerous natives, the Canaanites and Perizzites (13:7). Yet Abram is ready to risk everything to rescue; not a nephew, deserving or not, but a kinsman for whom ethos and ethics preclude a denial of responsibility.

The focus is on Abram and his readiness to act. We have been alerted in the previous verse that he is allied to three Amorite chieftains. We have every right to assume that in his pursuit of and assault upon a superior force he would have called upon his allies. But to keep the focus on Abram, to suggest that had he no allies it would have made no difference in his resolve, the allies are not even mentioned at a second opportunity in verse 15. And were he taxed with this omission, the narrator could point to the description for the pincers attack by night in verse 15. The separation of the attacking party into two forces we translated by *he and his slaves*. But the last word can also be servants, followers, vassals, and therefore apply even to the allied forces under his command.

The enemy completely routed, the allied forces now returning at a pace slowed by the recovered goods and captives, word would have been sped to Hebron and Sodom about the success of the mission; else the king of Sodom could not know that the returning host was retracing the invasion route, east of the Jordan. We shall hold in abeyance consideration of verses 18–20 a parenthetic aside marked by the hypotactic construction signaled by the nominal clause that begins verse 18. Upon meeting up with Abram at some point in Level Valley, later to be known as King's Vale, the King of Sodom—presumably after congratulations have been exchanged (as in the intervening parenthesis)—makes Abram an offer. "Let me have the captives [lit., the living (entities)] and the [material] property keep for yourself." We do not know the ancient protocols governing war and peace, the sharing of loot, the restoration of spoil to the despoiled by a third party that had spoiled the despoilers.[5] Chances are that might determined policy then as today and, given the forewarning of the character of Sodom's magistrates in 13:13 as reinforced in Chapter 19, we have no reason to assume that the offer was a generous one. The king of Sodom has been defeated in battle, his army scattered, his city pauperized, and he is in no position to haggle with the victors, whose motives in the pursuit were anything but mercenary. That being the case, it is likely that the victors might have claimed, if only as a debt for future repayment, the ransom value of the captives extorted from Sodom (and presumably, its sister cities). Just as the king of Sodom represents the other defeated kings who survived, so now—as before— Abram is pictured as the sole commander-in-chief, free to dispose as he wills of the prizes he has won. No further mention is made of Lot. Given the character drawn of Abram, no charge was laid on Lot for his freedom and that of his family, nor for the property restored to him. But Lot is kinsman, and not, as we shall learn a few chapters later on, party to the depraved ethos of his Sodomite hosts. The king of Sodom, however, is neither kin nor kith. Abram owes him nothing. All the more interesting then is Abram's statement that he has foresworn (literally) any profit at the king of Sodom's expense. One question we shall soon consider is why Abram takes an oath when a simple "no, thank you" would have sufficed. A second question is why the hyperbole as to the degree of abnegation. The merism for any part of any garment (cloth or leather, i.e., "thread or lace") is utterly at home in biblical Hebrew, but why this "by so much as a hair" when the reason is so that he, king of Sodom, may have no cause "to muse/say, it is I who have made that Abram rich"?

This bit of direct discourse attributed to Abram is liable to several constructions on the part of the reader. One, and the least likely for its picturing of an arrogant Abram jeering at a rival in his misfortune, is: "I want neither your riches nor your envy." A second construction would picture Abram as less confident, and even fearful of a Sodom that has recovered its former strength, "I'll not give you occasion to dream of recovering by force what was torn from you and ended, unfairly to your narrow mind, in my possession." This interpretation is much closer to the reassurance offered by YHWH in the very next chapter, two verses later. The fear that YHWH is addressing in Abram is, as Rashi understood, retaliation on the part of parties injured in the recently concluded hostilities. But even this construction is less than fully congruent with Abram's concluding words to Sodom's king. Starting with the word *bil'āday* "nothing for me," as correctly and for the first time translated by Speiser, Abram reiterates his abnegation, but in what follows he disabuses his hearers of any notion that his own renunciation of profit means no loss to Sodom. While he passes up his *shares* in the loot, he is not so silly as to reject recompense for the expense the campaign has cost him. Literally, "save for what my lads have eaten," for the lads (Hebrew definite article often serving for the possessive pronoun) he has in mind, being slaves, receive no shares of their own. Finally he concludes with the item that incidentally fills in the gap noted earlier (on the matter of his allies' participation in the campaign), that his allied chieftains—named again to heighten their importance and thereby to suggest that these shares must be substantial—must receive the full bounty fairly owing to them.

The gapping that we discussed does not seem particularly vital (in terms of narrative strategy); it could have been avoided by the insertion of two words *ubaᵃaley-bᵉrītō* "and his allies" in verse 14 after the number of his own troops. But this detail having been omitted, there does not seem to be any compelling poetic need to close the gap; as for example, there is no closing of the gap in regard to the treatment or disposition of expenses or bounty shares in respect to Lot and to his twice-mentioned property (taken in verse 12, recovered in verse 16). If, further, this spelling out in detail of what Abram will or will not accept for himself, of what he in fact demands for his allies (whose recompense it was certainly not in his prerogative and probably not in his power to forego), is in the interest of precluding hostile designs on the part of Sodom, then we should have to judge the narrative's ending as an anticlimax, and a very unfunny one at that.

This leads us to consider a third way of construing Abram's oath to forego profit but not expenses for himself, and neither the one or the other for his allies. *That you cannot say, it is I who have made Abram rich* is equivalent to rejecting what in economics or games-theory is called zero-sum thinking; here: *your gain is my loss.* Every system is closed, every plus is balanced by a corresponding minus and vice versa. It is such a view of reality that Abram is rejecting, and not for its entertainment by the king of Sodom, but for its entertainment by any and every reader of this story. And to that end our narrator resorts to the gapping strategy at the beginning of the pursuit so that he can close the gap at the story's ending. The entire story is an example of what Meir Sternberg has demonstrated again and again for the multi-partied, frequently separated, often overlapping play of perspectives in relation both to literary artistry and the reality that the Scriptural artist explores in the postulations of his ideological narrative. One of the perspectives that Sternberg frequently identifies is God's. He is totally absent from this narrative except for being invoked in the parenthesis we have yet to consider, once in praise and once in oath. We have the perspective of the narrator, sometimes speaking for himself in omniscient and not to be questioned judgment, as for example, in the names he gives the kings of Sodom and Gomorrah; sometimes in (implied) free indirect discourse, as in the self-images of Lot and Abram; sometimes as uninvolved reporter who, in merely recording the direct discourse of a king of Sodom or an Abram, permits the reader a direct, unmediated perception of the perspective(s) of each of these personae. There are also other perspectives, that of the implied reader whose perspectival sympathy may coincide in part or totally with any of the aforementioned ones, and who may possibly be won over to the moral view that is the kerygma or preachment of the narrative.

The moral economy of the universe, in the minds of most people—Lot, the king of Sodom, Abram's Amorite allies, and (most of the time) you and me—is zero-sum in nature. A review of the contrast between pagan and Scriptural theology drawn in Chapter 2 will bear out, I believe, this additional distinction: In paganism, the immanence of the gods in the same sphere as humankind (and other life forms) renders them co-contestants with humanity in the zero-sum game of life. In biblical religion, that sphere—absent autonomous divinities—is the creation of God, and the limits of its blessings are infinitely expandable or contractible by the will and decree of that God. Earth can be one Edenic garden, as was "the entire Jordan plain so thoroughly watered—before YHWH's laying waste of Sodom and Gomorrah—like YHWH's own garden" (13:10), or it can be like the barrens around the Salt Sea after that action. So now the affirmation of Abram that he will not allow credit for his prosperity to the fickle fortunes of war. Whatever material goods he is possessed of are the dispensations of the God who uprooted him from Mesopotamia, promising him great blessing (12:1–3), who by his intervention on behalf of this vulnerable alien in the land of Egypt arranged his escaping with his life, his wife, and, in addition, "herds and flocks and jackasses, male and female slaves, and jenny asses and camels" (12:16). Others may attribute their gains to their own wit or prowess or even to chance, the luck of the draw. Not so Abram. And so it is that his affirmation to the contrary, in respect to his own condition—he will not speak for others—is expressed in an oath, that most somber of asseverations, binding himself at the hazard of punishment by the God in whom he reposes such faith. And the name of that God is . . . what?

It is this question that brings us back to the most peculiar feature of the entire narrative, the parenthesis inserted between the king of Sodom's coming to greet Abram at King's Vale and that king's proposal to Abram as to the disposition of the recovered property. In terms of plot, whether in respect to the redistribution of the loot or any aspect of the campaign that was waged, this parenthetic event is totally without relevance. Melchizedek himself is never again heard of except in Psalm

110, where the name is a reflex of this single appearance in Genesis 14. The bread and wine which Melchizedek produces is clearly a symbolic religious gesture, for a victorious host comes laden with the provisions taken from the defeated enemy. Lest we forget this commonplace at this critical interpretive juncture, the narrator has jogged our memory in advance when in verse 11 he explicitly includes "their victuals" in the tribute wrested from Sodom. The bread and wine are symbolic therefore of the divine source of all sustenance, necessities and luxuries alike. But how did this priest-king of ancient Salem, later to be known as Jerusalem the earthly seat of Israel's God, learn of Abram's triumphant return? Why and how did he make that trek from his mountain fortress (presumably via the road to Jericho, then down to a ford of the Jordan and across it) in time so precisely calculated to meet up with the returning hero? And the motivation behind this arduous journey by the priest-king of a great city to congratulate upon a successful foray the land-less, cityless cattle breeding chieftain called Abram the Hebrew? Could he have anticipated that for a blessing invoked of a hitherto unknown god named El Elyon, and for attributing the victory to this god, a grateful Abram would hand over a tithe of all the regained spoil?

None of these questions calls for answers, for they are rhetorical, pointing up the improbability that this incident is intended either as history, or even historical fiction. But even as expressive of ideological fiction, how are we to read this intro-duction of a presumably pagan priest, whose mediating status between the divine and human realms is not only acknowledged by Abram but accorded an enormous tribute? The answer to these questions must lie in the function of this parenthetic episode in relation to the main plot line, into which it is so pointedly interjected. On two scores it is proleptic of elements in the main plot that follows. One is the divine name El Elyon, two words appearing three times in staccato fashion within a space of fourteen words altogether, declared by Melchizedek to be creator of heaven and earth. The other is the division of the spoil, in the tithe given to Melchizedek.

Let us take up the latter first. The entire parenthesis takes place, so to speak, off-stage, the only witnesses to it being the narrator, the reader, and the two principals, Abram and Melchizedek. The entire scene therefore is played out for the benefit of the reader and the reader alone. The king of Sodom, for example, knows not at all that the proposal he is about to make can apply only to 90 percent of the spoils, 10 percent having already been allotted. That allotment, we must understand, is not for Melchizedek in his private capacity, but like the canonical Levitical tithe, for services rendered to God. This then supplies the element which we have hitherto in our discussion not located in the text: the God who grants victory and blessing in a reward and punishment economy that is not based on zero-sum assumptions. Hence when Abram reaffirms Melchizedek's declaration of faith, that reaffirmation is only recognized as such by the reader who recognizes in Abram's oath the same divine name invoked by Melchizedek; the kerygmatic preachment is totally lost on the king of Sodom, to whom the direct discourse is formally addressed. So also must it be totally lost on any reader who can come to terms with a historiographic narrative that comes to a climax in Abram as an arrogant warlord gratuitously jeer-ing at the petition of a king brought low; only to be succeeded by a concluding

anticlimax in which the lordly generosity of his abnegation is nullified by a concern for the recovery of his expenses and for the shares due to his allied chieftains,
who cannot speak for themselves.

There is one more nicety of formulation in Abram's declination of the king of
Sodom's proposal. The normal way of expressing an oath in direct discourse is the
particle *ḥēy/ḥāy*, followed by the first person pronoun or a divine name followed by
ʾim "if." "By my life / the life of DN [Divine Name] if . . ." The act of swearing then
is in the present tense, which is what we would expect in Abram's address to
Sodom's king. Instead we have direct discourse as indicated by the *ʾim* "if," and a
hand gesture bespeaking the taking of an oath. This taking of the oath, however, is
in the past tense. The oath then is not Abram's spontaneous response to the king
of Sodom. He anticipated the problem of the distribution of the loot long before
this meeting, and made the decision in regard to his own profiting by the campaign. The past tense of the swearing points back then to the parenthesis, to the
honoring of God through the tithe given to his priest, as the parenthetic episode—
introducing God into the narrative for the first time—points forward and informs
on the significance of the dialogue between Abram and the king. (Note how reasoned is the placement of the parenthesis between the king's arrival at Abram's
camp and his making of the proposal.) That the act of supererogation is to give
honor to God (and not to win honor or security for himself) is, to be sure, the
point of the oath (rather than a simple asseveration) on Abram's part. But there is
further and subtle purpose to the idiom that the narrator chooses (or invents) for
the oath taking. Instead of the normal *nišbaʿtī* "I have sworn," he puts into Abram's
mouth a circumlocution for "swear" (never elsewhere attested)[6] that compels
Abram to make explicit what is always implicit in an oath, the invocation of a
higher power to punish the oath-taker if the statement made is false or if the
promise made is broken. And this explication of the invocation of this higher
power involves Abram's use of the name of or an expression for a deity, which outside this chapter appears only once again in all Scripture. And which within this
chapter appears three times, in the parenthesis preceding Abram's use of it, in the
mouth of the (presumably pagan) king of Salem. This dictional link between the
hypotactic parenthesis and the paratactically formulated main narrative thus points
to a secondary or sub-kerygma, or perhaps an embroidery on the kerygma that we
have already discerned.

On the name El Elyon, Speiser, in a note ad loc., and leaning heavily on Marvin
Pope's *El in the Ugaritic Texts*,[7] affirms that the elements *ʾel* and *ʾelyōn*, which "occur
as names of specific deities," are combined in the Aramaic inscription from Sujin
into a compound name. This attestation would seem to be the basis for his conclusion in his Comment that Melchizedek "invokes an authentic Canaanite deity (see
Note) as a good Canaanite priest would be expected to do." The establishing of El
Elyon as the authentic name of an authentic pagan deity invoked by an authentic
Canaanite priest is, of course, in the interest of supporting his view (and that of
most biblicists) as to the historiographic nature of Chapter 14. His last sentence
reads, "The narrative itself has all the ingredients of historicity." Aside from the
questionability of literary citations to bolster arguments as to historiography, this
particular argument of Speiser's is questionable on the ground of the judiciousness

of a methodology which can affirm the existence of a god on the basis of a single instance. In the case of the one instance here, in the inscription from Sujin, the name El Elyon may not be present at all, for as Speiser himself observes, these two words are both appellatives, "god" and "supreme" respectively. Thus in extra-biblical cultures where El is indeed the name of a god, 'El 'elyōn may be simply El (is) (the) supreme one. In Scripture, where 'el is rarely a proper noun, 'El 'Elyon as applied to the One and Only Deity might exist, but only as a playful name, for in itself it is a tautology = God Supreme.

We suggested earlier in connection with Exodus 6:2–3 that the names 'El Shaddai and Shaddai deserved a poetical study in themselves. We would now make the same statement for the names 'El 'Elyon and Elyon, which are so striking a parallel to the former pair. But both of these statements are unconscionably restrictive and, when made by me, open me to the suspicion that I regard my own chapter 1 and the followups in the succeeding exegetical essays as more than the scratchy beginnings of the poetical study of the names, appellations, epithets, and attributives disposed of in Scripture with (and for) the one referent, the one and only autonomous creator and lord of all that is. In no Book of Scripture is this literary challenge so fascinatingly displayed as in the five books that make up the Psalter. To sketch a few examples: the statistical distribution of the names YHWH and 'Elōhim in each of these five books; the psalmic dittograms featuring the one or the other name respectively; the appearance of consonantal ^{a}dōnāy where we would expect the Tetragrammaton; the use of šem in construct with one of the names for Deity.

Perhaps most germane to my immediate preoccupation with Genesis 14 is Psalm 78, the only text other than Genesis 14 in which the name El Elyon appears (and only once, at that, in parallelism with Elohim [verse 35]). In this psalm of seventy-two verses, one or another term for Deity appears twenty times. These terms are, in the order of their appearance, reading across the rows:

YHWH	Elohim	'el	'el rūhō	Elohim
Elyon	'el	Elohim	'el	YHWH
Elohim	Elohim	'el	Elohim	El Elyon
'el	q^{e}dōš yisrael	Elohim Elyon	Elohim	^{a}dōnāy

Six of these terms appear in the table in italic type, as indication of a special feature inhering in it. Of the two biblical names (i.e., proper nouns) of Deity, YHWH appears twice and Elohim appears seven times. In addition, the term 'el appears five times. Since every one of these twenty occurrences is to the same one and only Divine referent, this term 'el—despite my earlier statement that, unlike Ugarit El, it is rarely a *name* for God—certainly functions as a proper name, alongside YHWH and Elohim. This statement holds equally true for the (consonantal) ^{a}dōnāy of line 4; and of the appellative 'el rūhō "the god of his [i.e., Israel's] spirit" in line 1, where the 'el element, being in the construct, can only be a common noun. That leaves us with the three other terms functioning (at least) as proper names: Elyōn, which is essentially a substantive adjective, "highest One" in line 1; 'El Elyōn "highest d/Divinity" of Genesis 14 fame in line 3; and in line 4 a mimicking of *ʾEl Elyōn* in the one and only occurrence *ᵉlōhīm ʿelyōn* "highest g/God."

The literary play of the poet's imagination in the alternation of proper noun (YHWH), common noun become proper noun (*ᵉlōhīm*), common noun in construct with another noun (*ʾel rūhō, qᵉdoš yisrāʾel*), the vocable substituted for the Tetragrammaton (*ᵃdōnāy*) in place of the original YHWH, together with the subset of "names" featuring *ʿelyōn* alone or in combination: this play is so ingenious that its poetical study promises to fill many pages. For our present purposes this creative play on the part of a Scriptural poet will serve to confirm what I suggested earlier in respect to the equally imaginative author of the narrative in Genesis 14. Unconcerned with historiography, crafting plot and character in the interest of ideational kerygmas, he has inserted a priest of the ancient city that is destined centuries after his time to become the earthly seat of Israel's God YHWH. This king bears the good and well-omened Hebrew name, which as Speiser has pointed out means "the king is legitimate," and is one way in which our omniscient narrator commends him to our sympathetic reception. The name of the god to whom he is dedicated priest, *ʾEl Elyon*, is no more a documented "authentic" deity-persona in the world of Father Abraham or any of his remote descendants than is the king who invokes him. This deity is invoked as the *qōnē* (first meaning "possessor, owner," second meaning by metonymy of result for cause "creator") of heaven and earth without any suggestion that he has any associates or rivals. This god, he declares, is the one by whom the fortunate Abram has been blessed, perhaps also whose continued blessing is invoked upon Abraham, and who is then credited with the specific blessing, the victory of Abram over his enemies. The narrator's recommendation (to the reader) of Melchizedek is thus seconded and reinforced by the Abram who, in granting him and his god a tithe of the spoil, is acknowledging this god as indeed the grantor of his victory, the source of his material prosperity, this in contrast, as we have seen, with the one-time possessor of the goods Abram has recovered, namely the king of Sodom, who generously offers Abram what is neither in his power nor his prerogative to give. Inasmuch as there is no hint that the Abram of Chapter 14 has undergone a momentary lapse from his presumed (and properly so) monotheism, there would appear to be a question as to whether we had any right early on to presume that Melchizedek was a pagan, indeed to assume that he worshiped more gods than did Abram and, consequently, whether there is any justification for spelling his Deity with a lower case "g."

So much for Melchizedek, legitimate king, legitimate priest of a legitimate Deity (note capital D, and with indefinite article) named El Elyon. What does this have to do with Abram's invocation of Deity in his dialogue with the king of Sodom, the dialogue in which he seems to invoke Deity by the same name? In terms of plot, nothing. For Melchizedek's use of that name is in a parenthetic episode in which the king of Sodom is not present, and to which neither he nor anyone other than Melchizedek and Abram is witness. As far as the plot line of the narrative is concerned Abram has merely disposed of the same name and epithet as had Melchizedek in an offstage episode. But this last statement is not altogether—at least demonstrably—true. Abram does not invoke Deity by the same *name*, he invokes him by the name YHWH, to which he adds two expressions, one of which in

Melchizedek's speech is a name and the other an epithet, but both of which in Abram's speech are epithets. Abram then invokes YHWH, God Supreme, Owner of Heaven and Earth.

The play then is on an expression for Deity, which from Melchizedek's perspective is a name and from Abram's perspective is an epithet. From a third perspective, that of the authoritative narrator, these two points of view constitute an identification of Abram's God with Melchizedek's God, of YHWH with El Elyon. And the reader, for whom narrative and parenthesis are played out, will recognize that this perspective of the narrator's is the point of view or kerygma that he is asked to adopt as his own (as, indeed, it is so adopted by the author of Psalm 78, among many other Scriptural authors).

The student of the history of religions will immediately associate this kerygma with the term syncretism, an association which in this context *may* be wrong, but is certainly misleading. This term bespeaks a union of two parties or principles (usually conflicting) into a single harmonious one. In the context of the religions of antiquity, however, this term refers to the fusion of two gods from two different and polytheistic systems. And there is nothing in Genesis that explicitly identifies any of the descendants of Shem, Ham, and Japheth as polytheists. To the contrary, as we have stressed earlier, the first couple and the serpent-tempter, Cain and Noah, all know only the one God. And none of the malefactors—victims of the Deluge, builders of Babel, sinners of Sodom—in any of the narratives hitherto treated is charged with idolatry or other cultic offense; every sin is a breach of morality, not one the violation of a cultic taboo. For all that Joshua in Chapter 24 declares in God's name that Abram's father Terah was among the ancestors who worshipped "other gods," not only is such a charge absent in Genesis in regard to the line of Shem (or, for that matter, of his brothers), but also in regard to Abimelech of Gerar, who is acknowledged by God as blameless in the matter of Sarah (ch. 20), and who recognizes YHWH as Isaac's divine sponsor, hailing him as "YHWH's blessed one" (ch. 26). Given the continual tirades against Israel for its lapses into "idolatry" or apostasy in other books of Scripture, it is understandable that these practices are read back into Genesis with the assumption that the pagan practices of their neighbors were challenge to Israel's ancestors of the patriarchal age. But these assumptions, erroneous for the Book of Genesis, make for almost insuperable difficulties as we seek to understand the kerygmas of such stories as Jacob's traffic with sub-gods, vying with them in night-long struggles, or paying them homage at the behest of God himself. A more serious consequence of these assumptions is that we are conditioned to miss the metaphors in which Scripture formulates loyalty to or apostasy from the one God of nature and humanity. Among the literal understandings that are most seriously distortive of Scripture's perspective on true and false religion is the proliferation of names for gods and God, and for seeing supernal entities in rivalry with God everywhere we come across uncanonical names or priests of such uncanonical "gods," be they in Midian or Salem. The purpose of the kerygma in the play on divine names and divine attributes in Genesis 14 is to arm us against such misconceptions in our encounters with the righteous of the Gentiles and the unrighteous of Israel.

THE COVENANT (CONCLUDED) BETWEEN
THE (ANIMAL) PARTS

Episode A

(1) After these events it was that YHWH's word came to Abram in a vision: "Have no fear, Abram. I am your shield. Very great, indeed, will your reward be." (2) Abram said, "My lord YHWH, what can you give me as long as I continue destitute and the favorite of my household is Damascene Eliezer." (3) [The meaning of what] Abram said: "Lo, to me You have granted no issue, so lo, a homeborn slave succeeds to my estate." (4) And lo, just as quick YHWH's response to him, "Not that one will succeed you; none but one from your loins sprung, only such a one will succeed you." (5) Thereupon He drew him out into the open and said, "Look heavenwards and count the stars, if count them you can." Thus did He promise, "So (numerous) will your progeny be."

(6) And trust YHWH he did—so that He reckoned it to his credit.) (Genesis 15:1–6)

Episode B

(7) [The preceding took place as follows:] He said to him, "I am YHWH, who drew you forth from Ur Kasdim to give you this land as inheritance." (8) Said he, "My lord YHWH, by what token may I know that inherit it I shall?" (9) Said he to him, "Fetch me a heifer in her third year, and a nanny-goat in her third year, and a ram in his third year, and dove and squab." (10) He fetched Him all these. He split them down the middle, placed each animal-side opposite its other half; but the birds he did not divide. (11) When the vultures made descent upon the carrion, Abram shooed them away. (12) Just as the sun had all but set, lo, a trance overcame Abram and at that moment a deep dark dread was overwhelming him. (13) He said to Abram, "Know of a certainty that your issue will live as aliens in a land not their own, will be subject to them and they [the hosts] will oppress them, for 400 years. (14) The nation which they shall serve do I also hold in judgment, so that thereafter they shall go free with rich possessions. (15) You yourself **now** will peacefully join your ancestors, receive burial in old and happy age. (16) The fourth generation **now** will return hither—for till then, incomplete the full tale of Amorite doom-incurring iniquity." (17) The sun then set, there was a darkness impenetrable, and **then**—a firepot spewing smoke and fiery blaze which coursed between those cadaver parts. (Genesis 15:7–17)

Coda

(18) At that time it was that YHWH made covenant with Abram, promising: To your issue have I granted this land, from the river of Egypt to the great river, River Euphrates, (19) [land then of] the Kenite and Kenizzite and Kadmonite, (20) and Hittite and Perizzite and the Rephaites, (21) and Amorite and Canaanite and Girgashite and Jebusite. (Genesis 15:18–21)

It is in this chapter that source-criticism divines for the first time the hand of that author labeled E (for his use of ᵉlōhīm for God, let us remember). This despite the consistent appearance of the name YHWH and the absence of any stylistic fingerprints that could not possibly belong to J. The insinuation of E elements into a predominantly J narrative is the answer that this school of literary analysis offers to the many problems in this text, which if seen as the work of a single author would brand that author as singularly inept. And so the reputation of that author (J in this case) is salvaged by these critics, who seem to be unaware that this service to the author is at the expense of the editor who is responsible for such unilluminating splicing.

The problems identified in this chapter may be classified under the headings of inconsistencies, discrepancies, and excrescent repetitions. Thus, for example, under the first heading the revelation to Abram could, according to verse 5, only have taken place at night; yet according to verses 12 and 17 YHWH's appearance occurred in the daytime. Under the second heading there is YHWH's self-introduction in verse 7, when it would have been most natural in verse 1; the "suspiciousness" of the Ur Kasdim in a J context;[8] the perplexing transition from verse 6 (which seems to conclude the question of Abram's doubts) to verse 8 (where Abram asks for YHWH's help in dispelling them); the preoccupation with the promise of progeny in verses 1–5 and in verses 7–12 with the promise of land, and this shift without any indication of a transition; the collocation of four hundred years of servitude in verse 13 and the return from exile in the fourth generation, implying an equation (never attested elsewhere) of a generation and a century. Under the third heading at the beginning of verses 2 and 4, is the appearance of *wayyōmer* "he said" when both verbs have the same subject and nothing intervenes between the direct discourse of that character in the two verses.

However scornful we may be of the conflation of sources as a reasonable solution to these problems in the text before us, such is not our stance in regard to the problems themselves. To the extent that we hew to the most literal lines of translation—for example, in rendering every waw-conversive followed by an imperfect as paratactic in function as well as in form—to that extent we harden the problems and are driven to cast about for metaliterary solutions.[9] Thus, for example, compare the Authorized Version (AV) rendering of *wayyōmer Àbrām* at the beginning of verse 2 and verse 3 "And Abram said" (in both instances) with NJPS "But Abram said" (verse 2) and "Abram said further" (verse 3). As superior as is the rendering of NJPS to the mechanical one of AV, it falls short of the narrator's intent as explicated in our own translation. For in the second statement Abram is not continuing to speak; rather the narrator is telling us what the thought of Abram was in his one and only statement.[10] Our own original translation, and closer to the Hebrew, read "Abram's thought was . . ."

All the problems of pointless repetition, inconsistency, and discrepancy fall away when we pay close attention to the subtle resources of biblical Hebrew (in regard to diction and syntax) and the author's masterful deployment of these resources in his poetic repertory of narrative and dialogue: direct and indirect discourse, actual and implied, strict and free; shifts in point of view and perspective; depiction of events in a seemingly direct time flow, and the ambiguation of both events and their chronological order in episodic techniques such as the synoptic-conclusive/resumptive-expansive. In the case of the chapter before us, a review of the problems as they emerge from so literal a translation as that of AV will reveal how few of these remain when the text is rendered as in our translation. But let us review text and translation options with a view to analyzing the poetic operations of our artist and synthesizing the kerygma or kerygmas he achieves by the maneuvers so intricate in the Hebrew and so simplistically flattened out by the mangle of literal translation.

EPISODE A: REVELATION, PROMISE (AND TRUST)

The opening sentence of this story does not begin with a waw-conversive imperfect tense verbal clause, the normal (or at least most frequent) narrative option (as for example in the first verse of these chapters in Genesis: 2, 6–9, 11–14, 17–20, 22). Nor does it begin with a nominal clause, a copulative waw attached to a noun, followed by a verb in the perfect tense, and expressive of a parenthetic notice prefatory to the narrative that will ensue momentarily with a waw-conversive construction (as in the first verse of these chapters in Genesis: 3, 4, 16, 21). It begins without a waw. It begins with an adverbial phrase *aḥar hadd^ebārīm hā^aellē* "after these events," this followed by a verb in the perfect tense followed by its subject. This adverbial phrase appears another seven times in Scripture. In five of these instances (Genesis 22:1, 39:7, 40:1, 1 Kings 17:17, 21:1) this phrase is preceded by the waw-conversive construction of *way^ehī* "it was." An examination of these contexts will disclose that in each case the duration of time between the previous events and the event(s) about to be related is indefinite or hazy, which is to say that the force of this adverbial transition is "now it happened some (indeterminate) time after these events . . ." In only two instances does this adverbial phrase appear as in our opening verse (Genesis 15:1) without the preceding *way^ehī*. And in these two instances (Esther 2:1, 3:1) it is quite clear from the context that the force of the clause is, "*Shortly after/hard upon these events* [Proper Noun] did such-and-such." Thus the adverbial usage here in 15:1 is to connect the revelatory assurance of YHWH to Abram with the hazards survived in the immediately preceding tale of war, rapine, loot, retaliation, restoration, and disposition of the profits.[11]

The introduction of this story of divine revelation (now that its circumstances have been provided by the adverbial phrase) is unique on a number of scores. Similar stories featuring Abram and other human recipients of divine oracles begin with the simple *wayyo'mer* [Divine Name] *'el* "Deity (by one or another name or rubric) said to . . ." (So, for example, Genesis 6:13, 7:1, 12:1.) In other instances which we shall examine (Genesis 17:1, 18:1) "YHWH appeared" (*wayyērā' YHWH*), and we are then given to understand that this appearance of God was in the guise of messenger(s) human or numen. In the place of *God said* we have many instances of the verb "to be" (*hāyā/way^ehī*) with *d^ebar YHWH* "YHWH's word" (1 Samuel 15:10, 2 Samuel 7:4, 1 Kings 6:11, Isaiah 38:4, Jeremiah 25:3) as here, but never with the addition as here of "in a vision." We shall soon see the reasons for these unique features.

The word of YHWH in this instance is given in direct discourse, three terse statements. The first relates to the hazards of war (such as the one just waged, and hostilities likely to be encountered). Abram has no cause for fear. YHWH will continue to protect him from enemies. Better yet, great reward is yet in store for him. This last promise gives Abram his opening. Reward is a matter of material possessions enjoyed in good health over a long lifetime. What good he asks are such "goods" to a man like himself who is barren. He then makes oblique reference to the heir he does not have in a pun on the person and status of the person who is likely to dispose of his estate after his death. The ambiguities and nuances in this pun-centered identification are lost on us and may have been opaque to much of the biblical audience that read or heard it. It may also bespeak timidity in its indirection, and an (understandable) avoidance of a challenge to the God who promises him generalities when his need is so obviously specific as to not require specification, especially to an all-knowing God. Having placed this opacity of expression in Abram's mouth, the narrator then goes on to enlighten his readers with a pointed explication of what Abram thought but feared to express. Everybody knows that "a son of one's house" is not a chattel-slave, with all the brute unfeelingness associated with such status. He is as "slave" deracinated from the family of his biological origin, but an adopted member of the religion-family whose line is his line, and the line that he may propagate as senior "son" and heir. Alas, it is a human weakness (and will be so admitted by any adoptive parent) not to grant to such an adopted heir the full depth of sentiment one would repose in a genetic son. Now the narrator glosses "the favorite of my household" as "my slave-son, Damascene Eliezer," as "the one who will inherit my estate," pointing in both epithets to the complaint "to me have you granted no seed (of my own body)." For all that the narrator is thus glossing what Abram has said, the glossing is presented as though it were indeed Abram's speech, and the plaintiveness of his question (which is really a plea or a challenge) is brought out by the two "lo" clauses. And it is to these two *lo*'s, attributed to Abram, that the narrator now has YHWH responding, a response that he introduces with a countering *lo*, introducing YHWH's response to the complaint intended though never uttered. "And lo, the *word of YHWH* to him," which is to say, "the word of YHWH," which is the subject of verse 1. That word, however, is twofold; first, that not that [adopted] one but [seed] issue of your own body will constitute your heir(s) and second, the innumerable multitude that will constitute those heirs. But that "word of YHWH's" came to Abram "in a vision." What was that vision, that sign in which context the words were sounded? Was it the sight of the stars in their myriads to which YHWH drew his attention as he emerged from behind his tent's entrance-flap? No, it was not that literal sight, normally expressed by *marē*, but a *maḥ^azē* "a prophetic vision/scenario." This scenario will be presented to us in the resumptive-expansive episode that begins with verse 7. (We shall defer our discussion of the seemingly parenthetic verse 6, formulated in the hypotactic construction of nominal clause with verb in the perfect tense.)

EPISODE B: HOW THE COVENANT WAS MADE

The narrative strategy of the synoptic-resumptive technique so unique to Scripture is the telling of one incident or event twice, in two successive episodes. The first episode, almost always the shorter of the two, provides the gist of the event and its conclusion. In the second episode, the narrator backs up in time, so to speak, resumes the event's beginning, and—expanding on the synoptic version of the event—describes how the conclusion (or bottom line) was arrived at. A problem is raised in this chapter by the sudden switch from normal narrative paratactic syntax in verse 5 to the hypotactic (normally parenthetic) syntax in verse 6. The question, whether the bottom line, toward the resolution of which Episode B will move, is represented in verse 5, or verse 6 must await the analysis of this second episode.

The episode begins with a resumption of the direct discourse of YHWH to Abram. In Episode A that discourse begins directly with the divine reassurance and with a gapping of the question as to whether Abram was told explicitly the name or epithet of the divine source whence the message was emanating. This gap is quickly bridged, however, by Abram's direct discourse address to that source as *adōnāy YHWH*, consonantally equal to "my Lordship, YHWH," but vocalized to be read aloud as *adōnāy elōhīm* "my Lordship, God." In Episode B, there is neither gapping nor bridging. The divine speaker identifies himself as YHWH (or uses the Tetragrammaton in apposition: "I, YHWH, am [the one] that drew you forth"). Abram's address (as in the first episode) to *adōnāy YHWH* after his self-identification is the first expansion of Episode A, telling us how it was that Abram knew to address the source by name.

The poetical purpose of YHWH's self-identification here is not, however, to disclose a name to a mortal who has hitherto been ignorant of it. It is to link the God who initiated the process of election by extracting him from his native land with the God who will complete the process by giving him possession of the land in which he is now a sojourner. The fulfillment of the promise, however, will not be to Abram in his own person and lifetime, but in the person of his progeny centuries after his death. It is this time factor (and the identification of ancestral felicity with the felicity of their posterity) that makes the promise of progeny and the promise of land a single promise, but one with two aspects. The first aspect has been dealt with in Episode A, where Abram's (implied) insistence on his posterity being biological, not just adoptive, has been received favorably by God. The second aspect is now brought into focus in YHWH's self-identification as the God who had him turn his back on his native land in favor of this new territory. This promise is seized upon by Abram: "What assurance can I have that I [in my seed centuries hence] will indeed come into possession of it?" And what follows in the episode must be or contain YHWH's response to this question.

And what follows is, as explicated in verse 18—the recapitulative coda—the enactment of a *berīt* "agreement, pact, covenant, contract, treaty." Yes, the Hebrew word means all these but it also means something else. Whereas all these terms presuppose a relationship between two parties, that relationship may bespeak parity or inequality as between the two parties. Thus a treaty of friendship or nonaggression may suggest a near equality in the matter of power, while a peace treaty or vassal-treaty will reflect the imposition of the will of the strong on the weaker, often recently defeated, party. Within a given polity, it is the state that enforces contracts by penalizing the party that violates the terms of the agreement. Where the nature of the agreement is such that the agreement is not amenable to enforcement by society (state or tribal authority), recourse will often be had to the oath, the invocation of a higher power, to exact a penalty from the possibly unfaithful party. So too in the case of international treaties, in the absence of a super-state (or *imperium*) which might play this role, God (or, in particular, the gods of the subjected party) will be invoked to punish the treaty violator; this in anticipation that, the balance of power having shifted, the treaty partner on whom the promises or pledges have been imposed may feel that it may abrogate them with impunity. The additional meaning of the word *bᵉrīt*, a meaning that in one sense is less and in another sense more than that of *compact*, is *promise*, an undertaking by one party to behave in a certain manner, usually in regard to a second party. This sense of *bᵉrīt* (even while in a given context the promise is implicitly contingent) is probably due to metonymy (of the whole for the part, in that every compact contains one or more promise). But this *promise* may be pronounced without invocation of sanctions, implicit or explicit; it may be completely voluntative, requiring no assent from the party benefited, and made by a stronger party to a weaker party without any expectation of reciprocity. When, then, in the Bible, God "makes a *bᵉrīt* with," which is to say "a promise to"—as for example, in Genesis 6:18, 9:9—Noah, humanity, or all living creatures, the mechanical translation of *bᵉrīt* as covenant rather than promise will occasion many an otiose line of exegesis. For all the foregoing, the answer of God to Abram's question in verse 8 is in every respect a promise, in no respect a compact, and yet in form and imagery altogether expressive of a covenant, indeed of a treaty, and (for all the presumed probity of the promisor) not at all of a mere promise.

One of the more thorny problems in our story is the feature of the animal carcasses and their division (or non-division) into halves. The minimum number of animal parts seems to be eight, six halves of the domestic beasts and one each of the two birds, which, for lack of better information, we have translated as "dove and squab." Since these two birds are undivided and, unlike the animal halves, not counterparts of one another, it is likely that these two nouns are collectives standing for an indeterminate number, and the two nouns are a merism or hendiadys standing for any species of barnyard fowl. If we had to guess at the total number, we would suggest six birds corresponding to the six animal halves for a total of two aisles, each consisting of three animal halves and three birds, the total of twelve, then, suggestive of the twelve tribes that Abram's chosen progeny will constitute.

It is now fairly common knowledge that both the killing of an animal and the identification of the slaughtered victim with one of the human parties are features of treaty-making ceremonies in the ancient Near East. Thus, for example, among the Amorites from Mari on the middle Euphrates, where the animal ritually slain was an ass, an idiom for "to enter a compact" is "to slay an ass." In the text of one such treaty text from Syria the symbolism is explicit: "The (slain) goat," it reads in reference to the subjected party, "is you!"[12] The symbolism of the fate of treaty-violator as invoked in the treaty partner's walking between the parts of the animal victim is also attested in Israel. Jeremiah regards the prohibition in Exodus 21 of one Israelite keeping another in indentured service for more than six years as one of the terms of the covenant made between Israel and her God. In Jeremiah, in the context of pronouncing doom on the Judean gentry, who have kept their brethren in indefinite subjection, God says:

I will make the gentry who are transgressing My covenant, who have not fulfilled the covenant they made in My presence, the bullock which they cut into two and passed between its halves. (Jeremiah 34:18)

YHWH will make the transgressors, not like,[13] but into, the slain bullock. Exactly as in the treaty from Syria ("this goat is you") the slain animal is a metaphor for the fate of the covenant violator. In the two verses following, the Judean parties to the covenant are identified and their fate is evoked in the very imagery of the vultures that Abram frightened off from the exposed halves of the cadavers:

The chieftains of Judah and the chieftains of Jerusalem, the chamberlains and the priests and the assemblymen—those who passed between the bullock's halves—them will I hand over to their enemies, to those who seek their deaths, so that their carcasses be food for the birds of the sky and the beasts of the earth. (Jeremiah 34:19–20)

In the Jeremiah passage there is a play on the verb 'br, which appears in the sense of "passing" between the halves and "transgressing" the covenant; the word for "halves" is precisely the one appearing in Genesis 15; and the very term for enacting a covenant in biblical Hebrew is not "to make" a covenant but "to cut" it. The covenant symbolism in Chapter 15 could hardly be more lucid. But what of the element of the firepot flaming and smoking, which passes between the parts?

The answer to this last question would long ago have been apparent if it were not for our reluctance to credit Scripture's authors with a capacity for metaphor of breathtaking boldness. During Israel's years of wandering in the wilderness, God led the way as "a pillar of cloud by day and a pillar of fire at night." The firepot (or oven or brazier) that passes between the animals' parts is emblematic of God. Although God is the suzerain and Abram the vassal, in this episode it is the former who binds himself. Abram asked for a token by which he in the present could be confident that his distant offspring would take possession of the promised land. God's response is merely a reaffirmation of the promise in the strongest terms available. Not just by an oath, in which God—as the Ultimate Power—must swear by himself, invoke sanctions upon himself, but by the most solemn context of an oath, the "cutting" of a covenant. God binds himself by the covenant symbolism, invoking upon himself—metaphorically speaking, how else?—the punishment invoked upon the violator of a treaty. Bold symbolism indeed! And, on the literal level, nonsense. Is God's word not enough? What more is added to Abram's ability to believe, to have faith, by the granting of a vision in which God resorts to such symbolism? The answer is that God did the most he could—short of robbing Abram of his freedom to trust or not—to reassure Abram. The rest was up to Abram himself. He remained free to doubt. And in the end, he trusted . . . And for this merit the reward was reaped, the trust vindicated, by his descendants to whom the story is addressed.

But despite the bottom line of Abram's faith and the vindication of that faith, the progression to the realization of the promise was to be neither easy nor of short duration. For one thing, it will require several generations before Abram's progeny in the line of Isaac and Jacob can become numerous enough to constitute a people who can attain the status of a nation upon its own territory. And YHWH is a god of justice. The accumulating sins of the Amorites will require some centuries yet before they reach critical mass, warrant for the irruption into their midst of YHWH's agents, the people of Israel who will dispossess them.

The birds of prey that descend upon the carcass parts—six animal halves, and perhaps, six undivided birds—are in themselves a grim omen. Abram protects the flesh from the scavengers until the sun is about to sink below the horizon. It is with the sudden chill and dark of that moment that Abram is gripped by the trance and a sense of deep dark dread. Although the premonition of God's presence about to make itself felt might give rise to a feeling of awe, dread is a different emotion. And the dread may well relate to the oppression of four hundred years duration that Abram's descendants will have to endure in an alien land before their return (to "this" land where Abram's vision takes place) in the fourth generation.[14] What cannot be ruled out, however, is that in the dread which he imputes to Abram, the narrator may be expressing his own sense of awe at the manifestation of a Deity whom he so often seems to conjure up at will; and particularly a God so generous in benevolence, so forbearing with humanity, that he will forgive the hybris of a poet so daring as to portray God himself, evoking the image of his own death in self-invoked punishment should he fail to make good his word to a doubting mortal.

If we review the contents of the episodes, recalling the problems of repetition and inconsistency discerned in and between the two episodes, we shall see how both (seemingly gratuitous) repetition and (seemingly irreconcilable) discrepancy dovetail in Episode B's function as resumptive and expansive of Episode A. Thus the word of YHWH in reassurance to Abram appears in verse 1 in A, and verse 7 in B. But neither of these assurances are given in or relate to the *maḥᵃzē* "vision" of verse 1. That *maḥᵃzē* is the vision of God moving between the carrion parts. That vision does not begin until Abram has slaughtered the victims and shooed away the vultures, this in compliance with YHWH's bidding and in broad daylight. The vision begins only after the trance overtakes Abram (as the sun is sinking, verse 12) and the episode thus concludes at night (with sunset completed and the fall of impenetrable darkness, verse 17), this in concordance with the conclusion of Episode A, at night (verse 5). But as Episode A ends not with the promise in YHWH's direct discourse in verse 5, but with the omniscient narrator's observation in verse 6 (in hypotactic construction), so does Episode B end not with the description of the vision in verse 17 but with the narrator's recapitulation, in explication of that vision, in the first part of verse 18 (in hypotactic construction), "At that time it was that YHWH made covenant with Abram, to the effect, 'To your seed have I granted this land.'" This recapitulative explication—without it one would not even guess that the vision was in expression of a covenant—we have, perhaps misleadingly, assigned to the recapitulative Coda. For it is the boundaries of the land grant in verses 18b–20 in supplementation of the promise, presenting a new item of information, and presenting a far from minor problem, which requires that the recapitulation and supplementation be marked off as a separate compositional unit. (For the discussion of this unit see Structures, in chapter 7 of this volume.)

But let us return to the concluding verse in Episode A. The verse tells us that Abram trusted in YHWH, which is to say, he trusted YHWH to keep his promise.

The first question is why we are told this at all. Were we not told this, would it occur to anyone that the reverse might be the case, that Abram did not so trust in his God? The answer to this question is, of course, in the narrative strategy of the storyteller. He raises the question of doubt obliquely in this synoptic conclusion by negating it, so that he may resume this theme of faith and doubt in the following episode, so that he can describe just how it came about that Abram did repose such trust in God. The resumption of the question is in Abram's not so much expressing lack of trust (something that would be unthinkable even if he were addressing a mortal king, let alone the almighty sovereign of the universe) as in his wheedling for some token of reassurance, a need on the part of a short-lived human to catch a glimpse of the realization of his hope (this promise) over a span of centuries, which is but a moment in the scheme of the lord of infinity. And the response of YHWH to this cajoling, for all the daring and dreadful imagery of God invoking his own demise—of the vassal-treaty imagery in which the sovereign assumes the role of the vassal—this response is basically the human narrator's self-mockery, mockery of the species to which he belongs and to whose frailness he is as subject as any. But a gentle mockery on the part of a God who, were he less than benevolent and tolerant, might well express umbrage at the distrust masked as a childish whine. "So you want to be sure? Sure that I really mean what I am saying. Well, I'll tell you what—I'll do what you would do if you were in my place. I'll cross my heart and hope to . . . die."

This then is the kerygma, or one version of the kerygma, or part of the kerygma of this chapter. But there may well be more to it than this. And the pointer to the additional kerygma is signaled by both content and form. The content is that rare narratorial statement that a human had faith in God. The form—which jerks us to attention to the strangeness of what is coming—is the sudden narratorial switch to hypotaxis. Normal narrative practice, even in the conclusionary sentence of a synoptic episode, is the waw-conversive verbal clause. Instead of *wayya^{a}mīn b^{e}YHWH* (cf. Exodus 14:31) "he (Abram) had faith in YHWH," we have, "he **now** (Abram) had faith in YHWH," and then—in normal paratactic syntax—the strange conclusion of the omniscient narrator that "he (YHWH) reckoned it to his (Abram's) credit." Whether our readers will agree that the purport of this conclusion is strange may depend on their willingness to read a philosophical issue into a narrative text. Whether they can entertain our suggestion as to the kerygma of this philosophical "aside" may depend on the limits they are inclined to set on the scriptural author's sophistication.

Rather than argue our exegesis at length, we shall reproduce our discussion of this verse in an earlier essay:[15]

> How did God speak to Abraham? In Chapter 15 of Genesis we are told that the word of God came to the childless Abraham in a vision . . . drawing him out-of-doors and directing his gaze to the numberless stars of heaven, the Lord said, "So numerous will your issue be." Whereupon Scripture notes, *w^{e}he ^{e}min b-YHWH wayyaḥsh^{e}veha lo ṣ^{e}daqa* "And he believed/trusted in the Lord Who accounted it to his merit." The question we must raise is, "Pray, what merit?" If it is meritorious in man to believe in God, to trust Him, the degree of merit should be in proportion to the difficulties, to the obstacles in the way of faith. But in this narrative Abraham has experienced a

revelation, YHWH has appeared to him in a vision and promised him his heart's desire. And yet Scripture finds it necessary to make explicit what one should have thought to be obvious, that a divine revelation engendered faith in the first of the Patriarchs; and indeed deems it important to underscore this faith as being particularly meritorious!

Let us attempt another formulation. Meritoriousness (or its opposite, for that matter) can only be attributed to an act in the absence of compulsion. Faith in God is a meritorious act. Ergo, faith in God cannot be compelled. But Abraham had faith in God in the context of a divine revelation. Ergo, divine revelation does not compel faith. Does this not constitute a paradox—that one may experience God and yet be free to disbelieve in Him? Our answer is no, there is no paradox. Scripture is drawing our attention to the phenomena of revelation and faith and to the relation between them: Every revelation is a human experience; whatever its manner or form, its degree or content, it is a discrete event; it takes place in time—it has a beginning and an end. And after the event man is free—to remember or to forget; to formulate in words the impact of the event or message—if any; to accept it or— yes—to question its reality. Was it a dream, a figment, a chimera, an illusion, a delusion, a hallucination?

The lesson Scripture would teach us would be far more accessible to us were it not for our habit of assigning our faith-experiences to one realm and those of yesterday's spiritual giants to another; to see the biblical protagonists as having received communication from and having experienced the presence of a God who has ceased to show himself and has left off speaking to man; to confess our own faith as derivative and vacillating, flawed by periods of guilty doubts and anxious skepticism, while picturing the faith of the ancients as absolute and uninterrupted, whole and without blemish, rooted in a never-to-be-questioned experience of the divine. ("On Faith and Revelation in the Hebrew Bible." HUCA 39 (1968): 35–53.

ABRAM'S OTHER WIFE

The chapter immediately following that of the *Covenant (Enacted) between the Parts* tells of the first fulfillment of the promise that those descendants of Abram's who will one day possess that great tract of territory stretching from the Nile to the Euphrates will spring from his own biological issue. That issue is universally read as referring to a single line, that of Jacob/Israel through Isaac. This reading, as we show in our discussion of the Coda of Chapter 15,[16] is mistaken. Abraham's biological issue is begotten first of an Egyptian lass named Hagar, then of his First Wife Sarah, and after Sarah's demise of a wife named Keturah (as well as, it would seem, unnamed sons of unnamed concubines, cf. Genesis 25:1–5 and 25:6).

We shall proceed to treat this Chapter 16, and then alongside it the continuing story of Hagar and her progeny in Chapter 21:1–21. These two stories featuring the one heroine in desperate plight and vouchsafed a divine revelation are regarded as doublets, if not duplicates, by source criticism. Not only do the two accounts feature the Deity under the name YHWH in the former account and Elohim in the latter, betraying two different authorial hands, but there are other stylistic distinctions (to which we confess ourselves blind) that make it possible to assign the latter story to E rather than to P.

Hagar's Flight from Home—and Her Revelation

(1) **Now** Sarai, Abram's wife, had borne him no child. She did, however, possess a slave-girl, an Egyptian, Hagar by name. (2) So it was that Sarai said to Abram, "Lo now—YHWH has kept me from bearing—cohabit with my slave-girl; perhaps I may yet through her continue my line. Abram agreed to Sarai's suggestion. (3) So it was that Sarai, Abram's wife, took Hagar the Egyptian, her slave-girl, some ten years after Abram's settling in the land of Canaan, and gave her to her husband Abram to be wife to him.

(4) He cohabited with Hagar and she conceived. When she realized that she was with child, her mistress become lowered in her esteem. (5) Sarai then said to Abram, "Yours is the onus for the wrong I suffer. I, for my part, bestowed my maid to your embrace. The moment she realized herself with child I fell in her esteem. YHWH judge between me and you!" (6) Said Abram to Sarai, "Lo, your maid is at your disposition. Do with her as you please." So Sarai degraded her till she fled from her presence.

(7) An angel of YHWH's came upon her by a certain spring in the wilderness, the spring on the road to Shur. (8) He declared, "Hagar, slave-girl of Sarai's, whence come you here, whither are you headed?" "From Sarai my mistress," she replied, "I have taken flight." (9) YHWH's angel said to her, "Go back to your mistress, endure abasement at her hands." (10) [Yes,] YHWH's angel promised her [in His name], "So numerous will I make your offspring that they will be beyond counting." (11) [The gist of] what YHWH's angel said, "Lo, with child you are, a son will you bear. You are to name him Ishmael [meaning, God has heard]; that is to say, YHWH has paid heed to your plight. (12) He **now** will be a wild ass of a man, his hand against everyone and everyone's hand against him. Over against all his kinsmen shall he his dwelling secure." (13) So she thus designated YHWH, He Who was addressing her, "*El-roï* is Who You are"—her thought being "Have I to such point been given sight, beyond my [gift of?] sight?"[17] (14) Hence is that spring named *Bᵉer-laḥai-roi*—there yet today, between Kadesh and Bered.

(15) So it was that Hagar bore Abram a son. This son born to him by Hagar, Abram named Ishmael. (16) Abram **now** being 86 years old when Hagar bore Ishmael to Abram. (Genesis 16:1–16)

The hypotactic construction of verse 1 ties this narrative beginning to the theme of Abram's childlessness, so central to that in the immediately preceding chapter, the promise of an end to that barrenness. The content of this narrative, its plot if you will, points to the realization of that promise—its first realization—in the heir who will spring from Abram's loins, but not from Sarai's. Yet—for all that the plot will focus on that heir's mother—the construction in verse 1 also serves to foreground Sarai as the initiator of the step that will end Abram's barrenness (and, in a sense, her own). In addition to foregrounding Sarai by naming her at the narrative's very beginning and immediately thereafter underlining that the Egyptian slave-girl is hers, not Abram's, the narrator will continue to stress the distances (and proximities) of the characters from (and to) one another as also from (and to) the God who personally presides over the destiny of this family he has chosen for his purposes. He will do this by deploying the name YHWH throughout the narrative in both his own voice and in Sarai's direct discourse, by having Hagar addressed not by YHWH himself but by *YHWH's angel*, and finally by making it clear in his own narratorial voice and in immediate conjunction with Hagar's direct discourse that, unlike Sarai, Hagar does not, perhaps may not, dispose of that name; perhaps because she lacks the requisite awareness of the significance inhering in that name. The status of the characters and their importance—in varying degrees—to YHWH, to Abram, and to one another, is further underlined by the narrator's (sometimes repetitious) use of the personae's proper names and their epithets, frequently redundant in context and as information. Thus in the narrative's first clause, the identification of Sarai as *Abram's wife*.

The appearance of YHWH everywhere in this chapter as in the preceding one, the *Covenant (Enacted) Between the Parts*, as well as the proximity and order of the two chapters, should alert us to the problems in Scriptural composition that cannot be resolved by recourse to the genetic theory of multiple authorship. The problem comes to the fore in Sarai's proposal to Abram. It is YHWH, she says, who has kept her from giving birth. Not a problem this, if (in keeping with our suggestion) that name is a metaphor for the One and Only source of life and determiner of all destinies. But is it conceivable that Abram has not told her of the promise vouchsafed to him by YHWH in yesterday's vision? Or is the story of the promise and the vision, itself a metaphor (and intended for the reader rather than the personae of patriarch and matriarch) irrelevant for the consciousness or perspectives of these personae as they cast about for ways to achieve their longed-for heir, despite Heaven's seeming unconcern with their barrenness? Or may we indeed infer that Sarai has been informed of the promise, knows now that an heir will spring from Abram's loins, if not from her own? But what matter if she too may have her line perpetuated by a son who will be hers (*ibbānē*) though conceived in the foster womb of her slave-girl?

Abram accedes to Sarai's proposal. But in the next verse it is once again Sarai *Abram's wife* who takes Hagar *the Egyptian, her slave* and makes her over to Abram *her husband* to be *wife to him*. Thus the one and only wife transfers her chattel to her husband, but in the process that lowly slave ceases to be her property, a mere proxy-womb for the production of an heir to her husband and herself; hers now is the status of wife, secondary wife to be sure, but wife nonetheless to her lady's husband. We need not review here the legal background for the domestic web of status-relationships that is provided by researchers[18] of the cuneiform literature. Suffice it to say that even if we could recover the store of legal expertise in the mind of the Scriptural author, we might still be at a loss to ascertain how much of that lore he would have attributed to his contemporary readers. Yet there is enough in the narrative for us to judge the narrator's own judgment as to the rights and wrongs in the case. Hagar, upon conceiving, feels that the social gap between herself as wife number two and her former owner has now narrowed significantly; it is likely that the sense of her lady's becoming "lower in her eyes" is an expression for her own growing self-esteem. Whether her new sense of self was conveyed to Sarai by acts of commission or omission or only by indications of less then wonted subservience, the narrator chooses not to inform us. It is enough that Sarai regards the slight to herself as totally illicit, bespeaking ingratitude (if nothing else) on the part of the handmaid promoted to consortship with her lord, and of the lord who has been presented with this odalisque by his wife of many decades. That Heaven itself should be outraged by her husband's tolerance of such disrespect is evident in her appeal to YHWH's judgment. Abram for his part either acknowledges Sarai to be in the right or assumes that Sarai had all along the latitude to deal with the ungrateful servant, which he now makes explicit. Sarai acts in accordance with the discretion allowed her, and whether that entailed a diminution in her wifely entitlements (see Exodus 21:10) or reduction to chambermaid status, the newly abused (or disabused) Hagar opts to decamp for Negeb steppe.

The perspective of the omniscient narrator, as Sternberg has disclosed, is sometimes separable from that of God's and sometimes virtually identical with it. In this instance the direct discourse of YHWH's angel is in accord with the distinctly unjudgmental voice of the narrator. Not a one of the three protagonists is blamed, not a one is upheld. Whatever the affections and disaffections, hopes and piques, vanities and aspirations of the three flesh-and-blood personae, those are of no account as against the Heaven-destined histories of the posterities they foreshadow. However unrealistic in existential terms, the Egyptian runaway expresses no surprise at an address that can only be divine in its recognition of her by name, the address that identifies her not as wife or concubine to Abram but as *Sarai's slave girl*. Knowing this about her, the interrogator surely needs no further information from her. But the questions are rhetorical: "Wheresoever have you come from, whithersoever are you bound?" To which she replies that destination has she none, her flight senseless, and fugitive she is from her legitimate *mistress Sarai*.

My translation of the next three verses (for which I offer no apology) conceals the fact that the Hebrew opens each verse with the same four words *wayyōmer lāh malak YHWH* "YHWH's angel said to her." The first statement thus introduced picks up Hagar's confession of rebellion against legitimate authority. She is directed to return to her lady and accept subjugation. The second statement provides her with incentive to obey and consolation for the miseries yet in store: promise (made to none of the matriarchs) of innumerable posterity. The third statement then bridges the content and time-span between the instruction to submit to degradation now and the promise of glorious destiny in a far-off future. Drawing attention to her pregnancy, the prediction is made that the issue will be male, and she is instructed to name him *Yishmael* "El hears," a name whose purport is immediately glossed as "YHWH has heard (taken sympathetic notice of) your suffering." This is then followed by an aside, in hypotactic construction which need not detain us here.[19] There can be little doubt that for all the solicitude of God for Hagar and her issue, the distancing of God from this wife of Abram's is expressed in her being addressed by an angel of YHWH's rather than by YHWH himself. This is the point of the three divine statements, each featuring this representation of YHWH, of the theophorical element El "God" in the name Heaven-chosen for her son, yet of that theophoric element's being immediately glossed as *YHWH*. And all these nuanced emphases on the names and terms for the One God of Scripture are brought to a head in the construction that literally has Hagar "naming YHWH," who, being YHWH, cannot be named anything else. Such a literal translation is, of course, ruled out by good sense, as also by the sense of "she said of the one addressing her (through the angel), 'You are *el roi*.'"[20] When one adds to these options the (literal) unlikelihood of a well being named after a designation for a benevolent numen/deity/God in the mouth of a runaway slave-girl, the kerygmatic options in this word-play are almost inexhaustible. In addition to this there must be some significance to the information that this place named after the experience of Ishmael's mother is twice identified as the Negeb haunt of Isaac (Genesis 24:62, 25:11). The return of Hagar to her home is gapped in characteristic biblical narrative economy. The coda brings Abram back to front and center, carrying out the naming instruction, which could only have been retailed to him by Hagar in a full account of her experience. To overlook this invitation to the gap-recognizing and gap-filling capacity of the reader is to overlook the discrepancy between the instruction to the woman and the instruction's fulfillment by the man. If the reader, identifying himself with the yet-unborn ancestor Isaac, has missed the point of YHWH's concern for Hagar, the Egyptian mother of Uncle Ishmael, the narrator exploits the coda to stress the ties between Grandfather Abram and the young woman who mothered his firstborn. Three times in two verses it is *Hagar* who bears to *Abram* (four times) a *son* (twice) named *Ishmael* (twice), the naming—an acknowledgment of God's favor in the granting of this son—performed by the patriarch himself.

Hagar's Expulsion—and Her Revelation

(1) YHWH **now** took note of Sarah as He had promised. YHWH dealt with Sarah according to his declaration. (2) Thus it was that Sarah conceived and bore Abraham a son in his old age, at the set time that God had specified. (3) Abraham named this son of his, just born to him, he whom Sarah had borne to him, Isaac. (4) Abraham circumcised his son Isaac at the age of eight days as God had charged him. (5) Abraham **now** was 100 years old when Isaac his son was born to him. (6) Sarah thought, "Smiles has God produced for me. Any one hearing [the news] will smile over/for me." (7) [The thought behind what] Sarah thought: "Who would have predicted [such a moment] for Abraham: *Sarah has given suck to child,* that I should have indeed born him a son in his old age!"

(8) The lad grew older, reached weaning age. And Abraham held a great feast at the time of Isaac's weaning. (9) Sarah spied the son of Hagar the Egyptian, (the one) whom she had born to Abraham, making merry. (10) Said she to Abraham, "Drive out that slavegirl—along with that son of hers." Her thought (*ki*): *No son of that slavegirl shall be an heir alongside my son, not alongside (my) Isaac.* (11) This turn was most unwelcome to Abraham, troubled for his son. (12) But God said to Abraham, "Be not distressed on account of the youngster nor of your maidservant. Precisely as Sarah proposes to you, even so do her bidding. Verily it is through Isaac that your line will continue.[21] (13) For all that, this maidservant's son will I also make into a nation, he too being your issue."

(14) Forthwith at morn Abraham fetched food and a skin of water. These he handed to Hagar—he loaded [them] on her back—and the lad as well, and sent her away. So she proceeded to wander in the wasteland beyond Beersheba. (15) When the water was drained from the skin, she left the lad alone under some bush or other, (16) herself went on a stretch and sat down a good bowshot's distance away, her

thought being, "I won't look on at the child's death throes." Thus settled at a distance
she broke into loud sobbing. (17) God took heed of the youngster's call. An angel of
God called to Hagar from heaven, "What troubles you, Hagar? Have no fear. Verily,
God has taken heed of the lad, yes of the plight that he is in. (18) Up now, rouse up
the lad, take him firmly by the hand. Of a truth, a great nation will I make of him."
(19) God then cleared her sight and she beheld a spring of water. She proceeded to
fill the skin with water and gave drink to the lad. (20) Thus did God attend the
youngster and he grew to maturity. He kept to wilderness haunts and became a skillful
archer. (21) He settled in the wilderness of Paran. And his mother got a wife for him
from the land of Egypt. (Genesis 21:1–21)

Source-criticism assigns verse 1 to J, having no other option for the appearance
twice of the Tetragrammaton. Verses 2–5, featuring ᵉlōhīm twice, might well have
been assigned to E, to whom the rest of the story through verse 20 is credited since
he, like P, shuns the use of YHWH in Genesis. But a concern for numbers and
dates, as for such cultic matters as circumcision, being hallmarks of P's stationery,
this source prevails over any possible claim for E. Speiser refuses to translate the
second YHWH in verse 1 (replacing it by the pronoun "he," noting: "The second
half of the verse duplicates the first. It appears to stem from P, with a secondary
change of Elohim to Yahweh, induced by the preceding clause." We find it characteristic of source-critical manipulations and typical of its fast-and-loose concepts of
the editorial process to deny a human editor the leeway to iron out a discrepancy,
even while it permits the dead weight of "a preceding clause" to *induce* a pointless
change of P's *elohim* to J's *YHWH*. We shall cite his further *Comment* to serve as foil
to our own reading:

> Except for the first five verses, the narrative is the work of E. The proof goes deeper
> then the external evidence from the consistent use of Elohim (6, 12, 17, 19, 20). The
> present account duplicates ch. xvi. More significant, however is the fact that the rea-
> son for Hagar's departure is not at all the same as in the earlier story by J, nor does the
> personality of Hagar as here depicted bear any resemblance to that of her namesake in
> the other story. So complete a dichotomy would be inconceivable in the work of the
> same author, or in a fixed written tradition. (Genesis p. 156)

To say that "the present account duplicates ch. xvi" is slovenly use of language,
for the verb suggests exact correspondence. But this lapse is understandable on the
part of a comparative Semitist newly fallen under the spell of source-critical solution of narrative doublets via assignment to different hands. What is not so com-
prehensible is how the differences between the doublets are seen as proof of two
authors rather than of one author telling similar yet different stories.

The characters are identical except for their names. In the first story Abram,
Sarai, Hagar and—waiting in the wings, so to speak—Ishmael and Isaac; while
Deity is always referred to as YHWH, even His agent is not just an angel but
YHWH's angel. In the second story Abraham, Sarah, Hagar, Ishmael and Isaac;
while Deity appears first as YHWH and then as God, even to his agent's being
called God's angel. Both stories begin with a focus on the matriarch. In the first it
is Sarai who gives her slave over to Abram's embrace, that she—Sarai—may obtain a child by proxy (as Speiser convincingly demonstrates). In the second, it is

the sight of that child, in his seventeenth year at the least, that arouses her jealous fears for the newly weaned child who issued from her own womb. In both stories, Hagar, in a situation dangerous or desperate in a barren steppe, is vouchsafed a divine revelation in the vicinity of a spring or cistern of life-giving water. In both revelations the providential care of Deity is assured the mother: her son shall become a great nation. The martial skills of that nation-to-be, implicitly or explicitly dwelling in the steppe-lands and at odds with his more civilized kinsmen and neighbors, is symbolized in the second story by his masterful archery; in the first story, the second part of the oracle, predicting the untameable nature of the Ishmaelite race and its bellicose destiny, could hardly have been comforting to his mother; it is therefore, in all probability, another instance of free direct discourse, seemingly addressed to Hagar, actually intended for an Israelite audience in a future centuries away (from Hagar's time, that is, not from the narrator's time).

Having done fair justice to the similarities we turn now to the differences, differences that will reveal that the two narratives are neither duplicates of nor inconsistent with one another, that each is meaningful in its own context and is complementary to the other. In the first story the child that Hagar is carrying in her womb is the child of Sarai. Sarai would only be spiting herself if she drove from home the bearer of her future hope. Her complaint is that an incubator sees herself as agent rather than instrument, full-wife or sultana to Abram rather than odalisque subject to her royal mistress (16:4 g^ebirtāh). The flight to the Negev (Does she hope to make it back to Egypt? And to what status or fate there?) is all Hagar's idea. And had not Deity intervened to turn her back when she was but a few hours gone from Abram's tenting grounds, who could doubt but that the resourceful Abram would have retrieved her, even restored her to a chastened mistress who would not again risk bringing to despair the young woman bearing her heir and her husband's. What need then at all for YHWH's intervention? One might as reasonably ask why God gave tongue to church-bell clappers and turned gongs into words in a young man's ears, "Dick Whittington, Dick Whittington, thrice Lord Mayor of London-town!" YHWH has promised Abram a countless posterity. In Chapter 15 the territory promised to his descendants was to extend from "the river of Egypt to the Great river, Euphrates." In neither direction, as we noted, did historic Israel ever attain — perhaps even aspire to — such distant borders. But YHWH never limited his promise to a single branch nor even to two or three branches of Abram's line. In Chapter 17, which we have yet to discuss, the promise is explicitly formulated in terms of several nations and separate dynasties in separate kingdoms. YHWH's concern then for Egyptian Hagar — her origin twice stressed in chapter 16 (again in ch. 21, and again in the notice there of her obtaining from the land of Egypt a wife for Ishmael) — is also an expression of care and concern for Abram in the matter of his posterity, not only through the child yet to issue from Sarai's womb but through that of his wife Hagar.[22] So long as Sarai remains barren (and at age 75, cf. 16:5, her recourse to Hagar as her proxy is as realistic as the desperation it bespeaks) the child in Hagar's womb is the one and only conduit to a future line sprung from Abraham's loins.

Let us note that it is the source-critical assignment of 16:15–16 to P in an otherwise J narrative, of Chapter 17 to P, of Chapter 18 to J, and most of Chapter 21 to E, which masks from our poetical appreciation the unity, harmony, indeed the suspenseful buildup to a climax of the progressively emerging promise and fulfill-ment of that promise to Abraham. It starts with the most broad and general formu-lation in Chapter 12 of his becoming "a great nation," continues with offspring "like grains of earth" in 13:16, to the assurance in 15:4 that his line will continue through his own biological issue, that assurance beginning of realization in Hagar's womb—the mother *de jure* being Sarai—and then with the promise in Chapter 17 that while Ishmael's branch will thrive, the main growth of Abram's line will be from yet another son, a biological son of Sarai as well as of Abram, all the forego-ing culminating in the bearing of Isaac by a ninety-year old (renamed) Sarah to a (renamed) Abraham aged 100, and now with that child's weaning marking his suc-cessful passage through the risks of infancy.

Now, her maternal drive satisfied, having come to accept that the miraculous-ness of her having given birth was not merely a stroke of luck, confident now that the God who wrought this for her will continue to preserve her newly weaned child, Sarah suddenly sees Ishmael through different eyes. The cheerful teenager enjoying the festivity of his younger brother's celebration is no longer her own child, he is son to that Egyptian slave-girl; he is indeed his father's firstborn heir. But that is now a source of anxiety to her. Even if she could have been privy to the preachment of Deuteronomy 21:15–17, that would not have affected her or Isaac, for there could never be any question as to which child was the principal heir. No, her concern is lest Ishmael share at all, diminish by a fraction the totality of the in-heritance that will fall to her one-and-only son Isaac. The judgment on the ruth-lessness of Sarah's maternal loyalties is present for us in the pain of Abraham when confronted by the demand of wife number one that he send away both his first-born son and the mother who bore him. And which of us—the readers—would not concur in that judgement, could not but identify with Abraham in his pain, and—forgetting that Sarah's protective parental stance is perhaps a slightly hyper-bolic reflection of our own short-sighted normality—would not see her as the stock evil stepmother of fairy tales?

Two elements in the plot, however, may strike us as less than credible. One, how can the God of Scripture, champion of justice, endorse Sarah's decree, even seek to assuage the pain of Abraham over the loss of his flesh and blood son by the promise that his main line will be reckoned through Isaac? Two, assuming that Sarah must have her way—disinheritance of Ishmael is after all her goal—could that goal not have been achieved by finding a home for mother and child under some kinsman's aegis (or since Lot has been removed from the scene, perhaps in the encampments of the allied Amorite brothers, Mamre, Eshkol, and Aner [14:13])?

Both perplexities dissolve when we remind ourselves that the biblical author constantly performs feats of literary legerdemain as he shades his personae from three dimensional humans in an historic and never repeatable past to symbolic foreshadowings of ethnic and political entities. And the bridge between these two narrative poles, perhaps better the fulcrum of the seesaw, is the role played by God. Thus it is no unfeeling Deity who seconds Sarah's bidding to Abraham. God is here, to an extent, a fully realized character, a powerful and long-lived participant in the lives of succeeding generations, who at this point—without approving of

Sarah's deplorable self-centeredness nor condemnation of Abraham for even vacillating in the face of so cruel an ultimatum—relieves Abraham of responsibility for a decision. He himself will take over now, as guardian and guarantor of the future. Sarah's bidding is now God's command, and Abraham cannot but obey. His continuing concern for Hagar and Ishmael is symbolized in the quantity of food and water he "loads" her with. Despite the troubles Speiser (among others) finds with verse 14, the text is not obscure, nor is the "middle of the sentence . . . now distorted." The three Hebrew words "placed on her shoulder" are a normal asyndetic hypotactic construction expressing a parenthetic aside, drawing attention to the quantity of provisions he gave her and leaving her hands free to grasp her son's, as she will be bidden to do (again) in verse 18.[23] Whereas the pregnant Hagar, who was a runaway from home, must have had some sense of the direction she should take (she did make it as far west and south as Beer-lahai-roi, which must have been situated at a point very close to today's border between Israel's Negev and Egypt's Sinai), the expelled Hagar wanders aimlessly in the steppe of Beersheba. Aside from the normal characteristic of economy in biblical narrative, it would certainly strike a false note to have Abraham consoling Hagar upon her banishment by assuring her that God would be watching over her. And so we have the heart-wrenching scene of a despairing mother, giving no thought to her own thirst, sobbing as she waits for her only son to breathe his last. It is a scene that drives home to us the heartlessness of good people, of parents fixed on the welfare of their biological issue to the unnecessary exclusion of the loves and hopes, the aspirations for life and fulfillment of those who in the last analysis are, if not our own children in every sense, the children of our brothers and sisters. And it reminds us as well that a God who cares for us must also care for them.

Ishmael's birth to a one-time slave girl is but one aspect of his ancillary role in the story of Abraham's family. A question that cannot but tease our curiosity, for all our knowledge that answer can there be none, is what if anything our biblical author owed to a received tradition in creating this character or representing his sketchy history? To be sure, that question can equally be asked of Abraham himself. But whatever fraction of the Abraham presented to us owes to historic fact or family tradition or poetic fancy, his representation as the ideal ancestor of an ideal Israel, friend of God, and ancestor of many nations is clear. What by comparison can we say of Ishmael? He barely exists as a character, he barely draws a breath or two on the story's stage. He is born and he is circumcised. We catch sight of him laughing once (through Sarah's eyes), hear him gasping once (through Hagar's ears), and have the narrator's word for his skill at archery. As brother-rival to our own ancestor Isaac, we tend to see in him a foreshadowing of a sociopolitical entity, contesting with our own sociopolitical ancestral stock in a later generation, very much as we see Esau-Edom as a polity contesting with Jacob-Israel. But is that the way that the biblical author intends us to view Ishmael?

The question I am posing is a literary one: how the biblical author when crafting his story, perhaps as late as the sixth or even the fifth century, related to the Ishmael he was presenting or representing as person and as ethnic prefigurement. For clues to the answer we can focus on two antipodes: one, an exclusively poetical focus on the story itself; and two, an essentially meta-literary or "historical" focus on the historic entity called Ishmael, from the first appearance of that grouping to its latest datable one.

In regard to the poetical focus, we have already said almost everything that can be said in pointing out the sketchiness, the nebulousness of Ishmael as a persona. The significance of this can be better appreciated if we compare Ishmael and Esau as *dramatis personae*. "Esau the outdoorsman skilled in the hunt" of 25:27 may be a roughneck compared to the Jacob who is "an unwily man keeping to home." But that is a far cry from the violent cutthroat he is made out to be in some rabbinic sources. In the deprivation by deceit of his father's favored-son blessing he is the innocent and wronged party, done in by a mother's treachery and a brother's moral spinelessness.[24] Yet is he goaded by his loss into a murderous resolve, restrained for the moment by unwillingness to bring pain to his father, a resolve discerned by his mother. And as she reads this mood correctly so does she also read correctly the character of this elder son, which will with the passage of time bring him "to forget how you [Jacob] treated him"(27:45). And for all the double entendres and ambivalent emotions, the play of tensions, of resentment and forgiveness, guilt and contrition in the confrontation of Jacob and Esau on the former's return from Aram, the bottom line is that the two are reconciled. Yet are they depicted as brothers destined from the womb to struggle for mastery, and for all Esau's martial professionalism he [in his progeny] is fated to be subjugated by his brother until a time comes when he will throw off that yoke of servitude (25:23, 27:40). Ishmael, like Esau, is more sinned against than sinning (a misleading understatement, since he does nothing at all). If he is destined to be (in his progeny) untameable, and to stand alone against all and to hold his own against all his kinsmen (16:12), this may be as much due to his kinsmen's debarring him from fertile settlements as to an innate preference for steppe existence and the marauding it encourages.

The texts that enable us to focus on Esau and Ishmael as meta-literary or historical entities, which is to say as ethnic, national, or political entities with which the monarchies of Israel in the north and Judah in the south related on terms of amity or hostility, are examined in the section of this book devoted to Structures (see chapter 7). Nothing in that examination runs counter to these observations: Unlike the eponymous children of Lot, Moab, and Ammon, Ishmael is never a political eponym; and whatever pastoral or bedouin tribes may be identified as descendants of this brother of Isaac and son of Abraham, these are never featured as hostile, making incursions against the descendants of Jacob. (The latter in contrast with Midian, Abraham's son by Keturah, and Amalek, grandson of Esau, neither of whom become eponymous of polities, but both of whom figure as steppe-raiders victimizing Jacob's descendants.) The case is somewhat more complicated with respect to Esau, for strictly speaking he too, like Ishmael, is not a political eponym, although he is identified as legendary leader of the proto-polity that became the state (sometimes ruled by a king) of Edom. Thus in respect to the descendants of these two descendants of Abraham's, one a son and the other a grandson of his, there are no *Benē Esau* or *Benē Yishmael* (comparable to *Benē Ya*ᵃ*kob* or *Benē Yisrā'el*, although there are the gentilics *'Edōmī* and *Yišmā'ēlī.*)

It would seem, therefore, some basis for assimilating—as literary prototypes— the totally unrealized persona of Ishmael with the more fully realized, although sketchy nonetheless, persona of Esau. Or, to be more specific as to our intent, to see both these (essentially fictional) protagonists as rival protagonists to the personae with whom we identify as posterity to ancestor, exploited by Scripture to teach a lesson to us of the *bet Yaᵘakob* or *BᵉnēYisraʹel*. No one reading the story of the two brothers, Esau and Jacob—particularly Chapter 27, on the purloined blessing—would fail to realize, unless he had already identified with Jacob, that the narrator's sympathies are totally with the victimized Esau, with the flesh and blood person Esau, not with the historic abstraction Edom or Seir. Whatever our judgments on such questions as the good sense or fair-mindedness of Mother Rebecca's favoring one son over the other, or of the good sense or obtuseness of Father Isaac, who is so easily fooled, any defect in the verisimilitude of either of these parents as personae is compensated for by their functioning as prophetic foreshadowings. Thus Rebecca's role serves both to shift much of the moral guilt from Jacob who, acting on his own, would have been an altogether unforgivable scoundrel, and to make her an unwitting historic factor or signpost, to the dominance of Israel over Edom. So too is Father Isaac, more blind in wisdom than in eyesight, in possession of all his other sense-faculties but as unperceptive as he is lacking in sensitivity, a historic factor or signpost. When the storyteller has Isaac responding to Esau's arrival with the dish of venison, he prefaces the response by a notice that Isaac was gripped by spasms of trembling. He tells Esau that an unnamed other has brought him food and received a blessing. He is then made to add what is as unnatural a conclusion as was his intrusion of peoples and nations to be subjugated to his son into that blessing. "I blessed him" he says, and then adds, as though he has just been given a glimpse of the portentousness of his blessing for future history, "and blessed will he surely be!" The notion that a blessing extracted from a father by fraud is irrevocable is, of course, nonsense. But not the notion that a father may, in invoking blessing upon a son, be the unwitting harbinger of divine will. Esau expresses the nonsense of the former by asking his father, "Did you not *reserve* a blessing for me?" Which is to say, since you have *alienated* the blessing owing to me, can you not give me the blessing that you must have reserved for my brother? (This delicious bit of free direct discourse lies in the use of ʂl "alienate," where "alienate" makes no sense and must be rendered by what the context demands, i.e., "reserve, hold back.") Similarly, Esau's incredulous question and plea: "Have you but a single blessing, father mine? Bless me, me too, father mine." In these words the narrator expresses not only the common sense of Esau, and the anguish of a mortal son of a divine Father, whose beneficent resources must be limitless, but also the ineluctable vagaries of God's way in history. For as surely as Esau did nothing to warrant his posterity's subjugation in time to come, so surely had Jacob done nothing to warrant the success of his posterity, Israel, in time to come. And there is the moral intended for us, the seed of undeserving Jacob, himself through Isaac—the undeserving younger son by Sarah—the destiny-favored son of Abraham. And that too—the felicity that we, the posterity of Isaac, enjoy in our sovereign state and territory, as over against the hard lot of our steppe-dwelling cousins—is ours by grace and not desert. But for accident of birth, we might be roaming the wilderness while grandfather Abraham's merit carried down to his grandchildren via another branch.

THE NAMES OF GOD IN GENESIS, CHAPTERS 16 AND 21

The regular appearance of YHWH in the story of Hagar's flight and of Elohim in the story of Hagar's expulsion might be seen as an almost mechanical reflection of the disposition to deploy the former in context of intimacy with the patriarch Abram/ Abraham and his chosen line through Isaac and Jacob, and of the latter in contexts of outsiders to/of that chosen line. Thus in Chapter 16 the intimacy of Sarai's (free direct discourse)[25] invocation of the Tetragrammaton, as against Hagar's (free indirect discourse)[26] naming of a Deity known to narrator and reader as YHWH, but altogether (seemingly) unknown to her. Yet this Hagar, wife to Abram and proxy-womb of Sarai, bearing their future child, is very much within the chosen family's parameters, and so even when her greater distance (from the "God of Abram and Sarai") is marked by an angel's appearance, it is nonetheless an angel of YHWH. In Chapter 21, by contrast, with Isaac now arrived as the bearer of the chosen line, Yishmael now dispensable—in Sarah's mind, at least, if not in Abraham's—the Hagar in whose expulsion the Deity concurs (but whose flight in Chapter 16 is vetoed) is the concern not of YHWH but of Elohim, and the revelation to her is made by the mediating angel of Elohim. And whereas in 16:11 YHWH's angel (in free direct discourse) tells Hagar that YHWH had heeded her plight, in 21:17 Elohim's angel tells her that Elohim has heeded the plaint of her son.

For all the cogency of the foregoing, we would stress that to see these correspondences as mechanical is to render more problematic those texts where the contexts do not conform so agreeably to our desire as critics to control the author by the imposition upon him of the formulas we have devised. Thus, for example, the double appearance of YHWH in 21:1 and the sudden switch to Elohim in the following verse. To this we shall return after examining a few more pertinent pericopes.

THE ANNUNCIATION OF ISAAC'S BIRTH: TWO VERSIONS

Midst Covenant and Circumcision

Episode A

(1) Abram was ninety and nine years old when YHWH appeared to Abram and said to him, "I am El Shaddai. Conduct yourself according to my will, sustain your integrity. (2) Then will I endow you with this covenant-promise of mine—making you oh so populous." (3) Abram fell face down.

God addressed him as follows, "For my part—here is my compact with you: (4) You are to become father to a mass of nations. (5) No longer will your name be Abram, rather will Abraham be your name, betokening: Father to a mass of nations have I destined you to be. (6) As I make you so very fruitful, and make you into nations, so will kings spring from you. (7) I shall fulfill my pact with you and with your seed after your lifetime for ongoing generations, an ever continuing pact, to be god to you as also to your seed, your succession. (8) [That is,] I do grant to you and your successor seed the land of your sojourning, even all the land of Canaan, for a holding in perpetuity. Their god will I be."

(9) God said further to Abraham, "You for your part are to keep my pact, you and

your successor seed down the generations. (10) This now is the covenant [rite] which you are to observe, between me and all of you, that is, your seed succeeding you: the circumcision of every one of your males. (11) When you circumcise your foreskins, that will be the mark of the covenant between me and all of you. (12) At the age of eight days shall every one of your males in all your generations be circumcised, [yes, even] homeborn slaves as also those whom you acquire by purchase of any alien race, any not of your very own issue. (13) Take care to the circumcision of slave homeborn or purchased that the covenant [mark] be on your flesh as [mark of] the covenant-in-perpetuity. (14) As for any uncircumcised male, one who has failed to have his foreskin circumcised, that person shall be cut off from his kin: My covenant has he breached." (Genesis 17:1–14)

Episode B

(15) Further said God to Abraham, "Your wife Sarai—no longer are you to call her Sarai; rather—Sarah is her name. (16) I will bless her, by her also will I grant you a son, yes by my blessing of her will she become nations, yea kings of [different] peoples will from her come to be."

(17) Abraham [as told above] fell face down. He smiled as he thought to himself, "Will child be born to a hundred-year-old man? And by Sarah—will a ninety-year-old woman bear child? (18) And so he said to the Divinity, "Pray, let Ishmael thrive by your grace." (19) God said, "But [attend,] it is indeed your wife Sarah who is to bear you a son—Isaac you are to name him—with whom I shall fulfill my covenant-promise, a covenant-promise enduring to his issue in his aftertime. (20) As for Ishmael, I have heeded you: lo, I have decreed blessing for him, a fertility so rich, a posterity so numerous—twelve chieftainships will he sire—destining him to be a great nation. (21) But my covenant-promise, I shall fulfill with Isaac, he whom Sarah will bear to you at this time in the coming year." (22) So, having finished his address to him, God took off from Abraham. (Genesis 17:15–22)

Episode C

(23) Abraham then took his son Ishmael and all his homeborn and all his purchased slaves, every male of the members of Abraham's family, and circumcised their foreskins—on that very same day, just as God had addressed him. (24) Abraham, **now** was ninety-nine years old when his foreskin was circumcised, (25) and his son Ishmael was thirteen years old when his foreskin was circumcised. (26) On that very same day was Abraham circumcised as well as his son Ishmael. (27) And all the members of his family, homeborn and purchased of alien race, were circumcised along with him. (Genesis 17:23–27)

The very fact of two annunciations of one and the same birth to one and the same father in two successive chapters would seem to add decisive weight to an argument that has already advanced other criteria for assigning the two parallel narratives to two different authors or sources. Thus, for example, Speiser, who concurs with the assignment of the second narrative (18:1–15) to J comments on this first one:

> The entire chapter is from the hand of P. As a unit of considerable length, and richer in content than the genealogical lists, this section offers a better picture of P's scope

and approach. At the same time, the contrast with other sources stands out all the more sharply in view of J's parallel treatment of the covenant theme in xv.

P's concern about chronological detail is reaffirmed at the outset (vs. 1); and it is worth stressing that all other statistics about Abraham or Sarah stem from the same source. . . . If J was familiar with these computations, he did not consider them germane to his story.

The most striking difference, however, between P and J lies, here and elsewhere, in their contrasting treatments of the same event and their dissimilar approach to the individual. Both here and in xv [The Covenant between the Parts] the central theme is the covenant. J saw the covenant as a future factor in world history. It was set against a fearsome background which helped to bring out the numinous character of YHWH's partnership with Abraham. Yet for all his bewilderment, Abraham was presented as a sensitive participant in an intensely dramatic process. Just as in the Eden account, J's handling of the episode was earth-centered. In the present account by P, on the other hand, the overriding feature of the covenant is circumcision. And much of the chapter is devoted to a formal pronouncement by God. P's approach, in short, is ritualistic and impersonal.[27]

The above citation, typical of source-critical analysis, reveals upon closer examination that the criteria for distinguishing between the two sources (J and P) are remarkably vague and hardly contrastive. Thus "contrasting treatments of the same event," assumes that the central theme in the two narratives is covenant, whereas we would see the central theme of this narrative as the annunciation of Isaac's birth and compare it to the following chapter, which features that same theme. Then, "their dissimilar approach to the individual." Speiser goes on to see J's Abraham of Chapter 15 as "for all his bewilderment . . . a sensitive participant in an intensely dramatic process," and "the handling of the episode . . . earth centered," while in our narrative "by P . . . the overriding feature is circumcision . . . much of the chapter is devoted to a formal pronouncement by God. P's approach, in short, is ritualistic and impersonal." Questions: In what way is Abraham in Chapter 15 more sensitive a participant than the Abraham in Chapter 17? How is the revelation in Chapter 15 a more intense process than the revelation in Chapter 17? And what does dramatic intensity have to do with source-assignment? In what way is the episode of the covenant-between-the-parts more earth-centered than the ordination of circumcision in Chapter 17 as human-centered token of adherence to the covenant? If P's approach in Chapter 17 is ritualistic and impersonal, is the slaughtering of animals and the procession between the parts not ritualistic, and is the smoking firepot more personal than the God who commands in Chapter 17? And while Deity as subject appears in Chapter 17 as ʾĕlōhīm some half-dozen times, how did the meticulous editor who preserved P's compulsion to avoid the Tetragrammaton slip up in the opening verse 1? And, further, why should P, who pretends not to know that God has a name until the disclosure in Exodus 6, feel a need to have that God introduce Himself to Abraham by the name—if name it is—El Shaddai? And why, when Abraham addresses God in verse 18, does P decide that he did not address ʾElōhīm [God: a proper name) but haʾĕlōhīm "the divinity" (god: a common noun)?

The most important difference between my own approach to this Chapter 17 and Speiser's is in how I view its central theme. Despite the omnipresence of the covenant themes in this chapter, and the unarguable stress on the importance of the circumcision rite ordained by God for Abraham's descendants as mark of their loyalty to that covenant, I see all this as setting for the central theme. This theme is not covenant as such, which has appeared in several revelatory episodes, but with whom in particular the covenant is to be continued, on the parts of both God and man. Hence my own view of the necessity to compare this episode with its parallel in Chapter 18, a parallel strangely unnoticed by Speiser, who discerned "duplication" in the two stories of Hagar in the wilderness.

And as a matter of poetical address, particularly because there is no quarrel as to Chapter 17's owing to one hand, we must address the really remarkable amount of repetition in the first fourteen verses. The term *b^erīt* "promise, covenant-sign" appears ten times. The reciprocal aspect of covenant, the *betweenness*, appears four times; the single-vector aspect of *b^erīt*, as from God to man or from man to God — often indicated by prepositional particles, sometimes direct and sometimes indirect, such as *'et, ōt, l^e* — appears almost a dozen times. Abraham, as the individual with whom God is establishing His pact, is featured seven times; five times the covenant is with both Abraham and his posterity. The emphasis on posterity appears eleven times: five times under the rubric *'ah^arey-*, three times under *l^edōrōt-*, and three times under *ōlām*.

And, once again, an assumption of purposiveness on the part of the author, especially in the deployment of redundancy, will eventuate in an exegesis and a kerygma that will in turn vindicate that assumption.

The narrative begins with a synoptic episode, verses 1–3a. Except for the specific of the El Shaddai self-introductory rubric, and for the appearance of the specific term for covenant(-promise) *b^erīt*, which is, however, implicit in every promise of God's to his servants, the urging of Abraham to continue in his fidelity to God's ways and the promise of proliferation as reward is a broad formulation substantially the same as in the first revelation to Abram in 12:1–2. The bottom line, however, is clear.

The resumptive episode begins with 3b, with the expansion of proliferation in terms of "a mass of nations," resuming also the *nations* of 12:2. The word for *mass* or multitude provides in a pun-like manner for an additional consonant to be inserted into the name Abram. This new name, incorporating the nuance of agglomeration or conglomeration, is then explicated not only in terms of nations but of kings; hence the element of royal dynasties points not to changing dynastic lines in one nation but to many dynasties in many nations. Thus far the promise to Abraham in his own person, from God to him in verses 2, 4, and 6. Verse 7 begins with the assurance of the fulfillment of the promise as not just from God to Abraham, but to his seed after his lifetime for long generations; the specificity of the promise is that this Deity (who has identified Himself as El Shaddai) will be god (= protector) to Abraham and to them. This promise to continue as god or protector, to Abraham first and then to his posterity, is then expanded to include the grant of the territory of Canaan to Abraham (to whom in his person it will never be other than "the land of his sojourning") and to his posterity, whose "holding in perpetuity" it will be, because he will continue to guard them as their *^elōhīm*. Inasmuch as *posterity, for long generations*, constituting national entities, must inevitably refer to descendants "after (your) lifetime," we have translated the second appearance of *zar*ᵃ*kā* ʾ*a*ʰʳᵉ*kā* by "your seed, your succession." Let us note that in English, all those who come after us are in one sense our successors, and so too in Hebrew. On the other hand, in both languages, not all of our posterity will continue as our "successors," in the sense of preserving our traditions and being heir to our dignities. If we will then recall our discussion of Ishmael, he who is fulfillment of the promise to Abram in 15:4 that only one "sprung from his loins will heir to you be," and further, anticipate that Ishmael in his descendants will not be successors to this promise of land, we shall be alert to the ambiguity in the promise. For all its seeming specificity, the promise, which to Abraham at this point could only have been intended for his successor Ishmael, does not in so many words specify Ishmael as the heir. And there is the rub!

It may prove helpful at this point to divide the resumptive episode of this revelation into separate phases. Thus Phase 1, verses 4–6, addressed to Abraham as the immediate persona who has earned the covenant-promise, and verses 7–8, the extension of the promise to his progeny and specification of the grant of territory now called the land of Canaan. Phase 2, introduced by *vayyōʾmer* ᵉ*lōhīm* ʾ*el Abrāhām* in verse 9, "God said further to Abraham," has the dialogue beginning with *w*ᵉ*attā* "you, for your part," balancing the beginning of God's dialogue in Phase 1, verse 4, ʾ*anī* "I, for My part." This now combines with the obligation of Abraham and his descendants to observe their part of the covenant (in general) and specifically to mark their obedience by the circumcision rite. The continuity with Phase 2 is thus the notice of verses 23–27 of Abraham's punctilious carrying out of this commanded rite. But this notice is the result of and not part of the revelation. The last phase of the revelation then, Phase 3, is verses 15–22, which we mark off as a separate episode, with verse 23 constituting a rather unusual *dixit atque exit* in conclusion of a biblical revelation.

Phase 3, verse 15—exactly like Phase 2, verse 9—begins with "God said further to Abraham." But the dialogue quickly signals that this is a continuation of the first part of Phase 2. It is exactly parallel to the promise to Abraham as a persona: Sarai's name, like Abram's, undergoes a slight but significant symbolic alteration. Sarah too is to have a son. No, not quite. Sarah too—like Hagar before—is instrument for God's beneficence to Abraham. Her blessing is twofold. First, "I shall bless her, granting to you a son by her also." Second, "I shall bless her, in that she will become nations, kings of [different] peoples will from her come to be."

Abraham's response to this announcement is to fall to earth face down. Since he fell face down in verse 3 and has not risen since, this notice would seem to call for comment both on the grounds of repetitiveness and inconsistency. But it poses no difficulty for us if we are alert to the subtle effects achievable by the synoptic-resumptive narrative technique. Indeed, in this present example of that narrative strategy, the second notice of Abraham's throwing himself upon his face is the narrator's way of indicating just when—at what point—in the revelation, which is synoptically told in Episode A and extensively developed in Episode B, Abraham did so. The assumption of this posture, one which expresses self-abasement before a higher power, may betoken a range of differing attitudes. Thus, for example, in 2 Samuel 14:4 it bespeaks the humility of the petitioner; in Ruth 2:10 the acknowledgement of a boon graciously bestowed; and in Numbers 14:5 acknowledgment of the complaint of the people they serve by leaders who do not deserve such repudiation. That Abraham's assumption of this posture is expressive of thanks for the boon announced is unquestionable. But this response would be equally fitting at the end of the promise in verse 8. The point of locating this act of grateful obeisance at this juncture is to signal a skepticism on Abraham's part, a skepticism explicitly thought, yet a skepticism which might have betrayed itself to an observer by the merest twitch of a lip, had not such observation been precluded by Abraham's kneeling or lying face to the ground. But—the narrator informs us—that numinous figure speaking for God (who has called himself El Shaddai), that manifestation referred to in verse 18 as *haᵉlōhīm* "the d/Divinity," is quick to read Abraham's mind and heart, to interpret correctly Abraham's prayer on Ishmael's behalf, this in response to the promise of a son by Sarah, as equivalent to a mild demurrer: *a bird in hand is worth two in the bush.* It is to this almost-expressed skepticism that God replies, introducing his statement with the adverbial conjunction *ᵃbāl* "nevertheless, for all that, contrary to the foregoing." Which is to say, "Despite your doubts and misgivings, it is Sarah your wife who will bear you a son;" and not just *a* son, indeed, but *the* son, through whom the blessing of possession of Canaan and the special protection of God will be fulfilled.

Midst Feasting and Mission Grim

(1) YHWH appeared to him at Mamre's Oaks—he sitting in the tent opening as the day waxed hot. (2) Looking up, he saw a sight: three personages looming over him. At the sight he ran toward them from the tent entrance, then stretched to the ground in obeisance. (3) He said, "My Lord, if I have won Your [*sing.*] favor, do not pass Your [*sing.*] servant by. (4) Let some water be fetched, rinse your [*pl.*] feet, and take your [*pl.*] ease under that tree. (5) Let me fetch a morsel of bread, and take you [*pl.*] some refreshment. Then go on your [*pl.*] way. Surely 'tis not by chance you [*pl.*] come this way, by your servant." They replied, "Do so, just as you have proposed."

(6) Abraham dashed to the tents, to Sarah, and said, "Quick, three *seā-* measures of choice flour, knead, make loaves." (7) Then to the herd Abraham himself ran, picked a yearling, tender and choice, handed it over to a hand who hastened to dress it. (8) He fetched curds and milk, and the yearling [meat] that had been readied and set these before them—he himself standing attendance upon them while they dined.

(9) They addressed him then, "Where now is Sarah, your wife?" "There, in the tent," he replied. (10) Thereupon He declared, "I shall be back with you, be sure, at gestation's term—and Sarah your wife shall have a son!" (Sarah, **now** was listening from the tent entrance, it [the tent] to His back. (11) Abraham and Sarah were elderly, well on in years—Sarah's menses had come to an end. (12) Sarah smiled to herself: *So long dried up, should I again have known conjugal delight—and my husband so old?* (13) Said YHWH to Abraham, "What means this scoff of Sarah's: *Am I really to bear child, being myself so old:* (14) Is anything so wondrous as to be beyond YHWH['s doing]? On schedule will I come back to you, at gestation's term, and Sarah shall have a son." (15) Sarah dissembled—so intimidated was she—*I did not scoff.* But He said, "No, you scoffed indeed." (Genesis 18:1–15)

This story of the annunciation of Isaac's birth is in so many ways repetitious of the annunciation in Chapter 17 as to contain no feature of novelty for source-critics who assign the first account to P and this second one to J. There are, on the other hand, enough dissimilarities to raise the interpretive possibility that Chapter 17, itself made up of synoptic and resumptive episodes, may in itself constitute a synoptic forerunner of a resumptive episode, that is, the text of 18:1–15. Militating against such a hypothesis is a feature of the synoptic-resumptive mechanism that is not easily discerned as between these two narratives. In every instance that we have studied, the resumptive episode provides a significant element of plot development or moral twist that is not present in the synoptic episode. Thus the addition in the resumptive episode is never trivial, idle, or even just whimsical. What significant lesson is there in Chapter 18 that is absent in Chapter 17? A clue to the answer to this question may lie in the setting, or ambience, or mood of the parallel narrations. This factor is suggested in my own captions for the two stories.

In the case of Chapter 18, the episode of the annunciation, the episode of Abraham's intercession in respect to Sodom, as well as the aftermath of that city's destruction do indeed, in Speiser's words, "present a continuous and closely integrated narrative." And unless we can discern a light or humorous side to Abraham's pleading for the life of an entire city, or to the grim story of that city's overthrow and of the righteous escapee's besotted involvement in incest, there would seem to be a contrast between the first and the next two episodes. Three angels feast in the first episode, at an indolent pace, and almost incidentally announce a birth to come; in the second episode, one of the three tarries with Abraham in a life-and-death debate, while his two companions continue their downhill journey to extract Lot from the city before they reduce it with fire and brimstone.

In the case of Chapter 17, the element of the covenant is not new. What is new is the introduction of the circumcision-rite as a mark of the covenant to be observed by Abraham and his descendants. True, the covenant element functions as the framework for the emerging realization that God intends the covenant line to continue through the yet unborn Isaac and not the thirteen-year-old Ishmael. But it is this Ishmael, along with Abraham and the bound members of Abraham's family, who undergoes circumcision. What, in terms of the steadily developing story of Abraham's many begettings, and the narrowing of his religion-line down to Isaac, is the point of the introduction of the circumcision-rite at this juncture? To answer this question we must raise a meta-literary consideration, the historical question of when circumcision became a sine qua non rite of Israel's religion. Or since this question will surely remain unanswerable, not when we today believe that rite originated in Israel but when the biblical author himself believed it to have originated. To the objection that we have just been told in Chapter 17 what the biblical author's belief is, my reply is no; what we are asking, the meta-literary consideration we are raising, is whether the author is (as most of us, believing religionists and skeptical scholars alike, assume) intent on conveying historic information to us with a view to satisfying our antiquarian curiosity, or to impressing upon us the critical importance of this surgical rite.

This last motivation for a putative historiographical narrative intention is open to doubt on a number of scores. One, a normative prescription, apodictically or ca-

suistically formulated, legalistic or perceptive, for all that it is open to interpretation as to degree of literalistic or metaphoric intent,[28] is nonetheless a less ambiguous form of instruction than a narrative. (The Cain and Abel story assumes that
murder is an atrocity, it does not enact it as a crime.) And nowhere in the rich deposits of biblical *halakha* does the rite of circumcision appear as a self-standing
command from God.[29] Two, such narratives as the perplexing assault of YHWH on
Moses in Exodus 4:24–26; the treacherous exploitation by Simeon and Levi of the
circumcision of the newly-covenanted Shechemites; the distinction in Joshua 5
between the circumcised Israelites, who left Egypt to die in the wilderness, and the
uncircumcised Israelites—who were born in the wilderness and survived to cross
the Jordan—suggest another kerygmatic intent in these narrations: that this criti-
cally important rite in the eyes of Israelites at large might be featured in prophetic
narrative to contrast external obedience to time-honored rites with unblinkered
perception of and obedience to God's will. Such indeed is the force of such
metaphors as circumcision of the heart (= mind) in Deuteronomy 10:16, 30:6 and
the jeer of Jeremiah against the circumcised of foreskin but not of heart among
Egyptians and Judeans, Edomites, Ammorites, Moabites, and sundry dwellers of the
steppe (9:24–25). Third and particularly significant in light of this last passage
from Jeremiah is the explicit testimony of Chapter 17 that the Ishmael who under-
went the rite at the age of thirteen years was born to an uncircumcised father,
while Isaac, first to undergo circumcision at the legislated age of eight days (21:4)
was born to a father who had himself been circumcised. While the foregoing may
strike some as facetious and perhaps not in the best of taste, the literary critic may
not close his eyes to the possibility of a bit of ribaldry in an otherwise essentially
somber text. But the point I am driving at is that one of the background facts of
this literary composition is that the author knew that circumcision was not an exclusively Israelite rite, and that although it was practiced by non-Israelite descendants (at least by this author's construction) of Abraham such as Ishmaelite and
Keturah-ite steppe-dwellers, and by the Isaac-descended Edomites, it was also a
critical practice for unrelated Egyptians, and for two peoples, descended—as he
will tell us—from Abraham's uncircumcised nephew Lot.

    In any case, we have come as far as we can in contrasting the plot settings of the
two annunciations. Let us now more closely examine this second narrative. It begins, as did the previous one, with the narrator informing us that YHWH appeared
to Abraham. But whereas in Chapter 17 the form of this Divine appearance was
thereafter characterized by an indeterminate *ᵉlōhīm*, once (verse 17) called *the*
ᵉlōhīm (who presented himself as El Shaddai), in this Chapter 18 the form of that
Divine appearance is specific. YHWH this time has chosen to present himself in
the guise of three personages, mortals to all appearances. Yet for all this, the narrator has skillfully and unambiguously indicated for all but the literalism-blinded
source critic that Abraham had from the moment he espied them recognized that
these "three men" were stand-ins for YHWH. This recognition is expressed in his
immediate run to greet them and his prostration before them.

    The most self-depreciating of hospitable etiquettes does not call for host to
so abase himself, especially before unexpected callers who accept such homage
as their due. How—are we to understand—were they garbed? Rich dress, even

princely headdress, might have stamped them as nobility, but not as representations of Divinity. This is indicated by the suddenness of the apparition. They do
not appear at a distance, even as hazy figures growing larger and more clear in outline as they emerge from the shimmering heat waves. One moment there is nothing unfamiliar in Abraham's vista; the next moment they are "looming over him,"
figuratively speaking of course, for they are yet at a distance, and it is their numinous dignity, not their physical size, that makes them extraordinary. Another clue
to Abraham's recognition of the nature of his visitors is the narrator's repetition of
a detail. Verse 1 starts in normal waw-conversive narrative style with the fact of
YHWH's self-revelation, and this notice is immediately explicated in the paratactic clause, in that same narrative style, of what met Abraham's eyes when he
looked up. In between these two clauses is the hypotactic parenthetic clause—subject followed by participial verb—telling us that Abraham at the time was sitting
at this tent opening. Now in verse 2 the narrator tells us that it was from the tent's
opening that Abraham ran to greet them. Whence else? The point, of course, is
that normal etiquette would have been satisfied by Abraham's rising, perhaps, and
waiting for them at the entrance to his tent. My explication (in my translation) of
singular and plural pronouns in Abraham's address to his visitor(s) is necessary for
the reader to appreciate that Abraham recognizes all three to be numina in YHWH's
service, even while he addresses the leader of the three as my Lord. My capitalization of this word, for Hebrew 'adōnāy, is to indicate that Abraham knew the nature
of the Persona he was addressing. The Masoretic textual tradition, as I pointed out
in chapter 1, supplies the regular Hebrew consonants for the common noun "my
lords" (pl. of majesty), but in providing the pointed vocalization for the term,
which their tradition dictates as substitute for the ineffable Tetragrammaton, they
lengthen the final patah of 'adōnay to qāmeṣ ('adōnāy); this to indicate to the reader
that speaker and addressee are cognizant that this "my Lordship" has YHWH as
referent.

The content of Abraham's address to his visitors is also pregnant with meanings,
which seem to have eluded so astute a translator and commentator as Speiser. First,
the formulation for please, "if I have found favor in your eyes." Speiser departs from
this literal translation to render the Hebrew by "if I may beg of you this favor."
While this rendering cannot be called wrong, it does in its use of the present tense
conceal another clue as to Abraham's recognition of his visitor's divinity; the past
tense in the literal expression is yet another indication that Abraham knows this
deity/Deity as (the) one/One with whom he has had experience on previous occasions. Then, also, the request that divinity tarry a while. Abraham's knowledge
that not even extraordinary mortals could have slipped by the many hands guard-
ing his flocks on an oft-contested range and penetrated without warning to his
headquarters should alert us to the possibility of a response to divine appearance altogether different from Abraham's. But Abraham's words show that he has not for a
moment entertained a fear that God could be other than friendly to him. Our
translation of 'al ken ᵃbartem is closer to the Hebrew than any of the renderings we
have come across, and further, catches the spirit of Abraham's response: "I know
you are friendly to me, your coming by is an expression of that friendliness, show
me even greater honor and friendship by letting me play the host."

There is surely a playful or even humorous whimsy in the notion of a mortal's playing host to Him whose guests all creatures are. And perhaps that note of whimsy is struck in the acceptance of the invitation, not by the one addressed, but by the entire company. The pivotal clue to the whimsy lies, however—and one can only marvel that it has for so long been overlooked—in Abraham's specification to Sarah of the bread she is to prepare. The *seā* measure seems to have equaled about eleven of our dry quarts. Three of these measures then—some sixty-five pounds of flour, when mixed with water and baked, would have yielded double or triple that weight in bread—to feed three men? And whereas in another revelation (Judges 13) an angel when offered food pointedly does not eat, here the men—soon to be called angels (*mal'ākīm*)—do eat, and inasmuch as there is no complaint that the host is overdoing things, presumably finish off over a hundred pounds of bread, an entire bullock, and a generous quantity of yoghurt and milk! The repast—which Abraham had proposed as "a morsel of bread"—now over, the guests ask Sarah's whereabouts. Despite Abraham's response, "There in the tent" (where else should she be?), the question is essentially free direct discourse: the question's purport is not to question her not having waited upon the guests, nor to her presence inside or outside, in one tent or another; it is to focus the reader's attention upon her in a certain locus on stage, and to alert us to the fun yet to come. The Deity now speaks in the singular. Having, so to speak, brought Sarah to center stage, He announces that in some nine months' time, when He will appear again, Sarah will have borne a son.

This announcement, substantially the same as in 17:21 in regard to the timing of the birth, is now followed by two or three hypotactic parentheses. One, that Sarah was eavesdropping from the tent entrance, which tent was to the speaker's back, and that Abraham and Sarah were well on in years, Sarah being beyond her climacteric. Now this second piece of information we have already been given in 17:17, in Abraham's thought at the moment of annunciation that he was a year short of a hundred and Sarah a year short of ninety. Similarly, the aside that Sarah was standing at the opening of the tent, which was situated behind the numen's back, is functionally parallel to Abraham's lying face to the ground in Chapter 17: in neither case could an expression on the face of the mortal have betrayed to the numen an inkling of what was going on in that mortal's mind. Having set the stage now for the reader, the narrator resumes the paratactic sequence with the notice of what was indeed going on in Sarah's mind. As in 17:17 Abraham, fallen with face to the ground *smiled and thought in his heart*, so here in 18:12 Sarah, standing at tent-entrance behind the numen *smiled and thought within herself*. The smile in each case is a wry smile, to be sure; a skeptical smile, expressing disbelief in a promise the mortal so desperately would want to believe, and the negative force of "jeer" or even "scoff" is perhaps too strong to convey the skepticism of a smile on the part of one receiving tidings too good to be true.

There is also a parallel in the sensitivity expressed in the skeptical thought of both Abraham and Sarah. Abraham in 17:17 first reacted to the unlikelihood of a ninety-nine-year-old man being capable of siring, and then went on (with an implicit *and were that difficulty overcome*) with the unlikelihood of an eighty-nine-year-old woman becoming pregnant. Sarah, too, begins with her own inadequacy, and only then thinks of her husband's. But in between the two thoughts the narrator has recourse to the perfect tense, which, seemingly untranslatable as a past tense in the context, is regularly ignored by translators, who blithely treat it as if it were a simple future tense. Her thought is, essentially, *I am dried up . . . [and were that not impediment enough,] my husband is old.* But the formulation of this internal dialogue, starting with a prepositional phrase and continuing with a perfect tense —expressive of completed action in a future time[30]—is a masterful touch by the narrator. A literal translation is, "After my being worn out shall I have had pleasure, and my husband old?" It is a masterful and delicate touch, for it points to an act that must take place preliminary to the fulfillment of the prophecy. Why delicate? Surely it is not in the best of taste to evoke our parents in the intimate act that led to our birth; perhaps even less so the evocation of grandparents coupling to conceive our parents. And in this case! Our great-great-grandparents doing so at so advanced an age! But our storyteller is no prude, and his smile is a kindly one, tinged with ancestral pride: They were old, Grandpa Abraham and Grandma Sarah, but (by Providential grace) there was still some juice in the old folks when Papa Isaac was conceived, and—doubtless—no little joy at his making.

As Abraham and Sarah are alter egos in the matter of their skepticism about the son promised them, the son whose name will always recall their suppressed smiles of doubt, so are they equally vulnerable on the score of their lack of faith in God's promise. Abraham is chided for being remiss in Chapter 17, where God indicates to Abraham that He has understood the true meaning of his plea for Ishmael. In this chapter Sarah, who was not privy to the first revelation and promise of a son to come from her own womb, and who reacts to it even as did Abraham before, is the target of the reproof. But interestingly, the reproof is not made directly to her. As in the previous chapter, the address—not by the numen but by YHWH—is only to Abraham. And just as He knows what is going on in the mind of Sarah, of whose location in the tent behind him the numen has been informed by Abraham, so does his rhetorical question to Abraham partake of poetic license in the assumption that Abraham too could know what was going on in Sarah's mind. How—he asks the husband who had earlier harbored the same reservation—how can Sarah be skeptical about a promise of YHWH's? And to doubt such a promise's fulfillment on the strength of human incapacity! (And let us note that the rabbis are engaged in a close reading of the text, not overinterpreting, when in the reformulation of Sarah's thought in his question to Abraham, He pictures her as doubting only her own capacity to bear, with no suggestion at all of her aged husband's impotence.) Does Sarah think that the God who opens or closes all wombs is not up to bestowing fertility upon a woman who has so long been sterile? And at that, a woman who will be fertilized by a husband whose single act of procreation was performed fourteen years earlier, and even then at the advanced age of eighty-five!

And now the narrator shifts his attention from Abraham to Sarah. Abraham was given no opportunity to respond to God's gentle chiding of him for his disbelief. Here, too, no response from Abraham, but a response from Sarah. To the note of reproof in YHWH's question regarding a thought she never uttered, she responds guiltily—speaking as much for Abraham as herself—with a denial. A denial that is not a lie, for neither she nor Abraham actually expressed the doubt in word or smile, but which is not quite true either. And to this denial, no more spoken aloud than her first sad doubt, it is a benign and paternal YHWH who responds. "I did not really doubt," she says, and hears His gentle reproof, "Not so, you really did."

On this note our story ends. Further commentary would seem bound to be superfluous and anticlimactic. But, this being a story told in Scripture, we must as always raise the question: Delightful as it is, why is it told at all? Why entertain ourselves at the expense of our first grandparents? And the answer would have to include the assumption implied in the question: that any entertainment or sheer esthetic pleasure derived from a Scriptural story is a bonus for the reader, a by-product of the author's art. The essential object of that artist is (was) to convey a message. In the case of the many stories of patriarchs or matriarchs who were unable to sire or to conceive, and then did so at an unbelievably advanced age, we have metaphoric variations on the theme of the vagaries that attend not just pro-creation, or continuance of line to guarantee ancestral afterlife, but the continu-ance of one out of many lines. One line that, seeking to vindicate its ethnocentric place as God's favorite, is ever taught to see itself as called to be the worthy vessel of God's purpose in the unfolding story of times and history.

One aspect of the theme is a noble or royal couple who cannot conceive. An-other is the husband's capacity to sire, but by a commoner in his harem, not by his equally royal consort; and then, when past childbearing time, the queen miracu-lously becomes a mother. And when this pattern is repeated in several succeeding generations, one can only marvel at the providential grace that, late but surely, provided the long prayed-for scion of both royal parents. In the case of our patriar-chal great-grandparents, their own royal status is assured by their being the elect of God, but they themselves were sojourners in a land not their own. In their survival of perils as posed by haughty kings, xenophobic natives, or international hostilities, we would have to be blind to miss the guardian care of God. And so too—witness the three tales of a matriarch barely escaping the embrace of a foreign potentate— must we realize that the purity of our descent, the prevention of interloping alien genes, is something that could not have been but for the guarantee of an ever-wakeful God.

Our own tendency to single out the distinguished ancestor from whom we reckon our descent—be he a Mayflower passenger or she a daughter of the Ameri-can Revolution—will show how literally humans can construe the whole question of descent and pedigree. If each offspring of a single line produces only two (male) children who so reproduce in turn, there will be one thousand male descendants in the tenth generation, and the multiple of that by a thousand every ten generations thereafter; so that the resultant number will be a billion in the fortieth and a tril-lion in the fiftieth generation. (Allowing twenty years for a generation, we need only ten centuries to achieve this fiftieth generation.) Reversing the direction of our gaze, consider the fatuity of the passion to pass on our genes or our fortunes to our posterity when a great-grandchild carries (on average) but one-eighth of our genes, and one two generations later less than 2 percent. How many are there who deny any belief in *any kind of immortality* who will yet devote all their time and energy to the amassing of a fame, if not a fortune, that may not endure even a few decades after their death? Is it our own myopia, or inconsistency, or self-contradictions, that—blinding us to our own blindness—lead us to deny to the biblical authors the rudimentary considerations or simple arithmetic calculations that we have just been entertaining? A review of Psalm 105 will leave no doubt that the poet who identifies his ethnic and national and personal identity with patriarchs from Abraham to Joseph, and servants of YHWH such as Moses and Aaron, saw the (hi)story of the forefathers through the lenses of metaphor:

4. Seek YHWH and his resources . . .
5. Recall the wonders he has performed . . .
8. He has kept his covenant in mind enduringly, the matter he ordained for a thousand generations
9. The one he made with Abraham, his oath to Isaac
10. Rearing it as a decree for Jacob, for Israel an enduring covenant, to wit:
11. "To you [sing.] do I grant Canaan land, the territorial borders of your heritage."
12. When they were in number a handful, barely—and only sojourners there,
13. They traveled from one nation to another, from one kingdom to another people.
14. He permitted no ordinary man to take advantage of them, and kings he chastised on their account:
15. "Touch not mine anointed ones, to my prophets do no harm!"
    [YHWH redeems Israel from Egypt, and into the promised land]
44. He granted them the territories of nations, the store of many polities they took as theirs,
45. All to one end: That they observe his decrees, that they preserve his teachings.

Let us return now to our two stories of the annunciation. In both of them, faith in the destined future is at the core of the narrative and the dialogue. In both the ancestral avatar—if I may borrow an apposite metaphor—appears less than steadfast in faith. In the context of a divine revelation the promise of an event is greeted with skepticism. Not because it is unwelcome, but rather because it is so desperately longed for. In the case of Chapter 17 the Abraham who now has a thirteen-year-old heir by Hagar, an heir he took to be the promised one of an earlier revelation, is prompted by the promise of an heir by Sarah to think how tenuous is anyone's hold on life, and to entreat for the welfare of Ishmael. A mere fourteen years before, when Abraham was eighty-five years old (16:16), ten years after his departure for Canaan (12:4), neither Sarah nor he thought it unlikely that he should sire a child by a young woman. And now in Chapter 18 it is Sarah, who cites not her menopause alone but Abraham's presumed impotence. That YHWH's reproof of Sarah—as also the implied reproof of Abraham in Chapter 17—was not in anger should be clear from the whimsical tone of the story, from the fulfillment of the promise, and from an additional item in the narrative sequence. Between the promise and the notice of the promise's fulfillment in Sarah's conception in 21:2, we have two stories intervening. In one we learn how fares the line of nephew Lot, how he came to be the father of nations, two of them through the less than licit cohabitation with his own daughters. In the other we have the 89-year-old Sarah, so restored in youthful beauty (or had she never shown her age to begin with?) that God Himself must keep her inviolate, intervene to threaten the life of a king and his realm, to keep that king from succumbing to the ravishing seductiveness of this ageless matriarch.

Given, then, the genius of Scripture's authors for metaphor, metaphors strung together like gems on single or parallel strands, the poetical design remaining consistent for the complementariness and harmoniousness of the various kerygmas, we have again in both these stories a teaching on the nature of faith, of faith in a God whose beneficence is witnessed in a thousand manifestations, and which is often shaky in proportion to the strength of our desire to believe. The message of these stories is that in relation to God, Abraham and Sarah, old as they were and wise as they may have been, were children. As we are, all of us, no matter what depth of maturity we attain, in the matter of faith. God, however, is patient and gracious.

ANNUNCIATION'S AFTERMATH

If we reexamine the narratives in chapters 17 and 18, focusing on the annunciatory elements in each, and specifically in terms of the narrower announcement of the future birth of a son by Sarah to Abraham, we cannot but be struck by the little space that is actually accorded to that announcement. In both narratives, much more attention is paid to the reaction of the human protagonists to that announcement and to the divine response to that reaction; in both cases, the response is either complaisant or consolatory. In chapter 17, out of a total of twenty-seven verses, only three deal with Isaac's birth (verses 16, 19, 21). The rest deal with the *bᵉrīt* "covenant" that God is making with Abram and the circumcisional sign or witness to that covenant. And although the males circumcised that day feature Ishmael and Abraham, it is "with [the yet unborn] Isaac [as over against Ishmael] that I will fulfill my covenant" says the Deity in verses 20–21. Thus the context compels the recognition that the focus of this announcement is on Sarah's son's personification of the covenant-people-to-be, and not on the persona of that son Isaac.

Similarly in the fifteen-verse narration of that same annunciation in Chapter 18. Here only half of a single verse deals with the announcement. The rest of the narrative deals with the tableau of the Deity's representations for the annunciation (in striking parallelism to the opening tableau in Chapter 19), the response of Sarah to the announcement, and YHWH's reaction to that response. YHWH's reaction—sounding in Abraham's mind or, possibly, spoken by one of the visitors—is the last word of the episode, for the next verse begins with the visitors' departure. The context then, in terms of Isaac, who will father the covenant-line, is the line of Uncle Lot, whose seed will constitute the eastern neighbors of the covenant-people. And the covenant itself—which is not mentioned here explicitly, either in substance or ritual token—what of it? It is there implicitly in the verse that explains the whole point of that covenant, verse 19. This verse defines the choice of Abraham and his line through Isaac in terms of their divinely destined role to embody, enact, and champion the cause of that justice, the outrage of which is symbolized in Sodom and Gomorrah, the cities—note, both of them!—in which Lot had taken up residence (19:29).

Let us then proceed to that dialogue that is the bridge between annunciation and doom, between hope for the future and the depravity of the past, between Isaac's line as the covenant-people and the non-covenant-people who, for all that they do not share that line's moral dignity, have survived, and who will continue to survive as the tutorial charges of the seed, in whom they too will find blessing.

YHWH AND ABRAHAM IN A DIALOGUE ON GOD'S JUSTICE

(16) The personages picked up from there [to an elevation whence] they looked down on Sodom's expanse—Abraham going with them to see them off.

(17) YHWH, **now**, had thought, "Can I keep hidden from Abraham what it is I am about to do? (18) In view of Abraham's sure destiny to become a great and populous nation in whom all earth's nations are to achieve blessing: (19) in that I have singled him out for one purpose, to charge his children and his line in succession with the keeping of YHWH's way, the practice of justice—to the end that YHWH may bring about for Abraham the promise he bespoke for him!" (20) YHWH's thought was: the outcries against Sodom and Gomorrah are so many, the offenses charged to them so grave, (21) I must go down to conclude, to consider whether or not they have so ruthlessly behaved as is the shriek of protest which has come to my attention.[31]

(22) From there [the place of overlook] the personages [two of them] turned to make their way down to Sodom—Abraham remaining behind in YHWH's presence.

(23) Abraham came forward; he said, "Will you really sweep away the innocent along with the guilty? (24) Suppose that there are fifty within the city who are innocent, will you make a clean sweep rather than forbear in regard to the entire place for the sake of the innocent fifty within it? (25) Perish forbid that you do such a thing; putting the innocent to death along with the guilty, so that the innocent and the guilty fare alike. Perish forbid it to you! Shall the governor of all earth not exercise judgment?"

(26) YHWH replied, "If in Sodom, I find within the city fifty innocent, I shall forbear in regard to all that place on their account."

(27) Abraham spoke up, "Lo, I have already presumed to address my Lord, I who am but dust and ashes—(28) Suppose that the fifty innocent are short by five, will you—on account of this five—destroy the entire city?"

He replied, "I will not destroy it if I find there forty-five."

(29) Once again he addressed him, "Suppose there are only forty?"

He replied, "I will do nothing, on account of the forty."

(30) He said, "Let my Lord not be vexed if I persist: What if there are thirty there?"

He replied, "I will do nothing if I find thirty there."

(31) He said, "I have presumed to venture with my Lord [this far]—suppose there are twenty there?"

"I shall not act on account of the twenty," he said.

(32) Then he said, "Let it not vex my Lord that I speak this one time more: What if there be only ten there?"

He replied, "I will not destroy, for the sake of the ten."

(33) YHWH, bringing his audience with Abraham to a close, departed; and Abraham went back, to his place. (Genesis 18:16–33)

Among the many interpretations of this second episode in Chapter 18 I will cite two as contrasts to my own reading of it. And, as I have repeatedly stressed, competing interpretations of an artistic product need not be contradictory or mutually exclusive. The differences often inhere not in whether certain messages are at all present in the artwork before us, but in what is the central message, the kerygma that lies at its core. Thus, Sheldon Blank implies an eloquent case for this dialogue as a daring championing of justice by a mortal, in defiance of a deity who is not, or possibly may not be, guided by the strict canons of justice; in short, a parallel to Prometheus's defiance of Zeus.[32] Speiser in his commentary sees the issue not so much as between justice and injustice, but as between justice and grace: "The patriarch . . . in his resolute and insistent appeal on behalf of Sodom, seeks to establish for the meritorious individual the privilege of saving an otherwise worthless community." (Apparently the "meritorious individual" in this case would be Lot, not Abraham himself.) Then citing the "correlation between merit and fate" treated in Mesopotamian literature and in the Book of Job, Speiser goes on to declare that "J's own answer is an emphatic affirmation of the saving grace of the just. And even though the deserving minority proves to be in this instance too small to affect the fate of the sinful majority, the innocent—here Lot and his daughters— are ultimately spared."[33]

A crucial factor in determining the development of the narrative theme in this story (as in so many others we have studied) is the temporal logic of the narrative and the deployment of the Hebrew tenses in paratactic and/or hypotactic sequence. Our translation divides the narrative into two episodes, each followed by a nominal sentence in parenthetic and parallel hypotaxis.

Thus in the first episode we have the three visitors proceeding from Abraham's tenting-ground to a spot whence they can look down on the plain of Sodom. Abraham's accompanying them is expressed in the hypotactic parenthesis, as is also the explanation for YHWH's permitting Abraham to come along: his intention to disclose to Abraham what "I am about to do." This last project is then explicated in (paratactic) formulation in verses 20–21: that is, not a judgment already arrived at, but a decision to "go down" to investigate in order to arrive at a judgment.

In the second episode, two of the visitors turn to make their winding way down the slope, this in paratactic formulation, while the following notice in hypotactic formulation has the third visitor, YHWH Himself, standing at cliff-edge with Abraham. And Abraham it is who initiates the discussion, thus indicating that the content of verses 19–20 have already been made known to Abraham.

The dialogue itself, in which the mortal does seem to challenge the Divinity, would indeed be in place in a pagan ambience whose theology does not identify deity and justice. But is it in place in the Scriptural theology that indissolubly unites justice (or even grace) with power as attributes of God? This question points to a feature of the dialogue that is shared by the preceding narrative, namely its playfulness. At first reading, if the playfulness is not discerned, it does seem as though the question at issue is whether justice is better served by the sparing of a host of criminals in order that a few innocents not be punished, or contrariwise, to overlook the unmerited punishment of a few innocents who are either blind to the company they are keeping or so confident in their righteousness that they can feel secure in their health, despite their residence in a barrel of rotten apples. But the play on the numbers of the hypothetically righteous inhabitants of Sodom is just that. The number is steadily reduced from fifty to ten, and ten serves as a metaphor for three, two, or one. For in any event, it turns out that only Lot is truly righteous, and that by virtue of his merit even his Sodomite sons-in-law would have been delivered with him had they been conscious enough of their fellow-citizens' crimes to take Lot seriously.

Abraham begins with the possibility of fifty innocents in a city of perhaps a hundred times that number. God's answer is straightfaced (no disrespect intended): he will forbear for the sake of fifty. Does God's repetition of this number mean that he would desist only for a minimum of fifty? Abraham has his opening. What if there are only forty-five? But he does not ask whether God will spare Sodom for the sake of forty-five: he asks whether God will destroy for the paltry five non-existent innocents. God accepts Abraham's argument as to what would be proper judgment. He does not, however, let Abraham's sly debating tactic pass unremarked. He will spare for the sake of forty-five innocents. Eventually, Abraham dispenses with tricks and, having apparently won his point, returns home. But only after two of the personages representing YHWH have turned to take the trail that winds down to Sodom, and the third personage—seemingly YHWH in person—has ended the audience and similarly departed. What has escaped notice is that the departure of the two "men," leaving the third with Abraham (in verse 22), and the departure of the third in verse 33, are the brackets for the revelatory dialogue here and only here. Other accounts of revelation may signal the beginning of the audience or its end, but not both. Thus for example, the departure of the numen heavenward in 17:22, but not his arrival at the beginning of the chapter. Why is this account unique in this respect?

The clue lies in verse 22, where two of YHWH's agents depart while the third figure, representing YHWH himself, remains behind with Abraham. Abraham, then, does not remain behind, for he is going nowhere. Yet the text reads, "Abraham remaining standing before YHWH." Rabbinic tradition, however, records that this wording is one of the *tiqqunē sōferīm* "scribal emendations," a substitution for the original "while YHWH remained standing before Abraham." (Cf. Midrash Rabba) Inasmuch as it is the arraigned or his attorney who stands before the judge, not vice versa, the reversal of positions was substituted out of respect to Deity. And we must be grateful to the transmitters of the text that their reverence for its sanctity is such that they record the occasions when they have felt impelled to tamper with it. For it is this original and bold anthropomorphism, which reverses the dignities of mortal and divine, which militates against a Promethean purport as the dialogue's central kerygma. Verses 17–19, perhaps as eloquent a parenthesis as exists in Scripture, reveal that the entire dialogue took place only at God's invitation. And that invitation calls for Abraham, as father of the justice-dedicated seed-to-be, Israel, to act the role of paraclete, humanity's supporter, advocate, and intercessor. The entire dialogue is thus a didactic device. YHWH had not yet passed sentence. There is no effrontery in Abraham's seeming challenge, "Will the Magistrate of all the world not exercise judgment?" It is not challenge at all, but a rhetorical question, the strongest way to make a statement, a statement borne out by the outcome that every single innocent is given a chance to escape the doomed city. Unlike the divine magistrates of paganism, the capricious gods who are sentenced by God in Psalm 82, the God of Scripture cannot ever be anything but just.[34]

Our story is didactic, but not (like our commentary, perhaps) pedantic. And this is disclosed in the storyteller's bold imagery, an imagery in keeping with the rabbinic indulgence of *chutzpah* "effrontery," even toward Heaven, in the interest of justice. The imagery, of course, is in the picture of YHWH "stationing Himself before Abraham," putting himself in the dock, so to speak, so that his attribute of justice may stand examination.

The stage is cleared. The curtain drops. The next act will take place in Sodom. And despite the awfulness of entire populations to be wiped out, the drama there is not tragedy, for the innocent will be extracted, the guilty punished. And a sensitive reading of Chapter 19 will find the comic note struck more than once. But our discussion of Chapter 18 is not complete. The chapter is a single narrative, featuring the same characters (except for Sarah) in two episodes. How are the two related? The one vein that runs through both episodes is the playfulness, the light touch, the note of humor that is encapsulated in the name of the son who is to be the propagator of the chosen seed. *Yitzhak* means "he smiles, he laughs." And the subject of that sentence is God. This is the God who reveals himself simultaneously as One and three, three men—never called angels—who put away a feast worthy of Rabelais' Gargantua or Pantagruel; who splits himself into two parties: one a party of two heading for Sodom, the other a party of one remaining behind, to be engaged by Abraham in a debate on justice, a debate in which he permits himself to be arraigned before the mortal. Yes, this is a God who is full of surprises. The first episode ends on a note of mild reproof directed to the faith of Sarah, whose unseen smile (like that of her husband in Chapter 17) bespeaks skepticism that YHWH can restore potency to a man nearing his hundredth birthday, or fertility to a woman approaching her ninetieth. The Hebrew term *pele'*, appearing in the question of God's capacity to do *wonders* or *miracles*, has the sense of "surprise," and while it is the mortals who are mocked for their surprise, it is YHWH who displays the humor and is the author of all the surprises. The very situation or the drama that is strung out through a series of synoptic and resumptive episodes—repeated promises of blessing and posterity, partly but never quite satisfactorily fulfilled for both Sarah and Abraham—is what should occasion surprise in the audience. Why the suspense? Why the dragging out of the process? Why would (or should, or did) the Almighty YHWH make Sarah and Abraham wait so long, that the fulfillment when it comes appears miraculous? The answer, of course, is the extended metaphor (extended also in the long duration of barrenness for the matriarchs Rebekah and Rachel) of the joy in the achieving of the long longed-for, of the providential care, which, moving so slowly, moves inexorably nonetheless, and moves in apparent zigzags as firstborn after firstborn (Ishmael, Esau, Reuben, to name but a few) proves not to be the vessel of destiny. And if faith in an ultimately benevolent God can be so sorely tried, what can be said about the ultimately overwhelming nature of the faith that one is indeed the chosen vessel of destiny? Unlike his more dogmatic followers, therefore, YHWH must exercise forbearance and humor when his chosen ones experience lapses of faith. And shocking as it may seem to the sensibilities of the inquisitorial believer, the ultimate sin may derive from the blasphemous notion that would deny a sense of humor to the God who created man with that highly esteemed sense.

THE STORY OF LOT

Episode A: Sodom Shows Its True Colors

(1) The two emissaries arrived at Sodom in the evening—Lot **then** sitting in Sodom's gateway—Lot at first sight [of them] rose to greet them. He made obeisance to them, face to the ground. (2) He said, "I pray you, my lords, turn aside to your servant's house for lodging. Wash there the dust from your feet, and as early as you please resume your mission." They said, "Not so. Out-of-doors we'll spend the night." (3) But he importuned them so vigorously that they did turn aside and entered his home. He prepared high tea for them, had cakes fresh-baked, and they dined. (4) Just about to retire, they, when the townsmen of the city—Sodom's townsmen—besieged the house, minions and elders, all the citizenry of every degree. (5) Calling to Lot, they addressed him, "How now the men, those overnight guests of yours—bring them out to us that we may become intimate with them." (6) Lot went out to them in the entrance-way, having the door behind him barred shut. (7) Said he, "No my brothers, commit no mischief. (8) I have at hand two daughters who have never had intimacy with man. Let me deliver them to you, and deal with them as you see fit. But those personages you are not to touch. Verily, it is for shelter they took haven under my roof." (9) Some said, "Come closer—move away!" Others said, "This lone alien came to sojourn and now plays the magistrate!" "Now then, we'll do you mischief worse than [what we had in mind] for them." They pressed hard on this gentleman Lot. Some came close to break in the door. (10) The [two] dignitaries now took a hand [in the matter]. They pulled Lot back inside with them—the door **now** they [re-] locked. (11) As for those [Sodomite] worthies at the entrance, them they had assailed with sight-searing light, minion and elder—they were unable to obtain entry. (Genesis 19:1–11)

Episode B: Last Chance for Lot's In-Laws

(12) Now said the men to Lot, "Any kin or kith you have in this place, be they son-in-law, [grand]son or [grand]daughter, anyone of your own in this city—get them out of this place! (13) Verily, we are about to devastate this area— so great the charge against them in YHWH's judgment, YHWH has dispatched us to lay it waste. (14) Lot went forth and spoke to his sons-in-law, those who had taken his daughters in wedlock. He said, "Quick now, get out of this area. Verily, YHWH is about to devastate the city." But in the eyes of his sons-in-law he could only have been joking. (Genesis 19:12–14)

Episode C: The Escape from Sodom

(15) **Now then** just as the morning-star had risen, the emissaries urged Lot on, to wit, "Quick now, take your wife and your two daughters that are here at hand, if you would not be swept away in the doom of the city." (16) When he yet dilly-dallied the men gripped him by hand and his wife by hand as also the two daughters each by a

hand—[this only] by the grace of YHWH's pity on him—they brought him out and deposited him outside the city. (17) And just as he was bringing them outside [it], he said, "Flee on for your very life, cast no glance behind you, come to no halt anywhere in the plain, to the hills make good your flight if you would not be swept away!" (18) Said Lot to them, "Please, not so, my Lordship. (19) Look now—your servant has indeed found favor in your eyes, and greatly have you extended your merciful dealings with me in the interest of prolonging my life. But I, for my part, just cannot make my escape all the way to the hill country. Lest the cataclysm overtake me and I die, [I propose]—(20) Look now, that town yonder is close enough for me to make good my flight there. And it is such a wee place. Let me, pray, make escape thither—such a wee place it is—and let me survive." (21) He said to him, "Now in this particular too I have hereby granted you great face, not to destroy that city as you have proposed. (22) Make haste now to escape there, for till you reach that spot I can undertake nothing." (This now is why the city is name Zoar ["Trifle"].) Genesis (19:15–22)

Episode D: The Doom of Sodom and the Fate of Lot's Wife

(23) (The sun **now** had fully risen over the horizon just as Lot reached Zoar.) (24) (YHWH **then** precipitated on Sodom and Gomorrah a rain of blazing sulfur, [a rain] from heaven, from YHWH himself.) (25) Thus he reduced those cities and that entire plain, together with the populations of the cities and every growth of the soil. (26) His wife, however, looked back past him and became a salt statue. (Genesis 19:23–26)

Episode E: What Abraham Saw

(27) Early that morning Abraham hied to the spot where he had stood in YHWH's presence. (28) He looked down upon the vista of Sodom and Gomorrah and of all that area of the plain. And there before his gaze: a fog had arisen over that area like that rising from a furnace. (29) Thus it was that when God laid waste the Cities of the Plain, God was mindful of Abraham and dispatched Lot from within the area [doomed to be] devastated when he was reducing the cities wherein Lot had taken up residence. (Genesis 19:27–29)

Episode F: The Issue of Lot

(30) Lot then moved upland from Zoar and settled down in the hill-country, his two daughters with him—so fearful he of staying on in Zoar. He lived in a cave, he and his two daughters. (31) The elder said to the younger, "Our father is old. And male there is none to cover us in nature's universal way. (32) Come now, let us ply our father with wine, bed with him and of our father keep posterity live." (33) So they plied their father with wine that night. The elder girl made bold to lie with her father—he **now** unconscious of her coming and going. (34) Upon the morrow the elder said to the younger, "Lo, I did lie yestereve with Father. Let us ply him with wine tonight again, and you enter and lie with him; thus may we [both] keep of our father posterity live. (35) So that night again they plied their father with wine. The younger then proceeded to lie with him, he unconscious of her coming or going. (36) So did the two daughters of Lot conceive by their father. (37) The elder bore a son, named him Moab, he the ancestor of the [people of] Moab of our own day. (38) And the younger

girl, she also **now** bore a son, named him Ben-ammi, he the ancestor of the Ammonites of our own time. (Genesis 19:30–38)

A review of the narratives treated in *Toward a Grammar* will bear out the following: the full force of a story's kerygma is only realized at the very end of that story. But "story" itself is a literary category with meanings both denotative and connotative, sometimes—in keeping with context—independent of one another, sometimes overlapping, and sometimes antipodal, if not contradictory. In the case of the literature of our time, two opposed categories bear names in English making for a kind of confusion, which coordinate nomenclature in another language does not. Thus, for example, French *comte/histoire/nouvelle* and *roman*, as contrasted with English *short story/novella* and *novel*. The category *short story* has very little to do with length; many such will contain many more words than constitute a work universally recognized as a *novel*. Indeed, in contemporary publishing practice a short story will often appear first in a journal, anthology, or a single author's collection, and then (virtually) unaltered as a chapter in a novel; while a single chapter may be excerpted from a novel and be republished as a short story. Thus a novel may have a *story* to tell in the very same sense as a short story does, even while it (the *novel*) contains stories in a sense unlikely to appear in a short story.[35]

If therefore, we view Genesis 19 as essentially a short story, essentially giving us the story of Lot, we should have to judge verses 27–29 as an excrescence, which were well excised (from a literary point of view). And the kerygma of Lot's story would lie in the rise of two neighboring peoples and polities in trans-Jordan, both sharing a single male ancestor, both begotten by an incestuous coupling.

But if this Chapter 19 is a short story, featuring Lot as its hero and concluding in the birth of his two sons, destined to become national entities, it is nonetheless a chapter in a novel; a novel featuring Abraham as its hero, utilizing the person and the character, the story and the progeny of Lot as foils to set off the person, the character, the story, and the progeny of his uncle Abraham. For this chapter is not a freestanding narrative. The story of Lot begins with his role as tagalong to uncle Abram in Chapter 12, with his parting from his uncle in Chapter 13 for the green fields of Sodom and Gomorrah,[36] and with his rescue by Abram from the clutches of Sodom's despoilers. This concluding chapter of Lot's life, too, is—like the preceding notices about him—subordinate and ancillary to the life of Abraham. It is anticipated in the three divine emissaries representing YHWH, the one who will represent YHWH in the debate over the fate of the morally depraved citizenry of the Cities of the Plain, and the two who extract the foursome of Lot, wife, and two daughters before calling down the rain of searing sulfur. And, before the conclusion of the short story centering on Lot and featuring him as that story's protagonist, the narrator will gap the event of the cities' destruction in the paratactic narrative sequence, that is, verses 23–25, by casting this event in the parenthetic hypotactic narrative sequence. No translator before has attended to this abrupt departure from normal narrative style; thus the translations are not only unfaithful to the Hebrew original, but have Lot's wife in verse 26 not only looking "behind"—not "her(self)" but "behind him," the masculine accusative pronoun having no antecedent!

But we have not yet done full justice to the stylistic ingenuity of our narrator.

After the conclusion of verse 23, where the destination of Lot's desire is both (implicitly) named and the name "etiologically" explained, there appear (not one but) two parenthetic statements, as indicated by two successive nominal clauses. The first gives the time of day when Lot arrives at the settlement, which has been spared for his sake. The second, verse 24, emphasizes the extraordinary destructive rain as stemming from the will of YHWH, an emphasis that in itself would seem rather pointless. Yet it does provide the only narrative assertion of the actual manner of the reduction of the Cities of the Plain and their lush fields to the salt-and-alkaline wastes that greet the reader's eye today as they did the eye of the narrator's audience in the times of monarchical Israel or Judah. This second hypotactically formulated notice is then followed by two verses in paratactic formulation. The first of these, verse 25, serves as a resumptive coda to the parenthetic verse 24, or merely completes the narrative interrupted after verse 23, to wit: "Then did he (YHWH or his representative) reduce . . ." The second paratactic formulation, verse 26, together with verse 23, gives us a picture of Lot herding wife and daughters from behind them, and his wife looking back past him at the home and possessions she will never see again.

The story of Lot himself resumes in verse 30, to end with his siring of Moab and Ammon. But between the notice of the demise of Mrs. Lot by instantaneous petrification in verse 26 and the resumptions of Lot's trek in verse 30, we have an episode interpolated that does not center on Lot, which features no divine emissaries, and whose function in this narrative is rarely raised. What the narrator achieves in this episode, however, is the introduction of a new point of view, featuring neither the human protagonists nor the divine representatives in the plot. It is the point of view of the novel's protagonist, Abraham, and provides in its suggestiveness a powerful lesson for the reader, who shares the role of the patriarch, the concerned but personally untouched observer.

Let us now proceed to a close reading of this chapter:

Episode A: Sodom Shows Its True Colors

(1) The two emissaries arrived at Sodom in the evening—Lot **then** sitting in Sodom's gateway—Lot at first sight [of them] rose to greet them. He made obeisance to them, face to the ground. (2) He said, "I pray you, my lords, turn aside to your servant's house for lodging. Wash there the dust from your feet, and as early as you please resume your mission." They said, "Not so. Out-of-doors we'll spend the night." (3) But he importuned them so vigorously that they did turn aside and entered his home. He prepared high tea for them, had cakes fresh-baked, and they dined. (4) Just about to retire, they, when the townsmen of the city—Sodom's townsmen—besieged the house, minions and elders, all the citizenry of every degree. (5) Calling to Lot, they addressed him, "How now the men, those overnight guests of yours—bring them out to us that we may become intimate with them." (6) Lot went out to them in the entrance-way, having the door behind him barred shut. (7) Said he, "No my brothers, commit no mischief. (8) I have at hand two daughters who have never had intimacy with man. Let me deliver them to you, and deal with them as you see fit. But those personages you are not to touch. Verily, it is for shelter they took haven under my

roof." (9) Some said, "Come closer—move away!" Others said, "This lone alien came to sojourn and now plays the magistrate!" "Now then, we'll do you mischief worse than [what we had in mind] for them." They pressed hard on this gentleman Lot. Some came close to break in the door. (10) The [two] dignitaries now took a hand [in the matter]. They pulled Lot back inside with them—the door now they [re-] locked. (11) As for those [Sodomite] worthies at the entrance, them they had assailed with sight-searing light, minion and elder—they were unable to obtain entry. (Genesis 19:1–11)

Abraham's three visitors of the previous chapter are referred to as ^{a}nāšīm (18:1, 16, 22) by the narrator, a term whose connotative range extends from the neutral "men, individuals," through the more respectful "adult males, persons," to the honorific "personages, burghers, magistrates." Abraham, as we saw, recognized their standing immediately, and as indicated by the pointed vocalization of 'dny in verse 3 and his act of obeisance in the preceding verse (wayyištaḥū ʾārᵉṣā), the numinous nature of their dignity as well. The two of these visitors who enter Sodom's gateway are for the first time identified by the narrator as malʾākīm "emissaries"—of YHWH, to be sure—but this numinous aspect of their dignity is not immediately perceived by Lot. One indication of this difference between his perception and Abraham's is the differently pointed vocalization of 'dny in verse 2. (The long qameṣ under the n in 18:3 signaling the recognition of YHWH's "presence," versus the pataḥ under that consonant in 19:2 indicating the normal plural "my lords.")[37] Any question as to the correctness of the Masoretic reading of the unvocalized text will be dispelled by attending to the difference in number in the continuing addresses of Abraham and Lot to the visitors. Abraham's address is in the singular when he requests that the visitor(s) tarry before he goes on to treat them as mortals to whom hospitality may be offered; Lot, by contrast, addresses both of the "emissaries" in an immediate offer of hospitality.

Such close reading of the two texts is virtually dictated by the almost identical series in the opening of the two narratives:

ABRAHAM	LOT
. . . he **now** sitting at the opening . . .	. . . [he] **now** sitting in the gateway . . .
he saw . . . he ran towards them . . .	he saw . . . he *rose* towards them . . .
he did obeisance to the ground . . .	he did obeisance *nose* to the ground
"do not pass by" . . .	. . . "*turn aside*" . . .
. . . your [*sing.*] servant . . . bathe your [*pl.*] feet . . . [have a bite to eat]	. . . your [*pl.*] servant's . . . bathe your [*pl.*] feet . . .
. . . only then continue on your way	
. . . they ate.	. . . resume your way . . . they ate.

Some of the differences between the two accounts are a function of the time of day and (unbeknownst to the mortal host) the mission of the visitors. Thus Abraham's request that they take a brief pause for refreshment al fresco, as against Lot's invitation to come indoors and spend the night. Such is probably the point also of the leisurely preparation of a meat dinner in Abraham's story as contrasted with the pita-and-drinks of Lot's supper. Other differences, however, serve to contrast the char-

acters of Abraham and Lot. Abraham *runs* to his divine visitors and does obeisance, bowing (by definition) earthward, while Lot's *rising* to greet the visitors is
slower, and perhaps more studied. Taking in their rich caparison, presuming perhaps on a comparable munificence, but taking them nonetheless for mortals, he yet
proceeds to outdo Abraham in subservience: his obeisance is *with nose to the*
ground.

Further indication of the differences in perception and stance on the parts of
Abraham and Lot may be gleaned from the different ways the two men assure the
visitors that they may terminate the proffered hospitality as soon as they will, and
the response of the visitors to the invitations. Abraham's is immediately accepted,
and Lot's is as promptly declined. The manner of that declination is pointedly puzzling. An invitation to home hospitality may be declined on delicate grounds, such
as a reluctance to impose. But it would be churlish, and gratuitously so, to express a
preference for a park bench, so to speak. And if taken at face value, such a response
would have precluded a renewal of the invitation. The visitors' response, therefore,
is ambiguous, multivalent, and readable on several levels and expressive of different points of view. From the point of view of the narrator, (and, as Sternberg would
point out, from that of the God whose point of view is frequently identical with
that of the narrator),[38] the response reflects the following: an awareness that the
reader will shortly, if he does not already, share, that Sodom's thoroughfares are
risky after dark; and the irony yet to transpire of YHWH's invulnerable agents
being asked to seek haven in the home of the man they have come to protect.
From the point of view of Lot, the response is at the metaphoric end of the spectrum: We'll lodge in the public facilities. And, *vying* with the inns or hostels for the
custom of these opulent visitors, he begs for the privilege of accommodating them.
Hence his assurance to the two humans, who have been compelled by approaching
darkness to break their journey, and this in the course of his first invitation, that
they may resume their journey/mission as early as they like, "Go early on your
way/enterprise." By contrast, the direct discourse of the Abraham who does know
that "the men" are YHWH's agents features the term *'br* three times, in seemingly
pointless redundancy. The term meaning "pass on, pass by, pass over, pass without
stopping," to mention but a few, expresses here the following, "Please do not [*sing.*],
my Lord [*ᵃdōnāy* = YHWH] pass your servant by." *I beg the boon of your presence a*
while. "Refresh *yourselves*—afterwards you [*pl.*] may pass on." *I do not pretend to be*
your central or only concern. "Surely with purpose have you come by your servant."
You must have some word for me, else you would not have come this way.

We may thus infer that there might have been but one basis for the eventuation
of the delegation's passing him by: an unworthiness on Abraham's part, symbolized
in his failure to recognize the divine presence. Such eventuality is precluded by
Abraham's first use of the term *'br.* But then, his request that divinity honor him, in
reward for his merit in recognizing divinity's presence, may itself be taken as an act
of *hybris*: not one agent, nor two, but three, on a mission to a single mortal.[39]
Hence his disavowal of such conceit in the second deployment of *'br*, and his
awareness that no action of Deity is capricious in his third use of that term. By contrast then, Lot's invitation, featuring the term *sūr* "to turn aside, make a detour"
emphasizing his lesser perceptivity, hinting at a mercenary motive in his offer, is

declined; and only after his importunacy strengthens the suggestion of venality (what other motive might he have?) do the emissaries agree to "turn aside" to the home of the unperceptive mortal whose person and welfare are a (perhaps *the*) principal point of their mission.

The sense of the two visitors constituting a treasure of sorts is borne out by the question, "Where are your two guests," which can only be rhetorical; then by "produce them/hand them over to us;" and last, by Lot's coming outside to treat with the extortionists while having the safe-door, so to speak, locked behind him. His fearlessness to expose his own person to danger may further the sense of the far greater value inhering in the persons of the visitors or, like the hyperbolic and ambiguous merism for the men of Sodom, "young and old/minor and adult/commoner and senator," point to other expressions as metaphoric rather than literal. Thus the words "that we may know/be intimate with them" in its unquestioned denotation of sexual congress, which has resulted in the variously defined sexual felonies subsumed under *sodomy*. This sexual denotation is pointed up by Lot's offer to substitute the persons of his two virgin daughters ("who have *known* no man"). On the other hand, the addition of "deal with them as you see fit," as opposed to his response to the Sodomites' designs on the emissaries ("No, *my brothers*, do no wrong/mischief") would reveal him as not only a monstrously unfeeling father, but as a man who regarded womankind in general as a less than human species. And perhaps that is the very intent of the narrator who puts these words into his mouth. But, however extreme the male chauvinism that is often attributed to the biblical authors in their valuation of the female sex, no such grossly atrocious dehumanization of half of the human race has ever been demonstrated to have been harbored by any pagan—let alone the biblical—normative ethos. The effect of the narrative then is to indict Lot for his insensitivity to his own children's pain, dignity, life, even as it seems to show that his concern for the safety of his guests excepts him from inclusion in the ethos of his Sodomite hosts, whom he cajoles as "my brothers."

The *free direct discourse* in the Sodomites' response to Lot's proposal has never been given a translation faithful to the Hebrew original. (But context alone indicates it as a rejection of his proposal, and hence allows us to conclude that the citizens of Sodom were more hell-bent on sodomizing two visiting males than on taking their pleasure with two nubile females.) The two initial words of speech, a verb *geš* "draw near" and an adverb *hāleʾā* "[move] back, away," are of course opposite in meaning. The introductory *wayyōmerū* "some said" thus indicates not a univocal chorus but a mixture of shouts, some calling *stand back* and others *come closer* (*-if you dare*). So too, the second *wayyōmerū* "others said" introduces two different "voices." One merely expressed astonishment that this lone (*hāʾḥād*) outsider admitted on sufferance dares to pose as the arbiter of morals; the other addresses his urging that no wrong be done. *Whatever mischief we might have had in mind for your guests, we shall now exceed in abusing you [in a manner far more serious] than [what we had in mind for] them.* Note carefully the ellipsis represented by our words in brackets: free direct discourse; the intent of the speakers, the gist of their raucous rioting is what the narrator *shows* (as opposed to *tells*) in the dialogue, which is at one and the same time both free and direct, featuring both the drama of speech and the stylistic thrift of biblical expression. Having achieved this in dialogue, the narrator resumes the story in his own voice, employing two verbs whose force we may have missed in their first appearances: The verb pṣr appears in its denotative sense of "press hard," describing the action of the Sodomites in respect to Lot. This informs on the sense of almost physical exertion in Lot's persistency with the visitors in verse 2, where our rendering "importuned" for that same verb seems now almost a euphemism. And the verb ngš for their "drawing near" or "closing in" to break down the door, which at the beginning of this verse was so incongruously attached to the adverb for "back, away." What follows can serve as a textbook example of the biblical deployment of parataxis and hypotaxis. Verse 10, in paratactic syntax, has the angels pulling the hapless Lot back into the safety of the house and barring again the door that they had unbarred to retrieve him. Thus we have the conclusion of this episode with the rescue of the endangered host by the supposedly help-less guests, whom he sought to deliver from danger. This verse is, however, fol-lowed by another notice, which is regularly rendered as if it were also formulated paratactically in the Hebrew, that is, by a rendering of the tenses as in normal nar-rative sequence. Were this the purport of the Hebrew, we should be at a loss to un-derstand how the rioters could have failed to reach their vulnerable target, the Lot who had foolishly locked himself out "in the cold," and how they could have failed to pour through the doorway, which the angels had unblocked to pull in their host. But no. The hypotactic verse 11, nominal clause with subject followed by a perfect verb, is a parenthetic flashback, the verb bespeaking action in the past perfect sense: the blinding of the Sodomites with the dazzling light had preceded the un-barring of the door. If the reader will review our translation it will be clear that the hypotactic parenthesis begins with the last three words (in Hebrew) of verse 10, and ends before the last three words of verse 11. These last three words, resuming the paratactic sequence of the first two clauses of verse 10, thus are the real conclu-sion of this episode: a statement in narrative sequence that the rioters were unable to find the dwelling's entrance, the reason for the futility having been provided in the parenthetic insertion between the paratactic formulation of the first two clauses in verse 10 and the last clause of verse 11.

Episode B: Last Chance for Lot's In-Laws

> (12) Now said the men to Lot, "Any kin or kith you have in this place, be they son-in-law, [grand]son or [grand]daughter, anyone of your own in this city—get them out of this place! (13) Verily, we are about to devastate this area—so great the charge against them in YHWH's judgment, YHWH has dispatched us to lay it waste. (14) Lot went forth and spoke to his sons-in-law, those who had taken his daughters in wedlock. He said, "Quick now, get out of this area. Verily, YHWH is about to devas-tate the city." But in the eyes of his sons-in-law he could only have been joking. (Genesis 19:12–14)

The Sodomites having now demonstrated their moral depravity—to the Deity who had received complaints of their behavior, to the emissaries who represent him, and to the reader and all other interested parties—the narrative may proceed to the extrication of Lot and the destruction of the Plain. Given the economy, frugality even, of biblical narrative, what would we have missed if in place of these three verses we had the narrator's bald statement that Lot was told by the angels the purpose of their mission? In a passage of which dialogue constitutes at least 75 percent, we are informed three times of the impending doom, that Lot had intermarried with the citizens of Sodom so that he had sons-in-law and probably grandchildren as well, and that these in-laws jeered at the warning that would have saved their lives.

The dialogue in verse 13 sandwiches two mentions of the impending doom around the reason for it. *We are about to destroy—so great the indictment before YHWH—that YHWH dispatched us to destroy.* The reference to the indictment resonates in sense and diction with the double appearance of the term for "complaint, protest, charge" (*z̦q/ṣ̌q*) in verses 20–21 of the preceding chapter. If we turn back to our translation of that passage we shall see that it is part of a considerably longer hypotactic parenthesis (beginning with verse 17) explaining the how and the why of the following dialogue between Abraham and YHWH. The import of this parenthesis is that Deity had received the complaint, had not yet investigated it, and hence had not yet given verdict or pronounced sentence; had he done any of the last it would have impaired the dignity of Abraham by having him plead in a case where the conclusion has been foreclosed. Now in verse 13 of our chapter, we have the conclusion that had not yet been reached in the dialogue between Abraham and YHWH. The term for "destroy/doom" (*šḥt*), appearing here twice, appears four times in that dialogue. The complaint (*z̦q/ṣ̌q*), which in 18:21 is characterized by YHWH as *habbāʾā ʾēlay* "the one reaching me," the one which calls for me to go down to see for myself, is characterized in 19:13 as *ʾet-pney YHWH* "in YHWH's judgment." Thus in this verse of dense yet seemingly repetitive free direct discourse we are given to understand that the investigation of the complaint by YHWH is represented in the angelic representatives' experience of the Sodomites' designs upon them, the verdict now being unquestionably *guilty on all counts* (18:21, *hakkeṣaʿaqātā . . . ʾāśū kālā*), and the angels' mission has now become to lay the city waste.

The verb *šḥt* in this verse also resonates with the four appearances of this same term in Genesis 6:11–12, where the equivalent term for *ṣaʿqā* "criminal charge" is *ḥāmās* "lawlessness." These intertextual connections with the flood story we shall soon take up again. But for the present, let us note that the opportunity to save themselves and their families afforded Lot's sons-in-law is in fulfillment of the promise made by YHWH in his concluding word to Abraham "I shall not destroy (*šḥt*) on account of (any) ten (innocents)." There being no ten such in Sodom, the city is doomed. But the sons-in-law of Lot would have been extricated along with him from the city had they not shared the immoral ethos that doomed their fellow citizens. That they might have indeed been of a different stripe is suggested by the pleonastic explication in verse 14 that Lot's sons-in-law were *lōqeḥē benōtāw*; they had seen fit to take his daughters to wife. That they were cast in the same moral mold as their neighbors is, however, demonstrated by their regarding as ridiculous the warning of a death-sentence having been pronounced on their city; a sentence that must be ridiculous because the criminal charge against the city is ridiculous.

And this the judgment of men who, if the events centering on Lot's home and guests had somehow escaped them, would have been informed of them by their victimized father-in-law, himself a (resident-) alien in Sodom and—for all his greed, selfishness, and deracination—alien to the murderous ethos of that city.

A final word about a dictional element: the perplexing designation of Deity as YHWH in the speech of the angels to Lot and in the speech of Lot to his sons-in-law. It would seem to be perplexing on a number of counts and (for different reasons) for both our own poetical approach to the names of God as well as the approach of source criticism. For us, the presence of YHWH bespeaking his special and intimate relationship to his people Israel, or to the patriarchs who sired this people as against Elohim in contexts of his dealings with outsiders of the lineage, would seem to face serious challenge here. For Lot is not an ancestor of Israel, and his Sodomite sons-in-law would hardly have known who this YHWH was whom Lot specified by name as the god—one of many, to be sure, if his Sodomite son-in-laws were polytheistic pagans—who was about to destroy their city. But this latter literary absurdity is equally such for the J author posited by source criticism! And, let us remember, while P, according to the tenets of source criticism, must eschew the name YHWH, there is nothing in its tenets to preclude J from identifying the Deity as Elohim when that usage makes better sense in context.

This perplexity, and its resolution as well, will illustrate the point we made in connection with the various nuances that can frequently be characterized as inhering in or accounting for the deployment by the biblical author(s) of either YHWH or God (or, for that matter, of any other name): to wit, literary composition is art, not science, nor technology; as a literary creator does not write according to formula, so does literary criticism not perform its analyses according to formula(s); always and everywhere; and so also in respect to biblical literature and the specific lexical alternatives for Deity's proper name, literary criticism is never inductive, never predictive, and though it is in a sense empirical it is so ex post facto, the "fact" being the literary corpus under examination.

In the case of our pericope, the appearance of YHWH in the dialogue of angels with Lot and Lot with his sons-in-law must be seen as a studied contrast to the name Elohim as twice deployed in our chapter's verse 29: once in connection with the negative and destructive devastation of the cities of the plain, and once in the positive and salvific connection with God's remembering Abraham and rescuing Lot. That verse, the resumptive conclusion of Episode E, as well as the episodes which precede it, will be discussed in place. We mention it here to highlight our contention that this name of God would have occasioned none of the problems raised by the use of YHWH, and therefore points to the deliberateness of this deployment.

First, we must recognize that the speech of both angels and Lot represent free direct discourse, which is to say direct discourse in form, but in substance either more or less than what is said, betraying the *intrusive narrator's* signal to the reader to interpret the element that is a departure from (what would have been) precise or strict direct discourse. In this case that element is the name of God, YHWH. We suggested in our opening chapter that very often the expression *šem-YHWH* "the name YHWH" does not mean the name "YHWH" at all; that it serves as a metaphor for a non-explicit term for the one and only Deity of Scripture, the purport of the metaphor being that by whatever name the Deity was invoked or referred to, the character invoking or referring to that Deity correctly understood that one and only God, which is to say, imputed to "Him" the attributes that Scripture does, implicitly or explicitly.[40]

As we have noted in regard to the terms šḥt and ṣ'q of verse 13 their resonance with those terms in 18:20–21, so too must we note that the attribute of justice is the chief attribute of the YHWH, who in 18:19 describes his singling out of Abraham to instill in his progeny the "way of YHWH," which is glossed as the doing of justice. So it is that here in 19:13 the charge that has been accepted as true on high—'et penē-YHWH—would not have been so judged by the ᵉlōhīm, "gods" of pagan Sodom. And the warning of Lot to his sons-in-law that YHWH it is who is about to destroy the city heightens in their eyes the absurdity of a god they could not recognize—by this name or any other—whose chiefest demand is justice, and who exacts retribution when that demand is outraged.

Episode C: The Escape from Sodom

(15) **Now then** just as the morning-star had risen, the emissaries urged Lot on, to wit, "Quick now, take your wife and your two daughters that are here at hand, if you would not be swept away in the doom of the city." (16) When he yet dilly-dallied the men gripped him by hand and his wife by hand as also the two daughters each by a hand—[this only] by the grace of YHWH's pity on him—they brought him out and deposited him outside the city. (17) And just as he was bringing them outside [it], he said, "Flee on for your very life, cast no glance behind you, come to no halt anywhere in the plain, to the hills make good your flight if you would not be swept away!" (18) Said Lot to them, "Please, not so, my Lordship. (19) Look now—your servant has indeed found favor in your eyes, and greatly have you extended your merciful dealings with me in the interest of prolonging my life. But I, for my part, just cannot make my escape all the way to the hill country. Lest the cataclysm overtake me and I die, [I propose]—(20) Look now, that town yonder is close enough for me to make good my flight there. And it is such a wee place. Let me, pray, make escape thither—such a wee place it is—and let me survive." (21) He said to him, "Now in this particular too I have hereby granted you great face, not to destroy that city as you have proposed. (22) Make haste now to escape there, for till you reach that spot I can undertake nothing." (This now is why the city is named Zoar ["Trifle"].) (Genesis 19:15–22)

The return of Lot from his sons-in-law's home is *gapped* in our narrative. The futility of his mission has been encapsulated in the last words of the previous episode. But the rising of the morning star, an hour or so before dawn, is significant. The riot around Lot's home having begun just as the family was about to retire for the night, we can bridge the gap between the striking of the rioter's blind and the angel's prodding of Lot to get started with evocation of Lot's night-long pleading with his in-laws. The direct-discourse of that prodding, characterizing his two daughters as *hannimṣā'ōt* "those present," evokes the pain of the father who now must perforce leave behind the married daughters, a pain that would be in no way eased even had he come to acknowledge that he had really lost them when they were taken in marriage by men of Sodom. Still he hesitates. Can it be that he wonders whether a life without his treasures is worth saving? If so, and left to his own devices, his vacillation would indeed have cost him his life, with only himself to blame. But the angels intervene with physical force, this by reason of YHWH's supererogatory compassion, and the four—each gripped by an angelic hand—are literally dragged out of the city. From there on, they are told, it is all up to their own efforts. They are not to cast a look backward, not to come to an even momentary halt anywhere on the Plain. They must make good their flight to the hills (which, given today's topography, as that of the biblical writer's generation, can only be to the north or northeast).

Lot, however, demurs, "No, please, my lordship." But this time this last word in Hebrew is vocalized with a *qāmeṣ*, in recognition that this time—unlike at his first encounter with the angels in verse 2—he knows and acknowledges them as representative of the One God, YHWH. That this Masoretic vocalization is intrinsic to the text is, as we saw the case was in 18:3, proven by the string of second personal pronouns in Lot's continued address in verse 19. Thus, in verse 18, "Lot said to *them*, *ᵃdōnāy*," and he now continues with "*your* (s.) servant, *your* (s.) dealings, which *you* (s.) have dealt with me." This entire section of dialogue, which could without loss have been omitted, may indeed have been primarily designed to impress upon the reader this switch from the address in the plural to the address in the singular.

The direct discourse serves another purpose. Lot's initial speech features the immediacy of *hinnē-nā* "look now," and he now repeats that phrase in reference to the tiny settlement to which he proposes to flee as against the hill-country recommended by the angel. The point of this is to impress upon us that whatever was the location of that mythical Sodom (anywhere in the once lush semi-circular Plain, which, now a wasteland, extends to the east and south and west of the Salt Sea), Lot from his vantage point outside Sodom's walls is able to see and point to the settlement, which is so much nearer than are the hills. But let us recall that this settlement, so tiny that Deity may exclude it from his destructive program, this settlement to which Lot will give its name in this "etiological" account, this Zoar has been twice brought to our attention, in 13:10–13 and in 14:1–9. In the former account, Lot envisages the whole Jordan Plain, which, the narrator informs us, was so well-watered—this, to be sure, before YHWH laid waste to Sodom and Gomorrah—as to resemble the land of Egypt, this lushness then visible from the vantage point of Zoar and beyond.

We come across the second instance of Zoar's appearance in Chapter 14. The tiny settlement referred to by Lot and (implicitly) named by him for its contemptible size is, however, in that chapter one of the five great Cities of the Plain that rebelled against their Mesopotamian overlords and sent troops to engage them "in the Vale of Siddim, that is [now] the Salt Sea" (14:4). This discrepancy then adds to the never-never-land aura of both these chapters. On the other hand, an out-and-out contradiction that would trouble any literalist is avoided as between these two chapters by their author. The city, which received its name only after Lot's plea to the angel in Chapter 19, could hardly be the city that stood up to Amraphel's armies. Oh yes it can, our author has anticipated with a smile. It can, but under another name. Note, of the five Cities of the Plain twice listed in Chapter 14, only one appears without its king being named: that ruler is "the king of Bela, that is [today] Zoar" (verses 2, 8).

Episode D: *The Doom of Sodom and the Fate of Lot's Wife*

(23) The sun **now** had just risen over the horizon just as Lot reached Zoar.) (24) YHWH **then** precipitated on Sodom and Gomorrah a rain of blazing sulfur, [a rain] from YHWH, from the sky.) (25) Thus did he reduce those cities and the entire plain, together with the populations of the cities and every growth of the soil. (26) His wife, however, looked back past him and became a salt statue. (Genesis 19:23–26)

The effect of the two hypotactic sentences at the beginning is to give the reader a sense of the dramatic timing occasioned by the schedule of the angels, the dallying of Lot, and his escape by a hair's breadth, arriving in the agreed-upon haven just as the sun arose like thunder in the east, the direction whence Lot had fled. A glance ahead to 32:24–33 will support our suspicion that an ancient convention is implied, and (perhaps) spoofed in the morning star's rising, constituting a warning to supernatural agents that they must vacate earth's premises before the sun rises. Be that as it may, the second hypotactic sentence suggests that the rain of brimstone was brief, perhaps lasting from the first appearance of the sun's upper rim until the appearance of the lower rim "on the earth horizon." The short story of Lot's escape from the doomed plain is thus concluded in verse 25 with the paratactic coda of the vast devastation, except for one last notice, harking back to the preceding episode, the warning of the angels to Lot to stop not a moment, to cast no wishful regretful glance backward. To look back with rue upon life in an ambience so sinful that it incurred YHWH's damnation, to express a longing for a condemned past—even while escaping the consequences of that past by the grace of an ever so gracious and patient God—is perhaps to forfeit a share in the new life that is opening up. The removal of Lot's wife from the scene is, of course, a narrative necessity for the enactment of Episode F. But it is a storytelling genius that exploits the metaphor of sterility in salt, the eerie salt and alkali rock foundations sculpted by the wind in the cliffs overlooking the Salt Sea, and the circumstances that make for regrets over the past entailing foreclosing of the future, all these to end this part of the story with an enigmatic "pillar of salt."

Episode E: *What Abraham Saw*

(27) Early that morning Abraham hied to the spot where he had stood in YHWH's presence. (28) He looked down upon the vista of Sodom and Gomorrah and that of all the plain area and beheld, lo a fog had arisen over that area like that emanating from a furnace. (29) Thus it was that at the time of God's laying waste the Cities of the Plain, God was mindful of Abraham and dispatched Lot from within the cataclysm area, yes that upheaval of the cities among which Lot had dwelt. (Genesis 19:27–29)

We have earlier discussed this second concluding episode, a resumptive winding up of Lot's story from the point of view of the novel's hero, Lot's uncle Abraham. Although Lot's name never appeared in the dialogue between God and Abraham anent the fate of the guilty and the innocent in the depraved cities, no one would question that he was uppermost in the minds of both parties to that dialogue. For all that, it is not at all clear whether this consciousness of Lot or concern for him in either or both the minds of God and Abraham relates to him on a personal level as a flesh-and-blood individual (a *round character*) or as a useful counterpoise to the character of Abraham and to those moral attributes of his which made him the elect of God. For all his copious speech in this chapter, Lot remains the flattest of *flat characters*.[41] Although I have stressed the mercenary motive in Lot's invitation to the strangers in Sodom's gate, one cannot be at all confident that the merit of hospitableness is to be denied to him. We saw that the contrast between Abraham's hospitality to the three visitors and Lot's to the two does not hinge at all on the generosity of the one against the other; but rather on the recognition or failure to recognize them as God's representatives. Similarly, Lot's coming forth to confront his Sodomite neighbors may bespeak an arrogant self-confidence, and his locking the door behind him a bit of foolishness, or a brave attempt to face down the mob and, come what may, keep his visitors secure behind the barred door. And even the offer of his daughters as substitute victims—even as it impugns him as an unfeeling father and his sensitivity to the pain and degradation of woman as person rather than commodity—may yet bespeak his determination to honor the obligation of host to those to whom he has extended "the shade of my roof-beam." Finally, there is the ambiguity in Lot's plea that Zoar be spared and God's (amused?) acceptance of the plea. On a literal level there is his assumption that the God who can paralyze a mob and lay waste to a string of cities in a single brief upheaval could underestimate the stamina required to reach the hills. On the moral level, the symbolism of even a small settlement of inveterate sinners being spared for the sake of an innocent (note in verse 29 the metaphoric purpose of all the Plain Cities as the residence of Lot) is an alternative that if ruled out for Sodom is equally ruled out for Zoar. If the dialogue between God and Abraham rules out anything it is quantity (of the guilty or innocent) as a significant factor in arriving at a verdict or exercise of sentence. To be sure, Lot was not privy to that dialogue, but God was. And that raises the question of why God would spare the fewer sinners of Zoar for the sake of Lot, and not the greater number of, but no more sinful, inhabitants of a larger city.

This blurring of the moral outlines of Lot's character is what accounts for the debate that will continue long after our discussion of the question: Was Lot spared for his merits? Which is to say, that for all his human weaknesses he was as morally superior to the sinners of the Plain Cities as was, let us say, Noah to his doomed contemporaries. (See 6:9, *ṣaddīq . . . bᵉdōrōtāw* "innocent [despite, or given the standards] of those of his generation.") Or was Lot spared on the score of his uncle Abraham's merits? This second alternative is the one that many point to as the purport of our episode's last sentence, the connection between God's mindfulness of Abraham and extricating of Lot being taken as a causal one. Possible, even likely, as this interpretation is, it does not necessarily rule out the first alternative:

God's mindfulness of Abraham may be a metonymic metaphor for the kerygma of his dialogue with Abraham.

My own reading of this chapter is that it deliberately ambiguates the question of Lot's moral merit and, therefore, the degree to which (if any at all) his rescue is attributable to Abraham's merit. There certainly is an attribution of some such merit to Lot, for no merit of Abraham's would extend so far as to offer an option of escape to Lot's Sodomite sons-in-law, an option touching Lot because of the fate of his married daughters, this subtlety suggested by the seeming pleonastic gloss (in verse 13) of "his sons-in-law" as "the takers-in-marriage of his daughters." There is the further hint that the Deity's stock of good will is fast being used up as Lot pleads with his in-laws into the wee hours, and then continues to respond with vacillation to the angels' importunacy. (The verb *ūṣ* in verse 15 is a synonym for the verb *pṣr* appearing with Lot as subject and the angels as object in verse 3, and, in verse 9, with the Sodomites as subject and *the personage*, Lot as object.) Thus the physical dragging of Lot and his remaining family by the angels is characterized as being due (not to desert but) to YHWH's compassion for him. And still Lot continues to tax the elasticity of divine grace and pity, pleading and winning divine assent for the sparing of the wicked (in the settlement in which he would take haven), an assent that is not present in the kerygma of Abraham's dialogue with YHWH. Nor for that matter is there so fine or final a resolution of the problem of felicity and suffering, reward and punishment, in any of the many Scriptural loci where the metaphor of God's presence in history clashes with the ubiquitous Scriptural assumption of all humans' free will.[42]

And as this episode at its close leaves us uncertain as to the reasons in the mind of God or of the narrator for Lot's survival, so the episode also closes for Abraham the chapter of his involvement with his nephew, and cloaks the resolution of the equation of his nephew's merits as against the entropic factor of Sodom's sinfulness. The pall of mist or smoke, of fog or smog, thick like the emission from a furnace, but (unlike such a column) rising everywhere over the plain that he only yesterday viewed in all its green lushness, gives him the answer as to whether or not there were enough innocents to compensate for the wickedness of the many. But how far the devastation extends he cannot see. Nor can he know that Lot has—by reason of his merit, or the merit of his uncle, or the requirements of further history—survived somewhere beyond the limits of that awful cataclysm. The book on Lot has been closed for him, but not for us, the readers. Another episode awaits us before the book closes for us on Lot the person, the Lot who as a person will be lost also to us and to history, until he reemerges to the gaze of historic Israel in his progeny, two of the tribal polities with whom the polities of Abraham's progeny will have to deal.

Episode F: The Issue of Lot

(30) Lot then moved upland from Zoar and settled down in the hill-country, his two daughters with him—so fearful he of staying on in Zoar. He lived in a cave, he and his two daughters. (31) The elder said to the younger, "Our father is old. And male there is none to cover us in nature's universal way. (32) Come now, let us ply our fa-

ther with wine, bed with him and of our father keep posterity live." (33) So they plied
their father with wine that night. The elder girl made bold to lie with her father—he
now unconscious of her coming and going. (34) Upon the morrow the elder said to
the younger, "Lo, I did lie yestereve with Father. Let us ply him with wine tonight
again, and you enter and lie with him; thus may we [both] keep of our father posterity
live." (35) So that night again they plied their father with wine. The younger then
proceeded to lie with him, he unconscious of her coming or going. (36) So did the
two daughters of Lot conceive by their father. (37) The elder bore a son, named him
Moab, he the ancestor of the [people of] Moab of our own day. (38) And the younger
girl, she also **now** bore a son, named him Ben-ammi, he the ancestor of the Ammonites of our own time. (Genesis 19:30–38)

Having pleaded for an exemption of Zoar from the scheduled fate of its sister
Cities of the Plain, having won Deity over to his plea, and having made good his
escape there, Lot now decides that his place of refuge is no longer a safe haven and
leaves it for the hill-country, which the angels had initially suggested as a proper
destination when he had to flee from Sodom. Zoar, as we suggested earlier, can only
be the locale of that name, which is (in Deuteronomy 34:1–4) the southernmost
border of the area constituting Israel's promised land, the area scanned for Moses
by YHWH as he stands on Moab's Mount Nebo, this southern area described as the
Negev, the Plain, the valley of Jericho . . . as far as Zoar. The fear of Lot for his
safety there would have to be traced to one of two dangers. Either the saved remnant of Zoarites, having learned nothing from the cataclysm, are showing Sodomite tendencies, or Lot fears that the immunity he had won for Zoar was only a
reprieve, and that he had better continue on to the destination in the hills to the
north first pointed to by the angels. This second alternative would seem to be a
likely inference from the words and actions of Lot's daughters. They seem to think
that no male other than their father has survived, the inhabitants of Zoar having
now succumbed to another of Heaven's fireballs. They and their father alone are,
like Noah—but Noah without wife or sons—the last hope for the human race:
"Let us lie with him, and beget life by our father['s semen]." (More literally, the Hebrew reads, "keep seed alive of our father.") The stress on Lot's not knowing of his
daughters' lying down with him nor their arising may suggest that had he known of
his daughters' intentions he could have disabused them of their assumptions.
Along this line too, his daughters' resorting to stupefying him with the beverage
discovered by Noah would bespeak their determination to keep the race alive despite the inhibitions to be expected of an older—may I use the word "effete"—
generation. Whatever the sneer or jeer of the biblical narrator in this tale of contaminated coupling that produced Israel's YHWH-protected cousins in their tribal
lands to the east (see Deuteronomy 2), the preservation of Lot's lines would appear
to have had God's tacit assent. As for the incest on a literal level, it presents no
more perplexing a problem than the consanguinity of the wives of Cain and Seth.

What is the kerygma of this short story of Lot? Or, if more than one, what are
the kerygmas, and which is the central one? Some of the possible answers such as,
for example, the resolution of the question of how divine justice operates when it
comes to the separation of (white) sheep from the (black) goats, are implicit in our

discussion of the story up to this point, and others have been and will continue to be put forward. Our own enterprise in analysis and interpretation does not call upon us to attempt an answer, and definitely not a definitive answer to such questions. But it probably goes without saying that an important factor in reaching one or another conclusion on these questions would be the judgment as to whether Episode F is the culmination or climax of this story, or whether—the climax having been reached in Episode D—this episode represents a kind of Postlude to the story of Lot, which serves a useful purpose in the embracing novel of Father Abraham and his descendants, the latter culminating in the people and polities of Israel and Judah.

Our readers, whatever their own conclusions on these questions, will not be surprised that our own judgment will be based on our crediting to the biblical writer that interpretation which is seen to be on the highest level of abstraction. And that level is certainly that of the never-finally-resolved enigma of a God who is by definition absolutely just, by characterization ever-interfering in human history, and somehow without complicity in the manifest injustices represented by the disastrous rains of radioactive or volcanic ash yet the immediate cause of the precipitation, rational biped or inanimate volcano. What then is the secondary kerygma, that of Episode F? My opinion on this appears in the section on Structures (in chapter 7). I cannot complete my discussion of this story, however, without taking up again the deployment here of the names of God.

THE NAMES OF GOD IN GENESIS, CHAPTERS 18 AND 19

In plot and structure (cf. the openings of the two chapters) the stories of the annunciation to Abraham and the extrication of Lot are inseparable. The Deity appears to Abraham in the guise of three human visitors, in whom Abraham recognizes the presence of the one and only God, identified by the narrator (six times) as YHWH, by Himself in dialogue (twice) as YHWH, and once by Abraham as Àdōnāy, a plural of majesty bespeaking the singular lordship of the one and only YHWH, yet a pointed (as we shall see) avoidance of YHWH in Abraham's speech. The three men are accompanied by Abraham to a vantage point overlooking the plain of Sodom, two of them continuing on the way winding downward toward the doomed valley, the third—identified as YHWH—remaining behind to engage Abraham in a discussion on the considerations that might make for a sparing of a morally depraved city. This chapter ends with the departure of YHWH at the interview's close and Abraham's return home (to Mamre's Oaks, Hebron).

The two men, now designated as mal'ākīm "agents, angels, emissaries," arrive in Sodom and are recognized as persons of high standing by Lot, but not until they have displayed their awesome power as agents of Deity. Now, for the first time in this chapter, the Deity is mentioned by name. Three times the name YHWH appears, twice in the speech of "the men" and once in that of Lot. And each time that appearance must strike us as strange; especially so for the incompatibility of this name's poetical function as divined by Cassuto (and refined by us). The visitors in their dialogue with Abraham never refer to Deity as YHWH, nor does Abraham his intimate. Yet in their dialogue with Lot the visitors do so refer to him, as does Lot himself, and—were this not strange enough in itself—in address to his Sodomite sons-in-law! The deliberateness of this deployment of the Tetragrammaton is underlined by the pleonastic second appearance of this name in the mouth of the angels (verse 13: "for we are about to devastate this place, so great the indictment in YHWH's judgment that he, YHWH, has dispatched us to devastate it"). The meticulous care of the text in this matter of the deployment of the names for Deity evinces itself again in Lot's second direct address to his divine visitor(s). In his first address (verse 2) he said, "My lords, [ᵃdōnay] please turn aside [pl.] to your [pl.] servant's house." In his second address (verses 18–19), like Abraham before him, he says, "My lordship [ᵃdōnāy]," and continues consistently with the second person singular.

The shift of the narrator's focus from Lot to Abraham is clear in verse 27, which opens Episode E. The back-reference to the dialogue between Deity and Abraham is equally clear in "to the spot where he had stood in YHWH's presence." All the more surprising then that in verse 29, which concludes this episode, and also—so to speak—wraps up the story of the plain's devastation and Lot's escape, the name for the Deity is Elohim. And, as in verse 13 YHWH appears twice, the second time pleonastically, so in this verse Elohim appears twice, the second time pleonastically: "Thus it was, when God was laying waste the Cities of the Plain, that he, God, was mindful of Abraham and dispatched Lot from the cataclysmic event." Here again the context is, according to the Cassuto-Brichto hypothesis, appropriate for the appearance of YHWH, not Elohim.

If the aforementioned hypothesis were a formula, the deployment of both the names, YHWH and Elohim, in this Chapter 19 would constitute an invalidation of that formula. But, as I stressed earlier, it is not a formula but a guide to a number of nuances in the contexts in which these names may variously appear; which is to say, separately, in association and in contrast with one another, or in association and in contrast with yet other names or terms for Deity, or even not at all, this last a zero instance that is not to be ignored as insignificant. In addition to the nuances discussed in Chapter 1 are others (sometimes complementary, sometimes supplementary to them) whose functions as poetic ploys have been devised by the writer, and which stand as challenges to the reader in what Sternberg explores under the rubric *the drama of reading*.

Thus, for example, the subtle shifts in point-of-view, which Sternberg charts under the rubric *free indirect discourse* (explicit and implied), may be mustered for the interpretation of many a Scriptural passage with special reference to the term(s) or name(s) deployed for Deity. In the case of our verse 13, the double presence of YHWH would seem to us to be an instance of *free direct discourse*, the Tetragrammaton conveying the sense of the angels that it is the God of Justice who has judged the city and has sent them to execute sentence; so too, perhaps not altogether wittingly, the Tetragrammaton in Lot's address to his sons-in-law. These latter, who would have been informed by Lot of their fellow Sodomites' designs on the visitors (had they not already known of the assault) show themselves as true Sodomites by their incredulity in the existence of a Deity possessing such an attribute and intervening in the affairs of mortals. And in verse 29, the generic term for deity that has become in Scripture's monotheistic theology the most comprehensive name, God, is the narrator's device for redirecting our attention—should we have missed it at first reading—to the significance of the Tetragrammaton's appearances in verses 13 and 14.

My readers must judge for themselves, here as everywhere, the persuasiveness of my interpretation. But one thing must be clear: the genetic hypothesis of two narrative traditions, that of J and that of P, offers no solution to the problems I have raised. For even if verse 29 represents a sudden irruption of P into our text, the author named J is admittedly free to dispose of the name Elohim as well as the Tetragrammaton; that author would have known how inappropriate would be the Tetragrammaton in the mouths of YHWH's emissaries addressing Lot, or in Lot's mouth addressing Sodomites; and that author would therefore have opted for Elohim in the direct discourse of angels and Lot, as indeed he did in 3:1–5, in the direct discourse of the serpent and the woman in the matter of the tree significant for its connection with the knowledge of good and bad.

THREE DOMESTIC TRIANGLES

The Triangle in Egypt

(10) A famine occurred in that area, so Abram went down to Egypt for a short stay there—so severe in the area was the famine. (11) When he was close to reaching Egypt he said to his wife Sarai, "Attend me: Well do I appreciate how beautiful a woman you are. (12) It may well be then that when the Egyptians catch sight of you and presume, 'that's his wife, that one,' that they take my life that they may have you alive. (13) Do you then bruit, it's my sister you are, to the end that it go well with me, thanks to you, that my neck is saved, by your grace."

(14) And so it came about when Abram entered Egypt, the Egyptians on beholding this woman were struck—how exceedingly beautiful she is. (15) When Pharaoh's lieutenants beheld her, they praised her to Pharaoh and so this woman was taken into Pharaoh's household. (16) With Abram **now** it went very well indeed, thanks to her, so that there accrued to him flocks and herds, jackasses and male slaves and female slaves and jenny asses and camels.) (17) YHWH then afflicted Pharaoh with great afflictions and his household as well on account of Sarai, Abram's wife. (18) Pharaoh summoned Abram. He declared, "How could you do such a thing to me! Why did you not tell me that it's your wife she is? (19) Why did you declare, 'My sister—she?' So that I took her for myself as wife! Now then, here's your wife, take [her] and get!" (20) Thus Pharaoh put him under official charge and deported him and his wife and everyone/thing his. (Genesis 12:10–20)

Were this episode a chapter in a biographical novel centering on Abram we, the modern reader, would find a number of details in plot and character so incongruous with our own life experience as to lead us either to stamp the author as inept, or to be pulling our leg, or to be indulging in fantasy of a particularly unverisimilitudinous nature.

There is, to begin with, the matter of chronology. A glance at Table 7-1 in part II will show that at the time of this descent to Egypt Sarai was sixty-five years old, at the least. This of course is not a problem for source-critics, who find these chronological notices as P's (mindless) irruption into the narratives spun by the talented J. But the poetician may not so lightly dispose of it, and we may have to accept the rabbinic suggestion that Mother Sarai's beauty did not age or stale.

A second problem centers on the descent to Egypt. Was it a matter of life and death for Abram and his immediate family? Or, as in most cases of biblical famines, was it a matter of prosperity, of keeping his livestock in flourishing condition? It is normally assumed that Abram was already a stockman in his native land. But this is nowhere stated. And it may well be the intent of our narrator in the parenthetic verse 16 of this episode to trace the beginning of Abram's fortune to the stock, steeds, and servants that accrued to him largely in consequence of his standing as Pharaoh's brother-in-law. The narrator may indeed be signaling such intent in the words he puts into Abram's mouth in verse 13. Having expressed his fear that his life will be in danger if he is taken as her husband, but not if she declares him her brother, the follow-up to his petition would simply be something along the line of *umalṭi ʾet napšī* "and thus save my life." Instead Abram expresses first a desire for general good fortune, and then a reference to his life by *napšī*, a noun whose denotation is "throat, gullet" (hence our translation "neck"), together with the verb *ḥyh*, whose connotation is "be alive," but which also bears such nuances as "be well, be healthy, recover, prosper, flourish."[43] Thus, although our translation "my neck be saved" = "that I do not die" (*nepeš* with the pronominal endings also serves for the personal pronouns) the words may just as correctly be rendered, "that my life be enhanced." Both expressions for a happy outcome are attached to expressions that mean "on your account," and not "by virtue of your action." Abram's words thus prophetically, although unconsciously, foreshadow the actual result of the lie whose design it is to mislead the Egyptians.

The reasoning behind the lie is also puzzling. On the face of it, it seems to suggest that the Egyptians would shrink from committing adultery with the wife of an alien, but not from the act of murdering an alien in order to have their way with the victim's widow, she now effectively freed from conjugal taboos. Anthropologists specializing in law and mores agree that the two acts considered criminal in the most primitive societies are murder and adultery. None, as far as I know, cite a case where the greater of the two crimes is adultery.[44] But assuming that Abram did indeed fear that either his life or wife would be at risk in Egypt, why would he take such chances there rather than with the scarcity in Canaan? Or, if passing off his wife as sister would render her courtable by her Egyptian hosts, was he ready to surrender her as price for escaping the consequences of famine? And what of Sarai's mind on this matter? Abram's petition to her makes it explicit that her consent and collaboration were critical to engaging in the ruse.

This last observation, that the narrative explicates the responsibility of both Abram and Sarai for the trigger mechanism of the plot entanglement, directs our attention to the third party in this romantic triangle: Pharaoh. A number of gapping features in the narration may serve to ambiguate the question of Pharaoh's responsibility, complicity, or even guilt. The parenthetic detail of verse 16—which both in the matter of time-setting and plot development would seem to be clearly out of place—occupies a gap without filling it. How much time elapsed between the removal of Sarai to Pharaoh's harem and YHWH's initiation of the "great afflictions?" How many days or weeks intervened between Sarai's entry into the king's household and her being fetched to his bed? If indeed fetched to his bed she ever was! And was this fetching without ceremony, whether of courting consent or hymeneal celebration? Would even a woman who was only the sister of Abram have been denied co-wife status, treated as merely an alluring odalisque? And if so indeed would Sarai at the last moment not have blurted out the truth? Or was it at the moment before that moment that YHWH's intervention rendered her confession unnecessary? Or is it conceivable that there was no confession in desperation, and that the afflictions began only after Sarai's virtue was sullied? And how did Pharaoh learn that not only he but his entire household had suffered affliction(s) in common? And how did he discover that the afflicting power was none other than an (or the) avenging d/Deity? Or, if the proper adjective is *minatory* rather than *avenging*, how did Pharaoh learn that the warning related to "Sarai wife of Abram" (verse 17)? But learn he certainly did, and his response to his discovery, in the dialogue placed in his mouth and in the absence of response from Abram, would indicate that whatever happened or did not happen or almost happened, the responsibility was entirely Abram's. Pharaoh himself is not only blameless, he is the victim of Abram's scandalous deportment. His series of rhetorical questions begins with the wrong done to him by Abram. The second and third questions would normally have been reversed: first, why did you say she was your sister, resulting in my taking her to wife? Second, why did you not tell me that she was your wife, not your sister? By ordering the questions as he does, the narrator informs us that even after Sarai had been taken to the palace Abram kept his silence, and that the meaning of the verb *āmar*, literally "said," is a metaphoric expression for "give the impression," or in my translation "bruit (it about)."

The answers to most of the gapping questions—the gaps themselves unbridgeable on the basis of this one narrative episode—may perhaps emerge from a study of the remaining two romantic-triangle stories.[45] The answer to one question, however, emerges from an examination of the verb *lāqaḥ*, which appears three times in this narrative. The denotation of this verb is "take;" its connotations extend to a remarkable range of nuances: static or dynamic, positive or negative, licit or illicit. Thus, for example: take = accept, share, partake; take possession of, purchase, carry off; marry (take in marriage), take as concubine, take (a woman by force), rape; fetch, take back, remove, seize, capture, take a bribe, extort; receive an oracle. The first appearance of this verb in verse 15 is a passive qal: Sarai was "brought, introduced into" with no indication of the agent (the implication of Sarai's being praised in his presence is of course that the action had Pharaoh's consent). But with the word *bayit* "house, home, palace, household, family," except for the limitations imposed by Pharaoh's dialogue, the expression can run the gamut from "abducted into the palace" to "was taken as a wife." The second appearance of this verb is with "to wive" or "to wife," the difference between the two being the question of whether the intent had yet been consummated. In its third appearance (*qaḥ*) imperative (without an object) in Pharaoh's curt command, and followed by another monolithic imperative (*lek*) "git, scram," it is preceded by, "here, now, is this wife of yours," equivalent to "mine she never became!" The concluding sentence, in the narrator's voice but reflecting the perspective of Pharaoh, and in the absence of a challenge to that perspective, paints so sorry a picture of Abram that the reader—conditioned to accept him as hero-ancestor—finds it almost impossible to credit. The divine power that protected Sarai's chastity bars Pharaoh from any punitive action against his treacherous guest, but it cannot require a continuing hospitality. Pharaoh places Abram under guard ("honor guard," if you insist, but guard nonetheless) and—the piel *šlḥ* "to release, speed, drive out, expel, divorce"—has him, his wife, and every thing attaching to him escorted to the border. Good riddance to bad garbage!

The Triangle in Gerar

(1) From there [Mamre's Oaks] Abraham traveled toward the Negev area and settled down between Kadesh and Shur. When he took up temporary residence in Gerar, (2) Abraham said of his wife Sarah, "my sister—she." Abimelech, king of Gerar, sent [a delegation] and took Sarah. (3) In a dream by night came God to Abimelech and said to him, "'Tis a dead man you are, by reason of the woman/wife you have taken—she being of a husband possessed. (4) (Abimelech **now** had made no physical advance to her.) He declared, "My Lord, will you slay a nation innocent though it be? (5) Was it not he himself said to me, 'My sister—she,' and she, yes she herself said, 'My brother —he.' With intent all innocent and hands clean of wrong doing did I this thing." (6) Then the numen in the dream said to him, "I too know that in all innocent intent you did this. And I held you back, yes I [held] you [back] from offending me. For this reason I allowed you not to make contact with her. (7) Now then restore the man's wife. Verily, he is a prophet, let him intercede for you and you, recover. But if you do not restore, know that you will of a certainty die, you and all your [people]."

(8) Early that morning Abimelech summoned all his courtiers and made them privy to all these details. These personages were terribly frightened. (9) Abimelech then summoned Abraham and said to him, "What have you brought upon us—and what the offense of mine against you—that you brought upon me and upon my realm such great punishment! Deeds unthinkable have you done in your dealings with me." (10) Another question Abimelech posed to Abraham: "Just what did you experience [among us] that brought you to commit such a deed?"

(11) Abraham declared, "[Nothing indeed] only that it was my supposition: There is surely no reverence here for Divinity['s norms]: they might well kill me on account of my wife. (12) And indeed she is, of a truth, my sister—my father's daughter she, but not my mother's daughter, and so became wife to me. (13) It was when Providence caused me to roam from my father's home that I said to her, 'This act of fidelity I would have you do for me: at any place where we arrive, say of me, that one is my brother.'"

(14) Abimelech fetched flocks and herds, male slaves and female slaves and presented [them] to Abraham, and restored to him his wife Sarah. (15) Said Abimelech, "My territory lies at your disposal, settle wherever you please." (16) To Sarah he said, "Go now, I have given a thousand-weight of silver to your brother. That now serves you as eye-veil for all in your company, that is, in every respect your position is set aright." (17) Abraham then interceded with the Deity. God then provided remedy for

Abimelech, that is to say for his wife and all his female subjects: they gave birth. (18) Yes indeed, YHWH had placed restraining bar across every womb in Abimelech's realm, on account of Sarah, Abraham's wife. (Genesis 20:1–18)

The similar features of this story and the one in Egypt are as follows. The decision to seek hospitality in a foreign kingdom is Abraham's and his alone. No divine source recommends this option. The lie (or half-truth, which comes to the same thing) about Sarah's status originates with the patriarch, out of fear for his life; it requires that he win consent of his wife who does not share the same vulnerability as to life, yet must be ready to forgo the respect due to a married woman and to risk assault on her sexual honor. The reasoning behind the lie is the assumption of the patriarch as to the immorality of Egyptians and Gerarites, an assumption implicit in the first story and explicit in the second; an assumption, furthermore, not only unsupported in the narrator's voice, but contravened by the dialogue in which the host kings express their shock over the mischief-making lie. Both kings are absolved of any serious wrongdoing in their arrogation (not, let us note, usurpation) of the beauteous matriarch, yet both suffer grievous punishment at the hands of God and both (apparently) extend reparations in one form or another, whether willingly or unwillingly, which enrich the undeserving patriarch. Finally, in both cases the affliction of the king is not limited to his own person, but extends to his household, court, or even nation.

The second story, more than twice as long as the first, provides details that, if extrapolated for the first, will bridge a number of gaps we have noted, and thus extend the list of similarities in the two narratives. (But even as we note these additional similarities, let us remember that a full poetical analysis would require a discerning of why what is gapped in the one account is made explicit in the other.) The appearance of God (ᵉlōhīm, verse 3) in the undescribed form of a numen (hāᵉ-lōhīm, verse 6) to advise Abimelech that the danger impending is owing to his taking of Abraham's wife enables us to understand that Pharaoh too received an oracle to warn him that the "great afflictions" were on account of the matriarch, and for the same reason. So too Abimelech's characterizing himself as innocent both in intent and deed, characterizing himself (and his nation) as ṣaddīq "upright, moral, righteous, innocent," this defense corroborated by the narrator in his own voice that no physical contact had occurred (verse 4), and again by the numen's indicating that some divine action was responsible for that failure to approach Sarah. All this informs us that the punishment, which is not made explicit until verses 17–18, had already begun before the oracular dream, and thus points to the same conclusion in the case of Pharaoh. The warning, which he received in the form of "great afflictions" upon himself and his household or court, came before he had a chance to sully Sarah and before the oracular response traced his troubles to her presence in his harem.

The nature of these great afflictions, unspecified in the first story, is suggested in the second. A fitting affliction (the idiom *poetic justice* comes to mind), and particularly efficacious for the achieving of Deity's objective would, of course, be impotence. A sudden and continuing loss of virility afflicting all the males in the kingdom would be remedy for the hybris of the dominant males who assume that the place for female beauties is the noble's harem. And it would also explain Abimelech's implication that the continuance of an entire nation is at stake (verse 4), as well as the point in verse 8 of Abimelech's involving all the lords of the court, as well as their great and collective fright. The last two verses, which serve as an illuminating epilogue, stress another side of the fertility equation and, in a context of humor, prepare us for the possibility that the affliction was not only miraculous and bizarre, but even fantastical. The humor begins in verses 6–7. The numen representing God first acknowledges Abimelech's innocence in the matter of the abduction into his seraglio, cites this knowledge on his part from the very beginning, and takes the credit for preventing Abimelech from compromising the honor of the strangely reticent wife of another man, which is to say, takes credit for Abimelech's affliction. This is followed, as though the impending death sentence on an entire nation were not enough, by an exhortation to restore the woman to her husband, and by another threat that the failure to do so would entail his death and that of all who appertain to him. The point of the seemingly otiose exhortation and the equally superfluous threat is what comes in between: the restoration to the husband of his wife is necessary to achieve this husband's prophetic intercession, without which intercession presumably Deity cannot act. And it is this critical intercession (duly noted in verse 17 as addressed to *hā^elōhīm* "the numen") by Abraham that results in God's (*^elōhīm*) curing not only Abimelech but also his wife and all his female subjects. We have speculated on Abimelech's malady, but what ailed the women? All of them? No speculation required: the text tells us explicitly. God himself, designated by the name that marks him as the tutelary and protective genius of Abraham and his line to come — YHWH — had rendered them barren. Incapable of conceiving? No, not quite. The time factor, never explicitly referred to in the narrative, implicitly rules out this specific aspect of barrenness. For barrenness to be recognized as a punishment or warning imposed by Deity to protect the honor of a woman newly introduced to the roster of royal wives, the fact of the barrenness would have to be as immediately recognizable as the conjectured impotence. And the expression for the barrenness is that YHWH had imposed a restraint, a bar — so to speak — "across every womb in Abimelech's court." And the conclusion of verse 17's notice that God cured the women is not that they were able to conceive (*wattāh^arū*), but *wayyēlēdū* "and they gave birth." The one condition that would seem to fit all the clinical and plot requirements here is false pregnancy, a swollen belly signaling a near-term pregnancy that never results in a delivery. This medical pathology has been recognized elsewhere in Scripture,[46] but it does not qualify here. For false pregnancy is just that: an external appearance of gravidity, but no fetus within. In the case of Abimelech's women, and perhaps by inference of Pharaoh's as well, women arrived at pregnancy's term — and no small number of such — were barred from giving birth.

Similarities in two narratives sharing an identical plot occasion no surprise. Differences, standing out in greater relief by reason of the similarities, must provide the clues to why two stories appear at all. In order of their appearance then, the patriarch's fear for his life is given in the first story as explanation for the lie, but not in the second. This may be due to the assumption of this detail in the second story. But it may also or alternatively be traced to the differing circumstances. In the first,

Abram's descent to Egypt to escape the famine in Canaan gives the impression of compulsion; in the second, the sojourn in Gerar is casual and voluntary, which would render his fear rather silly. Why then resort to the lie to begin with? Similarly, neither Sarah's beauty nor Abraham's petition that she corroborate the lie appear at the beginning of the second story. Where these details do appear, in story one, they are realized in the praise of the woman to Pharaoh and in her being fetched to his palace, yet this last act is formulated in the passive voice, without an agent, as though the narrator, reflecting Pharaoh's perspective, denies responsibility for his pandering ministers' concern for his pleasure. By contrast, Abimelech himself sends a delegation, and it is he who fetches Sarah to court. Pharaoh is abruptly smitten with afflictions, the source and cause of which he must ferret out for himself, a search not difficult for a king whose court is fabled for its diviners and wizards. And, there being no explicit mention of reparations, the paying of which is tantamount to an acceptance of some guilt, the fact of such reparations is perhaps buried in the parenthetic aside, verse 16, explicating Abram's material gains by the Pharaoh's arrogation of Sarai. Abimelech is not left to wonder about the cause of his troubles. Even before these are made explicit, he is declared innocent of encroachment by the narrator, and is vouchsafed a divine revelation confirming his innocence and affirming divinity's favorable disposition. As for Abimelech's own disposition in the matter of reparations, the story concludes with his own voluntary making of amends. To this we shall return.

In contrast to Pharaoh's unanswered monologue, assaultive in tone for all its justification, and followed by the contemptuous banishment of the patriarchal family from his borders, is the extended dialogue between Abimelech and Abraham, subtle yet eloquent in its undertones and overtones, these borne out in Abimelech's treatment of his troublesome guest. Abimelech's address to Abraham is given in two sections, the first consisting of three segments. 1) *What have you brought upon us?* Note the plural accusative pronoun, which can include Abraham in his lie's victimization, as against Pharaoh's *me*, and the absence of the Pharaoh's accusatory *zōt* "this awful thing." 2) *What offense have I done to you?* Note the two singular pronouns and the assumption that there must be some exculpating reason for Abraham's damaging behavior. This reason—an offense unknowingly and unintentionally committed or likely to be committed by host against his guest—both excuses and accuses Abraham at once. His damaging conduct was not without reason (excuse). But in this formulation there is also the perverse hyperbole of *obliqueness*: the implication that Abraham, having good cause for rancor, had perpetrated his deed with intent and malice, in aggression and not self-defense. *That you have brought upon me and my kingdom so great a punishment.* This last word (*ḥetāā*) has the primary denotation of "offense," and by metonymic extension (cause for effect) "punishment." In Abimelech's mouth this word carries both meanings. Thus: What offense have I committed against you that you brought us to commit an offense entailing such punishment? The courtesy of this overstatement of his own possible fault and understatement of Abraham's fault then concludes with a cajoling appeal to Abraham to acknowledge the full enormity of his lie, literally: 3) *Deeds undoable have you done [in your dealings] with me.* The second section of Abimelech's address to Abraham gives another version of or nuance to his question about the motivation behind Abraham's lie. Abandoning false presumption about his own possible provocation of this assaultive behavior, he now gets to the heart of the matter; he recognizes that Abraham's fear of danger to himself, occasioned by his wife's beauty, that is, the fear that Abimelech's subjects will not be able to resist the temptation to commit a morally barbarous act, is why Abraham had recourse to the lie. And so he asks what evidence Abraham had for judging the Gerarites so lacking in elementary decency: *Just what did you observe that you behaved as you did?*

Abraham's response is to this last question. His suspicion as to the lack of moral standards was only that, an unsupported presumption! He then offers a lame excuse: his statement that Sarah's is his sister is technically true.[47] This, of course, is no mitigating argument for his action (nor Sarah's), for the crux of the deception lies in the denial, implicit if not explicit, that she is his wife. Nevertheless, this technical truth was what made it possible for him to ask Sarah to identify him as her brother. The point of his statement, not in the narrator's voice at the story's beginning as in the first story, but at story's end and in Abraham's voice, is that this confession too—like the technical truth of the brother-sister relationship—is apologetic in tone. The suspicion about the lack of morality was not pointedly directed to the citizens of Gerar. It came to Abraham's mind when first he left the safety (and civilized morality?) of his father's home city, extended to every locale that the patriarch might hit upon, and alas—the inference that Abimelech and reader are asked to make—it was the misfortune of Gerar to fall within the penumbra of Abraham's sojourning and xenophobic, perhaps paranoid, distrust.

From these differences in the two stories—monologue in one and dialogue in the other; the favor of Deity expressed in revelatory oracle and assurance of remedy; gapping in the one and explication in the other; the ordering and circumstance of the information supplied to the reader—from all these emerges a vivid contrast between Pharaoh and Abimelech. The former is arrogant and brusque, self-righteous and unsympathetic to the vulnerabilities of a stranger. Abimelech is the opposite in every respect. And his closing action and words are in consistent contrast with Pharaoh's parting shots. Whereas the latter may have had an indemnity extorted from him (as witness hypotactic verse 12:16), and drives his guests back to famine-ridden Canaan, Abimelech volunteers a princely gift in herds, flocks, and slaves male and female. These same categories appear in 12:16 with a difference: here there is the addition of male asses to the flocks and herds and, anomalously placed—after slaves male and female—she-assess and camels. The close reader will not miss the point: the beasts of burden will be required to carry the patriarchal freight back across the Sinai's sands. Abimelech's gift is pointedly associated (verse 14) with the return of Sarah to Abraham. This is immediately followed by Abimelech's address to Abram as a cherished guest: *the freedom of all my realm is yours.* And then, sensitive to any fears she may have about loss of face in the eyes of her company, he assures her that the huge indemnity paid over to *her brother* will set straight the matter of her honor in everyone's eyes.[48] With this assurance by the gracious Abimelech, and with the conclusionary curing of the king and the afflicted women of his realm, the reader too is relieved of any anxiety as to whether Mother Sarah's person was or was not touched in the privacy of the harem. When

God intervenes in behalf of the pure, it is axiomatic that the intervention will take place before that purity can be compromised.

For all the enlightenment we have achieved by our comparison of these two narratives, there remains a number of questions raised earlier: the problem of Abraham's projecting onto his new neighbors a morality that precludes adultery but not murder, and the readiness of both Abraham and Sarah to hold silent when Sarah's chastity is in momentary danger of violation. To these we must now add a third. Is it conceivable that the patriarchal couple, some twenty-three years after the adventure in Egypt—Sarah now being about eighty-nine years old, and having declared herself withered and past the age of sexual activity—would again feel compelled to play out the triangle-scenario with a foreign king, having learned nothing from their first experience? The question of the matriarch's sudden new lease on youth and beauty such as to captivate Abimelech poses a particularly vexing problem for the poetical critic who maintains a single authorial voice for both narratives. How must he envy the documentary approach, which so neatly solves at least these last mentioned problems. The chronological data stemming from P is irrelevant for our narratives. The first adventure in Egypt is from the hand of J, as attested by the presence of YHWH in 12:17, and the second, in Gerar, is from the hand of E, here attested by the consistent use of ᵉlohim. To be sure it would have been helpful if in the concluding verse 20:18 that consistency were maintained. But—not to worry—the appearance of YHWH now and then is an understandable contamination in the E source, which is so often wedded to J's embrace as to be beyond disentanglement.

Another Triangle in Gerar

(1) Now a famine occurred in the area—apart from the earlier famine that occurred in the time of Abraham—so Isaac went to Abimelech, king of the Philistines, at Gerar.

(2) [This happened so:] YHWH appeared to him and said, "Do not go down to Egypt. Abide in the area that I designate to you. (3) Sojourn in this land, that I be with you and bless you. For it is to you and your seed that I grant all these lands. Thus will I fulfil the oath that I swore to your father Abraham. (4) That I will make your seed as numerous as the stars of heaven, and that I will grant to your seed all these lands so that by [i.e., by example of] your seed will all the nations on earth invoke blessing upon themselves. (5) [This] on account of the obedience that Abraham gave to my bidding, in that he kept my charge, my commands, my decrees and my instructions." (6) So Isaac settled in Gerar.

(7) When the people of that place asked about his wife, he said, "My sister, she!"—fearful of saying "My wife" lest "the townsmen of this place kill me over Rebecca," so great a beauty she. (8) As the number of his days there lengthened it came to pass that Abimelech, king of the Philistines, looked down from a window and beheld, there was Isaac dallying with Rebecca his wife. (9) Abimelech summoned Isaac and declared, "Your wife and that alone is she. How could you then say, 'my sister, she'!" Said Isaac to him, "My thought was: let me not die because of her." (10) Abimelech said, "How could you treat us so! How close an escape! Had one of ours bedded

your wife—then would you have brought upon us retribution." (11) Abimelech thereupon laid a charge upon the citizenry, to wit, "Anyone who so much as touches this man or his wife pays with his life!"

(12) Isaac sowed in that area and realized that year a hundredfold return. Thus did YHWH bless him. (Genesis 26:1–12)

In addition to the problems of plot, centering on the sister-wife ploy, which this third story shares with the first two stories, this story features a number of odd formulations, so odd indeed as to warrant our characterizing them as gratuitously and perversely illogical, almost in defiance of any postulation of a grammar of rhetoric. Let us review these features in the order of their appearance:

1. *There was a famine in the area apart from the former famine that occurred in Abraham's time.* The earlier famine took place in Abram's early years in Canaan; the second famine, even if (despite the narrative order) it occurred prior to Rebecca's conception of the twins, was some eighty years later. That the narrator might want us to associate the latter with the former is understandable. But why does he formulate the comparison, not in an assimilatory mode (*like* the famine, *as severe* as the famine), but in a dissociative mode, which is also absurdly gratuitous by reason of temporal and existential logic.

2. *So Isaac went to Abimelech, king of the Philistines, at Gerar.* Philistia and Canaan share a dependency on rain, unlike Nile-sufficient Egypt. Isaac's going to Abimelech for respite from a shared drought-caused famine makes no sense whatsoever. Speiser solves this problem in his departure from the standard translations of the verbs introducing verse 2. He renders them as pluperfects, thus rendering verses 2–6 anterior in time to Isaac's decision to "go to Abimelech at Gerar." Thus he makes sense of the passage at the expense of ignoring the paratactic tense construction in verse 2. My translation, pointing to the *synoptic-resumptive* narrative device by the words supplied in brackets, suggests also why the narrator resorted to this device here, rather than to the hypotactic option of a nominal clause with verb in the perfect tense. The bottom line was indeed that Isaac, although he had (like his father before him) set out for the hospitality of Egypt, sought the hospitality of Abimelech. This parenthetic resumptive episode, however, constituting a full third of the narrative, requires explanation. Why the divine veto of his (but not his father's) descent in to Egypt? And why the insertion here (as a subordinate theme) of the blessing of Isaac as the son, through whom the blessing promised to Abram will be transmitted? And why the stress here, not on YHWH's self-willed graciousness in his dealings with Abraham, but on Abraham's deserts; these merits being one: obedience; and this obedience explicated in terms normally reserved for prescriptive and exhortatory contexts: *mišmeret* "a duty charged upon someone," *miṣwā* "commandment," *ḥuqqā* "decree, statute," *tōrā* "(oracular) instruction, teaching."

3. The repeated alternation in narrator's voice and direct dialogue in verse 7: *When the citizens of that place asked after his wife he said, "my sister, she," he fearful of saying, "my wife," for fear that "the citizens of this place may yet kill me over Rebecca"— she being of such dazzling appearance.*

4. *Abimelech summoned Isaac and said, "But [ʾak, not ʾāken "ah so!"—expressive of recognition, new awareness]—So, it's your wife she is."*

5. *Abimelech said, "How could you treat us so! How close an escape! Had one of ours bedded your wife then would you have brought upon us retribution."* Just how free my translation is will emerge from comparison with a literal rendering: "What a thing this that you have done to us! Had one of our people barely bedded your wife then would you have brought upon us guilt." Since nothing happened, Isaac did nothing "to us." A man can no more barely/scarcely/hardly (*kim'at*) have intercourse with a woman than a woman can barely/scarcely/hardly be pregnant. And what Abimelech would have feared (in retrospective prospect, or is it prospective retrospect?) is not guilt (*āšām*) but the consequence of guilt, punishment in the form of a required indemnity (*āšām*).

6. One more example of peculiar expression relates to the geographical place names and the verbs for human presence there. Whereas Gerar is the city where Isaac receives his revelation (verse 1), and Egypt is the land where YHWH forbids him to go (verse 2), the alternative to this descent is not that he remain in Gerar but that he "reside/take up residence (*škn*) in the land which I shall designate to you." The command then continues in verse 3, "sojourn/reside temporarily (*gūr*) in this land." In obedience to this bidding, we are told in verse 6, "Isaac *settled down* (*yšb*) [i.e., instead of pursuing his original intention to move on] *in Gerar*." Yet in verse 7, where we should have expected that name to reappear, we have instead, once in the narrator's voice and once in Isaac's, "the place."

In addition to these peculiar features of diction, we are faced in this narrative with a number of the questions in respect to plot that we have faced in one or both of the two earlier triangle-narratives: The question of assuming that the host populations of the peripatetic patriarchs would shrink from engaging in sex with a married woman, but not from murdering a husband to clear the way for engaging in sex with the now husbandless widow; the nature of the guilt of the monarch, who takes into his household the unmarried sister of an honored guest; the rationale for an indemnification extorted from an innocent victim payable to a prevaricating poltroon responsible for the near outrage, outrage only prevented by the near intervention of Deity; the resort of the patriarchal couple to the treacherous ruse with Abimelech, after having experienced its consequences when played on Pharaoh; and now Abimelech, apparently ignorant of Isaac's kinship with Abraham and Sarah, not the least bit suspicious of yet another traveling couple, content—both of them—to cohabit as brother and sister, each without possessing a spouse; and now, learning by indirection that the couple are indeed man and wife, remonstrates to this guest on the strength of what might have happened, as though in utter forgetfulness that the same shabby game had been played with him some sixty years earlier.

THE KEYS TO THE SOLUTION of every problem in every narrative so far treated have been the following: recognition of metaphor in single words and phrases as well as in character and plot delineation; a discerning of the range of diction in terms of normal, metonymic, and abnormal, the last often to the point of the absurd or grotesque; and the problem-solving technique common to riddle and detective-story whodunit, this last item based on the assumptions of a single artist-author behind every narrative, spinning his story so as to allow for various levels of meaning according to the perceptive capacity of different readerships, this last reader-choice often defined in terms of predilection for one end or the other, or the middle of the literal-figurative spectrum. Such predilections may eventuate in the most abstract or philosophic of kerygmatic interpretations at the figurative end, or—at the most literal   in the total absence of kerygma: a historiographic tale told because it happened, or was believed to have happened, and thus has no true author other than the transmission process, one often going back to a preliterate origin.

In the case of our three triangle-narratives, even the most literal interpretations would have to read a moral into the plot, ranging from an answer to why the event took place three times to why the story is told three times, or why three versions of one event were preserved by tradition. The one answer on which all seem to agree is that it is to drill into the minds of the patriarch's descendants that their forbears, despite their vulnerability as aliens in the lands of their wanderings, were of noble standing, the purity of their line guaranteed by the God who watched over them day and night. Resonances of this kerygma in the words "prophet" (*nābī*) and "touch/afflict" (*ng*), "nation" (*goy*), "sojourn" (*gūr*), and "barely" (*kim'aṭ*), are only to be expected in a hymn that rehearses YHWH's care:

> When they were few in number, barely able to *sojourn* therein,
> Moving from *nation* to *nation*, from [one] kingdom to another people,
> He allowed no one to oppress them, on their behalf disciplined *kings* [saying,]
> Touch not my anointed ones,
> To my *prophets* do no harm. (Psalm 105:12–15)

However, strongly as this kerygma may recommend itself to us, it does not answer such questions as the patriarch's failure to ask for oracular guidance, to petition for divine intervention, and to resort twice to a ruse that had failed on a similar occasion. Furthermore it may be urged that the kerygma simply does not appear, explicitly at least, in the third story. For one thing, nothing happens to either the matriarch or patriarch, and so there is no occasion for God to intervene to protect them. YHWH does put in an appearance, but to Isaac, not Abimelech. And if YHWH's command to Isaac that he remain in Gerar despite the famine, together with the subsequent blessing, implies YHWH's protection, as it surely does, that protection is not in connection with Isaac's fear for wife or life, or rather fear for life on account of wife. The absence of any concupiscent move on Rebecca thus renders the suggested kerygma as at best peripheral to this narrative.

Let us then review the problems with diction in this third story with a view to what metaphors may have eluded our appreciation.

There was a famine in the area apart from the former famine that occurred in Abraham's time. It is most unlikely that the point of this sentence is to remind the reader of the story that he had read six chapters earlier. It is much more likely that the narrator, aware of the reader's problems with the events of Chapter 20, following the similar events in Chapter 12, is anticipating the reader's initial sense of déja vu at the story's opening words, "There was a famine in the area." And therefore assuring the reader: yes, indeed, there were two famines. But that would call for a simile, a comparison of similarities employing a preposition *like, similar to*. Instead we have (as noted) a dissociative preposition introducing a *simile of negation* (if I may indulge in the pomposity of expanding the register of rhetorical categories). And this abjuration of simile is underlined by another (and absurd) figure, the pleonasm of an *earlier famine, in the time of Abraham*, as if a famine in the father's time might have occurred later then the one in the son's lifetime.[49]

The solution of this figurative conundrum involves such novelty that my reader may be tempted to dismiss it out of hand. I therefore take the precaution of reminding that reader that the novelty lies in the poetic creativity of the biblical master of metaphor, and not in an academic critic straining at a gnat. Simply put, the dissociative preposition *millebad* "apart from, aside from" may in its negation of not-likeness, facing one antipode, signify not-*like* because different; or facing the other antipode, signify not-*like* because identical. Yes the famine is one and the same, as Abimelech the king of Gerar is the same, as the patriarch son and father are one and the same, which is to say, for all the seeming dissimilarities in *personae* and *plot*, the *characters* and the *plots* are kerygmatically identical. To resort to an analogy from a discipline that is as much art as it is science, as independent of reality as it is useful in structuring it, as concrete in its particulars as it is abstract in its universals, as quantitative as arithmetic and as argumentative as rhetoric, narratives 2 and 3 are as congruent as triangles having identical angles opposite legs of equal length. When superimposed on one another, or whether facing one another in seeming confrontation or aligned in the same direction, their similarities and juxtapositions inform on one another.[50]

Thus the identity of Abimelech of Gerar in both tales, not because personal name and city name are identical, but because as morally sensitive and generous character in both tales he stands out in contrast with the Pharaoh of the first story. Isaac in Gerar in a year of famine is the Abraham in Gerar in a year when famine there is none (as there was indeed in the year he went down to Egypt). In the blessing of YHWH to Isaac, reassuring the patriarch that nothing untoward will happen if he stays in Gerar, there are echoes of earlier promises made by God to Abram/Abraham:

TO ABRAHAM	TO ISAAC
1. I shall bless you (12:2) [both in the imperfect with waw conjunctive;]	I shall bless you (26:3)
2. to the land that I shall show you (12:1), on a mountain top that I shall designate to you (22:2),	in the land that I shall designate to you (26:2);
3. for all this territory that you view, I give to you and to your seed (13:15),	verily to you and your seed to I give all these territories (26:3);
4. count the stars if count them you can . . . so may will your seed be (15:5 cf., also 33:18),	I will make your seed as numerous as the stars of heaven (26:4);
5. I shall give you, that is to say [deictic waw] to your seed after you the land of your sojourning (17:2),	I shall give to your seed all these lands (26:4);
6. by [example of] your seed will all the nations of earth invoke blessing on themselves (12:3).	as consequence of your obedience to my bidding (26:5–6).

Most striking in respect to these echoes of the blessings of the father in the blessings of the son is that the seed through whom Abram/Abraham's blessing is to be fulfilled is not specified to Abraham until 19:2, but once this only heir of the promise is specified there as Isaac, the reiteration of the promise to Isaac in Chapter 26 is supererogatory if not pleonastic, except for the implied exhortation to Isaac to be obedient as his father was, as though the promise to Abraham concerning Isaac were conditional on his being indeed the avatar of his father.

The identity of father and son is most strongly suggested in the parallel between the instructions in item 2 above, the command to Abram to go to, and the command to Isaac to dwell in, the land that God will yet indicate. The reason for the indefiniteness of Abram's destination is twofold. Some of the areas through which he will travel will constitute the territory promised to his posterity; other areas fall outside that grant. It is this distinction that lies behind the three verbs and the terms for territory in verses 2–6. The "reside in the land that I shall designate to you" (škn b'arṣ) is in contrast to Egypt, to which he is forbidden to descend (verse 2). But the sense of permanence in the verb škn and the as yet undefined "land," that is, Israel's future territory, is in contrast to "sojourn in this land" (gūr bāāreṣ hazzō't) in verse 3, that is, the territory of Philistia (Gerar), which never became nor was claimed as Israelite territory in biblical times. Thus Philistia too is in contrast with both Egypt and (promised) Israelite territory. And thus it is that in verse 6, "Isaac settling down in Gerar" (wyšb yṣḥq bgrr) is his *remaining* where he is, a guest in a land not destined for his posterity, and this—perhaps—because of the generosity of the hospitality and moral decency that characterize the Philistine host of Abram-Isaac.

But this praiseworthy aspect of Gerar-Philistia is from the perspective of the narrator, a perspective he has made available to the reader here, and will yet share with the reader and with Isaac in the denouement of story two that follows.[51] But until that happens, the perspective of Isaac in regard to his host city and its citizens, colored by his suspicion and fear, is the purport of the distancing expressions, "men of that place" twice in verse 7 and "there" (šām) in verse 8.

It is such play on perspective that lies behind the alternation of narrator's voice and character's voice (dialogue) in verse 7. When the citizens *of that place* ask after *his wife*, this reflects the point of view of narrator and reader who share this information about Rebecca's status, but it does not reflect the point of view of the Gerarites, who know her as the lady of the household but not her status; and it is the knowledge of Isaac, which he is immediately to falsify in dialogue: "My sister, she." The narrator points to this falsehood in attributing the lie to Isaac's fear (twice, *ki yāre'* and *pen*) to acknowledge the truth "my wife (she)" and his craven self-concern "they may yet kill me"—not "for my wife" but "over Rebecca." This name, expressive of endearment in Isaac's dialogue, is then brought into sardonic juxtaposition with the narrator's addition that the endearing factor of her beauty has been transformed in his mind from blessing to curse.

Time puts prevarication to the test. The longer its duration, the more difficult to maintain the stance required by a ruse. And so in an unguarded moment Isaac is caught out by Abimelech in an unbrotherly caress of *Rebecca*, who has thus been betrayed as "his wife." This apperception on Abimelech's part is expressed in *free indirect discourse* ("and lo," expressing Abimelech's *internal dialogue*). But again the narrator interjects his own, if not quite sardonic, at least jeering pun on *Isaac* [(root *ṣḥq* "smile, laugh, play, amuse, sport, disport, wanton, dally, dilly-dally, diddle" and his activity] *isaaking Rebecca—his wife.* Respect for the sensibilities of others who share my reverence for my common grandparents is behind my translation, "Isaac dallying with Rebecca." But respect for a *meta-literary* convention (our relationship to Isaac and Rebecca), pious virtue as that is, may also constitute the literary sin of bowdlerization, if—as in our case—the narrator intended and wrote, "Abimelech, king (hence arbiter) of Philistines, looked down from his window and caught sight, "*There!* Diddler diddling Rebecca—oho! his wife!"

The one-sentence dialogue of Abimelech to Isaac is divided into two parts, introduced respectively by *'ak* "but" and *(we)'eik* "how." The first, *'ak*, must be rendered to reflect aposiopesis, a rhetorical nicety that expresses both what Abimelech thought and what he said and did not say. "But[—you've been lying]—It's your wife she is." Having broken off his sentence in mid-thought, he then mitigates the accusation, which is implicitly there but has not been voiced, in a question that may be read as informational or rhetorical, "How is it you said, 'My sister, she?'" Isaac's response, like Abraham's in 20:11 (note "in this place") is a confession of guilt and offers suspicious fear as excuse for the lie, leaving moot the question of whether he had grounds for that suspicion. Abimelech's answer to this confession puts the blame squarely on Isaac in the hyperbolic, "What thing is this you did to us," yet it is in both denial and confirmation of grounds for the suspicion of immorality. His *kim'at* "almost" = *"had but"* anyone bedded your wife acknowledges that immoral riffraff are to be found in every land and in every stratum of society, but his entire stance, and in particular his acknowledgment that the entire society would be held responsible for a single offense, prove the probity of his nation. Indeed, what this denouement adds to that in the second story is further confirmation of his own supererogatory moral sensitivity. He is horrified by the might-have-been consequences of a fear-induced lie. He acknowledges personal responsibility for the uprightness of all his subjects. Since no offense whatsoever against his guest was registered there can be no volunteering of indemnity, but YHWH makes up for this by his blessing of the patriarch. Isaac remains in Philistia as an honored guest. Whether he literally rented or purchased land for sowing, or whether this is a metaphor for the general and sensational success of his enterprises, whatever their nature, must remain moot. But blessed he was, at YHWH's instance, in the territory of Philistia where YHWH had bidden him to sojourn; the famine must have come to an abrupt end.

One final question must be addressed in this narrative. What is the meaning of verse 11? *Abimelech laid a charge on all his people: Anyone who but lays hand on this man or his wife pays with his life!* That no Gerarite made a move on Rebecca, unmarried sister of Isaac as was thought, rules out a fear on the king's part that anything so untoward might now be attempted against her, now known to be wedded wife, or—as Isaac feared—against Isaac on her account. The motivation behind Abimelech's charge must be his reading of his subjects' mind. When they learned of the near retribution they might have suffered for a single morally irresponsible act that might have been committed by one of their number, they too would have marveled at the lie which had abetted that behavior. And learning of the slur upon their ethos and their honor implicit in the gratuitous suspicion of the guest they had welcomed, to what acts of retaliation might their indignation have led? Thus, once again the narrator makes a case for Abimelech's righteousness. Even righteous indignation against an overweeningly judgmental alien will not mitigate the least of hostile acts. In all three narratives, and climactically in this third one, one moral hero emerges: Abimelech king of Gerar.

It is this last conclusion that points us in the direction where the kerygma of this tripartite narrative riddle must lie. The three stories are one and, if we except YHWH, there are only two *dramatis personae* in the cast. YHWH can be left out because he plays no real role in the third story, and very little role in the first; he, so to speak, stands outside the action. The patriarchal couple are, for the purposes of role-identification, one. That is to say, each couple is a unity, but since Isaac(-Rebecca) and Abraham(-Sarah) are one, there is only one patriarch(-matriarch) role or persona in all three stories. Similarly, the three foreign kings together constitute but a single persona. For the two Abimelechs are one by identity, and the Pharaoh functions only as counterfoil to establish the differing and different character of Abimelech; this comes through clearly in story two, and climactically in story three. If then, Abimelech is the moral hero of the riddle-narrative, what is the patriarch-matriarch, the villain? This is hard to swallow! Then how about the antihero? Yes, but in what sense? Well, only in the sense that Abimelech is hero, in the moral sense. Fine, but then we must come up with the moral of the narrative, and let us remember that kerygma is another term for the *moral* of a fabulary narrative.

One of the factors that militates against viewing the patriarch-matriarch as villain is that YHWH is clearly on their side, protector of the matriarch's virtue in the first two stories, and the power behind their material enrichment in all three. Another factor is the meta-literary fact (a fact created by Scripture's literary artistry) that the reader relates to Israel and Israel's forebears as descendant to ancestors. It is inconceivable therefore that the ancestral story reflect shame rather than glory on our venerable and venerated grandparents. A brief reflection on the narrative sweep of Israel's "history" will, however, compel us to reconsider whether the un-qualified nature of this bias on the part of the filial reader is justified. Hardly a single ancestral hero or heroine, from Abram and Sarai through Jacob and Rachel, Moses and Miriam, Gideon and Samson, David and Solomon, and Jonah and Jeremiah, is without serious or even fatal flaw. Indeed, prototypical Israel is not the ideal saved and saving remnant, it is the weak-of-faith to faithless generations of wilderness wanderings and the invasion of Canaan, of the periods of Judges, monarchical dynasties, Exile and Return. And, to be sure, the ancestral shortcomings and backslidings are the time-warp mirrors of our own deficiencies in faith and conduct, even as the shine of ancestral virtues so dims the luster of our own, and renders us craven petitioners for the grace of God in the name of ancestral merit. Here, then, lies one clue to ancestors, so often models for emulation, yet again and again cast in antihero roles for our self-identification and moral correction.

Another factor that makes it difficult for us to relate to Israel's ancestors as anti-heroes is the mind-set we have about Scripture's attitude to their non-Israelite contemporaries. The ancestors are monotheists (or striving to be), all others are pagan.

The ancestors are moral, decent, peaceable, chaste. Their opposite numbers are immoral, bellicose, xenophobic, and lewd. This mind-set of ours, as I will show in a moment, is wrong, utterly wrong. And yet this mind-set does derive from Scripture, if not from the thrust of the stories of the family that became the people and the nation of Israel. The history of Israel's polity in the monarchical period is, vis-à-vis the non-Israelite world, largely a story of success, despite the disastrous end of the Northern Kingdom almost three hundred years and of the Judean kingdom a little more than four hundred years, after the rise of monarchy. Yet it is the conquest of the two kingdoms—by the rapacious empires in the east—that dominates our picture of Israel's history. And the villains are the godless pagans who sent the northern tribes into the oblivion of exile and who razed the sacred shrine on Zion's mount, this despite prophetic assurance in the historical narratives and the oracles of the writing prophets that the author of the calamities was Israel's God, and the reason for the sentence the disobedience and faithlessness of his people.

The premonarchical history is even more surely a success story, a tribesmen mob breaking out of Sinai's desert to destroy ancient Amorite kingdoms east of the Jordan, fording the river and dispossessing the autochthonous populations, in the words of Deuteronomy 9:1, "greatly more numerous than you," and making their own "great cities fortified into the very skies." It is more surely a success story, in that this invasion culminates in the monarchy's rise. Yet these few centuries of history too are overhung by a lugubrious pall: Israel's newly settled tribesmen being ever subject to Canaanite attack from the north, Midianite camel-riding kings from the east, Philistine exacters of tribute from the west; the very rise of the monarchy itself being the desperate recourse of fractious tribes to impose upon themselves a defensive unity, which had eluded the theoretical rule of a single God.

A third factor is the rationale behind the atrocity that still bewilders the moralists who in almost all other respects are the heirs of biblical morality: genocide, perpetrated by Israel in obedience to the demand of YHWH, the benign God of Israel, and of all humankind. What is overlooked is that this element of Israel's success story is, narratively and prescriptively speaking, altogether post facto. It is the proscription of inveterate, hopelessly and incorrigibly immoral defilers of Deity by a righteous Judge, who waited until "the Amorite iniquity was full to the brim" and a possibly more promising seed was available to sow the territories about to be vacated. The proscription and the execution of sentence both took place—from the vantage point of the biblical "historiographer"—in a time at least centuries ago. The last ḥerem-war sanctioned by God was botched by Israel's first king, Saul, against an Amalekite population now extinct. The kindred peoples of Moab, Ammon, and Edom are not to be goaded into war. The kindred peoples of Aram entered into non-aggression treaties with Israel's ancestors. The Hamitic Egyptians were—for all the oppressive nature of a polity that reduced natural subjects as well as guests to servitude—the hosts of Israelites for many generations, and are not to be treated as abhorrent (Deuteronomy 23:8). The Hamitic inhabitants of Philistia, hosts to David and the patriarchs long before him, allies of Judah against Assyria as late as the time of King Hezekiah, agreed to legitimate borders between their own unviolated territories and the adjacent southern territories of a yet unborn and unconceived Judah, this in treaties with the patriarchs Abraham and Isaac (Genesis

21:22–34; 26:12–33).[52] Let us now consider the non-Abrahamitic personae in the first twenty-six chapters of Genesis with a view to determining the extent to which they are pictured as pagan, immoral, bellicose, lewd, and xenophobic. In respect to paganism or polytheism, Adam, Eve and the serpent, Cain, Noah and his three sons, Lot, Melchizedek, Pharaoh, and Abimelech—not a one of all of these relates to the divine realm as if it consists of more than one member. Nor in the remaining thirty-six chapters of this book will we come across any suggestion as to proscribed divinities (or idols, material representations of them) except in connection with the numens to whom Jacob relates; namely, in connection with God's approving reference in 35:1 to one such numinal representative, and Jacob's bidding to his household to turn in the "alien gods" in their midst; which gods (together with his family members' earrings) he buries under a terebinth in the neighborhood of Shechem. The clearly immoral inhabitants of the world are the humanity destroyed in the flood, the Amorites of 15:16 whose iniquity has not yet earned a sentence of extermination, and the Sodomites and Gomorrans who enact their depravity in the presence of the messengers God has sent to destroy them once Lot has been extracted from their midst. Lewdness can be ascribed only to the Hamitic branch of humanity as personified in Ham-Canaan in 9:20–27, but by the same token the Japhethite and Shemite branches are free of this particular moral twist. As for bellicosity and xenophobia, the patriarchs wander in a remarkably unthreatening world, and if aggression is a necessary ingredient of illicit belligerence, even the kings of the five cities of the Plain cannot be faulted on this score. If there is a single case of unwarranted war-making, it is that at least twice-condemned action of Simon and Levi against the invalided males of Shechem. The seduction (or perhaps statutory rape) of their sister Dinah, which leads to the Shechemite slaughter, is pictured as the loss of control on the part of a love-smitten youth for which he, father, and subjects are ready to make whatever amends are demanded.

In the light of all this, one can only stand in awe before the achievement of this literary work of ideational and moralistic fiction, which propagates doctrine without ever becoming doctrinaire; which purports to be the saga of a God-chosen people, yet never loses sight of the role designed for this particular people, that it be model for the humanity of which it is a part and which, alas, it does not excel in virtue, yet exemplifies in vice. Hence it is that every moral hero, of the Abrahamitic line or outside it, is a model for emulation; that every antihero of that line or outside it embodies traits that are to be shunned; and the most meaningful of lessons for us, the seed of Abraham and Sarah, are in the deficiencies in the best of our ancestral heroes of faith. More cogent for us than the plague-defying Pharaoh who knows not YHWH are the Israelite complainers in the wilderness who do acknowledge him; more cogent for us the callous judgmental stance of a Jonah toward Ninevites than the loving one of a Jeremiah lamenting "the slain of the daughter of my people."

And so finally to the moral of the three romantic triangles. A moral for a people that has learned to see itself more as victim of history than fashioner of it; as outsider to the congress of nations rather than, in Judah Halevi's phrase, heart of the nations; and finally that in a world of xenophobic pagans finds itself singled out for special exhortation to know the heart of the stranger and to treat him as one's own.

One of the absurdities that we have not hitherto raised in regard to the triangle plot is the presence of God in all three, acting on behalf of his chosen ones in all three, and in the third, in a revelation directing the patriarch to stay where he is, and assuring him on the promise of the land to his numberless descendants. This revelation and promise precedes the first journey of Abram to Egypt in Chapter 12. Revelation and promise precede in Chapter 18 the journey, in Chapter 19, from Mamre's Oaks to Gerar. That second story, coming after the promise of Isaac's birth and immediately before the fulfillment of that promise in Chapter 21, seems designed by placement to underline God's guaranteeing of Abraham's paternity. What seems absurd then is the readiness in all three stories of the patriarch-matriarch to head off danger by recourse to a lie, rather than to rely on God to keep his promise. (Well, let us remember that even in these days when such personal revelations are rare, those of us who are yet strong in faith in God's saving promise will resort to wiles and stratagems against the designs of our faithless neighbors; and why not, since it is well known that God helps those who help themselves!) And to be sure the God whose help has not been petitioned comes through for his elect despite this seeming slight.

Another perplexity that I have raised several times is the fear or suspicion that the xenophobic natives may commit murder to avoid the sin of adultery. If an important element of the moral is that a sense of our own righteousness as against the iniquity of our neighbors may lead us to dissemble, lie, deny our own most sacred relationships; and, further, that such resort to subterfuge and scheming may, so to speak, hoist us on own petard and bring about the very danger we feared, the invasion of our rights to property and person; if this, there must be some verisimilitude to the suspicion and fear of the patriarch, which seems to be the same in all three stories. This is to say that the suspicion of the patriarch about the ethos of his host-peoples must realistically correspond to our own experience of the ethos of the non-Bible-oriented communities with whom we share this island-universe. And nowhere is the taboo of adultery stronger than that of murder. We must therefore seek in the three formulations of the patriarch's fear the metaphoric sense—be it hyperbole, metonymy or other trope—that has escaped us. And in reexamining the diction which expresses that fear, we shall come first to realize that while our translations are faithful, our restatements in paraphrase of the texts have been misleadingly incorrect. First, the term for "murder" (rṣḥ) never appears. Second, we have failed to distinguish, in each narrative, the nuance which attaches to the expression of the suspicion by virtue of its diction, its timing, and its addressee.

In story one, and in this story alone, it is the beauty of the matriarch that is stated and stressed as the ultimate factor in the patriarch's fear. (Once made explicit here, it will be implicit in the two stories to follow.) The fact and significance of her beauty appears at the very opening of the narrative in Abraham's statement to his wife Sarai of his awareness of her beauty, the term for this last featuring the stem rʾh "see" (active) "be seen, appear" (passive): ypt-mrʾh "comely to the sight." When the Egyptians *see* you, he goes on (leaving an easily filled gap) they will/may kill me and let you live. This judgment of Abram's as to Sarai's appearance is then twice confirmed by the narrator: first, when the Egyptians *see the woman* it is to realize how very beautiful she is; and then when Pharaoh's ministers *see her* and *praise her* to Pharaoh, whereupon she is *taken* into Pharaoh's household. The association of the perception *r'h*, the attractive (*ḥmd*) or beautiful (*yph*), frequent elsewhere in Scripture, is exemplified in the expression "attractive to the sight." The Hebrew for this, *neḥmad l^emar'e* in Gen. 2:9, is the characterization of what we call "shade trees" (in contrast to "fruit trees," which are *tōb l^ema^akāl* "good for eating"). These two terms then naturally eventuate in a third term, *lqḥ* "to take," and this last, as in the case of Sarai's being *taken* into Pharaoh's household, with a sense of illegitimacy. All three terms appear in Joshua 7:21, in the confession of Achan that it was he who brought down God's wrath on Israel by appropriating for himself the *ḥerem*-loot from the city of Jericho. "Upon *seeing* [the precious items], I *craved* (*ḥmd*) them and *took* them."

It is surely this existential process, from seeing, to desiring, to (mis)appropriation, that informs the last charge in the Decalogue. "You shall not covet (*ḥmd*) your fellow's estate (*byt*), you shall not covet your fellow's wife" (Exodus 20:17). "You shall not covet (*ḥmd*) your fellow's wife, nor shall you go a-lusting (*'wh*) after your fellow's estates" (Deuteronomy 5:21). This last verb, a durative hittpael, informs on the meaning here of *ḥmd*. The address is not to the purely emotional or passive aspect of desire, but to the nursing of cupidity and its eventuation in behavior aimed at achieving the desired goal. Hence, the force of the last commandment, in a sense a recapitulation of the preceding four prohibitions, is: *Make/harbor no designs* on your fellow's wife, house, etc.

Were the fear of the patriarch Abram for his life predicated on the assumption that outside Ur or Aram Neharayim no moral norms existed, it is doubtful that he should have left home to begin with. But the danger from stranger hosts in civilized lands is not from the unchecked practice of murder and rape; it is from the crafty designs of those who, secure in their own homes and governments and courts, will find ways to remove by one means or another the head of the household who stands in the way of their achieving of their illicit desires. Against such clandestine plotting, the patriarch takes the precaution embodied in the lie. And to be sure, the lie boomerangs in that it does away with the very inhibitions that would inform the actions of the most morally sensitive of kings and commoners. Once hoist on his own petard, his wife in the legitimate custody of his host country's supreme magistrate, what can the patriarch do but wait in silence for a greater magistrate to take a hand in the game?

Let us note how the patriarch informs his host of the reason for his lie. In the first story, he simply does not. The Pharaoh gives Abram no chance to answer his question, which thus becomes rhetorical. And well for Abram that he does not. For how would his answer do anything but exacerbate the righteous indignation for this monarch who does not suffer liars gladly? In the second story, as we saw, the possibility that a general lack of morality—for which lack Abraham had no evidence—might lead to his death "over the matter of my wife" is the patriarch's lame half-excuse, half-apology, the sting of the suspicion of Gerarites mitigated for its general application to people "anywhere." And in the third story, where the absence of any advance made to the matriarch underlines the gratuitousness of the suspicion voiced in the other two stories, the patriarch's response is untranslatable for the compounding of narrator's introduction and the direct discourse that follows. Our translation, "Said Isaac to him, 'My thought was: *let me not* die because of her'" simply does not reflect the Hebrew. The words in italics would be correct if the Hebrew word were *al*, the negative particle governing an imperfect in direct discourse. The Hebrew particle *pen* "lest, that not" introduces indirect discourse. The translation should therefore be along this line: Said Isaac to him "Truly, I thought" [thinking to avert the possibility] that, "I may yet come to grief [lit., *die, not be killed*] over her."

POETICAL REVIEW OF THE NAMES OF GOD

In story one the Deity appears only once, in verse 17, where it is YHWH, the personal and tutelary protector of the patriarchs, who afflicts the unfortunate Pharaoh. A quick glance at the exclusive appearance of YHWH in the preceding nine verses in Chapter 12 and in the eighteen verses of the following Chapter 13 will reveal how well the entire story is integrated into the flow of the surrounding narrative.

In story two, it is the (universal) God (Elohim) who appears to Abimelech (verse 3). The latter addresses him as "my lord(s)" the plural being that of majesty (verse 4). Yet the narrator signals that this "my lord" is the Deity to whom we of the Israelite tradition refer in writing as YHWH, but substitute for that unpronounceable spelling the Hebrew word for "my lord" (*ᵃdōnay*) except for the lengthening of the final vowel (*ᵃdōnāy*). This lengthening, let us remember, characterizing *ᵃdōnay* "my lord(s)" only when the reference is to YHWH, is purely a literary—which is to say, a *written*—sign, for the vowel, being a diphthong, cannot be further lengthened in speech. The appearance, then, of this (masked) Adonay-YHWH, first referred to as Elohim "God," is thereupon revealed to be a numen representing that God: *hāᵉlōhīm* (verse 6). Abraham, in his discourse with Abimelech, refers to the supernal power that sent him a-wandering as God (Elohim) in verse 13. But interesting, to be sure, is the narrator's voice in verse 17, informing us that Abraham did on Abimelech's behalf intercede with *hāᵉlōhīm*. This term can stand, as we have seen, for the abstract sense of Providence/Heaven or the particular representation of God in the form of a numen. Either sense is reasonable here, but the subtle nuances of the terms for Deity comes through immediately (if not with formulaic clarity) by the narrator's informing us that it was God (Elohim)—not the numen—who cured Abimelech and his female subjects, and then attaching in hypotactic formulation the gap-filling information that it was YHWH, who had acted on his protegé's behalf in placing a bar over every womb in Abimelech's realm (verse 18).

In the third story, there are no problems and no surprises. It is YHWH in verse 2 who reveals himself to Isaac in Gerar, and at story's conclusion it is YHWH who blesses Isaac with abundance (verse 12).

THE MADNESS OF FATHER ABRAHAM: GENESIS 22

The knotty question of this narrative's kerygma is in contrast with the simplicity of the plot and the straightforwardness of its telling. There is very little repetition, none that appears redundant, a simple vocabulary, and only one departure from paratactic syntax. A father receives a divine call to sacrifice his son, is prevented by divine intervention at the last moment, and is praised for his readiness to obey. The stumbling blocks to our discernment of the kerygma may be narrowed to the motivation or rationalization behind the first call of Divinity, and to the mortal's failure to question it. An answer of sorts to the first would seem to be present in the hypotactically formulated notice that Abraham was being put to a test. But what need does an all-knowing God have to subject a single person to such a test? As for the mortal's response, it is particularly perplexing in the case of an Abraham, who did not hesitate to haggle on behalf of a tiny percentage of possible innocents in Sodom's moral sinkhole.[53]

We may defer to another place discussion of the meta-literary question of the historic fact or frequency of child-sacrifice in antiquity, and the influence of this *interpretative factor* on the exegesis of this chapter.[54] But in the interest of clearing the way for our translation and impressionistic retelling of this story, it would be advisable to establish that this bizarre episode is in place within the overarching narrative of Abraham's career; which is to say, that it is not an intrusive fantasy awkwardly thrust into a verisimilitudinous history by an inept author or injudicious redactor. The last verse of our narrative in Chapter 22 has Abraham returning to Beersheba, which must therefore be his location when he receives the call. This is in keeping with the immediately preceding narrative (2:22–34), in which King Abimelech of Gerar cedes to Abraham the area around the Sheba Spring (= Beersheba), an area that is pictured as being Philistine territory at that time.[55] The following Chapter 23 begins with Sarah's death at Hebron, which, as verse 2 pointedly reminds us, was then known as Kiriath Arba, but more important, was located in what was then Canaanite territory.[56]

A grazing range from Beersheba in the south to Hebron some twenty miles north would not be overly extensive for someone of the patriarch's substance and status. If the story of the mission to Moriah took place shortly before Sarah's death, the matriarch—ailing, perhaps—might well have remained at the northern headquarters of the family's grazing grounds while her husband and son attended to business at the southern end. Thus the neat transition in terms of geography may serve as an implicit accounting for the absence of Sarah from the scene at Beersheba when Abraham, Isaac, and the two ranch hands depart for their fateful destination. She might well have been spared the knowledge of what almost happened to her beloved son. On the other hand, the celebration of Isaac's weaning and the subsequent expulsion of Hagar and Ishmael, as told in Chapter 21, are more likely in the setting of Beersheba than Hebron. So it might have been in Isaac's early years that the family moved north to Hebron, and subsequently left the matriarch there while the flocks were herded to the south. The absence of any definitive clue to the time-setting of the near-sacrifice is certainly no accident. We have been told that Sarah, ninety years old when she gave birth to Isaac, died thirty-seven years later. So Isaac may, at the time of the ordeal, have been anywhere from seven to thirty-seven.[57] This heightens the author's message to us. We have been given the vital facts about him: he was born, circumcised, weaned, and separated from brother Ishmael at the time of his weaning. Sometime between his weaning and his loss of mother took place the test, which—had he not already arrived at that status—must have jolted him into the emotional stage we call manhood.

The Text

(1) It was some time after these events—the Divinity **now** put Abraham to the test—He said to him, "Abraham!" "Yes sir," he answered. (2) He said, "Take now your son, your one-and-only, whom you cherish, Isaac; and betake yourself to the land of Moriah—there offer him up as a burnt offering on one of the heights that I shall indicate to you."

(3) Promptly that morning Abraham strapped [pannier on] his ass. Then taking two of his hands with him as well as his son Isaac, he split the wood for the burnt offering. Then he set out for the place which the Divinity had told him of. (4) On the third day, Abraham looked up, and sighted the place at a distance. (5) Abraham said to his boys, "Stay you here with the ass. I and the lad will go up yonder, we shall worship, and we shall come back to you."

(6) Abraham then took the wood for the burnt offering, loaded it on his son Isaac. In his own hand he took the fire[-pot] and the butcher-knife. The two of them walked on together. (7) Isaac spoke up to his father Abraham, "Father!" "Yes, my son," he answered. "Here," he said, "is the fire and the wood, but where is the sheep for the burnt offering?" (8) Abraham replied, "God will see to the sheep for the burnt offering for Himself, my son." And the two of them walked on together.

(9) They arrived at the place which the Divinity pointed out to him. There Abraham built up the altar. He laid out the wood. He bound his son Isaac. He laid him on the altar, on top of the wood. (10) He put out his hand, took up the butcher-knife to slaughter his son. (11) An angel of YHWH called out to him from heaven, "Abraham, Abraham!" "Yes sir," he said. (12) He said, "Do not thrust your hand against the lad, do him no harm! Now do I know how great a God-fearer you are—in that you withheld not from Me your son, your one-and-only."

(13) Abraham looked up and caught sight—there before his eyes a substitute ram, held fast in a thicket by its horns. Abraham went and took the ram and offered it up as a burnt offering in his son's stead. (14) Abraham named that place *YHWH-yire* ["YHWH provides"]—in today's parlance, "On YHWH's mount there is (pro)vision."

(15) YHWH's angel called again to Abraham from heaven, (16) "By Myself— swears YHWH—because you have so acted, withholding not your son, your one-and-only, (17) I will richly bless your offspring as numerous as the stars of heaven or the grains of sand on the seashore. Your offspring shall win the gateways of their enemies. (18) By your offspring will all nations of earth invoke blessing upon themselves—[all this] because you obeyed my command."

(19) Abraham then went back to his servants, and together they proceeded back to Beersheba. Abraham stayed on in Beersheba. (Genesis 22:1–19)

The story begins in the most casual manner, a transition (as we have noted) from the immediately preceding narrative of the treaty concluded between Abimelech and Abraham: *It was some time after these events.* What follows this introduction grammatically is the continuing paratactic formulation "that he [an anonymous subject] said, 'Abraham?'" This is what follows *grammatically*, but not actually. The narrator breaks off after the transitional temporal clause. He was going to continue (as indeed he does) with Heaven's call to Abraham. But he has suddenly remembered (so he would have us understand) what a shock the content of that call will occasion the reader. So he inserts an anticipatory parenthesis, which reassures us that what God asked of Abraham was not—as we would tell a child—"for real." It was only a test. As the narrator thus distances himself and the reader (but not poor Abraham) from the dreadful bidding that is about to come, so does he distance the subject of the call. That subject is not Elohim "God," certainly not YHWH, that name for Abraham's (and our) tutelary God, but *hāᵉlōhīm*, the definite article being the *hē* of abstraction, thus betokening "Heaven," or the *hē* of particularity, thus betokening a representative numen. This term *hāᵉlōhīm*, will appear twice more in an identical subordinate clause (verses 4, 9) as the subject of the perfect verb *ʾāmar* "said," while Abram will once refer to the Deity by Elohim. But it is noteworthy that the narrator exploits a third way of distancing the divine call(er). The voice that calls Abraham by name, the "He" implicit in the imperfect *wayyōmer*, is not identified. For the subject referent the reader must reach back, so to speak, into the parenthetic hypotactic clause for the ambiguous *hāᵉlōhīm*.[58]

Why, however, divide the call into two dialogic parts separated by Abraham's response? That response *hinnēnī*, literally "here I be," signifies the speaker's focused attention as, in verse 7, in that same response to Isaac's call, "Father?" But whereas that response on the part of a father to child (or master to servant) may betoken care, concern, or kindly condescension, on the part of servant to master or mortal to divinity, as here, it bespeaks respectful attention, even—"at your service"—an avowal of obedience. All of which serves to highlight the absence of any response —verbal response, that is—at the conclusion of the command from on high. In terms of dialogic response, there is only silence. But in terms of narratorial consecution, how eloquent is that silence! For that first avowal of obedience, before the command, is reaffirmed by the close-lipped obedience that follows the command without delay.

Alacrity to embark on the commission would occasion perplexity on the reader's part if the command were reported in indirect discourse or by a simple order, "Sacrifice your son on my altar." But the command as it is spelled out can only be read as *free direct discourse* if we are not to accept the speaker as demiurge. Four times, with a painful measured beat, grim if not sardonic, the voice—even before revealing what, if anything, is at stake—identifies who is at stake. The voice knows what it is asking. And a rabbinic midrash fills in, to an extent at least, the baffling vacuum of Abraham's silence. At the words, "Take your son," Abraham with premonition interrupts, "Which son? I have two!" "Your one-and-only." "But each," he answers, "is the only son of his mother." "The one whom you love!" "But I love them both." "Isaac!"

I will return to this question of Abraham's baffling silence on receipt of the heart-stopping command to incinerate his son on an altar to Divinity, and of the promptitude of his obedience. I will first attend to a number of other details in that command that I have characterized as free direct discourse. There is the name Moriah, appearing here as an area, and only once again. In 2 Chronicles 3:1 it is a mount (implicitly identified with the hill of Zion), explicitly identified with the rocky mesa that David purchased from Ornan the Jebusite, upon which Solomon might erect, in his father's stead, the Jerusalem temple.[59] The root of this name would appear to be *yrh* "aim, direct, let fly (a missile)," whence also the noun *tōrā* "instruction, oracle." But the name also resonates with *r'h* "to see" in the *qal* and "to appear, to reveal (one's self)" in the *niph'al*. Thus on both counts the name may connote Revelation: land/mount.[60] The second detail is the diction of the divine direct discourse. In all Scripture the command *lek* "go!" is followed immediately (or, better, attached to) the prepositional phrase *l'kā* "for yourself" only twice: here, and in YHWH's first command to Abraham in 12:1. This odd attachment of the (oddly named) *ethical dative* in two closely parallel contexts, where the semantic function of the ethical dative "to your interest, on your own behalf" is not only inappropriate, but—in the contexts—perversely so, is no accident. For the two commands have another feature in common. In both places, although the destination is known from the immediate context (in the first revelation, 11:3 and 12:5 "to go to the land of Canaan," and in the second 12:2 "go for yourself to Moriahland" and the paranomasia in 12:14) this destination is known to narrator and to reader but not, it would seem, to Abram/Abraham. For in both instances the destination is explicitly withheld from the hero. In 12:1 it is "the land which I shall disclose (*hiph'il r'h*) to you," and in 22:2, although *Moriah-land* has been specified, the destination is "on that one of the peaks which I shall designate (*'ōmar*) to you." It would be hard to overstate the richness of the exegetical and homilectical options (the two categories are not necessarily contradictory or oppositional) opened up by this feature in each case and in respect to one another. Two of the most obvious are: one, the mutually reinforcing sounding of the note of fatefulness in each call; and two, the reinforcing of the note of doom in the second call, the execution of which could only write finis to the hope and promise made explicit in the first.

With the last words of divinity still sounding in our ears (and perhaps in Abraham's), "Offer him up as a holocaust upon one of the peaks which I shall designate to you," the narrator resumes: "Prompt on the morn Abraham strapped his ass, fetched two of his hands to accompany him and Isaac his son, split the kindling for the holocaust and went forthwith towards the place that the divinity had declared to him." How far from Beersheba is that *territory*, never before or after heard of again, which in free direct discourse was named—for the reader, not for Abraham—*Moriah*? Did Abraham know for how long a journey he needed to pack provisions? An ass might easily be laden with enough foodstuff to keep four men and himself for a week or more. We might fill in this gap by presuming that Abraham played it safe in regard to such store. But the focus is on the kindling, a pyre sufficient to cremate a human body, no twigs, mind you, but split logs. But why carry coals to Newcastle? The answer can only be that firewood, scarce enough in Beersheba region as to require the combined efforts of father, son, and two servants, is anticipated to be even more scarce at the point of destination: a bleak crag in the arid wastes of the deep Negev. But who is the subject of that anticipation, if not Abraham? And so we have another clue to absence of transition from the direct discourse of the dread call to the narrator's telling of Abraham's response. *Early on the morn*—aha, the revelation took place at night!—Abraham prepares for the journey. And he asks no questions because everything he does, he does at the continuing prompting of that revelatory voice: what and how much to pack, how many asses to bear the load, how many attendants, in what direction to head *toward the place divinity had declared to him*.

On the third day—some forty-eight hours or so later, after two overnight camps—*Abraham, raising his eyes [to the horizon], beheld the place from afar.* Not quite so. Not, at any rate, literally so. Abraham had no idea as to destination, route, or landmarks. God had said he would indicate the place when he arrived in the vicinity. So God would have had to point out the peak, even as he would have had to guide him on the route. Once again the narrator presupposes that the reader must be aware that revelation—profound and real experience though it be—is also a metaphor; and that the sophisticated reader must be aware of the problems attending revelations and the maintenance of faith in them. The specific problem, for example, of maintaining faith in a revelation that was experienced in the past and is now only a memory. (And questioning memory is self-doubt, not calling God into question.) And, particularly, the problem of maintaining faith in a re-membered revelation whose content is inherently incredible, whose demand runs counter to everything we have been taught to believe—nay, to everything we know by faith—about the benevolence of God. The problem, here, of maintaining faith in a remembered command to butcher one's child.

In the extended time of the journey, in the recognition of the destined peak, in Abraham's unquestioning, unhesitant obedience—obedience to a demand on the part of God that would have to be unbelievable except in the revelatory moment's ineluctable knowledge that God is indeed speaking—in all these, our author is telling us that of all recorded revelations, this was surely the most remarkable, at least in the matter of its specificity and its continuity. From the moment of the first calling of his name, Abraham did not cease to receive instruction. At every fork in the road, God had to say "left" or "right." Abraham now stands before a range of hills, and as his eyes light upon one of them, the voice within says, "That's the one."

Does Abraham's stomach tighten into knots as he gazes upon that ominous height? We are not told. His address to his servants would seem to be as casual as that of a foreman instructing his ranch hands. But where a ranch-boss might have said any number of things—along the lines of "You set here, I'll take the boy yon-der for a look-see"—the author chooses to give Abraham a line that cannot but give the reader a jolt. "We will walk up yonder, we will worship, we will come back to you." What did the ranch hands make of this? Worship means sacrifice, of course. Well that explains the wood, knife, and firepot they will be taking with them. *This is to be a very private service: just the boss and his son. No victim for the sacrifice? Maybe the old man has something up his sleeve. Or is he becoming somewhat dotty? Come to think of it, he has been acting a little strange on this trip. Best not ask . . .*

What are we the readers to make of this statement? What does the author want us to believe? That Abraham is afraid that his servants may divine his intention? That, if they did so divine, they might even interfere to prevent him? That Abra-ham is justified in misleading them with what he knows to be a lie: "We will come back to you"?

Or, as rabbinic tradition long ago speculated, did Abraham's prophetic powers at that moment enable him to see that Isaac would indeed not be sacrificed? But surely that is absurd. Prophecy is but another biblical term for revelation. If God is sending a double message, commanding the sacrifice and at the same time assuring Abraham that Isaac will survive this experience, there is no real test at all; the whole thing would seem to be a charade! Perhaps not. Perhaps it is not so absurd. Perhaps we have here an insight into that human faith which is the experience of the martyr, one who bears witness to his faith by his willingness to die for it. But such a witness to biblical faith, faith in a God who is both all good and all-powerful, must know that his death—given that goodness and power—makes no sense, is something of a self-contradiction. And so in a significant sense he does not really believe that martyrdom will take place, until that last moment when it is too late. And then what sense is there in giving up faith? Having come this far with God, endure the pain and the perplexity a little longer: it is the price for a more glorious future, vindication in the afterlife in the presence of God.

But, it may be objected, Abraham is not a martyr; on the contrary, the martyr is Isaac, and Abraham is the instrument inflicting the martyrdom. Not so. The ancient concept of immortality (in Scripture, as in paganism), that felicity in the afterlife depends on leaving behind a son who will continue one's life on one's ancestral land, made it clear to the ancient audience (as it should be to us) that the test is indeed, as the opening verse announces, a test of Abraham. It is not a test of his readiness to take his son's life (although it is that too); it is a test of his readiness to commit suicide, suicide not alone in this world, in which his years are in any case numbered, but for all eternity, should Deity prove not to be either all good or all-powerful. Isaac and Isaac's descendants to come are Abraham's immortality.[61] And in taking the young Isaac's life on the altar of God, Abraham—if his faith is mistaken—will be destroying his own hope for all future time. The seemingly pointless detail of leaving the ass behind with the hands (or rather the reverse—"Stay you here with the ass"—is a device to evoke pathos, the pathos, in verse 6, of Isaac carrying the wood for his own funeral pyre. This pathos has often been noted; to the neglect, however, of the pathos of Abraham carrying the knife that will sever his immortality and the smoldering fire that will light the pyre on which his hope for eternity will be reduced to ashes. "The two of them walked on together," verse 6 concludes. Isaac then asks the question that the servants did not dare to raise: "Where is the sacrificial victim?" Abraham responds, using the Hebrew word which means "to see," but which also—as in Anglo-Saxon or Latinate English—is metaphorically extended to mean "see to, provide." *Elōhīm yirē* "God will see to" . . . what? The Hebrew word for the object of this verb, *śē*, stands for "a head" from the flock of any age or sex. Standing for the most common item for sacrificial slaughter—lamb, kid, ewe, ram, nanny or billy goat—it lends itself to metaphoric extension, to include the human victim, Isaac. Abraham's response then is, "God will see to the sacrificial victim for Himself, my son." The comma in this sentence—standing for a pause, a split-second of silence—is perhaps the most dramatic comma in all literature. It is the comma that introduces the vocative—the person addressed—and the appositional, the identification of the preceding noun. It means both, "God, my son, will provide Himself with a victim," and "God is providing Himself with a victim: my son." The reader must pronounce the sentence aloud, trying out the tonal variations that would make unmistakably for a vocative or an appositive, or for ambiguity.[62] And as he weighs the ambiguity, he must consider the meaning of the sentence that follows: "The two of them walked on together." Only twenty-five words in the Hebrew separate the first appearance of this sentence in verse 6 and its repetition in verse 8. Why this repetition? The author, we would suggest, wants the reader to ask the question that must have exercised him as he spun his tale: At what point did Isaac realize the role for which he was intended? Was it not until his father began to tie him up? He apparently did not flinch or demur at that point. Could he have guessed earlier? Was he able to read the perplexed sorrow in his father's eyes, the agonized quaver in his father's utterance of the ambiguous "my son"? And having walked, first, in the blessed and trusting innocence of a child with his father, did he, the second time, walk with him— knowing, suddenly matured, accepting—at one with his father in resolve, faith, and destiny?

"Thus they arrived at the spot which the Divinity had pointed out to him. There Abraham built up the altar. He arranged the wood. He bound his son, Isaac. He placed him on the altar. On top of the wood." Every one of the five verbs in paratactic sequence must resound to an invisible drum beating a tattoo such as, the cinematographers would have us believe, preceded every drop of guillotine blade during the Reign of Terror. But in this biblical scene there are no gendarmes or drummers, no executioners to fit neck into groove and collar, no spectators cheering or jeering. There are only a father and a son. And if we challenge our imagination to introduce such lifelike touches of pseudoreality as might be attempted in a Hollywood studio, we shall quickly realize that our narrator's diction is designed to convey the eeriness of fantasy, the unverisimilitudinousness of characters in a trancelike evocation of a cultic charade. First there is the altar. The Hebrew word is *mizbeaḥ*, its etymology suggesting "the place of slaughtering." The altar as rock or table on which the sacrificial victim is killed appears in a number of texts critical to the biblical concept of animal sacrifice.[63] But in all the cultic prescriptions involving a *mizbeaḥ*, the altar is a table on which (incense or) animal parts are burned as an offering presumably pleasing to Deity's olfactory sense. Never is an altar featured as both slaughtering-block and incendiary pyre. Except here! And note the narrator's care to emphasize that the bound Isaac was laid on top (not under or between) the firewood. The firewood that had been hauled on donkey-back from Beersheba but was shifted to Isaac's back for the last few miles walk to and up the Moriah peak, while servants and ass enjoyed a well-earned respite. And note the care of Abraham to lay out the wood (presumably in lattice layers) to insure a satisfactory blaze once the victim's throat is cut and torch applied to the kindling. And then there is the matter of the binding of the victim, natural enough if we think of a maverick being hog-tied or a malefactor prepared for gallows-noose or execution-block. But only the Hebraist will know that the verb for *bind* here never occurs again, so that rabbinic tradition can refer to this entire chapter as the *Akedah*, the (one and only) Binding. What does the rarity of this usage suggest? If nothing else, that the reader consider the reason for the binding. Was it done with Isaac's consent or despite his protest? Even if he had accepted the fate determined for him by his father's revelation, can we picture him not horror-stricken when his father begins to strap him down? Can there be any doubt that the midrash is engaged in close reading of the narrative (rather than in pious and incredible homily) when it pictures Isaac asking to be firmly bound lest an involuntary shudder cause him to deflect the knife and inflict upon himself a blemish that would disqualify him as candidate for immolation? On the other hand, if Isaac had not been one with his father in response to the divine call, how could we envisage the effectuality of the binding without changing the tenor of the story from high tragedy to ghoulish and—considering the personae—ludicrous horror? Whether Isaac was closer to age seven or thirty-seven at the time makes little difference: Picture a father, reve-lation-gripped and revelation-maddened, chasing down a terrified child or wrest-ling to the ground a slow-witted adult. And did this take place before or after the arranging of the kindling on the grill that is God's table? Our narrator's intent can-not be mooted: In this text Isaac is Abraham and Abraham is Isaac.[64]

As Abraham put out his hand, took up the butcher-knife to slaughter his son, an angel of YHWH called out to him from heaven . . . Not so fast! . . . and picked up the butcher-knife to slaughter his son—an angel of YHWH . . . Why consistently up to this point is the voice he hears that of the Divinity (or the numen) and suddenly a change: not God, but an angel; not of God's but of YHWH's? For one thing, I suggest, it is because the narrator is signaling that Abraham's activity was not interrupted by the angel's call. His activity stopped when the voice within stopped. Every step, every motion, had been to the accompaniment of that voice; else the trance would have been broken, the normalcy of nonrevelation restored, and time opened up for a question: "What am I doing?" When the receiver within fell silent, all motion stopped, the hand with the knife arrested in mid-swing. And the silence within is succeeded by a voice from without. No longer the impersonal, inscrutable, over-whelming Will of the cosmos: from heaven a messenger calls with the word from his personal Deity, YHWH his God and the God of Israel. The test is over, and Abraham has passed. The threat to the future is lifted. The future is open again, with a promise reiterated, renewed, reinforced, a promise told of before as act of gracious choice on the part of God, a promise that now has been earned, earned at a price at which YHWH himself seems to marvel: "Because you acted so, because you withheld not your son, your one-and-only."

The ram which Abraham espies, its horns entangled in a thicket, is modified by a word of three consonants, which is strange in this context: ḥr. If the third conso-nant were a daleth rather than a resh (the two characters being very similar in both the Old Hebrew and the later "square" alphabets), we should vocalize it 'eḥād and render it as "one" or "a" or "a certain." Or, adhering to the consonantal text, we might vocalize it 'aḥer, render it by "another," and see in it a syncopated metaphor 'ayil (= śē) 'aḥer "a ram [representing] another [i.e., substitute] victim." The image is clear enough. The pecus or head from the flock, whose absence was questioned by Isaac, whose place would (as context requires and Abraham's response makes ex-plicit), be filled by Isaac, has now indeed appeared: a śē literally, specifically a ram, and replacement victim for Isaac. How then to account for the consonantal text and the Masoretic pointing, which express a term that is either adverb or preposi-tion, neither of them appropriate to the context? Since neither the original author nor the tradition that transmitted the story can be impugned on the score of faulty knowledge of Hebrew, it is likely that we have here a deliberately inserted interpre-tive crux. A word that the reader would first anticipate to be the indefinite article (the need for it being a matter of the author's option) then turns out to be an anomalously vocalized word for "another = substitute," designed to make us pull up short, to invite us to dwell a moment on this recognition: that the Abraham who had prophesied, "We shall return to you" even as he had prophesied, "God will provide a victim," has now been vindicated (if not in the sense he had originally intended) on the score of both prophecies. The God who had provided Abraham with his son Isaac, who asked that Isaac be returned to him on an altar, has now restored Isaac to his father, providing a vicarious offering for himself, thus rounding out the extended metaphor.

Abraham sacrifices this ram provided by God and gives the spot a sentence-name: *YHWH-yirē* "YHWH Sees, YHWH Provides." There then follows an explanation, as it were, by the narrator of Abraham's intent in so naming it. The clause introducing this explanation is not the normal Hebrew expression for "as it is said today" or "whence the present saying." The spot did not continue to be known in Israelite tradition, and so there was no variation in the name, nor was there "a present saying" about a place whose location was unknown. Our own translation ("in today's parlance") is closer to the Hebrew; a variation, perhaps closer to the original, is "as one might say today." The place name *YHWH Sees* or *YHWH Provides* is in the active voice. The "explanation" adds the reminder that the place named is a mountain height, a height special to YHWH, and that furthermore, the name may also be understood in a passive and general sense: On YHWH's Mountain *He Appears*, or *There Is Revelation*, or *There is Vision*, or *There is Provision*; perhaps even *There is Providence*. What is this Vision or Provision? Perhaps the Providence-willed role of the people Israel. Perhaps the whole point of this strange experience of Israel's forebears, Abraham and Isaac.

The Point of the Story

What *is* the point of this story? The one thing that it certainly is not is the interpretation most commonly proffered: a protest against the pagan practice of child sacrifice. For one thing, the evidence for the meta-literary convention of child sacrifice, certainly as a widespread practice, is flimsy. For another, there is no note of protest struck in the course of the narrative and, to quote Speiser (who accepts the rite of child sacrifice as a practice known in Scripture and in Mesopotamia), "If the author had intended to expose a barbaric custom, he would surely have gone about it in another way." How can one read such a repudiation of child sacrifice into a story in which the central theme throughout is Abraham's readiness to make the sacrifice, and in the denouement of which that readiness of Abraham's is explicitly hailed as meritorious and certain to elicit reward?[65]

With what then are we left? With the unequivocal statement of the meritoriousness of Abraham, of his faith so strong as to override all other considerations when called on to slay his son and foreclose his future. But with whom is Abraham, in his meritorious faith, to be compared? Not with his pagan contemporaries, who did not know the benevolent God of Scripture in the first place; and who did not, in all probability, regularly sacrifice their children to their gods. The answer, by a process of elimination, comes down to this: he is to be compared with the audience for whom the story is intended, the seed of Abraham and Isaac called Israel, extending from the time the story was first told to the present heirs of the biblical (or

Judeo-Christian) tradition, and to all who in the future will lay claim to constituting the ideal Israel.

The story is told to us, and it is told to us in a context. As little as we know of the Isaac who walked first with his father in blissful ignorance, then perhaps in knowledge and acquiescence, we do know him to be our ancestor, the long-awaited, repeatedly promised bearer-to-be of that line of Abraham that is to culminate in us. Let us now remind ourselves that this fixing of the intended audience is a metaliterary consideration, and that another metaliterary prejudice, which we have had to repeatedly overcome, is the denial to the ancient author of an elementary intelligence or sophistication comparable to that which we credit to today's hoi polloi. And then, proceeding from the assumption that it is not for us to insult the intelligence of the author of the Binding of Isaac, we arrive at the corollary that neither is that author to be seen as insulting our intelligence, the intelligence of his intended audience. God's command to Abraham, which if carried out would have made of him a liar and treaty-breaker, is acted upon by Abraham in a faith-contradicting-faith obedience. Are we expected to accept at face value such a seeming absurdity? Without question or demurrer? And also to remain supinely silent in the face of this challenge to the quality of our own faith? A challenge in which our meritoriousness is to be measured against that of a great-grandfather who would have slaughtered our grandfather, and thus have precluded our very existence? Are we being asked to measure our faith by the faith of one whom, in our heart of hearts and unclouded rationality, we can only judge to be a madman?

This last is the only honest response that could be expected of any rational person, whether or not that person considers himself a paragon of faith. Let us conjure up a scene in which one observes a neighbor and his son packing their station wagon for what is clearly a hunting and fishing trip; and then being told in confidence that the boy is headed for a butcher block at God's behest. Be that observer simple or wise, atheist or fideist, even priest, pastor or rabbi, is there any question that he might fail to call the police? Or that the father would be committed to a secure hospital ward for observation?

No, there can be no question that the normal, honest, and rational reaction of audience to Abraham's obedience is the judgment that, in the forty-eight to seventy-two hours from call to slay to command to desist, he was a madman. And it follows therefore that this is precisely the response that the author is inviting. Inviting the response, and inviting consideration of the reason for the invitation. How long should it take before we try to change places with the author? The reader exclaims, "But he must have been mad, Father Abraham!" And we, the author, respond with a riposte that pins him on the point of our metaphor: "Mad, was he? Well, well. Mad, compared to whom? Shall we compare his sanity to the sanity of your neighbors, or to your own? Yes, he was prepared to sacrifice his son, his future, his eternity. Are you never prepared—ever—to do so? He did not, in the final event, make the sacrifice. Have you, or your neighbors, perhaps your own parents, not actually committed such acts of sacrifice? Abraham's readiness was in response to the God who is Ultimate Reality, who calls us into being and gives meaning to our existence. When and where, to the call of what authority, in loyalty to what cause, in the name of what values, is it your wont to sacrifice your children—and yourself?" And we need continue no further. Let him contemplate those moments when sanity succumbs to Eros' fevering of the flesh, when Mammon wafts his fool's gold into our eyes, when the state recruits for war, when the lust for fame or another lure of "the bitch-goddess Success" anesthetizes us to pain or sensibility and we lay everything down on the altar of public opinion.

The lesson, the kerygma, of the Binding of Isaac is that if you will not make the ultimate sacrifice except at the call of Scripture's god, you will never hear that call. For he is the God of life and blessing. But if you think that to respond to such a call from God—were it ever to come—would be madness, you will find that the call will come indeed. But it will come from the domain of the less than ultimate. And it will come with an importunacy you will not withstand.

COMPARING THE AKEDA WITH ANOTHER BINDING

Martyrdom is a word from the vocabulary of religion, not patriotism; yet for every Jew or Christian who was given a choice of apostasy or death and accepted martyrdom, how many tens of thousands have died for the flag on battlefields far removed from their country's borders?

The biblical ethos is not pacifism. Its life-affirming thrust does not preclude its sanctioning of civil war in the cause of an exclusive YHWH worship, nor does it condemn many an Israelitish imperialist war, much less armed defense of one's territory. But warfare is the phenomenon that, for its frequency and fatality, best lends itself to illustrate the metaphor of Isaac's Binding, the legitimacy of the surrender of one's children's lives for the sake of a value whose ultimacy must somehow entail its being the precondition for life. And it was a British war poet, Wilfred Owen, killed in action in 1918 at the age of twenty-five, who penetrated the metaphor and exploited it:

The Parable of the Old Man and the Young

So Abram rose, and clave the wood, and went
And took the fire with him, and a knife.
And as they sojourned both of them together,
Isaac the first-born spake and said, My Father
Behold the preparations, fire and iron,
But where the lamb for this burnt-offering?
Then Abram bound the youth with belts and straps,
And builded parapets and trenches there,
And stretched forth the knife to slay his son.
When lo! an angel called him out of heaven,
Saying, Lay not thy hand upon the lad,
Neither do anything to him. Behold,
A ram, caught in a thicket by its horns;
Offer the Ram of Pride instead of him.
But the old man would not so, but slew his son,
And half the seed of Europe, one by one.

The Abram of Wilfred Owen's poem is a murderous old man indeed. But except for the initial undertaking of the sacrifice, he is not the Abraham of Scripture. He is the very opposite of Scripture's patriarch. Whatever the cause or reason for his undertaking to begin with—and the first three words of the poem require an antecedent call from without, whether real or imagined—this Abram is under no external compulsion, once the angel calls to him "out of heaven." But compulsion there must be for him to reject the call of heaven, and the nature of that compulsion is explicit: It is Pride. Rather than surrender that Ram, he will slay not only his own son, but "half the seed of Europe, one by one."

So much is clear. What remains less than clear is the point of Owen's poem, as the point of Scripture's story will remain subject for debate despite our confident exposition of its purport. And, indeed, I betrayed my own understanding of Owen's poem when I wrote that he, in this poem, penetrated and exploited the metaphor of Scripture's story. That is to say, Owen understood that the call from heaven forbids the slaughter, and that that irrational impetus within which he calls Pride proves stronger (or at least, proved stronger in World War I) than Heaven's call. Thus the point of Owen's poem, while not the point of the Akeda, is in total consonance with the point of the Akeda as we see it. The Abraham of Scripture did not need to sacrifice his son because the God in whom he had such faith is one who by definition could not require such a doom. Even as deep in his being he knew that Isaac would survive the call, which he had to obey when it pointed in one direction, so was he ready for the call which reversed that direction. But Owen's Abram—who would certainly have rejected a call to a celibate priesthood, for himself or his son—could not attend the call to preserve his son, committed as he is to the ram of his own pride. For such a consonance to obtain, however, between the two inventions (if we may call them that without denying truth to either), the Abraham and Isaac who are one inseparable persona (as we have seen) in Scripture's story, sharing one faith and one destiny, must also be that in Owen's poem. And the Abraham who bound his son in the belts and straps of a soldier's uniform and put him on the altar of Mars, "the parapets and trenches," in so doing committed self-slaughter as well.

But not everyone will acquiesce in this reading of Owen's poem. During the upheavals in this country in the late 1960s and early 1970s, the years of the generation gap and protests against restrictions of civil rights and conscription for service in the jungles of Vietnam, this poem was presented for interpretation to several classes of seminarians and graduate students. And overwhelmingly, the consensus was that Abraham was the slaughterer and his son the victim. No solidarity between the two. No sharing of vision, of values or sense of interdependence. And what better evidence that this Abram represented the parental generation, smug in comfort and smugly complacent, feeding the defenseless young into the maw of the war-machine, than the concluding line. For this Abram "slew his son"—yes, but also—"And half the seed of Europe, one by one."

Literary criticism, interpretation, exegesis being what it is—art and not science—there can be no final adjudication between the two interpretations of Owen's poem that will satisfy (or be true for) everybody. In trying to win a majority over to my side, I might plead that my interpretation is a deeper reading of the poet's intention; that the message—applying to all peoples and all age groups, children and parents alike—is more universal, hence more likely than the competing interpretation. On the poetical level, I might cite the larger literary corpus of Wilfred Owen, one which is characterized by a general horror at the blindnesses leading to and generated by warfare. I might also argue that Owen's insertion of "The Parable of" into his poem's title is not due to a pedant's fear that his reader could possibly miss the metaphors of "belts and straps" and "parapets and trenches" for the binding of Isaac on the altar. The "parable" reminder is against taking literally the victimization of one generation by the other. And, finally, militating against an indictment of the older generation's victimization of the young is a consideration of a datum about the poet himself (which perhaps even the New Criticism would admit as relevant): he, like his friend and brother-poet in the lyrical war against war, Siegfried Sassoon, had enlisted for combat, served in the trenches as a commissioned officer; returned to combat after the publication-scandal of his pacifist protest; and met his death as a company commander in the last week of a war which, as all knew, was winding down to an end.

Our introduction, for comparison, of Owen's "Parable" patently owes to a hope that enlisting one poet as exegetical expert on the work of another poet might impress even the disciplined, "objective" academician. And even the awareness that the poet-expert's testimony itself may be taken as moot, as also the awareness that contesting interpretations need not be mutually exclusive does not deter me from proceeding with this exercise in comparative study. For in the case of the kerygma of Genesis 22, I am driven not so much by a desire to convince my readers as to the correctness of my reading, as by a desperate hope that my colleagues can be opened up to contemplate my reading of the kerygma as worthy of consideration as one of its possible meanings. And this because no interpretation of a biblical narrative I have put forth has met with such skepticism and quarrel as has this one, on the part of students and colleagues alike. My collegial friends, in particular, have tried to soften the skeptic's jeer by praising the homiletical brilliance of my reading. But such praise, characterizing as imaginative exegesis what is put forward as sober exegesis, is cold comfort at best to the exegete.

No, I must insist that both brilliance and imaginative invention lie in Scripture's metaphor and not in the homily of a derivative preacher. And so I must seek to account for the unwillingness of so many to entertain an interpretation for Scripture's *Akeda* so close to the one that is regarded as at least plausible for Owen's version of *The Binding*. A number of factors may be operative here. For one, there is the deeply implanted prejudice of literal-mindedness, ascribed to the ancient author but actually characteristic of our own thinking, and particularly in regard to the ready recourse of the ancients to devote their children to bloody cults. For another, there is the assumption of the ancient storyteller's primitiveness. (How, for example, ascribe a philosophical parable to an author who believes that the world's animate populations were saved from extinction by means of a capacious wooden ark!) For others there may be a deeply rooted reluctance to have so marvelous a numinous mystery cleared up so that a child may understand it. Such simplification may even seem to be a depreciation of a fable appreciable only in terms of Kierkegaard's profound analysis and its resolution in the kerygma of "the leap of faith." My own suspicion, however, is that the most potent factor in our resistance to this interpretation is that we cannot but resent being trapped by the ancient author's genius for parable: the profundity of the mythos is, paradoxically, subverted by its simplicity, by the moral's lying so close to the surface; for if each of us is Abraham, each of us is touched in an excruciatingly sensitive nerve. It is not only the Roman mother who gives ultimatum to her son: *Come back, bearing your shield or being carried upon it*. It is not only the predominance in each of us of the shame culture as over the moral code. It is—in every one of us—that particular area of shallow values where we play the hypocrite, those values we actually live by as against the values we profess. Life and literature are replete with the king (or businessman) who will do anything to preserve his dynasty except to retire a year early in favor of son and heir apparent; the father who will give his life for his son, so long as this son does not compete for the woman they both love; the salvation-centered clergyman whose life's dearest ambition is, as it turns out, to enable his daughter "to marry up." Yes, every one of us could go on adding to this list, and feel little or no pain, until someone whom he loves best and who knows him best suggests the area of his own hypocritical vulnerability.

If I am close to the truth in this last suspicion of mine, then I would do well, in pleading for my interpretation, to abandon the ubiquitous and mundane applications or extensions of the metaphor of the *Akeda*, and return to the narrower, less frequently self-indicting lesson in regard to war and pacifism. Most of us are not implicated as an everyday matter in the defense of our nation's territories, nor in the recruitment of our children for its defense forces. And, from this perspective, we may find an instructive comparison in a pacifist invention from antiquity, a drama from ancient Greece—no, not the comedy *Lysistrata* of Aristophanes, but one that, remarkably enough, is listed among the tragedies: Euripides' *Iphigenia in Aulis*.

Euripides wrote his *Iphigenia in Aulis* within a few centuries of the composition of the Binding of Isaac. And the story he tells is, bizarrely enough, accepted as one of the attestations that the ancients sacrificed their children to their gods. Let us review the plot.

Before the play begins, the Greek armies have gathered at Aulis for embarkation for the assault on Troy. The fleet long becalmed and the soldiers growing restless, Agamemnon, king of Argos, the commander-in-chief of the allied armies, has sent for his eldest daughter, Iphigenia. An oracle has informed him that favoring winds will not rise unless he sacrifices this daughter to Artemis, she who is goddess of chastity, of the hunt, and of the locality of Aulis. The pretext for bringing Iphigenia to Aulis is marriage to Achilles, the hero who has no idea that his name is being thus used.

The action begins with Agamemnon summoning a servant to take a letter to Argos to his wife Clytemnestra. The message countermands the earlier summons of Iphigenia; her father has thought better of the demanded sacrifice, and will instead dismiss the assembled host. The letter, however, is intercepted by Menelaus, brother of Agamemnon and husband of Helen, whose abduction by Prince Paris of Troy has precipitated the gathering of the Greek armies. Menelaus, having read the letter, and bent on compelling his brother to abide by his original intention, accuses Agamemnon of weakness unbefitting the man who aspired to lead the allied hosts of Hellas. A messenger arrives with the news that Clytemnestra and Iphigenia have arrived. Menelaus relents, withdraws his words, and declares to Agamemnon, "I cannot bid you slay your child for me."

Agamemnon now declares it is too late to save his child. In addition to the seer Calchas, who delivered the oracle, the cunning Odysseus has knowledge of it. Calchas' mouth can be stopped: "he is base, ambitious, like every prophet born." But Odysseus can be counted on to inform the armies that the aborting of the campaign is due to their leader's refusal to sacrifice his daughter for the cause; he will goad the men to kill their generals and sacrifice Iphigenia, or if they flee, to pursue them to Argos, and raze its walls in revenge.

Achilles arrives and is astounded to learn from Clytemnestra that the bride he never sued for is here. The puzzle is cleared up when the two of them learn of the ruse that brought Iphigenia to Aulis for sacrifice. Achilles declares that he has been irrevocably implicated by the use of his name to decoy Iphigenia to her death, that "I needs must bear the stain of murder if she perish thus," and vows to protect her even against the entire army. Better, however, if Clytemnestra can prevail upon her husband to reconsider. She pleads with her husband. Iphigenia pleads. Agamemnon protests that he is no madman, that he loves his children, but that he is bound. Achilles appears with news that the army knows, and is howling for the sacrifice; his own men have turned against him save for a few; he yet stands ready to snatch Iphigenia from the altar steps. Now Iphigenia speaks. She rejects a sacrificial defense of herself by Achilles. Ten thousand soldiers are on fire to die for Greece. She will not stand in the way. Her victory will be her fame. By her death she will have won freedom for Hellas.

At Iphigenia's bidding, Clytemnestra remains behind in the tent while she, with one attendant, makes for the altar, the chorus hailing her as the conqueror of Troy.

In the last scene a messenger appears to Clytemnestra. He informs her of a miracle that has just taken place in full view of the Achaean army. The priest-prophet Calchas raised his knife and struck with it at the neck of Iphigenia. But none saw the blade reach its target. Instead, where Iphigenia had lain on the altar, a doe now lay in the victim's place, dripping blood from the sacrificial wound. Artemis, so declares Calchas, has taken the girl to herself and provided the panting hind as substitute. News of this wonder has been sent to her by her lord, Agamemnon, so that she may lay aside grief for her child and anger against her husband. The leader of the chorus expresses joy at the tidings, "Your daughter lives, he tells us, with the gods." Not so Clytemnestra. "Stolen, my child, by the gods? What gods? . . . An idle story to cheat my sorrow." Agamemnon comes on stage to tell his unbelieving wife that they have cause for joy in their daughter's being now with the gods. He sends her home to Argos with the gift of a youngling steer, while he himself faces the beckoning sea. He promises to send news from the battlefront, "Farewell. From Troy I will send word. May all go well with you." And the chorus sings him off:

> Rejoice, O king, go forth in joy.
> In joy return to us, bringing rich booty,
> Home again from captured Troy. (lines 1627–1629; tr. F. M. Stawell)

To label such a play a tragedy! A play with so happy an ending? The chorus it-self concluding on so joyous a note and in anticipation of greater triumphs and richer rewards to attend the hero's return!

In *Toward a Grammer* (pp. 25–26) I animadverted upon the genres of dramatic tragedy and comedy with brief reference to the universal deployment of these liter-ary conventions, despite the absence of agreement as to critical aspects of their definitions. It was doubtless the incongruity of the happy ending of this play that led the translator whose version I have been using to determine that the original drama ended with the chorus' praise of Iphigenia as she leaves the stage altar-bound. But if the last scene (which the translator labels "an epilogue") is original, and if thereby the play is excluded from the category of tragedy, must we commit the absurdity of calling it a comedy? No, whatever the conventions of the ancient Greek theatre, we must make room for a dramatic genre in which the ludicrousness of human antics bring us close to laughter even as the grimness of these antics' consequences renders tears and tearing of flesh a beggarly response. And the closest we can come to a literary invention whose main thrust is to hold up human folly to scorn is satire.

The version of the Iphigenia tale which accepts as literal her being wafted away by Artemis from the altar in Aulis is treated by Euripides in another drama, *Iphige-nia in Tauris*. In this barbarous locale we find Iphigenia, years after the fall of Troy, repaying her divine benefactress by presiding as priestess over the altar on which there is offered to Artemis the life of every Greek who strays into this worshipful territory. So much for a literal belief on the part of the ancient Greeks in human sacrifice in general and child sacrifice in particular. But let us return to the Iphige-nia who was slaughtered in Aulis. That maiden who goes (and so willingly!) to her death as "the conqueror of Troy" before a single ship is launched is the symbol of every warrior, Greek or Amazon, who fell before the walls of Troy. As Agamemnon is every father who is "forced by circumstance" to sacrifice his offspring on the altar of personal pride and national honor. The question the poet is raising is how many battles would be fought if the commander-in-chief had to sacrifice his own child before sounding the charge. And he is not sanguine about the answer.

Patriotism is love for the extended family. The family earns that love by being the womb from which one springs, the nurturing bosom, the enfolding protecting arms. To turn the family into an abstraction of ultimate value, which breeds only to aggrandize itself, and aggrandizes by sacrificing its issue, is one of humanity's great-est absurdities. All war is madness. The best that can be said for a defensive war is that the madness originates with the aggressors. The defenders fight under compul-sion, to protect life and liberty, which would be forfeited by surrender.

But consider when the poet introduces the theme of defense of country and freedom. The entire play consists of some fifteen hundred lines. It is with line 1255 that Agamemnon begins his richly ironic reply to wife and daughter:

I know the touch of pity, know it well:
I love my children—I am no madman, wife.
It is a fearful thing to do this deed,
Yet fearful not to do it: I am bound.

(*He turns to Iphigenia*)

You see this host of ships and mail-clad men —
They cannot reach the towers of Ilium,
They cannot take the far-famed steep of Troy,
Unless I sacrifice you as he bids,
Calchas, the prophet. And our Greeks are hot
To smite the foe, nor let them steal our wives.
If I refuse the Goddess, they will come
To Argos, kill your sisters, you and me!
I am no slave of Menelaus, child;
I do not bow to him, I bow to Hellas,
As bow I must, whether I will or no.
She is the greater. For her we live, my child,
To guard her freedom. Foreigners must not rule
Our land, nor tear our women from their homes. (lines 1255–1277; tr. F.M. Stawell)

Could Aristophanes (who composed his own lampoon on war in *Lysistrata*) have outdone the tragedian in painting the speaker as a buffoon? Twice the same pathetic note is struck, in the middle and the final line: "nor let them steal our wives." "nor tear our women from their homes." The first quote follows, "Our Greeks are hot to smite the foe." That is to say, we are fighting a war of aggression; our justification, however, is to teach the enemy not to come a thousand kilometers to seduce our women. The second quote follows, "Foreigners must not rule our land." Is that the threat to Greece from Troy? And "tear our women from our homes"? Is that what Paris did? Clytemnestra flung the reason for the Trojan campaign into Agamemnon's teeth, "To win back Helen! Your own child for a wanton, your dearest for a foe!" Helen, wife to Menelaus, is Clytemnestra's sister-in-law. But, let us remember, she is also Clytemnestra's sister; they are both Leda's daughters. Who, better than her sister, would know Helen's whorish heart, or the disloyalty that stamps her not just as frump, but foe!

The irony does not stop here, however. When Agamemnon says that he is not bowing to Menelaus' determination to win back his strumpet wife, he speaks truth; for Euripides had pictured Menelaus earlier as relenting of his purpose. Agamemnon is indeed bowing to the will of Hellas, a Hellas that does not exist except as cities warring against one another, but for this one occasion when they have united to win the greater spoil of Troy. "She is the greater." To be sure; by reason of force, not virtue. But to add, "For her we live, my child"? Hellas is the threat! "To guard her freedom"? From whom? "Foreigners must not rule our land"? The land in danger is not Greece, But Agamemnon's Argos. And the foreigners are not Trojans, but the very Greeks over whom he exercises so shaky a command.

ISAAC AND IPHIGENIA, ABRAHAM AND AGAMEMNON: A COMPARISON

The Binding of Isaac and *Iphigenia in Aulis*, deriving from two widely separated cultures, each with its distinctive ethos, make for instructive comparison. There are marked similarities and differences. Both are supreme creations. One, a short story in the fabulary genre of Scripture; the other a play in the lofty tradition of Greek tragedy. Jerusalem and Athens, the two major founts of Western civilization, both dealing with essentially the same phenomenon in the human condition: the absurdities of human response to a ubiquitous and ever-present dilemma. Life is the highest of values, for it is the bearer of all values. Without life there is neither goodness nor evil, neither beauty nor ugliness, neither triumph nor defeat. Yet the defense of values highly cherished by man often requires the taking of life and its surrender. When—for the defense of which values, and in the face of how grave a danger to these values—is it justified to sacrifice life itself, even the life that represents our future, our immortality? Only, it would seem, for a value without which life itself becomes meaningless, and when that value is threatened with extinction. How often is such the case?

In both The Binding and *Iphigenia*, the call comes from the divine in a form of revelation. Abraham receives the call directly, Agamemnon through an intermediary. Abraham cannot doubt his inner ear. Agamemnon, in desperate ambition, accepts the word of the prophet intermediary, whom he himself describes as "base, ambitious, like every prophet born," and concerning whom Menelaus agrees, "They do no good; they are never any use." The God whom Abraham obeys is the source of all goodness and the guarantor of the future. The deity who summons Agamemnon is one of middling importance. The God who calls to Abraham initiates the action; the human must respond. There is no call to Agamemnon: he asks for an oracle, and the divine response poses for him a dilemma of his own making. The demand of the divine upon Abraham is unconditional. Abraham must obey or deny the ground of his faith and hope. There is no demand upon Agamemnon, if he wants something from the goddess—a wind to speed him on his ambition of conquest—he must give her something in return; unfortunately for him, the goddess drives a hard bargain. But he is under no compulsion to do business at all. Abraham's faith results in the affirmation of life, the preclusion of sacrifice. Agamemnon's vacillation leads to a sacrifice, which opens the way to many more deaths. Abraham's God is the one we want to believe in, the One whom many of us claim to worship. Agamemnon's gods are those we deny with our lips and to whom we render ourselves slave. Abraham is the protagonist we would want to be. Agamemnon is the one we are.

And so we wallow in the welter of our absurdities. In action, in philosophy, in reading the texts from our antique heritage, we—in the words of the prophet Isaiah—"call evil good and good evil; present darkness as light and light as darkness, make the bitter sweet and the sweet bitter" (5:20). Every fiber of our being is woven into the cloth of Abraham's faith; we tear it and ourselves to tatters. The faith of Abraham is the moral force of gravity that anchors us to life; the leap we make is not into faith but out of it, and such is its ease and regularity that we do not discern it as a leap at all.

This, at least, is what Scripture is telling us. Had Euripides Scripture before him, what chance that he would disagree?

PART II

STRUCTURES

SEVEN

STRUCTURES AS A BIBLICAL LITERARY PHENOMENON

The division of this book into two sections, one on stories and one on structures, is both occasioned by and reflective of the uniqueness of Scripture (in general, and of Genesis or the Pentateuch in particular) in respect to the question of literary genre.

Genre is a matter of classification, and classification is a highly subjective human organization of its perceptions. Every system of classification is assessable, not in terms of true or false or valid or invalid, but rather in terms of usefulness or idleness, weightiness or frivolity. Thus one broad literary distinction is that between prose and poetry, a classification so obvious that to refer to them as *genres* verges on the pedantic, and makes for the ridicule of Moliere's newly arrived gentleman who is thrilled to discover that all his life he has been talking prose. Another broad literary distinction not normally considered as genre-distinction is that between history and fiction; fiction itself almost preempting title to constituting *literature*, and history being promoted to a transcendent class of narrative; the former creative and entertaining, the latter verisimilitudinous and edifying, the former a tolerable recreation, the latter the sober pursuit of savants and scientists. Thus, whereas maps and charts and graphs and statistical tables are seen as indigenous to history writing, the appearance of such in the text of a creative narrative would be regarded as literary excrescence, or indeed be read as a purport of historiographic rather than fictive authorial intent.

Such indeed has been the case in regard to Scriptural narrative. The interpolations of genealogies and chronologies in particular, inclusive of toponyms and ethnonyms known to us from other sources, contribute greatly to the assumption alike of pious reader and scholarly investigator that—correct or accurate in outline or detail or not—these narratives are intended as history.[1] Both pietist and scholarly researcher will recognize here and there in the narrative the presence of meta-phoric rather than literalistic intention on the author's part. But it is in the structures (for the pietists, revealed by God; for the scholar, collected from oral and written tradition) that both will find the firmest basis for and confirmation of the literalistic or historiographic purport of the narrative.

The poetic approach to literature is essentially confined to compositions at the imaginative and metaphoric end of the narrative spectrum.[2] This being so, the material embodied in narrative ambiance that we call structures constitutes perhaps the most formidable challenge to poetic analysis: the longer the list of items in these structures and the more specific the details, the heavier the onus on the poetician to demonstrate that the structure contributes to, or even supports and extends, the kerygma of the framing narrative.

The essential elements of story are personae and plot (or action) arranged in a meaningful time-sequence, acting and being acted upon. Structures are properly patterns or designs, arranged data rather than personae acting and being acted upon. Scripture's intricate ways of weaving these structural elements into its narratives, or interpolating into these structures characterization or dialogue—hallmarks of narrative, especially fictive—may often make it difficult to decide whether a given pericope should be treated under the heading of story or structure.[3] Ideally a structural element should be treated in close conjunction with the narrative which it abuts and whose kerygma it furthers. Unfortunately the details of these structures are so often related in pattern and function to the structures which attend other narratives, that extended argumentation might overtax the patience of the reader, who is wrestling with the persuasiveness or cogency of a single narrative's exegesis and the kerygma proposed for it. Hence, my extrapolation of structural pericopes and treatment of them together under the separate heading of Structures.

Another problem relating to structures is the vagueness of definition of this category as a literary phenomenon. A code or a partial code of law or ethics, or of cultic prescriptions or proscriptions, when incorporated in a narrative framework, is a far different phenomenon than when confronted outside such a context. Such formulations then are to be treated as constituent elements within a composition, susceptible to poetic treatment in terms of the kerygmatic function in the overarching narrative context. I have long argued that "biblical law" is not to be (mis)taken for the legal code of ancient Israel's society, and that such legal formulations are to be interpreted in terms of their formulaic patterns as kerygmatic vectors, and not in comparison and contrast with similar formulations in neighboring cuneiform societies.[4] It is on the basis then of such poetical thinking and poetic analysis that I have felt free to include examples of poetic expression—narrative and lyrical— and of legal(istic) formulations to support the plausibility of a kerygmatic conception or line of thought as it emerges from my reading of narrative texts and related structures.

GENEALOGIES AND CHRONOLOGIES OF CAIN AND SETH

Cain's Descendants, Their Genius

(17) Cain had relations [knowledge, experience] with his wife; she conceived and gave birth to Enoch. He [Cain] engaged in building a settlement [*lit.*, city], named the settlement after his son, Enoch. (18) To Enoch was born Irad; Irad begot Mehujael; Mehujael begot Methusael; Methusael begot Lamech. (19) Lamech took two wives, one named Adah, the other named Zillah. (20) Adah gave birth to Jabal—he became ancestor of tent-dweller and livestock[-keeper]; (21) while his brother, his name Jubal, became ancestor of all who ply string or wind instruments. (22) Now Zillah, she too, gave birth—to Tubal-Cain, sharp-blade-maker of smiths in copper or iron; Tubal-Cain's sister was Naamah.

(23) Lamech declared to his wives,
"Adah and Zillah, hear my cry,
Wives of Lamech, heed my word:
Truly, A man have I slain for a wound I suffered,
A young brave—for an injury I sustained.
(24) Truly, if vengeance for Cain be sevenfold,
Then for Lamech seventy-and sevenfold!" (Genesis 4:17–24)

The foregoing eight verses constitute a pericope in that its subject matter is clearly separable from what precedes it and what follows. If we try to put a genre-label on this snippet of text we will quickly see the problems of form, substance, purpose, and purport confronting the literary analyst, especially one who seeks to fix its poetical function within the overarching narrative. Thus as narrative, the notice of Cain propagating is hardly an aesthetically satisfying conclusion to the story of history's first murderer, the story whose last scene had this murderer winning from God a protection against infliction upon him of the sentence he so richly deserved. Further, there would seem to be a pointlessness in informing us that he named his son Enoch, which name no person in Scripture's story will ever again carry,[5] and that he named after him a city of which we have never otherwise heard nor of which any trace has been left. And this aside from the incongruity of a father building a "city," settlement for a community that consists only of himself, his wife, this one son Enoch, and—possibly—the one son whom Enoch will sire on the wife whose provenance is as mysterious as that of his father's wife. The naming of three culture-heroes as incidental detail or aside within an apposite narrative context might be understandable, but such a narrative context we do not have here. And what is the point of the intrusive taunt-song with which this pericope concludes? If, on the other hand, this pericope is not so much narrative as snippets of tradition included here to preserve some legendary lore, why would the biblical author be concerned to record for posterity the names of mythical personae (appearing elsewhere as Hephaestos or Orpheus) who never figure in biblical narrative or lyric? And if further, the essential point of preserving this tradition reflects the preoccupation of a historian or antiquarian—that is to say, the recording of a historic family line—why obtrude these anthropological notices into a genealogy? And, lastly, just what is the significance of this family-line in the history of the human race?

The answer to this last question provides, I believe—in the raising of another question—the clue to the solution of this literary puzzle. The answer to this last question is: no significance whatsoever! The line of Cain came to an end in the universal Flood, as did the entire line of his brother Seth (whose birth and line follows hard upon this pericope) except for that of his one descendant, Noah. Well in that case, what need of the entire story of Cain or of his doomed descendants?

The answer to this question was given at the end of the section titled "Aftermath of Eden: Second Generation, Second Banishment." *And Cain had to live, in this allegory, to father the human race. So that the moral be not lost—Cain, ancestor of all mankind, is your father and mine.* If we retrace the narrative of our text we will appreciate that the choice made by Adam and Eve—for sex, procreation, history (and death)—culminated in that aspect of history that is symbolized in the Cain and Abel story: the atrocity of (fratricidal) murder. Thus there were two sons in the Second Generation: one the killer, the other his victim. The power of the moral depends, however, on our recognizing that the meaning—the *moral*—is for us, not for some unrelated race of humanoids on earth or on Mars: that we have in us the gene, so to speak, for murder, our legacy from Father Cain. Cain must, therefore, by the logic of the allegory, be our ancestor.

But let us remember that, anomalously enough, we are in moral terms—also the *victims* of murder—the descendants of descendantless Abel. That anomaly, however, is not troublesome; for we focus as readers on the crucial aspect of the allegory: *De te fabula narratur.* And the *te*, the *you* addressed by the narrator, the *us* of the audience, is clearly in this fable the descendants of Cain. Fine! Except that this resolution goes contrary to the demands of justice, unless, at least, the murderer becomes a true repentant. What was the case with Cain? Not a *soupçon* of remorse is attributed to him by the narrator. He accepts God's stay of sentence as if it were an unqualified and timeless guarantee. In his own person he goes to the land of Nod "Transience" in contrapoise to the stability and permanence of Eden (*qidmat Eden*). As the second Adam, so to speak, Cain suffers, for forcing mother-matrix earth ("earth-clod you are, to earth-clod will you revert") to drink his brother's blood, the same curse earned by the first Adam for his disobedience: the earth will prove recalcitrant to his cultivation of her. Is there then not a contradiction between the decreed fate of his becoming "a wanderer ever on the move" (*nā ᶜnād*) and a builder of a city in the Land of Transience Across from Eden? No, for even settlements, small or large (*ᶜīr* "city") are not guaranteed regular and rich crops from the fields about them so laboriously tilled. And as for Cain as City-Builder, the metaphor here for the generation inaugurating civilization will be more readily appreciable if we remind ourselves that the word *civilization* in our own speech—antonym of the state of primitivism, savagery, barbarism, boorism, what-have-you—is virtually synonymous with urbanization. (The *civis* is citizen of an *urbs/civitas*.) And the continuity of the civilizing process is expressed in the "naming" "of the city" after Cain's only son Enoch.

So much for Cain in his own career, *in propria persona.* But what about remorse or repentance for his crime? Well, the last generation of the Cainite line—the three sons named Jabal, Jubal, and Tubal—these are the ones who as eponymous ancestors epitomize the civilized human race: Jabal, those far-from-uncivilized pastoral folk who, like Israel's patriarchs, dwell in tents and keep livestock; Jubal, those artistic folk who enhance life with culture's refinements; and Tubal, his name hyphenated with that of his murderous ancestor so that he is now Tubal-Cain, represents the technologists of forge and smithy who are featured for production—not of such instruments of peace as pruning-hooks and ploughshares, but—of life-taking blades of sword or ax. And as this last male descendant evokes the image of executioner's blade, so does the father of this final generation of the Cainite line, express again the murderous genetic heritage of Grandfather Cain: so Lamech, in boast of macho vendetta and scorn of justice. In Tubal-Cain's technology of menace, in his father Lamech's joy in violence, we have the culmination of the Cainite character that doomed the line of Cain. But metaphor, let us remember, is not mathematics, for all its similarities to equations. And as Lamech fathers the peaceful ancestors, Jabal and Jubal, on one wife, Ada, so does he father on his second wife, Zillah, not only blade-making Tubal-Cain, but the one and only daughter of this primordial line, she—perhaps symbolizing in her sex all her sisters—expressed in her name Na'amah "Pleasantness, Dulcea."

What an achievement of rhetoric! Eight verses, disguised as a genealogy, with four seemingly pointless asides, with the final two verses a savage monologue so out-of-place in its context, all to build in a density of separate yet related metaphor to the culminating metaphor of the justice-serving end of a human line, a metaphor for that line as the human line, all to the end that—having served its metaphorical purpose—the entire metaphor be literally abandoned in the notice that follows. That notice, now put before us, is that there were three sons—not two— in the Second Generation. One died childless, victim of murder. One, perpetrator of the murder, was given the chance to breed better than his performance might augur; that hope, in the end unfulfilled, that line died out; hence, provision by God (see 4:25 below) of a third son in that generation, Seth, of whose many branched lines only one will culminate in the race that was given a third chance—so to speak—in the generation of Noah. Let us now examine the text.

Seth and His Descendants: On Seth Himself

(25) Adam had relations again with his wife. She bore a son whom she named Seth, her thought being, "God has allotted me another issue," [i.e.] in place of Abel . . . he whom Cain killed. (26) To Seth, in turn, a son was born, whom he named Enosh.— Back then it was that YHWH was first invoked.

(1) Now this is the register of Adam's descendants—When God created Man, it was in the likeness of God that He made him. (2) Male and female did he create them. He blessed them, naming them Man at the time of their creation —

(3) Adam lived to the age of 130 years. He sired—in his very likeness and image—and named him Seth. (4) After siring Seth, Adam's years amounted to 800 in number. (He sired [other] sons and daughters.) (5) Thus the total of Adam's lifetime came to 930 years. Then he died.

(6) Seth lived to the age of 105 years. He sired Enosh. (7) After siring Enosh Seth lived 807 years. (He sired other sons and daughters.) (8) Thus the total of Seth's lifetime was 912 years. Then he died.

(9) Enosh lived 90 years. He sired Kenan. (10) After siring Kenan Enosh lived 815 years. (He sired other sons and daughters.) (11) Thus the total of Enosh's lifetime was 905 years. Then he died.

(12) Kenan lived 70 years. He sired Mahalalel. (13) After siring Mahalalel he lived 840 years. (He sired other sons and daughters.) (14) Thus the total lifetime of Kenan was 910 years. Then he died.

(15) Mahalalel lived 65 years. He sired Jared. (16) After the birth of Jared, Mahalalel lived 830 years. (He sired other sons and daughters.) (17) Thus the total lifetime of Mahalalel was 895 years. Then he died.

(18) Jared lived 162 years. He sired Enoch. (19) After siring Enoch, Jared lived 800 years. (He sired other sons and daughters.) (20) Thus the total lifetime of Jared was 962 years. Then he died.

(21) Enoch lived 65 years. He sired Methuselah. (22) Enoch was obedient to God, after he sired Methuselah, 300 years. (He sired other sons and daughters.) (23) Thus the total lifetime of Enoch was 365 years. (24) [Yes] Enoch was obedient to God. Yet he was gone, God having taken him.

(25) Methuselah lived 187 years. He sired Lamech. (26) After siring Lamech, Methuselah lived 782 years. (He sired other sons and daughters.) (27) Thus the total lifetime of Methuselah was 969 years. Then he died.

(28) Lamech lived 182 years. He sired a son. (29) He named him Noah, intending, "This one will bring us consolation for the grievous toil of our hands out of the soil which YHWH has placed under a ban." (30) After siring Noah, Lamech lived 595 years. (He sired other sons and daughters.) (31) Thus the total lifetime of Lamech was 777 years. Then he died.

(32) Noah was 500 years of age. Noah sired Shem, Ham, and Japheth. (Genesis 4:25–5:32)

It could not be clearer that verses 25 and 26, concluding chapter 4, are the coda of the Cain and Abel pericope, bridging the way to the line of Adam and Eve, which would survive through Seth, as their line through Cain would not.[6] An example of the precision of the biblical author's diction (and the fidelity of the process that transmitted the text to us) is the formulation in verse 25 of the thinking behind Eve's naming of her third son. This precision in the Hebrew text is lost on the reader who—even if the Hebrew is accessible to him—reads the text under the influence of the commentaries implicit in translations of the text. Let us examine three such translations: AV, NJPS, and Speiser:

1. . . . his name Seth: *For* God, said she, hath appointed me another seed instead of Abel, *whom* Cain slew. (AV)
2. . . . named him Seth, *meaning*, "God has provided me with another offspring in place of Abel," *for* Cain had killed him. (NJPS)
3. . . . she called Seth, *meaning*, "God has granted me other issue, *because* Cain killed Abel." (Speiser)

Let us note first that the name Seth is followed in the Hebrew by the particle *ki*, which is rendered as a kind of deictic by 2 and 3 ("meaning") and by its functional equivalent by 1; thus AV, faithful to the old tradition that renders *ki* as causal ("for"), achieves the deictic force by inserting a phrase ("said she") which, though it may indeed be implicit, does not appear in the Hebrew. The last clause in this verse is also introduced by the particle *ki*, rendered by "for" in 2 and "because" in 3. In the translations above I have italicized the renderings of these two instances of *ki* in the three translations. Let it be noted that 1 does not render this second *ki* at all; it sidesteps the particle, and not at all illegitimately, by telescoping it into the suffix objective of killed, that is, *whom* = "*that* he killed *him*."

Of further interest in this verse is its exemplification of our discussion of the fundamental place of punctuation in the poetical approach.[7] AV, like the Hebrew original, supplies no punctuation marks. Therefore, whether the motivation of Eve in naming Seth is rendered as direct discourse (as in 1) or as internal dialogue (as in 2 and 3), AV leaves us in the dark as to where Eve's thought begins and ends, which is also to say, where Eve ends and the narrator resumes. NJPS and Speiser, providing quotation marks, define the dialogic stretch. Thus Speiser (3) assigns everything to Eve's thought: Eve knows that Cain killed Abel, and somehow interprets God's replacement of this son with Seth as having a causal connection with the lost son's having been killed by his brother. Whether Speiser intended this meaning or not, it is the meaning clearly conveyed by his deployment of quotation marks. Let us note further that Speiser in his translation altogether omits the Hebrew words rendered in the other two versions by "instead/in place of Abel."[8] NJPS, which is not guilty of such omission, puts quotation marks after these words, indicating that these words are the end of Eve's thought; hence the reason, "for Cain had killed him," is the editor's assumption of a causal connection, or else a redundancy of information on his part. Since we have just read of the murder and the sentence upon the murderer, why should we need to be reminded of what we have had no time to forget?

I will now cite my own translation: "*God has allotted me another issue*," [i.e.] *in place of Abel . . . he whom Cain killed.* Eve's thought, according to this rendering, is confined to this third birth as an additional boon by God's grace. But instead of one of the normal Hebrew terms for additional (such as *nōsāf* or *'ōd*) the author has her using the term *'aḥer* "an other/another," implying an antecedent referent. In this context that "other" referent can be either Cain or Abel. The narrator goes on to explain her thought: the referent is Abel, who has disappeared. No one (save God and Cain), certainly not Eve, knows that he is dead. For who would have told her? But gone (like Enoch in 5:24) he is, and the new child she sees as a compensation provided to her by God. Compare her acknowledgment of God's grace in 4:1 in regard to Cain's birth. Cain is not the referent because, for one thing, he is still around. But, for another, the narrator reminds us, Cain's survival—which would normally render a third son unnecessary—does not so operate. For Cain, the murderer of Abel, is himself under a death sentence called for by justice, a death sentence suspended for him in his own person, but foreshadowed though undetermined yet for his line. That is, as we have seen, in the implicit end of that line in Noah's time, an end that is merited by the death-dealing blades forged by his descendant Tubal-Cain, by the self-confessed blood-lust of Tubal-Cain's father Lamech, both carrying the gene for violence inherited from fratricidal ancestor, Cain.

In *Toward a Grammar* (pp. 5–7) I discussed the economy of biblical style, which has been remarked upon by others. I suggested that the economy was such that *thrifty* was a term more apposite to this style. We can now see this adjective vindicated and more: biblical style is not only thrifty, it is dense, frugally dense. Metaphor itself, generally speaking, is a thrifty figure, for it achieves its effect by omitting the "like" (the comparing element) in simile, and makes bold to substitute an identification where none exists—literally, that is. The density of biblical metaphor—as we have now repeatedly seen, in 4:17–24 and again in this verse 25—challenges compare in any other literature, from antiquity to our own time.

Seth and His Descendants: Seth's Line

A chapter heading, had such a device been available to the author of Genesis, could hardly have served better to mark off Chapter 5 from Chapter 4, as we divide the text today, than verse 1 of this chapter. For the biblical author, of course, his Chapter 1 would correspond to our 1:1–2:4a; his Chapter 2 to our 2:4b–4:26. His Chapter 3 beginning with our 5:1–3 is signaled to us as a resumption of the narrative in Chapter 1 by 1) the use of the verb *br* "create" (as in 1:27); 2) of *dᵉmūt* *ᵉlōhīm* "likeness of God" (as in 1:26); 3) of "male and female created He them" (as in 1:27); and 4) of "he blessed them" as in 1:28. A fifth signal in verse 2 is, "He named them *ādām*—Man—*at the time that he created them.*" Although no such naming as a separate action appears in Chapter 1, this naming—at the time of their creation—is a reference to 1:26, "God said, 'Let us make Man.'"

The register of the begettings, then, begins (after the narrator's superscription in verses 1–2) in verse 3 with Adam, at the age of 300, siring Seth. But here in the register and never again, with the additional notice that this siring of Seth was "in his very own likeness and image." How subtle a touch! Another example of Scripture's metaphorical density: This begetting of Seth—unlike the begetting of Cain—eventuates in the true and enduring line of the Adam whom God blessed.

The chronological features that distinguish this register of the Sethite line of Adam from the Cainite line in Genesis 4 will be discussed in the context of a similar register in Chapter 11, below. I would like to conclude this chapter with some observations on the treatment of the Cainite and Sethite genealogies in source-critical scholarship. My reference point to the latter will be the discussion by E. A. Speiser in his *Genesis*. I have chosen this typical commentary for a number of reasons: One, it is lucid and comparatively simple. Two, Speiser had no part in originating or developing the source-analytic approach. Himself a comparative Semitist and cultural historian of genius, he modestly and respectfully—in this venture into biblical studies—accepts the approach of what he would have labeled the *consensus of scientific study*, and which we would formulate as the then and hitherto *state of the art* of critical literary study of Scripture. Three, in my argument in favor of a poetical approach, and this in opposition to and rebuttal of the source-critical one, my diction may sometimes seem acerbic. It is my hope that any suggestion or appearance of disrespect for the school I am criticizing will be discounted for my choosing as its champion my own revered teacher, for whom my appreciation mounts even as I lengthen the distance traveled from that fork in the road where we—so long ago and only yesterday—parted.

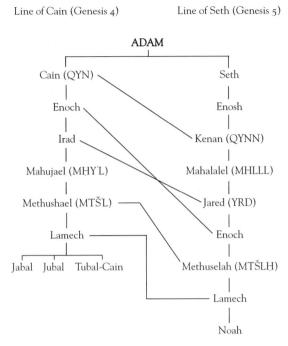

FIGURE 7-1 The Lines of Adam

Speiser assigns the biblical author's Chapter 1 to P, his Chapter 2 to J, and his Chapter 3 to P again. Verses 25–26 of our Chapter 4 he assigns to J, despite his awareness that "some critics would attribute verses 25–26 to P in view of the fact that verse 25 speaks of 'Adam' (instead of "the man") as is P's custom (see verses 1 ff.), aside from mentioning Elohim." Yet he assigns 5:29 to J, indicating in a note on that verse, "*He named him Noah.* This clause must have been present in P as well as in J, to whom the verse is attributed in view of the reference to Yahweh."

Let us now turn to figure 7-1, a graphic representation of the names in the two genealogies, which source-criticism finds irreconcilable with one another as the work of one author. The two lists have these features in common:

1. a beginning with Adam
2. ten names
3. the names Enoch and Lamech
4. the singling out of Enoch for special notice

The most notable difference between the two lists is that in Genesis 5 the ten names represent successive generations, while in Genesis 4 the ten names represent seven successive generations plus an eighth consisting of three siblings.

As has often been noted, the number of similarities indeed are rather remarkable. Of the eight descendants of Seth, only two names are altogether without correspondents in the line of Cain: Noah, being the sole survivor of the flood, cannot have a correspondent in Cain's line, for the last of this line perished in that flood;

Enos (in Hebrew "mortal, human") is the only one who might have a correspondent, yet does not. One name, Adam, is an identity; two names are borne by different step-descendants in both lists; and examination of consonants and semantic elements in the original Hebrew will reveal striking similarities in the remaining four pairs.

From the similarities modern scholarship concludes that the two lists cannot have been altogether unrelated, and that at least one of them was not the imaginative creation of the author. From the differences it concludes that neither list was copied from the other; hence neither of the lists is an independent creation. It therefore seems to follow that we have two versions of a single tradition. Both lists probably culminated, in their original versions, in Noah. The editor who patched these conflicting traditions together must have tampered with the original list in Genesis 4 so that "Noah" would derive from only one father.

For the traditionalist literalists who assume that both genealogies were dictated by God to Moses, the conclusions of modern scholarship are, of course, unacceptable. God can have only one version, and that one beyond question as to correctness. Study the two genealogies, they say, and you will see that the two are altogether compatible. Two lines issued from Adam, one through Cain, the other through Seth. The line of Seth culminates in the tenth generation (from Adam) in Noah, son of Lamech, through whom the race of mankind was preserved. The line of Cain culminates in the eighth generation (from Adam) in the three sons of another Lamech; these three—and their children, if any—died before the flood or perished in it. As for the coincidence of the names Enoch and Lamech appearing in both lists—how absurd to assume the coincidence to be improbable! They belong, after all to one family; why is the reappearance of a name or two cause for perplexity? A brief study of figure 7-1 will show that the two Enochs are first cousins four times removed, while the two Lamechs are fifth cousins twice removed. Not convinced? Let us try another formulation. The Lamech in the line of Seth had a grandfather, Enoch, who had a fifth cousin (in the line of Cain) by the name of Lamech. The Enoch of the line of Cain had a first cousin, Enos, whose great-great-grandson was also named Enoch. No improbability, no basis for skepticism.

If this flawless reasoning of the traditionalist literalist imposes a strain on credulity, what shall our judgment be on the ratiocinative acrobatics displayed in source-criticism? Chapter 2:4b through Chapter 4:24 is a unit ascribed to an author named J. This author naively collected primitive legends in which snakes talked and blood cried out and God jealously denied immortality to man, even as he showed arbitrary favor to the shepherd over the farmer. Centuries later another author, called P, wrote 1:1–2:4a and Chapter 5. This author was far more sophisticated theologically, hence, for example, his concentration on the cultic institution of the Sabbath; and for a reason not at all clear, his advanced interest in cultic matters went hand in hand with a concern for chronology, as exemplified in this one, the generations through Seth from Adam to Noah. For all his sophistication this author, Mr. P, was an imaginative dullard and an indifferent stylist, especially when compared to the inventiveness and charming style of our rather primitive Mr. J. Some time later an editor came along and combined these chapters from different hands. Whenever this editor (or R, for redactor) could, he harmonized the contradictions. When he could not, for one reason or another (both unfathomable) do so—which is most of the time—he let the stitches show (presumably with a prayer that no one would notice them). And this is only the broad basic outline of what this school of "literary criticism" has posited; its adherents have so refined their methods that they claim—with ever-mounting success in the last hundred years—to have isolated the original narrative units and sub-units and to have reconstructed the history of the Bible's composition and redaction, if not quite the history of the naive oral traditions that lie behind the compositions.

All this instead of trying an alternative set of assumptions: that the authors of the compositions were neither naive nor literal-minded; that the redactors of these compositions were neither naive nor literal-minded; and finally, that the redactors did not assume that the authors were naive nor literal-minded, nor did they assume that future generations would think them so. Many of the absurdities of modern Bible scholarship, as indeed the very development of the source-critical school, can be traced in large measure to one factor: the spell of literal-mindedness, which differs little in respect to grip from its hold on those fundamentalists who uphold the literal as a matter of dogmatic faith.[9]

In the case of the two genealogies under discussion, no religious issue or principle of logic or science hangs on the authenticity of the names, on whether five generations intervened between Adam and a descendant named Lamech (as in Genesis 4) or seven (as in Genesis 5). Thus, we may hope that neither dogmatic religionist nor scientific biblicist will be barred from perceiving the ten names in each list as an interesting literary device, whether they fall into eight generations or ten. Once the author of the Eden and Cain and Abel myths has gotten his moral across to us that we are (metaphorically) all descended from a murderer, Cain, he can dispense with the Cainite genealogy and let this murderous line of Cain and boastful killer grandson Lamech come to an end in the great flood. And the human race can make a fresh start with Noah, descendant of Seth, "*whom God granted me (Eve) in place of Abel*"—*whom Cain slew* (4:25).

And if further evidence be desired that a single author crafted both genealogies, playing with names and narrative asides to provide the clues to the metaphoric nature of both lists, let us note the following. In addition to the similarities that I have noted above as between the two lists there is an additional one, that the Lamech in each genealogy is the final progenitor of that generation which came to an end (except for Noah) in the flood. But there are other similarities as well. As we have seen in the case of the pun in the glossing of Cain's name (and this same phenomenon will be repeated often in the narratives that follow), two out of three shared consonants is not considered too puny a pun for the biblical author's purpose. Thus Cain (*qyn* and *qnh*) is in assonance with Kenan (*Qyn* and *Qynn*), Irad with Jared (*'rd* and *yrd*), Mehujael with Mahalalel (*Mhyl* and *Mhlll*), Methushael with Methuselah (*Mtšl* and *Mtšlḥ*).[10]

Finally, let us note the play on *'ab* "father, ancestor, principal, heading or fount," in the account of the Cainite line. Cain himself, at the time the only descendant of the first couple in the second generation, is already City-Builder, who names his first city after his son—now, both city and son (Enoch) lost—and the three sons of Lamech respectively are "ancestors" of the pastoral way of life, musicians of every sort, and smiths of every kind. To anyone who takes these notices literally, we might address the question: How could they be ancestors of anybody if all their descendants died out in the flood? And even a literalist might answer: The word *'ab* need not be ancestor, it may mean the first to live or practice in a certain manner; while trades and crafts—of shepherd, musician, and smith—may indeed be passed on by father to son, even in the event of a father's line coming to an end, his skill and lore may yet be retrieved by a nephew or a cousin several times removed in an agnate line. As for the scholar who will smile tolerantly in the awareness that such ancestral names as culture-heroes are that well-known phenomenon of eponyms, I would ask him to remind himself: That biblical author of long ago also knew what an eponym is; however else it may serve, the eponym is also a metaphor; and in his figurative disposition of such eponyms the biblical author is signaling: Artist at Work—Look Out for Flying Metaphors.

The Line of Noah: Through Japheth, Ham, and Shem

(1) These **now** are the issues of Noah's sons, Shem, Ham, and Japheth. Sons were born to them after the Deluge:

(2) The sons of Japheth: Gomer, and Magog, and Madai, and Javan, and Tubal, and Meshech, and Tiras.

(3) The sons of Gomer: Ashkenaz, and Riphath, and Togarmah.

(4) The sons of Javan: Elishah, and Tarshish, Kittim, and Dodanites.

(5) From these branched out the coastlands of [sundry] national entities within their territories, each idiosyncratic as to its language, by their families within their nationalities.

(6) And the sons of Ham (were): Cush, and Mizraim, and Put, and Canaan.

(7) And the sons of Cush: Seba, and Havilah, and Raamah, and Sabteca. And Raamah's sons (were): Sheba and Dedan.

[(8) Cush **now** bore Nimrod. He was the first one to be the mightiest on earth. (9) He was, by YHWH's grace, mighty in the hunt, hence is it said, "Like Nimrod, by YHWH's grace, mighty in the hunt."

(10) The mainspring of his kingdom was Babel, and Erech and Akkad and Calneh in Shinar-land.

(11) From that country sprang Asshur, and he builded Nineveh, and Rehoboth-Ir, and Calah,

(12) and Resen between Nineveh and Calah—that one being the greatest city.]

(13) And Mizraim bore Ludites, and Anamites, and Lehabites, and Naphtuhites, (14) and Patrusites, and Kasluhites, whence came forth Philistines and Caphtorites.

(15) And Canaan bore Sidon, his eldest, and Heth, (16) and the Jebusites, and the Amorites, and the Girgashites, (17) and the Hivites and the Arkites and the Sinites; (18) and the Arvadites, and the Zemarites, and the Hamathites, and after [what or whom?] did the families of the Canaanites disperse: (19) Thus was the Canaanite border from Sidon—on your way to Gerar—as far as Gaza; on your way to Sodom and Gomorrah and Admah and Zeboim, as far as Lesha.

(20) These [aforementioned] the Hamites, according to their families and their
tongues within their lands, within their nationalities.)

(21) And there was born to Shem—yes, he too—[he] the ancestor of all the
Eberites, the elder brother of Japheth . . . (22) The sons of Shem: Elam, and Asshur,
and Arpachshad, and Lud, and Aram.

(23) And the sons of Aram: Uz, and Hul, and Gether, and Mash.

(24) And Arpachshad bore Shelah
and Shelah bore Eber,
(25) and to Eber was born a twosome of sons, the name of one Peleg—to wit:
in his lifetime was earth['s population] splintered—and the name of his brother
was Joktan.
(26) And Joktan bore Almodad, and Sheleph, and Hazarmaveth, and
Jerah, (27) and Hadoram, and Uzal, and Diklah, (28) and Obal, and Abi-
mael, and Sheba, (29) and Ophir, and Havilah, and Jobab. All these the
sons of Joktan. (30) Their area of settlement was from Mesha—on your
way to Sefar—the Eastern Mountain.

(31) These are the sons of Shem, according to their families and their tongues, in
their territories according to their nationalities.

(32) These are the families of the sons of Noah, according to their begettings, in
their nationalities. And from these [three] did the nations branch out on earth after
the Deluge. (Genesis 10:1–32)

The scholarly approach to these early genealogies of the human race, reading
literal—which is to say, historiographic—intent into the minds of the biblical
writers responsible for them, is fairly reflected in Speiser's Comment on them.[11]
The notion that these writers—in respect to the genealogies we cannot call them
authors—collected ancient traditions, going back to the earliest generations of the
human species is, of course, subject to neither confirmation nor rebuttal. My own
approach, which views the biblical writers as the authors indeed of the genealogical trees, as of the framing narratives, derives from peculiarities of style and diction,
of composition and constituent onomastic data, which are generally ignored in
scholarly commentaries. Inasmuch as the poetic investigator assumes that the literary material before him is the product of a competent, not to say artistic, crafts-
man, he cannot allow that such peculiarities are explainable as slips of the pen in
the hands of a nodding Homer. These peculiarities then are intentional, designed
to serve as flags for the close and careful reader, flags as to what the author really intends—as also, what he certainly cannot intend—by the structures that he is
putting before us.

One peculiar feature of diction in this chapter is the regular appearance of the
verb wld/yld in the qal with an apparently masculine subject.[12] The qal verb has the
sense of "to bear a child," a biological activity confined to the female sex. The corresponding activity for the male sex is the same verb in the hiphil conjugation hōlīd
"to sire, cause (a woman) to bear." It is perhaps due to this exceptional use of the
qal stem in this chapter, in clear contrast with the hiphil stem in the genealogy of
Chapter 11, that led the early translators of Scripture into English to opt for the
gender-neutral "begat" for both these stems in the genealogies. The anomalous fea-

turing of the qal stem in this genealogy is almost certainly due to the peculiar characteristic of the "begetters." In contrast to the begetters in chapters 5 and 11, who are individuals, male ancestors of the human race (who therefore *sire* their progeny), the names of the begetters in this "genealogy" are eponyms, that is, they represent hypothetical ancestors to whom or to which are traced the name of an existing family or tribe, city or nationality. Thus these names represent not biological forebears but political origins; the originators are metaphoric.

To deny to the biblical author the consciousness of the difference between a personal name, a place name, an ethnic name, and a political name is in flagrant (if unthinking and unintentional) disrespect of—even insulting to—his intelligence. And it is not out of disrespect for his reader's intelligence, nor of his grasp of Hebrew, that our author challenges our attention by scrambling the subject of the verb. The Hebrew word *'iy*, meaning coastland, is of course a geographical term, and *goy* "nation" is a political term. Peoples and polities, like rivers and tributaries, may separate from one another or branch out; not so, islands or headlands. Yet instead of having the *goy(y)ē hā'iyyim* "the nations of the coastlands" branching out, he has the *'iyyē haggoyīm* "the coastlands of the nations" doing so. This then is another signal that a *table* of nations masquerading as a family tree can only be a metaphor. And, let us note, it is not these named entities that are branching out in a welter of ethnic, linguistic, geographic, and political groups; it is rather that out of these named entities there branch out other such in such numbers as not to be nameable!

The most glaring peculiarity in this Table of Nations projected as a genealogy is the insertion of a pericope, verses 8–12, which in substance and manner identifies itself as both extraneous and intrusive. For one thing, it begins with the first appearance of a masculine subject governing the qal verb *yālad*. The subject is Cush, whose "sons" are listed in the preceding verse, five of them, along with two "grandsons." Thus the question arises, why was the son he "birthed" not included with the five in the preceding verse? The answer, to be sure, lies in the name of this son, for this Nimrod is clearly an individual not an eponym. His individuality and personhood is affirmed by three notices in regard to him.

1. He was the first (of an implied succession of conquerors, each like Nimrod) "mighty one on earth."
2. He was so great a hunter as to have his preeminence in this sport of kings attributed to a special grace vouchsafed upon him by God; no, not by God, but by YHWH; the citation of this name attributable, so we are asked to believe, to the currency in ancient Israel, at the time of this pericope's writing, of a proverbial expression for hunting prowess, "like Nimrod a mighty hunter—by the (very) grace of YHWH."
3. The mainstays of this mighty ruler's dominion in the land of Shinar (lower Mesopotamia) were four in number. The first mentioned, Babel/Babylon, must have been known to the most rustic of the writer's Israelite or Judean contemporaries. The second, Erech/Uruk, once great but in the writer's time a Mesopotamian backwater town, would have been known only to one versed in a cuneiform history. The third, Accad/Akkad/Agade, its site today unknown, was already a legendary imperial capital in the time of Moses. The fourth, Calneh, is unattested elsewhere in the Bible or in cuneiform.

The author of our intrusive pericope continues now with an ambiguity-laden notice that "from that land," that is, the land of Shinar, "there came forth/issued/sprung" an individual/a polity named Asshur, the same name which—along with other polities in or near Mesopotamia—appears in verse 22 as (eponymous) descendants of Shem. This Asshur, now, sprung from southern Mesopotamia, built four cities, two of them renowned capitals of Assyria (Nineveh and Calah), and two (like the mysterious Calah in Shinar) totally unknown to us. It is hardly credible that there existed three cities in Mesopotamia that were known to the biblical author but unattested in the huge trove of cuneiform writings available to us today. So too is it hard to believe that a biblical writer who knew of Uruk and Akkad did not know that Cush was a name common to two widely separated polities, the Cossaea of the Kassites (who ruled Babylon for five and a half centuries) in the east, and the Cush of the southwest, inclusive of Ethiopia, Sudan, and part of the Sinai. In view of this the entire pericope, serving as a flag as to the figurative function of this entire Table of Nations, is compounded of real place names and polities, as well as of onomastic figments ingeniously formulated to caution the close and knowing reader. If there were a Calneh in Shinar, its insignificance would deny it a place alongside of Babel, Uruk, and Akkad. (But if there is a fourth name of historic fame that might have been included, would it not be the mighty center called Ur?) So too, if there were an insignificant town between Nineveh and Calah. And as for Rehoboth-Ir, the never-heard-of city placed between Nineveh and Calah (the latter being "the great city" in the writer's time), if its signification is (as Speiser suggests) city of broad streets, the Hebrew should be (cf. coastlands of the nations in verse 5 above) 'Ir-Rehoboth.

I will not attempt to exhaust all the peculiarities in this chapter. But let us note, in sequential order, that following the niphal of wld "there were born" in verse 1, we have the formula bᵉnē-PN "sons of" at the beginnings of verses 2, 3, 4, 6, and 7. This series is broken off with PN yālad "PN bore" at the beginning of the intrusive Cush pericope, verse 8. This formula now continues at the beginnings of verses 13 and 15. Verse 15 is peculiar for having Mizraim (Egypt) bearing six—not eponymous individuals but—gentilic plurals, and then treating these six (or is it only the last of these six, the Kasluhites?) as a *place whence* rather than an *ancestry from which* "there sprung Philistines and Caphtorites (Cretans)." Surprising in verse 15 is the notice that Canaan bore Sidon and Heth. Sidon, a well-known city, is designated as Canaan's firstborn, making prominent by absence (if we may be permitted an oxymoron) the far more important Tyre; and Heth is an eponym for the ethnic group elsewhere termed Ḥitti or Bᵉnē-Ḥet "Hittites" or "Heth-ites." There then follow nine (grammatical) gentilics, including two otherwise unknown Canaanite groups—the Arkites and Sinites, omitting the well-known Perizzites, and including the inhabitants of two cities, Arvad—a neighbor of Sidon and the famous Hamath in northern Syria. Stranger yet, however, is the following sketch of "the Canaanite border" extending from Sidon—hence ignoring both Tyre on the coast to the north and Hamath to the northeast—southward to Gaza (inclusive of historically insignificant but patriarchally prominent Gerar) and somehow—although obscurely—raising up the names of the four Cities of the Plain, which, destroyed in the days of Father Abraham, their sites hidden from human eyes for at least a millennium at the time of this pericope's writing, cannot possible serve as signposts to ethnic border markings. Why then include these legendary—or should we say, mythic—reminders of human depravity and divine sentence? And to add to these unlocateable four a hitherto unheard-of fifth city, Lesha, to make for a pentapolis of perversion? Again, I would suggest, by tying in to the figurative significance of *illo tempore*, to remind the reader that data of ethnicity and polity, geography and chronological priority are of no significance whatever for the human condition. Why then this charade of a historical structure? Again, we shall have to wait until we review a few more peculiarities.

The sons of Noah, in the order of their births, are Shem, Ham, and Japheth. The listing of their descendant genetic, ethnic, political, and geographically situated entities in reverse order is to focus our attention on the line, the climactic line—so to speak—of the eldest. The Shemite branch of the human race is introduced in verse 21, a sentence altogether unnecessary (cf. the beginning of verse 22 with that of verse 2 and verse 6) and featuring two peculiar epithets or characterizations of Shem. The characterization of this patriarch as the elder brother of Japheth, as if he were not the elder brother of Ham, is discussed in this chapter. The other characterization of him is as ancestor to the descendants of his grandson Eber, as if he were not the ancestor as well of his grandsons Uz, Hul, Gether, and Mash.

A long-ago discovery that has become a staple of biblical scholarship is the intertextual connection between this Chapter 10 of Genesis and Deuteronomy 32:8. This last passage reads:

> When Elyon (the One on High) allotted [lands] to nations,
> When he caused humankind to branch out,
> He fixed the boundaries of peoples
> According to the number of the sons of Israel.

The number of the "sons of Israel"—seventy—appears in Exodus 1:5: "All the souls (*nepeš*) springing from Jacob's loins made for a sum of 70 souls." This number seventy is accounted for in Genesis 46:8–27, which concludes, "All the souls of Jacob's household that came to Egypt were 70 (in number)." Corresponding to this number are the descendants of Shem, Ham, and Japheth. The reader may easily check this out by reference to figure 7-2. The descendants of Japheth number fourteen, of Ham thirty, and of Shem twenty-six, for a total of seventy.[13]

That this play of number as between the seventy descendants of Noah's three sons and the seventy descendants of Jacob, respectively the *benē-'Ādām* and the *benē Yiśrā'el* of Deuteronomy 32:8, reflects accurately the intent of the biblical author(s) is hardly to be doubted. But that these descendants of Noah's sons represent—all of them—*nations*, or that Deity set the borders for these *peoples*, can be accepted only if we see in these juxtapositions another kind of play, a whimsical playfulness. For even if we grant ethnic and national status to all the other names in figure 7-2, it is not easily granted that the same may be said for the line of Shem through Arpachshad, Shela, Eber, and Peleg. There are no Arpachshadites, Shelaites, or Pelegites in Scripture. These are, as we shall soon see, incontrovertibly individual personae. There are, however, Eberites: the *benē-'Eber* of verse 21, which we have just discussed. These Eberites, however, are neither an ethnic nor a political entity.

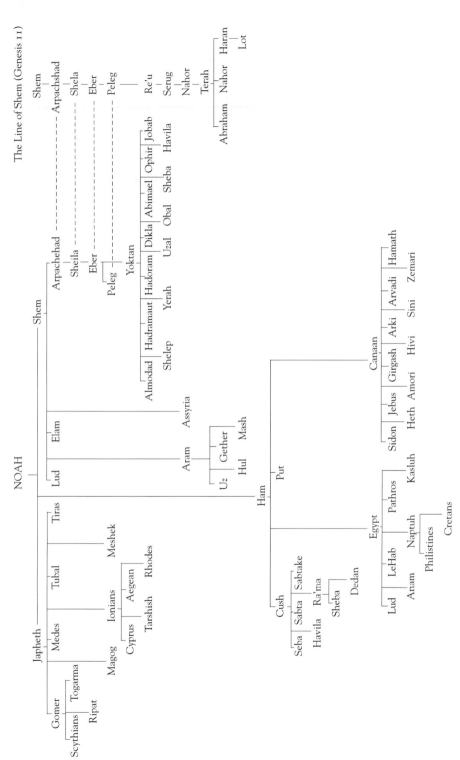

FIGURE 7-2 The Lines of Noah (Genesis 10)

These "sons of Eber" are the descendants (if any—none mentioned in this chapter) of Peleg, and the thirteen listed for Yoktan. Thus Eber cannot be counted among "the seventy nations," nor can Canaan, for that matter, for it will not do to count him twice—once as a self-standing ethnological entity, and once as embodied in his eleven descendant ethno-polities. And the same holds true for other progenitors, such as Japheth's son Gomer, and Egypt (particularly in regard to Philistines and Caphtorites) and Cush. The mention of these last two brings up yet another peculiarity, which is that in a tree that is not so much a genealogy as a table of nations and their national offshoots, out of a total of seventy names, there are three pairs of identical names. Egypt produces a Lud and his uncle Shem does likewise. Cush produces a grandson Sheba, and his uncle Shem produces a Sheba in the fourth generation. And, furthermore, the Cushite Sheba has an uncle Havila, while the Shemite Sheba has a brother Havila. Or can it be that the framer of our table knows of a single Sheba and a single Havila in that neighborhood where Hamites and Shemites abut one another, and that he is signaling that to sort out the true ancestry of these two is a task beyond his capability or, perhaps, desire? We will yet come across similar ancestral perplexities in succeeding genealogies.

Before we turn to our next structure, which is not only a genealogy but a chronology as well, let us note the last two verses in this chapter. Verse 31 is a coda summing up the begettings of Shem, as verses 5 and 20 did respectively for the lines of Japheth and Ham. Verse 32 is the summational coda for the begettings of all three. "These are the families of the sons of Noah—in respect to their begettings, by their national entities—yes, from these did the nations branch out on earth after the Deluge." *Yes, from these,* which is to say the sons of Noah, he the second Adam, do all human societies—whatever their political configurations, however they trace their ethnicities—derive. And that moral (if not demonstrable biologic or historic) reality is, like the derivation of Noah from the line of Seth and Enosh (Humanity), the implicit kerygma of this structure.

GENEALOGIES CONTINUED: THE LINE OF SHEM

(10) These are the issue of Shem, Shem [then] 100 years old. He sired Arpachshad two years after the Deluge. (11) After siring Arpachshad he lived 500 years. He sired [additional] sons, and daughters.

(12) Now Arpachshad lived 35 years. He sired Shelah. (13) After siring Shelah, Arpachshad lived 403 years. He sired [additional] sons, and daughters.

(14) Now Shelah lived 30 years. He sired Eber. (15) After siring Eber, Shelah lived 403 years. He sired [additional] sons, and daughters.

(16) Eber lived 34 years. He sired Peleg. (17) After siring Peleg Eber lived 430 years. He sired [additional] sons, and daughters.

(18) Peleg lived 30 years. He sired Reu. (19) After siring Reu, Peleg lived 209 years. He sired [additional] sons, and daughters.

(20) Reu lived 32 years. He sired Serug. (21) After siring Serug, Reu lived 207 years. He sired [additional] sons, and daughters.

(22) Serug lived 30 years. He sired Nahor. (23) After siring Nahor, Serug lived 200 years. He sired [additional] sons, and daughters.

(24) Nahor lived 29 years. He sired Terah. (25) After siring Terah, Nahor lived 119 years. He sired [additional] sons, and daughters.

(26) Terah lived 70 years. He sired Abram, Nahor and Haran—

(27) Now these are the issue of Terah: Terah sired Abram, Nahor and Haran; and Haran now sired Lot. (28) Haran died in the lifetime of his father Terah, in the land of his birth, in Ur Kasdim. (29) Abram and Nahor took themselves wives, the name of Abram's wife Sarai, and the name of Nahor's wife Milcah daughter of Haran, [he] father of Milcah and [also] father of Iscah. (30) Sarai was barren, had no child whatsoever. . . . (32) Terah's lifetime was 205 years. Terah died in Haran. (Genesis 11:10–30, 32)

The figurative nature of the seventy descendant names of the three lines of Noah as detailed in Chapter 10 is underscored by the genealogy in Chapter 11. In Chapter 10, although the thirteen descendants of Yoktan are given, the line of his brother Peleg is not. Peleg, whose name means Division or Split, was so named for it was "in his days that earth['s population] was split apart. The reference is, of course, to the event at Babel that follows the genealogy in Chapter 10—the dissolution of humankind's unity—and is followed by the resumption of Shem's line through Arpachshad to Peleg, and continues with Peleg's line through the sons of Terah. Thus metaphor is again signaled by Peleg's name, for the Great Division could hardly have been foreseen by the parents who named him. All this can be reviewed in a glance at figure 7-2.

I have at this point inserted figure 7-3, a list of Terah's line, in order to facilitate a grasp of our author's inventiveness in forcing upon our attention the kerygmatic meanings (or at least one of them) by his disposition of names. Thus the sibling ancestors of two peoples known to the biblical author's world, Sheba and Dedan. Assignable to the Hamite line of Cush or the Shemite line of Arpachshad-Yoktan, as we saw before, was Sheba. (figure 7-2) But now the siblings Sheba and Dedan are both seen as assigned to the Hamite line in Figure 7-2, and in Figure 7-3 appear as grandchildren, descendants of our own Father Abraham!

Such a duplication of a pair of ancestors, some ten generations apart and in two different branches, can hardly be credibly explained as the product of an absent-minded author (or one consciously yet slavishly tied to his "source") whose inattention (or slavishness) is not caught by his dull-sighted (or equally slavish) editor. But even if such explanation were not, as Lewis Carroll would have put it, too much of a muchness, this duplication is not provided for its own sake. Dedan is not a prominent biblical ethnos (although Isaiah in 21:13 lists the Dedanites among steppe-traveling caravaneers), and Sheba, better known—especially for her queen's liaison with Solomon—impinges but slightly upon Israelite or Judean neighbors. But this duplicated pair in branches and generations so far apart is but a signal to a far more perplexing duplication of ethnic lines far more closely tied to Israel's patriarchs.

Thus in Figure 7-2, Arpachshad's brother is Aram, and Aram is father to Uz (the land of Job, he great among the Kedemites). Yet in Figure 7-3, Uz is the first-born of Abram's brother Nahor. This Uz has no children, but he does have two brothers. One is Kesed, obviously eponymous ancestor of the Kasdim. The other is Kemuel, who sires a son, Aram. Thus the Aram, father of Uz in Figure 7-2 is the

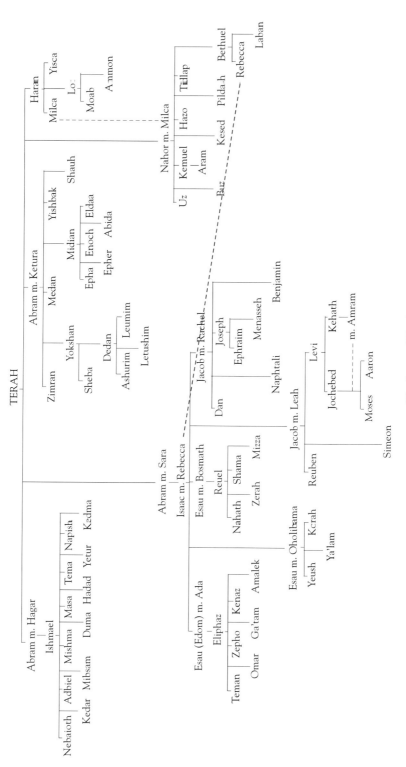

FIGURE 7-3 The Lines of Terah

Aram, nephew of Uz in Figure 7-3. But that is not all. Uz in Figure 7-3 has a brother named Bethuel, the father of Rebecca and Laban, and this Bethuel, like his son Laban, is identified by the gentilic "the Aramean," which would seem appropriate only to the children of the Aram who is their nephew and cousin (Genesis 25:20, 28:5, 31:30, 31:24).

THE CHRONOLOGIES OF THE LINES OF SETH AND SHEM

The genealogy of Adam in the line of Cain in Chapter 4 is assigned by modern scholarship to the author or source labeled J. The other three genealogies are, except for a few interpolations attributed to J, all assigned to the Priestly Source, or P for short. These three are: 1) The line of Adam through Seth in Chapter 5; 2) The line of Noah through his three sons in Chapter 10; 3) That line of Seth which ends in Abram in Chapter 11. Of these three, the first and the last provide details of chronology, the middle one does not. The reason for the absence of such detail in this second genealogy is, or ought to be, obvious. As there is no chronology for the line of Cain, which comes to an abrupt end in the all-destroying Deluge, so in the case of the line of all mankind—as known to, or imaginatively constructed by, the biblical writers—there is no compelling reason for chronology. Scripture's interest in chronology relates to the line of Adam as it culminates in Noah, as Noah's culminates in Abram. This is why the third genealogy resumes the line of Shem and continues it, with chronological detail, through Eber's son, Peleg (but not Eber's son, Yoktan), until the generation of Abram. It is also why these genealogies make it explicit that each progenitor had other children, who are not named because our interest is not in ancillary lines. (The existence of these other children, their progeny not explicitly included in the categories of the names making up the Table of Nations in Chapter 10 [cf. Genesis 48:5–6] is, of course, yet another signal as to the metaphoric nature of that table/genealogy.)

But why the need for chronology altogether? Source-critics have assumed that priests—for a reason that is as obvious to them as it is unfathomable to us—are by nature interested in chronology, at least to a degree not shared by the laity. And so, by a process of circular reasoning, they are satisfied that a priestly source, which is by definition concerned with chronology, should take pains to preserve and transmit chronological details. But chronology is either invented by humans, in which case the numbers may constitute a cipher, a message in code—written by humans for other humans to decipher—or it is determined by God, the Author of life and death; and humans have faithfully preserved the record in the hope that God's motives in prolonging one life and shortening another may one day be discerned. The numbers in these lists have been studied over the centuries with less than gratifying results. The most insightful conclusions appear in ancient rabbinic commentaries called *midrash*, but since so much of this literature is playful and frankly eisegetical, they have been largely overlooked by scholars. The least conclusive results have been yielded by studies employing computers.

On the assumption that the chronology is as much part of the biblical message as the narratives for which it provides the framework, we have reduced the data to graphic form in table 7-1. The method of the biblical genealogist is to give the age

TABLE 7-1 Chronologies, Adam to Joseph

	Adam	Seth	Enosh	Kenan	Mahalalel	Jared	Enoch	Methusela	Lamech	Noah	Shem	Arpachshad	Shelah	Eber	Peleg	Reu	Serug	Nahor	Terah	Abram	Isaac	Jacob	Joseph
50																							
100																							
150		130																					
250			235																				
300																							
350				325																			
400																							
450					395																		
500						460																	
550	930																						
600																							
650		912					622																
700			905					687															
750				910			365																
800					895																		
850																							
900						962			874														
950	930						987																
1000																							
1050		1042								1056													
1100																							
1150			1140																				
1200								969	777														
1250				1235																			
1300					1290																		
1350																							
1400						1422																	
1450																							

Genealogical timeline chart (Genesis patriarchs). Rows = years (Anno Mundi), columns = names. Circled numbers (shown here in parentheses) are ages/lifespans; underlined numbers are dates.

Year	Adam	Seth	Enosh	Kenan	Mahalalel	Jared	Enoch	Methusela	Lamech	Noah	Shem	Arpachshad	Shelah	Eber	Peleg	Reu	Serug	Nahor	Terah	Abram	Isaac	Jacob	Joseph
1500																							
1550										(950)	1556												
1600																							
1650								1656	1651			1658											
1700													1693										
1750														1723	1757								
1800																1787	1819						
1850											(600)	(438)	(433)					1849	1878				
1900														(464)	(239)								
1950														1996		(239)	(230)	(148) 1997	(205)	1948			
2000										2006						2026	2049				2048		
2050												2093							2083	(175)			
2100													2126							2123		2108	
2150											2156			2187									
2200																				2199	(180) 2228	(147)	
2250																						2255	(110)
2300																							2309
Generational Overlap	8	7	7	6	5	4	2	3	2	10	11	9	9	8	5	4	4	2	2	2	2	2	3

of each progenitor at the time he sired the one son who continues this one line of many. Starting with zero for the day of Adam's birth, we have then the descending step arrangement, which gives us the birth-year of each generation. But the genealogist also tells us how many years the progenitor lived after siring this son. He thereby makes it possible for us to plot the year of each generation's death. In Chapter 5, the text also provides the total lifetime of each generation, thus emphasizing a significance implicit in these data, while Chapter 11, leaving to us the addition necessary to arrive at the total lifetime, underlines the redundancy, hence the significance, of these data. Just what is that significance? The circled numbers in the table represent the total lifetimes of the individuals listed. What significance can there be to such data as, for example, that the otherwise unremarkable Methuselah outlived the next longest-lived, Noah, by nineteen years, while Noah lived twenty years more than did Adam?

The answer, I suggest, lies in the one feature that would be impossible to retrieve unless both birth-year and year of death were given: the overlap of lifetimes, a feature with which the Rabbis play in midrash, and which modern scholarship has largely ignored. It is this feature that yields a significant pattern. How many generations of descendants did a given ancestor live to see? The numbers are given at the bottom of the columns. Thus, for example, Adam was still alive when Lamech, the eighth generation after Adam, was born; indeed it was only in the fifty-sixth year of Lamech's life that Adam died. Lamech, however, witnessed the smallest number of his descendants' generations. He lived to see his grandchild Shem (and, of course, Ham and Japheth also). The Deluge took place in the year 1656, the six hundredth year of Noah's life, and Lamech died five years before that. Since Noah's sons had no children until after the flood, poor Lamech alone in the first ten generations was denied the joy of great-grandchildren. Alone, that is, except for his own grandfather Enoch, who, shortest-lived by far of the first generations, died before a child was born to Lamech. The pattern is clear: earlier ancestors witnessed the larger number of descendants, the later ones the fewest, with but one exception, Enoch—the righteous!

The next ten generations are from Shem to Abram. This second series of generations is distinguished from the first series in the matter of longevity. Shem, the longest-lived, has a lifetime only two-thirds of the average lifetime of his predecessors; and as his line continues, the lifetimes of his descendants show a pattern of decline so that Abram, in the tenth generation, enjoys not even a third of the span of years that were granted to Shem. The decline in lifetimes is fairly regular. The one exception is Abram's grandfather Nahor, whose lifetime is the shortest in these ten generations. And Nahor—like Enoch before him—is also the one exception in the pattern of the declining numbers of descendant generations that the ancestors live to see. Noah, the tenth generation from Adam, lived to see the tenth generation of his descendants. Shem saw eleven. And then again the pattern is one of decline. Terah and Abram and Nahor only live to see grandchildren, while all their predecessors lived to see at least great-great-grandchildren.

Long life and numerous offspring are in Scripture the most desirable of blessings. Proverbs 16:31 says, "Hoary age is a glorious crown, to be achieved by righteous living," while Proverbs 17:6 affirms, "Grandchildren are the crown of the elderly."

In Psalm 127, such blessings are traced to the Source of all life: "Children are a legacy from YHWH, the fruit of the womb is reward. Like arrows in a warrior's hand, so are children of [one's] youth. Fortunate the one who has a quiver full of them."[14] The declining felicity, then, in each of the series of ten generations, would seem to be an indication of declining merit or virtue. It is questionable whether the biblical authors would have wanted us to draw as a necessary conclusion that the individuals of the second set of ten generations were—as judged by their so much shorter lifetimes—so greatly inferior in virtue to those in the first set of ten. Though the lifetime of Shem is considerably less than that of his predecessors, Shem—like his father Noah—lived to see more generations of his descendants than did Adam. The pattern is there, the pattern is suggestive, but it must not be read mechanically, literally, or as a one-to-one correspondence between evidence of reward and assumption of comparable virtue.

The Sumerian King List, preserved by Semitic heirs of Sumerian culture, attributes lifetimes averaging more that thirty thousand years to the kings who reigned before the flood. The long lifetimes of the biblical antediluvians is certainly reflective of that Mesopotamian tradition. But whatever those monstrous lifetimes symbolized to the Mesopotamians, the biblical tradition has incorporated the feature of longevity, modified it to a more reasonable scale, and adapted it for its own metaphoric purpose. Enoch, who lived fewer years by far than those before or after him, and who saw no great grandchildren, is singled out for notice in 5:24: "Enoch was faithful to [literally, "walked with"] God—and disappeared, for God had taken him." Here is an explicit warning not to read the signs mechanically: Enoch may have been the most virtuous of the first ten for all his brief career. Similarly, we have no reason to assume that Nahor, Abram's short-lived grandfather, died young for his sins.

I have added Isaac, Jacob, and Joseph to my graphic figure for a number of reasons. For one, it was necessary to show that Abram lived only to see grandchildren, in this respect like his father before him, and Isaac and Jacob after him. Yet his son Isaac lived five years longer than he did, and his grandson Joseph lived to see great-grandchildren. And it is by no accident that we come by this last item of information. The penultimate notice about Joseph in the last chapter of Genesis is that he lived to see the grandchildren of both his sons: "Joseph saw the third generation of [his] descendants, [grandchildren] of Ephraim; and, as well, the children of Machir son of Manasseh were born on Joseph's knees" (50:23).

After Abram, we must reconstruct the overlap of the generations from widely scattered notices. But we must remember that the notices are provided in the text, and provided for us to use and to draw those conclusions that our wits may construe. Thus, for example, in 21:5, Abraham was one hundred years old when Isaac was born; in 25:26, Isaac was sixty when the twins Esau and Jacob were born. In the case of Jacob and Joseph, we are not informed of Jacob's age at the time that Joseph was born. But we can arrive at the year by working backward from data that is supplied, and supplied in so apparently off-handed a manner as to conceal that its purpose is to make our calculation possible. Thus, for example, the curious notice in 41:46 that Joseph was thirty years old when he became viceroy of Egypt. From the ages of Abram when Isaac was born and the age of Isaac when the twins were born we get 2108 as the year of Jacob's birth. In 47:28 we are given the total lifetime of Jacob as 147, the last seventeen years spent in Egypt. Jacob, then, died in 2255, and came to Egypt in 2238. In 45:11 Joseph mentions to his brothers that there are yet five years of the famine to come. Since he came to office at the age of thirty, and seven years of plenty and two years of famine have passed, he is then thirty-nine years old, and must have been born in 2199.

In the introduction to the flood, which features the miscegenation of male divinities and human women resulting in the births of the "mighty men of renown in time of yore," God determines to set an upper limit of 120 years to the human lifetime. This notice can hardly be disassociated from the antediluvians' longevity, but the limit does not take effect immediately. On the contrary, the ten post-diluvians' lifetimes decline from the 600 years of Shem to the 175 years of Abram. Yet Isaac lives five more years than did his father Abram; and Jacob, the last of the patriarchs—who, at the age of 130 years characterizes them to Pharaoh as having been "few and hard," and prophetically, "nor do they come up to the lifespans of my fathers"—is already ten years past the 120-year limit when he comes down to Egypt. Joseph is the first Israelite ancestor who falls within the limit; he dies at the age of 110. But that there can be no one-to-one correspondence consistently drawn from longevity to virtue is indicated by the age reported in Exodus 6 for Joseph's brother Levi (137). Amram is the father of Aaron, who lived to the age of 123 (Numbers 33:39), and of Moses who (according to Deuteronomy 34:7) died in the prime of life (at the divinely decreed limit), at the age of 120, "his eyes undimmed, his vitality undiminished."

A number of other conclusions of piquant interest may be drawn from a study of our chronicler's chronology. Methuselah, the longest-lived of all, dies in 1656, the six hundredth year of Noah's life, which is the year of the Deluge. Are we to understand that he died in that cataclysm, or was saved from such a fate by a natural death at the age of 969? Perhaps more meaningful is the death of Isaac in 2228, twelve years after Joseph was sold into slavery (at the age of seventeen; cf. 37:2) and ten years before Jacob's reunion with his son in Egypt. The last verses of Chapter 35, which tell us—at the end of the Jacob story, before the Joseph story begins—of Isaac's last breath, also tell us that "Jacob came to his father Isaac . . ." at Hebron where Isaac "was gathered to his kin in ripe old age; and he was buried by his sons Esau and Jacob." But what about his wife and their mother, Rebekah? The biblical author who takes pains to tell us (in 35:8) of the death and burial of Deborah, Rebekah's nurse, does not see fit to tell us anything of Rebekah's own demise. Apparently the mother who took it upon herself to delude her husband Isaac, to instigate the younger twin to steal his elder brother's blessing, died before Jacob returned from his exile in Paddan-Aram. For her intrigue, she saw one son turn against the other in murderous rage, and her favorite son take flight from that wrath, never for her to set eyes on him again; while Isaac—who thought himself close to death when he undertook to bless his eldest son—lived on for many years, lived to witness Jacob's loss of a son (blessed irony not to know that this loss too owed to brothers' wrath) and died knowing that both his sons, now reconciled, would be there to close his eyes and lay him to rest.

So much for the poetic unity of structural patterns and narrative plotting across the chapters of (as well as across "the documents" or "sources" of) Genesis, and indeed of Exodus, as well as consistency of voice in these books and in the Books of Psalms and Proverbs. The above examples, however, far from exhaust the intricate play of numbers and narrative in Scripture's literary art. The following section will present two examples of how chronological items, genealogical redundancy (and even narrative strategy in dialogic "showing" and authorial "telling") can provide allusive plot elements just where a less than respectful critic finds nothing or an egregiously pointless detail.

CHRONOLOGY AS CLUE TO NARRATIVE: THE MISSING YEARS IN JACOB'S LIFE

While working out the chronology of Jacob's life, I came up with two questions I could not answer. One of these had to do with a period of years during which I could not account for the patriarch's whereabouts. Recalling a Talmudic tradition about Jacob having studied for a number of years in the academy of Shem-Eber, I looked up that tradition, and found that the rabbis had come up with a solution to my problem that at first glance seemed even more fanciful than I remembered, and which upon second thought seemed worthy of serious consideration as to the intriguing intent of Scripture's chronology and genealogic formulations. I will present my own reasoning and the argument of the Talmud. To help the reader follow the two tracks of similar but different steps, I have prepared table 7-2. The items in the left-hand column show my own reconstruction, those in the right-hand column the reconstruction of the rabbis. The dates in the left-hand column are those I arrived at on my own; there is no discrepancy between any of these dates and the rabbinic calculations. The dates in the right-hand column are those arrived at by the rabbis; here, too, there is no discrepancy with my calculations.

Most of my date-items, as arrived at, are discussed in the preceding sections. Item 6 is based on 26:34, the notice that Esau was forty years old when he took his first two wives. Assuming that a year intervened between the two marriages, I assumed further that he was forty at the time of his first marriage. No serious effect on my calculations would be occasioned by having the second marriage take place at his age forty and in the year 2149 for the year. What is new in my table 7-2 are items 11–25, dates at which I arrived by working backward from item 25. The year 2206 for Jacob's flight from Laban was arrived at on the basis of 30:25: Jacob's address to Laban comes after the birth of Joseph, at the end of his fourteen years of service for his wives, and it results in six additional years of service for wages (in kind). This total of fourteen plus six is explicit in 31:41, and the date, six years after Joseph's birth, is confirmed by the date of 2201 for Joseph's birth, at which I had arrived on the basis of other notices.[15] The birth of Jacob's twelve children (eleven sons and one daughter (told in 29:31–30:24) was then plotted backward, allowing for one birth a year, resulting in Reuben's birth in 2188, three years after Jacob's arrival at Padan Aram, and Levi's birth in 2190. Had we begun with 2185, and had Reuben been born in 2186, then Levi would have been born in 2188.[16] The dates are approximate (±2) and need not be any more exact. The crucial prob-

TABLE 7-2

	Dates Derived from Text	Rabbinical Tradition
1. Abram born	1948	
2. Ishmael born		2035
3. Isaac born	2048	
4. Jacob born (also Esau)	2108	
5. Abraham dies	(2123)	
6. Esau marries (first 2 wives)	2149	
7. Isaac's Blessing	?	2171
8. Esau's third marriage	?	2171
9. Ishmael dies		2171
10. Jacob leaves Eber		2185
11. Jacob arrives chez Laban	2185	
12. Eber dies	(2187)	2187
13. Reuben is born (1) (to Leah)	2188	
14. Simeon is born (2) (to Leah)	2189	
15. Levi is born (3) (to Leah)	2190	
16. Judah is born (4) (to Leah)	2191	
17. Dan is born (5) (to Bilhah)	2192	
18. Naphtali is born (6) (to Bilhah)	2193	
19. Gad is born (7) (to Zilpah)	2194	
20. Asher is born (8) (to Zilpah)	2195	
21. Issachar is born (9) (to Leah)	2196	
22. Zebulon is born (10) (to Leah)	2197	
23. Dinah is born (11) (to Leah)	2198	
24. Joseph is born (12) (to Rachel)	2199	
25. Jacob leaves Laban	2205	
26. Joseph is sold	2216	
27. Isaac dies	(2228)	
28. Joseph becomes viceroy	2229	
29. Jacob comes to Egypt	2238	
30. Jacob dies	2255	

lem is that, since the last notice before Isaac's blessing of his sons is that of Esau's marriages at the age of forty (item 6), we have a period of thirty-six years between that date and the year of Jacob's arrival at Padan Aram. If the Blessing occurred in 2149—and Jacob's flight from home a few days after it is a narrative necessity—where did Jacob spend those thirty-six years? The alternative—that the Blessing occurred in 2185—would seem an acceptable one, indeed the acceptable one, were it not for two notices that I had ignored, but which the rabbis had not. One is that Esau takes a third wife, the daughter of Uncle Ishmael, immediately after Jacob is sent packing northward to Uncle Laban on the pretext that otherwise he might follow brother Esau's example and take a Hittite wife (27:46–28:9). A second notice is the gratuitous detail of Ishmael's death at the age of 137 (25:17). This detail, coming at the end of Ishmael's descendant clans, is—for example—without correspondence for Esau in the listing of his tribal and clan descendants in Chapter 36. A second gratuitous detail noted by the rabbis is the identification of Ishmael's daughter, taken in marriage by Esau, as being the sister of her eldest brother Nebaioth (28:9). Let us now review the rabbinic account in Bab. Tal. *Megillah* 17a (the Talmud speaks only in terms of age; I will provide the year from creation in parentheses, as well as chapter and verse in Genesis):

> Why does Scripture give us the years of Ishmael's life? We are told that Ishmael was 14 years older than Isaac, in that Abram was 86 when Hagar bore Ishmael (16:16) and 100 when Isaac was born (21:5). Since Isaac was 60 years old when the twins were born (25:26), Ishmael was then 74. Inasmuch as he died at the age of 137 (25:17), he had 63 years to go. A tradition is then cited that Jacob was 63 years old when his father blessed him. (That year of the Blessing coincides then with the year of Ishmael's death, 2171.) [Whence, now, the tradition of the year of the Blessing?] We are told that [in the year of the Blessing] Esau took Ishmael's daughter Mahalath, she being the sister of Nebaioth (28:6–9). Why this mention of her father's eldest son and the unnecessary reminder that he was her brother? The answer is that Esau proposed the marriage to Ishmael who agreed to affiance her to his nephew. When the time came to follow up the betrothal with the consummating marriage, Ishmael had died and Nebaioth (now head of the family) gave her in marriage.
>
> Jacob was with Laban 14 years when Joseph was born (30:25). If we add 63 (Jacob's age in the year of Blessing) to this 14(th year of residence with Laban) we get 77. Joseph was 30 when he became viceroy (41:46). 77 + 30 = 107. Add 9 to this total—7 years of plenty and 2 years of famine when Jacob came to Egypt (45:6)—and you have 116 as Jacob's age when he came to Egypt. But his age that year is explicitly given as 130 (47:9). We therefore have 14 years to account for, between the year of Blessing (2171), [which was the year of departure from home] and his arrival at Uncle Laban's in Padan Aram. He spent those years with grandfather (in the 8th generation) Eber. As we have been taught: Two years after Jacob left for Aram Naharaim, Eber died. [That year—see the chart in Table 7-2—was 2187, two years after Jacob's arrival, 2185.)[17] This jibes with another tradition—that Jacob (63 when blessed) was 77 when he stood by the well near Haran (chapter 29).

So much for the rabbinic tradition. It answers all the questions. It explains the reason for two seemingly pointless dates and one pointless kinship explication. If we do not, for all this, find it convincing (or even persuasive), it stands as a challenge for us to better. If we do find it plausible, we might wonder: Did the rabbis receive the sacred scripts together with a complementing oral commentary? Or did they too make inferences after the closest of readings, readings that—if not informed by a consciously detailed poetical methodology—were at the least based on an assumption of the unity and thrift of Scripture's formulations?

HOW FOUR HUNDRED YEARS CAN EQUAL FOUR GENERATIONS

In the treatment of the Covenant between the Parts (Genesis 15), I deferred consideration of YHWH's warning to Abram that the fulfillment of the promise of felicity entailed a dread period of suffering for his posterity. For four hundred years they will be aliens "in a land not their own"—will be subject for those long four centuries to degrading servitude. YHWH will, however, pass judgment on the oppressing host population, and "the fourth generation [of Abram's posterity] will return hither." The word *dōr* "generation" may be a referent for twenty years (from birth to mature nubility) or for the seventy years of a normal life-span; not, however, for one hundred years. Hence the problem of squaring four hundred years with a return to Canaan in or by the fourth generation, a problem that has never been satisfactorily resolved. Another outstanding problem in connection with this number, four hundred years, is that it is discrepant with Exodus 12 where, in a pointedly redundant repetition, the sojourn in Egypt is given as 430 years:

(40) The stay **now** of the Israelites which they stayed in Egypt was 430 years.) (41) At the end of 430 years—yes it was at this exact time—did all of YHWH's hosts make exit from the land of Egypt. (Exodus 12:40–41)

I will tend to this second problem, it being the easier of the two, first; but both problems require me to reproduce a number of significant dates from table 7-2, with the addition of a last item, the date for Joseph's death, the basis for which is provided in Genesis 50:22, the years of Joseph's lifetime:

2108 Jacob is born.
2199 Joseph is born.
2216 Joseph is sold.
2229 Joseph becomes viceroy.
2238 Jacob and his sons come to Egypt.
2255 Jacob dies.
2309 Joseph dies.

The answer to the second question, the discrepancy between the four hundred years of Genesis 15 and the 430 years of Exodus 12:40–41, is that there is no discrepancy at all. The number four hundred refers explicitly to the period of servitude, the number 430 refers to the number of years of the Egyptian sojourn. Thus the date of the exodus, 430 years after Jacob's arrival in Egypt, is 2668. The figure of four hundred years for the period of servitude, however, makes it possible to date the beginning of that oppression, thirty years after Jacob's arrival in Egypt, to the year 2268, thirteen years after Jacob's death.

Joseph was then sixty-nine years old and would live another forty-one years, during which he would witness the evil consequences of his brothers' having sold him into slavery; his brother Levi, who—as we have seen—was eleven years older than Joseph and who died at the age of 137, would witness this retribution for fifty-seven years. That this is built into the narrative plot is confirmed by two notices. In Chapter 49 we are told of Jacob's deathbed wish to be buried in the ancestral cave in Machpelah field. More than half of the following chapter is devoted to the fulfillment of that wish, with Pharaoh himself giving Joseph and his brethren leave to be part of the burial cortege. Joseph himself is denied similar honors, as surely as he would have welcomed them. When in 50:24 he addresses his brothers, he breaks off his words in mid-sentence, as if—to conform to the classic definition of aposiopesis—reluctant to express his thought: "I am about to die—and may God take note of you, and bring you up from *this* land, to the land He swore to Abraham, to Isaac, to Jacob." The next verse continues: "Thus did Joseph [in effect] adjure the Israelites, '[When] God takes note of you, then you bring up my bones from this _____ ' ". The reluctance to name the land once hospitable, now hateful; the reluctance to complete the thought or to make explicit the adjuration—for the Israelites could hardly bring up the bones of all their ancestors who died in Egypt—

all point to the meaning of Exod. 1:8, normally rendered, "A new king arose over Egypt who did not know Joseph." The verb *yd* "to have experience of, to come to know" also connotes "to acknowledge, know one's worth, give preferment to." And this new king brought Joseph's preferment to an end.

The rabbis, having worked out the biblical chronology as we have done, were aware of this meaning, of the sons of Jacob living to experience the consequence of their dreadful rivalry. What, to the best of my knowledge, has not been pointed out is the significance of Joseph's petition to the Pharaoh, whom he will—according to our calculations—probably serve for another thirteen years. In asking permission to bury his father in Canaan, Joseph says, "Let me, pray, go up and bury my father, whereafter *I shall return*." The italics, needless to say, are ours. Pharaoh gives him leave—in the singular—to go up. But the next verse informs us that "When Joseph went up to bury his father, there went up with him all of Pharaoh's courtiers, the elders (senators, nobles) of his palace and all the elders of the land of Egypt." After a verse (8) in hypotactic formulation, the narrator continues, "And there went up with him even horse-and-chariotry, so that the army [*lit.*, "encampment"] was enormous." The hypotactic verse 8 reads, "as well as the whole family of Joseph and his brothers, that is his father's entire family—only their *young children, flocks and herds* did they leave behind in the Goshen territory." Now these two classes of entities, human young (*tap*) and livestock, figure twice in Exodus 10 in Pharaoh's vacillating bargaining with Moses as to what hostages Israel is to leave behind in Egypt as surety for their return from their wilderness worship-site. It would seem then from all the above that the new king who ended Joseph's preferment had already come to the throne by the year 2255 when Jacob died. Joseph may already have yielded his vice-gerent's sceptre some thirteen years before this Pharaoh initiated the oppression. Whether he did or did not do so is, however, not critical. What is clear from the texts, narrative and structure, is that the young and cattle of Jacob's children were held hostage for the return of the brothers to Egypt, and that the Egyptian army, which accompanied them to their father's burial-site, was more warden than honor guard.[18]

FOR THE RESOLUTION OF the problem of four generations equivalent to four hundred years, we shall have to have recourse to a genealogical passage, Exodus 6:14–26, which is strange in itself, and strange for its apparently purposeless interruption of narrative flow. It begins with an announcement that what follows are the principal clan's (*beit ᵃbōt*, resumptively referred to as *mišpāhōt* "families") and then lists for the Reubenites the same four names as in Genesis 46:9; then for the Simeonites the same six names as in Genesis 46:10; then for the Levites, the same three names as in Genesis 46:11. But unlike the genealogy in Genesis 46, this list never goes on to the lines of Judah and the other sons of Israel. What follows is the lifetime of Levi (127 years), and the descendants for a few generations of Levi's three sons. In respect to two of Levi's descendants, their lifetimes are also given: Kehath, middle son of Levi, lived 133 years, and Amram, son of Kehath, lived 137 years.

The data of this register appear in figure 7-4. (For reasons that will appear later, the line of Levi has been supplemented with a single branch of the line of Judah, one that culminates in Elisheba who, according to Exodus 6:23, became wife to Aaron.)

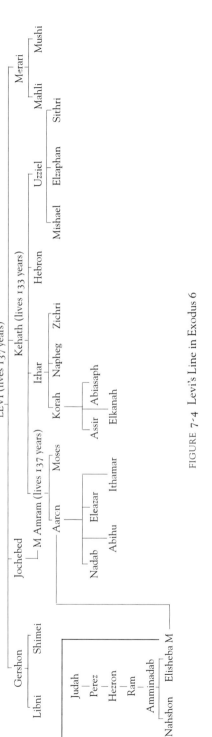

FIGURE 7-4 Levi's Line in Exodus 6

If we begin the count of the generations subject to servitude with that of Levi's children, then, the third generation—that of his great-grandchildren—is the generation of Moses and Aaron, which died out in the wilderness. The following generation, that of Aaron's son and successor Eleazar, is the fourth generation that did enter Canaan!

As for the lifetimes given for Levi, Kohath, and Amram—137, 133, and 137, respectively—these add up to 407 years. As we have seen (table 7-2), Joseph—born in Jacob's fourteenth year with Laban—is the twelfth child born to Jacob. Levi, the third born, would have been eleven years older than Joseph, which would have him fifty years old when he brought his family to Egypt. In counting the years of Israelitic residence in Egypt, we should have to subtract these fifty years from the total of 407, as also a year or two from the lifetime of Kehath, inasmuch as he and his younger brother Merari were among those who came to Egypt with their father (Genesis 46:8–11). This would reduce our total to 356. Add the eighty years of Moses' age in the year of the exodus (Exodus 7:7), and our total is 436 years; that is, the 430 years of residence in Egypt with six years to spare. This margin of six years is, to be sure, a very narrow one, for if Kehath's fourth son Uzziel were born posthumously, the eldest, Amram, could only have been sired three years earlier; that would allow then for Amram himself to sire Moses in his last year, and Aaron some two years before his death. This is close figuring to be sure, but it does allow for the 430 years of residence in Egypt (along with the promised return of "the fourth generation").

Had the biblical author not given us these chronological notices, we should hardly have missed them. Had he foreseen the conclusions of source-criticism, he might have scattered these notices across Genesis and Exodus in order to fortify an argument (such as ours) for poetic consistency and unity of authorship. Since such a motivation is less than likely, we have to ask again: Why the chronology? And, if chronology, why such close figuring? The answer lies in the nature and character of our author's purposes in narrative and the strategies he deploys to these ends. His purposes are to show, or intimate, the ways of God with the world of men, particularly the ways of YHWH with the children of Israel, and the ways of men, particularly the chosen seed of Abraham, with the God with whom they covenant, YHWH. What elements he drew for his historical fiction (or is it fictional history?) from a received tradition, what elements were his figments alone, we shall for the most part never know. But where is the loss? The truths he preaches through the norms he teaches and the tales he tells are the truths of metaphor and metaphysics, and not the facts of annals or arithmetic. And his wondrous imagination allows him to point to large generalizations and high levels of abstraction, even as he can marshal numbers: adding and subtracting ages, plotting births and deaths in calendrical succession, sometimes mundane and otiose, sometimes of fantastic coincidence, and well-nigh incredible in terms of statistical probability. Such, I believe, is the key to the playfulness of matching four generations with 430 years, when he well could have added generations or lengthened lifetimes so as not to require a father and son to produce their posterity each in the last three years of a lifetime that began more than 130 years before. But, as we shall see, even this drollery is a continuation of a theme that begins much earlier: how the promised progeny arrives

TABLE 7-3 From Entry to Exodus

Col. 1	Col. 2	Col. 3	Col. 4	Col. 5	Col. 6
1. 2188	Levi is born.	Levi			
2. 2199	Joseph is born.				
3. 2239	Joseph becomes viceroy.				
4. 2235	Levi sires Gershon.	50 years			Inset
5. 2236	Levi sires Kehath.		Kehath		87
6. 2237	Levi sires Merari.				131
7. 2238	Israelites come to Egypt.				133
	Among them Levi.				+ 79
8. 2255	A new Pharaoh (?). Jacob dies.				430
9. 2268	The oppression begins.	87 years			
10. 2309	Joseph dies.		131 yrs.		
11. 2325	Levi dies.				
12. 2365	Kehath sires Amram.			Amram	
13. 2366	Kehath sires Izhar.				
14. 2367	Kehath sires Hebron.				
15. 2368	Kehath sires Uzziel.				
16. 2369	Kehath dies.				
17. 2498	Amram sires Aaron.			133 yrs.	
18. 2501	Amram sires Moses				Moses
19. 2502	Amram dies.				
20. 2581	Moses is 80? Year of exodus?				
21. 2668	Year of Exodus!!!!				

just when despair seems justified, and how fruitful in old age is the line of those of YHWH blessed.[19]

Let us note the following about the dates and the count in table 7-3.

Item 1: In table 7-2 I listed 2190 as Levi's birth date, having worked backward a year at a time from Joseph's birth in the fourteenth year of Jacob's stay with Laban. It will be recalled that twelve children were sired by Jacob in fourteen years. A more reasonable distribution, however, beginning with Jacob's arrival in Padan-Aram in 2185 and allowing an average interval of fourteen months between the births, would have the third son, Levi, born in 2188.

Items 6 and 7: Genesis 46:8 begins the list of the sixty-six children and grandchildren who came to Egypt in 2238. Among them are Levi's three sons. Allowing for the birth of the youngest, Merari, in the previous year (2237), I assigned the birth of Kehath to the year before that.

Columns 3 and 4: Since Levi was fifty in 2038 and lived to the age of 137, his residence in Egypt totaled eighty-seven years. Kehath, arriving in Egypt at the age of two, and attaining 133 years, his residence in Egypt was 131 years.

Items 12–16: I assigned the year before Kehath's death as the birth year for his youngest son Uzziel, and worked back one year at a time to Amram's birth in 2365, four years before his father's death.

Column 5: Since these four years of Amram's life overlap the last four years of Kehath's residence in Egypt, only 133 of his 137 years are counted toward the total of generational years of Egyptian residence.

Column 6: A similar overlap of one year of the lifetimes of Amram and Moses, cf. Items 18 and 19, reduces the residence count of Moses in his eightieth year to seventy-nine years.

The total of these years of residence was, in the rough estimate I made earlier, seen to be 430 plus six years to spare, in keeping with the numbers of years of that residence in Genesis 15:13 (four hundred years of oppression, thirty years—implicit—before that) and in Exodus 12:40–41. The finer working out of the genealogical scheme in figure 7-4, together with the extrapolation of birthyears from the chronological information in that genealogical list in Table 7-3 now gives us exactly 430 years as shown in that figure's Inset.

The rub, however, comes in Item 20. For the birthdate of Moses in the year 2501 makes him eighty years old in the year 2581, whereas Exodus 7:7 explicitly makes him eighty years old in the year of the exodus. And that year, 430 years after the entry into Egypt in 2238, must be 2668. The discrepancy in dates, the difference between 2668 and 2581, is eighty-seven years. If we look down the vertical columns we find that number in column 3, the number of years of Levi's residence in Egypt. And if we look right to column 4, we see that these eighty-seven years overlap the 131 years of Kehath in Egypt, an overlap for which I did not allow. The total residence in Egypt, according to table 7-3, based on the data in Exodus 6, is 430 minus eighty-seven, or 343.

The question before us now is whether the biblical author made the same mistake that I did in my initial calculations, a possibility made plausible by the observation that—to the best of my knowledge—no commentator has caught up with his error, or whether his calculations are intentional; which is to say, that he deliberately manipulated his persons and figures so as to leave us with the impression that the four generations and four hundred years of oppression (plus thirty years of privileged guest status) could be fitted together, when he knew full well that they could not. And if the latter, why would he want to do such a thing?

On the side of the author's intentional deployment of a mathematical trap is the accumulated evidence, reflected in the various figures and our discussions centering on them, that the author had a precise control of the arithmetic processes of addition and subtraction. I noted in my earlier discussion of figure 7-3 that the metaphoric message of the calculations behind this Figure 7-3 is embodied in the requirement that Kehath and Amram both sire sons beyond the age of 130, thus exceeding the wondrous grace of God in the instance of Abraham's siring Isaac at the age of one hundred. (But not exceeding Abraham's continuing virility, for whereas Amram sired Moses at the age of 136, Abraham—who was 137 when Sarah dies [23:1]—took another wife after Sarah's death and sired upon her six additional sons [25:1–5].)

An additional pointer to the (hyperbolic) metaphor of fecundity in old age is the notice in the genealogy in Exodus 6 that Amram took as wife Jochebed *dōdātō* "his aunt." Now while it is possible to argue that *dōdā* may be a metonym for a close relative, not necessarily an aunt, the context—which includes the detail that Aaron married the sister of Nahshon b. Aminadab (tribal head of Judah)—would seem to indicate that if she were a cousin, we would be told whether she was daughter of Gershon or Merari. Moses' parents are first introduced, without names, in Exodus 2:1: "A certain man of Levi's family went and took to wife the daughter of Levi." Should we be inclined to see a metonym also in the word *bat* "daughter," the third (and seemingly superfluous) notice of the parents of Miriam, Aaron, and Moses in Numbers 26:59 is doubly explicit: "Now the name of Amram's wife was Jochebed, the daughter of Levi, who was born to Levi in Egypt." Assuming the latest possible date (short of a posthumous one) for Jochebed's birth, in the year 2325 when Levi died, Jochebed was forty years older than her husband. That would make her 176 in the year that she bore Moses. (And Sarah thought it past belief to bear a child at ninety by a husband aged one hundred!)

Further, and perhaps conclusive, argument in favor of our author's intention to make 343 years look like 430—at first blush, so to speak—is this consideration: Having determined to make 430 years congruent with four generations, and feeling free to have fathers siring sons in advanced old age (and a mother bearing one at an even more advanced age), he could have done so without the erroneous overlap of eighty-seven years. There is no compelling reason for Levi's sons to be born before the entry to Egypt. If Kehath, for example, were born two years before Levi's death, along the patterns of siring by Kehath and Amram, there would be only thirty-seven years to account for, a number easily achievable by lengthening each of these patriarch's lives by twelve or thirteen years.

The question before us then is why? Why does the biblical author play this number game, almost a matching of wits with the reader, in which neither gains by winning and neither gains by losing? If the reader does not see through to the mistake, he can still see the vindication of Genesis 15 and the metaphor for God's grace to the line of Levi; the author has made his point, but has gained nothing except a superior smile at his reader's ineptitude for arithmetic. If the reader does penetrate to the error, Genesis 15 remains a puzzle, and he marvels at the author's lame attempt to solve it; in the process he may lose sight of the metaphor as well, and so he wins nothing by his acuity, and the author loses perhaps a little of the reader's respect for his ingenuity.

The answer must lie in the author's consciousness of the various levels of readership in his audience. The most literal-minded will accept the genealogy and the chronology, along with God's forewarning to Abraham, as simply a narrative of what happened—that is, history—and will not trouble about the numbers one way or another. The Israelites were fated to spend four hundred years in Egyptian subjugation for one or more good reasons (explicit or implied in various Scriptural contexts). And so they did spend them until God redeemed his promise to the ancestors. The more careful reader, trusting in the depths of meaning with which all the inspired text is pregnant, or seeking to divine the purposes of a deeply serious preacher who works through artful narration, will seek hints and clues in seeming redundancies, or inconsistencies, or contradictions, or otiose details. He will follow the spoor of one plot line, into a tangle with another plot line, and track the second back until he comes upon a crux where it intersects with the early stages of the first. He will take every detail of genealogy and chronology seriously—not as facts of history, but as facts of a purposeful art—and, when these details become overwhelming, attempt to plot them on a graph to see how these literary facts contribute to a literary pattern or structure, whose meaning is not in the verisimilitude of the details, nor in the credibility of the structure as a photograph of shapes and shadows of a once existent material monument. And as he grasps the metaphoric intent of each genealogy or collocation of genealogies, he will find again and again a discrepancy or contradiction or fantastic coincidence, unresolvable and clearly intentional, which can have had only one purpose: to remind the reader that when presented with the kind of details that most resemble the stuff of historiography, these details—like the narrative in which they are imbedded—serve the ends of theology, not of history.

We have seen this in connection with the line of Cain, who is and is not the ancestor of the human race. We have seen this in the chronological plotting of the lives of Shem and Eber so that both of them may be available to their descendant, Jacob, in the tenth or eighth generation, while the two intervening ancestors, Arpachshad and Shelah, had died scores of years before. These are but a few examples of what we have seen and of what remains to be discerned. The crucial thing to recognize is the poetical awareness—on some level of consciousness or subconsciousness—of the author that the more successful he is in his fictive or semifictive constructions, and therefore the less strain on the reader's willingness to suspend disbelief, the more likely that the reader will read literal intent on the part of the narrative's author, will indeed see him as historiographer rather than theologian, as chronicler of man's story, *history*, and not God's story, theology. Is it not true that the success of Tolstoi or Flaubert may be seen in the measure that we see them as the historians of the lives of Anna Karenina or Emma Bovary? But such success on the part of the biblical author may frustrate the critical purport of his designs: this story is not about what happened yesterday to them; it is about what is going on in your life and mine today.

In the case of our immediate context, the years between the descent to Egypt and the ascent toward the promised land, let us note that the metaphor of long-lived ancestors producing progeny in their last years is in existential contradiction with the notice that the Israelites multiplied so rapidly as to terrify the Pharaoh. For rapid reproduction requires early mating, early and continuing procreation. The force of this contradiction, however, is as nothing compared to a metaphor taken as history that runs counter to anything in our experience, even perhaps defies our capacity to imagine: the providential deposit by Deity of a single family into the midst of a mighty kingdom, where over a period of 430 years it might—despite oppression—multiply into a nation of millions who might erupt into history as the conquerors of the land scouted by a handful of ancestors; 430 years during which a national or ethnic consciousness and loyalty would be preserved without a homeland, without a political constitution, without a distinctive religion or established clergy, and—all the while—maintaining tribal and clan divisions immune to assimilation to one another or to the native population.

PLAYING THE BIBLE'S NUMBER GAME: ANOTHER SOLUTION

In the discussion just concluded, the solution to the problem of four hundred years = four generations led to an arithmetic contradiction as to the date of the exodus, and to an arithmetic calculation of an incredible age for Jochebed when she was delivered of her three famous children. That this last item did not escape the notice of the rabbis is attested by a disagreement between two commentators, Rashi and Ibn Ezra, on the credibility of Jochebed's giving birth at double the age of Mother Sarah when she was delivered of Isaac. The issue of credibility hangs not so much on the length of the years of barrenness as on that of the upstaging, so to speak, of the older matriarch by the younger. And the more sanguine of our commentators explains away this seeming absurdity by denying any upstaging at all: once Mother Sarah broke through the propagative time-barrier, the breaking of her record by Jochebed was no longer a matter of the miraculous, substantively speaking, to be sure. For those of us who yet incline to the side of incredulity, both as to the intrusion of an endogamous marriage in which bride and groom are so far apart in age and the deliberate obtrusion of a calculation that is egregiously erroneous, there is another rabbinic interpretation and calculation as to the four hundred years of servitude. The four hundred years of servitude, prophesied by God to Abram in Genesis 15, begin (according to Genesis Rab. 44, 21), not with the descent of Jacob and his children to Egypt, but with the birth of Isaac.

Given such an assumption, with Isaac born in 2048 (see table 7-2), the exodus—which is to say, the end of the oppression—must date to the year 2448. The period then between the Israelites' descent to Egypt in 2238 (see table 7-3) and the year of the exodus is only 210 years.[20] Subtracting the eighty years of Moses' age at the time of the exodus, we now have a mere 130 years over which to apportion the sirings of Amram by Kehath and of Moses by Amram. Thus, for example, if Levi sired Kehath at the age of forty-eight (2236), and Kehath sired Amram at the age of forty-five (2281), Amram would have sired Moses in the year 2368 (eighty years before the exodus) at the age of eighty-three. And if his wife Jochebed were sired by Levi in the year of his death 2325, she would have been forty-four years her husband's senior and a mere 127 when she gave birth to Moses.

Now, whereas it is easy to understand how rabbis concerned with the problem of Jochebed's breaking Sarah's record age at birthing a son might clutch at any straw to rewrite the chronology, it is not so easy to commend such desperate recourse to a modern poeticist. How could the period of Egyptian servitude announced by God to Father Abraham have been intended by him to start with the birth of Isaac, the Isaac who as may be seen in Chapter 26 never did himself enter Egypt, forbidden by God himself to do so? And, furthermore, how could the Israelite stay in Egypt, 430 years in duration according to Exodus 12:40, have started thirty years before the birth of Isaac, a date which (since Abram was seventy-five when he left Haran and one hundred when Isaac was born) is five years earlier than Abram's arrival in Canaan?

A reexamination of the relevant biblical passages will reveal, I believe, that however fanciful the implications of biblical chronology may be, however fanciful the rabbinic manipulations of that chronology, the rabbis did not cavalierly contravene the Scriptural texts and, indeed, that those texts were so formulated by their author(s) as to render the rabbinic constructions a creditable and credible option:

(13) He (/someone) said to Abram: "You are hereby put on notice that a [?] stranger/sojourner will your seed [sing.] be in a land not theirs, and they will be sub-

ject to them, and they will oppress them for 400 years. (14) Also the nation to whom they are subject do I hold in judgment—so that after this [period] they shall go free, with massive acquisitions. (15) You, for your part, however, will go to your ancestors safe and sound, receive burial in a happy old age. (16) And [as for them, your seed] the fourth generation will return hither. (Genesis 15:13–16)

The implicit subject in verse 13 is God or one of his agents. Yet the absence of an explicit subject—and we have to go back six verses for that subject, "YHWH [the god] that brought you out from Ur Kasdim"—distances the benevolent Providence of this chapter of promise from the god who must nevertheless inform Abram of the centuries of suffering that will precede the fulfillment of the promise. The use of the singular "seed" for posterity is regular, but only here does the predicate appear as *ger* "sojourner." Hence the subject "seed" can be a true (rather than a collective) singular and refer to a single descendant. This singular (i.e., both "seed" and sojourner) is therefore rather startlingly followed by "a land not theirs" rather than "a land not *his*," where the his/its could refer to either an individual or the collective posterity. I need not overemphasize the redundant nature of the phrase, namely, that a sojourner can only be that in a land not his own, for the redundancy here is quite natural. Except for one thing: the redundance is due to the pointed failure to specify the land of sojourning. And, indeed, there are two such different lands: Canaan and Egypt. And the signal that the specific land intended is Egypt only comes in the following two clauses, where the object of the first clause's verb and the subject of the second clause's verb are an indefinite *them, they* respectively. The only signal of specificity is contextual: it is only in Egypt that Abram's posterity is subject and subjected to hard treatment. If, however, we take the three words *wa᾿abādūm wᵉinnu ōtam* as parenthetic "they will be subject to them and they will oppress them," we have four hundred years of sojourning (in land or lands unspecified), and either the specific rigor of Egyptian bondage or the general condition of being vulnerable guest rather than master in one's own territory. Verse 14, on the other hand, is unambiguous in its pointing to Egypt. That God is *also* judging the oppressors points—as the rabbis were aware—to the oppression, as the price paid for the brothers' sale of Joseph (into Egyptian servitude). So also the extraction of wealth from Egypt in compensation for generations-long unpaid toil. And there is a sudden interpolation of a blessed fate for Abram in his own person, this before a reversion to the posterity that will return to Canaan in the fourth generation.

In *Toward a Grammar* we saw in a number of instances how the biblical author, dwelling on the role or function or symbolic identity of two or more personae, will (in anticipation almost of cinematic photomontage) overlay one persona over another and even that of the second over a third persona.[21] In this volume we have even more striking examples in the overlay of the identities of Terah and Abram and of Abraham and Isaac, Sarah and Rebekah. And all these are apart from the eponymous ancestor and collective ethnos or polity in such examples as Esau/Seir/Edom, Jacob/Israelites, and Israel/Jacobites. So, in the passage under discussion, the association of Abram with the seed (implicit) of Israel and dissociation from them in personal felicity, of Isaac the sojourner (like his father before and his child after him) associated as territorial alien but dissociated from his seed in respect to servitude and oppression. From the perspective of such montage-like strategies we gain a deeper appreciation of such explicit narrative details as the burial of Abraham by Ishmael and Isaac, the burial of Isaac by Esau and Jacob, even the burial of Jacob by his twelve sons, the details of the deaths and burials of Sarah and Rachel, and the failure even to mention the death of Rebekah. One begins to wonder how many details of plot and structure we have altogether missed. But let us go on to the formulation in Exodus 12 of the period of 430 years of Egyptian "residence," and the relationship of that number to the years of servitude:

> (40) The *stay/residence now* of the Israelites that they *stayed/resided* in Egypt [was in duration] 430 years. (41) It was at the close of 430 years, [yes] it was on this very day [that] all the hosts of YHWH went out/went free from the land of Egypt. (42) A night of watchkeeping [was] that for YHWH, that he might bring them out/deliver them from the land of Egypt. That [one/day]—this night—belongs to YHWH, a watchkeeping/observance [owed by] all Israelites for all their generations. (Exodus 12:40–42)

The number and variety of redundancies in these three verses would be remarkable even in a literature not unique for its economy of style. The substance of (paratactic) verse 41 is in no way different from that of (hypotactic) verse 40. Within verse 40 the verb with cognate accusative ("the residence they resided") is artificial. The 430 years of the stay in verse 40 guarantees that the going forth in verse 41 was at the end of 430 years; the second *wayehī* in 41 (note our rendering "[yes,] it was") is superfluous, and in order to find the antecedent for "this very day" we have to go back in the chapter to the "this day" in verse 14, which itself has its antecedent in verse 6 ("the 14th day of this [first] month"). And this backtracking will remind us of the iterations "on this night" (verses 8 and 12), "this day" (verses 12, 14, 17), "on this very day" (verses 17 and 51), and the "drawing forth/delivery" (verses 17 and 51), together with the characterization in both these verses of the Israelites as *ṣb't* "hosts." To these I might add the "that (night) . . . that (night) . . . this night" in verse 42, together with the repetition of *šimmūrīm*, the first time with the sense of the *safekeeping* activity on God's part with Israel as object, the second time with the annual memorial *observance* of this day owed by Israel's descendants to their deliverer.

All these redundancies in this Chapter 12 of Exodus relate directly to our three verses (40–42). The exceptionally long chapter, unquestionably constituting a pericope, contains many other repetitions, many of them redundant. While a study of these is not appropriate here, the fact of this feature is relevant to the most glaring redundancy in the entire chapter, the repetition in verses 41–42 of the 430 years of Israelite residence in Egypt. Do the many other repetitions in the surrounding text serve to concentrate the reader's attention on this particular redundancy or to distract him from it? The question, as to effect as also as to authorial design, is difficult to determine. What is certain, however, is that the close reader of Scripture—mindful of the apparent contradiction between the four hundred years prophesied in Genesis 15:13 and the 430 years on this passage in Exodus— would have expected two different notices in verses 41 and 42. One would have reference to the four hundred years of servitude, the other to the 430 years of residence. And, indeed, the frustration of that expectation is doubly highlighted: once by the sense of emancipation in the term *yṣʾ* "to go free" rather than mere directional movement "to go out;" the other is the specificity of "on this very day"—an adverbial clause without an antecedent—and provoking the question, to which "very day?" To the very day of the entry to Egypt, or of subjection to servitude? And since no other notice is given of that day, is this to imply that it was on the fourteenth day of the first month (Nisan) that Jacob crossed the boundary into Egypt, or that the Pharaonic decree of subjection was issued on that day, or perhaps both? Which is to say: such a triple coincidence of a single calendrical date for entry into Egyptian residence, entry into Egyptian servitude, and exodus from both, could only have been by providential design, as, indeed, foreshadowed in God's word to Abram in Genesis 15:13–16.

But, for all this, the textual fact remains that verses 40–41 both refer to the 430 years of residence, and neither refers to the four hundred years of servitude. For the theory of the rabbis who calculate the first year of subjection as coinciding with the birth of Isaac (and for those of us willing to entertain that as a symbolic, if literally implausible, option), verses 40–41 would seem to administer the coup de grace. For, as we saw, that option would require the entry of Abram into Egypt, thirty years before Isaac's birth, as told in Chapter 12, to have taken place five years before Abram left Haran at the age of seventy-five.

Not so! Not, that is, necessarily so. The reasoning is based on the assumption that the narrator of these histories and chronologies is both omniscient and altogether reliable. But, as Sternberg has pointed out, the narrator's perspective may often reflect God's, and therefore be impeccable, or his own, and therefore mistaken in one respect or another. We have seen how the juxtaposition of the data from the texts of Genesis 15 and Exodus 6 and 13 led to an arithmetic error of eighty-seven years, as well as a number of existential absurdities, a strategy whereby the *author* impeaches the reliability of the *narrator*, and thereby impels the rabbis to seek for an alternative way to number the years and centuries of servitude, the alternative we are in the process of examining. Is it possible that now again the narrator's reliability is undergoing impeachment? This time the discrepancy is merely a matter of five years. Simply put, how might the narrator have erred in making Abraham seventy-five years old, when all calculations require him to be only seventy years old in the year he left Haran and entered Egypt? Let us suppose that the narrator's chronology was based on a graph, like ours in table 7-1, tracing the year dates from zero of Adam's birth to 1879 for the year of Terah's birth. Extrapolating the figures from table 7-1, we have fixed dates as follows:

1878   Terah is born
1948   Abram is born. Terah is seventy.
   ?   Year of departure from Ur Kasdim.
   ?   Year of departure from Haran.
2048   Isaac is born. Abraham is one hundred.

Now let us suppose that the move of Terah's entire family from Ur to Haran occurred in the same year that Abram departed from Haran at the instance of God, leaving behind Terah (and brother Nahor). There is nothing inherently implausible in this, and the closing of the time-gap between the departure from Ur and that from Haran renders somewhat more explicable YHWH's identifying himself as the god "who brought you [Abram] out of Ur Kasdim." Let us further assume that that year of fateful departures was—on the timeline before the narrator—seventy-five years after the birth of Terah's eldest son, which is to say the year 2023. Entering this date in lines 3 and 4, we have the following timeline, totally consistent with the data before us in chapters 11 and 12:

1878   Terah is born
1948   *Abram is born.* Terah is seventy.
2023   Departure from Ur Kasdim.
2023   Departure from Haran. *Abram is seventy-five.*
2048   *Isaac is born. Abraham is one hundred.*

But, let us remember, our assumption is that not every line-event and year on our narrator's time line need have been given, as, for example, the reader is not given the year-dates in lines 3 and 4, but only the underlined description in line 4. Suppose then that the narrator's timeline did not include the underlined element in line 2, nor did it include the date or the underlined description in line 5. Line 5 then would be a logical conclusion on the part of the narrator, a fill-in—so to speak—deriving from Abraham's age. But that age, the underlined element in line 4, is a consequence of the underlined element in line 2, an element that again may have been filled in on a prior assumption, that assumption being that Abraham was Terah's firstborn; a reasonable assumption, to be sure, but nonetheless an *assumption* because it is not explicitly stated in the biblical text. This assumption is shared by a number of the ancient rabbis as expressed in two midrashim that I will cite; yet at least one of the two midrashim may be seen as expressing some dubiety about the assumption.

On the second clause in Genesis 23:2, "Abraham came to offer the funerary rites for Sarah," Midrash Rabba asks, "Whence did he come?" Rabbi Levi's answer is, "He came to Sarah from the interment of [his father] Terah." Rabbi Jose raises this objection: "But is it not the case that Terah's interment preceded Sarah's by a full two years?" Inasmuch as Abraham is ten years older than Sarah, who died at the age of 127, Abram was 137 at the time. His father, who lived 205 years and sired Abraham at the age of seventy, must have been buried when Abram was 135, two years before the death of Sarah.[22]

The other text in Midrash Rabba is a comment on Genesis 11:29, "Abraham took, and Nahor also, wives to themselves." "Abram was the elder of Nahor by a year; and Nahor was older than Haran by a year; hence Abraham was two years older than Haran. [Allow] a year for the gestation of Milcah and a year for the gestation of Iscah and lo [one finds that] Haran sired [his first] child at the age of 6. Yet Abram does not sire at all [until the age of 86 or 100]. Wondrous indeed!"[23] Thus this text too assumes Abram to be Terah's firstborn. The reasoning here is that Sarah, being ten years younger than Abraham, must have been conceived when Abraham was nine years old and Haran seven, the elder Milcah having been conceived when Haran was six. (Lot therefore was Haran's youngest child, at least eleven years younger than his uncle Abraham.

The wonder of Haran's virility at so early an age would be mitigated if Haran were the firstborn, say five years older than Abraham. For Sarah then would have been conceived when Haran was fourteen years old and Milcah when he was thirteen. The basis for the possibility that Abram was not the firstborn of Terah is 11:26: "Terah lived 70 years; he then sired Abram, and Nahor, and Haran." The question then is, in ascending or descending order? Was Abram necessarily the firstborn, the presumption as to his primogeniture being borne out by the same order of names in the resumptive hypotactic formulation of verse 27? Some may see a case for this interpretation made by the one striking parallel to 11:26. In 5:32 we read, "Noah lived 500 years old; he sired Shem, and Ham, and Japheth."

In neither case is the assumption made that the individual sired triplets. At a certain age he sired a son, then two more in years following. But the first mentioned son need not have been the first born. His priority in the listing may be due to his importance rather than age. And it is clear that both Shem and Abram were the most important of the two sets of three siblings. In the genealogical listing of Noah's sons in Chapter 10, the first verse begins pointedly with the order of Shem, Ham, and Japheth, and immediately continues with a reversal of that order, the posterity of Japheth being given first, then that of Ham, and finally that of Shem. Here, too, the order points to Shem as cynosure, for his placement as the last progenitor brings his line into narrower, more intense focus. His line is not completed in this chapter. It ends with a single branch of his line, that of Yoktan son of Eber, and breaks off another branch, Peleg son of Eber, to resume Peleg's line after the narrative of the tower of Babel. That Shem is, indeed, the eldest, seems guaranteed by the introduction of his line in 10:21, a verse that contains the somewhat puzzling characterization of Shem as "the elder brother of Japheth." This notice we have interpreted as stressing the affinity between Shem and Japheth to the exclusion of Ham. It would therefore establish the primogeniture of Shem, but would not in itself be relevant for Abram, for whom no such notice exists. An additional counter to this argument is the possibility that Shem too is the youngest of his siblings, for the syntax of the Hebrew notice does not rule out the translation of ²ḥī Yepet haggādōl by "the brother of Japheth, the eldest." If I am correct in this, I would have to conclude that the parallel formulations as to the sirings of Noah and Terah, and the ambiguity as to the rendering of Shem as the older brother of Japheth, or as the brother of the older Japheth point to these interconnections as deliberate ambiguations. Ambiguations on the part of an author who mocks the importance of chronological priority and the significance we all attach to genetic propinquity and distance, even as he seems to define historic origins with the added precision of mathematics, that adjunct of both the empirical and the social sciences so popularly treasured because its "figures never lie."[24]

Now let us examine the arithmetic implication of the assumption that Abram, the most important of Terah's sons, was also the youngest. For one thing, it would, as I have already noted, ease the perplexity occasioned by the youngest son, Haran, siring a daughter at the age of six. For another, it requires an adjustment in our timeline so that Abram is born in 1953 (when Terah is seventy-five), and enters Canaan (and Egypt) in 2023 at the age of seventy. Thus the beginning of the mōšāb "the residing" in Egypt of the Israelites coincides with Abraham's entry there. And 430 years after that residential or sojournal beginning, after four hundred years (after the birth of Isaac) of "Egyptian" subjection, the exodus takes place, in the year 2383.

IF THE MODEST SAGE Agur of Proverbs 30 had assayed a foray into literary criticism, he might have added to the four ways (or operations) that excited him to awe a fifth: the way of an author with a metaphor.

Of the structural metaphors we have been exploring—in Genesis 11, 12, and 15; in Exodus 6 and 12—we have recognized metaphor within metaphor and metaphor upon metaphor, particularly in relation to two temporal constructs, two durations: one of four hundred years, one of 430 years; one of residence, one of servitude. Two possible interpretations of this pair of constructs have been explored, each with its own strengths and each with its own problematic features. An overarching metaphor of the two pairs of constructs was seen to be the deliberate ambiguation on the author's part, involving impeachment of the narrator's reliability, yet providing clues for the reader to correct for that unreliability. In respect to the construct which orients the two durations to the descent of Jacob and his sons into Egypt, the numbers are straightforward, present no need for metaphoric interpretation, yet turn out to be ludicrously off in respect to equating four generations with four hundred years. In respect to the other construct, which orients the durations to Isaac's birth and to Abram's first descent into Egypt, only one number is problematic, that one susceptible to explanation and emendation, but these orientation points seem so bizarre as to demand a metaphoric reading and, at that, one that will strike many a reader as stretching metaphor to its breaking point. What was the "residence" of the *Israelites* in Egypt if it began with a great-grandfather whose name never became their eponym unless we admit under that rubric "the seed of Abraham" in a few poetic passages (Isaiah 41:8, Psalm 105:6); whose stay was brief, and who was—much like his Israelite descendants at the end—expelled from the land; and whose "residence" there by his seed was not resumed until 210 years after his own expulsion? What was the servitude (and to whom?) that did not include the thirty years of Abraham's life before the birth of Isaac, and—to jibe with the four hundred years of Genesis 5:13 and the 430 (minus thirty) years of Exodus 12:40–41—had to begin when Isaac drew his first breath.

Most of us who have, for the sake of a deeper understanding of the biblical experience, steeped ourselves in the history of Egypt and Mesopotamia as it reaches us through the independent writings in hieroglyphics and cuneiform, will find it hard to resist the temptation to ask how close to our own knowledge of that ancient world was the knowledge of the biblical authors. Did they know, as we do, or as we think we do, that for the greater part of that age we call "patriarchal" the greater part of the land we call Canaan (vague though its boundaries be) was for all practical purposes a fiefdom of Pharaonic hegemony? That certainly subject to that hegemony was the Philistine coastal strip, and perhaps of little interest to Egypt (as to the Mesopotamian imperialists of Genesis 14) were the highland settlements south of the Jebusite fortress (called Salem in Genesis 14)? And might the biblical author, therefore, have exploited Egyptian dominance over the larger area of the patriarchal sojournings to stretch the boundaries of his metaphors for durations of subjection and durations of residence?

Such speculation is not unreasonable, and may even prove to be instructive. Yet for my own part I must confess to a conviction that few of the ancients (and the Israelites among them) shared my own passion for historiography or my own conviction that a deeper understanding of the past may help us to avoid the pitfalls to which our unhistoriographic predecessors fell victim. As far as the biblical authors are concerned, it is the arithmetic of human experience, the rhythms of moral concern, indifference, or outrage, rather than the tides of empire or periodization of polities' preeminence, which are the determinants of human misery or felicity, frustration or fulfillment. And so it is that in their treatment of "history" these authors indulge in playfulness, whimsy, and even levity where the subject—according to our mentality—demands earnestness, sobriety, and rigorous discipline. For us history writing is least suspect when it is dry and quantitative, and elegance of style and recourse to figuration make us wonder uneasily (and perhaps rightly) what sins against unbiased research and academic objectivity are concealed by such cosmeticians of historical practice as Edward Gibbon or Thomas Babington Macaulay.

But consider how the biblical historian manages to paint a picture of an entire nation enslaved, groaning under cruel taskmasters at nigh-unbearable labor, and yet on the morrow of liberation ready to exchange freedom for a return to the spicier diet that is unobtainable in the wilderness. And what indeed was the nature of the subjection or servitude in Egypt? Chattel slavery it was not, for not only were the Israelites never reduced to the status of property, they managed to own flocks and herds, rights to the grazing grounds of the delta where they had settled, and, as in the case of sister Miriam spying on her brother's basket-boat among the bulrushes or the adult Aaron and Moses, had easy freedom of movement even near the palace precincts. The tally-masters who oversaw the corvee-labor they performed for the Pharaoh were themselves Israelites, and, until the interference of Moses and Aaron, were supplied with the material wherewithal for the construction projects assigned to them. Their good repute among their native Egyptian neighbors resulted in loans of precious raiment and gold and silver on the eve of their departure, and nothing in the parenthetic verse Exodus 12:36 suggests that the YHWH-prompted amity of Egyptian for Israelite represented an emancipation-eve conversion. And, finally, the amity that God prescribes as Israel's stance towards Egyptians, in contrast to the distance recommended between them and kindred Ammonites and Moabites, is based on the hospitality extended there to their ancestors, "for alien you were in his land."

Surely the nature and tendency, the bias and moral kerygma of such biblical literature as we are pleased to call "history" should not be considered as settled before we subject it to comparison and contrast with our own popular histories of the reception our ancestors received at the hands of the natives of the New World, and the melancholy tale of our reciprocation.

ABRAM'S ROOTS AND UPROOTINGS

Abram's Antecedents

(26) Terah lived 70 years. He sired Abram, Nahor and Haran. (27) This **now** is the story of Terah. Terah sired Abram, Nahor and Haran; Haran sired Lot. (28) But

Haran died in the lifetime of his father Terah, in his native land, in Ur of the Chaldees. (29) Abram and Nahor took wives, the name of Abram's wife Sarai, and the name of Nahor's wife Milcah, [she] daughter of Haran, father of Milcah and father [also] of Iscah. (30) Sarai was barren, child had she none. (31) Terah gathered his son Abram, and Lot son of Haran, his grandson, as well as his daughter-in-law Sarai, wife of his son Abram, and there went forth [others] with them from Ur Kasdim bound for the land of Canaan. They came as far as Haran and settled there. (32) The days of Terah were 205 years when Terah died in Haran. (Genesis 11:26–32)

Abram's Departure

(1) YHWH addressed Abram. "Betake yourself from your native land and from your father's house to the land that I shall reveal to you . . . (4) Abram went according to YHWH's address to him. Lot went with him, (Abram then being 75 years old when he left Haran). (5) Abraham gathered his wife Sarai, and his nephew Lot and all the property which they had acquired and the living creatures which they had amassed in Haran. They went forth bound for Canaan-land. They arrived in Canaan land. (Genesis 12:1, 4, 5)

The Data and the Poetic Problems

The "facts," or perhaps better, the data provided in this pericope are clear. Terah had three sons, all born to him in a city called Ur, further characterized as appertaining to a people called Kasdim in the Bible, known to us as the Chaldeans. The youngest of these sons, Haran by name, dies prematurely, leaving three orphans, one a son named Lot, and two daughters. One of these, Milcah ("Queen"), is taken to wife by her paternal uncle Nahor, the second of Terah's sons. The other daughter, Iscah, is never heard of again. For reasons unknown Terah leaves Ur bound for Canaan-land, but gets no further than the city of Haran (where he dies). Leaving behind in Ur his son Nahor and Milcah (his daughter-in-law, Heb. *kallā*), he takes with him to Haran his (firstborn?) Abram, the daughter-in-law (*kallā*) to whom Abram is married, Sarai (Heb. "Princess"), and his orphaned grandson Lot. Thus the great mystery in this familial constellation is, "Whatever happened to Iscah?" If she died unmarried and childless, why is she mentioned at all? If she was married off, by whom and to whom?

The indirection, the less than logical order of the presentation of these data, the redundancy of details, the seemingly unnecessary artlessness on the part of the narrator, combined with the never-bridged gap of an insignificant granddaughter's nameless fate, all these cry aloud for a poetic explanation. Why is Ur Kasdim, where Haran dies, characterized as his native land (*'ereṣ mōledet*), a datum provided by the context? Why are we told in verse 29 first, that Abram and Nahor married; second, the name of Abram's wife, giving her no antecedents; and third, the name of Nahor's wife together with her ancestry, but in such a way that her father is incidentally revealed as the sire of a sister? Why, since no mention is made of progeny born to Nahor and Milcah, is the barrenness of Sarai mentioned here, she identified by name alone and without reference to her status as Abram's wife? The last question in contrast to verse 31, where Terah gathers Abram, who is explicated as his son, Lot, who is explicated as both his grandson and Haran's son, and Sarai explicated as both his daughter-in-law and wife of his son, explicated as Abram! Finally, how does the narrator know that Terah's destination upon first setting out was the land of Canaan? And if this question is a silly one to ask of an omniscient narrator, why does he not tell us—since he must know this also—why Terah settled in Haran instead of pressing on to his original goal?

The Scholarly Problem as to Locale

Needless to say, none of the problems raised above are treated seriously, if at all, by the modern critical approach, which assumes historiography as the minimal intent of the biblical author(s), and seeks to isolate/separate oral traditions, written sources, and the biblical heirs of such traditions who are responsible for the various "documents" that constitute (if not most of Scripture at least) the Pentateuch. In the matter of locating the geographical origin of the patriarch's family, source-division is of no help in resolving the textual problems, and the problem of the text's historicity becomes ever knottier in proportion to the increase in our knowledge of the ancient Near East. Thus, for example, in the early years of this century, scholarship generally identified the biblical Ur (of the patriarchs) with a center of great renown, the city of Ur located on the right bank of the Euphrates about 125 miles southeast of Babylon; and the biblical city of Haran with the great commercial center of Haran in northwest Mesopotamia, situated seventy miles north of the Euphrates alongside its tributary stream, the Bali. The removal of Terah from Ur to Haran would thus have constituted quite a trek, and renders more perplexing the call of YHWH in 12:1 to Abram to leave his native land: Inasmuch as the context of 11:26–32 places Abram in Haran at the time of the call, how could the call specify the departure point as his native land, when that native land was Ur Kasdim, explicitly identified in 11:28 as *the native land* where his brother Haran died, before the removal to Haran? From a poetic perspective the repetition of *'ereṣ moledet* "native land" just five verses apart, explicitly referring to Ur Kasdim in 11:28 and implicitly referring to Haran in 12:1, would seem to be a deliberately concocted conundrum. A step in the direction of solving this puzzle is the recognition that the biblical Ur is not the renowned Ur of southern Babylonia but a yet-to-be-located site in Northwestern Mesopotamia, not far from Haran, in the general area of that city, an area that is consistently referred to in the subsequent stories of the patriarchs as Aram Naharaim (once) or Paddan Aram (ten times). The very qualification of Ur as (being in the territory) "of the Kasdim" suggests (as was long ago recognized) that the narrator is dissociating the native town of Haran and Abram and Nahor from the famous city of that name in southern Babylonia. Thus there would be no contradiction between 12:1 and 11:31, for both the birth-town of Ur-Kasdim and the nearby city of Haran where Abram is settled (according to 11:31) are included in the "native land," which Abram (in 12:1) is bidden to leave. That native territory is "Aram Naharaim," wherein according to 24:10 is located the "city of Nahor." Far more often, however, that native territory is called "Paddan Aram," and Nahor's city is, in those contexts, explicitly Haran. Were Ur-Kasdim and Haran separated by hundreds of miles, this last datum would create another problem for, as is implicit in

11:26–32, Nahor was left behind in Ur Kasdim when his father Terah and brother Abram removed to Haran. But if Ur-Kasdim is merely a suburb, so to speak, and part of Greater Haran, then no discrepancy exists in the subsequent location of Nahor in (Greater) Haran. The poetic problem would, however, remain. If Ur (of the Kasdim) never appears in a cuneiform document because it was historically assimilated to abutting Haran, why does our narrator take pains to perform the act of dissimilation? Or is it possible that Ur-Kasdim is a figment dreamed up by our narrator in the interest of a metaphor whose presence has never been suspected by readers who, taking the narrative(s) as essentially historic, would laugh to scorn the notion that a geographic datum, a place name, could have been included for reasons other than its historic existence (its existence, that is, as both place and place-name)?

The Mystery of the Missing Iscah

Before we continue our search for such a metaphor, let us address the question of the mysterious Iscah, who exists only here and only as a name. Only one possibility has been advanced that makes any sense whatsoever, one that so fine a scholar as John Skinner peremptorily dismisses:

> Of yiscā nothing is known. The Rabbinical fiction that she is Sarah under another name . . . is worthless. Ewald's conjecture that she was the wife of Lot is plausible, but baseless.[25]

Ewald's conjecture that Yiscā was the wife of Lot is truly implausible, for Yiscā like Milcā is Lot's biological sister, apparently by the same unpedigreed wife of his father Haran. A number of the peculiarities that I have noted may indicate that more serious consideration should be given to the rabbinic identification of Iscah and Sarah. One is the repetition of the names of Terah's sons in verses 26 and 27. The genealogies and chronologies of the twenty generations antecedent and subsequent to the flood are discussed above. Of direct relevance to our passage is that verse 26 follows the pattern of the preceding verses, which (beginning with verse 16) exhibit this pattern: "PN lived [to the age of] x years, whereupon he sired PN. PN lived after siring PN [an additional] y years. He sired [additional] sons and daughters [as well]." But verse 26 conforms to that pattern only in its first five words (in the Hebrew), "Terah lived [to the age of] 70 years, whereupon he sired Abram." The next words "and Nahor and Haran [as well]" mark a departure from the pattern (in which only one son is named) and that pattern is never resumed. Having thus broken with the pattern, the narrator signals the start of a new narrative with a nominal clause in hypotactic contrast to what precedes. The Hebrew word tōleḏōt denoting "births, sirings, generations" or connoting "entailments, results, events, history" is admirably suited to our narrator's requirements at this juncture, to mark the beginning of Terah's story (in contrast to his predecessors, whose only story is the name of the first born son sired), and to encapsulate his story, so to speak, in his begetting of three sons and their issue. That issue is disclosed in what at first looks like a reverse order, the siring of a son, Lot, by the youngest son, Haran; this last disclosure in a hypotactic nominal clause, parallel to the hypotactic nominal clause of father Terah's begettings.

STRUCTURES AS A BIBLICAL LITERARY PHENOMENON 349

It quickly becomes apparent, however, that there is no reversal, that is, the begettings of the youngest son preceding those of his older brothers, for his older brothers do not (at this point in the narrative) do any begettings at all. This is to say that no progeny is produced by middle brother Nahor, while the wife of (elder?) brother Abram, Sarai, is explicitly and emphatically characterized as "barren, [yes] child had she none." But this information about the (implicit) childlessness of Nahor and the (explicit) childlessness of Abram does not immediately follow the notice of Haran's siring of a son. First we are told of the death of Ḥārān-ʾăbī-Lōṭ (Haran Lot's father), this death taking place during his father's lifetime (which we would have understood from the developing context without being told) and in Ur Kasdim (which we should also have known from context), that town being charac-terized as (in?) the land of his birth (which we might also have guessed), an expli-cation of no conceivable significance for Haran, or for his father Terah, or for his son Lot. The placement of this death notice becomes quickly understandable, for the following sentence—telling us of the marriages of Abram and Nahor (two brothers who in the normal course of events would take wives before their younger brother did, and) who apparently led lives of bachelorhood until their brother's death—tells us also that the wife whom one of them took was none other than a daughter of Haran, this Haran being father of Lady Milcah (to be sure), but also of Lady Iscah.

When we are then told that Terah, on departing from Ur Kasdim, took with him his son Abram (but not his son Nahor), his grandson Lot Haranson (the only one he had), and his daughter-in-law Sarai, *wife to his son Abram* (but not his daughter-in-law Milcah, wife to his son Nahor), we are not far from divining that upon his son Haran's death, Terah took his three orphaned grandchildren in ward. His youngest grandchild, Lot, he therefore took with him to Haran; his grand-daughter Milcah he had married off to his son Nahor. But what did he do with Iscah? Or better still, why did he not marry her off to his other son, Abram, rather than let him take to wife an unpedigreed Sarai? Or if he did do just that, and his granddaughter and daughter-in-law Iscah is masked under the name Sarai, to what end is the narrator playing this game with his readers?

The answer I would suggest lies ahead in Chapter 20. There Abraham has got-ten Abimelech, king of Gerar, into trouble with God by permitting that king to take into his harem Abraham's wife Sarah, the king having been led to believe that Sarah is Abraham's sister. When Abimelech taxes Abraham with his duplicity, Abraham replies that he has not lied: "And of a truth my sister she is, my father's daughter but not my mother's daughter. And so she came to be my wife" (20:12). Now it would appear strange indeed if the narrator of 11:26, who risks redundancy to stress that Sarai is Terah's daughter-in-law, this by virtue of her being wife to Abram (which we have been told), who is Terah's son (which we have also been told), would have omitted the datum that she was also his daughter by a second wife; especially strange in view of that narrator's providing the pointless datum that Terah's son Haran had, in addition to the daughter who became his brother Nahor's wife, another daughter, never to be heard of again.

Strange as such an omission would be (and, let us remember, gapping is an es-tablished narrative strategy in Scripture) it would be stranger yet if the narrator of

Genesis 11:26–32 had made it explicit that Abram had taken to wife a half-sister, in contravention of Leviticus 18:9, which forbids marriage to a half-sister of any parentage. But is it not equally strange that Abraham confesses to that very contravention in 20:12? No, stranger yet! For Abraham seems to be confessing to incest (or what will be regarded as such in the reader's time) to escape the charge of prevarication!

All the strangenesses disappear when we realize that Abraham is telling the truth in 20:12, yet that truth does not entail Sarah's being his half-sister. Upon the death of his son Haran, as we noted earlier, Terah took his three orphaned grandchildren as wards. In more technical language he "adopted" them as his own. He married off his two granddaughters (now his "daughters") to his two sons. Thus Abram and Nahor in taking their nieces to wife are also marrying their father's "daughters," who by that technicality of adoption are also their "sisters." Sisters only on the strength of their having been adopted by paterfamilias Terah, but not by his wife, who had borne him all three sons. As for the question of why the narrator concealed Sarai's/Sarah's parentage under the cover of the name Iscah, how else might he have tucked away in Genesis 11 the clue for solving the puzzle, which comes as such a jolt to us upon first hearing in Genesis 20 Abraham's confession that his wife is also his sister?

But this is not all. Our pericope in Genesis 11 provides us with a few more clues to narratorial niceties in chapters to follow. One of them is the death of Terah in Haran at the age of 205 years. Let us cite from Skinner's commentary on Genesis the view that is generally shared in modern scholarship:

> The migration from Ur-Kasdim to Canaan is accomplished in two stages. Terah, as patriarchal head of the family, conducts the expedition as far as Haran, where he dies. The obvious implication is that after his death the journey is resumed by Abram (12:5); although [the Samaritan text] alone gives a chronology consistent with this view (v. *supra*). Nāḥor, we are left to infer, remained behind in Ur-Kasdīm; and in the subsequent narrative P (in opposition to J) seems careful to avoid any suggestion of a connexion between Nāḥōr and the city of Ḥaran.[26]

What Skinner has in mind when he asserts that only the Samaritan version accords with the view that Abram resumed the journey to Canaan after his father's death is that the Samaritan text gives Terah a lifetime of 145 years as against MT's 205 years. In dropping this matter without further consideration Skinner misses the following:

1. The discrepancy between MT and the Samaritan text is a prime example of the reasoning behind the text-critical rule *lectio difficilior praestat*. Terah was seventy years old when he sired Abram (11:26), and Abram was seventy-five years old when he left Haran. Thus Terah was 145 years old when Abram left Haran. Thus, according to MT, Terah lived another sixty years after Abram's departure. This is deemed unlikely for two reasons. First, the statement that Terah died (11:32) precedes the telling of Abram's departure from Haran. Second, why would Terah have remained behind in Haran, having set out for Canaan-land in the first place? Therefore, reasons the Samaritan editor, MT is in error on the year of Terah's death, and he corrects it so that Abram will leave Haran in the year that Terah dies.

2. The MT is not in error. The statement as to Terah's lifetime concludes his story (*tēlᵉdōt*, 11:27), and is of no relevance for the chronology of what follows. As for the perplexity of Terah's pointless abandoning of his intention to go to Canaan, in his lifetime's full vigor, this only serves to underline the perplexity of his original intention and that of his abandoning that intention inspired at Ur Kasdim, which (as we have reasoned) is so close to Haran as to be virtually assimilated to it. To this we shall return in a moment.

3. When Abram leaves Haran he takes with him—and, certainly, not without his guardian's (father's) permission—the ward of his father, Lot. This Lot, who must have been close in years to his sisters Milcah and Iscah-Sarah, is—as we are now in a position to appreciate—not only Abram's nephew but the ward he has taken over from his father and, as well, the brother of his wife Sarai. This double or triple kinship bond (with his younger brother's orphaned son, his father's adopted son, and his wife's younger brother) will then underline Abram's generosity and Lot's ingratitude when the two of them come to a parting of the ways. That parting, in Chapter 13, is ascribed to the wealth in livestock owned by both parties, and to Lot's inability or refusal to restrain his shepherds out of deference to his protector, this despite the greater security they would have enjoyed as a unit vis-à-vis the native Canaanites and Perizzites, who "were then the settled population in the land." (The preceding considerations are neither overinterpretation nor idle conjecture. The narrator has signaled us to read between the lines by referring to the Canaanites and Perizzites in 13:7—as against the Canaanites alone in 12:6—and embracing them in a singular participle *yōšeb*; in contrast to this the brothers-in-law's crowding of one another is why in 13:6 "the area would not bear their abiding together." The Hebrew for the last two words *šebet yaḥdāw* appears in the apparently pointless repetition in that same verse, "so they could not [i.e., found themselves unable to] abide together." Appearing in Deuteronomy 25:5 and Psalm 133:1 with *'aḥīm* "brothers, kinsmen" as subject, this dwelling together of brothers was recognized by Speiser[27] as an idiom for an extended family living in union, as a unit, in solidarity, often on a father's (or ancestor's) undivided estate.

The Problem of Ur Kasdim-Haran

Let us review now our argument for Ur Kasdim-Haran as twin cities, which are virtually one, both of them in what is implicitly the *native land* of father Terah. Ur Kasdim is explicitly (in) *the native land* of Haran, where he dies before his father leaves it and is implicitly (in) the land of Nahor, the brother who (implicitly) remains there when his father leaves it. Haran is implicitly (in) the native land of Abram, for it is in that town that Abram in 12:1 receives the divine call to leave his *native land* and explicitly that in 12:4, where he leaves upon receipt of the revelation. And, as we saw from the chronology, "his father's house" at Haran, which he is told to leave, would be perplexing if his father had died before Abram's leaving for Canaan, for with father dead there would be no father's house to leave in Haran, inasmuch as the rest of Terah's family is in Ur Kasdim. (Needless to say, even if Terah had died before Abram's departure, there would still be "a father's house" in Haran if it were virtually indistinguishable from brother Nahor's Ur Kas-

dim.) And Haran—in the following stories of Isaac and Jacob—is three times explicitly and thirteen times implicitly the home of Nahor, to whose family (Abram's
bēt ābī "father's house" in 24:38, 40) repair is made for suitable brides.

Now let us restate the poetic problem. In view of the above, why is the insignificant suburb, Ur Kasdim, introduced to begin with, (1) entailing Terah's and
Abram's move, (2) characterized as the *native land* of Haran Terah's son (11:28),
(3) this last seeming to clash with the identification of Abram's *native land* (12:1),
and (4) with Abram's characterization of Haran, the city of his brother Nahor, as
his own *native land* (24:38, 40)?

The solution, we propose, must lie in the only additional appearance of Ur Kasdim in the book of Genesis, in a chapter to which we give a very close reading, but
one of whose problems may be profitably treated here. In 15:7, an episode of a revelation to Abram begins, "He said to him, 'I am YHWH, [the one] who fetched you
out from Ur Kasdim, to grant to you this land, to take possession of it.'" If ever one
biblical text appeared in clear contradiction to another (or to others) it is these
words put into the mouth of YHWH himself. For if the statements in 11:27–12:5
make anything unambiguous, even at the price of repeated redundancies, it is that
YHWH did not fetch Abram out of Ur Kasdim, but out of Haran. It was father
Terah who initiated the move from Ur Kasdim in the direction of Canaan, taking
Abram along with him, and breaking off his intended itinerary in Haran; in Haran
where Abram receives the call to go on to the land "which I shall reveal to you."
And it is from Haran that Abram explicitly departs at the age of seventy-five, and
it is in Haran that Abram had amassed the treasure and the living creatures that he
took with him as he set out.

It is not only the fact of 15:7's blatant contradiction of 11:27–12:5, but the gratuitousness of the contradicting element "from Ur Kasdim" that points to its deployment here as an essential piece of the jigsaw-like puzzle of the Ur Kasdim-
Ḥaran landscape. For in the place of "Ur Kasdim" in YHWH's dialogue we might
have had "your native land" or "your father's house" or—less likely (looking forward to chapters 24-48)—"Aram-naharaim" or "Paddan Aram." Thus we must
have here a Scriptural category of poetic design, which (with a bow to Tertullian)
we may label the *quia absurdum est*: The appearance of an element pointless in itself, serving no poetic purpose in regard to plot or setting, and in a conjunction of
texts where it can only be described as egregiously dysfunctional, hence an element
that importunes us for a solution.[28]

A father, taking part of his family with him, moves from a location A (never
otherwise heard of), headed for a foreign territory B for an unguessable reason. He
interrupts his itinerary a few miles from his starting point and settles in a famed
commercial center C, which will subsequently so overcloud location A as to be referred to as the home of that part of the family that never left A. In this famous locale C, the son who has accompanied his father there, and who is to figure thereafter as the paramount heroic protagonist of our story, receives a revelation from
the Deity himself, who instructs him to leave C and make his way to territory B,
which had been his father's initial destination when he left A. Our hero obeys, and
continues the trek into territory B and even beyond it to the kingdom that became
the famed and wealthy empire at the western end of the Fertile Crescent. After

hobnobbing with royalty and surviving a contretemps there by the grace of the Deity, he returns to territory B, where he had earlier become allied with a powerful native family. From the far north, an army from the Empire of the East descends upon the royal city-states to the south of our hero's ranging grounds, to punish them for violating the terms of their vassal treaties with that Empire. Laden with spoil from the defeated cities, the imperial army returns homeward, among their captives the nephew who had accompanied our hero in his departure from C. Our hero and his native allies give pursuit to the withdrawing army, put it to rout in a night battle, and return home with all the loot and captives restored. This then is the context for another divine revelation, one in which the Deity reiterates the promise to grant the as yet unborn progeny of our hero possession of the territories of B, where he is a successful but nevertheless only recently arrived alien. But a puzzling feature of this revelational narrative is that the Deity, who had appeared to him in city C of his native land, introduces himself as the Deity who had brought him out of town A in that native land.

As we seek for some meaningful moral or lesson or kerygma in this conundrum, let us remind ourselves of the nature of this library called Scripture. It is an ideological, ideational, religious, theological, moralistic literature of preachment. And while precepts and laws and prophetic oracles and exhortations make up a significant portion of this literature, perhaps as much as two-thirds of it is in the form of story, that is, narratives, which—whatever else their content and interest—focus on aspects of the relationship between humans and God, how God reveals his will to humans, and how they respond to the revelations of that will. In short, the very question of revelation and revelations, their nature and avenues, their certainties and dubieties, are again and again at the center of so many of these narratives that feature a God who speaks, the how of his speaking, and the people whom he rarely ceases to address.

The features then that relate to the theme of revelation and response are as follows:

1. A father who leaves home A to go to land B, taking one son with him; they get as far as C, where their trip ends.
2. The son in C receives God's summons to go on to land B, where a great destiny awaits him and his descendants.
3. The son obeys, departs from C, arrives at B, where God appears again and reiterates the promise of national glory, specifying this time that land B will be the national territory of the hero's descendants.
4. After two risky adventures, in which God explicitly or implicitly acts on behalf of the hero, another revelation is vouchsafed the hero, one in which God declares himself as the one who had brought the hero forth, not from C, but from A to give him possession of land B.

The nexus of the matter lies then in some kind of identification or superimposition of son and father, in which the intention of the latter (uninspired by God) to go from A to land B is transformed by God into a command to the former to fulfil the original intent of his father. When God, in a subsequent revelation, has reference to the first one, he talks as if the command to the son to go from C to B had really been expressed in the departure (of father and son) from A with B as the(ir?)

purposed destination. The assimilation of one persona to another, or the dissimilation—so to speak—of one character into two personae, or the identification of a person or place by two different names, are so frequent an occurrence, and function so meaningfully in a variety of narrative strategies as not to require extended comment at this point.[29] But what would be the moral or kerygma of this intricate play of place names, departure points, intended or ordained destinations, and the assimilation of a father's caprice and his son's divinely inspired compulsion? The only one that I can suggest is a lesson that human beings may, in the pursuit of their private designs or hunches, initiate actions or movements that are, unbeknownst to them, parts of a much larger and purposive design, the author of which is God. Thus Terah, in heading for Canaan, is doing God's will. And, perhaps, because he fails to acknowledge God's interest in his initiatives, never manages to reach his own purposed destination while his son, who is on such intimate terms with Deity, resumes the journey at God's instance, and in reaching his destination earns the glorious destiny that God has in mind for him in the persons of his multitudinous progeny.

If the reader find himself less than impressed by this kerygmatic solution to a riddle that has been so painstakingly constructed and whose elements are spread over five (or thirty-five) chapters, he is of the same mind as I am. It is such a sense of this kerygma's lameness that sends us back to our text, to review the many peculiar problems of diction, grammar, gapping, contextual redundancies, and superfluous explications, in search for clues that we may have missed.

The following alignment of two remarkably parallel verses in the Hebrew features the following, in order to facilitate comparison and contrast: 1) literal translation; 2) linear arrangement, wherever possible, to emphasize similar formulation or identical matter; 3) the rendering in italics of material that is informationally redundant; 4) the prefixing to 12:5 of the immediately preceding verse, which renders verse 5 even more redundant:

GENESIS 11:31	GENESIS 12:(4 &) 5
	(4. Abram went as YHWH had charged him. And Lot went with him.)
Terah	Abram
took	took
Abram, *his son*, and	Sarai, *his wife*, and
Lot, *son of Haran, his grandson,* and	Lot, *his brother's son and*
Sarai, *his daughter-in-law, wife of Abram, his son,* and	
	all the property they had amassed and the creatures they had made in Haran, and
they/*there* went forth *with them*	they went forth
to go to the land of Canaan.	to go to the land of Canaan.
(They arrived in Canaan land.)	(They arrived in Canaan land.)

Inasmuch as wives are either too greatly cherished or too substantial a part of one's identity to be lightly abandoned, no one reading verse 12:4 would ever assume other than that Abram's going according to God's charge included his wife as well. Hence, the first part of verse 5 would appear to be redundant, in that Lot's accompanying Abram has just been told in verse 4. And so too the rather supererogatory notice that the patriarchal figures did not make charitable disbursement of their wealth before their emigration, and the equally supererogatory notice that as they took along their inanimate property, so did they also take the animate—the word *nepeš* "creature, animal" connoting either humans or beasts or both—which they had *made*; this last verb reinforcing the incongruity of the entire context, for human beings may acquire other creatures. They do not, even when they purposefully cohabit for reproduction, "*make* a baby."

This peculiar insertion in 12:5 is matched by an equally peculiar intrusive redundancy in 11:31. The second clauses of both verses are identical, except for the baffling addition of *tm*. This prepositional phrase is vocalized in MT as *ʾittām* "with them;" a different vocalization would yield *ōtām* "(accusative) them." Modern scholarship is agreed that this *tm* represents a textual error, and remedies it by one or another implicit emendation of the text. Thus Speiser, for example, translated the clause "they all left" and provides this note:

> MT literally "and they left with them" which is obviously in error; either, "he brought them out" (with Sam., LXX, Old Latin, Vulg.) or "he went with them" (with Syr.) which is idiomatically the same as "he took them."[30]

Interestingly, all these cited "versions"[31] testify to the presence in this Hebrew text of *tm*, the former emending the verb to a singular (transitive) hiphil with an accusative *ōtām*, and the latter to a singular intransitive with a prepositional dative *ʾittām*. (Both these changes, incidentally, are rendered dubious by the plural verb in the verse's third [and informationally redundant] clause, "and/so they arrived in Canaan land.")

Given then the testimony that the early translators had a Vorlage that did not essentially differ from MT's consonantal text, why did the original text include *tm*, which, however vocalized, is superfluous if the verb is singular, and silly if the verb is plural? Our answer is presented in the alternative translation "and there went forth with them [others]." Who then could have been these unmentioned "others" who left Ur Kasdim together with Terah and Abram and Lot and Sarai? Why, none other than Nahor (and his niece-wife, Milcah, sister of Lot and Iscah-Sarai, and like the latter, natural granddaughter and adopted daughter of Terah). Yes, Nahor, who will never again be associated with Ur Kasdim. Nahor who, with his descendant family, is located a dozen times in Paddan Aram and three times at Haran; and once has his name cited in connection with that specific settlement in Aram Naharaim, "the city of Nahor."

If that be the case, however—which is to say, if the author-narrator of this snippet of Patriarchal history wants us to divine that Nahor and his family also left Ur Kasdim with Father Terah and settled with him at Haran, there to raise the children and grandchildren, among whom will be the Rebekah who becomes wife to Isaac and the daughters of her brother Laban, who become wives to Jacob—why is the information not put forward straightforwardly? Why encode the information in a cipher? Once we ask the question in this way, we come to realize that at the heart of the code lies the cipher of the two place names, Haran and Ur Kasdim. Haran/ Ḥarranum, which is the last great stronghold of Assyria to fall to the armies that we dub Neo-Babylonian, but are known to Jeremiah as *Kasdim*; to Jeremiah who heard of Haran's fall to the Kasdim and witnessed the fall to them of Jerusalem only fiifteen years later. And Ur of the Kasdim, not the great city of Ur, which flourished as imperial city in southern Babylonia more than 1,100 years before Jeremiah's time, already a legend before the rise of the (to us) legendary Hammurabi of Babylon, but a never-heard-of settlement close enough to Haran to be, like Haran, in the area called Aram of the Two Rivers, these two streams being the Euphrates and the Baliḥ. Why then this apparent invention of a suburb of Haran proper, to be credited as the place of Abram's begetting, as the birth place abandoned by his father, yet identified by God himself as the place from which he drew him out rather than from Haran, the place where he first revealed himself to Abram? Clearly, to make Aram Naharaim the indigenous homeland of the patriarchs, yet deny to its capital, Haran, the honor or prestige of being the first patriarch's birthplace.

And this eclipsing of the historic record, so to speak, this ambiguation of names —of places and people, personalities and polities—is in keeping with the scriptural author's(/authors') attempt ever to keep his readership (or, at least, one level of that readership) from reading his story as historiography rather than as metaphor. The examples of this throughout the Hebrew Scriptures are almost too numerous to be counted. Among them, the actual mountain peak of revelation called Mount of God, Horeb, Sinai; the sacred plateau shrine identified as Jerusalem, Zion, Moriah; the ancestral lines of Mordecai and Haman; the original place names of Bethel and Hebron and Shechem, and so on; the contradictory ethnonyms and eponyms and toponyms in genealogic tables; the arcane metathetic identification of Aaron and Moses, Moses and Aaron—identification with whom or what?—at the beginning and end of Exodus 6:26 and 6:27.

Such ubiquitous reminders of the figurative, rather than literal—which is to say, historiographic—purport of biblical story are balanced by the symbolism, so frequently playful, in such names as Cain (*Qayin* = Blacksmith), Abel (*Hebel* = Windpuff), Enos (*'Enosh* = Human), Noah (*Noᵃḥ* = Ease, Relief), Abram (= High Father), Isaac (*Yiṣḥāq* = One Smiles), and Jacob (*Yaᵃqob* = Heel-dodger/Supplanter). But the deliberate repudiation of literalism in the names that figure in what appear so deceptively to be historical narratives is the more telling witness to the biblical authors' awareness that the most common expression of heresy or blasphemy is that form of idolatry which we may call historicism: the sanctification of past events, people, and places—mere meaningless data—at the expense of theology, which reads moral meaning out of and into history. Today's sophisticate will smile condescendingly at the patriot who will search out the inn where George Washington slept, or at the pietist at the peak where yet abides the keel of Noah's ark, yet stand in rapt bemusement before the pottery lamps and cruses that served our biblical ancestors to light up their darkness and store their oil. The sophistication of the biblical authors was such that they were aware, and could warn us, of the danger of knowing the spot where Moses was buried or received a revelation. They who knew what power humans attribute to the word of man, could signal to us the danger of presuming that we were privy to *the* name of God. And we, for our part, scorn such evidence by attributing to them the most absurdly childish of literalistic credulities. Consider the words put into the mouth of Moses in Deuteronomy 3, and search out the commentaries for a suggestion that Moses (or the narrator for whom he speaks) is laughing to gentle scorn the literalist argumentation of simple and sophisticate alike. Moses is bent on awing his audience with the stupendousness of their victories over the titanic Og king of Bashan, the last of the surviving Rephaites. Making mention of one border of his territory, Mt. Hermon, he breaks off his impassioned tale of victory with the aside that there are other names for this peak—the Sidonians calling it Sirion and the Amorites calling it Senir—and then goes on to cite the evidence (or is this the narrator breaking in to address his contemporary audience?) for his physical stature, "Lo his bedstead, a bedstead (made) of iron, is it not [there to be seen yet] in Rabbah of the Ammonites, nine cubits in length and four cubits in breadth, by [measure of] a hero's cubit" (3:11). Talk of a king-size bed!

Let us return now to the two verses from chapters 11 and 12, which I aligned in parallel columns a few pages back. They are preceded in the biblical text by the various notices of the begettings of Terah and his son Haran, formulated in a way to ambiguate the pedigree of the wife of Abram while specifying that of his brother Nahor, making explicit the childlessness of Sarai while leaving implicit that condition of Nahor's wife. Ambiguated also is the chronological order of the births of Terah's three sons, which makes for a chronological problem that I discussed earlier in this chapter. Perplexing also, as we have seen, is the laconic notice of Terah's removal from Ur Kasdim, a motiveless move, with a suggestion that the destination for the move was the land of Canaan. What is not explicit is whether the intentionality of that destination is in the mind of Terah, or—unbeknownst to him—only in the mind of God.

That the latter might indeed be the case in the mind of the ambiguating narrator is in the notice of the revelatory command of YHWH to Abram to leave patrimonial home in native land for a destination clearly ambiguated by "to the land I shall reveal to you" (12:1). Abram's departure for this destination in obedience to the command is then told twice, the first time in 12:4, which gives his age at the time of departure from Haran, but not with knowledge as to his destination (12:4); and then (in 12:5) with the notice that (as in the case of Terah in 11:31) the destination was the land of Canaan, but with the same abiguation as to whether Abram knew his God-chosen destination at the time of his departure.[32]

That Nahor was left behind in Ur Kasdim has been almost universally inferred from the omission of information that he too accompanied his father to Haran. But this inference, logical as it is, is neither necessary nor correct. Not correct, as is the testimony of every subsequent reference to the location of his residence. And the omission of Nahor's participation in the move from Ur Kasdim to Haran may indeed be twice rectified, once in 11:31 in "there went forth with them [others]," and again in 12:5 in "the creatures they had made in Haran." Now while every one assumes that the subject of *ʿāśū* "they had made" must be the members of Abram's party, the fact is that the only grammatical subject is Abram; the plural verb then constituting a hint that the subject of *'āśū* is the collective/plural family of Terah. The reference then in the *nepeš* "creature(s)" that Abram took with him is to exclude the brother and sister-in-law (and niece) who were *produced* not in Haran but in Ur Kasdim.

But again, why formulate the information so as to obscure what could be so obvious, and then encipher the obvious in the murk of allusive formulation? A specific, and partial, answer is that the inclusion of Lot in both 11:31 and 12:4–5 (twice), together with the informationally redundant details as to his relationship with Terah and Abram, is suggestively emphasized by the omission of Nahor (and wife) from the list of those accompanying Terah. And the placing of Lot in the list of Terah's accompaniers between Abram and Sarai rather than after Terah's (son and) son's wife Sarai (11:31), as his accompanying Uncle Abram and sister Sarai to Canaan (12:4–5), both suggest the reason for the placing of the information as to Sarai's childlessness in verse 11:30. In the face of the complex web of relationships occasioned by a father, Terah, adopting as wards the three children of his deceased son, Haran, marrying off one granddaughter (Milcah) to son Nahor and a second granddaughter Sarai to son Abram, and allowing that son Abram to take over the guardianship of his grandson as he sets out for his Heaven-determined destiny, we have apparently lost sight of the fact that Lot, the nephew of Abram by his dead brother Haran, and also the brother-in-law of Abram by virtue of being brother to Abram's niece-wife Sarai, would, by law and sentiment, be the heir-apparent of the childless couple. (And, incidentally, this adds to the picture of Lot's churlishness, content as he is to abandon his natural sister and uncle, guardian and foster or adoptive parent, to their childlessness as he sets out to aggrandize his material fortune in the lush and corrupt Edenic plain.)

The larger and overarching answer addresses the sum total of ambiguations in regard to names and relationships of personae, of places, of motivations—self-originated or Providence prompted—and how these further the purposes of the biblical narrator who invents, so to speak, the history of humankind, of one branch of humankind called Israel, relating that branch to cognate branches in terms of genetics, geographical origins, stances of amity, sympathy, and antipathy, and at the same time sends his audience signals that these structures and patterns are to be read as figurative—emblematic of the human condition and illustrative of the options open to those who share in this condition—and not as the stultifying raw data as to who came from where, produced what segment of humanity, and won or lost the favor of Providence, which is to say, of a moral Governance of humanity and its destinies, universal and particular.[33] The assimilation in verses 11:31 and 12:5 of Terah to Abram, as the assimilation of Abraham and Isaac in the narratives of the romantic triangles and the well of Beersheba, as the assimilation of father and son in the Binding of Isaac, of the personae of Moses, Elijah, and Elisha,[34] the assimilation of Adam and Seth and Noah and (the latter's son) Enos, should by now have become a metaphoric narrative pattern. Who we are (as genetic or ethnic) identities is a consideration of nugatory value as against what we are in terms of moral commitment.

As I pointed out earlier in this chapter, it is not at all clear whether Abram is the oldest or youngest or middle son of Terah, nor does it make any difference. Neither primogeniture nor autochthony, nor—for that matter—genetic provenance, ancestral virtue or vice, are determinant for the ethos an individual or a people will choose to live by and, consequently, for their felicity or misfortune. This kerygma, building slowly and surely in the narratives and structures of what we are pleased to call the Primeval History of Genesis, continuing in Abram and his seed, to Egyptian bondage and deliverance and wilderness wandering and divinely revealed structures of normative behavior in the following books of Pentateuch and Prophets, is all encapsulated in a single chapter (9) in the Book of Nehemiah, in which the faithful remnant returned to Jerusalem is urged to confess and affirm the destiny expressed in the choice—by the sole Creator and Lord of the cosmos—of an ancestor Abram calling him forth from a place called Ur Kasdim and renaming him Abraham (9:7).[35]

ABRAHAM'S REVELATIONS AND ALTARS

No figure in biblical narrative (except, perhaps Moses) is the subject of so many revelational events as is Abraham. Most of these narrative events are in connection with the development of the thematic kerygma, or a critical plot element, for the purposes of which the appearance of God to the patriarch is indispensable. Thus, for example, the narrative events treated in the Life of Abraham: The Covenant between the Parts (Ch. 15); Covenant and Circumcision (Ch. 17); The Annunciation of Isaac's Birth and the Dialogue on God's Justice (Ch. 18); and The Binding of Isaac (Ch. 22). Similarly indispensable would appear to be the revelation to Abram in Haran, which launches the patriarch upon his career:

(1) YHWH addressed Abram,
Betake yourself from your native land and your father's house
To the land I shall reveal to you.
(2) That I may make you into a great nation,
that I may bless you and make great your name.
[You,] Be a blessing—
(3) So will I bless those who [lit. bless] are good to you,
And whoever mistreats you will I damn—
And by you[r felicity] will all earth's families bless themselves. (Genesis 12:1–3)

For all its generality and its terseness (the Hebrew is shorter by 60 percent), this promise includes all the elements of subsequent promises to Abraham and Isaac, numerous progeny constituting a flourishing polity within the secure boundaries of ancestral territory.

In perplexing contrast to these revelations, significant in themselves and in the context of plot, are two revelations, both of which feature—although in different formulation—essentially the same promise of progeny and land. The fact then of these two revelations is informationally redundant. Why should God make an appearance, rather two appearances, to repeat himself? To add to our perplexity, these two revelations are arranged in association with three historically important geographic sites, at each of which Abraham builds an altar to YHWH. In addition to the lack of coordination of revelation-sites (two) and altars built (three), our attempts to arrange these pericopes according to the one number or the other are further complicated by the following two considerations: 1) one of these sites is featured twice; the first time as the place where the altar is built, but with no revelation mentioned, the second time as the place where the altar is revisited (and invocation of YHWH-name is made for the second time), this *followed* by a revelation; 2) the telling of this last incident is not in normal paratactic formulation, but in a hypotactic formulation that somehow seems to serve as bridge between what takes place at this second visit at this location and the third notice of an altar built at a third site, this last item formulated in paratactic syntax.

Let us proceed with our not altogether successful attempt to arrange these texts in quasi-episodic fashion:

A. *First Revelation (Promise) in Canaan. First Altar*

(5b) Upon this arrival in the land of Canaan, (6) Abram traversed the land until the vicinity of Shechem, to Elon Moreh. (The Canaanites were at that time [dominant] in the land.)

(7) YHWH appeared to Abram. He said, "To your seed will I give this land." He erected there an altar to YHWH [the god] who was appearing to him. (Genesis 12:5b–7)

B. *Journey South. Second Altar*

(8) From there he moved on to the hill-country to the east of Bethel. He pitched his tents with Bethel to the west and Ai to the east. There he erected an altar to YHWH. And he made invocation in YHWH-name.

(9) Abram then journeyed on, moving steadily toward the Negeb. (Genesis 12:8–9)

[First Triangle Narrative, in Egypt (Genesis 12:10–20)]

C1. *Intermezzo: Return to Bethel-Ai. Parting with Lot*

(1) Abram went up from Egypt, he and his wife and everyone his—and Lot with him—to the Negeb. (2) Abram **now** great of substance in livestock, in silver and gold.) (3) He then moved by stages from the Negeb to Bethel, to that very place where his tents were located early on, between Bethel and Ai, (4) to the site of the altar he had made there at the outset, and where [or, *there*] Abram made invocation by YHWH-name.

(5) Lot **now**, accompanying Abram, was also possessed of flocks and herds and [many] tents, (6) so that the area did not allow them to abide as a unit, their possessions so great they could not live on together, [to wit:]

(7) Quarrel arose between Abram's stockherders and Lot's stockherders (and [remember,] Canaanites and Perizzites were then inhabiting that land). (8) Abram said to Lot, "Let there be no contest between me and you, between my herders and yours, close kinsmen that we are. (9) Of a surety the whole territory lies at your disposal. Do part company with me. If to the north, I'll to the south. If to the south, I'll to the north."

(10) Raising his eyes to the horizons, Lot envisioned the entire Jordan plain, so

abundantly watered—[this] before YHWH's devastation of Sodom and Gomorrah—
like YHWH's own garden, [yes,] like the land of Egypt—[the then Jordan plain] from
Zoar onwards. (11) So Lot chose for himself the entire Jordan plain. Thus did Lot in
that time of yore set off on his own journey, the two kinsman parting company with
one another: (12) Abram **then** took up residence in Canaan-land, while Lot **then**
took up residence in the Cities of Plain. He pitched his tents all the way to Sodom—
(13) the townsmen of Sodom **now** being wicked, yes inveterate sinners against
YHWH['s will].) (Genesis 13:1–13)

C2. Second Revelation. Third Altar

(14) YHWH **now** said to Abram, after Lot's parting company with him, "Raise your
eyes to the horizons and envision from this vantage point where you are, northwards
and southwards, eastwards and westwards. (15) Verily, all the land that you envision
to you I grant, that is, to your seed enduringly. (16) Like the particles of earth shall I
make your seed: if anyone there be capable of counting earth's particles, so too will
there be taken up the sum total of your seed. (17) Come now, make your way through
the land, lengthwise and breadthwise—lo, to you I grant it."

(18) So it was that Abram pitched his tents (here and there) until he arrived and
settled at Mamre's Oaks, which is in Hebron's territory. There he built an altar to
YHWH. (Genesis 13:14–18)

Sacrifice, the ritual offering made to one's god, is the essential act and metaphor
of biblical worship. Hence the building of an altar bespeaks the worship of the
deity to whom the altar is dedicated or to whom prayer is addressed at that altar.
Worship is acknowledgment of the deity's power, and prayer—or address to the
power acknowledged—may be subsumed under two categories: petition (for favor
desired) and thanks (for favor shown).

It would appear that in Episode A, the building of the altar to YHWH, following the promise made in the revelation, bespeaks Abram's gratitude for that favor.
So too would appear to be the sense behind the building of the third altar at Hebron, that dedication following the (second) revelation and promise in Episode
C2. That leaves, for interpretation, the building of the second altar between Bethel
and Ai in Episode B. Since this altar's dedication is not preceded by a revelatory
promise, we might reasonably suppose that this altar's building bespeaks Abram's
petitioning God for the continuance of his favor. And this supposition would be
supported by the appearance here—for the first time—of the notice "and he made
invocation in YHWH-name." The point, then, of Abram's return to the Bethel-Ai
altar site is that there/where (note the ambiguity in our translation of verse 3) is
merely a reminder of his first invocation in petition (i.e., "where he had invoked
YHWH-name") or, independent of that first invocation notice, "and there he
[again] invoked in YHWH-name." Needless to say, this second invocation of his
god, preceded by the favor shown to him by YHWH in Egypt, would then bespeak
his gratitude for his deliverance and prosperity, the note on which Episode C1 begins. This now would explain the two hypotactic (syntactical) constructions in this
episode's two parts: first at the beginning of verse 5, second, at the beginning of
verse 14, both identified by the **now** in boldface.

The successful return from Egypt to Bethel-Ai is, of course, an occasion of good omen. But the very prosperity that is part of that good omen becomes the opposite when friction arises between uncle and nephew over the grazing and watering needs of their swollen livestock. The generosity of the uncle in his self-abnegating proposal to his nephew is matched by the greed of the nephew in his choice of the then-lush plain. The good omen of this fertility is then overshadowed for the reader by the notice of the sinfulness of the neighbors whom Lot has chosen, a sinfulness the reader knows as the reason for the aridity of that plain in his own time. The good omen of the plain's fertility will also be balanced by the temptation of its riches to the imperial predators from the east in Chapter 14. But for the present, Abram is settled in the less-favored but better-omened hill country around Hebron, explicitly identified as Canaan-land, while—we are thereby given to understand—the once lush, now sterile area around the Dead Sea never was envisioned as part of the land of promise reserved for Abram's Israelitic descendants.

We should remind ourselves at this point, in connection with the various structures exploited by the biblical author, how artistically they complement the ongoing narrative. Thus, for example, the insertion of the parting from Lot in hypotactic narrative style—like his central yet secondary role in Chapter 14—serves as foreground to the story of Abraham in regard to land promised to his posterity, even while Lot, as persona and ancestor of two ethnic polities to the north and east of the Dead Sea, serves as contrasting foil in terms of character, moral merit, and historical destiny. The meaningfulness of this design is all the more impressive in the context of a seemingly arbitrary jumble of peregrinations and revelations, altar erections, and invocations of Deity in Chapters 13 and 14, which—unedifying in themselves—have hitherto been explained as traditional accretions from a factually historic past. For all this, the meanings of these seemingly annalistic notices have not yet been exhausted. I will return to them at the conclusion of the next set of structures: on the digging of wells, the making of treaties, and the "etiological" tracing of a topographical name.

DIGGING WELLS IN PHILISTIA

Abraham, Philistines, and Beersheba

Episode A

(22) It was at that time that Abimelech—and Pikol his marshal—addressed Abraham as follows, "God is with you in everything that you undertake. (23) Now therefore [I ask]: Swear to me by God, herewith, that you will not deal falsely with me, with my son and with any grandson of mine. As faithfully gracious as I have been in my dealings with you, so shall you deal with me and with the land in which you have sojourned." (24) Abraham said, "I do so swear." (Genesis 21:22–24)

Episode B

(25) Abraham, **however,** did first tax Abimelech with the robbery of a certain well committed by Abimelech's minions. (26) Abimelech declared, "I had no inkling!

That anyone could have done such a thing! You, for your part, never told me; I, for mine, hear of it only now." (27) Abraham fetched cattle small and large, gave [them] over to Abimelech, and the two of them concluded a pact. (Genesis 21:25–27)

Episode C

(28) [What happened was:] Abraham set apart seven ewes from the flock. (29) Abimelech said to Abraham, "What portend these seven ewes that you have set apart?" (30) He said, "Just so—you now accept from my hand these seven ewes as token-testimony that it was I who dug this well." (31) Hence is it that that site is called Beersheba (Seven-Well/Oath-Well), which is to say, there did the two take oath.

(32) Thus it was that they concluded the pact at Beersheba. Abimelech proceeded—and Pikol his marshal also—and they returned to Philistia; (33) while he [Abraham] planted a tamarisk at Beersheba and made invocation there by YHWH-name, Deity Eternal 'el 'ōlām. (34) Abraham sojourned in Philistia many years. (Genesis 21:28–34)

The opening words of this story, an abrupt address by Abimelech to Abraham without specification of place and with a vague temporal indicator ("at that time"), requires us to backtrack in the narrative to fix these details as to the circumstance. The time is provided in the previous Chapter 21. It takes place after the birth of Isaac to Sarah and the expulsion of Hagar and Ishmael, which follows hard upon the weaning of Isaac. A clue as to the story's location is also suggested in the notice that the draining of Hagar's water-skin took place in the steppe of Beersheba (verses 14–15). Prior to this is the sister-wife imbroglio in Gerar, culminating in Abimelech's invitation to Abraham to settle anywhere in his land. Thus Abimelech's opening to Abraham is made within the territorial domain of Gerar, at or near the site of Beersheba.

Abimelech's proposal to Abraham does not relate to his immediate present nor to his private personal concern. The awareness that Abraham is God's favorite and that this protegé status is likely to be inherited by his heirs is what lies behind his concern for his own descendants. That this concern is, furthermore, not just for individual lines of posterity but for two future polities is the burden of "and with the realm in which you have been sojourning" (verse 23), and by the specification of the official accompanying him to the negotiations. This official, normally rendered "captain of his host/troops," may connote a range of responsibility not restricted to the military, inasmuch as ṣb' has the general denotation of multitude and is attested in the sense of throng, work-force, etc. The name of this official, who is assimilated grammatically into the person of Abimelech (note the singular verbs in verses 22 and 32), may therefore symbolize the populus identified with the person of the king, pī-kōl signifying literally "everybody's mouth/the voice of all." Despite these pointers to representation of two political entities, which would call for mutual oaths of nonaggression, this episode ends with Abraham's accession to the proposal: ānōkī 'iššābe'a "I, for my part, do hereby (or stand ready to, or will so) swear." Since, as we shall soon see, an oath is also (implicitly) exacted of Abimelech, the force of this conclusion is to underline the significance of Abimelech's proposal: for all that he, representing Philistia, is the dominant power, it is the future dominant power—Abraham's posterity—that is sworn not to commit aggression.

This conclusion, followed by a parenthetic clause in hypotactic construction, reveals an interesting variation on the synoptic-resumptive narrative technique, for Episode B, which is in a sense a resumptive-conclusion of Episode A, ending in the conclusion of a *bᵉrīt* "treaty" (verse 27), is as well a synoptic episode, followed by its own resumptive, Episode C. In the (resumptive-synoptic) Episode B Abimelech shows the same righteousness and generosity that characterize him in the brother-sister imbroglio in Chapter 20. His response to Abraham's complaint about the misappropriated well is a plea of guilty, mitigated by the fact of his ignorance of his minions' malfeasance. What follows is a narrational gapping. For we would expect here a response on Abraham's part as to why he had not complained earlier, and/or perhaps an offer of amends on the part of Abimelech. Instead we have a gift or payment of substantial value on the part of the plaintiff Abraham to Abimelech the defendant who is the petitioner, suing Abraham for a nonaggression pact. The payment is followed by the bottom line of Episode B (as also of Episode C) that the two parties concluded the petitioned pact. All this points to verse 28 as the beginning of a resumptive episode, in which the gap will have to be bridged.

Episode C begins with the notice of (not an indefinite but) a determined "seven ewes" set apart from the flock by Abraham; set apart, that is, from the flock of sheep and goats as well as the herd that (in verse 27) Abraham made over to Abimelech prior to the treaty's conclusion. The point of the payment of seven ewes is that Abimelech, in accepting them, is yielding something in exchange. That something is claim to the well, which according to Abraham had been "robbed," which is to say, illicitly appropriated by Abimelech's minions; a charge that Abimelech himself had conceded to be just. Why then should Abraham pay for that which both sides agree belongs to him by virtue of his enterprise? If, further, sense can be made of this seemingly supererogatory payment on Abraham's part, what is the point of the far larger payment of herd and flock from which the seven ewes had been set apart?

Perhaps a clue to the functions of the divided payment lies in the opposed implications of two notices in verses 32 and 34. In the former verse Abimelech and Pikol return "to the land of the Philistines," implying that the area that they are leaving, the vicinity of Beersheba, is not part of Philistia proper. In the latter verse, which comes after Abraham's planting of a tamarisk at Beersheba and invoking there by YHWH-name, the narrator tells us that "Abraham *sojourned* in the land of the Philistines for many days," from which we may infer that Beersheba was indeed part of Philistia proper. The solution to this seeming opposition, if not contradiction, would then lie in the two temporal levels of the narrative, the present time of Abimelech and Abraham, and the future time of their political posterities, Israel and Philistia, which is the present time of the narrator. Thus the freedom of his realm, which Abimelech grants to Abraham in 20:15, secures to the latter the benefits of any enterprise, such as the water-rights to wells of his digging, without conveying to him any land title. Abimelech's minions would thus have robbed Abraham of his rights if they had driven their own stock to the well, thereby denying the water to Abraham's stock.

The gap that we noted in Episode B, the failure of Abraham to respond to Abimelech conceding the justice of his complaint, is filled by Abimelech's acceptance of the seven-ewes payment that Abraham imposes upon him, "serving me as testimony that I dug this well." Thus the territory (*'ereṣ*) of Beersheba was, for the lifetime of Abraham and perhaps of Isaac, effectively sundered from the land (*'ereṣ*) of the Philistines, to which Abimelech and Pikol return upon the pact's conclusion. The actual title, however, was to the water-rights of Beersheba, the area itself remaining Philistine territory in which the patriarchs stayed on as sojourners. The larger part of Abraham's payment in flock and herd was in payment indeed for the land title in the future, the time of Abraham's descendants of the southern kingdom of Judah when, in the present time of the narrator, Philistia is a confederacy of five cities (not including Gerar) on a narrow coastal strip to the west of Judean Beersheba; a confederacy that constitutes no threat to its powerful neighbor to the east, and one upon whose territory neither Judah nor its sister-kingdom to the north ever encroaches.

If this interpretation of this three-episode narrative be at all persuasive, it still leaves unanswered the question of its kerygma. As a Judean story in support of its claim to hinterland territory once belonging to Philistia, it would carry no weight with putative Philistine rivals. These putative rivals in any case inhabit the cities of Ashdod, Askalon, Gaza, Gath, and Ekron, and may never have heard of a legendary Philistine capital called Gerar (a place name never appearing in Scripture outside of these early chapters of Genesis, except for a legendary area by that name, not associated with Philistia, in 2 Chronicles 14:12–14). As for serving to warn off possible Israelite or Judean encroachment, the story of an ancestral pact made with an ancient and generous royal host pales as motivation when compared to a direct divine command such as the one not to trouble the kindred peoples of Edom, Moab, and Ammon, peoples whom Israel and Judah did nonetheless force into subjugation.

Two remaining problems we shall reconsider after our treatment of the Beersheba narrative featuring Isaac. One is the naming of the town which in the time of Israel's monarchies was the last major settlement in the south before the topographical descent to the Negev wastelands. Were it not for the etiological explanations (as modern biblical scholarship characterizes such namings) in our two narratives, we would assume that Sheba', a common biblical surname, is the genitive with "well" in the construct case: thus, *Sheba's Well* along the lines of Mamre's Oaks. Our translation of the verb *qārā* as a passive (= "one called it") is in keeping with most modern translations, but it should not rule out the older renderings, "he [Abraham] named it." The problem, however, lies not in the verbal construction but in the name itself, for *šeba'* means *seven* (as in verse 20 *šeba' kᵉbāśot* "the seven ewes"), and never "oath," for which the Hebrew is *šᵉbū'ā*. Yet the point of the naming is given as "to wit, (*kī*) there the two of them took oath," this seeming to intentionally ignore the seven ewes that were a feature in the swearing-narrative.

The second problem is that in three other places (12:7, Elon Moreh/Shechem; 12:8, between Bethel and Ai; and 13:18, Mamre's Oaks/Hebron) Abraham builds an altar dedicated to (*lᵉ*) YHWH; at one of these places, between Bethel and Ai, he twice invokes in YHWH-name. Yet here Abraham "invokes in YHWH-name" but builds no altar; instead he plants a tamarisk. Why the planting of a tree in a context where we have been conditioned to anticipate the erection of an altar?

Isaac, Philistines, and Beersheba

Episode A

(12b) YHWH blessed him so that (13) that personage [Isaac] waxed great [in wealth]. He continued waxing ever greater until he was magnate indeed. (14) He owned stock of flocks and stock of herds and a great work-force so that Philistines begrudged him.

(15) **Now** all the wells which his father's minions had dug in the time of Abraham his father had Philistines stopped up, which is to say, they filled them in with earth.)

(16) Abimelech said to Isaac; "Betake yourself elsewhere—you have become much too numerous for us." (17) So Isaac departed thence, made camp in Wadi Gerar. There he settled down. (18) Isaac then dug out again the water wells which they had dug in the time of Abraham his father, and which Philistines had stopped up after Abraham's death. He gave them names like the names that his father had given them. (Genesis 26:12b–18)

Episode B

(19) As the minions of Isaac dug in the wadi they struck there a flowing spring. (20) Gerarite shepherds quarreled with Isaac's shepherds, claiming, "The water belongs to us." He named the well Wrangle for they wrangled with him. (21) They dug another well and they quarreled over it also. He named it Hostility. (22) He moved on from there, he dug yet another well, and they did not contest it, so he named it Expanse, his thought, Now indeed has YHWH given us broad expanse, that we may flourish in the land. (23) From there he moved up to Beersheba. (Genesis 26:19–23)

Episode C

(24) That night YHWH appeared to him. He said, "I am the God of your father Abraham. Be not fearful for I am with you, I shall bless you and make your posterity numerous for the sake of Abraham, my servant." (25) He built an altar there and invoked in YHWH-name, and pitched his tents there. There, Isaac's minions dug a well. (Genesis 26:24–25)

Digression

(26) Abimelech **now** went to him from Gerar—and [with him] Ahuzath his intimate and Pikol his marshal. (27) Isaac addressed them, "How comes it that you come to me a-visiting seeing it was you who rejected me and dismissed me from your company!" (28) Said they, "We came to an inescapable conclusion, that it was YHWH who was with you. Hence have we have come to propose, Let sanctions be invoked between our two parties, between us and you—that is to say, we should like to conclude a pact with you—(29) that you will not deal injuriously with us, just as we have not touched you, indeed just as we have dealt most amicably with you, sending you off safe and sound—yes, you now [clearly] blessed favorite of YHWH." (30) He treated them to a feast. They ate and drank. (31) Promptly on the morn they took oaths to one an-

other, Isaac saw them off and they parted from him safe and sound. (Genesis 26:26–31)

Episode D

(32) It was at that time that Isaac's minions came and told him about the well they had dug, announcing to him, "We have struck water!" He named it *Shib'-ā* [Seven/ Swearing], hence the town's name to this very day: Beersheba [Seven Spring / Swear Spring]. (Genesis 26:32)

This story is a continuation of Isaac's story in Gerar, under the protection of its punctilious and hospitable king Abimelech. The conclusion of that first episode is that Isaac's enterprise in the Gerar area netted him a hundredfold return. The two last words of verse 2 *wayyebārekēhū YHWH* introduce a new narrative. Due to YHWH's favor, the hero of our story becomes so rich and powerful as to give rise to envy and even misgiving on the part of many of his Philistine hosts. Three or four elements in the diction of verses 13–14 contribute to an aura of naiveté and fantasy, akin to what is achieved in English story-telling by the "Once upon a time" opening. The hero's sudden rise to wealth and power is expressed in an eight-word verse whose flavor is totally misrepresented by my translation. Featuring three occurrences of the term *gdl* "big," two occurrences of the verb *hlk* "to go," a one-word subject, one preposition, and one adverb, the flavor of the Hebrew is better captured by a literal rendering: "The man became big, he went on going bigger until so big he became indeed." The subject of the sentence is not *Isaac* (our vulnerable ancestor sojourning in lands that may someday centuries later become ours), but *the Man* and the word *'abuddā* "hacienda, that is, works, establishment" appears only once more in Scripture (and in connection with enormous quantities of livestock). The book of Job begins "A Man there was, and that Man was . . ." Along with herds and flocks, camels and asses, his estate constitutes an *'abuddā rabbā* "an extensive hacienda," so that that Man was *bigger than (gādol mi[n])* any of his ancient contemporaries (Job 1:1–3). The final element of diction is the curious grammatical fact that, alone among the many ethnic groups in Scripture, *Philistine(s)* is regularly definite, without the definite article (perhaps 97 percent of all occurrences). Thus in the matter of these Philistines, envious of Isaac in verse 14 and responsible for the stopping up of Abraham's wells in the parenthetic verse 15, the ambiguity as to definiteness serves to ambiguate the personal stance of Abimelech and that of his courtiers in respect to their inordinately prosperous guest.

Thus it is that when Abimelech in verse 16 advises Isaac that the time has come for him to leave the city of Gerar, we do not know whether he is acting under popular pressure, or possibly expressing his own lately developed rancor as well. In verse 17 Isaac leaves Gerar and encamps in Wadi Gerar, in which valley he redigs the wells first dug by his father Abraham. This last repetition of the content of parenthetic verse 15 raises two questions. First, why the repetition to begin with? And second, assuming we can come up with a reason for the repetition, why should the parenthetic notice not precede verse 17, where it would logically seem to belong? The second question is easily answered. By placing the parenthesis between the end of the (verse 14) Philistine begrudgment of Isaac's success, and (verse 16) the consequence of that envy in Abimelech's request to Isaac to leave Gerar, the narrator suggests to us that for all the friendship shown by Abimelech to Abraham and then to Isaac, the Philistine grudge dated back to Abraham's time. It further points up the nature of the Philistine affect: not fear or anxiety, but rather dog-in-the-manger envy. For the stopping up of wells expresses spite and spite alone. Otherwise one would exploit the wells for one's own benefit. When this item of information is repeated in verse 17, it is with the explication of what the reader may or may not have sensed in the parenthesis, that the filling in of the wells took place "after the death of Abraham." The reaction of (the) Philistines to Isaac's redigging of the wells is omitted (gapped) in this first episode; it will be provided in the resumptive Episode B. The synoptic Episode A ends with the enigmatic statement that, having redug the wells excavated by his father, "he gave them names *like* the names which his father had given them." The word we italicized, like, means *similar*, and not, as Speiser renders it, *the same* (names). In what ways would the names, reported in Episode B, be similar to yet not the same as the unreported names given to the wells by Abraham? And, for that matter, aside from the reported detail so cherished by the antiquarian historian, what is the purport of these names? Why have they been preserved for us? And why in the "similar" version of Isaac's and not the original one of Abraham's?

Episode B begins with verse 19's resumptions of the prior episode's verse 18, the digging of the wells—well, not quite—with the digging of the first of several wells where water was struck. Our translation *struck there a flowing spring* is a close and defensible rendering of the Hebrew, faithful to both the English and Hebrew idioms. But while an idiomatic rendering may be faithful to a/the metaphor inherent in the original idiom, it may lead us astray from another metaphoric purport in the original idiom. I hasten therefore to remind my readers that other translations, close to the literal, may open up the field of metaphoric options. The Hebrew is *wayyimṣeʿū - šām beʿer mayīm ḥayyīm*. American Standard Version reads "and found there a well of springing water;" NJPS "found there a well of spring water." Thus old and new translations agree on "find" as translation of *mṣ*, one with which we can find no fault here as long as we remember that the meaning of "find" is *to come upon* (by chance, or after search) something which is there (where it is) by chance or by choice. The English word "well" may denote a spring (welling up from a subterranean source), or it may connote a pit or hole sunk into the earth in search for water, as in the case of a dry well. One can therefore dig down until one reaches the water table, and obtain water by lowering a container by rope into that underground flow. Or one might strike a flow where the internal pressure will bring water spurting toward the surface, as in the case of an artesian well. And such a vigorous flow may be all that is intended by the Hebrew, "brimming water" as opposed to stagnant. On the other hand, *mayīm ḥayyīm*, literally "living water" or "life-giving water," may have some special signification in this context.

The claim of the Gerarite shepherds is pointedly in direct discourse; the well is not theirs, for they did no digging. But the water is theirs, which is to say that any water struck on Gerarite territory belongs to them. Such blatant denial of earnings to the laborers reverberates with the charge of Abraham to Abimelech in 21:25 that his minions had *robbed* him (*gzl*) of a *water-well*. As for the naming of this well, it points up the inanity of *etiology* as an explanatory category. No such place-name appears again, and the root of the verb from which the name is derived never appears again in Scripture. All translations of it are pure conjecture based on a sense of what might be contextually appropriate. The name of the second well derives from a root more often attested, yet still only rarely, and such renderings as our own (or others, such as Opposition, Challenge) all derive from the general assumption that *(the) Satan* means Adversary. Needless to say, no such place name appears again in Scripture. Of clear relevance to our story is the omission of any information as to the resolution of these two contests for water-rights, as also the absence of contest for the third well. The naming of this third well, featuring a well-known root, is clearly in expression of good omen, in contrast with the circumstances attending the naming of the first two wells, but this place-name is also unique. What then is the point of these unedifying particulars in the life and travels of this patriarch, whose career—as has so often been noted—is distinguished for the absence of event?

Episode B ends with the purport of Isaac's name for the third well: it is a sign of YHWH's favor and presage of a flourishing posterity. He then moves up from the Philistine littoral to the Beersheba plateau. Episode C begins with YHWH's revelation to him, apparently on the first night of his arrival there, that the presentiment he had experienced at Rehoboth was not an idle one. For the sake of "my (faithful) servant Abraham" he would continue to favor Isaac, particularly in respect to numerous progeny. Isaac then proceeds to erect at Beersheba an altar (such as Abraham had erected at Shechem, Bethel and Hebron, but—pointedly—not at Beersheba). He invokes in YHWH-name, as did Abraham before him at Beersheba (as well as at Bethel). The episode ends with Isaac's servants digging a well once again. But this theme is broken off, to be resumed in verse 32 with the announcement of water being struck there, and Isaac's naming of the spring, a name to which the settlement there in the narrator's time owes its name.

That verses 26–31 represent a digression—with the associated sense of *oddity* in respect to the composition within which it appears, hence to which it must somehow and significantly *relate*—is unquestioned. The event told in this digression is preceded by the notice that Isaac's minions' are digging a well, and it is followed by the same diggers report to Isaac that they have struck water. The oddity of this particular digression is reinforced by its content, plot, and characters almost duplicating those of the freestanding narrative, Genesis 21:22–34. The king of Gerar, Abimelech, and Pikol his marshal would appear to be the same who, having broached a nonaggression treaty to Abraham, now broach the same proposal to Abraham's son, Isaac. This, as if the treaty concluded with the father—which explicitly referred to posterity of the two parties—did not already apply to or bind Isaac. The only addition, to Abimelech's party, is an intimate associate by the name *Ahuzzath*. The meaning of this word, with an alternate feminine ending (*'ahuzzā*, see Genesis 23:20) is *land-holding, real estate ownership*, and it, therefore, reinforces the Philistine collectivity represented in the first narrative by the king and his marshal, *Pikol* "Voice of All."

In the freestanding narrative featuring Abraham, Philistine hostility seems to be almost nugatory, confined perhaps to the greed of those who had infringed on Abraham's well water unbeknownst to Abimelech. Yet a consciousness of adversarial interests may be read into Abimelech's very proposal of the nonaggression treaty. In the Isaac narrative, by contrast, the patriarch taxes the Philistines with the unfriendliness that forced his departure from the city of Gerar. And the hostility is open and explicit in the claim of the Gerarite shepherds to the water of two of the three springs dug or redug by Isaac's shepherds. Although Isaac does not bring up to Abimelech the actions of the Gerarite shepherds, hence allows for no disavowal by the king as to his sanctioning their behavior, there is no reason to involve the sovereign in the fault of his subjects. Isaac, for his part, accepts Abimelech's compliment that he is Heaven's favorite, and accedes to the petition for a nonaggression pact. He treats his visitors to a feast. On the morrow oaths are exchanged, and Isaac sees his visitors off. There may be something ironic in the concluding notion that his visitors "parted from him safe and sound" (bešālōm), corresponding to the visitors' claim that they had "seen him off safe and sound" (wannešalēḥakā bešālōm, verse 29), when he departed from Gerar. For the Isaac with whom they are treating is hardly in a position to oppose them with physical force. On the other hand, šālōm also has the sense of "amity," so the point of the second bešālōm may merely be that the guests left in a spirit of good feeling. The amicable conclusion of both narratives would seem to point to the same kerygma: the descendants of Abraham-Isaac, in secure possession of Beersheba and the wadis leading from it to the Philistine coastal plain, are by ancient treaty bound not to commit aggression against those ancient neighbors.

Militating against acceptance of this kerygmatic interpretation of these two patriarchal narratives is the mindset of the heirs of the biblical tradition (be these heirs the early rabbis or modern biblicists) on the one hand, and on the other, the likely mindset of the Israel-Judah populations that the biblical author (authors) was (were) addressing.

The heirs of the tradition are conditioned by the historical fate of the household of Israel, a history culminating in the destruction of the northern kingdom (and the "lost" ten tribes), in the destruction of the southern kingdom less than a century and a half later (and the "exile" of the Judean population), both disasters followed by the renewal of a precariously maintained priestly city-state centered on a rebuilt shrine in Jerusalem. This is to say that from the point of view of temporal hegemony, we cannot but view the history of Israel's states as a tale of defeat and failure. Far, far different was the view of the audience addressed by the first of the writing prophets, Amos. A close reexamination of, for example, Chapters 6 and 11 of this book, will show that his audience of both kingdoms were aflush with a sense of power, victory, success; and with this sense, inclined to a confidence in a stable future as surely as the present is rooted in a promise-fulfilled past. It is to counter such a rosy and smug mindset that Amos stresses the transitory nature of all polities, this before he goes on to prophesy the end of the sinful state(s), but not of the Israelite people. Unterritoried Cushites (= Midianite-like bedouin) have in the mind of YHWH, says Amos, equal status with Israelites. And the act of bringing up Israel from Egypt (not, be it noted, from Ur Kasdim or Haran) is not to be viewed as unique. For the one and the same and only god it was who fetched the (uncircumcised) Philistines from (ancestral) Crete as he did that collectivity called Aram from a far-distant Kir.

Given such a sense on the part of a polity and a populace, confident in its present well-merited success and concomitant notions such as national probity and manifest destiny, we can appreciate why a narrative warning one's own against encroaching on an ancient rival's territory should be told twice, each telling featuring the same ancestral antecedents and their respective legitimate territories.

So much for the similarities and identities in the two narratives. What of the differences? One is in the matter of the digging of wells. Abraham digs only one, that one at Beersheba.[36] This spring, its water rights contested by Abimelech's subjects, is central to the narrative, and—for all the play on the root *šb'* = seven—is cited in its sense of "swearing" in the naming of it, (seemingly by Abraham) Beersheba. In the Isaac narrative the spring at Beersheba is not at all related in terms of plot (though it is so in terms of narrative structure) to the oaths exchanged between patriarch and Philistines. As the site of the swearing between the two parties it later comes by the name Beersheba. This name, however, is not here associated with the *swearing* sense of *šb'* but with the name given to it by Isaac after the Philistines' departure, *šibā* "Seven." This cannot but point to the *seven*-sheep payment made by Abraham to Abimelech, an informational detail not to be credited to Isaac's consciousness, but provided by the narrator to the reader who *is* privy to the first narrative, and in the recesses of whose mind there still lurks the question as to the meaning of the names given by Isaac to the (redug) wells of his father, to which he "gives names *like* (but not identical with) those which his father had given them." Thus, whereas Abraham had named it *Sheba* (as in Beersheba), meaning (according to the explication in 21:31) Swearing Well, yet with an allusion to the *seven*-sheep payment, Isaac named it *Shibā* (Seven)—for reasons known to God alone—yet in doing so came so close to the name (apparently) given to it by his father!

But what is the point of this naming rigmarole? If the well had been named Beersheba by his father, then that would have been it for Isaac (and for the rest of us). But that could not have "been it" for Isaac, inasmuch as no such well existed in his time. He merely (or inadvertently) hit upon a name for a well that, unbeknownst to him, had been dug by his father, filled in by Philistines, and was thus "redug" by his own servants (inadvertently) and by Providential arrangement turned out to be the same site where both he and his father pledged nonaggression to the Philistine descendants of their legendary lord, known to the patriarchs (if not to either descendants of either or both) as Abimelech, king of Gerar.

The point of all this rigmarole is, of course, that when a narrative or a (nearly) twice-told narrative adds up to nonsense when taken as history, one must look for its meaning in terms of the fictive; ideological fiction, to be precise. And this brings us back to Isaac's redigging of his father's wells. One can no more redig filled-in wells in a wadi than one can retrace an oceanic voyage without a pilot's router. And the notice that the stopping-up of Abraham's wells took place *after his death* certifies that the father, anticipating no such meanness, would not have left a map for his son's benefit. But why does the second narrative feature such a pointless action on the part of Philistine herdsman, who—apparently—had no use for the water themselves? The answer points to another item of contradictory information in this narrative doublet. Whereas, as we saw, in the Abraham narrative the

Beersheba area lies implicitly in Philistine territory, no such territorial ownership is credited to the Philistines in the Isaac narrative. On the contrary, for all that Isaac takes up residence in Wadi Gerar, that name is no more attestation to that valley's ownership than, say, for the Ohio River valley's being the territory of the State of Ohio. Indeed, the very point of the failure of the Gerarites to contest ownership of the third well may be that Isaac has now moved beyond the ambit claimed by the Philistines. Hence, Isaac's name for the third well (Rehoboth = Expansiveness, Broad Scope). Isaac is no longer crowding or being crowded by rivals. That Isaac is now in his own uncontested territory is also borne out by his question to his Philistine visitors: "Why have you come now *to me* (in my bailiwick) when you drove me out *mēittᵉkem* "from your own jurisdiction?" So also, by the absence of any payment on his part to his Philistine contemporaries.

Assuming then (and we have no reason not to) a single narrator for both stories, we have a narrator who may be characterized as *reliably unreliable*. He is unreliable as to the historical information: in the matter of whether Beersheba did or did not in patriarchal times constitute part of Philistine territory. So too is he unreliable in tracing the name Sheba to one root or another, to one patriarch or the other, if—indeed—to either. He is, however, altogether reliable in that he takes such pains to deny the reliability of that information. Whatever was the case in that respect, the double narrative leaves no question in our (Israelitish) minds: We are solemnly bound by ancestral oath to refrain from aggression against our uncircumcised neighbors on the coast.

Why do we obtrude the detail as to circumcisional practice, a detail apparently irrelevant for our narrator himself? Just so: to remind ourselves that this detail, of a surgically unimpacted male organ, appears in narratives, not as an epithet betokening hatred, but rather contempt. It bespeaks the condescension of the insider to the outsider. But such a stance requires no concomitant sense of fear, hatred, hostility. Esau's first born son Eliphaz numbered among his sons one borne to him by a concubine. This great-grandson of Isaac, presumably circumcised in infancy, becomes—for all his insider, indeed, kindred status—inveterate foe of Israel. So too the presumably circumcised descendants of Midian, Abram's son by Keturah. Seemingly wiped out in a ḥerem-war at the behest of YHWH or Moses (see Numbers 31:1–3 and 31:44ff.), a branch of these cousins survives as implacable foes to the time of Gideon.[37] But the Philistines—despite our different perception of them—are never portrayed as vindictive, atrocity-committing enemy. As enemy of Samson (who intermarried with them), they are more victim than perpetrator. As enemy of Saul, they defeat him in fair battle. In David's time they are subdued by the king, whom they befriended when he was outlaw and fugitive from Saul. Just when in historic time their few coastal enclaves were so weak as to tempt Israelite or Judean aggression is a matter for speculation. But that such temptation was once a historic fact, and vetoed by the narrative traditions in Genesis—if not by the God of Israel himself—is the kerygmatic testimony of this narrative doublet.

I HAVE LEFT UNANSWERED an implicit problem I raised in connection with a significant difference as between the Abraham and Isaac narratives centering on Beersheba: Isaac builds one altar only, the one at Beersheba, while Abraham builds three altars, none of them at Beersheba. In connection with the altar between Bethel and Ai, we have twice the informationally redundant "and he called in YHWH-name." As if to call our attention to Abraham's planting a tamarisk at Beersheba, rather than erecting an altar there, the notice of this planting features, for a third time, the notice "and he called in YHWH-name." There must therefore be a pointed meaning to Isaac's building an altar at Beersheba, the one site out of four where Abram did not do so. And that meaning, altogether in keeping with the kerygma of the two Beersheba narratives, leaps to mind if we recall from elsewhere in Scripture a unique feature of altars built legitimately for the worship of YHWH.

Sacrifice to YHWH, even before the attempt to restrict it to the one central altar in Jerusalem (this according to biblical "historiography"), was restricted to that part of Israel's territory that—envisaged as God's original grant to the patriarchs—was sacred or pure soil. Only on such tracts might altars to YHWH be erected, not only to achieve his favor but to avoid incurring his wrath. Thus, to cite three examples antedating Jerusalem's conquest by King David: the altar for show but not for ritual practice in trans-Jordan (Joshua 22); the charge of David to Saul that his driving his loyal vassal from YHWH's *territory* (to Philistia, let us recall) is depriving YHWH of a worshiper (1 Samuel 26:18–20); and the petition of Naaman, who fills the same role for the king of Aram as did Pikol for the king of Gerar (*śar ṣᵉbā'ō*), for two mule loads of soil so that he may offer sacrifice to YHWH in Aramean territory (2 Kings 5:17).[38]

Thus, for the structurings or the patternings of altars built and not built by Abraham, of invocations of YHWH and tamarisk-planting, of wells dug by Abraham and Isaac, and an altar reared by Isaac at the one site where Abram erected none; from all this emerges the meaning of the pacts concluded at Beersheba that we have discerned hitherto. The title to the territory around Beersheba, its water-rights ceded to Abraham, remained with Philistia during Abraham's lifetime. Hence Abraham could build no altar there to YHWH, though he might (as he did) invoke there in YHWH-name, YHWH name here glossed as *'El 'ōlām* "God Eternal." The payment of flocks and herds made by Abraham to Abimelech (in addition to the seven sheep in attestation to his own rights to the water) was for title right to accrue to his posterity. The symbolism of that accrual to Abraham's progeny is thus metaphorically if not historiographically present in Beersheba's no longer constituting Gerarite territory in the lifetime of Abraham's son, Isaac, who "did build an altar there, invoking in YHWH-name, pitching there his tent." All this, let us be careful to note, in paratactically formulated verse 26:25, before the visit of the Gerarites, which begins in hypotactically formulated verse 26:26, which—had it been formulated paratactically (as, indeed, the continuing narrative is)—might have been read by us, mistakenly to be sure, as a resumptive-expansive episode.

ADDENDUM: TWO MORE GENEALOGIES AND ANOTHER NUMBERS GAME

We discussed earlier (see p. 316) the seventy names in the lines of Shem, Ham, and Japheth, the same number of names attributed to the descendants of Jacob/

Israel in Genesis 46, and the allusion to these numbers in Deuteronomy 32:8 in the Song of Moses. The pericope that contains the line of Jacob's descendants, Genesis 46:8–27, is replete with features of diction, repetition, variations on formulas, and lists of names with incongruent numbers attached to them, such as to pose a formidable challenge to the poetical critic. (Needless to say, the point of the genealogy and the numbers and the dictional and arithmetic perplexities are largely ignored by source-critics.)

I will present a translation of this pericope, and provide a graph of the genealogical tree (figure 7-5) to help the reader to retrace with me the features of a craftily designed puzzle, altogether in keeping with the playfulness that, as we have seen, characterizes the number play in three preceding sections. The stylistic features in the text upon which I will focus my attention in the following discussion will appear in italics or boldface. And the line-by-line arrangement of the verses will be such as to highlight the similarities and differences in what purports to be a genealogical table.

Superscription

(8) There *then* are the names of the *children of Israel, those arriving* in Egypt: *Jacob* and his children: (Genesis 46:8)

The Line through Leah

The firstborn of *Jacob* was Reuben.
(9) **Now** the children of Reuben were
Enoch, and Pallu, and Hezron and Carmi
(10) And the children of Simeon were
Yemuel, and Yamin, and Ohad, and Yachin, and Zohar,
and Saul son of a Canaanite woman.
(11) And the children of Levi were
Gershon, Kehath, and Merari.
(12) And the children of Judah were
Er, and Onan, and Shelah, and Perez, and Zerah.
Er and Onan died in the land of Canaan.
The children of Perez were Hezron and Hamul.
(13) And the children of Issachar were
Tola, and Puwah, and Yob, and Shimron.
(14) And the children of Zebulon were
Sered, and Elon, and Yahleel.
(15) These *the sons of Leah*, that she bore to *Jacob* in Paddan-Aram, as well as his daughter Dinah; all souls, *sons and daughters*: 33. (Genesis 46:9–15)

The Line through Zilpah

(16) And the children of Gad were
Ziphion, and Haggi, Shuni, and Ezbon, Eri, and Arodi, and Areli.
(17) And the children of Asher were
Yimnah, and Yishwa, and Yishwi, and Beriah, and *their sister Serah*. And the children of Beriah were Heber and Malchiel.

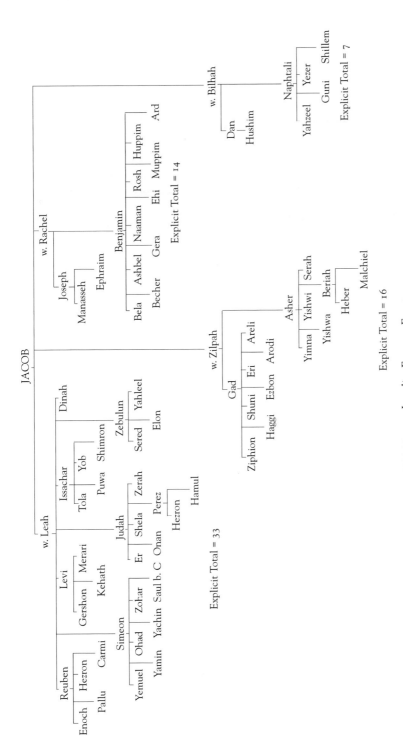

FIGURE 7-5 Israelite Entry to Egypt

(18) These the children of Zilpah, she whom Laban gave to his daughter Leah. These she bore to Jacob: 16 souls. (Genesis 46:16–18)

The Line through Rachel

(19) The sons of Rachel, *Jacob's wife* were
Joseph and Benjamin.
(20) Children were born to Joseph in the land of Egypt, [those] born to him by Asenath daughter of Poti-phera, priest of On: namely, Manasseh and Ephraim.
(21) And the children of Benjamin were
Bela, and Becher, and Ashbel, Gera and Naaman, Ehi and Rosh, Muppim and Huppim and Ard.
(22) These the children of Rachel, that were born to *Jacob*, all souls: 14. (Genesis 46:19–22)

The Line through Bilhah

(23) And the children of Dan—Hushim.
(24) And the children of Naphtali were
Yahzeel, and Guni, and Yezer, and Shillem.
(25) These the children of Bilhah, she whom Laban gave to his daughter Rachel. These she bore to *Jacob*, all souls: 7.
(26) All the souls that arrived—of *Jacob's*—in Egypt, sprung of his own loins ([that is,] excluding the wives of *Jacob's* sons), all souls: 66; (27) plus the children of Joseph that were born to him in Egypt: 2 souls; all the souls of the line (*bēt*) of *Jacob* arriving in Egypt: 70. (Genesis 46: 23–27)

Let us first note the following features of diction in respect to (1) the appearance of the two names, Israel and Jacob, for the ancestor by whose name(s) the chosen people are called; (2) the distribution of the term *bānīm*, particularly in the construct (*beē*), a term that may denote *sons, children* (i.e., both sons and daughters); *issue* (even if there is only one such); *descendants* (i.e., children and grandchildren); an ethnos or polity traced to an eponymous ancestor and expressed in English by the addition to that ancestral name of the suffix *-ite* or *-ites*; and (3) the identification of some or most of the descendants of the patriarch by the determined participle of *bō* "those arriving," either in the plural masculine (with *benē*-PN) or in the feminine singular collective with the feminine noun *nepeš* "person(s), soul(s)." Needless perhaps to say, the importance of the application of one or another denotation to these terms in the context of this pericope is due to the perplexing counts in three contexts: verse 15—the 33 descendants of Leah; verse 26—the 66 descendants of Jacob arriving in Egypt; verse 27—the total number of persons, 70, arriving in Egypt.

In the superscription in verse 8 the names to come in the following list are those of the *benē-Yiśrāʾel*, which might bear almost all the connotations in 2 above, a statement that might be made with almost equal truth if the term *benē-Yaʿqob* appeared (see 1 above). Almost, but not quite, because these *benē-Yiśrāʾel* are immediately glossed by the narrator as "those who arrived in Egypt, *Jacob and his* offspring." The patriarch in his own person might *as Jacob* (perhaps stretching a little) be included in the gentilic for the nation-yet-to be, the gentilic *bᵉnē-Yiśrā'el*, but the same cannot be said in respect to the inclusion of *Jacob* among *the issue of Jacob*. The overwhelming preponderance of the gentilic Israel/Israelite over the gentilic Jacob/Jacobite is an additional datum that supports the sense of the patriarch's personhood in the name Jacob, and of eponym in the name Israel. Such then is the reason for the presence of Jacob as person in our verses 8 (twice), 15, 18, 19, 20, 25, 26 (twice); the information in these verses being so redundant as to make us question the point of these repetitions. If the point of these is to underline the inclusion of Jacob among the "Israelites" who came to Egypt (in verse 8), we should then have to address the final appearance of the name Jacob in verse 27. Here in contrast to *lᵉYaᵃqob* "of Jacob's" we have *lebēt-Yaᵃqob* "of the house/family/line of Jacob," an expression always referring to the people or nation. It would seem then that in this verse the number 70 would be inclusive of the patriarch Jacob himself.

Now to the numbers. The listed offspring of Jacob—inclusive of sons, grandchildren, and great-grandchildren—are explicitly numbered as follows: Leah's descendants, 33; Zilpah's, 16; Rachel's, 14; and Bilhah's, 7. These numbers add up to 70, an addition that the narrator does not perform here (as he does elsewhere, see, e.g., Genesis 5). But there is, further, this peculiarity: the 33 names of Leah's children and grandchildren do not include her daughter Dinah. Thus the recapitulation in verse 15 refers to the *bᵉnē-Lēā* "sons [not children] of Leah . . . and in addition (*wᵉt*) his daughter Leah." This is immediately followed by "all souls, sons and daughters, 33." This is manifestly wrong, for the names—inclusive of Dinah—would add up to 34. (That the narrator is deliberately introducing a red herring here is attested to by the names in Asher's line. Included among the *bᵉnē* Asher is his *daughter* Serah, a name that must be included in the total given for Zilpah's descendants: 16.) Thus the only way to understand the narrator's arithmetic at this point is to read verse 15 as follows. "These the *sons* of Leah, whom she bore to Jacob in Paddan-Aram—plus his daughter Dinah—all souls, sons and daughters [except for the bracketed daughter], 33." The poetical question, then, is why the narrator proceeds in such circuitous fashion: to list 33 male names, to add a 34th name—this one a female, to announce that the sum about to be given is inclusive of both male and female, and then to provide that number—not 34, but 33! And then to further perplex the close reader, to add the names of the descendants of other three wives, respectively 16, 14, 7, which numbers he explicitly provides without, however, making explicit that the addition will show a total of 70.

Instead, continuing in his seemingly pointless roundabout manner, he provides two parallel formulations of summation, one at the beginning of verse 26, the other at the end of verse 27.

VERSE 26A	VERSE 27B
All the souls arriving—of Jacob's— in Egypt . . . all the souls: 66	All the souls of Jacob's line arriving in Egypt: 70

The juxtaposition of these formulations virtually guarantees that the two numbers 66 and 70 must be congruent with one another. The incongruent factor, the difference represented by the number 4, must therefore be resolved by elements in the text explicit or implicit. The explicit element is that two of Jacob's grandsons—having been born to Joseph in Egypt—cannot be said to have been among "those arriving in Egypt." (So verse 27a and verse 20.) What about the remaining discrepancy, now the number 2? No problem. Implicit in verse 26 ("all arriving in Egypt") and explicit in verse 12 are the two of Jacob's grandsons who, having died in the land of Canaan (verse 12), could also not have been among "those arriving in Egypt." Thus, we might conclude, the congruence between the 66 souls in verse 26 and the 70 souls in verse 27 has been restored.

Such a conclusion would be wrong on a number of counts. For one, the 70 souls "who arrive in Egypt" in verse 27 cannot possibly include Er and Onan, the two sons of Judah who died in Canaan without issue. (The two sons of Joseph, however, despite their birth in Egypt, might be included in the 70; the word "arrived" can have a metaphoric sense without a geographic terminus. In this context specifically the sense of "accrue" can certainly inhere in the verb $bō$ '. Consider, in verse 26, "all the souls *accruing* to Jacob," and compare the usage in Exodus 22:14. Thus, in verse 26, the double entente—*accruing to Jacob* and *arriving in Egypt*—achieved by the placing of *leYaᵃqob* after *habbāʼā* and before *Miṣraimā* (instead of, as in verse 27, the normal order). Thus we would have to find another two souls to complement the number 70 in verse 27.

The clues to clear up this mystery will also resolve a few additional perplexities that we have noted. The Jacob in verse 26 to whom souls accrue, all sprung from his loins, is the patriarch in his own persona, and therefore is not, and cannot be, counted in his 66 descendants. But in verse 27 the 70 souls of *bēt-Yaᵃqob*—this last term, *like bēt-Yiśrāʼel*, or like the *benē-Yisrāʼel . . . i.e., Jacob and his children*—are members of a family, one of which can be and is the patriarch himself. Thus we now have another problem. The name-lists of the matriarchs' descendants added up (implicitly) to the number 70, inclusive of Er and Onan and Manasseh and Ephraim. None of these four grandsons, having indeed been descended from Jacob, can be subtracted from the list of 70. If we now add Jacob himself to the list (in keeping with verse 8) and his daughter Dinah (in keeping with verse 15), we have arrived at a total of 72 souls! Two souls must be subtracted from this total to achieve the number 70. Who are they? The answer is—as hinted at by the (redundant) exclusion of *the wives of the sons of (/children of) Jacob* from *those who sprung from his loins*, in verse 26—the two women (women never counting as continuers of the patrilineal lines), Dinah and Serah; the former never included in the names that total 70; the latter included in the names that total 70. But now we know why the narrator never provided the explicit addition of the names of the matriarchs' descendants: Had he done so, he would have had to subtract Serah and come up with a total of 69!

Have we then resolved all the problems of the names listed, numbered, once untotaled, once totaled to yield 66, once totaled to yield 70? No, we have not. For the total of 66 in verse 26 (not inclusive of Manasseh and Ephraim, Er and Onan) is implicitly based on the list of names of children (sons) and grandchildren of Jacob in verses 2–25, a list that adds up to 70 names inclusive of granddaughter Serah. Thus by including this one grandchild in the list and by excluding daughter Dinah from it our narrator guarantees that, however we process the information he so ingeniously formulates, we shall fall short by one, or find that we have one too many, in respect to the targeted number 70. What is the point of this baffling design?

Before we go on to address this question, I will ask the reader to bear with me as I present two riddles from my own period's recreational arithmetic:

> An Arab whose estate consists of a herd of 17 camels dies, leaving a will which specifies that the eldest son is to inherit $\frac{1}{2}$ the herd, the middle son $\frac{1}{3}$, and the youngest $\frac{1}{9}$. Simple division reveals that this amounts to $8\frac{1}{2}$ camels for the eldest, $5\frac{2}{3}$ camels for the middle son, and $1\frac{8}{9}$ camels for the youngest. Since a camel cannot be divided into fractions without serious impairment of its monetary value, the heirs have recourse to the tribal sheikh. This gentleman, after mulling over the problem for several minutes, volunteers to enrich the deceased's estate with a camel from his own herd. He then allots 9 camels to the eldest, 6 to the middle son and 2 to the youngest—each thus receiving more than the allotment of his father's will. The allotted camels, 9 + 6 + 2 adding up to 17, the sheikh then rides off on the camel which he has repossessed . . . The sheikh's trick? None at all. The enigma is cleared up when after laborious calculation we arrive at the awareness which the sheikh reached so quickly. The common denominator of $\frac{1}{2}$, $\frac{1}{3}$, and $\frac{1}{8}$ is 18, and the fractions add up to $\frac{9}{18} + \frac{6}{18} + \frac{2}{18}$ for a total of $\frac{17}{18}$. The deceased father had not distributed the sum total of his estate. From this undistributed portion, $\frac{1}{18}$, the sheikh was able to satisfy all parties.
>
> A night-clerk rents out his hotel's last unoccupied room to three salesman for $10 per person. A few minutes later, realizing that he has overcharged them for a $25 room, he summons the bellhop, explains his mistake, and hands him five singles to be returned to the three salesmen in Room 819. On his way up to the eighth floor, the bellhop—anticipating the difficultly of three men dividing 5 singles—decides to ease their perplexity. He pockets two dollars, and returns the remaining three to the salesmen. Each of these guests, having paid ten dollars and gotten one dollar back, the three together have now paid 27 dollars (3 × 9=27) for a room which should have cost them 25. But it did cost them 27 dollars and the bellhop kept 2 dollars (27 + 2=29). What, then, happened to the 30th dollar? . . . Answer: Nothing. The question is misleading. The 27 dollars paid by the salesmen included the 2 pocketed by the bellhop (they paid, in effect, 25 dollars for the room and 2 for the bellhop's dishonesty). Hence the 2 dollars pocketed must be subtracted from the 27 paid, to make for the $25 room charge, and cannot be added to the 27 as was done to create the problem.

Why have I cited these two riddles? Because this, being a poetical enterprise, must depend on comparative literary study for its argumentation. And such structures as these genealogical lists and the number-play associated with them simply do not figure largely, if at all, in the sparse literature from antiquity or in the spate of it in modern times. Comparing then the number-play in the Bible—specifically that in Genesis 46—and in the cited examples, I would have to concede that the authors or "narrators" are in both cases in complete control of their material and their craft. I would further have to agree that the formulation of the two cited riddles, like that in Genesis 46, is a poetical factor. Which is to say that the way in which the riddle is formulated has a great deal to do with the challenge posed for the reader or hearer. Consider, for example, the following formulation of the first riddle: Three brothers inheriting respectively one-half, one-third and one-ninth of a flock of 17 sheep worked out the fractions due to them as 8½, 5⅔, and 1⅞. They then rounded off each share to the nearest highest integer, and so divided the flock into shares consisting of 9, 6, and 2, for a total of 17. How was this operation possible?

The difference between the biblical and the modern riddles is striking. The information given in the modern riddles is minimal, and the necessary arithmetic operations are simple, linear, and compel a single answer. Only the presentation of the plot or the formulation of the question may be characterized, to some extent, as misleading. In the biblical riddle(s) the data may appear in one or more parallel contexts or sets, the items sometimes identical, sometimes variant, sometimes strangely inconsistent with (if not contradictory to) one another. The data may or may not include numeration, explicit process of addition, implicit process of subtraction; and the totals given in two different sets of such arithmetic processes are often such that the conclusion that will satisfy one set of data will be contraindicated by the data in the second set, and vice versa.

We have seen the above in the seven preceding sections dealing with structures of one kind or another. In the case of Genesis 46, we have a single genealogy, with a cunning conflation of personal names pointing either to a single individual or to an ethnic polity. All the data culminate in the bewilderingly clashing implications of the two different arithmetic summations in two successive verses, one yielding a count of 66, the other a count of 70. But another clue to the overarching design of the biblical author would be overlooked if we continued, as we have done so far, to be preoccupied only with the numbers and arithmetic operations in connection with this genealogy in Genesis 46, this line of Jacob. For another, swollen version of this genealogy appears in Numbers 26.

In characterizing this last genealogy as swollen we have two things in mind. One is the sleep-inducing or, if you will, mesmerizing drone of the census-taker as he names first each clan's eponymous ancestor from whom derives the clan that is named — how else? — after him. Thus: "(belonging) to Nemuel, the family/clan of the Nemuel-ites; (belonging) to Yamin, the clan of the Yamin-ites; belonging to Yachin, the clan of Yachin-ites," and so on and so on for perhaps half a hundred clans. That such a litany-like recital of (putative) ancestral clan names is testimony to the piety of the recorder, or to his sacerdotal status (P, being a priest, is naturally dedicated to preserving and transmitting archival data), is as reasonable as the conclusion that an arranger who set the names of St. Peter's successors to the strains of a Gregorian chant must have been a pious adherent of the Roman church, possibly himself ordained a priest, and drawing his material from Vatican archives.

The other element of swollenness is the differences in names in the census of Numbers 26. These are for the most part additions in the Numbers list of grandchildren and great-grandchildren of Jacob's sons. The two lists being 90 percent identical, I will not reproduce the second list here. Instead I will note the differences. In the Numbers list:

1. Reuben's son, Pallu, sires Eliab, who in turn sires Nemuel, Dathan, and Abiram. Dathan and Abiram are pointedly identified as the two Reubenites who joined the faction of Korah, and paid for it with their lives. Thus we can understand their leaving no clan-descendants behind. But this only draws (or should draw) our attention to the datum that neither their brother Nemuel nor their father Eliab left behind clans named after themselves. Why then are they included in this census-list to begin with?

2. Simeon's eldest is not Yemuel but Nemuel (like his Reubenite great-nephew, Eliab's surviving son). The third son, Ohad, is missing. In place of Zohar ($ṣhr$) the next to youngest son is Zerah (zrh)—like Judah's last mentioned son—and so we have the improbable phenomenon of two Zarhi clans in Israel, one Simeonite, the other Judahite. Finally, the last son Saul, ancestor of the Saulite clan, is not singled out here for having had a Canaanite mother.

3. Gad's seven sons are the same except for Ziphion, who appears as Zaphon, and Ezbon, who appears as Ozni.

4. Issachar's third son is not Yob (yb) but Yashub ($yšb$).

5. Joseph's two sons are each provided with three or two generations of sons, each of whom constitutes an eponymous clan ancestor. Thus:

Manasseh			Ephraim		
Machir(ites)			Shutelah(ites)	Becher(ites)	Tahan(ites)
Gilead(ites)			Eran(ites)		
Iezer(ites)		Hepher(ites)			
Helek(ites)	Shemida(ites)				
Ashriel(ites)	Shechem(ites)				

6. In place of Benjamin's ten sons there are only five. Two of these are, as in the Genesis list (but also constituting clan ancestors): Bela(ites), Ashbel(ites). Two of them bear names suggestive of sons in the Genesis list: Shephupham (Shuphamites), cf. Genesis *Muppim*, and Hupham(ites), cf. Genesis *Huppim*. A fifth son, absent in Genesis, is Abiram(ites). But two sons of Benjamin in the Genesis list, Naaman and Ard, appear as eponymous clan ancestors, they the sons of Benjamin's firstborn son, Bela.

7. In place of the one son of Dan in Genesis, Hushim ($ḥšm$), there appears a single son by the name Shuham ($šḥm$).

8. The five sons of Asher are reduced to four (Yishwa got lost, probably to the relief of his brother Yishwi). But the youngest son Beriah (himself here the clan ancestor of the Beriaites) is also father (as in Genesis) of the clan ancestors Heber and Malchiel (of the Heberites and Malchielites, to be sure). But perhaps the most interesting item in a comparison of the two lists is that Asher (the eighth son in order of appearance in Genesis, i.e., the second son of Leah's maid Zilpah, following the six sons of Leah herself) is the next-to-last of the tribal ancestors in the clan-list. And, interesting enough, despite this being a (patrilineal) clan-list, the last notice in respect to this Asher is that "the name of his daughter was Serah."

It will be of interest to note the comments on these two lists of two source-critics, both of them assuming (in varying degrees of rigidity) that such genealogies represent historiographic or historiographically intended reconstructions of Israel's ancestry. Thus Speiser in footnotes ad. loc. and in his notes to Chapter 46 does the following: He confidently assumes that the yob (Job) of Issachar's line is a textual error for the *yšwb* (Yashub) of Numbers 26:24, and so emends the name in his translation. He prefers the Numbers 26:15 "Zephon" to Gad's firstborn "Ziphion" in Genesis 46:16. The names "Ehi, Rosh, Mupppim, and Huppim" ought, he thinks, to be corrected to the "Abiram, Shephupham, Huppim" of Numbers 26:39f. He also refers us to 1 Chronicles 8:4f, which, however, does not comport with either of the two lists we are examining. Now his argumentation: Jemuel (our Yemuel), eldest son of Simeon in Genesis 46:10, is inferior to the Nemuel of Numbers 26:12 and 1 Chronicles 4:24, "because (1) Numbers 26 had "proved dependable on many counts" (What, we would ask, are the criteria for dependability of Numbers, or of the undependability of Genesis?), "and (2) Heb n will be mistaken for *y* more readily than the other way about." (Which is to say, given the shapes of the Hebrew letters, that the closing square bracket] is more readily mistaken for half that bracket ¬ than the other way about. On this point we should like to hear our readers' opinions.) Similar to the preceding is his apodictic, rather than reasoned, judgment that the "list of Benjamin's sons has been mangled in the present version. . . . Aside from mechanical textual corruptions which can be corrected on the basis of parallel passages. . . . All of which serves to point up the secondary character of the list before us." From Gerhard von Rad's discussion of the Genesis 46 genealogy I will cite only his conclusion:

> In distinction from the list in Numbers 26:5ff., for example, which must be considered a historically accurate statement of the generations from the period before the formation of the state, our list has to be thought of as the work of very late and theoretical erudition. It is the product of erudite occupation with ancient traditions and belongs, therefore, to a theological Priestly literature of which there is much in the Old Testament (cf. Num., ch. 7) but the actual life and real purpose of which is only recognizable with difficulty behind the hard, dry shell with which it is covered.[39]

It would serve no purpose to enter into detailed debate with these two notable scholars. (The fault may, in any case, lie with my own perverse mentality: I understand hardly a single word in this last citation from von Rad.) My citation of these historiographically oriented approaches to biblical genealogies is in the interest of contrasting them with my own poetical approach. For all the differences in the two lists, the uniformities and similarities in them are even more striking (as, for example, we have seen in the case of the genealogies provided for two different ancestors, Cain and Seth). And many of the differences are, given the different purports of the two lists, not at all problematic. Thus, for example, the list in Genesis 46, albeit in the guise of a genealogy, is a list of human beings in a single family who arrived in Egypt, a list adding up to 70 (or 66, depending on whether one includes one arrival or more, and paterfamilias, and one female but not another). One could not, therefore, include grandchildren or great-grandchildren who were not yet born at the time of Jacob's descent to Egypt, or who would have disturbed the count culminating in the number 70. Not so, however, the list in Numbers 26, which, albeit in the guise of a genealogy, is a list of clans (and sub-clans?) constituting the tribes of Israel. Number is not relevant here, hence the tracing of clan ancestry to an eponym in the second or third (or fifth, for that matter) generation constitutes no problem. But the similarities in the context of the differences are resolvable only on poetical grounds. Thus, for example, even if we could figure out why two "Priestly" lists would have been piously preserved despite their differences, which would seem to impeach the historical authenticity of one or the other, or both, we should have to explain the following: the appearance in either list of two descendants of Jacob (Er and Onan) who, having died young, were precluded from either arriving in Egypt or from becoming clan ancestors. And this is of course even more strikingly the case in respect to the inclusion of the female grandchild Serah in both lists, she who by virtue of patrilineal descent cannot be counted in the 70 of Genesis 46 and, not constituting a clan ancestor, has no place in Numbers 26.

The telling consideration, in connection with questions of historicity or invention, authenticity or fabrication, is the significant number of compositional absurdities in both the lists, given the explicit and different purport of each. Let us review some of these in each list.

In Numbers 26, verse 8—coming after the count of 43,730 males of military age in the Reubenite clans of Enochites, Palluites, Hezronites, and Carmites—provides these totally irrelevant data: Pallu had a son named Eliab (who never became an eponym), and he in turn had three sons, none of whom became eponyms. Dathan and Abiram might have become eponyms if they had not committed the fatal error of joining Korah's company. Eliab's third son, the surviving Nemuel, would have caused a problem had he sired a clan, for then there would have been two Nemuelite clans, one Reubenite, the other Simeonite. Of course this problem could not have arisen if the firstborn of Simeon were named Yemuel, as in Genesis 46. On the other hand, one might retort that such conjectural thinking is utterly absurd, in that Simeon's son Zerah (zrḥ)—and not, as in Genesis 46, Zohar (zhr)— is the father of the Simeonite Zarhites, despite the existence of the Zarhites, descended from Judah through his son Zerah.

A more incongruous element in a list of tribes and their constituent clans is the listing of two clans deriving from sons of Zerah's brother (the Judaite Zerah) Perez. These two sons, Hezron and Hamul, have given rise to the clans of the Hezroni and the Hamuli, but their father Perez gave rise to a separate clan, the Parzi. Could the "families" of the Hezroni and Hamuli represent sub-clans of the Parzi clan? If they can, however, be so regarded, who would be those members of the Parzi (main) clan who are not also either Hezroni or Hamuli? The same problem presents itself with Ephraim's son Shutelah and Shutelah's son Eran, who somehow constitute two separate clan groupings who must somehow be identical; for if the Eranites are only "sub-clan" derived from Shutela, then the only Shutelah-ites who exist must be Eranites as well. Similarly for the Ardite and Naamanite clans deriving from the Belaite clan of Benjamin. But on a much more ludicrous scale for the Menasseh-ite clans, which are descended from Gilead (who also constitutes a clan), he the son of Machir (who also constitutes a clan), he the son of Manasseh, who like his brother Ephraim enjoys full tribal status. That the above problems could not have escaped the notice of the biblical author is guaranteed by the notice in Genesis 48:6–7. When Jacob adopts these two of Joseph's sons as his own, raising them to tribal status on a par with Reuben and Simeon, he specifies that any other lines of children "that you have [better, *that you will have*] sired after them [sic] will be yours, [but] under the names of their brethren will they be called/summoned/listed in respect to their [tribal] heritage of real estate." Thus there are no Josephites, only Manaasites and Ephraimites, and just how the descendants of sons of Joseph other than these two came to or into their patrimonies is left to our imagination.

The clan-line of Manasseh through Machir, his son Gilead, and the six sons of Gilead must be the focus of our attention for yet another reason. Gilead is almost always elsewhere in Scripture a place name, not a personal name, a toponym and not an eponym. So this name seems to represent an area of territory the name of which has been converted—and ever so openly—by the author of this clan list into a social grouping and its ancestor. And so too in the case of Shechem, the name of a city in Genesis 33:18, which is also the name of that city's prince; this young man's sire being Hamor, who is in this chapter and the next $^a b\bar{i}$ $\check{s}^e kem$, both "father of (Prince) Shechem" and "lord of Shechem (the city)." Thus the names of well-known cities and tracts of land on both sides of the Jordan—well known to us from narratives of the patriarchy, exodus, judges and monarchy—have become, in this wilderness period, full-fledged clans tracing their ancestry to grandchildren or great-grandchildren of Jacob, who must (presumably) have been born some time during the centuries-long stay in Egypt.

In summation, then, whatever else may be said of the Numbers list—and we have not even raised the matter of 601,730 men of fighting age in these clans, plus the 23,000 additional clansmen of Levi—there would seem little in it to support Speiser's judgment as to its "reliability" or von Rad's assessment of it as "a historically accurate statement of the generations from the period before the formation of the state."

Let us turn now to the incongruities in the Genesis 46 list. We have already dealt at length with the incongruities of much of the diction, with the difficulty of making two sets of addition square with one another, with the inclusion (in the count) of a granddaughter Serah, and the exclusion (from the count) of a daughter, Dinah. Additional elements for which there are good poetical rationales—yet which are, nevertheless, out of place in a list merely purporting to account for 70 Jacobitic family members arriving in Egypt—are such caritative narrative touches as the identification of Leah and Rachel as Laban's "daughters" and Rachel (but not Leah) as Jacob's "wife." Also extraneous in such a list are the two grandsons who died before the descent to Egypt, who are nevertheless included in the line of Leah's descendants and in the sum of them as 33, which explicit total along with the explicit totals of the other wives' descendants adds up—implicitly—to 70. To these we may now add the consideration (raised by Speiser) about the chronologically unlikely possibility that Perez could already have had two sons at a time of Jacob's migration to Egypt. And, finally, von Rad's apperception: "For Benjamin already to be the father of ten sons here does not fit into the narrative at all." If we review our own discussion of the chronology of Exodus 6 (see p. 331) these improbabilities caught by Speiser and von Rad will become even more glaring. For we have seen the improbabilities arising from an assumption that Levi's son Kehath could have been at most two years of age at the time of the descent, and here a son who might well have been a grandson of Judah is already possessed of two sons, both of whom are part of the Israelitic complement of 70, along with the sons of Benjamin, the youngest of whose sons must have been about the age of his Judahite cousin Hamul. Even more to the point, a comparison of our discussions on previous chronologies and genealogies will confirm a conclusion that we have previously drawn: All the improbabilities and incongruities (in Genesis 46 and Numbers 26) were as clear to the biblical narrator as they are to us, his readers.

A review of the kerygmas that we have discerned in the metaphors of the scriptural structures we have studied, kerygmas altogether in accord with those of their interlocking narratives, will disclose that the overarching lesson is this: Literalness, in respect to the events of the past, to the individual personalities who figured in the these events, to the time and place of these personae—in a word, historiography—is the least of Scripture's concerns. The concern of Scripture, being the nature of God and the conduct this God requires of humanity, is with the nature of humans as they have shown themselves in the past, in contrast with the moral potentialities of that nature. Among the constituent metaphors of this overarching one are: the supreme dignity of the human race, endowed with the knowledge of morality and the freedom to act in its despite; the oneness of humanity, a single race for all its differentiations, and kindred in the flesh and in the spirit for all the sins against kinship's moral imperatives; every human's descent from a murderer, and vulnerability to the role of victim or the temptation to perpetrate crime; the repeated failures of humanity to meet the challenges of divinely set morality, the grace of God in sparing a remnant so that the human species have another chance; the choice of a single ancestor, to sire a single family to serve as moral model for its kindred families and polities; the indeterminacy of genetic inheritance for moral or immoral or amoral careers; the vagaries of cherished ancestors as they confront the moral ambiguities and dilemmas in coping with siblings and strangers in the never-ending existential struggles for necessities and luxuries, for dominance or independence or redemption; and their struggles to achieve that charity which must begin at home while eschewing the xenophobic bias that is so often the other face of blood-tie loyalties.

At first blush it would seem—and perhaps correctly so—that we could hardly educe these kerygmas from structures unless we had them already before us in the form of narratives. On the other hand, is the kerygma of a narrative not often misread for the very reason that, ignorant of those structures that we call poetical principles or procedures or options, we ignore the importance of structure in the framing of the narrative? We are conditioned by experience to think of narrative as the core edifice, and external structures as the scaffolding built to expedite the rearing of the edifice. But the scaffolding is normally removed once the edifice is completed. In the case of Scripture, the ubiquity of structures (prescriptive, legalistic, cultic, poetic, along with the kinds on which we have focused) must be seen as (often) ingenious formal creations to direct the reader's attention to the blueprints that tell so much of the function(s) for which the edifice and its constituent parts were designed.

Thus, fitting into the kerygma that human pedigree means nothing in itself[40] is the identification in Genesis 46:10 of Simeon's son Saul as "son of that Canaanitess." This might have been read by many a loyalist Israelite as a slur on this grandson of Jacob's, perhaps an implication that he should not be included in the list of Jacob's true descendants (which would therefore further complicate the problem of count). Such a reading would, to be sure, imply the improbable assumption that the other grandchildren were born to other than Canaanite mothers, improbable in itself, and clearly contradicted in the case of Judah's progeny by Tamar, explicitly identified as the daughter of a Canaanite. It would further fly in the face of Scripture's exclusion of the males but not the females of certain groups with whom intermarriage is interdicted. Yet this datum too did not deter Miriam and Aaron from prejudice against Moses' Cushite wife (Numbers 12:1), nor did it rule out for the author of the Book of Ruth the importance of stressing that King David himself derived from a Moabite great-grandmother. Perhaps then, the countering of such a xenophobic or racist mentality is the whole point of making Saul Simeonson the issue of a Canaanite mother in Genesis 46, and listing him in Numbers 26 without his maternal origin as a constitutively legitimate clan ancestor in Israel.

The key to the overarching kerygma of the Table of 70 Nations in Genesis 10, the List of 70 members of Beth Jacob descending to Egypt (and its comparative and contrastive counterpart, the Clans of Israel in Numbers 26) could lie only in the explication of the connection between the two lists of 70 in the Song of Moses:

> (7) Take note of the days of the primordial past
> Consider the years of generations long, long gone;
> Ask your father, let him tell you,
> Your elders, let them confirm to you:
> (8) When Elyon allotted nations their heritage,
> In defining the lineages of humankind,
> He fixed the territories of peoples
> In the number of the descendants of Israel. (Deuteronomy 32:7–8)

Verse 7, the first imperative verb ($z^e kor$), translated "remember," is widely understood as an expression of the importance of the past (history) and an urging of the wilderness generation to repair to their parents and grandparents for their witness to the events of that past (historiography). Such a literalistic interpretation of this verse is incongruous with what it is that Israel is "to remember," or to retrieve from the memory-store of past generations. For witnesses of the Jacobite descent to Egypt there exist no more. And there never were witnesses to the "event" of mankind's separation into ethnic and national entities defined by their differing tongues and geographical boundaries. The appeal to Israel is to refer to parents and grandparents, not for their historical memories of Israel's ethno-political origins, nor to those of the far more remote beginnings of mankind's national origins, but for the core-article of Israel's faith, the central position of Israel in God's program for the world, its unique role in the economy of the universe. But this tenet too, as expressed in the metaphoric application of Deuteronomy 32:8 to the metaphoric structures of Genesis 10 and 46, is subject to a range of nuanced, even opposed, interpretations. The most chauvinistic of Israelites will be confident that the meaning is the commensurability of Israel on the one side and, on the other, of all the rest of humankind. At the other end of the interpretive range is the role of Israel to exemplify God's will for all humanity, to unify in God's name and as Abraham's seed a prideful human unity expressed and disrupted in the primordial division at Babel's baked-brick edifice.

SUPPLEMENTS,
CONCLUSIONS,
ANTICIPATIONS

EIGHT

+>===<+

POETICAL ODDS
AND ADDENDS

The poetic address to Scripture, departing in so many ways from the regnant schools of biblical literary criticism, necessarily entails the argumentative and disputatious nature of our discussion of texts, narrative and structural. I employ the first two adjectives in the older sense of reasoning, deducing, arriving at conclusions, without the newer overtones of quarrel or altercation. Nevertheless putting forth an alternative approach to one that has taken the stance of an orthodoxy is what occasions the ubiquitous exposition of the assumptions and presuppositions (and their justification) of a method which, by reason of its relative novelty, will appear as a challenge at best and contentious at worst. The (perhaps self-imposed) requirement to present not just an interpretation but an argument for it determined my decision to treat the narratives and structures separately. For all their mutually complementary design and function in pointing to and reinforcing the component and overarching kerygmas, the differing codes and strategies of story and structure would have made for tedious ensnarlment had they been pursued together. As it is, the poetic assumption of consistent compositional modalities across the books and genres of Scripture will be written off *ab initio* by those committed to the genetic approaches, with their axioms of source-provenance and diachronic development. And my marshaling of testimony from Psalms, for example, as relevant to the mentality of the author of the prose account of creation that opens the

Book of Genesis, will be regarded as methodologically inadmissible by many of today's biblicists (particularly so by those of my own generation).

Yet my recourse to biblical material across the lines of the prose-verse demarcation has been slight, indeed, minimal, when one considers how rich the lode of available and relevant text. So too have I held many considerations in abeyance of intertextual (biblical) connections and cross-genre (biblical) associations, not to speak of poetic factors that are cross-cultural or cross-temporal(/generational) in nature. Thus, for example, the very questions of the legitimacy of genre-division and the operation of meta-literary conventions of unproved value in the "literary" approaches to Scripture of the past hundred years or so.[1] Hence I have reserved for this section such odds and (add)ends as I feel are legitimately adducible for some of the texts we have been studying. Legitimate by the criteria of such poetic assumptions as that human talents, concerns, perplexities, and the expression of these in various kinds of writing may not have differed so significantly in the past few millennia of "civilization" as to preclude their enlistment for comparative and contrastive purposes in our quest to decipher the codes and messages of Scripture.

One more observation is in order before we go on to address specific problems in biblical study and to adduce concepts and mindsets from across the Hebrew scriptures (from Genesis to Chronicles), from across the ancient world (from the Fertile Crescent to the lands of classical antiquity), from across the time extending from the development of writing to the entrustment of such graphemes and glyphs to the bytes and digits of today's computers: Modern Bible study, modeling itself on the natural sciences, has consistently tried for the precision of formulation that these sciences achieve by dint of measurement and mathematics.

The appropriateness (rather, inappropriateness) of such emulation by investigators of phenomena that do not (or at least, do not yet) lend themselves to quantification is hardly moot. Yet the search for such precision in disciplines properly labeled the humanities or liberal arts has been abetted by the increasingly deductive proportion of reasoning (or concern) in those sciences in respect to which *empirical* and *inductive* were once regarded as virtually synonymous. Thus in the realm of physics, induction and experiment are the hallmarks of its inquiry into the microcosm, but in the macrocosm its inquiry is a matter of deduction. The heavens are "read," the record of the past is observed in terms of events measured in the durations of distances called light-years. In the present reading of the dynamics of the past, clues are searched for as to the shape of the future. Altogether deductive by contrast is biology, particularly that branch of it labeled paleontology: here too, the record of the past is read in terms of skeleton remains and fossil imprints, and informed guesses on structural functions are extrapolated to read the how, if not the why, of botanic or zoological development; the predictive element, as to the prognosis of the future of this or that life-form, is—except for playful speculation— altogether absent. Yet here too, the size of bones in limbs or crania and their relative proportion to one another and to extant life-forms now requires the deployment of mathematical measurements to a significant degree.

How different is the practice of the arts and humanities and, indeed, the critical analyses and syntheses attempted by researchers who study the cultural deposits of mankind's past? Quantification is irrelevant, perhaps almost absolutely so. Cause and affect as a relationship between two events may be tentatively proposed, nuanced but never asserted. The interpretation of such pairs of qualitatively, but not dichotomously, antonymous categories abound. To name but a few: discursive versus parenetic or homiletical; sequential versus analogic; explicitly referential versus allusive; dogmatic versus suggestive; formal versus substantive; sacred versus profane or secular; legal versus normative; universalistic versus particularistic; and mundane and political versus metaphysical and theological.

It has been my experience that minds indisposed to entertain arguments viewed as methodologically impudent (when they are merely novel or challenging) will often counter these arguments by deploying rigorously construed dichotomies to discredit them. Thus, for example:

1. There is a general tendency in modern biblical study to equate legally-formulated texts with positive law, hypothetically existent in the ancient Israelite polity; to treat precepts as laws, norms as decrees, theological prescriptions as "cultic legislation," and recommended paradigms as constitutionally fixed straitjackets, which, like the laws of the Medes and the Persians (according to the Scroll of Esther and to this book alone) cannot be amended or repealed. Against this reductive usage, and searching for an adjective that could subsume the whole range of law, prescriptives, norms, moral directives, and regulations of social and domestic etiquette, I found no alternative to *halakhic*, a rabbinic expression that subsumes all the foregoing items without being restricted to any of them. Some of the reactions to this categorical importation into biblical study have ranged from sneers at this "apologetically" motivated innovation to a rejection of a postbiblical concept that, presumably by definition, is intrinsically inapposite to the biblical text.

2. Another category-label that I borrowed (this time of Greek derivation, and deployed variously by exegetical schools of New Testament interpretation) has brought me hoots of derision or opprobrium from biblicist colleagues of my own denomination. It would seem that there is something confessionally inappropriate (and philologically illicit) in a Jewish Bible student's adoption of the term *kerygma* "proclamation, preachment." Why such a borrowing at all? Well, for one thing, because *preachment*, like *homily* and *sermonic*, carries objectionable overtones of tediousness, didacticism, even (alas!) of religious commitment, to the ears of Scriptural savants dedicated to the value-free objectivity of the scientific researcher. More important, however, is that I could find no one term to represent what is the moral in a fable; the proposition in a discourse disguised as a narrative; the lesson in a homily; the moral vectors in attributes assigned to the one god of Scripture; the hierarchy of values that are implicitly endorsed, depreciated, or scorned in the various codes that I have designated as *structures*.

3. Perhaps the most pernicious bent of the biblicist mind is that which assumes a hard disjunction as between the *exegetical* (i.e., my) or the *eisegetical* (i.e., your) interpretation(s) of any given passage. Another expression of this phenomenon is the assumption that agreement can be reached as to what constitutes the *plain meaning* of a text as opposed to other meanings, meanings that are less immediate, more adorned, less obvious, so more imaginative, and therefore less probable. In this connection it will be helpful to recall that a dichotomy can only exist as between two terms; yet we know that the alternative to *plain meaning* is not merely

non-plain meaning. Four categories of interpretation, discerned by the rabbis and comprised in the acronym *PaRDeS*, are *pᵉšāṭ* "plain meaning," *remez* "hint, implication," *dᵉrāš* "homiletical, allegorical," and *sod* "cipher, esoteric meaning." My translations of these four Hebrew terms are suggestive rather than precise, the terms being parametrical vis-à-vis one another and not definitional or definitive. Thus *pᵉšāṭ* "(most) literal meaning" may stand not for "plain or minimal meaning" but for "meaning closest to the surface," and may actually be ruled out in a metaphorical context by common sense; *remez* may be "allusive" as *dᵉrāš* may be also, and *dᵉrāš* "inference" would only differ from *remez* "implication" by virtue of directional orientation; *sōd*, finally, may in its sense of "code" differ not at all from that same sense in *remez*. It is thus the absence (and perhaps the impossibility) of definitional demarcations in the rabbinic tradition that points to these interpretive categories as not merely overlapping in sense, but to their teleology as well; to wit, to expand as far as possible the options of legitimate and concomitant interpretations. A review of some of the interpretations of narrative and (particularly of) structure, arrived at by ourselves, the rabbis, or both, might yield both entertainment and edification if we try to sort them out in terms of the *PaRDeS* categories.

In view of the foregoing, the reader who has attended thus far will not be surprised to find that in this final section I may unabashedly invoke homiletical values from my own time as having a bearing on the values of what is, after all, a literature of preachment; that I may compare, for hermeneutic purposes, not only the mythopoeic expressions of the metaphysics implied in pagan and biblical literature, but implied (or even explicit) in the mythopoeics and metaphysics of our own century's philosophers; that I adduce from my own practices of authorial or editorial revision motivations for such revisions in biblical texts that are alike enough to be viewed almost as dittographs, and different enough to be ascribed to competing talents of a Scripture that is far from monolithic.

Finally, I would avow my belief that for all the truths that may inhere in the generous or invidious comparisons of times and polities (such as East and West, Age of Faith and Age of Reason, Rome and Jerusalem, Hellenism and Hebraism), the human ethos, like the human condition, is more alike in contrasted antipodes, and more variegated within each of them. To cite but one case in point: the demand that justice triumph, however dire the cost to world or cosmos: The biblical expression of this is in the Bible a postulate in narrative and verse: not only human thrones but the throne of Heaven itself are founded on and contingent upon the practice of justice;[2] the rabbinic dictum is *yiqqob haddīn ʾet hāhār* "may justice pierce/bore through the mountain" (i.e., adamantine matter); the Roman version is *fiat iustitia pereat mundus ruant coeli* "may justice be done even if this entail the perishing of the world, the crashing down of the very heavens!" And the like sentiment is to be found today in the poetry of a hundred victimized peoples, in the idealistic passion of political anarchist and nihilist, in the readiness of nations great and small to risk universal nuclear doom rather than surrender their weapon of ultimate deterrence. And yet Armageddon has been staved off, human imitation of the suicidal lemming is homiletical hyperbole, and Scripture itself affirms that no atrocity of unfeeling Nature or demoniac polity in the recorded past or conceivable future can or must preclude the prophetic faith in a God who is both just and benevolent.[3]

IN RE GENESIS I: SCRIPTURE AND THE
MYTHOPOEIC IMAGINATION

The genetic approaches of modern biblical scholarship—source-analysis, redaction-history, and the like—justify their claim to the adjective *critical* in that they all begin with analysis of the text. They divide it into pericopes, sections, and documents, which—often parallel to one another—are in their relation to one another redundantly repetitious, inconsistent, or contradictory in plot or action. The one thing that these approaches do not do is synthesize. The synthesis is already present for them in the editorial amalgam of texts before them; their—the critics'—function is to uncover how the editorial process proceeded to produce the product before us. It is in respect to this (missing) second half of the enterprise of literary investigation (literary *criticism*, the latter term a synonym for *analysis*, is thus a label bespeaking only half the process) that the poetical approach differs in assumptions, procedure, and conclusions. Assuming that repetitions, inconsistencies, even contradictions, are among the devices employed by *poets* (literary artists) in the Greek sense—to gap, to bridge, to abridge, to inflate, to ambiguate, to enrich—the poetical approach is to proceed from critical analysis to an attempt at critical synthesis. How do separate sections, episodes, and documents interrelate to make up a unity that is greater than the sum of its parts?

This approach of modern scholarship to narrative passages in Scripture (to isolate them from one another) is even more pronounced in respect to its approach to the narrative and lyric, or prose and poetic components of Scripture vis-à-vis one another. (A parade example is the prose narrative of Sisera's downfall in Judges 4 and the poetic rendition of it in Judges 5.) Against this approach is my resort in chapter 2 to verse from Psalms or Ecclesiastes to clarify and amplify the creation narrative in Genesis 1. Behind the readiness to have such resort is the assumption (always, let us remember, as a hypothesis to be vindicated by the understanding achieved) of the poetic unity of Scripture as a whole, hence a poetic unity not just within narrative or lyric, but across the boundaries between the two as well. Another assumption, which we now must make explicit, is that the metaphoric, the figurative, and the creatively imaginative may (in Scripture at least) be as much the hallmark of prose as of poetry. And as we have been arguing for the metaphoric elements in the biblical creation story—and will continue to so argue them—so shall we, as we have already started to, attempt to do equal justice to the intellectual achievements as well as the artistic genius of the authors of the pagan classics. This is to say that the authors of the great pagan classics knew what they were doing when they portrayed their divine protagonists as inconsistent, silly, foolish, sly, rapacious, capricious, destructive, even evil. And as these pagan authors were not constrained by an inherited impiety to so render the supernal heroes of both sexes, so the biblical authors were under no constraint of piety when they demythologized creation in the narrative of Genesis 1, nor were they in breach of piety's canons or in rebellion against them when they made free use of mythic themes in anthems praising the one and only God of Creation and History. Simply put, the biblical writers were not ignorant of their pagan neighbors' myths, nor did they regard them as a taboo subject; no more, for example, than the Talmudic sages who bore the names of pagan deities, or Renaissance artists who could populate Christian palaces and churches with scenes featuring Madonnas and the godchild alongside nude goddesses and lecherous gods.

With this as foreword I may amplify my discussion on biblical anthropology, as evinced in narrative and lyric celebrations of the creation theme, with another poetic pericope illustrative of the freedom of a biblical spokesman to deploy the imagery of polytheistic myth in a diatribe against a pagan king; this king's attack on the Judean nation is read as deriving from disregard of the One God who is championed by and is the champion of the people. The appositeness of this passage to my theme in specific is its connection with the forces of chaos, which in Psalm 8 were seen as the personified adversary ("the ever-vengeful enemy") of humankind and of God ("Your enemies"). Such a superhuman embodiment of evil, personified in a role of unremitting opposition to God and his godly creatures, is epitomized for us in the figure of Satan. For all that this word is a biblical Hebrew term (verb and noun) bespeaking an adversarial or inimical stance, the personification of Satan is commonly supposed to be a postbiblical creation. And this supposition is strengthened by the paucity of reference to such a figure in the Hebrew Bible, except for an appearance in a vision of Zachariah,[4] the Hebrew noun śāṭān with the definite article—the Adversary—appears only once as a nonhuman person. In the prologue of the Book of Job, he plays the role of a member of God's celestial court—the other side of God, so to speak—whose cynical jeers at the possibility of human goodness and fidelity to God, save out of self-interest, prompt God to put Job to the test. But this figure is far removed from the fallen archangel who rebelled against God, the brilliant Lucifer (lit., *light bearer*) who became the satanic Prince of Darkness, as in Milton's portrayal of him in *Paradise Lost*. Yet it is clear that we have but a fraction of the mythological lore of the ancients, and little of that fraction derives from Scriptural sources. A fragment of such lore is preserved for us in an oracle of the prophet Isaiah. And lo, we have before us here the brilliant fallen Celestial in all his rebellious ambition and downfall.

In Chapter 14, Isaiah taunts a fallen "King of Babylon," his rhetorical device an envisaging of the reception this monarch receives on his arrival at netherworld Sheol:

(9) Sheol below bestirred herself for you, anticipating your arrival,
       Waking for you the shades—
       Yes, all of earth's titans—
       Rousing up from their thrones
       All the kings of nations.
(10) All of them speak up, address you:
       "What! Have you too, like us been stricken?
       Art become just like us?"
(11) Your lofty state lowered to Sheol?
       And the thrumming of your lutes?
       Worms a pallet beneath you,
       Maggots on top your blanket!

(12) What a fall you've taken from heaven,
  O Dazzling One, Son of Morningstar!
  Chopped down to earth, are you,
  O Predator of nations?"
(13) Yes you who nursed the thought,
  "To heaven I will mount.
  Higher than the stars of God [El]
  I will rear my throne,
  Take my seat on the Mount of [Divine] Assembly,
  On the upper reaches of Zaphon [the Olympus of the Levant].
(14) I will mount the billow of a cloud,
  I shall be the peer of the Most High." (Isaiah 14:9–14)

PAGANISM, ANCIENT AND MODERN: METAPHYSICS IN MYTH AND SCIENCE

The gods are powerful in paganism. And in Babylon, Marduk is the most powerful: the victor over chaos, the creator of the cosmos, king of the gods. When the Assyrians conquered Babylon and built a new seat of the empire in Mesopotamia, they appropriated the hymn *Enuma elish* for themselves, replacing Marduk with their own tutelary deity Aššur, but whether in Babylon or Assyria, Greece or Rome, the gods are part of the natural continuum. Immortals they may be called, but this is only to distinguish them from humankind. They are born, they may die, they may be brought back to life. They may be personifications or wielders of the powers of such natural phenomena as sun, moon and stars, ocean, land and sky, wind, rain, thunder and lightning. But their power derives from a source outside themselves, that all-embracing, all-permeating power-essence that we may call mana or the magical. It was by tapping into this dumb, mindless power—or energy, if you will —that the cosmos was created. As reflected in many a myth, it is by a malicious or irresponsible deployment of that power that the ordered world of nature may at any moment revert to chaos.

In Greek mythology Zeus succeeded to the throne of Olympus by overcoming his father Kronos. But Fate (a name for a penultimate power beyond the gods) has set a limit to the reign of Zeus as well. And it is in the hope to wrest from Prometheus the time and identity of his successor that Zeus puts the Titan to torture. It is intriguing that this secret is known to only one individual, and he the champion and benefactor of mankind, who stole knowledge—the fire from heaven—to narrow the gap between mortals and their Olympian overlords. Did the framers of that myth foresee that by dint of that fire from heaven mankind would in a few millennia topple Zeus from his throne and displace or replace his entire Olympian company? Or, might one argue, does the story itself, its invention and its rehearsal—the story of a divine king so fatuous that he believes in an ineluctable Fate to the extent that he can contradict its ineluctability if only he can learn who is fated to be its agent—suggest that the divine king has already been toppled from his throne and his successor is already at hand in the storyteller and in his audience? Let us permit ourselves a speculation. If, in its exploration of space, mankind comes upon a planet inhabited by humanoids whose science is at the level achieved by mankind in the fifteenth century (A.D.), how will our race appear to those humanoids? A race that makes light a weapon and a tool that in seconds transmit its voice and form through the trackless wastes of space; that can destroy a planet's life with one bomb; that has mastered the nucleus of the atom and is reaching out to the far-flung skirts of the galaxy! On one thing one might safely wager: this new race of gods will feel no more secure than did their Olympian predecessors. For what lies beyond?

In speculating on the nature of ultimate reality, our ultimate concern is with how that reality relates to mankind, to its hopes and aspirations, to its fear and dreads. The possibilities are limited: hostility, benevolence, indifference. In paganism man could find some lukewarm comfort in the notion that he was useful to the gods; perhaps a warmer hope that he might one day succeed to their eminence. But beyond even that there was only the mindless, purposeless play of Chance. In what critical way does the pagan view of ultimate reality differ from the metaphysics of scientism, that religion of questionable legitimacy that is one spawn of our scientific advance? The most eloquent expression of this new old faith is that of Bertrand Russell, who some fifty years ago had this to say in *A Free Man's Worship*:

> That man is the product of causes which had no prevision of the end they were achieving; that his origin, his growth, his hopes and fears, his loves and beliefs, are but the outcome of accidental collocation of atoms; that no fire, no heroism, no intensity of thought and feeling can preserve an individual life beyond the grave; that all the labor of the ages, all the devotion, all the inspiration, all the noonday brightness of human genius, is destined to extinction in the vast death of the solar system, and that the whole temple of Man's achievement must inevitably be buried beneath the debris of a universe in ruins—all these things, if not quite beyond dispute, are yet so nearly certain, that no philosophy which rejects them can hope to stand.[5]

Against paganism, old and new, Genesis affirms that the universe and all its laws, matter and energy, are not the eternal and infinite self-sufficient stuff of reality. Beyond them are a Cause and an Author, a Person—for only person can have a purpose—and the Person is friendly to mankind. God, in Genesis, is not part of the natural continuum but beyond it, as its Ground of Being. Biblical religion is indeed "supernatural." But it denies nothing natural, opposes no empirical science, when it affirms that the God of nature transcends nature.

It may be that Russell is correct. There may even be something admirable in the heroic quest to search out—in what time remains to us—all the secrets of a universe which, having no consciousness, does not know it has any secrets. And if, when the last glimmer of consciousness—and consciousness of consciousness—flickers out, there still remain some unfathomed secrets. It may be a comfort to us now to believe that there is no one laughing at the pretensions and frustration of mankind, this intellectual Don Quixote. But the paradoxes opened up by every scientific discovery should make us pause before we label Russell's faith as rational and biblical faith as mystic. Big-bang cosmology and an expanding universe, quarks and black holes, nuclear particles having enormous energy and zero mass, antimatter and parallel universes in time, the relativity of time itself and the curvature of space: all these point to the possibility of an open-ended universe. This is the possibility that Genesis affirms as theology: the God of Creation is the guarantee of Order, the repudiation of Accident or Chance. That it is a comforting theology is undeniable. Perhaps that is why it managed to sweep away a pagan theology—almost. But a comforting view of reality is not ipso facto an irrationality, nor an absurdity. And as truths or falsities are independent of whether they lead to hope or despair, so are the truth or falsities of the creation story in Genesis not contingent upon its assignability to the literary realm we call fiction. For a philosophical fiction is as respectable as the vision it holds forth as a possible option as to ultimate reality.

My first thought was to label this section "An Exegetical Sermon." It was not then, nor is it in my mind now, to persuade the reader that Scripture's God of Creation is the theology that he or she should accept. It is a sermon only to the extent that it attempts to update, so to speak, the Genesis message for our own time. Since our cultural ambience is not polytheistic paganism, its address must be to that in our Weltanschauung ambience that corresponds to ancient paganism, namely, the role of impersonal Chance in modern scientism; scientism, which is neither prerequisite for nor a necessary outcome of the scientific spirit or scientific method. The propriety of this section here is in its claim to be an acceptable exegesis, that is, the kerygma of the creation story in its affirmation of the nature of the natural and of the Source who transcends it.

THE SABBATH: ITS MEANING

The Sabbath in Relation to Cosmic Creation and Israel's Liberation

The Sabbath is a day. And a day is a unit of time. And time is what the sabbath is all about. The sabbath is a particular kind of time, sacred time. In the words of Genesis 2:3, "God then blessed the seventh day, He declared it holy." Which means that there is also non-sacred time, profane time, or secular time. What is the difference between the two kinds of time?

The sabbath is a unit of time called a day. But it is not just any day, it is a particular day: the seventh day, to be precise. But the seventh day of what? Well, for Genesis, obviously it is the seventh day of creation, the seventh day since the beginning of time. But that was the first seventh day. What of all the other seventh days that have been and will yet be? What are they the seventh day of? Why, the seventh day of the week, of course. Of course? What is "the week?" Why, the week is a unit of time too, a septet of days to be precise. And where did this unit come from? Well, was it not always there? As a matter of fact it was not always there, wherever "there" is. Somewhere, sometime, someone invented it.

Which is not to say that the inventor of the week invented time. No, it was a way of measuring time, of marking time off that was invented, unlike natural units of time, which were discovered but not invented. Such as the day, from sunrise to sunrise or sunset to sunset; or the month, from new moon to new moon or full moon to full moon; or the year, from any position of the sun in the heavens until the sun returns to that position, 365¼ days. Unlike these natural units of time, determined and measured by the movement in space of physical bodies—earth, moon, sun, and stars—are such arbitrary divisions of time as those called seconds, minutes, and hours. And we know who invented this system of division, and who inspired the division of a circle or a clock face into degrees. They are the same people who gave rise to the tradition of the *Enuma elish*: the Babylonians, or, perhaps, their Sumerian predecessors, whose mathematical reckoning proceeded according to a sexagesimal system, a system named for the Latin word for sixty; actually based on the number six and its multiples by itself or by ten: hence 6, 36, 60, 360, and so on.

Now it is all well and good—and, to be sure, eminently fair—to give credit where credit is due. One might even consider the fact that the septet of days we call a week is also based on the unit six, being six weekdays plus one sabbath, and go on to presume a Mesopotamian origin for this week. But this will not do. For nowhere in Mesopotamia, nor in Canaan (nor, for that matter, in Greece or Rome before contact was made with biblical concepts) is there to be found a shred of evidence for the seven-day week. The seven-day week, like the sabbath day itself, is a biblical invention. Indeed, it is likely that it was the concept of the sabbath day that eventuated in the week: after every six days of secular time, one day of sacred time. For if every seventh day is not *set apart* (and this is one of the senses basic to the meaning of the Hebrew word *qādōš* "holy") for some special observance, what earthly function does the week serve? Neither lunar months nor solar years lend themselves to division by seven-day units.

If we knew no more about the seventh day than what is given in Genesis, the likelihood is that we should never come to any satisfactory conclusion as to why this cultic institution of ancient Israel was attached to or associated with the story of creation. From the point of view of the sabbath as a cult institution, there is no intrinsic necessity for the association. For in one of the key biblical formulations enjoining the sabbath upon Israel as an obligation to its God, the rationale for this command is associated not with the creation story but with Israel's liberation from Egyptian bondage. Were there no alternative association of the sabbath with creation we should, therefore, never miss it. Indeed, if we were informed only of the contexts that prescribe this institution, and asked to guess which of the two rationales—cosmic creation or Israelite liberation—was the more appropriate, there is little question that we would opt for the latter. The Sabbath, after all, is an obligation enjoined on Israel and Israel alone; why associate it with the universal theme of creation when the rest of mankind is free of this obligation? Or is it possible that I am misreading the evidence, and that while the Sabbath is obligatory upon Israel explicitly, the biblical intent is that it is implicitly an obligation of all mankind as well?

The charge of the Sabbath's observance appears in almost identical formulation in the two versions of the decalogue in Exodus 20 and Deuteronomy 5:

> Six days you may work in pursuit of your every enterprise. The seventh day, however, is a Sabbath belonging [or owing] to YHWH, your God: [On it] you are to perform no work—neither you, your son nor daughter, your manservant or maidservant . . . your cattle, the alien in your jurisdiction.

The Exodus version goes on to cite the creation motif, while Deuteronomy continues with the motif of the liberation from Egypt. Many scholars have assumed
that the Deuteronomy version, being a later one, is an indication of the Deuteronomic editor's dissatisfaction with the rationale for the Sabbath as offered in Genesis and in Exodus. The Sabbath institution represents social legislation, an attempt
to secure relief from ceaseless labor for people subordinate to masters. The liberation theme is congruent with such a thrust, whereas the metaphysical or cosmic
theme is not at all so, or only to a lesser degree. In the excursus that follows I will
examine this argument more closely. For the present I would cite that part of Mat-
titiahu Tsevat's argument that is a conclusive rebuttal of the notion that social legislation is what lies at the heart of the Sabbath decree.[6] First, there is the emphasis
that the seventh day is "a Sabbath to YHWH," that is, it belongs to or is the due of
God. Second, social legislation applies to people in need of protection from abuse,
in this case, the imposition of ceaseless labor. But the master of an enterprise requires no protection from himself. Consider the case of a shopkeeper forbidden by
blue laws to be open for business. This is to guarantee that his employees have a
day off. But he himself may spend the day taking inventory, arranging his goods, or
even manufacturing goods for sale on the morrow. The decalogue charge puts repeated emphasis on the address to the Israelite freeman and paterfamilias. He himself is forbidden to work on the day owing to God, even as he is free to work to his
heart's content on the other six days.

Time is what the Sabbath is all about. Time, which is an abstraction, a concept,
a dimension of existence. Yet this abstraction can be viewed as property, something
to be disposed of freely or to have restrictions placed upon its disposal. The psalmist proclaims time as God's property: "Daytime belongs to You, nighttime also is
Yours." And—interestingly enough—this appears in the context of a reminiscence
of creation, making free use of the mythological personification of the forces of
chaos.

> (12) Yes, God, my king, [He] of yore
>   Performing feats of victory in Earth's innards!
> (13) You ['twas] cleaved by Your power Sea,
>   Smashed water-monsters' heads on the Waters.
> (14) You ['twas] crushed Leviathan's heads.
>   . . .
> (15) You ['twas] split open spring and wellhead,
>   You ['twas] dried up wellsprings primordial.
> (16) Yours the daytime, Yours the night,
>   You [Who] emplaced lamp(s), even sun.
> (17) You ['twas] hewed out all the boundaries of earth;
>   Summer and winter, You ['twas] fashioned them. (Psalm 74:12–17)

Time is God's property. Time is God's gift to mankind, but not in its entirety. For
six days man is free, free—not obliged—to dispose of time in pursuit of his own
needs and luxuries. The seventh day God reserves for Himself; it is "a Sabbath belonging to YHWH," and it is incumbent upon humankind to abstain from its own
pursuits on that day. For in thus marking the seventh day, man—declaring God's

lordship over Time—proclaims his acceptance of God's lordship over himself. Who can say whether the Exodus rationale of the Sabbath echoes the theme in the Genesis creation story, or whether the reverse is the case? The common theme of both passages is the cosmic significance of God's sovereignty. He is sovereign over all phenomena, for he is Creator of all that is. The one element that is not explicitly or specifically listed in the Genesis catalogue of creation is that abstraction, Time. Yet it is there, mythopoeically present in the succession of days; even the first day, the second day, the third day, before the creation of sun, moon, and stars on the fourth day. The Genesis creation story is structured on the theological time-frame of the seven-day week. The authors of Scripture were well aware that the theology of paganism was chained to the natural rhythms of time, even to the celestial deities, personified as Sun, Moon, Stars, and Constellations, which lorded it over the cycles of days and nights, months and seasons and years: personified powers of nature that are demoted in Genesis to mere artifacts, lamps rising and setting on command of the One Creator.

In its conclusion on the Sabbath theme, the biblical creation story is a parallel to the *Enuma elish* epic, which concludes with an anthem of praise to Marduk. The proclamation of his fifty names, ascribing to him the powers and attributes of the gods, comes across to us almost as a paradoxical paroxysm: polytheism straining for a monotheistic rebirth. In vesting all power and praise in Marduk, paganism comes close to abandoning polytheism altogether; like a number of hymns from ancient Egypt, it all but breaks through to a formulation of monotheism. But it was left to Israel to arrive at that formulation, to make the deity not only one, but Ultimate and Person, the formulation already presupposed in the first words of Genesis: "In the beginning, God . . ." The Sabbath passage is the creation story's doxology: a hymn of praise that is not so much an assertion of the oneness of Deity as a call to Israel to acknowledge that oneness, to affirm the lordship of that One over ourselves, over our person and our property, over our time and activity, which is to say, the uses to which we put time. This biblical paean to the One Creator, proclaiming the Seventh Day as "the Lord's/YHWH's Day" is anticipated in the first day. This day, and the five that follow it, are merely rungs necessary to arrive at the seventh. Thus, the very creation of the seven-day week is a poetic triumph of Israel's religious genius.

Why seven? Why not? It is a prime number, of convenient size in that it is larger than five and smaller than eleven. It is also six plus one. Yes, there is something arbitrary in the choice of the number seven. But the very arbitrariness, the choosing of a number that is unrelated to such natural phenomena as, for example, the phases of the moon, creates a new way of structuring time. Marking a break with the time-bound, nature-tied theology of paganism, this new time is meta-natural, metaphysical. In the sense of historic time—time as the measure of events—this new time is metahistorical. The seven-day week of Creation, to be observed by mankind in historic time—now that time itself has been created—this is the culminating praise of the Lord of matter and spirit and time. Were we to remove the days, the first six and the seventh, from the Genesis prose-poem, the tapestry of the Creation composition would fall apart; for we would be removing its very warp and woof. From beginning to end, in material and structure, in content and form, the

Genesis Creation composition is—like its Sabbath conclusion—a celebration of that Deity who transcends both Time and Nature.

The Sabbath in Connection with Freedom and Servitude

In a preceding paragraph we characterized the Sabbath-conclusion of the creation narrative as "a hymn of praise that is not so much an assertion of the oneness of Deity as a call to Israel to acknowledge that oneness, to affirm the lordship of that One over ourselves, over our persons and our property, over our time and activity." This characterization of the conclusion bears out the consonance of the composition's conclusion with what precedes it; the entirety is essentially a theological document, its message the nature of Deity. The Source and Ground of all being a God who is Person, the purposive Author of cosmos, nature and living creatures, even the hymn is a hymn in terms of function, not of form; for it—like the rest of the composition—is not an address to God, but an address to man by man. The author of the composition informs us that the relationship of this God to mankind is benevolent, a benevolence in stark contrast to the master-peon relationship that obtains between the gods and mankind in paganism. But whereas this Genesis author seems to characterize this divine benevolence as disinterested on the part of God—there is nothing he wants in return from his protegés—the implicit call to acknowledge his lordship constitutes an asseveration that mankind does owe something to his Creator. That something—be it praise in song, in ritual symbolism, in literal sacrifice of animals on his altar, in obedience to his will—is expressed in the language of Babylon, in the language of Israel, and in our own tongue, by terms that add up to the concept of *service*. In *Enuma elish*, man's service to the gods seems confined to providing the gods with their food, but this too may have become—by the time of the Epic's composition—a metaphor. Certain it is that the cult activities in Israel's shrines are called $^a b\bar{o}d\bar{a}$ or $'ab\bar{o}dat\ haqq\bar{o}de\check{s}$ "the sacred service."

Not to recognize that such worship is essentially a metaphor is to fail to appreciate that the quintessential characteristic of a biblical theology is its indissoluble tie to morality. Whatever the weight given to cultic obligations—that which man owes to God in terms of ritual—the heavy preponderance of obligation is in terms of morality, that which man owes to God in terms of obedience to God's will in connection with his behavior to his fellow man. This moral dimension of human service to God, in connection with the Sabbath concept, is the subject of the following excursus on additional structures modeled on the 6 + 1 = 7 equation.

THE SEPTETS OF (SOCIAL) MORALITY

The special relationship between the God of the Cosmos and the people of Israel is expressed in the imagery of a contract, a solemn pact or covenant into which the two parties enter. On God's part there is the promise of a special providential care of his covenant people. On the part of the latter there is the pledge to worship this God alone and to be faithful to his will. This will of God is, in a sense, epitomized in the decalogue, the Ten Words or Ten Commandments, but this will is expanded upon in the Pentateuch in a body of cultic and social regulations of considerable volume. Our address is to a number of these regulations, each of which features a septet of time units.

The Seventh-Year Release of Land

(10) Six years you may sow your land and harvest its crop. (11) But the seventh you must not work it or exercise ownership—so that the needy among your people may eat of it, and the wild animals eat what they leave. So also are you to treat your vineyard and your olive grove.

(12) Six days you may do your own work, but on the seventh day you must abstain from it, to the end that your ox and your ass may rest and your bondman and the alien achieve refreshment. (Exodus 23:10–12)

This passage, by so closely associating the seven-year cycle with the seven-day Sabbath cycle, seems to suggest that one basic concept lies behind both, the Sabbath regulation that has been treated previously in the biblical text several times (see Exodus 16 in particular), and the seven-year cycle that is first introduced here. In both cases the Israelite is free to devote his resources (of property or time) for his own gain for six units of time, and prohibited from so doing on the seventh. In the case of the seventh day, the abstention from normal business activity focuses on the obligation of the householder to allow his draft animals and bondservants a period of rest and refreshment. In the case of the seventh year, the focus seems to be on permitting the land to lay fallow, to grant the soil—as it was—a year of rest, a respite from cultivation.

This last, however, is not the rationale for the seventh-year regulation, though it may commend itself to our own sensibilities. A concern for inanimate nature and a sense of the rights of animals—such as, here, to a respite from the yoke—strikes a responsive chord in a generation long sensitized to the inhumane treatment of animals and, more recently, to the horrors of industrial man's assault on the ecology, fauna and flora. It is an anachronism to attribute such concerns to the biblical authors, even as it may be to attribute to them the knowledge that continuous cultivation of a soil may deplete it of ingredients necessary for fertility. A requirement that all farms in a single country lie fallow every seventh year, the same seventh year for all, cannot stem from the same knowledge and concern that led to the modern practice of crop rotation.

The clue to the central concern of the biblical legislator lies in the second part of the double prohibition in regard to the seventh agricultural year. The words in verse 11, which I rendered "you must not work it or exercise ownership," would most literally be rendered along the lines of "you shall release it and abandon it." The point of the passage is that a person who invests labor in a crop is entitled to reap the benefits; the injunction against reaping the harvest precludes the Israelite from cultivating the soil, for in the seventh year the land is not his to work or to harvest. Every seventh year the land reverts to its ultimate owner, God, and whatever grows on it by his grace is for him to distribute. The emphasis on the negative—that the after growth crop is not the householder's—comes through in the beneficiaries of the soil's yield: needy humans, yes, but also the beasts of the wild!

And as the seven-year cycle of verses 10–11 bespeaks God's lordship over matter, lands, real property—without an explicit word about ownership—so does the following passage (verse 12) about the seven-day week bespeak God's lordship over time, specifically over man's activities in time. What must be stressed is that the Sabbath is the prior institution, and its presence here is to suggest the symbolism of the Sabbath as the symbolism of the seventh-year release. The author assumes that the Sabbath symbolism is patent to all. And so it is not out of pedantry or repetitious didacticism but in the easy flow of pursuing his theme that he continues in verse 13: "Take careful heed of all that I have said to you. The name of any other god you are not to utter, it shall not be heard from your mouth." The reference here is to the homage implicit in oath and adjuration, for the Power called on to effectuate the imprecation is the Power that is acknowledged as sovereign. The passage then continues with the three pilgrim festivals when homage is to be paid to YHWH at His shrine(s).

The Seventh-Year Release of Servants

The most common form of servitude in ancient Israel was not chattel slavery but debt slavery. In the case of the former the slave is owned by his master; he is property. In the case of the latter, the "slave" is no slave at all, there is no ownership of one person by another; the bondservant is rather a servant indentured to his master until the outstanding debt is paid off. In order to preclude the possibility of lifetime peonage, Scripture (in Exodus 21:2–6 and Deuteronomy 15:12–18) limits such service to a maximum of six years. For all practical purposes therefore, the six years of service are regarded as payment, not only of interest accrued but of the capital amount of the debt. Unlike the Sabbath day or, possibly, the seventh year of noncultivation of the soil, this seventh year does not appear on the calendar. It is a calculation made for each bondservant, six full years from the day he enters into service (or, to use the legal term, distraint).

The Seventh-Year Remission of Debt

A seven-year cycle, not explicitly identified with the analogous cycle in connection with the land release of fallowness, is proposed in Deuteronomy 15:1–3. Every seventh year every creditor must remit the debts owed to him by any fellow Israelite. The framer of this piece of "social legislation" is aware that there is something utopian about this requirement, for he goes on to urge that well-to-do Israelites not refuse to make any loan whatsoever, especially as this seventh year of debt remission draws nearer. But the reinforcement of this regulation by the gratuitous formulation in verse 2, "No one shall dun his fellow kinsman—this remission proclamation being YHWH's," reveals the basic rationale: All property, not just real estate, belongs ultimately to Israel's Sovereign God.

The Jubilee Year: $7 \times 7 + 1 = 50$

Chapter 25 of Leviticus begins with what is essentially a restatement of the provision in Exodus 23:10–12, the release of the land from cultivation every seventh year, and the prohibition of the householder's harvesting of the after-growth. Here, however, this seventh year is characterized as "a Sabbath of complete rest, a Sabbath owing to YHWH." With verse 8 the text goes on to provide for yet another extension of the septet cycle, "You shall count off seven sabbatical years—seven times seven years—so that you have a full septet of sabbatical years, [a total of] forty-nine years." The fiftieth year is the Jubilee year. Behind this institution is the ubiquitous view of Scripture that God is the ultimate owner of the land. He it was who granted Israel title to that land and supervised its apportionment by lot to the various kinship units: tribes, clans, and families. Land thus allotted cannot be sold in perpetuity (our legal term for sale in perpetuity is *freehold* or *fee simple*); any sale of land is for a term only (in our terminology, *leasehold* or *fee tail*). Title remains vested in the family, in the carefully defined chain of heirs. No heirs are free in any generation to surrender the rights of future heirs to redeem the property from its "purchaser" tenants. The generations, however, are long, and memory is short. Given a large enough lapse of time, the purchaser-tenants will pass on the land to their own heirs and it will be alienated from the family line that alone holds true title to it.

Hence the Jubilee year, when all land returns—without payment of any redemption-price—to the original family of owners, and, in addition, any Israelite in indentured service (no matter how long he has been in distraint) goes free to rejoin his own family on the family property. Lest any Israelite regard this regulation of real estate ownership as arbitrary or unjust, he is reminded by God in verse 23, "the land may not be sold in perpetuity, for the land is Mine; you are but alien residents with Me." Similarly in regard to an Israelite indentured to a non-Israelite on Israel's soil, if no kinsman of his redeems him—as is his moral obligation—from servitude, he is forcibly released in the Jubilee year. Verse 55 gives the rationale: "For the Israelites are My subjects (or servants/slaves), My subjects they are in that I liberated them from the land of Egypt." Thus YHWH is Sovereign, Lord of land and persons. And as in the case of the Genesis formulation of the weekly Sabbath, the attribute of holiness applies to the Jubilee year: "You shall hallow the fiftieth year, proclaiming liberty (or release) throughout the land for all its inhabitants" (verse 10).

A graphic arrangement of the five septets (table 8.1) may be conducive to a number of conclusions in regard to the purely literary question of authorial/editorial provenience of the featured texts, and to the largely meta-literary question as to whether the septets were ever intended as controlling elements in ancient Israel's economy.

The distribution of the formulations of the five septets—sometimes separately, sometimes conjointly, sometimes isolated (in whole or in part), sometimes strongly allusive, sometimes unarguably cross-referential—is in itself explanation enough for the failure of the most ambitious source critics to line them up with narrative sources such as J, E, JE, P, H, HP, D, or legal corpora such as Covenant, Holiness, Priestly, and Deuteronomic. Absent clear substantive or stylistic criteria for demar-

TABLE 8-1 Septets of Reversion

A	B	C
	Theological Symbolism	The 7 as fixed or variable
1. *Sabbath Day* Exodus 23:12; Deuteronomy 5:12–15 6 days work permitted. 7th day work forbidden.	Homage is paid to God, the Creator of Time in Genesis 1 and the author of Israel's freedom in Deuteronomy 5:12–15, by human dedication of this 7th day to God's work.	Clearly the Sabbath day has to be the same day for the entire nation. It thus introduces the week into Israel's cultic calendar.
2. *Seventh Agricultural Year* Exodus 23:10–12 6 years fields may be worked and reaped. 7th year, work and reaping forbidden	Homage paid to God by withholding cultivation as symbol of earth's reversion to God's ownership. The lordship of God is reinforced by two elements: 1) the homage paid to YHWH alone in oaths and imprecations; and 2) the association with the 7th day of the Sabbath.	The association of this 7th year with the 7th day sabbath would seem to point to a national 7th year return of the land to God. On the other hand, this is not explicitly specified; and one might argue that to leave the soil untended by an entire nation (or the world for that matter is an absurdity; that the intent is that every farmer leave his fields untended one year out of every seven.
3. *Seventh Year Release of Persons* Exodus 21:2–6 6 years, indenture permitted. 7th year, indenture forbidden	As the first expansion of the Decalogue in the "Covenant Code," the limitation of servitude by one Israelite to another to six years, this provision effectually does away with chattel slavery. Israelites who have been redeemed from Egyptian bondage can be a chattel only to the God who had redeemed them "for himself."	Unambiguously variable: 6 full years from the day of entry into servitude.
4. *Seventh Year Remission of Debt* Deuteronomy 15:1–3, 9–10 6 years, a creditor may exact payments from a debtor. 7th year, debt is erased (?)	The individual Israelite is not free to ignore the 7th year remission, for it is YHWH's *remission*, i.e., decreed by the God who is the source of all prosperity. Obedience to the decree is homage to God's lordship.	The somewhat extraneous preachment that remission not be forestalled by a refusal to lend to begin with compels this 7th year as fixed. If the 7th year release of land is also fixed, we should have the improbability of two fixed years in every 7. On the other hand, every year of the six served in distraint is in payment of a debt; hence any debt chargeable to the distrainee should be expunged in the 7th year of debt-remission.

TABLE 8-1 (*continued*)

A	B	C
5. Jubilee Year: 7 x 7 + 1 = 50 Leviticus 25:8–26:2 49 years, real estate may be alienated in fee tail. 50th year, real estate reverts to the line of heirs in fee simple.	The acceptance of these provisions as expressive of homage to God's lordship of people and prosperity is explicit in verses 23, 38, 42, 55, and recapitulated in the coda Leviticus 26:1–2.	Unambiguously fixed. So the Jubilee, hence the seven 7th years are also fixed. To wit, the 7th agricultural year of Exodus 23:10–12.

cations of legal or halakhic corpora (or *membra disiecta* of such corpora) it is of little wonder that there are few attempts to date such regulations according to historical progression.

The substantive content of the regulations in the five items of (vertical column) A constitutes more than a similarity; they are an identity. So, too, the theological symbolism in the five items that constitute (vertical column) B. No reader coming across these texts for the first time without any idea as to their provenience in respect to time, place, and language would credit a suggestion that they did not derive from a single source. By way of contrast consider vertical column C. The sketchy discussion in the graph builds up to an impression—one that will upon further study exfoliate into a conviction—that the author is determined to frustrate the reader's search for logical congruity or suggestive patterning. Thus, for example, the formulation in item C1 derives its compelling necessity not from the formulation here but from other texts, which rule out a choice of Sabbath-days for every Israelite. So the sense of the formulation in item C2 is also moot. Item C3 is not moot due to the nature of the regulation, but it sets up the question of mootness in respect to item C4. And in respect to this last item, the identity of the year in item 4 could be without logical bar that same year in item 2, but the patterning of these two years-in-one (in Exodus and Deuteronomy respectively) in two widely scattered formulations becomes editorially (or authorially) incomprehensible. And there remains as well, the consideration raised in C4, that a fixed seventh-year remission of debt might effectively mean a maximal three-year term of service for any distrainee. Why then have the six-year limit at all? Why would anyone lend an amount commensurable with more than three years of indentured service?

All these perplexities come to a head (at least one, perhaps more) in Leviticus 25, of which our item C5 is only a snippet. Verse 20 raises a question that should have appeared after Exodus 23:10–12 (item A2), namely, how to make up the shortfall of the seventh year when both cultivation and harvesting are forbidden. The answer in verses 21–22 is God's providential care for the cultivated crop of every year six. Somehow, the harvest of one year to suffice for two years is made to appear even more miraculous by having its crop suffice for three years (i.e., the sixth year, the seventh year of fallowness, and the eighth year, which is the first year of the new seven-year cycle). It is nonsense to attribute the seed crop to the eighth year to this numeration. The seed crop is part and parcel of the crop for any given year. Not to reserve a seed crop for the eighth year from the *sāpīaḥ* of the seventh year would constitute agronomical suicide, for a seed crop held over for two years would result in a germination rate of less than half of seed planted from the crop of the immediately preceding year. For all that, 25:22 explicates "the three years" of verse 21 as inclusive of "the ninth year until its crop may be reaped." (The rabbinic tradition takes this ninth year as referring to the fiftieth year of the Jubilee cycle, a desperate interpretation, inasmuch as the question of sufficiency is raised only in respect to the seventh year; thus the formulation makes allusion even while it evades the question of how two consecutive years of fallowness could be survived.) An additional bit of nonsense is the formulation in verses 14–17 that forbids fraud or unfairness in the sale and purchase of land that is rendered into a leasehold for a maximum of forty-nine years, and so is no longer a (freehold) purchase at all. In the case of the price asked for the purchase of a plot any excessive demand would be unfair, whether the purchase is freehold or leasehold. And furthermore, such unfairness could only apply to a purchaser who is dealing with a seller so reduced as to sell his inheritance for a song. The seller cannot be accused of unfairness, be the sale freehold or leasehold, because no one is ever forced to buy land. This last consideration must bring us to the realization that one cannot, as the "biblical legislator" does indeed again and again, turn a moral demand into civil legislation by appeal to piety and bring on a messianic age by a communistic abolition of all property rights.

This entire discussion might very well have been considered in our chapter on structures, for laws and codes constitute by their nature a structuring of society and society's values. The biblical genius, from a literary point of view, is to enlist a plethora of themes and genres so that a structure may be the embodiment of a narrative's kerygma, a narrative may be transformed into a constitutive kerygma, and both structure and story be spun in driest prose or lyric verse.

Perhaps we can conclude in no better way than with the citation of two pericopes that immediately follow the conclusion of the jubilee year passage. Chapter 26:1–2 introduces a prohibition of idolatry, an injunction to observe the sabbaths and revere the sanctuary of YHWH. The text continues:

> If you follow my decrees and observe my commands, obeying them, I will provide your rains at their due time so that earth produces its bounty and your scattered trees yield their fruit: threshing will follow hard upon harvest, and harvest follow hard upon sowing, so that you consume your food to satiety and settle in comfort on your land. Peace shall I dower on your land, you will loll at ease upon your land with none to cause you fright. You will put your enemies to flight and they shall fall from before you by the sword. Five of you will rout a hundred and a hundred of you will rout ten thousand; by the sword shall they fall before you. I shall then turn about to you making you fruitful and many and shall fulfill my covenant with you. Long stored stores will you consume and ancient stores withdraw to make way for a new store. I shall fix my sanctuary in your midst and find you never distasteful. I shall move freely among you serving you as God and you shall be my own people. I YHWH, your God, in that I liberated you from Egypt-land that you serve them not as slaves, and broke apart the span of your yoke and led you forth head high and chin up. (Leviticus 26:3–13)

THE SABBATH DAY IN THE TWO DECALOGUES:
A POETICAL COMPARISON

This discussion of the poetic harmony of the various sabbath day and sabbath year texts would be notably incomplete if I did not address the problem of the two versions of the decalogue, which centers on the two different formulations of the sabbath day prescriptions in the two decalogues.

If we examine the two verses that immediately precede the Ten Commandments in Exodus, we must be struck by this: the text carefully, indeed, awkwardly, avoids any explicit statement that the words of God were directly received by Israel, gathered at the foot of Mount Sinai and forbidden to ascend it. In Deuteronomy, which is explicitly cast as the last address of Moses to the people he has led to the threshold of the Promised Land, Moses recapitulates the event at Horeb-Sinai when YHWH made His covenant with Israel. In Chapter 5:4 he says, "Face to face did the Lord speak with you at the mountain from amidst the fire." Now no one will insist that these words are to be taken literally—not even the most literalist of traditionalists—for God has no face. But even the metaphoric sense of "face to face"—in a direct confrontation—is applicable here at only a second remove. For Moses continues in verse 5, "I was stationed between YHWH and you at that time to tell you the word of YHWH, because you were so afraid of the fire that you did not ascend the mountain." This statement, which is repeated and expanded immediately following the words of the Decalogue, leaves us to conclude that Israel witnessed a fire blazing through an otherwise impenetrable cloud and recognized it as emblematic of the presence of God. They heard a sound from the fire and acknowledged it as the "voice" of God. But the words they heard were the words that issued from the mouth of Moses. The substance of the commandments is of God. The formulations—and the expansions of the commands—are those of Moses.

And Moses, the mediator of the covenant between God and Israel, is free to give one emphasis to the sabbath institution in Exodus, and to stress another one when he recapitulates the decalogue in Deuteronomy. There is no inconsistency nor incongruence in the two rationales for the Sabbath. On the contrary, the clue to Scripture's concept of time and freedom, hence to the sabbath celebration of God as the Creator of nature and time and as the Author of history and freedom, will appear in the following excursus on a halakhic passage.

Of Time and Freedom: A Poetical Reading of Halakha

The passage appears in Exodus in a body of laws, precepts, and admonitions that immediately follows the revelation of the decalogue. This body (chapters 21–22 and 23 in part, called "the Covenant Code" by modern scholars) begins with the previously discussed regulation, which limits the servitude of one Israelite to another to a maximum of six years; at the beginning of the seventh year the bondman must go free. There follow regulations concerning a woman subordinated to a master, homicide of a freeman, abuse of parents, and violent injury to a freeman. Our interest lies in the three regulations that follow.

Case A. Fatal and Non-Fatal Beating of a Bondservant

Should a man beat his bondservant, male or female, with a rod so that he dies then and there [literally, "under his hand"], vengeance is to be exacted. But if he survives a day or two, no vengeance is to be exacted—for, to be sure, he [is/represents] his [the master's] money-investment. (Exodus 21:20–21)

Case B. Violent Injury to a Pregnant Woman

In a case of men engaged in a brawl where a pregnant [passer-by] is struck a blow resulting in a miscarriage, no other damage ensuing [to the woman], the penalty must be in accordance with a judicial assessment taking into consideration the value claimed by the woman's husband. If, however, damage [to the woman] ensues, payment must be made [according to the principle]: life for life, eye for eye, tooth for tooth, hand for hand, foot for foot, burn for burn, wound for wound, bruise for bruise. (Exodus 21:22–25)

Case C. The Maiming of a Bondservant

Should a man strike a blow to the eye of his manservant or the eye of his maidservant which destroys it, he must grant him his freedom in repayment for the eye. And if it is a tooth of his manservant or a tooth of his maidservant that he knocks out, he must grant him his freedom in repayment for the tooth. (Exodus 21:26–27)

Case A leaves no room for doubt that the term *'ebed* here refers to a debt-slave or indentured servant. The master, who has an investment in him, may resort to force to compel him to work. Should the bondservant, however, die—his death unmistakably caused by such a beating—the master incurs the same penalty prescribed for the killing of a free citizen. In Case B the injury—if any—is to a free person. The fetus is clearly not regarded as a life, but rather as a property of the father, who must be compensated for his loss. If injury to a person occurs, it is only to the Israelite free woman, in which case the penalty is determined according to the principle of the *lex talionis*, the so-called "rule of retaliation:" a life for a life, an eye for an eye, a tooth for a tooth, and so on. This principle having been stated, the text reverts to injuries inflicted upon slave by master in the course of a disciplinary beating.

Case C provides first that for mayhem to a bondservant's eye, the master loses the services of that servant. It then goes on to state in a separate sentence that the penalty is the same in the case of mayhem to a tooth. The immediate question is, why the necessity for two sentences? Why does the text not state that for striking out eye or tooth of a slave the owner must release his servant? This question of form is overshadowed by one of substance: By what logic of arithmetic or retaliation does the text prescribe the same penalty or compensation for a lost tooth as for a lost eye? Surely, the loss of a tooth is trivial compared to the loss of an eye! A third question is why Case B, death or injury to a free person, is permitted to intervene between A and C, cases dealing respectively with death or injury dealt to bondservants.

These questions point to a single answer, an answer that discloses once again that biblical verses did not just get misplaced by chance, nor were they permitted to remain in disarray by later editors. The answer will also reveal how artfully the biblical author can express a philosophical concept by simple juxtaposition of several legal cases.

Case B differs from those surrounding it not only in the status of the person injured, free rather than "slave," but also in the accidental nature of the injury to the free person. This consideration alone should cause us to realize that the rabbis correctly interpreted the life for life, eye for eye formula as a principle of compensation, not of mindless, mechanical retaliation. What purpose would be served either as a preventive or punitive measure by imposing exactly the same injury upon the person who caused the injury by *accident*? And what comfort to the victim that the person accidentally causing his injury was similarly maimed? The "law of talion" is not to be read literally (neither here nor in Mesopotamian contexts!), not to be understood as a principle of retaliation at all. It is a prescription for payment for damages: The payment is to correspond to the gravity of the injury inflicted, the greatest payment for the loss of life, the smallest payment for a bruise (and in Case B, payment for the embryo lost on the basis of the value of the child-to-be, given the sex of the fetus, its closeness to term, possibly the husband's having other children or not).

The insertion of this principle at the point of its appearance is to serve us as a red flag, to alert us to the significance of what follows (Case C): In the case of a beating administered to a bondservant, where the beating is both intentional and legitimate but the maiming is unintentional, the principle of "talion," featured in Case B, does not apply. The penalty does not vary with the gravity of the injury. Whether the loss to the slave is so much as an eye or so little as a tooth, the slave wins his freedom and the master loses his services. Why? Because the slave is no slave at all. He is not the property of his master. He belongs to himself. The only claim the master has upon him is not on his person but on his *time*. And the slightest impairment of his person, the slightest invasion—so to speak—of his capital, must eventuate in the end of his servitude.

Poetic Congruence of the Sabbath Texts in the Decalogue

Time. Time is what the sabbath is all about: God's time and man's time. Sovereignty over time, which is freedom, and surrender of time, which is service. Let us turn now to the two Decalogue Sabbath texts:

EXODUS 20:8–11	DEUTERONOMY 5:12–15
1. *Mark* the Sabbath Day by sanctifying it.	*Observe* the Sabbath Day by sanctifying it, as *YHWH your God has bidden you*.
2. Six days you may work in pursuit of your every enterprise. The seventh day, however, is a Sabbath owing to YHWH, your God: (On it) you are to perform no work —neither you, your son nor daughter, your manservant or maidservant	*Six days you may work in pursuit of your every enterprise.* The seventh day, however is a Sabbath owing to YHWH, your God: (On it) you are to perform no work— neither you, your son nor daughter, your manservant or maidservant

3.
your cattle, the alien in your
jurisdiction.

4.

Your ox or ass—that is, any of
your cattle, the alien in your jurisdiction.
—That your manservant and maidservant *may rest as you do.*
Thus you will *mark* that you were subjugated in the land of Egypt,
whence YHWH delivered you by
unremitting force.

5. The reason: In six days YHWH
made heaven and earth, the seas
and everything in them, and rested
on the seventh day.

6. That is the reason YHWH *blessed
the Sabbath Day, sanctifying it.*

That is the reason that YHWH *your
God has charged you to enact the
Sabbath Day.*

In the first proclamation of the Decalogue, the emphasis is on the universal claim
of the Lord of Creation on the time (or service, or worship) of all his creatures. In
his review of the Decalogue in Deuteronomy, Moses stresses the particular claim of
God on the time of his particular people, the people he has redeemed from servitude
to human masters in Egypt, that they may covenant to be servants to Him and to
Him alone. The parallel columns of the two sabbath texts will help us note the telltale differences. In 1, Moses in his recapitulation uses the word *observe* in the place
of *mark*, and adds "as YHWH your God has bidden you"—an unnecessary reference
to this command in the Exodus decalogue except by way of reminding the reader
that Moses is speaking—quoting his own retailing of YHWH's command. In 3, in
place of "your cattle," he says, "your ox or ass, that is any of your cattle," thus specifying that the release from labor applies to draft animals; sheep and cows do not labor.
In 4, he adds to the Exodus charge the words, "that your manservant and maidservant *may rest as you do.*" By thus putting the emphasis on the charge to the Israelite
householder to abstain from work, he makes it clear that the call on the master of
his own time to *observe* God's time by not working is not social legislation, but
rather an obligation to God. This obligation, to show oneself as God's subject, is
also a privilege, thus a privilege-obligation that the master must allow his bondservants to share with him. Only then does Moses takes up the word "mark," which begins the Exodus version and continues with the theme that the Israelite master, by
sharing the cessation of work with his servants, *marks* his acknowledgment that his
own freedom as an Israelite is a gift from the God who liberated him from Egyptian
servitude, this liberation underlined as a feat performed on his behalf "with unremitting force." Finally, in 6, in place of Exodus' reference to Genesis, "the reason
that YHWH blessed and sanctified the Sabbath Day," he now states that this is the
reason why YHWH, who had at the time of Creation blessed and sanctified the
Sabbath, the liberating God who covenanted at Sinai that he be "your God," *did
then charge you (Israel) as His people to enact the Sabbath Day.*

In brief, the authors of Scripture had one term (*'bd*) which as verb means both *to
labor* and *to serve;* and which as noun (*'ebed*) means both *servant* and *slave.* They

had several words and additional metaphors for the concepts of sovereignty and freedom, which mean respectively the faculty to dispose of power and the faculty to dispose of time. The sovereign creator of time and matter had deputed of his sovereignty to the race of mankind. The return he asks for this boon is subjection to his will, this return he asks from Israel in particular, the people for whom he has wrought another feat: a re-creation, a rebirth into freedom. This return that he asks, particularly of Israel, symbolized in a weekly surrender of time to him, is not a heavy bondage. Theology abounds in paradoxes that make a peculiar sense: The purest freedom lies in being servant-slave to the Author of all that is, to the God who is the principle of freedom.

TWO MORE ADDENDS

These odds and addends have related mostly to the discussions in chapter 2 centering on the sabbath element in the biblical creation narrative. I will confine myself to two more addends, the one immediately following, entitled Excursus of Psalm 19, and a concluding addend that complements the Drunkenness of Noah in chapter 5. The excursus on Psalm 19 could well appear elsewhere: my determination to include it here is in the interests of several aspects of biblical poetics that we have been discussing. Specifically it is placed here in connection with the ways in which the solar orb figures and does not figure in the Genesis creation account. More generally, it is instructive as to how a theological statement that is only implied in the creation narrative is almost kerygmatically pronounced in the psalm, and how, further, the borders of the cosmos may appear figuratively in both narrative prose and lyric verse as primeval waters or the gauze-thin cosmic tent-walls. Finally, to be sure, is the mythopoeic nature of the narrative creation account, and the sly humor in the poetic paean to (the God behind) the created world, as well as the juxtaposition in the psalm of power, esthetics, and morality, and the relationship of these to one another and to the revelational capacities of mute nature and prophetic utterance.

Excursus on Psalm 19

> (2) The heavens do tell the glory of God,
>   The works of His hands the sky-sheet recounts.
> (3) Day by day it [Creation] wells forth utterance,
>   And night by night creates awareness. ['Tho -]
> (4) There is no utterance, there are no words—['Tho]
>   No sound from them is heard.
> (5) Through all the earth their cable-lines have stretched,
>   Even to world's end their guy-ropes.
>   For the Sun has he designated a tent within them [the heavens].
> (6) And he, like a bridegroom coming forth from his pavilion,
>   Rejoices, like an athlete, to run his race.
> (7) [Yes] from one of heavens' limits his coming forth
>   and to their [other] limits his arc
>   —from his heat there is no hiding.

(8) YHWH's guidance (tōrā) is of a piece—life-restoring;
    YHWH's rules are reliable—enlightening the most simple.
(9) YHWH's regulations are straightforward—illuminating the mind;
    YHWH's bidding is transparent—bringing lustre to our eyes.
(10) Reverence for YHWH, when pure, stands us ever in good stead;
    YHWH's norms are true, correct—each and all.
(11) More desirable than gold or riches great,
    Sweeter than fruit-honey and dripping nectar.
(12) How alert to them is your [obedient] servant—
    that great is the outcome of their observance.
(13) Can anyone be conscious of all error?
    Clear me then of unconscious [wrong doing].
(14) So, indeed, from wrong intention hold back your servant,
    Let them have no sway o'er me. Only then shall I be whole
    And so cleared of grave transgression.
(15) May these words of my mouth find favor,
    My inarticulate meditation—acceptance by you,
    YHWH, my Rock and my Redeemer. (Psalm 19:2–15)

The affinity of the first six verses (2–7) to Psalm 8 has not escaped the notice of scholars. The "work of His hands" recorded on the sky-sheet of heaven refers, of course, to the celestial phenomena as they appear to human sight. This visual perception is translated into an auditory one—a story "told," a feat proclaimed—despite "no sound from them," that is, the heavens, being literally heard. And as the "message" of what transpires up there regularly by day and by night is one that even a blind man may see or a deaf one hears, so is the utterance of that message assigned to time-divisions—abstract, mute, unconscious—day and night expressing, like antiphonal choristers, the meaning of their being in respect to the Power that created them. And even while the poet engages in personificatory imagery he makes double use of the preposition lᵉ "to," which also governs temporal periods, so that "day utters to day" even as it does so "day by day."

Several interpretive difficulties in verse 5, owing to a slavish fixation on words rather than imagery, interfere with an easy grasp of the psalmist's thought. What is the "line" (qaw) which has "gone out" through the earth and to whom or what does the possessive suffix refer? The general assumption is that the antecedent is day and night, and that parallel to the lines of day and night, is "their words" (milleyhem); since "their lines" referring to day and night makes dubious sense, and "their words" has a parallel in the words (dᵉbārīm) of verse 4, many scholars accept the emendation of qawwam "their line" to qowlam "their voice;" this latter despite the fact that verse 4 explicitly denies utterance (ōmer), words (dᵉbārīm), or voice/sound (qol) altogether. The only antecedent that makes sense however is the sky-sheet of the heavens, in which he (the only possible subject here is the Creator) has provided a tent for the sun. And the presence here of imagery for two different tents has thrown exegetes off the track: the bowl of heaven under which we live, this concave sky-sheet is one "tent," and at its eastern extremity, 'neath its stretched skirts, there is another tent that the Creator has pitched for the sun.

The biblical tent (*'ohel*) is in its narrowest denotation a sheltering enclosure of cloth or skin stretched over supporting beams, and in its broadest connotation a term for *home*; Hebrew *miskan* "residence" is a certain kind of tent, one in which the tent "walls" are further supported by board-panels. The area covered by the tent is its *māqōm* "site" or *ḥevel* "boundary." The "walls" of the tent are *yᵉrīˀōt* "drape-cloth," *salmā* "sheet," or "skin, integument," and *doq* "thin curtain." These walls extending from upright posts are attached to ropes (*qawwīm* "lines," *ḥᵃbālīm* "cords," *meytārīm* "anchor-ropes") at points on their vertical axis, these ropes stretching to points on a perimeter where their pegs (*ytd*) are hammered into the ground. The terms for pitching a tent are thus *tqˀ* "fix in place" (i.e., the pegs), *nth* "stretch" (i.e., the wall-curtains), *mtḥ* "pull taut." Thus, for example, when the prophet addresses Israel as a woman who has produced not a single child but is destined to mother a huge brood, he calls on her to prepare a tent large enough to accommodate her many children, a tent occupying a large area requiring longer ropes and reinforced pegging:

> Enlarge the *area* of your *tent*
> Let the wall panels of your pavilion stretch long
>   —do not stint —
> Make long your anchor-ropes
> And fix more firm your tent-pegs. (Isaiah 54:2)

Similarly all of Jerusalem, synonymous now with the pilgrim shrine called Zion, is pictured in a felicitous future as—by the grace of YHWH—one fixed and unbuffeted tent:

> A tranquil residence,
> A tent not to be relocated,
> Its pegs never to shift,
> Nor any of its ropes severed. (Isaiah 33:20)

This tent imagery we have come across in Psalms, where the Creator:

> Draped light like a sheet-cloth,
> Stretched the heavens out like a drape. (Psalm 104:2)

This imagery for the celestial expanse appears again in Isaiah, where God is pictured as:

> He who stretches out the heavens like gauze,
> And pulls them taut like a tent [made] for dwelling. (Isaiah 40:22)

Returning to verse 5 of our psalm, we see now that the *qawwīm* are the metaphoric cables anchoring the figurative tent-walls of heaven, and their *millīm* are an elsewhere-unattested term for some aspect of the tent-appurtenances (perhaps their skirts), stretching to (/beyond) the limits of the world (*'ereṣ*). The sheer magnitude of that stretch and the sights it presents to the senses by day and by night, mute but eloquent witnesses to the power of its Creator, is multiplied in imagination when one considers that for its Creator all this is, as it was, a child's playhouse ("the work of his fingers"). And tucked away at one edge of this circus-top tent-bubble is a smaller tent: the abode of the sun. And here this mighty object of the pagan's awe, personified as the god Šamaš (or Sol or Helios) resides, "He from whose heat there is no hiding." Except of course when he regularly and on schedule "sets." But it is at the point of his coming forth from his pavilion in the east that our psalmist chooses to make fun of this personified paragon of polytheistic paganism. For this epiphany is not the ordinary awakening of any superhuman male: this is of a *bridegroom* making his first emergence from under his nuptial canopy. The heroic virility of a long-abstinent groom in the chamber where he has first been treated "to a woman's task" is probably a staple of every human culture. Perhaps our earliest record of it is in Tablet I, iv of the Gilgamesh Epic, where the courtesan introduces the virgin Enkidu to a woman's task, welcoming his ardor:

> As his love was drawn unto her,
> For six days and seven nights Enkidu comes forth,
> Mating with the lass.
> After he had had (his) fill of her charms,
> He set his face toward his wild beasts.
> On seeing him, Enkidu, the gazelles ran off . . .
> Enkidu had to slacken his pace . . . (ANET p. 75 TAB. I iv. 20–25, 28)

So too our psalmist parodies the emergence of Sol, filled with a sense of his nightlong profusion of puissant potency, ready now to exert his leg muscles in another of the competitive sports.

The appositeness of these six verses to the general theme of the grandeur of creation, and to the particular one of putting paganism in its place by putting one of its gods in his, is clear. But to stop here is to miss a golden opportunity to open ourselves up to the full range of poetical resources and strategies available to Scripture's authors, whether in a figurative narration of creation's chronicles, or a celebratory resume of creational results as record and teaching of the theological significance of creation-history.

There can be no question that between the last three words (Hebrew) of verse 7 —*from his heat there is no hiding*, a seemingly pointless praise of heaven's overheated athlete—and the three words opening verse 8—*YHWH's tora is of a piece*, beginning a catalogue in praise of YHWH's teachings—there seems to be a semantic gap of huge proportion. So great indeed is the felt absence of a transitional phrase or two, that most scholars opt for the conclusion that two unrelated poems have been patched together. Even more impressive, however, is the number of readers who are not driven to this poetical conclusion. Which is perhaps to say that the very abrupt switch in themes as in rhythm between verse 2–7 and verse 8–10 has been perceived by many as a dramatic device to compel the reader to examine what implicit thought-link bridges the two pericopes. And a formulation of that thought, often cited, and as philosophically impressive as it is lucidly simple, is this sentence of Immanuel Kant's: "There are two things that fill my soul with holy reverence and ever-growing wonder—the spectacle of the starry sky that virtually annihilates us as physical beings, and the moral law that raises us to infinite dignity as intelligent agents."

It may be argued that the cosmic awe felt by modern man under the starry sky and the seemingly same emotions experienced by our predecessors in antiquity are essentially incommensurable, that a firework display, however breathtaking, cannot compare to the impact of such a display when the observer is also aware that each sparkling light is one of many billions of suns, most of them dwarfing our own sun. And, further, that the reduction of the solar phenomenon to a jeer at the macho male pretension would seem to weaken the equipoise of the man-reducing effect of cosmic vastness on the one hand, and on the other the man-elevating effect of moral dignity as, indeed, the intellectual grandeur of the consciousness of that dignity.

To the first of these challenges the following verses from Isaiah 40 would seem adequate testimony that the human appreciation of infinity is not enhanced or lessened when it is expanded or reduced by the power of *n*:

> (12) Who has measured [creation's] waters by handful[s],
> Or fixed heaven's distance by his handspan,
> Or collected earth's soil in a scale's pod
> Or taken the weight of the mountains in a [hand-held] scale,
> Or the heights in a balance!
> (13) Who has fixed [the magnitude of] YHWH's spirit,
> Is there anyone who can make known his blueprint!
> (14) Whom has he taken into his counsel,
> Given him all-embracing consciousness,
> Trained him in the way of judgment,
> Trained him in awareness,
> Made known to him the path of comprehension! (Isaiah 40:12–14)

The theme of God as Creator is resumed in verse 21:

> (21) Will you not acknowledge,
> Will you not pay heed?
> Have you not been told of the Beginning,
> Have you not been made aware of earth's Foundations?
> (22) Enthroned (*yṣb*)/he is o'er earth's sphere,
> Whose populations (*yṣbyh*) are grasshopper-like;
> He Who stretches out the heavens like gauze,
> Pulls them taut like a tent-habitation (*lṣbt*).
> (26) Look upwards—high up—and consider
> Who 'twas created all these . . . (Isaiah 40:21, 22, 26)

As for the second of our questions, the incongruous leap in Psalm 19 from macho Sun to awareness of YHWH's *tora*, let us note the parallel phenomenon in this pericope from Isaiah 40: The transition between verse 14 (the puniness of human understanding of creation's vastness) and the call to recognize the transcendent dimensions of creation's Creator (verse 21) is a jeer at paganism's attempt to portray divinity:

> (18) To whom will you liken God,
> And what likeness will you impute to him?

(19) The idol cast by the smelter
   Plated o'er by the smith in gold.
   Fastened together by the smith with silver? (Isaiah 40:18–19)

In theme and structure, Psalm 19 and Is. 40 share so much as to suggest a single composer or, perhaps, the variations of a Beethoven on a theme of Mozart's. It is not the sun as such, one of nature's many and great artifacts ("from whose heat there is no hiding"), which is laughed to scorn in the psalm, as the breathtaking sweep of heaven is not deprecated in itself by likening it to a mere tent's canopy. The mockery is directed not at nature but at the attempts of pagan imagination to personify aspects of nature, attempts that trivialize nature even as they deify its constituencies and veil from human appreciation the truly awesome transcendence of the Power and Intelligence for whom all nature is but a plaything. The attack on a pagan theology—whether in Isaiah 40:18–19, where a man-made idol is put forward as paganism's best effort to imageize the divine, or in taking the sun's daily trek across the sky as the literal race of a divine athlete—is jocular and condescending in mood, for how could so silly an ideology stir the perceptive mind to anger? And ultimately, of course, it is neither paganism nor its representation that is the object of derision for psalmist or prophet. The derision is reserved for the humans, and for Israelite humans at that, who fail to receive the thunderously mute message presented to their organs of sight and hearing for processing by the intelligence that these faculties are supposed to feed.

And who, asks the psalmist in 19:11, is the loser by this but the humans who so regularly forego the sweet-beyond-compare fruit of revelation. Not so the psalmist himself. He is alert and grateful for the revelation, he knows that the ultimate revelation of God's creative power is made to promote the revelation of God's moral purpose for the race he has created and placed at creation's center stage. But this consciousness and self-consciousness of the psalmist does not lead him to the hubris of self-preening in moral pride. For all his awareness of what God wants of him, he is aware of the moral myopia of the most clear-sighted of moralists. Whether from unconscious error or conscious actions performed in self-delusive wrongheadedness, he needs a deterrence that only God can supply. Only if God keeps him alert to the never-interrupted message can he aspire to moral innocence and integrity. And in the humility that alone is proof against even the pride of probity, the psalmist in the poem's last verse reviews the composition he has so truly ordered in praise of God, and recognizes that at its best it is but a weak articulation of the praise with which he would, if he could, do justice to the majesty of his God.

The Drunkenness of Noah

The Odds and Addends treated hitherto relate primarily to chapter 2, the content and function of the biblical creation account, and to poetical problems raised in connection with the cluster of sextets and septets akin to the seventh-day construction imposed on Israel's lunar-solar calendar. Much of the material might well have been considered in chapter 7 ("Structures") with emphasis on the function of scriptural structures that lend themselves to a poetic consideration of the similar (yet not same) formulations vis-à-vis the mythopoeic aspects in prose and in verse, and of the conceptual complementarity between work and rest, between work and recompense, and of the associative conceptions of dominion and subservience, of liberty and the prerogative to dispose of time. Hence I have reserved this discussion for this supplementary chapter. So, too, with respect to Psalm 19. The role of the sun (as we have discerned) as divine gymnast in this spoof of paganism segueing into the priority of morality in Scripture's monotheistic theology is in polar contrast to the source-critical school of "literary criticism," which can discern substantive conceptual conflict between aspects of the created world as pictured in verse versus prose; between pagan personification of natural forces infiltrating biblical poetry and the demythologization of cosmogony in the catechistic prose of Genesis 1.

I will conclude this chapter with an addendum on the Drunkenness of Noah (see chapter 5), resuming particularly with a conjecture as to the connection of the Canaan in Noah's curse with the Gibeonites of Joshua 9, who were destined in Joshua's words to be heavers of wood and drawers of water for his people Israel and for the house of his God.

A review of our discussion in chapter 5 will show that in verse 27 "he" of the sentence "may he reside in the tents of Shem" is generally taken to be the Japheth of the immediately preceding invocation "Broad scope may God to Japheth grant." I however, leaning upon Rashi's understanding, take the subject as the "God" who has been invoked to bless Japheth. It is a matter of happenstance that I arrived independently at the identities of the personae in the immediately preceding verse.

> (26) [What] he said, [in full];
>> "Praised be YHWH, god of Shem!
>> And slave to them may Canaan be! (Genesis 9:26)

These personae are YHWH, god of Shem, Shem, being a metonym for Israel, and the "them" to whom Canaan is to be slave are YHWH and his people, while the slave Canaan is a fore-reference to the Gibeonites of Joshua 9. It was quite some time later that I discovered that I had forgotten or altogether missed that these same identifications were made ad loc. by Obadiah Sforno. This recovery of Sforno's having preempted me in the Gibeonites/Canaanite identification bolsters me as I proceed to my less than pious or orthodox reading of Joshua, Chapter 9.

A. Prelude

(1) When all the kings across the Jordan in the hill country and the Shephela, on the entire coast of the Great Sea as far [north as] facing Mt. Lebanon—the Hittites, the Amorites, the Canaanites, the Perizzites, the Hivvites and the Jebusites—got word, (2) they mobilized for war with Joshua and with Israel in single accord.

B. The Plot

(3) The citizens of Gibeon **now** got word of what Joshua had done to Jericho and Ai.) (4) They, for their part also, behaved with guile. They went and constituted themselves an embassy. They fetched worn sacks for their asses, wineskins worn, split and resown, (5) footgear worn and patched and attired in worn out garb and all their edible provision stale and mold-flecked.

C. Execution of the Plot

(6) They went to Joshua, to the encampment at Gilgal. To him and the fighting men of Israel they said, "From a distant land have we come. Now then, conclude a pact with us." (7) The fighting men of Israel responded to the Hivvites, "Perhaps it is within my ambit you dwell. In which case, how can I make a pact with you?" (8) So they said to Joshua, "It is your liege-men we are." Whereupon he said to them, "Just who is it you are and just where do you come from?" (9) To him they said, "From a far distant land have your liege-men come, for the sake of your god YHWH. Truly we have heard report of him, yes of all his doings in Egypt, (10) And the whole of his execution of the two Amorite kings in trans-Jordan, to Sihon king of Heshbon and to Og king of Bashan, he that was of Ashtaroth. (11) Then it was that our elders and all our land's citizens said, 'Take food provision for your trek and go to encounter them. Say to them: *Your liege-men are we. Make a pact with us.*' (12) This food of ours—warm we provisioned ourselves with it from home that day we set out to journey toward you—and [look] now: dry and mold-flecked. (13) And these wineskins that new were when we filled them, [look] now: split open. And this garb of ours and our footwear, worn out by reason of our trek, so long, so long." (14) The [Israelite] leaders took samples of their provisions—but of YHWH['s] oracle they made no inquiry. (15) Thus did Joshua make amity with them. He made a pact assuring them survival. And the confederacy's chieftain's took oaths to them.

D. Discovery, March, and Absent Assault

(16) It was a threesome of days after they had made this pact with them that they got word: how near their distance to him, yes well within his ambit dwelling, they . . . (17) The Israelites moved out and on the day after the morrow arrived at their cities— these cities being Gibeon, Kephirah, Beerot and Kiriath-jearim. (18) Yet did the Israelites not attack them, for the confederacy's chieftains had taken oath to them by YHWH, god of Israel.

E. Chagrin and Reprisal Decree

The confederacy's rank-and-file grumbled against the chieftains. (19) The chieftains all addressed the confederate ranks, "We did take oath to them by YHWH, god of Israel. Hence, we may do them no harm. (20) This we must do to them—(you) guarantee their lives—only thus avert from ourselves [God's] wrath [in keeping] with the oath we took to them." (21) Thus did the chieftains decree to them: *They are to live.* And thus did they become hewers of wood and drawers of water for all the confederacy, in keeping with the declaration to them of the chieftains.

F. Resumption of Reprisal, Recapitulation of Decree

(22) Joshua summoned them and dressed them down, to wit: "Why did you deceive us, saying 'We are at a far far distance from you,' when you live well within our ambit's center. (23) Now, then: Under ban you are [decreed] to be. Never will there fail to be from among you slave, hewers of wood and drawers of water for the house of my god!" (24) In response to Joshua they said, "Verily it was told in detail to your servants that which your god YHWH ordained to his servant Moses, to grant you all this land and

exterminate on your account all the inhabitants of the land. In great fear for our lives were we on your account, hence we did what we did. (25) And, now, we are in your power. However it seems proper and upright in your opinion to treat us, do so!" (26) Thus did he do to them, as told, delivering them from the Israelite's power, so that they did not kill them. (27) Thus it was that Joshua dedicated them at that time as hewers of wood and drawers of water to the confederacy, and [or, that is] to the altar of YHWH—continuing to this very day—in the place that he chooses [for it]. (Joshua 9:1–27)

The economy of Scripture's narrative style would seem to be notably absent in this long chapter devoted to a single event in the context of Israel's invasion of the promised land. A single event that may be momentous for the hapless Hivvites of Gibeon, but of trivial significance to the Israelite conquerors or their descendants. A simple and straightforward telling of the story would omit the pericopes A and B altogether. It would start with C, the arrival of the Gibeonite embassy, present the reason for its mission, and omit the ambassadors' wearisome citation of the instructions delivered to them at home. The substance of pericopes D, E, and F could be given in a single pericope without another supererogatory explanation of the reason for the Gibeonite ruse, and with a single statement of the decree that appears three times, and with seeming inconsistency and redundant repetitiveness: once, seemingly, in the mouth of the chieftains, once in that of Joshua, and once in the voice of the narrator, assuring us that the decree was Joshua's.

Let us then proceed to a close rereading of our chapter to search for the poetic purposes of the narrational convolutions.

Episode A. Prelude

(1) When all the kings across the Jordan in the hill country and the Shephela, on the entire coast of the Great Sea as far [north as] facing Mt. Lebanon—the Hittites, the Amorites, the Canaanites, the Perizzites, the Hivvites and the Jebusites—got word, (2) they mobilized for war with Joshua and with Israel in single accord.

The prelude is, at first glance, totally irrelevant to the narrative that follows. It tells us of the unanimous reaction of the kings of Canaan to the Israelite threat, their mustering their armies into a single force to do battle with the invaders. And not another word to follow up this introduction appears until the Gibeonite narrative is concluded. This introduction is resumed with the first verses of chapters 10 and 11, which begin with the identical opening words of 9:1, *wayhī kišmoᵃ* "When [so and so] got word . . ." In 10:1 it is Adoni-zedek, king of Jerusalem, who gets word of Joshua's conquest of Ai and Jericho and his putting their populations and kings to the *ḥerem* ban; and word as well of the Gibeonite's preclusion of a similar fate for themselves by dint of their peace treaty with Israel. His rallying of a number of kings against the Gibeonites results in disaster for these royal city-states to the south and west of Gibeon. In 11:1 it is Jabin, king of Hazor, who gets word— presumably of the debacle of the Adoni-zedek coalition—and rallies the kings of northern Canaan, who meet a like fate at Joshua's hands. The list of defeated kings is resumed and enlarged in Chapter 12. It is important to note that the conquered populations subsumed in 12:8 are exactly those six nations, and in the identical order to their appearance, in our 9:1, "The Hittites, the Amorites, the Canaanites, the Perizzites, the Hivvites and the Jebusites."

Episode B. The Plot

(3) The citizens of Gibeon **now** got word of what Joshua had done to Jericho and Ai.) (4) They, for their part also, behaved with guile. They went and constituted themselves an embassy. They fetched worn sacks for their asses, wineskins worn, split and resewn, (5) footgear worn and patched and attired in worn out garb and all their edible provision stale and mold-flecked.

In contrast to 9:1, where the word reaching the cis-Jordanian kings is left unspecified, is the parenthetic hypotactic verse 3, which I have placed at the beginning of pericope B. This verse, serving as the transition between the prelude and the main narrative, specifies that the word received by the Gibeonites was of Joshua's treatment of Jericho and Ai. We shall see that this contrast in specification serves a significant poetic purpose in the narrative that follows. For our immediate focus, the significance of the prelude—whose train of thought is not picked up again until 10:1—is to contrast the action of the Gibeonites in verse 4 with the stance of their fellow autochthones.

The first verse proper of pericope B, verse 4, rendered by the Revised Version (RV) as "they also did work wilily and went and made as if they had been ambassadors," for all its fidelity to the Hebrew may be misleading on at least two counts. One, inasmuch as the comparison (contrast) in context is as between "all the kings" and the Gibeonites, one would think that the wiliness of the Gibeonites is in comparison with the wiliness of "all the kings." But these latter are not wily in the least. Their hostility and bellicosity is open and straightforward. Hence the comparison can only be with the third party, the Israelites. And the guile of the Gibeonites is in counterploy to the guile of Joshua at Ai. As he lured these foes from their fortress into a cunning ambuscade, so did the Gibeonites lure Israel into a cunningly contrived compact. The poetic question would then remain: Is the ruse of the Gibeonites, which guarantees their survival, being justified by comparison with the ruse of Joshua, which led to the extermination of Ai? Or is it likely that Joshua's own wiliness serves to highlight his folly in falling for the Gibeonite ruse?

The second misperception that may arise from RV's rendering is the implication that the Gibeonites pretended to be an embassy when they were not that in reality. This, of course, is nonsense. They did indeed constitute themselves an embassy— note my translation—the ruse was in how they dressed themselves up for that mission. The stem ṣyr appears a half-dozen times in the noun form with the contextually attested sense of "agent, representative, legate," but the hitpael verb form "set one's self up as legate" appears only here, and seems to be a deliberate approximation of the hitpael of the stem ṣyd "game, food, provisions" that appears in verse 12, "to provide oneself with food." This occurrence is similarly the only verbal occurrence of this stem. (It is perhaps recognition of this approximation of ṣyr/ṣyd that led LXX to render this verb in verse 4 exactly as it does the verb in verse 12.) The play on the two stems thus would suggest a portmanteau signification: *they pro-ceeded to provision themselves for an embassy role,* as detailed in the description that follows of worn pack-bags and wineskins, footgear and body-wraps and food stale and moldy.[7]

Episode C. Execution of the Plot

(6) They went to Joshua, to the encampment at Gilgal. To him and the fighting men of Israel they said, "From a distant land have we come. Now then, conclude a pact with us." (7) The fighting men of Israel responded to the Hivvites, "Perhaps it is within my ambit you dwell. In which case, how can I make a pact with you?" (8) So they said to Joshua, "It is your liege-men we are." Whereupon he said to them, "Just who is it you are and just where do you come from?" (9) To him they said, "From a far distant land have your liege-men come, for the sake of your god YHWH. Truly we have heard report of him, yes of all his doings in Egypt, (10) And the whole of his execution of the two Amorite kings in trans-Jordan, to Sihon king of Heshbon and to Og king of Bashan, he that was of Ashtaroth. (11) Then it was that our elders and all our land's citizen's said, 'Take food provision for your trek and go to encounter them. Say to them: *Your liege-men are we. Make a pact with us!*' (12) This food of ours—warm we provisioned ourselves with it from home that day we set out to journey toward you— and [look] now: dry and mold-flecked. (13) And these wineskins that new were when we filled them, [look] now: split open. And this garb of ours and our footwear, worn out by reason of our trek, so long, so long." (14) The [Israelite] leaders took samples of their provisions—but of YHWH['s] oracle they made no inquiry. (15) Thus did Joshua make amity with them. He made a pact assuring them survival. And the confederacy's chief-tain's took oaths to them.

The address of the embassy upon reaching the encampment at Gilgal is so terse that it can only be instance of *free direct discourse.* The far distance they have come suffices to identify themselves; their purpose in coming is to propose a treaty; the nature of the treaty is unspecified. The Israelite identity is constituted of at least four elements or entities, two of which appear in this pericope. There is Joshua (the commander-in-chief), then the *ʾîš yiśrāel.* The rendering of the fifty or so appearances of this phrase by "the men of Israel" leaves this singular collective construct altogether undifferentiated from the construct (bearing this meaning) featuring the plural form *ʾanšei.* This latter can have a number of connotations: simple distributive or plural with reference to the individuals, members, citizens, magistrates, freemen, soldiers of a given people, polity, or political group. The expression *ʾîš yiśrāel* (/or a specified tribe of Israel) is always in construction or context that guarantees that the term refers to warriors or a warrior class, whereas a similar sense for *ʾanšei* is achieved only by the addition of such terms as *milḥāmā* "war," *ṣābāʾ* "army." The sense too of a status or role, rather than an exemplary execution of that role, is suggested in a number of contexts where these *braves* of Israel are cowering from conflict or routed by the enemy.

This collectivity then, the "manhood of Israel," may be expressing a *macho* bravado when, in contrast to the plural address of the Gibeonites, it speaks of itself in the singular and addresses the embassy in the singular. (Note also Joshua's use of plurals for the Israelites and the Gibeonites in verse 20.) The narrator too prepares us for this switch in person number when he has "the manhood of Israel" speaking to "the Hivvite" (singular collective). Aside from the arrogation of self-importance in the first person singular address to the Hivvite embassy, there is certainly an overwhelming arrogance in speaking of the autochthonous population as living "in my midst," when that "midst" is confined to "the camp at Gilgal" (verse 6). And for all the presage of the victories at Jericho and Ai, the first of these fell to YHWH's miraculous intervention, and the second to a divinely inspired ruse.

To this *macho* address the Gibeonites make no answer. Having declared their origin in a distant land, the question is tantamount to a charge that they are lying. Rather than attempt a rebuttal, they turn to the commander Joshua and submit themselves to his mercy. And Joshua asks again for specifics as to their identity and land of origins, to which questions no answer is forthcoming. Instead we have a response implying that their land is too distant and their polity too insignificant to be meaningful to Israel. By contrast to this is what inspired them to come so far, the report that has resounded worldwide, the mighty acts of YHWH in Egypt, the destruction of the kings of Heshbon and Bashan, told as if it were ancient history, citation almost from the book of Deuteronomy. No mention, of course, of Ai and Jericho, for these are only events of yesterday, and the embassy entrusted to them by unanimous vote of elders and citizens alike took place oh so many moons ago!

To the implicit charge of the *'īš yiśrā'el* that they are telling less than the truth, they stress first the unqualified legitimacy of their legation. Their mission had the unanimous authority of their homeland's oligarchy and commons. They then point to the sad state of their dress, gear, and provisions as proof of the long trek that has eventuated in their arrival at the Gilgal encampment. This argument supportive of their veracity, an argument that they did not raise in pericope B, where that veracity is questioned by Israel's macho braves, leads to an examination of their dry and moldy provisions. This examination apparently accepted as attestation to the *bona fides* of the embassy leads to a conclusion that is formulated in verse 15 in three paratactically formulated clauses. In clause 1, Joshua concludes an amicable agreement with them. Despite the formal parataxis, the following clause 2 may be hypotactical in relation to it as far as meaning is concerned: the amity that Joshua had enacted was embodied in the treaty that he made with them, a treaty which specifically and explicitly guaranteed them—was it only, or among other things?—their survival. Clause 3 adds that the (Joshua-sponsored) treaty was confirmed by an oath taken by the *nᵉ śī ē hā ēdā* "the confederacy's chieftains." These *nᵉśī'īm* are the third constituent of the Israelite identity (after Joshua and the *'īš yiśrā'el*), and will be shortly differentiated from the rank-and-file of the confederacy (*kol-hā ēdā*) over which they preside (verses 18, 19, 21). These last then are the fourth of the Israelite constituency.

A fifth term, however, *hā⁽ā⁾nāšīm* "the men" ("leaders" in our translation) is the subject of the verb "took (samples) of" in verse 14, and it is unclear whether this term includes Joshua, the chieftains, or both. But the second clause of this verse, in hypotactic construction, is a pointed contrastive notice, an aside on the part of the narrator as to what these leaders might well have done but did not do: consult the oracle of YHWH. Had they done so—the inference is ineluctable—the outcome of the ruse and the fate of its initiators would have been altogether different. But was this failure to consult YHWH a moral lapse or a singular deficiency of judgment? From what follows, the sustained decision to abide by the consequence of the oath taken in YHWH-name, it would appear that the lapse, if any, was a trivial one compared to the far greater one that would have been constituted by a violation of the oath, for all that the oath had been extorted by a ruse.

If that then be the case, Joshua's decision and its endorsement by the confederacy's elders represents a lapse, not from obedience to God's will, but from ordinary common sense. And the absurdity of this foolishness on the part of Israel's constituted authorities is only heightened by the information that Israel's macho rank-and-file were not taken in by the ruse, as indicated not only by the initial skepticism of the *'īš yiśrā'el*, but by the subsequent criticism of the decision lodged by the rank-and-file of the confederacy (*hā'ēdā/kol-hā'ēda*) against the elders (*hann°śīm/ n°śī'ē hā'ēda*). What are we to make of this attribution of perspicacity to the hoi polloi and of gullibility to the magistrates? I will defer this question for a while. But let us note that the common sense of the reader should lead him, as critic, to question not only the implausibility in the plot of the ruse's success, but of its having been attempted to begin with. Worn shoes and stale bread are a testimony to the age of these commodities, and not to the time when they were first laced on or baked.[8] But the obvious silliness of the ruse is merely the icing on the entire confection of the Gibeonite claim to be from so distant a land. Can one imagine a narrative in which Mayan Indians from central America, pretending to be Esquimos, arrive at Pizzaro's headquarters in the Peruvian highlands, citing their knowledge of the Spaniards' ravaging of Montezuma's Halls and asking for a treaty which would spare them a like fate in their Arctic ranges?

Episode D. Discovery, March, and Absent Assault

> (16) It was a threesome of days after they had made this pact with them that they got word: how near their distance to him,[9] yes well within his ambit dwelling, they . . . (17) The Israelites moved out and on the day after the morrow arrived at their cities— these cities being Gibeon, Kephirah, Beerot and Kiriath-jearim. (18) Yet did the Israelites not attack them, for the confederacy's chieftains had taken oath to them by YHWH, god of Israel.

Only two days after the departure of the Gibeonite embassy, the treaty-grantors learn of the proximity of those to whom they have sworn immunity. And a mere two days later the Israeli hosts arrive at the Gibeonite homeland—no, not the city of Gibeon itself—but at Gibeon, and three other Gibeonite cities as well.[10] Arrive for what purpose? The verb at the beginning of verse 17 bespeaks the breaking of a camp and the purposeful setting out of a migrating horde. But this pericope continues and ends, not with a statement of the purpose of this breaking of camp, but with a hypotactic denial of what we might have expected as the purpose and eventuation of this move, an attack on the Gibeonites. The reason for this non-event is then given in the bottom line of this synoptic episode: it is the oath taken by the confederacy's chieftains by YHWH, Israel's god. Inasmuch as the narrator need not inform us as to what role YHWH fills for Israel, the addition of the name (missing in verse 15), the first notice of this oath, along with the attribution, may be confidently read as the narrator's signal that this decision to honor the oath was in keeping with what they owed to the god by whom they swore. The resumptive episode E begins with the last clause of verse 18, which informs us that the arrival at the bottom line was not a foregone conclusion.

Episode E. Chagrin and Reprisal Decree

> The confederacy's rank-and-file grumbled against the chieftains. (19) The chieftains all addressed the confederate ranks, "We did take oath to them by YHWH, god of Israel. Hence, we may do them no harm. (20) This we must do to them—(you) guarantee their lives—only thus avert from ourselves [God's] wrath [in keeping] with the oath we took to them." (21) Thus did the chieftains decree to them: *They are to live.* And thus did they become hewers of wood and drawers of water for all the confederacy, in keeping with the declaration to them of the chieftains.

The grumbling of the rank-and-file can only be against the chieftains' decision, which precludes an attack on the wily Gibeonites. Yet these chieftains hold fast to the oath sworn by them in YHWH-name, to do the Gibeonites no harm, the expression for the latter being literally "to touch/lay hand" upon them. This unit of direct discourse is unambiguous, and would appear sufficient response to the disgruntled ranks of Israel. But their discourse does not stop here. Instead we have a continuation of it in verse 20, which would appear not only repetitively redundant, but syntactically perversely awkward. Such translations as that of AV, ("This we will do to them and let them live"), while not unfaithful to the Hebrew original, conceal from the reader that there is a jerky succession of verbs, a first person plural imperfect expressive of a cohortative or obligatory modality (*This let us/must we do*) followed by a singular imperative, implicitly second person, collective (you, *allow them to live*). Hence my own translation, which begins with an elliptical statement in free direct discourse of how we (corporate Israel) may deal with them, this followed by the deictic waw and the imperative "that is, you [for your part] must agree to their safety from physical harm." This is then followed by the statement that only thus, that is, by your agreement to their survival and the implementation of our (gapped) proposal, can we achieve a goal mutually satisfactory to us, yet not incurring Heaven's wrath. By this two-pronged proposal, reports verse 21, did the chieftains succeed in decreeing the survival of the Gibeonites in Israel's midst. And the gapped proposal "this we must do" is now bridged or filled in by the conclusion of the verse, the bottom line of this resumptive episode E: the upshot of the matter was that the Gibeonites "became hewers of wood and drawers of water *for all the confederacy*—this *in keeping with the declaration to them* [to Gibeonites, to Israelites, or to both?] *of the chieftains.*"

Just how the rank-and-file demand that the Gibeonites be eliminated from Israel's midst is reconciled with their survival as menials for all the tribes of the confederacy is far from clear. At the least it would seem to require a reduction of sentence from extirpation to slavery and a distribution of the Gibeonite slaves among the tribes of Israel, these at the moment constituting a migratory horde, one not destined for decades or centuries to come into settled possessions "from Dan to Beersheba." The resolution of this problem will appear when we recognize that this last verse of Episode E is the bottom line of an episode that, while it functions as the resumptive of synoptic Episode D, functions also as the synoptic for the resumptive Episode F.

Episode F. Resumption of Reprisal, Recapitulation of Decree

(22) Joshua summoned them and dressed them down, to wit: "Why did you deceive us, saying 'We are at a far far distance from you,' when you live well within our ambit's center? (23) Now, then: Under ban you are [decreed] to be. Never will there fail to be from among you slave, hewers of wood and drawers of water for the house of my god!" (24) In response to Joshua they said, "Verily it was told in detail to your servants that which your god YHWH ordained to his servant Moses, to grant you all this land and exterminate on your account all the inhabitants of the land. In great fear for our lives were we on your account, hence we did what we did. (25) And, now, we are in your power. However it seems proper and upright in your opinion to treat us, do so!" (26) Thus did he do to them, as told, delivering them from the Israelite's power, so that they did not kill them. (27) Thus it was that Joshua dedicated them at that time as hewers of wood and drawers of water to the confederacy, and [or, that is] to the altar of YHWH—continuing to this very day—in the place that He chooses [for it].

The narrative logic of our story requires that the address of Joshua to the Gibeonites in verse 22 take place between verses 17 and 18; while the altercation between the chieftains and the rank-and-file of the confederacy and its resolution needs to have taken place before the action related in verse 17, the advance of the warriors of Israel from the camp at Gilgal to the territory of the Gibeonites. Further to be noted in this concluding episode is that the personae of Joshua and the confederacy's chieftains are assimilated to one another as a single protagonist as in verse 15 (pericope C), verse 18 (pericope D), and verses 18b–21 (pericope E); while similarly assimilated to one another as a single protagonist are the "hard-liners," the *ʾîš yiśrāʾel* of verses 6 and 7 (pericope B) and the *ʿēdā* of verses 18b and 19 (pericope E).

The proposal of the chieftains, gapped in verse 20 and expressed in verse 21, is then the verdict or decree pronounced by Joshua to the Gibeonites in verse 23. The formulation in the mouth of Joshua differs, however, both from the narrator's explication of the decree "They are to live" in verse 21—but only as "hewers of wood and drawers of water for all the confederacy"—and from the narrator's explication of Joshua's decree as well in the concluding verse 27. The two differing formulations in Episode F, of Joshua's in verse 23 and of the narrator's in verse 21, thus together resolve the questions we raised about the gap-filling formulation of the chieftains in Episode E (verse 21). The menial service to which the Gibeonites are doomed forever does not require the geographic dispersal of the Gibeonites throughout Israel. Their service "to the confederacy" in verse 27 is explicated by the deictic waw "that is"—"to the altar of YHWH." By fulfilling this function they will thus be "stand-ins" for the Israelite confederacy at large, who bear the burden of the central sanctuary's support. That Israel at large is to be relieved of this obligation for ongoing generations (verse 27, "continuing to this very day") is implicit in the formulation of the decree to the Gibeonites. The word *ārūr(īm)*, as I long ago argued, bespeaks a metaphorical wall or enclosure that separates one entity from another.[11] In this case, the simple sparing of the Gibeonites' lives would eventuate in their intermarriage with and assimilation into the Israelite folk. This eventuality is ruled out by the proposal of the chieftains and the decree of Joshua: the Gibeonites are not to become chattel slaves as individuals or *in toto*. Incorporated though they may be in the Israelite entity, they will constitute a separate entity that will not be permitted to intermarry and assimilate with Israel. They will thus constitute a caste within Israel—conducting their lives in normal fashion—but fated to maintain their separate identity so that in every generation they may supply the hierodules to whom will be assigned the necessary but less dignified service to "the altar of YHWH" than those acts performed by the authochtonous Israelite castes, the priests, and (other) Levites of the "sons of Levi."

No essentially contradictory exegesis to the foregoing can be (or at least, has been) proposed for the pregnant formulation that might equally well be rendered, "now then, outside the pale you are, in that there must never be cut off (i.e., cease to exist) from among you some one(s) in thrall, splitters of kindling and haulers of water for my god's temple." But the formulation of Joshua's direct discourse is notable for other significant features, which will not be lost on the ear trained to catch nuances in narrative style generally and biblical idiom in particular. As I have rendered the Hebrew, Joshua first asks a question, the response to which is so obvious to the student of the Bible as to prompt the question why it is raised at all. Joshua does not wait for the answer and proceeds immediately to the decree, which says in effect, *No answer will do, herewith I declare your punishment,* and only then are the Gibeonites allowed to answer the question that was asked of them.

If this were the purport or the only purport of Joshua's discourse, the "why" of the question "Why did you deceive us?" would be expressive of a rhetorical question rather than one for information. Wherever a question of *why* in biblical Hebrew is unquestionably and unequivocally rhetorical that word is *maddū^a* "how does it then transpire," expressive of surprise, astonishment, incredulity, consternation and—even—protest. The expression of *why* in a purely informational context, or tinged with some expression of surprise is *lāmā* appearing—as we should expect—almost four times as often as the more restrictive *maddū^a*. Hence, if in Joshua's expression to the Gibeonites, the *why* were followed by the condemnatory decree and nothing else, it would have been expressed by *maddū^a*. But the question—after the dialogue follow-up of condemnatory decree, which allows only for a strong rhetorical element in it—is followed by the response of the Gibeonites, treating the *lāmā* "why" as a request for explanation and providing that information. The explanation is that the Gibeonites were afraid of being exterminated in a *herem*-war. This explains their lying as to their origin, and their immediately following words accepting any decision of Joshua's is ambiguous in this respect: while in narrative order it follows the decree of Joshua, in chronological order it may have preceded it. In that case, verse 26 is understandable as a welcoming of the decree of Joshua, the negative aspect of imposition of caste and servitude being a nugatory consideration as against the alternative of annihilation: Thus he dealt (ken "as told"), delivering them from the power of the Israelites, so that they could not kill them.

As we suggested earlier, however, the question of why the Gibeonites resorted to lie and ruse to win a peace treaty would never have been asked by a student of the Pentateuch, who knows how often the extermination of the promised land's natives is ordained. And in that case, neither would it have been asked by Joshua, who was at least as well informed as we are. And the answer of the Gibeonites, "verily it was told to us"—that is, we had it on the best authority—requires examination on two counts, the one substantive: how did they get this reliable information; and the other stylistic: the strange formulation of the information they received. In respect to the latter, a more literal rendering of the Hebrew is, "that YHWH, your [Joshua] god charged his servant Moses to give you [the Israelites] all the land and to destroy all the land's inhabitants from your front." Now the Lord could *promise* Moses to give Israel the land, promise repeatedly expressed by *ʾāmar* "averred" or *nišbaʿ* "swore." But Moses was no more *commanded* (*ṣiwā*) to give *you* (pl.) the land than he was to *exterminate* (*hišmīd*) its inhabitants from your advance. Both the granting of the land and the clearing of its inhabitants (metaphorically speaking to be sure) are the activities of YHWH, promises to Moses, but not delegated to him for performance.

And this requires us to examine those texts in the Pentateuch that we so confidently assumed (or presumed) constitute the commands of YHWH that Israel commit genocide against the inhabitants of Canaan.

No command to such effect exists in Genesis. The one intimation of the necessity of Canaan's being vacated to make room for Israel's settlement is in 15:16: the accumulation of Amorite offenses will not add up to a sentence of extirpation for several generations yet to come. Against the notion that annihilation of a populace is a light matter for the god of Israel is the debate preceding the doom of Sodom in Genesis 18 and the rise of two nations from the loins of Lot, despite their incestuous origin in Chapter 19.

No command to such effect exists in Exodus. The Amalek who attack Israel in Chapter 17, a clan deriving from Esau, neither settled in territory promised to Israel nor constitutes one of the supposedly proscribed nations that must be cleared from Israel's path. The notice at this chapter's end, twice phrased and full of ambiguity, to be recorded in writing and dinned into Joshua's ears, is that it is YHWH who intends at some future time to blot out any trace of this ethnic group. And the reason, supplied in Deuteronomy 25:17–19, is that this treacherous attack by a kindred people was directed at the women and children and superannuated who brought up the rear of Israel's migrating multitude. The one pericope in this book that focuses on Israel's coming arrival at the territory of Amorite, Hittite, Perizzite, Canaanite, Hivvite, and Jebusite (23:20–33) features YHWH's clearing the way for Israel, by means of *ṣirʿā* (variously rendered as *hornet* or *pestilence*), which will *drive out* (*grš*) these natives. At that this process is to be a gradual one. The one prescription to Israel is not to make a treaty *lāhem wᵉlēʾlōhēhem* "with them along with their gods." The reason "they may not dwell in your land" is that they might *lure* you into *worshipping their gods*. But suppose they abjure their gods in favor of YHWH? This question is unanswered, for it is not raised.

No command to such effect exists in Numbers. In 10:29–33 Moses invites his Midianite brother-in-law Hobab, son of his father-in-law Reuel, to scout for Israel in their wilderness travels, promising to share with him the felicitous destiny in that *place* that YHWH has promised to grant them. Inasmuch as the invitation is first declined and then renewed without a second response from Hobab, it is not clear whether he relented or not. That this exchange is immediately followed by the notice that YHWH's cloud hovered above the Israelites during their daytime movements and by Moses' invocation to YHWH at every start to clear the way of their advance need not mean that Hobab was not moved from his intent to return "to my own native land." This because a separate metaphor may be intended here.[12] But what the text does make clear is that the native land of the Midianites is outside the Canaanite pale of settlement, and that Midianites are welcome in that territory destined for Israel's possession.

The story of the attack on Israel by the *Canaanite* king of Arad (in the Negeb) is witness either to this later Judaean territory not having been considered part of the promised land (an easily dismissable possibility) or that no destruction of the Canaanites there had been dictated by God. For Israel makes a vow to YHWH that it will put to the ḥerem-ban "them and their cities" if he delivers them to Israel! (Numbers 21:1–3) Since a vow is essentially a bribe offered to God if he will effectuate a human desire, the notion of a vow uttered to achieve God's help in carrying out an express mandate of God's is the height of absurdity. Inasmuch as the archaeological spade has uncovered no level antedating settlement at Arad prior to the time of the Judaean monarchy, this entire fictive notice would seem designed to contradict the notion of a divine command to exterminate the Canaanites.

Where a genocidal war seems to be indicated (as having taken place) in the Book of Numbers is in (the intriguingly separated) chapters 25 and 31. Chapter 25 begins with the ʿam (of Israel)—a term ambiguous in that it can stand for a populace or for the empowered council or parliament of that populace—committing harlotry with Moabite woman. Whatever acts, literally sexual or metaphorically "straying from fidelity," in the term for "harlotry" (znh), this activity involves participation in sacrificial feasts celebrated in tribute to the gods or ancestral spirits of the Moabites. This interfaith intercourse, characterized as Israel's "coupling with Baal Peor," ires YHWH to inflict upon Israel a pestilence that takes a toll of twenty-four thousand lives before it is abruptly halted by the enterprise of Phineas, grandson of Aaron, the priest. This enterprise is his spontaneous spearing of an Israelite noble together with the foreign woman in his embrace; a denouement not altogether congruent with the preceding notice of YHWH to Moses that the remedy for the harlotry-inspired pestilence is the public impalement of all the chieftains of the ʿam. The oddest feature of this account, however, is that the woman who is transfixed together with her Israelite lover is not a Moabite, but a Midianite princess. Moses is then instructed by YHWH to open hostilities against the Midianites in return for their hostile wiles which lured Israel into the embrace of Baal Peor.

Numbers 31 opens with a repetition of YHWH's command to initiate hostilities against the Midianites, this time the bidding formulated as the exaction of YHWH's vengeance, and as the last mission to be executed by Moses before he dies. Most of this chapter, verses 13–54, is devoted to the aftermath of the Midianite defeat, the division of the spoil and—of relevance to our theme—the slaughter of every male infant and of every female captive who had had intercourse with a man. Among the indications that this constitutes ḥerem-war are the following:

1. The casual blending or overlay of Moab and Midian as the enemy. This narrative strategy will have become familiar to those who have attended to the plays on personae and protagonists, individual and corporate, that I have hitherto noted in both narratives and structures.[13]

2. The recourse to two adversarial groups that are one, or to one which bifurcates into two begins in 22:1 with the Israelite's encampment at the Rifts of Moab on the east side of the Jordan across from Jericho. These rifts or wadis are no more the legitimate territory of Moab than the Wadi Gerar was that of Philistia.[14] For Israel has been forbidden to encroach upon Moabite sovereignty, and Moab makes no effort to repel an invasion of its soil. Rather, Balak the king of Moab, in his fear of what the Israelite borders may do to the ecology, sends for the warlock extraordinaire Balaam from his native territory Pethor, which is located on the Euphrates. But this only after he has addressed his fear of Israel, not to his own council, but to the elders of Midian. Now since the plot as it develops will require a war of extirpation, the enemy cannot be Moab, which has been granted immunity by YHWH (this element is, of course, gapped and only bridged in Deuteronomy), hence the Midianite complicity in the seduction of Israel's faithful to the Baal Peor horror.

3. The sexual liaisons between Israelites and Moabite women, which constitute the Peor sin against YHWH, segue into liaisons with Midianite women, thus provoking the ḥerem-war against this people, which—unlike Moab—has received no grant of immunity from YHWH.

4. This sudden transformation of Midianites from the friendly family into which Moses has married into virulent enemies, and their presence in huge numbers east of the Jordan River on territory occupied by Moab (whereas Moses' flight from Egypt to Midianite territory would place this people in the Sinai to the east of Egypt, or even to the southeast of that peninsula where Moses acquired his "Cushite" wife), is attended by other marvels of incongruity.

5. The loot taken by Israel includes 675,000 head of the flocks, 72,000 head of the herds, 61,000 asses, and the sole surviving humans: 32,000 virginal women. Of this spoil, the participating warriors (one thousand from each of the twelve tribes) receive half minus 0.02 percent, which goes to the priests; the rank and file of the confederacy receive half minus 0.2 percent, which goes to the Levites. Aside from such staggering wealth of the Midianites, the assignment of 1 percent to the Levites and one-tenth of a percent to the priests conforms to the legislation for later times apportioning to the Levites a tithe from all Israel and a tenth of that tithe to the priests from the Levites. But this assignment would appear to be out of all proportion to the ratio of 23,000 Levites (see Numbers 26:52) to the Aaronide priests Eleazar and his overlooked brother Ithamar.

6. Finally there is the seeming discrepancy between the notice of the parting of Balaam and Balak in 24:30 and the presence of Balaam among those who fell to Israelite sword in 31:8. The former verse reads "Balaam proceeded to go off, returning to his place; Balak now also went his own way." Apparently then Balaam's "place" in

this verse is not the *Pethor-on-the-[Euphrates-] River, and of his ethnic kindred* of 22:5, but among the Midianite elders addressed by Balak in 22:4. There he apparently remained a force for evil counsel in that 31:15 has Moses laying to his door the fatal luring of Israel's males to the Peor apostasy represented by their intercourse with the women of *Midian*.

7. The final discrepancy is not within this story itself but with chapters 6–8 in the Book of Judges. Whereas the war in Numbers eventuates in the total destruction of the five kings of Midian and all their followers, a few generations later the camelriders of Midian, organized under four kings, together with Amalekites (who are normally situated somewhere in Sinai) and other "children of the east," cross the Jordan from the east and commit their depredations as far west and south as Gaza. Their fighting men number at least 135,000. And from their ill-defined (or rather, totally undefined) precincts, which can be neither the Gilead of Israel's transJordanian tribesman, nor the steppes of Moab and Ammon (and what other territory is there?) they come not as raiding parties but as a migrating locust-like horde, together with their livestock and tents.

In Deuteronomy alone do we find any texts—and at that, only two—that may be fairly read as a command (deriving from Deity) to exterminate the native populations of the promised land. And here, too, the voice is that of Moses, and the formulation as well as the context of how these populations are to be treated need not at all add up to a sentence of extirpation:

(1) When YHWH your god brings you to the land into the possession of which you are about to enter, and casts off[15] from your advance great nations the Hittite, and the Girgashite, and the Amorite, and the Canaanite, and the Perizzite, and the Hivvite, and the Jebusite—seven nations greater and mightier than you—(2) and YHWH your god disposes them before you so that you defeat them: you shall put them to the *herem*-ban. Grant them no treaty and show them no grace. (3) Nor may you intermarry with them; do not give your daughter to his son, and take not his daughter for your son. (4) For he will turn your son away from obedience to me, and when they (thus) serve other gods YHWH's anger will blaze against you and he will make quick dispatch of you. (5) Thus and thus alone are you to treat them: their altars you are to break up, their pillars you are to smash, their Ashera posts you are to truncate and their carved images you are to put to the torch. (Deuteronomy 7:1–5)

The reading of Moses' instructions as an imperative to commit genocide is based on the assumption that the verb *haḥᵃrīm* entails the total destruction of the opposing populace, livestock, and artifactual spoils. But contrary to this, we have indications that even in the context of a prescribed *herem*-war virginal women may be taken and reserved for Israelite marriages, livestock my be herded to swell the store of YHWH's shrine, and utensils purified for use so long as their function is not specifically appropriate for idolatrous practice. Whereas the following command in verse 2—to make no treaty with the defeated enemy and offer him no reprieve— may be read as a rhetorically redundant but emphatic reaffirmation of the absoluteness of the *herem*-ban, the same cannot be said for verse 3. If males and females alike are to be slaughtered, including even female infants, there can be no question of intermarriage. But defeat of an enemy in the field does not mean the reduction of his cities, and the repeated assertions on YHWH's part that the indigenous populations will not be conquered in a generation, or perhaps two or three, confirms the picture of a contested land, much of it in the hands of the proscribed enemy, and the consequent temptations to come to terms with them or to contract marriage alliances in the periods of stalemate. Most telling, however, is the formulation of verse 5. Instead of specifying the proper ḥerem-war procedure of putting men, women, and children, old and young, to the sword, the contrary prescribed behavior is the destruction of pagan cult-practices, those cult-practices that are the reason for the ḥerem-ban of peace treaty or intermarriage: the fear that Israel might be seduced into imitating them.

The second passage in Deuteronomy having reference to ḥerem-war is verse 20:10–18. Its primary concern is conduct of war against an enemy outside the borders promised to Israel. If such a city accepts an offer of peace and surrenders, you may subject it to feudal obligations. If it rejects such an offer and, as a result of YHWH's help succumbs to a siege, then—according to most translations—*you are to put all its males to the sword*. Since such a prescription of execution for all the fighting males of a stubborn enemy serves the interests of neither YHWH nor his people, our suggestion is that the modality of the verb is permissive rather than imperative: *you are free to execute them as you please*. What follows, however, seems to give Israel permission to do what all would take for granted, namely, to enjoy the spoils of war. The point of this permission, however, as of the ambiguous modality of the verbal formula "to put to the sword," is to foreshadow the contrast with ḥerem-war:

> (14) However, the women, infants, cattle and whatever there be within the city, all its booty, you may appropriate as spoil, consuming whatever booty that your god YHWH has granted you. (15) So may you treat all cities outside your pale, those not of these nations [within your pale]. (16) However, of the cities of these peoples, the estate [of whom] YHWH your god is granting to you, you shall not spare any animate. (17)- Rather, to the ḥerem-ban must you put them—the Hittite, the Amorite, the Canaanite and the Perizzite, the Hivvite and the Jebusite—just as your god YHWH has commanded you, (18) for this reason, that they may not teach you to practice in keeping with all the abominations they practice with respect to their gods and thus [cause] you to commit offense against your god YHWH. (Deuteronomy 20:14–18)

Again, the reason for the ruthless removal of the land's indigenous inhabitants, (whether projected or performed) by YHWH''s act or instance or that of his people, intermittently or programmatically over generations or centuries, that reason is to immunize Israel from their abominable ways. But again, the question—unanswered, because it is never raised—that we posed in connection with Exodus 23:20–33: Suppose any of these populations abjure their gods and/or their heinous practices in favor of YHWH and his ordinances?

We would submit that it is this question that is implicit behind the convoluted narrative of Joshua 9. The inherent absurdities of a frightened population trying to persuade an invading horde that they should abstain from attacking a people whose home is beyond the farthest horizon; of a leadership being taken in by a ruse as transparent as it is hoary while the hoi polloi insightfully resist it; of the failure to consult a god whose oracles and miraculous interventions are responsible for the success of the invasion up to this point; of the binding force of a trick-induced oath or the presumption that the Deity will be more wrathful over a (broken) promise made in his name than in a direct contravention of his repeated and explicit and unqualified command to exterminate a population (which he has himself predicted will only die out over a long period of time); of the Gibeonites being privy to a mandate of genocide given by an unheard-of god called YHWH to a wilderness-wandering rabble leader called Moses, and trusting in the authenticity of such a revelation, as well as in the power to guarantee its success against a far more numerous population ensconced in cities fortified "to the skies;" the readiness of this as yet unconquered people to accept whatever fate is ordained for it by the invaders who have already sworn not to harm them; all these plot-absurdities point to the key element of the Gibeonites' posture, which is at the crux of the narrative. In the last response of these Hivvite pagans of Canaan to Joshua in verse 24, the *resumptive* response, which in narrative time comes before the *synoptic-conclusive* decree of Joshua, they confess their fear—hence, their faith—in the power of YHWH; a faith therefore that does not preclude his relenting in respect to those aboriginal Canaanites, who abandon their loathsome cults and adopt the god and the ways of Joshua and Israel. This response, let us note, was adumbrated in the Gibeonites' first response to Joshua. In verse 9, in response to the questions "Just who is it you are and just where do you come from?" they seem to be saying that these questions are irrelevant, inasmuch as it is, "for the sake of (*lᵉšem* "for the name of") your god YHWH we have come."

So much for an unqualified divine decree to commit genocide, this in the name of the "angry God of the Old Testament." A review of the pronouncements and narratives preceding Joshua 9,[16] as well as those narratives (particularly in Joshua but also in Judges and Samuel) that disclose the actual fates of the populations of the cities whose kings opposed Joshua, will disclose how cunningly the biblical narrators contrived to convey one impression as to the disappearance in monarchical times of the aboriginal races *then no longer in the land* and provide quite another reading in Joshua 9; a reading that must be traced back to primordial times in the prophetic narrative of Noah's drunkenness, and pursued further in the fate of the Gibeonites under Saul and David, the hierodule class of Nethinim in the time of Ezra and Nehemiah and the domiciling of the wilderness tabernacle in the city of Gibeon. Yet we shall have missed a significant link in the saga of the Gibeonites, or rather a critical element in their saga's kerygma, if we fail to attend to the last baffling clause that concludes the Book of Zechariah.

After YHWH's infliction of a crushing defeat on the peoples gathered to assail Jerusalem (14:12–15), the triumph of the one and only god expressed in the eschatological pericope, 14:6–11 ("At that time will YHWH become king of all the earth, at that time it will be YHWH alone and his name alone"), is followed by the consequences of this triumph for the cult center in Jerusalem (14:16–23).[17] I will paraphrase this passage, interpolating in brackets my own comments:

> The survivors, [particularly] from among those nations who had come [in hostility] against Jerusalem will ascend year in, year out, to do obeisance to King YHWH-hosts, [particularly] in celebration of the [Harvest] Feast of Tabernacles. And surely, if any of these families of Earth do not come up to Jerusalem to do obeisance to King YHWH-

hosts, no rain will fall [on their sown fields]. And if the Egyptian family [which, Nile-fed, needs no rain] fails to come up in pilgrimage, verily upon them will fall the afflic-tion with which YHWH will assail those nations [above mentioned] who [rain-depen-dent] yet do not come up to celebrate the Feast of Tabernacles. [Probably famine, such as afflicted Egypt in Joseph's time.] Such will be the punishment of Egypt or the pun-ishment of any of the nations that do not make pilgrimage for the celebration of the Feast of Tabernacles. At that time upon the head-ornaments of [even] the horses will be writ [the legend] "Holy to YHWH." And the wash-basins in YHWH's temple will be even as the sprinkling-bowls [used] at the altar. And [indeed] every cauldron [any-where] in Jerusalem or Judah will be—holy to YHWH-hosts. And [any and] all mak-ing sacrifice will come and, taking freely from among them, boil [their meat from the šelem-offerings] in them. Nor will there be any longer in the temple of YHWH-hosts—at that time—any Canaanite.

In this vision of Zechariah, more in keeping with our sense of *messianic* rather than *eschatalogical*, there will take place a universalization of YHWH worship, a de-mocratization—so to speak—of status in respect to aliens and Israelites, humans and beasts, laity and priesthood: this expressed in imagery deriving from the cult and its appurtenances. The caparisoned riding mounts shall bear upon their fore-heads the legend reserved (in Exodus 28:36, 39:30) for the forehead of the High Priest. The large vessels within the temple precincts, like the brass laver (Exodus 30:18) or cooking pots of even heavier base metal, will be equal (in value, sanctity) to the small vessels of precious metal like the sprinkling bowls into which is poured the blood for sprinkling the altar. Indeed the pots and kettles and cauldron from anywhere in Jerusalem and Judah will be as sacred (pure, fitting for containing sacral meat) as those within the temple's precincts, and any and every celebrant of the *shelamim*-offerings will be welcome to make use of them. And, finally, whether because the lowest caste in temple-service will be abolished, or whether invidious caste distinctions will no longer apply, no longer will there be in the temple of YHWH, a scion of that caste of Canaanite stock, the Hivvite Gibeonites dedicated as hierodules in the time of Joshua.

AFTERWORD

Now we are come to an end. These last paragraphs were dictated short days before death, hence the lack of summary or conclusions. Yet there is naught not said over and again in the preceding pages that would add to, or clarify, my father's approach and methodology, and it was ever his contention that to succeed, his work would be accepted as a beginning rather than an ending.

Herschel D. Brichto
January 1997

NOTES

PREFACE

1. Herbert Brichto, "On Faith and Revelation in the Bible," *HUCA* (Hebrew Union College Annual) 39 (1968): 37.

CHAPTER I

1. It is highly unlikely that even the most meticulous of reciters would ever try to distinguish between a dipthong in which the "a" is short and the one in which the "a" is long. Hence the lengthening of the *patah* here, as in the case in other instances of Masoretic notation, is a signal for the eye and the mind and not the mouth or the ear. (Which is also to say that *ketib* and *qere* are not to be taken literally as representing respectively written and oral phenomena.)

2. The presumptions and underpinnings of this methodology are spelled out in chapters 1 and 2 of H. C. Brichto, *Toward a Grammar of Biblical Poetics* (hereinafter designated by TAG), (Oxford: Oxford University Press, 1992). The method is exemplified in the Exegetical Essays, chs. 3–7, on prophetic narratives. Chapter 9 of that volume adumbrates the extension of the poetical treatment to the early chapters in the Book of Genesis. See also p. viii of TAG's preface.

3. On the adoption of this term, see TAG pp. 46, 57–9, and listings in the General Index.

4. See TAG, pp. 27ff.

5. See, for example, Genesis 20:18 and note *e*, ad loc. in E. A. Speiser, *Genesis*, vol. 1 of *The Anchor Bible* (Garden City, N.Y.: Doubleday, 1964). See also Speiser, ibid., on Genesis 21:21 and on Genesis 22:11, 14, 15, 16. See also R. N. Whybray, *The Making of the Pentateuch: A Methodological Study* (Sheffield: Journal for the Study of the Old Testament [hereafter JSOT], 1967). Cited

hereafter as *MP*. P. 65: "Even Eisfeldt admitted that 'sometimes an *Elohim* has intruded into a Yahweh stratum and a *Yahweh* into an *Elohim* stratum.'"

6. It is interesting (some would say appalling) to note how many advanced students still think the phrase "the exception proves the rule" means that the exception validates the rule rather than puts the rule to the test.

7. Whybray (*MP*, p. 64f.) on the avoidance of the name YHWH by P and E: "This theory is hardly convincing. Since both the author of E and P and their readers would themselves have been familiar with the name Yahweh, there is no reason why these writers should not from the very outset have used the proper name of God except when quoting the words of their characters." See also Whybray's citation of M. H. Segal's "demonstration that a variety of biblical authors of texts where a plurality of documentary sources is out of the question use both Yahweh and Elohim interchangeably (p. 67)."

8. See below, "On Terms for Divinity, Common and Proper," p. 16.

9. *Commentary on Genesis I*, transl. from Hebrew by Israel Abrams, (Jerusalem: Magnes Press, Hebrew University, 1961), pp. 87–88.

10. The point of the ass seeing what even a true prophet will not see when a film of gold is laid over his prophetic eyeglasses would be lost if there were any doubt about Balaam being such a prophet. That he is such is thus guaranteed by the consistent presence of the name *YHWH*.

11. On the problem of dichotomous analysis, see TAG, pp. 30–34.

12. This citation is from Matitiahu Tsevat's "God and the Gods in Assembly: An Interpretation of Psalm 82," *HUCA* vols. 40–41 (1969–70), p. 126. Whybray (*MP*, p. 69f.) is satisfied that the preponderance of Elohim in the Elohistic Psalter is "due to redactional or scribal activity." Questions never asked about this putative "psalter" is why it exists at all, what drove scribes or redactors to change YHWH to Elohim where they did, why they did not do so elsewhere, why they limited their activities to these psalms, and why they neglected other names of the Deity in their passion to displace the Tetragrammaton.

13. To speak of any translation of the Hebrew biblical text as a "version," be the translation old or recent, into a Semitic or Indo-European tongue, is to render a status and authority to that translation that has never—in any instance whatsoever—been justified. Needless to say, the promotion of such translations to the status of "version" multiplies the quantity of biblical text many times, offers opportunities of specialization to biblicists whose strengths may lie elsewhere than within the parameters of O. T. linguistics, and encourages the activities of emenders and glossators whose stance toward the *textus receptus* can only be described as jaundiced.

14. Speiser, *Genesis*, pp. XLIII–LII.

15. See chs. 2 and 4 in this volume.

16. Speiser, *Genesis*, pp. XLI–XLII.

17. And indeed in Canaan as well, witness the fine fragment of the Gilgamesh Epic found at Megiddo in a layer dated a century or two before the Israelite monarchical era.

18. Thus, for example, the mysterious numen with whom Jacob wrestles until the rising of the morning star by the ford of the Jabbok (Genesis 32:25–33) is not the only superhuman personage who serves as intermediary between this patriarch and the One God. In the scene at Bethel (28:10–22) there is a strong indication that it is through an angelic intermediary that this God identifies Himself to Jacob as YHWH. Yet Jacob makes a conditional vow—as though one can bargain with Deity—to acknowledge YHWH as his god, to establish a shrine at that site and, addressing the representative of YHWH, apparently, offer him—in the second person— "a tenth of whatever you grant to me." In Chapter 31 Jacob tells of an angel of God appearing to him in a dream, identifying himself as *ha'el bet-el* (the numen Beth-el), to whom vow had been made. In 35:1–7 it is God who bids Jacob to return to Bethel, to erect an altar there "to the god/numen (*ha'el*) who was appearing to you when you were fleeing from your brother Esau." In 48:15ff. Israel in blessing Joseph through his two sons seems in his invocation to identify "the God with whom my father walked" with "the God shepherding me" since early times, with "the angel who has been redeeming me from every trouble." The prophet Hosea then, in 12:4–7, identifies the numen with whom

Jacob wrestled at the Jabbok ford with the numen of Bethel "where he held converse with us"—all this despite the fact that YHWH is the *mark/name* (*zikrō*) of YHWH, God of Hosts.

These alternating manifestations of the One God YHWH through less than omnipotent intermediaries and seemingly separate numina blending into one another, alternately acknowledged without adverse bias by the One God, yet mildly chided by an early writing prophet, can only be the stuff of metaphor, and humorously tolerant metaphor at that, of a prefiguring ancestor and the descendants' in his likeness, groping their inconsistent way from glimpse of the One True God to particularistic lapses in which He becomes a tame and tutelary deity before He is recognized again as One, Unfathomable, Universal and Ineffable. (Cf., particularly in 35:2–4 the only mention of "alien gods" in the patriarchal period and their burial at Shechem.)

19. Speiser, *Genesis*, pp. xxii–xxiii.

20. See, for example, in S. R. Driver's *An Introduction to the Literature of the Old Testament* (Edinburgh: T. & T. Clark, 1909) pp. 27–28, the tortuous reasoning behind the source analysis of Exodus 7:14–11:10, the plague narratives.

21. See TAG, note 24 to chap. 4, p. 274.

22. Pointless, or illogical rather, as explained by source criticism. But not at all pointless if we consider its appearance from a poetical point of view. Genesis 4:17–24 presents the line of Cain, concluding in verse 24 with the taunt song of Lamech. This line (see my discussion ad loc.) died out in the Deluge. Verses 25 and 26 then introduce the line that will survive the flood, the line of Seth, father of Enos (Hebrew *ᵉnōš* "human, humanity"). The concluding notice in verse 26, the authorial aside that the Tetragrammaton was known to the first generation(s) of humanity, draws our attention to Eve's deployment of the name Elohim/God when in verse 25 she cites Heaven's grace in granting her a third son, while in the first verse of this chapter she deploys the name YHWH in citing the supernal grace that enabled her to produce her firstborn, Cain.

23. This is the popular and regularly used expression in spoken Hebrew. The Mishna itself, however, knows this expression not at all. Yoma 6:2 as we shall note below, reads *šem hammᵉfōraš* as discussed below.

24. Rabbinic Hebrew would probably use the stem *bṭ'*, modern Hebrew the verb *habbī͗ᵃ*, for "pronounce, enunciate."

25. The Mishna text does not qualify the noun *šem* "name" with the definite article (see note 23 above). The text thus features *šem* in the construct state and *hammᵉfōraš* is a genitive; thus: "the name of the expounded one," or "the name expounded." In his commentary on the alteration of the priest's invocation of God by *haššem* and *baššem*, Hanoch Albeck (*Šiššā Sidrei Mishnā*, Israel: Bialik-Dvir, 1958) indicates his understanding of the Expounded Name as a reference to God's own exposition of his name as betokening the *middot* "attributes" in Exodus 34:5–7. I suspect that Albeck is correct in this reading of the Mishna's intent, for the expression of the exposition as a prolonged statement (and not one bisyllabic word) is indicated by the use of several durative verbs in the past tense. "The priests and the populace standing in the courtyard, *as they were hearing* the name of the Expounded One *as it was issuing* from the High Priest's mouth, *were bending* knees, *worshipping falling prone* and *saying*, 'Praised be . . .'"

26. That is to say, there never existed a set of vowels designed to accompany any of the pronounced consonants whose letters, vocalic or consonantal, were Y-H-W-H. See my following argument.

27. For the importance of the distinction between literary and metaliterary conventions and assumptions for exegesis, see TAG, pp. 22–37.

28. Without claiming any additional weight for my argument I would cite as of interest the following: In the Elephantine texts the name for Israel's God is regularly and without exception *YHW*. The inscriptions of the divine Name on the two *pithoi* from Tel Ajrud are *YHW* on the one and on the second—it is not at all clear from the drawings—the letter after *YHW* does not look like a *he*. In any case, the case for a rebuttal of my argument would depend not on the fact of *YHWH* appearing epigraphically, but on the early dating of such an inscription. The sad history of the stone bearing Mesha's inscription rules out a collation to confirm or cast doubt on the supposed

appearance in it of the (full) Tetragrammaton. My own feeling is that it is unlikely that the *YHW* → *YHWH* transition would have already been so entrenched by the middle of the ninth century that a Moabite scribe would not know that Israel's god was named Yahu; hence the clear appearance of the Tetragrammaton on an early inscription, especially one authored by a non-Israelite, would be a significant witness to the improbability of my suggestion.

29. See TAG, pp. 27–34 for the fatal (in my view) effect on exegesis of the assumption that the biblical authors, like their contemporaries in the Near East (but perhaps not those in Greece), were no match in sophistication for "modern man."

30. See 2 Kings 3:4–24 and my exegetical essay on this narrative in TAG, pp. 201–209.

31. What could be clearer evidence that the "name YHWH" can figure in Scripture as metaphor for God's sovereignty and not a vocable in everyday speech? See the following argument for the sense of the construct *šem YHWH*.

CHAPTER 2

1. E. A. Speiser, *Genesis*, vol. 1 of *The Anchor Bible* (New York: Doubleday, 1964), pp. 9–10.

2. Alexander Heidel, *The Babylonian Genesis* (Chicago: University of Chicago Press, 1951), p. 101.

3. Cf. Speiser, *Genesis*, p. 12, for the well-argued case for reading the first clause as a dependent one. I would, however, take issue with his statement that "Hebrew permits a finite verb in this position"—this in reference to *bārā'* following the construct *berē'šīt*. The support he adduces (as already Rashi ad loc.) is Hosea 1:2, where the construct *tehillat* is followed by *dibber*-YHWH, where *dibber* is presumed to be the verb in the perfect tense. It is much more likely, however, that *dibber* here is the singular noun as in Jeremiah 5:13 (and plural in later Hebrew *dibberōt*). Since the Masoretes could have precluded the entire problem by vocalizing the opening preposition with a *qameṣ*, it is my suspicion that here (as so often elsewhere) the Masoretes preserved a deliberate ambiguation in the text. Whereas the dependent clause here as in 2:4b and the opening of *Enuma elish* is appropriate in context, there is a different kind of grandeur in the reading of the opening words as an independent sentence.

4. For further support of *r'h*, lit. "see," metonymically "conclude," see ch. 3, n. 6 in this volume.

5. *Day One, Day Two*, etc., are the only names in Hebrew for the days of the week.

6. My translation is based on taking the first pair as a hendiadys "for signs, i.e., of time-periods" and the second pair as a merism for longer and shorter periods, i.e. "of days and years."

7. The Masoretes who vocalized the Hebrew text must be regarded as participants in the authorial process of Scripture. This will strike many as a bold claim for the role of the "editors" whom we call Masoretes, for whom the *terminus a quo* is usually regarded as the earliest datable systems of vocalization, be they Babylonian or Tiberian. My own view is that the Masoretic text, i.e., the consonantal text as vocalized in the Rabbinic Bible, is our *textus receptus*, for without these vocalization aids much of the Hebrew text would be undecipherable. Thus, the majority of cases where MT provides for alternative readings (*ketib* and *qere*) should be expounded in terms of possibilities of *double entente* rather than adjudicated in terms of a correct versus an incorrect *Vorlage*. See, e.g., TAG, pp. 217–218, for a classic example of what I have in mind. Needless to say, the spellings *lō, lō', lū, lū', lōh* are prime examples of such interpretive lodes. Note also the comment in note 1 above.

8. See TAG, pp. 16–18.

9. See "Pagan and Biblical Anthropology: A Contrast," pp. 68 ff.

10. See "Paganism and Biblical Religion Compared and Contrasted," pp. 58–59.

11. Thus Speiser, ad loc., translating *'āpar* correctly by *clod* rather than the traditional and incorrect *dust*. In note 5 on this verse he comments on the play on words, a resort here to popular etymology by the writer "who was not interested in derivation as such." The notion that the etonym *'ādām* might have been a coinage of the biblical author's is one that he would have surely rejected. Such indeed was his reaction to my suggestion that the noun *šabbāt* might have been coined with allusion to the Babylonia *šappatum*, yet with "derivation" from the Hebrew verb *šbt* "to desist."

12. This question of literalness or figuration in respect to fauna that are by nature carnivorous must of course be raised in connection with Genesis 9:1–8 and Isaiah 11:6–7. See ch. 4, "Poetical Review of the Flood Story," p. 155 ff.

13. See Yehezkel Kaufmann's discussion.

14. See ch. 3 in this volume.

15. Indeed, the *wayᵉhī-ken* at the end of verse 30, coming after the food-provision for the beasts created on the sixth day, but also for the birds created on the fifth, may thus apply to all three classes of animates, hence rendering supererogatory LXX's insertion of this phrase in verse 20.

16. Speiser, *Genesis*, p. 11.

17. *Ancient Near Eastern Texts*, ed. J. B. Pritchard (Princeton, N.J.: Princeton University Press, 1955), p. 371, col. 1. Hereafter cited as *ANET*.

18. Another more extended and humorous lampoon of the sun as an anthropomorphic god appears in the context of a stately anthem in praise of the biblical God. See below, my interpretation of Psalm 19.

19. See Kaufmann, *Religion of Israel*, pp. 21–26.

20. For the durative hitpael, see E. A. Speiser, "The Durative Hitpaᶜel: A *tan* Form," from *Oriental and Biblical Studies*, ed. J. J. Finkelstein and M. Greenburg (Phildelphia: University of Pennsylvania Press, 1967), p. 506.

21. TAG, pp. 15–18.

22. M. Tsevat, "The Basic Meaning of the Biblical Sabbath," *Zeitschrift des deutschen Palaestina-Vereins* (Leipzig) 84 (1972), pp. 447–59.

CHAPTER 3

1. The term *miqqedem* as a directional preposition always connotes "from the east," never "in the east." When this sense is inappropriate in a given context, the sense of anteriority in time is usually the only meaningful option. The sense here of inserting "in that time of yore" is to indicate that the actions (of God) are not related in their chronological order; for surely God would have prepared the habitat for *hāʾādām* before he fashioned him. Thus the focus of the story—on this man-thing—is expressed in the initial telling of his creation, and the details of the habitat provided for him coming (in the telling but not in narrative-time) after he is fashioned.

2. Most grammarians would not hesitate to pronounce the definite article attached to *daʾat* as grammatically inadmissible in biblical Hebrew, on the ground that a term followed by a genitive construct cannot be definite, i.e., by attachment of prepositive article or postpositive suffix. Yet among the exceptions to this rule is the locative usage *mizᵉrḥa haššemeš* (Joshua 12:1, Judges 21:19), and the *tōb wārāʾ* may be in the accusative case governed by the verb-noun as in Isaiah 11:9 (cf. also Malachi 2:13). Thus E. A. Speiser, *Genesis*, vol. 1 of *The Anchor Bible* (Garden City, N.Y.: Doubleday, 1964), p. 26, notes that in 2:5 and 22, "the objective phrase 'knowing/to know good and bad' is faultless in terms of Heb. syntax. But the longer possessive construction 'the tree of knowledge of good and bad' (ii 9, 17) is otherwise without analogy in biblical Hebrew and may well be secondary." Or, we would argue, the "longer construction" may also be an "objective phrase."

3. See Speiser, *Genesis*, pp. 19–20. "The traditions involved [i.e., *edu* "flow" and *edinu* "plain"] must go back, therefore, to the oldest cultural stratum of Mesopotamia. Next comes the evidence from the location of Eden which is furnished by the notices about the rivers of that region. Recent data on the subject demonstrate that the physical background of the tale is authentic (see the writer's 'The Rivers of Paradise,' *Festschrift Johannes Friedrich*, pp. 473–485)." For all my admiration of the scholarship displayed in this article on Eden's rivers, my own evaluation of its relevance has changed in the degree of my growing commitment to the poetical as opposed to the historical or genetic approach to the biblical literature. We no longer understand just what Speiser could have had in mind by judging the "physical background of the tale" to be "authentic." He surely did not himself believe in the sometime existence of a Garden of Eden. Did he mean to convey a confidence that the biblical author himself believed in its existence, and took pains to locate it for

us, so that we might, perhaps, go looking for it? The poetical approach would dictate a further exploration of how the verisimilitudinous details in the setting contribute to the author's purpose in revealing or cloaking the meaning of the mythos of which this is a constitutive segment. See below in the text, "Poetical Review of Eden."

4. The metaphoric intent of this verse and the story behind it is certainly apprehended and expressed in one of the seven traditional benedictions of the Jewish wedding liturgy. God is invoked to provide joy to the newlyweds, just as he provided joy to his creature (singular) in Eden aforetime (*miqqedem*).

5. Julian Morganstern, *The Book of Genesis* (New York: Schocken, 1965), p. 45 ff.

6. See Speiser's discussion of the verb *yd'* in the sense of "experience" generally and "sexual experience" in particular, *Genesis*, pp. 31–32. Speiser cites the use of the Akkadian cognate of *yd'*, as well as "the analogous use of the Akk. verb *lamadum* 'to learn, experience,'" and cites his own earlier observation that, "The Hebrew stem *yd'* signifies not only 'to know,' but more especially "to experience, to come to know." It is this last sense as the primary meaning of *yd'* (as of its close synonym *lmd*) which I would like to underline. It is to this sense, I believe, that the phenomenon of *yd'* in the perfect tense = "I know" owes: "having experienced, I have come to know."

Further support for the primarily inchoative force of *yd'* appears in the *yd'=r'h* couplet. In 11 instances the order of the verbs testifies that *r'h* "realize/come to the conclusion" follows in time the act of *yd'*, which must therefore have the sense of "consider, experience, explore" parallel to the sense of *tm* in Psalm 34:9. (The instances are I Samuel 12:17, 14:38, 23:22, 24:11, 25:17; I Kings 20:7, 22; 2 Kings 5:7; Jeremiah 2:19, 23. Only in one instance is the order reversed, in I Samuel 23:23. In Jeremiah 5:1 the two verbs appear together but not as a couplet.) It is this sense of *r'h* "to conclude" which prompts me to render *wayyar' ki tob* as "approved," i.e., "concluded that it was good," in Genesis 1, and to render the same verb as "concluded" in Genesis 3:6.

7. Note this rendering for *miqqedem* here. There is no reason to suppose that there was only one entrance to the Garden—and that one from the east. Hence, as the plural *cherubim* suggests, any and all approaches to the Garden were guarded by these fantasy-creatures with ever-turning propeller-like blades.

8. TAG, pp. 25–27.

9. What people will eat and wear in various narratives comports with the conditions determined by the extended metaphors or symbolism of the individual narrative. Thus, for example, in Genesis 1, in prescribing a diet for herbivores, God in verse 29 specifies cereal grasses (the mainstay of bread-eating man) as well as fruit of trees (verse 29). In the Garden of Eden context, where the threshing, milling, and baking of civilized society would be inappropriate, trees are divided into shade and fruit trees, and the fruit of the latter is the only specific edible (2:9, 16). Like baked goods, textiles are a product of civilization. Animal hides, therefore, are appropriate for people leading eremitic lives on the steppe. Thus, Elijah in II Kings 1:8, and Gilgamesh on his quest through the wilds for the secret of immortality. The state before the use of animal hides is represented in the human couple's use of the broad fig-leaf to improvise loin-clouts; the state after the dress of hides in Enkidu's sharing the harlot's garments (*ANET* p. 77, ii 28–30), "becoming human" in conjunction with "putting on clothes" (p. 77, iii 25–26) and in Šamaš's response to his anger at the harlot who *in bringing him to his civilized state also rendered his death inevitable*; Šamaš says that Enkidu should be grateful to her who brought him "to eat food fit for divinity . . . drink fit for royalty," and clothed him in "noble garments" (p. 86, iii 36–38).

10. See preceding note 9 for the lines that immediately precede these.

11. My use of the term *mythos* rather than myth is occasioned by the following considerations: The noun *epic* is defined as a narrative poem dealing with heroic action and written in an elevated style; it therefore involves form as well as substance and cannot be applied to a heroic legend unless it is composed in verse. *Legend* is a term for a story coming down from the past, ostensibly historical, but whose historicity is unverifiable. A *myth*, like a legend, comes down from a remote past, but the chief characters are divine or semi-divine beings, whereas in legends the principal characters are human. A myth can usually be interpreted as explaining the origin of a natural phenomenon or of a

religious institution, belief, or practice. Because myths feature adventures of the gods, and the God of Hebrew Bible has no adventures, I employ the term *mythos* for a story which in symbolism, metaphor, or allegorical fashion attempts to convey a religious moral or vision of reality.

12. The standard and universal translation of *wayyō'mer Qayyin 'el Hebel 'āḥīw* "Cain said to his brother Abel" leaves us bereft of Cain's declaration. This lacuna is filled in the Greek and the Targum by, "Come, let us go out into the field." Speiser's acceptance of this filling for the perceived lacuna is particularly interesting in view of his awareness—and the importance of this awareness—that "The Hebrew stem *'mr* coincides by and large with the English verb 'to say.' But the Hebrew verb in question carries many other nuances: *to tell, promise, threaten, express fear, reflect* (speak to oneself), and the like." (*Genesis*, p. LXVII). My translation, based on the recognition that *'mr* here is not *said* but *thought, spoke to himself*, does away with the problem of a lacuna by recognizing the clause *'el Hebel 'āḥīw* as the object of *'mr*. My translation fails, however, to express the dramatic force of the clause in presupposing the clause as indirect discourse. The preposition *'el* actually introduces Cain's thought, internal dialogue, viz. "['Tis] to my [*lit., his*] brother [I owe this rebuff by God]." The thinness of the line between free direct and free indirect discourse (particularly in biblical Hebrew) is suggested in TAG, pp. 10–13. In this instance, in response to YHWH's having just told him that his fate is in his own hands, as it was before his niggardly offering—there is no third party in addition to himself and the temptation to sin—Cain nevertheless thinks *that it was all a matter of (being shown up by) his brother Abel* [indirect discourse] = thinks, "I lay it to his—my brother Abel's—door."

13. As frequently in the parenthetic aside signaled by the nominal (or formally hypotactical) clause. See TAG, pp. 16–19 and ch. 1, note 15.

14. See Speiser's discussion of this passage, and for further instructive detail on the plethora of benevolent and malignant spirits/demons the article cited in ch. 8, note 1 of TAG.

15. The general interpretation of the Pandora myth, that she, representing woman, opens the box because of her overweening curiosity, overlooks the vital significance of her name. She represents man, humankind, endowed with all the riches and blessings. The foible of curiosity is not her undoing, but avarice, fear that some precious blessing has been withheld.

16. See, e.g., Deuteronomy 22–27 for the significance of a forbidden act taking place in a frequented place (*'īr* lit., "city") rather than "in the field" (*baśśāde*).

17. See my discussion of this verb's meaning in *The Problem of "Curse" in the Hebrew Bible*, SBL Monograph Series 13 (1962).

18. See TAG, ch. 8, "The Sign on the Forehead," pp. 235ff.

19. For the reason God spared Cain, see below the discussion of the lines of Cain and Seth.

20. For the synoptic-resumptive episodic technique in biblical narrative, see TAG, pp. 13–17

21. See preceding note 3, particularly the last sentence.

22. See Ch. 1 of this volume.

23. See TAG Ch. 3, pp. 67–83. Note particularly n. 21, p. 269.

CHAPTER 4

1. See Sir Leonard Wooley, *Ur of the Chaldees*, (London: Penguin, 1954), ch. 1, particularly pp. 22–23: "There could be no doubt that the flood of which we had thus found the only possible evidence was the Flood of Sumerian history and legend, the Flood on which is based the story of Noah."

2. As implied in Wooley's statement cited in preceding note 1.

3. These citations are from Hermann Gunkel, *The Legends of Genesis* (New York: Schocken, 1966), pp. 14, 100, and 101 respectively. For an interesting example of how genre labels can be deployed to mystify rather than to enlighten (see TAG, pp. 26–30), see W. F. Albright's introduction to this Schocken volume, particularly pp. viii, xi–xii. Gunkel's standing in biblical scholarship is reflected in the Albright's comment: "His mistakes were inevitable two-thirds of a century ago, and do not detract from his epochal place in the history of scholarship" (op. cit., p. xi), and in Speiser's

reference to Gunkel's *Genesis* (the introduction to which has been translated and published in Schocken's *The Legends*) as "marked by the author's keen appreciation of literary quality." It would be nice to observe the injunction *De mortuis*. Alas, the continued awe in which Gunkel is held, and as a literary critic in particular, compels me to warn the reader: It would be hard to find literary pontifications so poorly argued, and so consistent a chain of silliness, as is to be found on every page, nay almost in every paragraph, of this "survey" (as Albright calls it) of the "legends" in Genesis.

4. Julian Morgenstern, *The Book of Genesis* (New York: Schocken, 1965), p. 83.

5. Note in this question and answer, as in the sentence that begins the immediately preceding paragraph, the subtle and often overlooked difference between the narrator and a character in the narration as separate centers of consciousness, possessed of different degrees of information and responsibility for the judgments made by one or the other or possibly both. Thus the narrator knows, as Utnapishtim does not, which dispatch will be the first and which the last. On the other hand, our sense of the correctness of the flying range of Utnapishtim's three birds, and of the appositeness of this judgment to the logic (or illogic) of the dispatch, will determine whether we regard the narrator as himself accepting responsibility for Utnapishtim's reasoning or loading the entire responsibility on his hapless protagonist's shoulders.

6. Morgenstern, *Book of Genesis*, p. 81, note on 5:14.

7. I make grateful acknowledgment to my cherished colleague and friend, Prof. Aaron Schaffer, for this reading of the Akkadian text.

8. Thus, for example, if only two birds were released, the sender, who had first dispatched the far-ranging dove, which returned, may have suspected that the shoreline might have appeared—but beyond even the dove's range. For the second dispatch, enough time after the first so that the shoreline if any would be even further from his grounded ship, he therefore chose the swallow, whose range exceeds even that of the dove. But in that case, why the choice of the no-range raven for the third dispatch? Utnapishtim's muddled mental processes are also reflected in his attributing the raven's failure to return not to the plenteous carrion available to him, but to his "seeing that the waters had diminished."

Another instance of Utnapishtim's obtuseness, not hitherto cited, begins with l. 200. Four lines are spoken by the narrator (not by Utnapishtim, as, for example, also implicitly in ll. 99–128). Gilgamesh falls asleep, and remains so for six days and seven nights. Utnapishtim mockingly points to this hero who seeks eternal life and cannot resist [the half-death of] sleep. Mr. Utnapishtim refuses to awaken Gilgamesh, as Mrs. Utnapishtim urges, for seven days. In order to prevent Gilgamesh from exercising his human wiles on her (lit., "Mankind being wicked, he will seek to deceive thee"), he proposes that Mrs. Utnapishtim bake for seven days; the various stages of staleness, sogginess, and mold in the bread—along with marks recording the number of days he sleeps—will make it impossible for Gilgamesh to "deceive" Mrs. Utnapishtim. But neither wickedness nor deceit is germane to the situation. What Utnapishtim really means is—as it actually transpires—that Gilgamesh will not, upon awakening, believe that he has dozed more than a few moments; the baked goods and the marks will then demonstrate that Mr. and Mrs. Utnapishtim are not lying. The fatuity of this lies further in that the device would prove nothing to a Gilgamesh who was bent on believing that the Utnapishtim's were trying to deceive him: Seven marks can be made in a moment, and bread—moldy or stale—can be retrieved from the garbage heap. A closely parallel biblical account in Joshua 9 makes similar mockery of the Israelites, who are taken in by the moldy bread and worn-out clothes and sandals preferred by the Gibeonites as evidence of their having been long on the road from their distant homeland. Lacking the common sense to see through the silly ruse themselves, or to question their own sagacity and to inquire of YHWH, they take an oath to spare these Canaanites who were slated for extinction. Cf. Brichto, *The Problem of "Curse"*, SBL Monograph 13 (1963), pp. 88 ff.

9. As Speiser points out in his preface to his translation of the *Atrahasis* Epic in *ANET* (p. 104), this name, its meaning " 'Exceeding Wise' is associated with more than one hero of the epic literature of Mesopotamia." The one use of this epithet, by Ea, to designate a protagonist who is hardly the brightest of mortals may be an antonymic euphemism (like Hebrew *berek* "bless" for

"curse," Aramaic *sagi nahor* "abundant of light" for a blind man), deployed here in the manner of the American folk convention to nickname people who are extremely tall, obese, or bald by the sobriquets, respectively: *Shorty, Slim,* and *Curly.*

10. Can this "secret of the gods" be the same as the one which Utnapishtim at the beginning of his tale promised to divulge to Gilgamesh? In the mouth of Ea—who can fool Enlil that in talking to the wall of the reed-hut he was not really addressing the "Man of Shuruppak, son of Ubar-Tutu"—the secret can indeed be the resolve of the gods to annihilate humankind and to keep their plan a surprise so that this enterprising race will not take measures to survive the cataclysm. (Witness Mr. U.'s example! Another twit of Enlil, who is the divine counterpart of this human Atrahasis!) This is so because Ea is speaking in the dim past, immediately after the Flood. Utnapishtim's address to Gilgamesh, however, takes place eons later when all humanity knows—and in many versions—of that cataclysm brought on by the revered pantheon. Does he, fool that he is, think that thousands of years after his own translation to "the mouth of the rivers," mankind at large is still in the dark as to who was responsible for that primordial flood? Or is it possible that in this twice-mentioned "secret of the gods" our cunning author is signaling to his readers the real point of the narrative: the absurd nature of that religion we call polytheism or paganism? See the next section, "The Babylonian Flood Story as a Critique of Paganism."

11. Cf. Speiser's brief comment (*Genesis*, pp. LV–LVI) on the "Babel and Bibel" controversy begun by Friedrich Delitzsch (which was continued by defenders of Scripture's originality at the expense of Babel's level of urbanity) and Speiser's own perception of how "subsequent [cuneiform] discoveries" have served to refute "the theory [Delitzsch's] itself by placing the whole subject in its true perspective." Compare then the difference between even Speiser's perspective and the one we present in the section "Noah's Deluge and Utnapishtim's: A Comparison." I believe that my poetical approach—though not designed with any such purpose in mind—enhances our respect and appreciation for both Scripture and its pagan ambience. To enhance our respect for the accomplishments and wisdom of our pagan ancestors is to sharpen our appreciation of the breakthrough represented by Scripture. To denigrate pagans and paganism is to create a straw-man foil for a platitudinous Scripture. One example: compare Speiser's discussion of the beginning of biblical monotheism (*Genesis* pp. XLIII–LII) with Ernst Renan's characterization of that monotheism as a reflection of the monotony of the desert. (Renan may have been an expert on monotony, but, as my explorer son Herschel asks, what did he know about deserts?)

12. E. A. Speiser, *Genesis*, vol. 1 of *The Anchor Bible* (Garden City, N.Y.: Doubleday, 1964), pp. 45–46.

13. This phenomenon is thus a reversion to the condition of the primeval waters in Genesis before God separated them; and although never so termed explicitly is, rather than the phenomenon in Noah's time, the referent in Ps. 29:10, the *mabbūl* "over which YHWH sat enthroned and remained enthroned as king for all time."

14. The narrator informs us that Noah dispatched the raven 40 days after Day 1 of Month 10. The interval between the first and third dispatch of the dove is 14 days. We are not told what the interval was between the dispatch of the raven and the first dispatch of the dove. If that interval were 4 days, the arithmetic would be 40 + 14 + 4 = 58 (i.e., two months of 29 days, or exactly two months after the first appearance of the mountain peaks (!) on Day 1 of Month 10.

15. Since the whole point of dispatching the birds was to ascertain whether it was sage to disembark, there is something silly about Noah's waiting yet another month—for the call of God—after the dove's failure to return had provided the desired information. This, too, is in furtherance of the wry humor (see the immediately following discussion) of God's invitation to Noah, sons and wives, and living creatures in all categories, to proceed to the reproductive *process on the earth* (four times in verses 15–19), which was forbidden them *at sea*, which is to say, for the duration of their confinement to the ark.

16. Cf. for a more detailed discussion, Brichto, "On Slaughter and Sacrifice, Blood and Atonement," *HUCA* 47 (1976), pp. 19–28.

17. Literalists, and scholars who insist on ascribing to the ancient author a naïveté that we

moderns have long outgrown, will insist that this is indeed the purport of the passage. This despite my own arguments to the contrary; despite the witness of Scripture to a polar ambivalence as to the value or efficacy of animal sacrifice; and despite—ironically—the attribution of the offense that precipitated the flood to that perversely literal, naïve, and wrongheaded perception of reality in whose imaginative bent (*yēṣer leb*, *yēṣer maḥšᵉbōt leb*) we moderns delight for its esthetic play and decry for the immorality of its values and for the polytheism we call paganism.

CHAPTER 5

1. Another indication that the genealogies of Seth and Cain are the work of one hand is that the Lamech in each line is the next to the last generation before the flood. In the Seth list he is the father of Noah, who experiences the flood, and in the Cain list he is the father of the three sons, who implicitly perish in it. These last three are culture heroes, as is Noah in the Seth list.

2. The sons of Noah did not sire children until after the flood. The wives they brought with them into the ark may well have been descendants of the Cain line, thus making him—despite all—an ancestor of the entire human race.

3. Cf. E. A. Speiser, *Genesis*, vol. 1 of *The Anchor Bible* (Garden City, N.Y.: Doubleday, 1964), p. 63.

4. The plausibility of dittography is reinforced by the additional coincidence that the God (of Shem) *'lhy* and the *tents* (of Shem) *'hly* are constituted of the identical four consonants, with only the order of the two middle consonants being different in the two terms.

5. In his note on verse 26. As we shall see, however, the author may achieve a powerful effect precisely by taking a direction that is contrary to our expectations. The poetical approach seeks the reason for the author's decision to frustrate our expectations; whereas the prevailing scholarly approach is to find fault with the text.

6. Speiser, *Genesis*, p. 63. Let us note how productive of speculation is the assumption of source analytic methodology. If the genealogical note could not be assigned to P and the text of the curse to J, this conjecture on Speiser's part—for all its apparent conformation to what we assume is the history of Canaan—would never have made it to the printed page.

7. My interpretation, which will be in support of those championing the Masoretic pointing, makes this crux a parade example of *lectio difficilior praestat*, extending the principle from the consonantal text to the traditional vocalization as well.

8. See TAG, ch. 7, tale 2, pp. 196–98.

9. This is the plain meaning of Exodus 25:2–8 "from any individual freely prompted . . . [only on such condition] will I take up residence among them." It is also the view everywhere in Scripture (as indeed in pagan Mesopotamia), concealed from us by our own tendency to read obligation to God where our ancient predecessors intended—and with better theological sense—privilege. See below, my discussion of the Tower of Babel. Note further the weight of our conception as a meta-literary factor in the (mis)interpretation of numerous biblical texts and contexts.

10. See below, ch. 8. Once again the poetical integrity of the biblical text, an underground linking of Genesis and Joshua (and not, let us note, of J and D, or whatever authorship to whom/which source analysis sees fit to assign the sixth book of the "hexateuch").

11. It is the assumption of an act perpetuated upon Noah that inspires the kinds of speculation we have just discussed. "To deal with" is as much a meaning of Hebrew *'sh* as of the English verb "to do," which may cover the "act" in our oxymoronic expression "act of omission."

12. What point of origin could the narrator have possibly had in mind as the starting point for humankind? It would thus seem that every appearance of *miqqedem* as an adverb is temporal (as in Psalm 74:12, see below, ch. 8), not a one is directional.

13. TAG, pp. 28–30.

14. Eretz: Israel V (Mazar Volume, 1958), pp. 32–36.

15. See preceding note 14.

16. See Brichto, "Kin, Cult, Land and Afterlife," *HUCA* XLIV, 1973, p.7, note 9.

17. I have in mind certain formulations in cuneiform epics, of which some biblical images or metaphors seem to be distorted yet recognizable echoes. Thus the creation of the human race from the body-stuff of Kingu (Enuma Elish, Tablet VI, ll. 5–33, *ANET* 68 b), Anu's begetting Ea (Nudimmud) in his own image (Tablet I, l. 16, *ANET* 60a), and man (Enkidu) as made of clay, yet in the divine image (of Anu) in Gilgamesh Epic (Tablet I ii, ll. 32–35, *ANET* 74a.) These are examples of the kind of imagistic conceptualizations that the biblical authors clearly inherited from an earlier literary tradition, but which they shaped into expressions emblematic of a human dignity that does not obtain in the cuneiform sources. Thus, the mankind created from the stuff of Kingu is of a lower order of beings created to serve the gods, and both Gilgamesh and Enkidu created by Aruru as "double of Anu" are heroic mortal champions, but not specifically symbolic of humanity's sharing in general in the dignity of the divine.

CHAPTER 6

1. E. A. Speiser, *Genesis*, vol. 1 of The *Anchor Bible* (New York: Doubleday, 1964), p. 106.

2. Thus, for example, the protagonist kings of the five cities of the Plain. In verse 2, where they are first introduced, four of them are given names, the fifth is anonymous. The five city-states are named in that verse, but never again do all five appear in the text. Sodom and Gomorrah are mentioned in verses 10 and 11, but thereafter only Sodom appears. The kings of the Five Cities of the Plain appear in verse 8, none of them named, but the four kings of the Empire of the East are named in verse 9. The rout of the five kings is presumably indicated by the plural verb in verse 10—*wayyānūsū* "they fled"— but the subject of this verb is an explicit singular, *the king of Sodom*, immediately ambiguated by the addition of *and of Gomorrah*, which of course has its own king. Of the five defeated kings only the king of Sodom appears again (in verses 17, 21–22). Clearly, then, the one king of Sodom represents the monarchy of both Sodom and Gomorrah, as well as of Admah and Zeboim, and of the fifth city, which is variously Bela or Zoar, a great city-state or an insignificant town in the story of Lot's escape from the doomed Plain. All this—unthinkable in a sober historian's account—is poetically of a piece with 19:28, where Abraham looks down upon the pall-covered "Sodom and Gomorrah and upon the entire surface of the Plain," and with 19:29, where God overthrows "the *cities* in which Lot had taken up resident."

3. Improbable, because anyone capable of translating from Akkadian to BH would know that *ina ûmē* → *enuma* is equal to Hebrew *bᵉyōm* "when" in a syntax that calls for a temporal conjunction. Unnecessary, because it is one of many ambiguations that cannot be laid at the door of an inept translator. See note 1 above.

4. See TAG, pp. 5–6 and p. 259, note 3.

5. Yochanan Muffs has gathered as much as is retrievable on this matter. See *Love and Joy: Language and Religion in Ancient Israel* (York, N.Y.: Jewish Theological Seminary of America, 1992), pp. 67–95.

6. The expression "to raise (the/one's) hand" in the sense of "take an oath" appears only here with the verb *hērīm*. The expression does appear, however, in that sense with the verb *nś'*. See Exodus 6:8, Numbers 14:30, Deuteronomy 32:40, Ezekiel 20:5–6, 15, 23, 28, and 42; Psalm 106:26, Nehemiah 9:15. Thus this singular departure from the idiomatic *nś' yd* is to draw our attention to something unique in the context. That uniquely significant element in this context is then, as we see it, the past tense of the verb, the time of the oath-taking having been in the preceding hypotactically formulated episode, or even earlier.

7. Marvin H. Pope, *El in the Ugaritic Texts* (Leiden: Brill, 1955).

8. See ch. 7, "Structures."

9. See TAG, pp. 13–14, with particular attention to n. 13 (p. 260).

10. The parallel and seemingly pointless repetitions of *wayyō'mer* are thus a frequent signal to a synoptic and an expansive sub-episode within a larger episode (synoptic or resumptive) constituting part of an overarching narrative. In terms of poetic subtlety, compare the bald statement in verse 2 with the bolder reading of Abram's intent in verse 3. It is one thing for Abram to hint that

Damascene Eliezer is not an acceptable heir, quite another to charge God with responsibility for his sterility in the aftermath of a great victory and in the context of a revelatory promise that greater reward is yet in store.

11. See the rabbinic commentators ad loc., particularly Rashi, for the close reading of subtly shaded meanings in the presence of the imperfect *vayᵉhī* in a verbal clause or of a perfect *hāyā* in what might also be regarded as a verbal clause, in that the verb precedes the subject.

12. See Fitzmyer, "The Aramaic Inscriptions of Sefire I and II," *Journal of the American Oriental Society* 81, no. 3 (Sept. 1961), 178–222, particularly FACE A, ll. 36–40.

13. Despite the many translations, which—knowing the biblical author's intent better than he, or perhaps than the mistaken editor responsible for the *textus receptus*—provide a preposition to make for a simile rather than the metaphor. Needless to day, the preservation of the metaphor points to the meaning of the text while its rendering the text, as a simile contributes to the obfuscation of the meaning.

14. The discussion of 400 years and four generations appears in ch. 7, "Structures."

15. "On Faith and Revelation in the Hebrew Bible," *HUCA* 39 (1968), 44–45.

16. See ch. 7, "Structures."

17. The number of variables in the naming activity here are such as to preclude a single satisfactory resolution of the problems in verses 13–14. First it is Hagar who gives a name to the d/Deity. This name, however, features an infinitive gerund with a first personal suffix, which may refer to the first person as subject or object: *the deity taking note of me/the deity whom I experience*. The narrator introducing this direct discourse says that [*the deity whose*] *name* [*is*] *YHWH she called* {you are} "*'El Ro'ī.*" The narrator then expands upon her intent in this appellation in a four-word sentence twice featuring the ambiguous verb *r'h*, with another instance of a first person pronominal suffix, which can be nominative or accusative, an ambiguous preposition "after/behind," which may be temporal or locative in sense, and a contextually puzzling adverb "to this point (in place or time)." Given all this, one must be pretentious indeed to succumb to the temptation to emend the *hᵃlom* "hither" to *'lhm* "God." The narrator then compounds his problematic "clarification" by tracing to Hagar's utterance the name by which the spring between Kadesh(-Barnea?) and Bered is (later?) called; this spring subsequently identified as the haunt of Isaac, not of her son Ishmael.

18. See Speiser, *Comment*, pp. 119–20.

19. The wild ass metaphor for Ishmael may bespeak admiration for the untameable spirit of the sharp-hoofed onager, along with lions the favorite game of royal Assyrian huntsmen. But what need to inform the mother of a future race of bedouin that violence will mark them off from settled agrarians and camel-riding kinsmen as well? This is, thus, a prime example of how free biblical free direct discourse can be; this entire aside is for reader, not for Mother Hagar. And the multi-valent assurance that for all his "home"-lessness he will abide *'al-pnē* "to the east of/to the rue of/in defiance of" *all his kinsmen* is to be read as having reference to the descendants of Father Abraham by other wives, be they the settled sons of Sarah or the roving ones of Keturah. See ch. 7, "Structures."

20. The meaning of this designation for a (or the) d/Deity, and the gloss on it, are obscured by the following variables: (1) The connotations of the verb *r'h* "to see, take note of, regard, have regard for, experience, witness, provide, etc."; (2) The differing punctuation of *rō'ī/r°ī*, the former a participle with first person pronoun suffix accusative, and the latter an infinitive verbal noun with the same suffix, but with the possibilities of subjective or objective genitive for the pronoun; or, the latter as a noun in which the final vowel is radical (not a suffix at all); (3) The connotations of *gam* (especially with the *he* interrogative): "indeed! also, really"; and of *'aḥᵃrē* "behind, beyond, after" in senses both temporal and positional; (4) The adverb *hᵃlom*, capable of expressing place nearby or far away "hither, thither."

21. *That your line will continue*, lit. *that seed will be called/attributed to you*. For the various nouns and verbs appearing in the metaphor for "the continuance of a person's line," see "Kin, Cult, Land and Afterlife: A Biblical Complex," *HUCA* 44 (1973), p. 22. The metaphor—in view of the Coda, Genesis 15:18–21—must be seen as just that, not in denial of Ishmael's descendants being Abraham's also. Isaac's line will be the elect.

22. See preceding note.

23. Note the artist's lexical control in verse 18. The verb *ḥzq* means "to be strong" in the qal; with *yad* "hand" as subject it is an idiom for "to be heartened, encouraged." In the piel with *yad* as object it means to encourage s.o. In the hiphil the verb alone means to grasp, and with s.o.'s hand as object "to grasp that person by his hand." Here the instruction to Hagar to grasp (in the hiphil) Ishmael's hand takes "your (Hagar's) hand" as the object, with Ishmael as the indirect object (*bō* "in/on him"). The hiphil *ḥzq* thus, intransitive though it is, takes on the elative force of "grasp firmly," even while it becomes a transitive (like the piel) in that your hand is object of the verb. Why this lexical *tour de force*? To express the metaphor that is first implicit in verse 14 *Abraham . . . took food and waterskin, gave [these] to Hagar—[that is,] he put [these] on her shoulder—and the lad as well*. Ishmael, being in his late teens, did not require his mother's handhold. But Ishmael as her future hope is abandoned by her in her despair. And the encouraging word of God's angel is that she is to turn from despair and to renew her hold on the son who is her hope.

24. That such is or may well be the stance of the biblical narrator in respect to his own ancestors is the burden of my exegesis of the *Three Domestic Triangles* below.

25. Free direct discourse, in her disposition of the name YHWH, when that name, unpronounced and unpronounceable, was not uttered by her. See ch. 1 of this volume.

26. Note that in 16:13 (and cf. preceding n. 17) the narrator tells of Hagar's designation of the Deity, whom he knows as YHWH, in Hagar's direct discourse, which is an address to that Deity: *You are ʾEl rᵒʾī*, as though he is being informed, rather than this free discourse constituting a metaphor for Hagar's sudden recognition that she is under the providential care of the one and only God—of Abraham and all humanity.

27. Speiser, *Genesis*, p. 126.

28. See, for example, my reading of the *lex talionis*, below.

29. I use the terms *halakha* and *halakhic* for the corpus of injunctions and regulations, legal or preceptual, secular or cultic, which prescribe the behavioral norms for biblical Israel. In regard to the prescription (rather than narratorial assumption) of circumcision as one of these divinely instituted norms, there is only one such instance: in Leviticus 12:3, where a male child's circumcision on the eighth day is a parenthetical aside in a pericope dealing with the period of impurity incurred by a woman after birthing. Another prescription, in Exodus 12:43–49, requires circumcision of a non-Israelite bondsman or freeman (*ger*) if that male is to partake of the paschal sacrifice.

30. See TAG, p. 16 and p. 261, n.15.

31. The content, the context, and the paratactic formulations of verse 16 and verse 22—together with the content and hypotactic formulation of verses 17–21—guarantee that verses 18–20 are a parenthetic flashback to bridge the gap between Abraham's presence on the elevation overlooking Sodom and his coming forward to address the Deity, now represented by the single remaining personage. This parenthesis is divided into two parts. The first, verses 17–19, explains why YHWH must make Abraham privy to the fateful decision he is about to make: it is, in a manner of speaking, a test to see if Abraham was properly chosen for the role ordained for him and his line; Abraham's passing of this test is indicated by his stepping forward to challenge the Deity. The second part, verses 20–21, still part of the parenthesis, despite the verbal clause beginning verse 20, is to indicate that the dialogue to come is not a mere charade. YHWH has not yet reached his verdict; in responding to Abraham's arguments he is not playing cat-and-mouse with him. All this from the perspective of the narrator *qua* narrator. From the perspective of theology which binds the Magistrate of all earth to strict justice, from the perspective of the narrator's audience, which knows the verdict (even, so to speak, before YHWH does), because it hears or reads the narrative centuries after the overthrow, the verdict was inevitable. Hence that audience will understand—perhaps as the narrator, for all his reliability, did not, or did not even question—why the embassy of YHWH on this occasion consisted of three personages: one to stand before Abraham on the elevation, two to get down to the plain on the mission made necessary by the inevitable verdict.

32. Sheldon Blank, *Prophetic Thought, Essays and Addresses* (Cincinnati: Hebrew Union College Press, 1977), pp. 91–99.

33. See Speiser, *Genesis*, p. 135.

34. See chapter 1 in this volume.

35. A *novella* is, therefore, a long short story, in length more like a novel, but a short story nonetheless for containing only a single story.

36. See "Abram the Noble Warrior," p. 189.

37. See ch. 1, "The Problem: A Preliminary Review," p. 3 ff., and ch. 6, "The Annunciation of Isaac's Birth: Two Versions," pp. 230–31.

38. See Meir Sternberg, *The Poetics of Biblical Narrative* (Bloomington: Indiana University Press, 1987).

39. The rabbis pick up on this problem of three angels on a single mission in their midrashic explanation that Deity assigns only one task to any one angel. Here in Genesis 18–19, one makes the announcement of Isaac's birth, one rescues Lot from Sodom, one destroys the Cities of the Plain.

40. See ch. 1 in this volume pp. 32–3.

41. On flat and round characters see TAG, pp. 6–8.

42. Whether that locus is in Genesis or Job, in Psalms, or Proverbs, or Ecclesiastes.

43. For this meaning, see TAG, p. 149. Closer to hand is Genesis 45:3. Whereas most renderings are along the line of, "Is my father yet alive?" Speiser's translation is, "Is Father still in good health?" The brothers have hitherto made it clear that Jacob is alive and well. The force then of the Hebrew, immediately following the announcement, "I am Joseph," is, *now that you know why I am so interested in your father, tell me—a loving son of a loving father—is my father really well?* Note the ambiguity that is opened up by the attachment of the first person pronominal suffix to "father." The clearly caritative force of this pronoun is expressed in Speiser's capitalization of this word and omission of the pronoun. This expression of commonality also betokens Joseph's assumption that his reconciliation with his brothers has now been consummated. But an equally valid reading—one that the brothers might well have construed—is that Joseph is still preening himself on his place as Papa's favorite.

44. An exception might be inferred from the Laws of Manu (see my "Kin, Cult, Land, and Afterlife, *HUCA* 44 [1973], p. 5) that an adulterer is worse than a murderer, for the latter kills only once, whereas the adulterer destroys an entire line. To cite this in this context would be, in my opinion, to misapply a metaphor.

45. As I will attempt to demonstrate in ch. 6.

46. See Brichto, "The Case of the Śōṭā," *HUCA* 46 (1975), p. 66 and note 11.

47. On this perplexing "truth" see ch. 7, "Structures."

48. Just how that payment of 1,000 pieces of silver serves as Sarah's "*kᵉsūt ʿeynayīm* in regard to all/everything pertaining to you, yes in all (respects) your (good name?) is altogether assured" is so ambiguously formulated as to defy a confident interpretation. A key however, may be the hypotactic formulation of this address to Sarah in verse 16. The intent may well be: To Sarah **now** he had said, (the 1,000 silver pieces I gave to your *brother* (as bride-price) guarantees your honor and dignity. (That is to say, you entered my household unbound to any man and in honorable circumstances.) Now (that you are reunited with your husband, nothing having transpired between you and me) your status is beyond reproach.

49. For a similar bit of seeming nonsense, see in ch. 7, "Structures," the naming by Isaac of wells, dug by his father and redug by himself, with names *like* his father [never] gave them.

50. Figure 6-1, the congruence of narratives two and three compared to the disposition of three congruent triangles.

51. See, on this matter of Philistine verse Israelite territory, ch. 7, "Structures."

52. For more on genocide, supposedly ordered by God and committed by Israel against the Canaanite population which preceded them, see ch. 8, "Two More Addends," pp. 428 ff.

53. See ch. 6, "YHWH and Abraham in a Dialogue on God's Justice," pp. 237 ff.

54. For the present see TAG, pp. 34–35, particularly items 7 and 8; ch. 7, 1, pp. 194–96; ch. 7, 4, pp. 201–209; and 5, pp. 209–14.

55. See ch. 7, "Structures."

56. Although the territory was *Canaanite*, and Abram's allies in the *Hebron* area (13:18) were *Amorites* (14:13), one of them giving his name to the locality of Mamre's Oaks (idem), itself indistinguishable from the *Hebron* which is *Kiryat Arba* (23:2), it is from the *Hethites* that the cave containing the field of Machpelah "over against/east of *Mamre*" (23:19–20) is purchased by Abraham. So much for gentilics and toponyms in Genesis. In Joshua 15:13–14 the eponymous Arba, whose stronghold was superseded by Hebron, is the ancestor of the Anakite titans, three of whom are dispossessed by Caleb ben Jephunneh. It is to Hebron that "Abraham came to perform for Sarah the rites of mourning and lamentation." Came from where? Clearly from Beersheba, where (in 22:19) we are told he had settled.

57. For the purposes of a more realistic setting for the near-sacrifice of Isaac, this near-event would have taken place early in Isaac's career, perhaps at the age of 13 (the age of Ishmael at the time of his circumcision), betokening his coming into age of responsibility. For the purposes of the continuing story, with Sarah buried at Machpelah in Chapter 23, and in Chapter 24 the mission of Abraham's steward to bring a bride for Isaac from Nahor's city in Aram Naharaim, Isaac should be 37 or 38 when that mission is successfully completed. Hence the significance of 24:62–67, the notices which are the denouement of the steward's mission. Abraham is (not so) strangely missing from the scene. The focus is on Isaac, who travels to Beer-lahai-roi in the Negev (where in 25:11 he settles some 35 years later after Abraham's death) and back (presumably to the Hebron-Beersheba region) to be on hand for the arrival of Rebekah and the servant. Isaac's taking his bride to his mother's tent, and the love of this bride consoling him in a measure for the doting mother whose death some months (rather than years) before, are thus in keeping with 25:20, the notice that Isaac was forty "when he took Rebekah, daughter of Betuel the Aramean, from Paddan Aram, the sister of Laban the Aramean, to himself to wife."

58. Such a phenomenon, the absence of the (implicit) subject in a paratactic (waw-conversive) verb, and the explicit appearance of that subject in a preceding hypotactic parenthesis, is quite regular. Perhaps the most celebrated instance is Leviticus 1:1, "He called to Moses, and YHWH spoke to him from the Tent of Encounter." This verse is a continuation of Exodus 40:34a, "The cloud covered the Tent of Encounter." Between these two paratactic verses there intervenes the hypotactic explanation of the significance of the presence of the cloud and of its departure from the Tent of Encounter, this hypotactic explanation beginning with 40:34b, "The presence of YHWH **now** was occupying the tabernacle."

59. The identification of Solomon's Temple site on the mount of Moriah in 2 Chronicles 3:1 is a midrashic embroidery on the "territory of Moriah" in Genesis 22:2. Similarly in the same verse's identification of that site with "the threshing floor of Ornan the Jebusite," the embroidery is an extension of the altar, which David erected there according to 2 Samuel 24:19–25. The Chronicles verse is usually mistranslated, along the lines of "at the place that David had appointed/had prepared." The Hebrew verb *hēkīn* has Solomon for its subject, and refers to the Temple "which he (Solomon, acting) in (his father) David's stead, erected on the threshing-floor of Ornan the Jebusite."

60. The vocalization of the preformative *mem* points to the root *yrh*, while in the following verse 14 the play is on the *qal* and *niph'al* conjugations of *rh*; as also in 2 Chronicles 3:1 on the *niph'al* of *r'h*, a back-reference to 2 Samuel 24:16–17, where the revelation is in the person of the punishing angel.

61. See "Kin, Cult, Land and Afterlife," *HUCA* 44 (1973), pp. 27–28.

62. Cf. our discussion of dialogue in writing intended for the eye, as contrasted with characters' lines in a drama intended for the ear, in TAG, pp. 11–13.

63. See "Slaughter, Sacrifice, Blood, and Atonement," *HUCA* 44 (1976), pp. 24–25.

64. Thus another instance of the pattern of the overlay or congruence of two characters into one.

65. Indeed, to regard child sacrifice as a common enough practice of pagan antiquity is to raise additional perplexities. Why would Scripture want to picture the first of the patriarchs, the friend of God and champion of divine justice, so ready to emulate his pagan contemporaries? Further-more, if Abraham's dedication to his God is no more singular than that of the pagans to their deities, what special merit would attach to Abraham's readiness to perform for the true God what his contemporaries are—in their lamentable benightedness—performing for their false gods?

CHAPTER 7

1. See, e.g., Meir Sternberg, *The Poetics of Biblical Narrative* (Bloomington: Indiana University Press, 1987), pp. 15–19, 30–38, and particularly p. 41, from which the following citation is ex-tracted: "The historiographic function surfaces in the frequent dating, in the commentary on names and places . . . in the genealogies and other items or even patterns, like chronology, that seem to re-sist assimilation to any higher order of coherence. . . . All these . . . serve as nodes or notices of larger configurations working below the surface to the same end: recording for its own sake."

2. Poetics may be relevant or applicable to such middle-of-the-spectrum genres as historical fiction or fictional history. It is unthinkable at the historiographic end of the narrative spectrum, which are called chronicles or annals. See TAG, pp. 30–37.

3. Thus for example, the many indications in ch. 2 in this volume that the Genesis (1–2:4a) creation "story" might more properly belong in the chapter on Structures.

4. See my study on Numbers 5:11–31 in *HUCA* (1975), pp. 55–70, the adducing of prescrip-tive texts for the interpretation of Scriptural narratives in TAG, pp. 53–55, 109, 119–21, 207–209; and now Joe M. Sprinkle, *"The Book of the Covenant": a Literary Approach*, Sheffield: JSOT Supplement Series 174, (1994).

5. Except, of course, for his namesake in the Sethite genealogy and the eponyms of clans in the genealogies of Midian (Genesis 25:4, 1 Chronicles 1:33) and of Reuben (Genesis 46:9, Exodus 6:14, Numbers 26:5–9, 1 Chronicles 5:3).

6. Some of my most perceptive students have found it difficult to accept the notion that a cre-ative author would go to such lengths to create two genealogies, both representing the human race, in order to convey to the reader that he is descended from a murderous forebear. Especially so, when that first line of human descent from a murderer turns out not to be the true line of human-ity, inasmuch as all of us (readers) are descended from Seth and not from the extinct line of Cain. I therefore take this recourse to expand my previous discussion and to supplement it with a discus-sion of the partially repetitive contents of verses 4:25 and 5:1.

(1) The entire line of Cain is presented (4:17–24) before the information in 4:25 that a third son was (or was yet to be) born to Adam and his wife. (2) The register of descent in Chapter 5 of-fers the first notice that the first pair (as indeed their descendants also) gave birth to daughters as well as sons. But the birth of females is cunningly anticipated in the birth of fair Na'ama/Dulcea to Lamech, son of Cain. Yet the wives of Lamech and the wife of Cain must also have been born, and Cain's wife could only have been his sister. The implication of the incestuousness of his marriage in the second generation should occasion no distress to pious readers of these details of their own mythopoeic origins, if they will recall that Cain and his wife were born to an originally androgy-nous entity who by a kind of mitosis separated into two in order to procreate in his/her/their image. This then raises the possibility that the line of Cain did not die out altogether. Only his descen-dants became extinct. His granddaughters, like Na'amah, may well have provided wives to the sons of Seth. (3) No rival metaphorical function for the vocational specifications of Urbanizer Cain and his descendant practitioners of the arts and crafts has been put forward. (4) Unlike the two ge-nealogical registers of Chapters 5 and 10, each characterized as *tōlᵉdōt* "begettings," the line of Cain is not similarly introduced. And even while the four culture-heroes suggest the line of a civilized humanity, the story of Killer Cain ends with the brutal boast of Killer Lamech. (5) There is no transition at all between this last boast and the notice of another son born to Adam and Eve. There is no explicit notice that Lamech is the last of Cain's line to sire offspring. Yet the inference

is ineluctable in the begetting of a son who will continue the human race as Cain and his sons will not. (6) That this third son will beget the true—true in a double sense—line of humanity is betokened by two notices in verse 26, Seth's son is Enosh "Human/Humanity." And it is in connection with this true line, true in that it will endure, and endure because it is true to the one and only God as expressed in the human invocation of that God properly understood, "in YHWH name." (7) Lest we miss the significance of these pointers to Seth's line as the true line, in contrast to Cain's, we have this driven home at least three more times in 5:1–3, the beginning of the Sethite genealogy: (a) "This is the register of Adam's (Man's) begettings," i.e., through Seth; (b) an almost verbatim repetition of 1:27–28a of Adam and Eve's creation in God's image and accompanying blessing; (c) the unique passing on of this (true) image by Adam to Seth, and (d) the notice—for the first time—that God *named* humankind Adam, which name is thus passed on to this son in naming him Seth, i.e., "Fixed, Established, Foundation."

7. TAG, p. 4.

8. He does, however, in his note on this verse explain his omission and provides an alternative translation without such omission.

9. See TAG, pp. 32–34.

10. The long-ago noted possible meaning of Methuselah (*mut-šelaḥ* "man of the sword") and Speiser's seeing in Methusael "components and formation . . . transparently Akkadian" (*mutu-ša-ili* "Man of God") embolden me to speculate on another possible word-play in these two names: Man of the Sword and Man of Death/Netherworld (*mut-šeʾôl*).

11. E. A. Spiser, *Genesis*, vol. 1 of the *Anchor Bible* (Garden City, N.Y. Doubleday, 1964), pp. 35–38, 41–43, 71, 73.

12. Not inconsistent with our following explanation of the qal with masculine subjects are such instances of metaphoric expression as Numbers 11:12 of Psalm 2:7, where the subject is, respectively, Moses or God.

13. This statement is not true: Japheth plus 13 descendants, Ham plus 29 descendants, and Shem plus 25 descendants make for a total of 70. For the metaphorical sense of the "seventy nations" implicit in Deuteronomy 32:8, corresponding to the (implicit 70) "sons of Israel" in Exodus 1:5, and the explicit (but problematic) 70 in Genesis 46:8–27, see ch. 7, "Addendum: Two More Genealogies and Another Numbers Game," pp. 373 ff.

14. Grandchildren are, of course, a metonym for the continuance of one's line that guarantees a felicitous Afterlife. See note 6. This concept was not peculiar to ancient Israel. From among the many possible citations in cuneiform the following from *ANET ANET³* (with supplements) "the mother of N" (tr. A. L. Oppenheim), Princeton University Press (1969), p. 561 is notable for its similarity to Genesis 50:23. Adad-guppi, mother of Nabonidus, is pictured as living to the age of 104 in the ninth year of Nabonidus, the only son whom she bore. Yet she is quoted as follows: "I saw my great-great-grandchildren, up to the fourth generation [how else!], in good health and (thus) had my fill of old age."

15. See "The Chronologies of the Lines of Seth and Shem," pp. 325 ff.

16. As in table 7-1.

17. The coincidence of these dates of the death of Eber constitute conclusive evidence that the rabbis must have prepared a chronological chart just as I did in table 7-1. Note also that in table 7-1 the son and grandson of Shem are out-lived by Shem: son Arpachshad by 59 years and grandson Shelah by 29 years. Thus we can understand the rabbinic tradition of the yeshiva-academy founded by Shem and its tradition, continued by Shem's great-grandson Eber. Jacob (born 2108) is 47. Jacob then would have arrived at Shem's yeshiva some 16 years after its founder's demise. The place of that yeshiva is implicitly in Mesopotamia, implicitly in the neighborhood of Ur (of the Chaldees), ? miles removed from Haran, home of Bethuel youngest son of Nahor, father of Laban and Rebekah, these last two also native to "the city of Nahor." See below on the question of how far Jacob would have had to travel from the yeshiva at Ur to the home of Laban in Haran.

18. On the question of the peculiar formulation of Pharaoh's concern in Exodus 1:9–10—is it

to prevent Egypt from being overcome by too numerous a population of Israelites, or is it to prevent a slave-labor force from leaving his domain? See TAG, p. 38.

19. Thus the tribesmen descending from Abraham through Hagar and the concubines, from Isaac through Esau. Yet the House of Israel, numbering 70 at the time of Jacob's descent to Egypt, is of questionable size when the Pharaoh who initiates the oppression tries to counter the fertility rate of Israel. On the one hand, the failed attempt to limit Israel's population increase by the command to the two midwives is followed by the command to expose all Israel's male infants on the Nile; this latter command serving as background for the exposure of the infant Moses 80 years before the Exodus, 350 years after Jacob's descent to Egypt. One can only commiserate with scholars who are set to the task of conjecturing on how several differing "historical" sources came to be edited into this chronology-defying pattern of Israelite barrenness, fertility, and desperate Pharaonic measures to limit the size of a labor-force he does not want to do without.

20. The 430 years since the descent to (or residence in) Egypt of the "Israelites" would begin 30 years before Isaac's birth, with Abram's descent to Egypt as told in Genesis 12. This would be a fine touch therefore on the narrator's part in placing this descent in the same year of Abram's departure from Haran and arrival in Canaan. But on this reckoning Abram should have been 70 years old (since Isaac was born when Abram was 100) instead of the 75 years ascribed to him in 12:4. This (arithmetical-poetic) problem is raised and resolved below, ch. 7, "Playing the Bible's Number Game: Another Solution," p. 337.

21. Thus, for example, the prophet as "embodiment" of YHWH (as Moses in Exodus 3; see ch. 1), TAG, pp. 158–165; Elijah and Elisha, both of them "the horse and chariot of Israel" = "YHWH, Israel's myriads of thousands;" TAG, pp. 143–145, the first featuring of the mantle of Elijah upon Elisha, and pp. 214–225, Elisha fulfilling the charge laid upon Elijah.

22. The differing assumptions (of R. Levi and R. Jose) are in regard to the intent of 11:26, "Terah lived 70 years. He sired Abram, Nahor and Haran." This difference does not (as does the following midrash, which we cite) directly attack the question of whether Abram or Haran was the firstborn: R. Levi assumes that the siring at 70 refers to Haran, the third of the three sons. Terah died at age 205—135 years *after Haran's birth* (205 – 70 = 135). Hence Abraham, who was 137 (10 years older than Sarah, who died at the age of 127) in the year when both Terah and Sarah died, must have been born when Terah was 68 (205 – 137 = 68). Thus Abram is the first born. R. Jose also accepts that Abram was 137 when Sarah died at the age of 127. But since he assumes that Terah's age 70 in 11:26 refers to the year of Abram's birth, the death of Terah at the age of 205 must have been two years earlier than Sarah's *when Abraham was* 135 (205 – 70 = 135). Thus Abraham could still be the first son, two years older than Haran.

23. Midrash Rabbah, Genesis (Noach) [XXXVIII, 14.]

24. The ambiguation is clear in the construction, which can read "elder brother of Japheth" or "brother of Japheth of elder." But the question of which of the two is the firstborn is determined for us by the seemingly pointless information in 11:10 that Shem at the age of 100 begat Arpachshad *two years after the flood['s onset]. . . .* Noah sired at the age of 500, 100 years before the flood's onset. That siring at age 500 can refer to Shem as the oldest, or—if Japheth was the oldest, to Japheth— in which case Shem would have been born when his father was 502. Since the flood began when Noah was 600 years old, the son who was 100 two years after the flood (after Noah was 602) has to be the one born when his father was 502 years old. That son then is Shem, the youngest. By analogy then Abraham, the first mentioned of the three sons of Terah, is like Shem, the first mentioned of the sons of Noah, the youngest of three siblings. Note: the dates for Shem's birth and death in table 7-1 and all the subsequent dates are off by 2 years.

That the Arpachshad of 11:10 was the eldest of Shem's five sons is a consequence of his birth two years after the flood('s onset). Noah brought no grandchildren into the ark. There was no conception aboard the ark; conception could only begin with the issuance of the ark's population a year (minus approximately six weeks) after the flood began. Hence Arpachshad could not have been preceded by a sibling. Note, however in table 7-2 that Arpachshad in the genealogy in Genesis 10 is the middle son, flanked on either side by two siblings. Only one of these, Aram, is here credited with descendants. These descendants of Aram are then listed first so that the line of Arpachshad can be listed last.

25. John Skinner, *The International Critical Commentary: Genesis* (New York: Scribner's, 1910), p. 238.

26. Skinner, *ICC*, p. 238.

27. Recognized but, like so many other insights of his adopted by the present writer, never published.

28. In the *quia absurdum est* poetical category are such apparently pointless items as the two mentions of Canaanites present in Canaan in Abram's time and, to be sure, the many chronological items—such as Ishmael's death age and Seth's siring "two years after the flood—which I expound in this discussion of Structures. See above, particularly n. 24.

29. See ch. 6, "Poetical Review of the Names of God," pp. 268–274, and ch. 7, "Abrahams Revelations and Altars," pp. 358 ff.

30. E. A. Speiser, *Genesis*, p. 79.

31. The use of the term "versions" for both the Hebrew masoretic text and translations of this text into other languages (be they Aramaic, Greek, Syraic, or Latin) creates a presumption for the authority of these translations' witness as to a hypothetical Vorlage in Hebrew that differed from our *textus receptus*, the MT. Such a presumption has never been justified by the fruits of the comparative textual methodology which it has spawned. An instance of the perniciousness of this methodology is the recourse to the differing numbers in genealogical chronologies in these so-called "versions." Thus cf., e.g., the age of Terah at his death in the Samaritan copy of a/the Hebrew text, and in the chronologies of Noah's descendants.

32. Or, for that matter, upon his arrival. Which is to say that Canaan-land may be a convenient nickname for a territory of indeterminate borders that was populated by a mix of Canaanites, Hittites, etc., which was more idea than place. Consider, for analogy, the United States of America in 1776, in 1886, and after the incorporation of the state of Hawaii.

33. See TAG, pp. 255–256.

34. See TAG, pp. 158–165.

35. Which is to say from a town whose significance is resonant of *Nowheresville*, and he is given a name so slight in difference from his prior name as to suggest that the significance lies not in the literal meaning of the names but in the fact of the name-change itself, as in the substitution of a regnal name for the one in use before the coronation. (So, too, the Sarai renamed Sarah who first comes to our attention as Iscah.)

36. Note how careful and consistent the biblical narrator (/author) is in regard to this place-name. It never appears in a protagonist's voice before the notice of its naming in 21:31, where the notice is formulated in the ambiguous (parenthetic) aside featuring a verb without an explicit subject: *qārā* "one called the place/the place was called." Earlier notices of events that must by reason of context take place near the oasis which became Beersheba are: (1) "the water-spot (*'ayn hammayīm,*), in the steppe-land the well (*'ayin*) on the way to Shur," where YHWH's angel comes upon the fugitive Hagar (16:7), which then becomes the wellspring (*bᵉer*), which then in 16:14 gets its name (*Bᵉer la-ḥay-rōʾī*), and is now located not as in 16:7 "on the way to Shur" but situate "between Qadesh and Bered." (2) From the site in Mamre's Oaks, where the three divine visitors enjoy Abraham's hospitality (18:1), Abraham moves to the Negeb territory, settling "between Qadesh and Shur," but sojourning on occasion in Gerar. (3) After the invitation of Abimelech in 20:15 to Abraham to settle anywhere in his land, Hagar and Ishmael are expelled and wander "in the steppe of Beersheba" (clearly known as such only to the narrator and his audience). This steppe-land (21:14–19) is waterless to Hagar until God opens to her sight a water-spring (*bᵉr mayīm*). The notice of the haunt of the adult Ishmael in 21:21 is pointedly not Beersheba (nor Isaac's haunt at *bᵉer la-ḥay-rōʾī*) but the more distant steppe-land of *Pāran*. Only now comes the visit of Abimelech and Phicol to Abraham at an unnamed site which will get its name Beersheba at some future time (21:31). (4) After the Binding of Isaac Abraham returns to Beersheba 22:19, twice mentioned in one narrator's breath, whence presumably he travels north to perform the obsequies for Sarah, who

died "in Qiryat Arba, that is Hebron, *in the territory of Canaan* (23:2). (5) Let us note that Abraham's dispatch of his major-domo to Aram Naharaim must have been from Hebron or the not-yet-named Beersheba, and that when the major-domo returns home with Isaac's bride it is to find the groom in a landscape from which Abraham is, narratively speaking, missing. As to the location of that particular steppe where Isaac is musing at even time just as the returning caravan comes into view, it is provided in 24:62, a parenthetic double hypotaxis, "Isaac **now** had come from coming [from] *bᵉer la-ḥay-rōʾī*, he now residing in Negeb territory."

37. Judges 6–8.

38. See TAG, pp. 265–66, notes 6 and 7.

39. Gerhard von Rad, *Genesis: A Commentary*, tr. J. H. Marks, (Philadelphia: Westminster Press, 1973), p. 403.

40. See also my essay in *Essays on Human Rights*, ed. David Sidorsky, JPS (1919), "The Hebrew Bible on Human Rights," particularly pp. 219–221.

CHAPTER 8

1. See TAG, pp. 19–36.

2. See TAG, p. 59.

3. See TAG, Chapter 7, Table 6 (pp. 214–220), with particular attention to the last paragraph on page 20.

4. See Zechariah 3:1.

5. Bertrand Russell, *Mysticism and Logic* (Totowa, N.J.: Barnes and Noble Books, 1981), p. 41.

6. See ch. 2 in this volume.

7. Note the absurdity in my translation of verse 5, "footgear worn and patched and attired in worn out garb"—as though the subject of attired is the footgear and not the people shod in this way. A literal translation, beginning in verse 4b, is: They took worn socks *for their asses*, worn wine-skins also split and resown, (5) and footgear worn and patched *on their feet* and worn out garb *upon themselves*, and all food *of their provision*—dry—was mold-flecked. The five expressions that I have italicized are all redundant for a) the sacks/sackcloths are not *for* the beasts of burden but burdens to be laden *upon* them; b) footgear/shoes are by definition for the feet, c) garb (*śimlā*) is a body-wrap; d) bread/food (*leḥem*) is synonymous with provision (*ṣayīd*) and e) since all these items are the objects of the opening "they took," the verb "to be," normally omitted even when implicit, is both syntactically and grammatically pleonastic. These egregious peculiarities in the storytelling, stylistically jarring and seemingly purposeless, along with the other peculiarities that I will show to be suggestively meaningful, thus provide further support of my contention (see TAG, pp. 37–44 on figures of speech and *translation*) that the more anomalous or gauche an expression in the biblical text, the more it is incumbent upon us to search for its purpose. Such respect for the biblical author's competence constitutes modesty on the reader's part, whereas the scholarly resort to emendation bespeaks either disrespect for the text or critical arrogance.

8. The ploy of bread—fresh baked, soggy, stale, and moldy—as an attestation of time's passage is exploited in Tablet XI of the Gilgamesh Epic. Utnapishtim has his wife bake bread and mark thus the six or seven days of Gilgamesh's unbroken sleep. The marks and the regressively deteriorated loaves are to prove to Gilgamesh upon his awakening that he has indeed slept a week rather than the moment he thinks he has. The humor in this episode extends beyond what I have just noted—the proffering of stale and moldy bread as proof of when a historical event began in a human's experience, when all it attests is to the objective duration of time since its baking. For one thing, nothing hinges on whether Gilgamesh will or will not accept Utnapishtim's account of the length of his sleep. For another, Gilgamesh's anticipated refusal to believe that he has slept so long is interpreted by Utnapishtim as an example of humanity's proclivity for deception—U. himself presumably no longer party to this human weakness by virtue of his accession to immortality/divinity. It is against such human wiliness that Mrs. U. must protect herself by the daily baking of bread. The failure of scholarship to credit the ancient authors with a sense of humor, hence to

overlook such clear examples of its presence in biblical and cuneiform writings, makes for the greatest impediment to the appreciation of the literature of the ancients. See TAG, pp. 28–29, 257–258, and in this volume ch. 4, "The Babylonian Flood Story," pp. 117–126.

9. Note this twice-deployed singular pronoun, whereas the referent subject is plural, the verbs having no explicit subject. That subject becomes explicit only after the implicit "they" and the explicit "him." This subject is the *benē-yiśra'el* "Israelites" of verses 17 and 18. What we must then recognize is that the collective pronoun *(to)* him/his reflects the viewpoint of the *macho* braves of verse 7 ("my ambit" . . . "how can I") which the *Israelites* of verses 17 and 18 are the entire people (thus a fifth term for this "identity") who move out against but—in the end—do not assault the Gibeonite confederacy. Yet a sixth term for this ancestral collective identity of ours is the "Israel" of verse 18 (YHWH god of Israel).

To review then the narrator's deployment of terms for his people in its totality or constituent elements, the broadest term is (1) *Israel*, the entire people through its history from its beginnings in the patriarch, who was given that secondary name through the foreseeable future (verses 3, 18); (2) the *Israelites*, the present generation that is entering the promised land (verses 17–18, 26); (3) the *assembly* or the *entire assembly* representing the whole people (verses 18, 19, 21, 27); (4) the *Chieftains*, or *chieftains presiding over the assembly* (verses 15, 18 [twice], 19, 21 [twice]); (5) the *warriors* (verses 6. 7. 16 [implicitly]); (6) the ambiguated "men/leaders" of verse 14.

10. The inclusion of three additional cities in the category of Gibeon must serve a poetic purpose. That purpose, as we shall see, in terms of this story's kerygma, is that the inhabitants of Hivvite Gibeon were not the sole survivors of the aboriginal stock. Cf. Joshua 15:63, where the narrator, supposedly engaged in outlining the borders which fall by lot in Joshua's time to Judah skips ahead (to the time of David's kingship in Jerusalem) ever so insouciently to report, "so for the Jebusite inhabitants of Jerusalem, the Judahites (ketib: are not able) were not able (gere) to dispossess them. [Why ever not?] and so the Jebusite(s) dwell with the Judahites in Jerusalem down to this very day.

11. See *Problem of "Curse" in the Hebrew Bible*, JBL Monograph 13 (1963), pp. 77–117.

12. Namely, that the cloud by day and the pillar of fire by night are not expressive of YHWH's literally showing Israel its path in the wilderness so much as of the accompanying gracious and protective presence of YHWH among his people. So too, the purport of Moses' prayer to God at the beginning and end of each "day's" march is Numbers 10:35–36. But the availability of the metaphor of God's personal function as guide in the wilderness raises the question as to why a human guide is invited to serve in this capacity. The only answer I can suggest therefore is to stress the welcome to the Midianites to share Israel's felicity in the land destined to be wrested from the Canaanites.

13. As, for example, Abraham and Isaac, Pharaoh and Abimelech. But consider also the caravaneers bound for Egypt in the Joseph story (Ishmaelites = Midianites = Medanites), or Potiphar, Joseph's master in 39:1 and his father-in-law Poti-phera' (41:45), priest of On, whose name includes the three of the pharaoh (*pr'*).

14. See ch. 7, "Digging Wells in Philistia," p. 543.

15. This rare root (*nšl*) appears only here and in 7:22 in the qal with the sense of removing an enemy; in the piel it appears in 2 Kings 16:6, with the Judeans as the population "removed" from Elat. But even here in Deuteronomy the usage is strange, for the first context (verse 2) requires the sense of "sweep from your path," and in the second context (verse 22) such a sense is ruled out by the adverbial modifier *me'at me'at* "little by little." The strangeness of this usage here thus reinforces the strangeness of the diction here in other respects.

16. Among the many implausibilities in the preceding chapters in Joshua: In Chapter 1 YHWH's repeated urging Joshua to be of good heart and to rely not on the unqualified support of God just promised, but on his obedience to the *Tōrā* of Moses; Joshua's charge to the people: limited to the preparation of food in the next few days preparatory to the fording of the Jordan and a campaign projected to endure for years, if not centuries; the picture of the entire Israelite horde massed at one point for the river crossing in sharp contrast to the 2½ trans-Jordanian tribes being

already settled on their homesteads and ranges, where the fighting men will abandon wives and children as they cross over for the war of conquest that endures beyond their lifetimes. In Chapter 2, the mission to scout out the weaknesses of a fortified city whose walls will collapse by divine fiat; the foreshadowing of the kerygma of Joshua 9 (as I discern it) in the exemption from the decree of extirpation of the family of a Canaanite ale-wife/madam who earns this reprieve by her faith in YHWH; the dwelling of Rahab set in the city wall, its window facing outward, from which window the faithful harlot is to signal with a red *thread* her habitation—this to the invaders who, having entered the city via the breaches in the wall, would need to see the red flag/thread from a window overlooking the city street. In 7:24 the animate and inanimate items consigned to the *ḥerem*-fire and the contrast with 6:24, where metals precious and base are deposited in the treasury of YHWH's sanctuary (*bayit*).

17. Such a follow-up to the absoluteness of the universal recognition of YHWH would in itself constitute a bathetic descent, how much the more so the conclusion of this pericope and the book with the picture of YHWH's house bereft now—and apparently for all future time—of a single Canaanite. Yet generations of translators and commentators can soberly propose that the Canaanite here is a metonym for "merchant." (Was it to fulfill this metonymically expressed messianic prophecy that Jesus is pictured driving the money-changers from the sacred precincts?)

SELECTED BIBLIOGRAPHY

Abrams, Israel Aaron. *The Fall of Judea*. Baltimore: Baltimore Talmud Torah, 1913.
———. *Commentary on Genesis 1*: Jerusalem: Magnes Press, Hebrew University, 1961.
Blank, Sheldon. *Prophet Thought, Essays and Addresses*. Cincinnati: Hebrew Union College Press, 1977.
Cassuto, Umberto. *La Questione della Genesi*. Florence: F. Le Monnier, 1934.
Danby, Herbert. *The Mishnah*. Oxford: Clarendon Press, 1933.
Driver, S. R. *An Introduction to the Literature of the Old Testament*. Edinburgh: T&T Clark, 1909.
Gunkel, Hermann. *The Stories of Genesis*. Translated by John J. Scullion; edited by William R. Scott. Vallejo, Calif.: BIBAL Press, 1994.
Heidel, Alexander. *The Babylonian Genesis: The Story of Creation*. Chicago: University of Chicago Press, 1963.
Kaufman, Yehezkel. *The Religion of Israel*. Chicago: University of Chicago Press, 1960.
Lane Fox, Rubin. *The Unauthorized Version: Truth and Fiction in the Bible*. New York: Viking, 1991.
Morgenstern, Julian. *The Book of Genesis: A Jewish Interpretation*. New York: Schocken Books, 1965.
Muffs, Yochanan. *Love and Joy: Law, Language, and Religion in Ancient Israel*. York, N.Y.: Jewish Theological Seminary of America, 1992.
Owen, Wilfred. *The Complete Poems and Fragments*. Edited by Jon Sallworthy. London: Chatto & Windus/Hogarth Press, 1983.
Pope, Marvin H. *El in the Ugaritic Texts*. Leiden: Brill, 1955.
Pritchard, James Bennett. *Ancient Near Eastern Texts Relating to the Old Testament*. Princeton, N.J.: Princeton University Press, 1950.
Rad, Gerhard von. *Genesis, A Commentary*. Translated by John H. Marks. London: SCM, 1972.
Rendsburg, Gary A. *The Redaction of Genesis*. Winona Lake, Ind.: Eisenbrauns, 1986.

Russell, Bertrand. *Mysticism and Logic*. Garden City, N.Y.: Doubleday Anchor Books, 1957.

Sidorsky, David. *Essays on Human Rights: Contemporary Issues and Jewish Perspectives*. Edited by David Sidorsky et al. Phildelphia: Jewish Publication Society of America, 1979.

Speiser, E. A. *Genesis*. Garden City, N.Y.: Doubleday, 1964.

Sprinkle, Joe M. *The Book of the Covenant: A Literary Approach*. Sheffield, Eng.: JSOT, 1992.

Sternberg, Meir. *The Poetics of Biblical Narrative: Ideological Literature and Drama of Reading*. Bloomington: Indiana University Press, 1985.

Tsevat, Matitiahu. "Gods and the Gods in Assembly: An Interpretation of Psalm 82" *Hebrew Union College Annual* vols. 40–41 (1969–70).

Whybray, R. N. *The Making of the Pentateuch: A Methodological Study*. Sheffield, Eng.: JSOT, 1967.

Wooley, Sir Leonard. *Ur of the Chaldees*. London: Penguin, 1954.

DICTIONARIES AND ENCYCLOPEDIAS

Millon Hadash. Evan Shoshan, Avraham. Jerusalem: Kiryat Sefer, 1958.

The Interpreters' Bible. Nashville: Abington, 1962.

The Interpreters' Dictionary of the Bible. Nashville: Abington, 1962.

The Random House Dictionary of the English Language. Unabridged ed. New York: Random House, 1966

Webster's Collegiate Dictionary. 5th ed. Springfield, Mass.: GSC Merriam, 1936.

INDEX

Allegory, 81, 98, 100, 108, 113, 138, 176, 304

Allusion, 183, 194, 358, 371, 374

Anthropology, 108, 111, 112

Anthropomorphism, 57, 71, 75, 84, 160, 239

Aposiopesis, 273, 330,

Apostasy, 183, 202, 290, 431

Apposition, 172, 207, 285, 415

Aristophanes, 79

Babylonian Creation Epic, 37–9, 50–57

Bathos, 55, 117, 122, 150–51, 153

Bᵉrīt, 207–8, 226, 364

Blake, William, 47, 62, 94

Blank, Sheldon, 238

Bowdlerization, 273

Cassuto, Umberto, 8–11, 103, 257–8

Chaos, 64, 394, 395

Character. See Persona

Chronology, 321, 333, 338

Comedy, 117, 122, 240, 295

Cosmogony, 50–52

Comparative-contrastive, 39, 52, 59, 64, 66

Cosmology, 50, 51, 59

Covenant, 26. See also Bᵉrīt

Decalogue, 278, 398, 401, 408–12

Dialogue
  internal, 47, 233
  direct, 268 (see also Direct discourse)

Dichotomy, 11, 103

Didactic, 239–40

Discourse
  direct, 46–7, 141, 196–7, 199, 204–5, 207, 210, 213, 215, 250–52, 259, 283, 368, 425, 427
  free direct, 110, 139, 204, 218, 222, 232, 247, 249, 282–3, 422, 425
  free indirect, 194, 204, 258, 273
  implied free direct, 193–4 204, 258

implied free indirect, 193, 197
  indirect, 282

Documentary hypothesis, 8, 71, 267. See also Source criticism

Doxology, 69

Enuma Elish, 37–62, 395, 398, 400

Eisegesis, 28, 391

Ellipsis, 247

Eponym, 174, 221, 304, 312, 319, 339, 344, 356, 376, 380, 383–4

Ethonym, 301, 356

Etiology, 88, 244, 252, 362, 365, 369

Etymology, 28–29, 77, 286

Euripedes, 293–6

Exegesis, 25, 28, 200, 226, 280, 291, 302, 391, 397, 427. See also Kerygma

Faith, 284, 289

gap bridging, 148, 207, 251, 261, 263, 346, 364, 425, 430

gap filling, 365, 426

Gapping, 115, 137–8, 140, 191–4, 196, 216, 243, 251, 260, 283, 368

Genetic
  analysis, 111
  division, 71
  hypothesis, 259
  theory, 214

Genocide, 428–33. See also Ḥerem

Genre, 112, 295, 301
  assignment, 88, 109
  distinction, 301
  division, 390
  fabulary, 297
  label, 177, 303
  oriented, 111

Gentilic, 221, 321, 377

Glossing, 206

Graf-Wellhausen, 13